ODYSSEY SERIES IN LITERATURE
ROBERT SHAFER, *General Editor*

D1231884

PARADISE REGAINED, THE MINOR POEMS
AND SAMSON AGONISTES

JOHN MILTON

Aged 21

From the portrait at Nuneham

JOHN MILTON

PARADISE REGAINED
THE MINOR POEMS
AND
SAMSON AGONISTES

Complete and Arranged Chronologically

Edited by MERRITT Y. HUGHES
Professor of English, University of Wisconsin

THE ODYSSEY PRESS
New York

Magistro meo

HERBERT J. C. GRIERSON

CONTENTS

CHRONOLOGY

1608, Dec. 9. Birth in Bread Street, Cheapside, London.

1620. Admission to St. Paul's School.

1625, Feb. 12. Matriculation at Christ's College, Cambridge.

1629, March. Promotion to B. A. degree.

1629, Dec. *On the Morning of Christ's Nativity.*

1632, July. Promotion to M. A. degree.

1632, July, to 1638, April. Residence in the house to which John Milton Sr. had retired in Horton, Buckinghamshire.

1634, Sept. 29. *A Mask* (*Comus*) performed.

1637, Nov. *Lycidas.*

1638, April. Departure for Italy.

1639, Aug. Return to England.

1639-40. Establishment in London and beginning of school-keeping.

1640-41. Plans for tragedies and epics on national and biblical themes in the Cambridge manuscript.

1641, late spring. *Of Reformation in England.*
Early summer. *Of Prelatical Episcopacy.*
Late summer. *Animadversions upon the Remonstrant's Defence against Smectymnuus.*

1642, Jan. to March. *The Reason of Church Government Urged against Prelaty.*
March to April. *Apology for Smectymnuus.*
Whitsuntide. Marriage with Mary Powell, separation following about a month later.

1643, Aug. 1. *The Doctrine and Discipline of Divorce* first published.

1644, June. *On Education.*
July. *The Judgment of Martin Bucer concerning Divorce.*
Nov. *Areopagitica.*

1645, March. *Tetrachordon* and *Colasterion*.

Late summer. Reconciliation with Mary Powell.

Autumn. Publication of the collected Minor Poems.

1645–46. Work begun on the *History of Britain* and on *De Doctrina Christiana*.

1649, Feb. *The Tenure of Kings and Magistrates*.

March. Appointment as Secretary for Foreign Tongues to the Council of State.

Oct. *Eikonoklastes*.

1651, March. *Defensio pro Populo Anglicano*.

1652, May. Death of Mary Powell.

1654, spring. *Defensio Secunda*.

1655. *Defensio pro se*.

1656, Nov. Marriage with Katherine Woodcock.

1658, Feb. Death of Katherine Woodcock.

1660, March. *The Ready and Easy Way to Establish a Free Commonwealth*.

1663, Feb. Marriage with Elizabeth Minshull, who survived him until 1727.

1667. *Paradise Lost* first published.

1671. *Paradise Regained* and *Samson Agonistes* first published.

1674, Nov. 8. Death.

INTRODUCTION

I. YOUTH—THE LATIN POEMS

1. If it is true, as Mr. John Crowe Ransom believes, that "the great repute of the Miltonic style is a consequence of the scarcity . . . of poets who have mastered the technique of Latin poetry before they have turned to their own," then Milton's Latin poems should be the most alluring of all the roads that an explorer of the poet can follow. So in recent years they have proved to the investigators who have given us "the new Milton." Modern interest has been focused less upon their art, however, than upon their revelation of Milton's mind and of the "unconscious" meaning of his English poetry. Analysis of "the man and thinker" has rather obscured the artist to whom Mr. Ransom would bring us back. Because in some of the elegies Milton poured himself out with less reserve or with a kind of unreserve distinctly other than that of his most amazingly personal prose, it has sometimes been assumed that they are confessions about his adolescence hardly less intimate than those of Mr. Wells about his callow years in *Experiment in Autobiography*. They are hardly that, though they are full of an engaging candour. Searchers for autobiography will find it there a-plenty and they may be fortunate enough to find some other things to boot. Even to the reader who has no Latin the prose translations in the present volume have much to say about the development of the poet's mind and still more to suggest about the growth of his art. Although Milton segregated them in a section of their own when he first collected his poems, English, Latin, Greek, and Italian, for publication in 1645, and kept them by themselves again in 1673, his careful dating indicates that he expected them to have the

lively interest of a portrait of the artist as a very young man. His odd way of using ordinal numbers—calling himself in his seventeenth year until his eighteenth birthday—*may* have been due to a desire to strain the excuse of youth with the puritanical public of 1645. Yet that was the year of the publication of *Tetrachordon* and *Colasterion,* his two final salvos in defence of liberal divorce laws; and in his dating of his youthful poems he can hardly have conceded more than a jot to the prejudices of his public. On his own account he seems to have looked back with some regret upon his confession of "love at first sight" in the seventh elegy; but, on the whole, he was proud of his Latin poems—proud of the "erotic" fifth elegy, proud of the record of his friendship with Charles Diodati in the first and sixth elegies and in *Damon's Epitaph,* proud of the record of his Italian triumphs in *Manso* and *Salzilli,* proud even of the horrific, schoolboy, mock epic *On the Fifth of November,* in which so good a classicist as Professor E. K. Rand sees more power than, and almost as much beauty as, he does in the epyllion that Virgil wrote as a boy of eighteen, the *Gnat.* In reconstructing Milton's life in terms of his poetry we have to reckon with his Latin verse all the way from the first elegy in 1625 or 1626 to *Epitaphium Damonis* in 1639 or 1640, two years later than *Lycidas.*

2. In Milton's boyhood everything seems to have conspired to make him a linguist and a poet, but his father was the archconspirator. Business acumen, musical tastes, extraordinary faith in his sons, and dominant religious interests marked the man into whose home at the sign of the Spread Eagle in Bread Street, London, the boy was born on the ninth of December, 1608. How stern his father's religious principles really were is open to question. He had broken with his father, Richard Milton, a loyal Roman Catholic who twice suffered the financial martyrdom of the fine for recusancy; but he may have been less of a Puritan than his famous son, for his forgotten son, Christopher, grew up with conservative principles both in politics and in religion and had his reward by being appointed to a judgeship under Charles II. Because

he was a scrivener, John Milton, Sr., is usually described as a kind of solicitor; but he was less a lawyer than a banker, and at heart—as Milton reminded him in the poem addressed to him—he was a musician and perhaps a poet too.

3. The careful education at home as well as at St. Paul's School—for which Milton so cordially thanks his father in that poem—seems to have been begun with the ministry as its goal. In a familiar passage in the preface to the second book of *The Reason of Church Government* Milton speaks as if he had come up to his final degree at Cambridge with the clear resolve to take orders and had then been disappointed and "church-outed" by the oath enjoining support of episcopacy, "which, unless he took with a conscience that would retch, he must either straight perjure, or split his faith." Long before he took his degree, however, he must have resolved, at least subconsciously, to live the life of a man of letters. The years of independent, post-graduate study which were given to him at Horton, followed by sixteen very handsomely subsidized months in Italy, prove that, on the whole, the older man shared his hopes and dreams. The sonnet *On his being Arrived to the Age of Twenty-three*—which Mr. W. R. Parker proposes to date a year later, *i.e.* in 1632, just after rather than before the residence in the paternal home in Horton began—was sent in a letter to an unknown friend who seems to have felt that he should have gone into the Church, but there is no reason for supposing that the friend spoke for his father. On the other hand, we have the evidence of the Latin poem addressed to his father that his education had been most liberally planned. The poem's record of the training which began with private tutors several years before he entered St. Paul's School at age twelve is strikingly like the ideal scheme of studies which he drew up at age thirty-six, for boys preparing to serve their country "justly, skilfully and magnanimously." Latin was the starting point and Greek was soon added, then Hebrew, and then Italian, French, and Spanish; but no language was treated as an end in itself. They were all keys to literature and life. His own Latin must have begun under tutors when he was a

very little boy, and he may have learned it like the child, Montaigne, who was allowed to hear little else spoken in the house. In any case, he learned it—as we gather from what he says to the most famous of his tutors, Thomas Young, in the fourth elegy—from highly trained and intelligent men with whom he built up a friendship as they rambled together on Parnassus. The Italian sonnets, which Mr. Smart proved to have been written certainly before, and probably long before, the Italian journey, show how articulate he was, perhaps while still an undergraduate, in the formal language of Petrarch; and the tributes to his spoken Italian, French, and Spanish by his admirers in Rome and Florence suggest a flexible command of contemporary idiom in all three languages. Yet it is clear that he had no interest in languages as such and despised a linguist who would "pride himself to have all the tongues that Babel cleft the world into, yet if he have not studied the solid things in them, as well as the words and lexicons, he were nothing so much to be esteemed a learned man, as any yeoman or tradesman competently wise in his mother dialect only." At school and at Cambridge he hated the ceaseless exercises in the classical languages, and in the tractate *Of Education* he condemned the "preposterous exaction [of] forcing the empty wits of children to compose themes, verses, and orations" in "miserable Latin and Greek." But a practical and even an artistic faculty for self-expression in Latin was a prime object in the scheme of education which he drew up in 1644. No twentieth-century schoolboy ever hated the drudgery of languages more than Milton did, but his hatred was born of impatience to go exploring through the realms of gold in half a dozen tongues and to find his feet as an artist in the common speech of all educated men—Latin.

4. The ability to write with poetic power in that language seems to have dawned upon him like an afflatus about 1626— the year which saw three of the elegies, the epyllion *On the Fifth of November* and several lesser poems. Except *On the Death of a Fair Infant,* he had written no English poetry of importance and he was to write very little more English verse

before the hymn *On the Morning of Christ's Nativity* in 1629.
Even after that marvellous success in English he was to go on
writing in Latin with increasing mastery for ten more years.
Then, deliberately, he stopped. Barring the ode *To John
Rous* and a few scraps of Latin verse scattered in his prose,
he chose thereafter to be an English poet. In 1638–9 his
hexameters of compliment to his Neapolitan host, Giovanni
Baptista Manso, look forward to an epic about the British
hero, Arthur, and in *Damon's Epitaph* (ll. 170–8), his last serious poem in Latin, he made explicit his resolve to write thenceforth in English. Looking backward a little more than two
years later, in the preface to Book II of *The Reason of Church
Government,* he explained that his motive had been "God's
glory by the Honour and Instruction of my Country. For
which Cause," he added, "and not only for that I knew it
would be hard to arrive at the second Rank among the Latins,
I applied myself to that Resolution which Ariosto followed
against the Persuasions of Bembo, to fix all the Industry and
Art I could unite to the adorning of my native Tongue."

  5. From our distance the resolve to honour God and England by writing in English looks self-complacent, but the admission of incapacity to reach the first rank among the Latins
cost Milton a pang. He was thinking less of the ancients than
of his own contemporaries; men like the Scot, George Buchanan, who had won a European reputation with Latin elegies
as Ovidian and gay as Milton's fifth, *On the Coming of Spring.*
Buchanan's satires on the Franciscans helped to provoke Milton's sallies in *On the Fifth of November* against the mendicant
friars in their "Cimmerian darkness." By "the Latins" he
meant, in the main, to refer to the great Italians whose mastery
of Latin verse had been hardly inferior to their fluency—figures
like Pontano, Vida, and Sannazaro. In elegies like Sannazaro's and in epics like his *De Partu Virginis* and Vida's
Christias Milton found a more personal and idiomatic Latin
than even he could command. Yet in spite of his regret that
he could never rank with these men, he was ready, in 1640,
to let them go their way while he went another and a very

different path. Even in the hands of men of genius, classical Latin was not a very flexible medium. For some subjects it might serve better than a living language, but to write it well a man had to steep himself so deeply in the poetry of one or more of the ancients that he submitted to a kind of personal domination—as Milton confessed in *Smectymnuus* that he had once done with Ovid. Indeed, the history of his development as a versifier in Latin is the record of his emancipation from Ovid to become a disciple and, in a way, a rival of Virgil. The elegies are a tissue of Ovidian reminiscences, but it was Virgil who moved him when he wrote *Ad Patrem* and the fine poem addressed to his famous host in Naples, Giovanni Baptista Manso, and *Epitaphium Damonis.* For a time he was interested in Horace, for he experimented with Horatian metres both in Latin and in English; in Latin when, for example, he wrote *On the Death of the Vice-Chancellor;* and in English— if I am right in believing that the late date traditionally assigned to the lines is incorrect—when he translated Horace's fifth ode, "almost word for word, without rhyme, according to the Latin measure." The Horatian mood in sonnets like that *To Mr. Lawrence* proves the survival of his affection for Horace in later years. But Ovid and Virgil were passions with him. Whenever he wrote poetry, they were always at hand, haunting his thoughts; yet in 1640 he was ready to relinquish their imitation in their own language to others.

6. Even after making due allowance for Dr. Johnson's principle that "nearly every . . . flourish of fine motive in Milton's life was an afterthought," I believe that he stopped writing in Latin for the reasons that he gave in *The Reason of Church Government;* but it is worth pausing to ask whether he might ever under any circumstances have tried to write a long poem in Latin for all Europe to read—the audience for which the *De Doctrina Christiana* was boldly intended. In Latin prose Milton was to feel himself sure of a public as long as he lived and in Latin prose he was utterly at ease in expressing himself. In verse he could not have the public that he desired, and he was beginning to feel the constraint of an art which involved

the combination of countless phrases from the classics, used for their idiomatic rather than their allusive value. Such a phrase was the greeting in Virgil's first eclogue to the peasant who has had the good fortune to escape in a general eviction of his neighbours from their farms—"Fortunate senex" (Fortunate old man!). Milton's use of the words to congratulate his famous Neapolitan host, Manso, upon the fame that he enjoyed as the patron of Torquato Tasso is apt, but the reminiscence does not help the meaning. More appropriate is the echo in his compliment to Manso of Virgil's saying in the *Aeneid* (VI, 130 and 730) that by virtue men mount the skies, and his use of Virgil's words in the *Georgics* (III, 9) to promise Manso an immortality of fame on the lips of men. Less appropriate is his reminiscence in *Epitaphium Damonis* of Virgil's description (*Georgics* III, 433) of a dangerous field snake that comes writhing on "with head erect and eyes of fire." At the climax of his dirge for Diodati Milton introduced the celestial Cupid with eyes of flame that dart their sparkles far and wide among the stars. Seemingly with no sense of incongruity, the god's fiery glances are described in virtually the very same words that Virgil used to describe the adder. The incongruity is really less than it seems, for the picture in the *Georgics* has drama and beauty. In his later Latin poems, however, Milton's echoes of the classics have a subtle, two-fold propriety. When he paused in his lament for Diodati to imagine a group of his friends calling him in vain to join their field sports, there was a reminiscence of a kindred passage in Virgil's *Eclogues* (X, 42–3):

> Hic gelidi fontes, hic mollia prata, Lycori,
> Hic nemus . . .[1]

In Virgil's lines there is a note of frustrated love which is a faintly heard undertone in Milton's. He was seeking a particular effect of allusive depth and distance and he achieved

---

[1]Come, see what pleasures in our plains abound,
The woods, the fountains, and the flow'ry ground.
                        (Dryden's translation.)

it; but at the price of imitating both Virgil and—if Mr. T. P. Harrison is correct in a recent surmise—Castiglione, who used the Virgilian motif with more than Virgilian pathos in one of the most famous of the pastoral elegies of the Renaissance, *Alcon*.

7. For most modern readers the least impressive of Milton's Latin poems is likely to be the little epic on the Gunpowder Plot, *In Quintum Novembris,* which he wrote at age seventeen. Its ties with *Paradise Lost* and with *L'Allegro* and *Il Penseroso* entitle it to a moment's consideration. It is a torso, for Milton outgrew it as he worked on it, and threw it aside with an apology for a conclusion. The events of the Plot's discovery are huddled into a few final lines. Milton was interested only in the preliminaries; Satan's inspection of the wide world, ending in the discovery of the happy island of England, and the steps for its undoing taken by the fiend. Warton compared the account in Ovid's *Metamorphoses* (II, 787–96) of the goddess Envy ranging over sea and land to fix at last upon the peaceful city of Athens for molestation. Envy gains her ends by whispering a crime into the ears of the sleeping Athenian princess, Aglauros; and Milton's Satan gains his by breathing the outrage of the Gunpowder Plot into those of the sleeping Roman prince, Pope Paul V. From the cave of Phonos in the bowels of the earth Paul convokes a frightful council of monsters—Murder, double-tongued Treachery, Craft, Contention, Calumny, Fury, Fear, and pale Horror—and the Plot is hatched. Behind the cave stretched a venerable tradition going back to Hesiod's account in the *Theogony* of Night and its horrid children; but its atmosphere was familiar in several popular poems such as *The Purple Island* of Milton's admired Phineas Fletcher. In Fletcher's satires, the *Locustae* and its English counterpart, *The Apollyonists,* Milton found a treatment of the Plot which justified all that is most extreme in his own poem. His glory in the premature glee of the diabolical consistory over the prospect of James and the Parliament blown sky-high together matches Fletcher's so closely that he might have been paraphrasing. Then, abruptly, he turned to a description of

the tower of the goddess Rumour and wove together his memories of Ovid's description of her seat with that of Chaucer in *The House of Fame*. After thirty lines on this congenial theme, Rumour is commissioned by the Almighty to spread a report of the Plot throughout England. She does so, and the little epic sags suddenly to an end.

II. *L'ALLEGRO* AND *IL PENSEROSO*

8. Recently Mr. Tillyard has thrown altogether new light upon *L'Allegro* with his evidence that it dates from Milton's later years at Cambridge. Its strange exordium—"Hence, loathed Melancholy," *etc.*—reads with a new meaning and gaiety if it is felt as some kind of reaction against the horrific monsters from the cave of Phonos which Milton evoked to celebrate his second fifth of November at the University. Certainly the Stygian cave with its horrid shapes, the brooding darkness, and the Cimmerian desert are the very stuff out of which *In Quintum Novembris* is concocted. For some time opinion has been moving away from the traditional view of *L'Allegro* and *Il Penseroso* as voicing the moods of the studious recluse at Horton as he drifted through the orchard lanes, inviting his soul. All the evidence indicates that Milton's life at Horton was that of a much more systematic student than he had been at Cambridge. At Horton, except *Comus* and *Lycidas*, he wrote little poetry and most of it was composed under the pressure of various occasions. Horton itself has been regarded as the occasion prompting the two companion poems, but a college exercise would serve that purpose just as well. Indeed, the tone of l'Allegro's walk in the country is quite in the mood of an undergraduate on holiday. It is just Milton's mood in the seventh elegy, where he strolls in the fields around London; and in the first, where he confesses to having used his rustication to haunt the fields and groves, and to having been as much disturbed by the passing bevies of girls as l'Allegro was by the starry "Cynosure of neighbouring eyes."

9. The evidence suggesting that the strange exorcisms which open *L'Allegro* and *Il Penseroso* flowed from undergraduate high spirits is still more cogent. In the first prolusion, or academic exercise, Milton had to make an address to his tutors and fellow students on the assigned question, "Whether Day is more excellent than Night." The result was a formal yet playful Latin oration which repeats Hesiod's account of the birth from Chaos of Erebus and Night and goes on—like Hesiod, and like Boccaccio in his *Genealogy of the Gods,* and like many later mythographers—to make Night the mother of a hideous brood; Tribulation, Envy, Fear, Guile, Poverty, Sickness, and others no less dire. The theme was traditional and Milton knew that his audience would be familiar with many treatments of it, from that in Hesiod to Shakespeare's

> O comfort-killing Night, image of hell!
> Dim register and notary of shame!
> Black stage for tragedies and murders fell!
> Vast sin-concealing chaos! nurse of blame!
> Blind muffled bawd! dark harbour for defame!
>   Grim cave of death! whispering conspirator
>   With close-tongu'd treason and the ravisher.[1]

Mr. Tillyard thinks that at the first line or two of either *L'Allegro* or *Il Penseroso* Milton's audience of undergraduates (reading his verses or hearing them as a part of some entertainment like that in which the lines *At a Vacation Exercise* are embedded) would scent parody of familiar themes and begin to grin. If his view of the matter is to prevail, there is still comfort for those who will grieve over the loss of the two poems as the fine flowering of "the Horton period" in the fact that a poet like Lovelace could use the same motif, at least half seriously, in a love lyric like *Night: To Lucasta:*

> Night! loathed jailor of the lock'd up sun, . . .
>   Thou dost arise our living hell,
>   With thee groans, terrors, furies dwell,
>   Until Lucasta doth awake,
> And with her beams these heavy chains off shake.

---

[1] *The Rape of Lucrece,* 764–70.

10. The formal contrast between the two poems is, in part, the opposition of day to night in the prolusion. Like *L'Allegro* —and, it may be added, like the schoolboy verses in the Commonplace Book—the prolusion pays its "ample tribute to the honour of Day." At sunrise the birds in the tree-tops hail the Dawn and the first of them to herald the light is the cock, as he is in *L'Allegro*. The sun wears the same splendour in which l'Allegro sees him rise and "the clouds in garments of diverse hues, with festal show, in long procession, appear to be handmaidens attending the rising god." In the poem Milton's couplets soon carried him far out of the realm of the prolusion into the bright English landscape which Nicholas Breton had explored at the same swift pace in *The Passionate Shepherd,* and which had been familiar to Englishmen since it was discovered by one of the contributors to Tottel's *Miscellany*. But in design, although it includes a tribute to the gay pleasures of evening, the poem is a survey of Day and its moods, just as *Il Penseroso* is a survey of Night.

11. The real contrast between the two poems is, of course, one of mood, and it is Milton who is both the gay and the thoughtful dreamer. There is no conflict or tension, for both poems are aspects of the contemporary impulse to hunt for new and richer interests than the past afforded, in terms of which to revalue the medieval ideal of the contemplative life. It is *Il Penseroso,* with the Cherub Contemplation and divinest Melancholy as its presiding genii, that is the longer, if not the more successful poem. Dr. Johnson was right when he said that its mood seemed to him to carry over into *L'Allegro*. If the Doctor had read his Burton's *Anatomy of Melancholy* to better purpose than he did, he might have understood why this was so. Today everyone knows that in the "Author's Abstract of Melancholy," which he prefixed to the *Anatomy,* Burton counted many of l'Allegro's pleasures among what he considered the prime satisfactions of melancholy:

> Methinks I hear, methinks I see,
> Sweet musick, wondrous melody,

Towns, Palaces, and Cities fine;
Here now, then there; the world is mine;
Rare beauties, gallant Ladies shine—
Whate'er is lovely or divine.
    All other joys to this are folly,
    None so sweet as melancholy.

Certainly *L'Allegro* is the least morbid poem ever written and
no passion for the theatre and the night life of a great city was
ever healthier than Milton's; yet Burton recognized such indulgence as his in day-dreams and "castles in the air" as one
of the symptoms of the disease whose victims "soothe up themselves with phantastical and pleasant humours."[1]   The fact is
that in *L'Allegro* no less than in *Il Penseroso,* like Jaques in
As You Like It, Milton courted a melancholy of his own.   It
is essentially romantic and entitled to Mr. E. E. Stoll's comparison of it with that of Keats's ode on *Melancholy* and of
Coleridge's on *Dejection* and of Shelley's *Stanzas Written in
Dejection near Naples.*   An alternative—though not a perfect
one—to this view is to recognize a vein of irony running consistently through *Il Penseroso.*   This, in accordance with his
theory that the poem was written to amuse an academic audience, is what I understand Mr. Tillyard to do.   To my ear, it
is not possible to catch the irony in its glorious roster of
Platonic and Hermetic studies and of classical and romantic
reading.   Yet it is a relief to have a touch of humour pointed
out in the conclusion and to realize that Milton could poke
fun at his most serious studies.   Many readers will be prepared
to follow Mr. Tillyard joyfully when he says of the prayer for
the "peaceful hermitage" in "weary age" which ends the
poem: "How charmingly callow, how perfectly appropriate to
an audience of boys!   It fits far worse the lips of a man who
has retired into studious quiet already."   If there is no irony
in the passage, it can hardly be cleared of the charge of senti-
mentality.   Englishmen must have had more than enough of
the debate between the active and the contemplative lives in

---

[1] *Anatomy,* I, ii, 2, 6.

which—as in Bacon's *Device on the Queen's Day*—the final
reward offered to the youth who chose to live in the garden
of the Muses was "the privilege of the Golden Age" and the
promise of a life that "leadeth the eye beyond the horizon of
time and giveth no obscure divinations of time to come."[1]
The more playfully Milton's boyish vision of his declining years
as spent in attaining to "something like prophetic strain" can
be read, the better for it as poetry.

12. The question of the date of *Il Penseroso* and *L'Allegro*
is a half-solved enigma. Tentatively, I have put down the
year 1631. Milton's pleasant summer in the country then
seems to me—as Mr. Parker has recently urged—a plausible
background for them; and, like Mr. Parker, I doubt whether,
after Milton's beloved master at St. Paul's School, Alexander
Gill, had publicly condemned Ben Jonson's plays (as he did
late in 1632), his loyal pupil would have paid a compliment
to the "learned sock." Certainly they must have been written
well within two years of *On the Morning of Christ's Nativity*.
They may have been written in close succession to it, or even
before it; for there is no compelling reason to accept them
in their entirety as a single creative act. Although they correspond closely and even dovetail verbally here and there, they
cannot have been hastily written and they give signs of organic
growth. *Il Penseroso* is sometimes pointed to as the original
nucleus, on the ground that it harmonizes exactly with Milton's
character; but no one who compares *L'Allegro* with the Latin
verses on the enjoyment of a summer morning in the Commonplace Book can doubt that its moods and images had long
been a part of his nature. We are not likely ever to know
just when the two poems were written. Perhaps there was no
"just when," for the resemblances in *L'Allegro* to the verses
in the Commonplace Book and to the passage on the theatre
in the first elegy may have arisen out of some earlier attempt
or attempts to express similar ideas in English verse. It is

---

[1] The speeches drawn up by Mr. Bacon for the Earl of Essex, in a
device exhibited by his lordship before Queen Elizabeth on the anniversary of her accession to the throne, Nov. 17, 1595.

sure, however, that the poems represent Milton as he was in
his later years at Cambridge. I have discussed them here before *On the Morning of Christ's Nativity;* not because I believe
that they antedated that poem; but because it seems to me
that they were virtually contemporary with it, and that we
should regard the impression which they give us of Milton's
personality as complementary to that given by his "birthday
present to Christ."

III. "THE DANCE OF LIFE"

13. Playful though Milton's references to the rewards of
scientific study may have been in *Il Penseroso,* "natural philosophy" fired him with Baconian ardour. As an undergraduate
he must have been an enthusiastic reader of *The Advancement of Learning;* or at least a keen admirer of the author and
his point of view. In his third prolusion he makes a bitter
attack upon the scholastic tradition at Cambridge for obliging
the students to chop arguments with the "philosophasters"
instead of coming to grips with history, physics, and biology.
The outburst is a young idealist's espousal of Bacon's revolt
against the dead hand of the past in education. Down with
the "joyous wrangling of old men," which was begotten either
in the cave of Trophonius or in the cells of the monks, is his
cry. There is more in the third prolusion, however, than a
clever undergraduate's wail at finding himself "mocked," as
the *Tractate on Education* says, "with ragged notions and
babblements while [he] expected worthy and delightful
knowledge." The prolusion goes on to lay out a program
of study such as Milton actually carried out at Horton, "a
tour, as it were, about the whole earth," in which historical
and geographical interests could be cultivated, while the main
purpose would be "to investigate and observe the natures of all
living creatures; from these to plunge the mind into the secret
essences of stones and plants . . . and to peer into the caskets
of the hail and to survey the arsenals of the thunderbolts."
Let none of Nature's secrets remain a mystery, he cries; "nor

let even the tiniest stars be hidden from you. . . . Nay," he concludes, "let not your mind suffer itself to be confined by the limits of the earth, but let it range far beyond the boundaries of the world."

14. His lively interest in science, as he understood it, ranged Milton with the moderns in the then just beginning war between the defenders and assailants of the new doctrine of the progress of organic nature and the human mind. His rather transcendental ideas on that subject emerge in the Latin poem, *Naturam non Pati Senium* (That Nature is not Subject to Old Age). The occasion was a formal academic one and the subject may have been traditional; but it was timely in 1628, because—as Masson first pointed out—the preceding year had seen the publication of George Hakewell's *Apologie or Declaration of the Power of God in the Government of the World, Consisting in an Examination and Censure of the Common Errour Touching Nature's Perpetual and Universal Decay*. Milton's thought in the poem broadly resembles Hakewell's reasoning for the perpetuity of nature's powers. There can be no doubt that at this time also, however he may have felt when he wrote *Paradise Lost,* he agreed with Hakewell and with Bacon that modern men are the heirs and therefore the superiors of the ancients. The poem is a challenge to the contemporary view, which John Donne expressed when he said that God had put into the world, "a reproof, a rebuke, lest it should seem eternal, which is a sensible decay and age in the whole frame of the world and every piece thereof."[1] For more than half a century before Milton wrote, this traditional, theological view had been corroborated by the belief—which had a small foundation in the observations of astronomers—that the sun—to use Spenser's words in the prologue to the fifth book of *The Faerie Queene*—"is miscarried with the other spheres," and sunk fully thirty "minutes" lower in the skies than its position when the first accurate measurements of the heights of the heavenly bodies were taken by Ptolemy. It is this notion that *Naturam*

[1]Sermon xxxvi, folio of 1640.

non Pati Senium[1] assails with most gusto. The real issue in the debate, and the point upon which his ambition made him most sensitive, although his verses do not mention it, was the question whether modern men can hope to equal the ancients. Donne quoted St. Cyprian in support of the contrary opinion, and the poet Henry Vaughan, in *Corruption,* traced the progress of human decay down the centuries until now

> man is sunk below
> The center, and his shrowd.
> All's in deep sleep and night; thick darkness lyes
> And hatcheth o'er thy people.

15. Against such defeatism Milton's revolt was instinctive. It sprang from his conception of nature as well as from the pride which made him compare himself in *Paradise Lost* to Homer and Virgil and to "Tiresias and Phineus, Prophets old." His feeling about nature transpires in the Latin poems; especially in the vision of the world as flooded with light and colour in the first elegy and as animated by sex in the fifth, *In Adventum Veris* (On the Coming of Spring). No one who is curious about the origin of his lyric inspiration should fail to read that poem. Its beauty is like that of Botticelli's treatment of the same theme in the *Primavera,* his symbolic painting of spring. "No other poet," says M. Denis Saurat, "has ever been so close to a feeling of nature's fecundity." The feeling makes a bond between him and many of the artists and poets of Renaissance Italy. His candour in drawing the unreluctant nymph pursued by the satyr, in an elegy which opens with a glimpse of the cloven summit of Mount Parnassus and, beyond, of Olympus itself, suggests in its small way the pervading sense of sex as an animating force in nature which overflows in the poetry of Pontano, even in his great, cosmic, religious poem, the *Urania.* To a reader who is familiar with the Neo-Platonic allegories of the Celestial Venus who, as the principle of Concord, unites the universe—the allegories which inspire many of Spenser's cantos—there should be nothing

---

[1]Ll. 33–44.

surprising here. Spenser learned, and Milton perhaps instinctively understood, how to sympathize with the harmony
and fertility of nature as a force both physical and spiritual.
The feeling ramifies through all his undergraduate poetry.
Even in the lines,

> And then at last our bliss
> Full and perfect is,
> But now begins,

in *On the Morning of Christ's Nativity* Mr. Tillyard sees
"something of sex"; yet something which "does not disturb
and irritate as it had done shortly before in *Elegia Quinta*:
on the contrary, it animates, not usurping the mind but stimu-
lating many other feelings into delightful activity." In the
elegy the consciousness of sex hardly seems to me to amount
to a disturbance or an irritant; but rather to be quite consistent
with the implied admiration for the "gaudy trim" which
Nature lays aside in the first stanza of the poem so that
she may sympathize with her "great Master" in his extraordinary humiliation. It is taken for granted that normally she
would like to dress and "wanton with the Sun, her lusty
Paramour." Certainly, Mr. Tillyard is right in recognizing
something of sex in "the dance of the stanzas" and in other,
less definable elements in the poem. And—with a difference
—it can hardly be denied in the symbolism which concludes
both *Comus* and *Epitaphium Damonis,* where the mystic
marriage of the soul with God is the reward of earthly chastity.
The feeling in these passages touches various readers very
differently. Psychologically, the emotions of sex and their
conscious control are not very far apart. It is easy to interpret
the conclusions of both the masque and the dirge as either
hypocritical or morbid, and both charges have been brought.
Postponing their discussion, we may stop to notice that Milton's poetical resolution of the emotional and intellectual
tangle of sex is by way of the symbol of the divine wedding
dance. He describes it—with a deliberate mixture of pagan
and Christian imagery—as submerging the spirit of Charles

Diodati in an ecstasy as wide as the sky. And over the dancing choruses of heaven waves the thyrsos, the wand which was carried by the Bacchantes in the orgiastic rites of Dionysus.

16. In *Paradise Lost* the eternal world is constantly described in figures of dancing. Every day of festival there is kept by the heavenly host

> In Song and dance about the sacred Hill.

Their "mystical dance" was both a symbol and an actuality to Milton. Not, of course, a literal reality, but something no less real than the "dance of life" which Mr. Havelock Ellis sees patterning the world. In both cases the metaphors, different though they are, sprang from an intuition of the harmony of the universe, a sense of its challenge to the individual as a spectator and perhaps as an actor in the chorus. Ellis's metaphor embodies a lifetime of study of anthropology. Milton's was a consequence of interest in the most venerable of astronomical theories, but one which had assumed a new importance in his time. His cosmos was a dance and harmony and song because he more than half identified his heavenly choruses with "yonder starry Sphere Of Planets," in whose

> motions harmony Divine
> So smooths her charming tones, that God's own ear
> Listens delighted.[1]

Behind this passage in *Paradise Lost* lies Plato's comparison[2] of the figures made by the planets as they meet and wheel in their orbits to a dance. Milton knew that the conception of the planets and stars as composing a mighty chorus of song and dance went beyond Plato and back to Pythagoras. We may be sure also that his undergraduate reading included Plato's myth of the celestial sirens, which motivates the final movement in *Arcades;* and he would be certain to know the famous passage in the *Metaphysics*[3] where Aristotle quotes the opinion

---

[1] Bk. V, 625–7.
[2] *Timaeus*, 40 c.
[3] Bk. XIV, chap. viii.

of "the ancients" that the harmonious movements of the stars are due to an intelligence or divinity in every one of them. It was to Pythagoras that he really ascribed the idea, for in the second prolusion, *On the Music of the Spheres,* expressly, and in *At a Solemn Music* by clear implication, he declares that if men had "hearts so pure, so stainless, so snowy, as once Pythagoras had," not only would they hear the music of the revolving stars, but "then all things would return immediately, as it were, to the Golden Age; then, at last, freed from miseries, we would spend our time in peace, happy and envied even by the gods."

IV. *ON THE MORNING OF CHRIST'S NATIVITY*

17. The interest of the second prolusion is greatest in connection with *On the Morning of Christ's Nativity,* for the central movement of that poem turns upon the thought in the passage from *On the Music of the Spheres* which is translated above. In stanza xii Milton refers to the music of the spheres in language reminiscent of the account of the creation in Job,[1] "When the morning stars sang together, and all the sons of God shouted for joy";

> Such music (as 'tis said)
> Before was never made,
>   But when of old the Sons of morning sung.

Then he goes on to bid the spheres ring out in concert with the "Angelic symphony" and concludes that

>   if such holy song
>   Enwrap our fancy long,
>   Time will run back and fetch the Age of Gold.

If the "full and perfect" bliss of the eighteenth stanza suggests a delight more sensuous than transcendental, it is because the poem as a whole is shot through with a keen yet religious sense of physical beauty. There is nothing mystical

---

[1] Chap. xxxviii, 7.

in this, for Milton was the least mystical of religious poets; yet the feeling resembles that in Donne's casual reference in one of his sermons[1] to God as "spread as an universal honeycomb over all." A consciousness of imminent divinity hovers over the world; not confused with it in a vague pantheism; but descending upon it

> 'gainst that season comes,
> Wherein our Saviour's birth is celebrated;

and driving away all evil spirits, as Marcellus in *Hamlet* reminds his friends on the battlements that it was supposed to do at Christmas—

> So hallow'd and so gracious is the time.

18. The secret of the beauty of the "Hymn" is its unfolding of the traditional faith which Shakespeare poured into Marcellus' speech. Its real theme, however, is the Christian-Platonic one of Christ as the incarnate Word, the Logos of St. John's Gospel, whose advent means the return of Truth and Justice to men. It is the theme of *Paradise Regained*. Yet Milton's conception of Christ was still orthodox and Mr. Belloc does not misrepresent the quality of the poem when he says, "The ode to the *Nativity* might have been written by a warm Catholic from beginning to end." In every sense of the word it is Catholic. If it lacks the fervour of Southwell's *Burning Babe,* and of Vaughan's *Christ's Nativity,* it has the genuine devotion of Herbert's *Christmas:*

> The shepherds sing; and shall I silent be?
> My God, no hymne for Thee?

It is Catholic also in its treatment of nature as the willing servant of God, hiding her face in her master's presence while the sun dims "his inferior flame" when he sees

> a greater sun appear
> Than his bright Throne or burning Axletree could bear.

These are not mere conceits, to be swept aside as errors of taste, due to the malign influence upon the immature poet of

---

[1] Sermon xxvi, folio of 1649.

the extravagant treatment of the subject by Sylvester in his translation of Du Bartas' *Divine Weeks* and by Giles Fletcher in *Christ's Victory and Triumph on Earth and in Heaven.* They are a part of the theme itself, just as the wildness of the time is a part of it. Upon that topic alone the Italian, Baptista Mantuano, wasted a wealth of fancy in his *Parthenicae*[1]— burying the earth at the first Christmas deep under frost and snow as far south as remotest India.

19. The most Catholic of all the elements in the "Hymn" is the Christian Platonism of the twelfth and the following stanzas. The return to earth of Peace, and of Truth and Justice with Mercy sitting between them, owes something to the allegorical pageantry of the court masque and something to the medieval doctrine of the Four Daughters of God, to which Giles Fletcher gave fresh currency in *Christ's Victory in Heaven.* But the essence of these stanzas is Platonic. Milton thought of Justice as the platonizing Latin father of the Church, Lactantius, defined it: "Justice, which is nothing else than the pious and religious worship of the one God."[2] It was to restore such justice, Lactantius said, that God's son was sent into the world. Today his idea may seem strange, and it becomes stranger still when we find its full significance in a chapter of *The City of God*[3] where St. Augustine defines justice as giving to every one his due, and then asks: "What justice is that, then, that takes man from the true God, and gives him unto the condemned fiends?" At the coming of Christ, says Lactantius, in a long and eloquent passage which it is very likely that Milton had read, a sentence of banishment from their shrines was laid upon the evil spirits who had long masqueraded as the gods of the pagan world. Here is the beginning of Milton's great march into oblivion of the deities of Greece and Rome and Egypt and Asia, all of whom feel

> from Juda's land
> The dreaded Infant's hand.

---

[1] Bk. III, 1.
[2] *Divine Institutes,* Bk. V, chap. vii.
[3] Bk. XV, chap. xxi. Healey's translation.

And here also is the beginning of the folk belief about Christmas which Marcellus recollects:

> And then, they say, no spirit dare stir abroad,
> The nights are wholesome, then no planets strike,
> No fairy takes, nor witch hath power to charm.

20. It is not important to settle the exact degree to which
Milton accepted the traditional belief about the "bad spirits" or
fallen angels, which "our Schoolmen and other Divines" (as
Robert Burton observed[1]) held to have assumed the names and
honours of "those false gods of the Gentiles, which were adored
heretofore in several Idols, and gave Oracles at Delphos and
elsewhere." In the seventeenth century most men believed,
like Sir Thomas Browne, that at least "in a qualified sense" the
oracles "ceased or grew mute at the coming of Christ."[2]
Plutarch's essay *On the Cessation of the Oracles* was the main
bulwark of the tradition; but for centuries it had been curiously
integrated with Christian-Neo-Platonic doctrines. The Florentine translator of Plato, Marsilio Ficino, gathered all the
strands of the tradition together in his book *On the Christian
Religion,*[3] where he described Christ as the bringer of truth
and the banisher of errors, and then assembled countless
authorities for the historic credibility of the story of the cessation of the oracles at the Incarnation. The theme, long before
it reached Milton, had made its way into poetry as well as into
philosophy. Milton may have been familiar with its panoramic treatment in the *Apotheosis* of Prudentius, back in the
fourth century; and perhaps he was attracted by Tasso's
slighter development of it in the canzone on the Chapel of
the Nativity which Pope Sixtus V erected in the church of
Santa Maria Maggiore. It is idle to look for his "sources," for
literature was strewn with references to the cessation of the
oracles. To most minds the theme was still full of mystery
and poetry, but scepticism was beginning to throw it—for

---

[1] *Anatomy of Melancholy,* I, ii, 1, 2.
[2] *Vulgar Errors,* Bk. VII, chap. xii.
[3] Chap. xxii.

educated minds—into just the perspective necessary for Milton's romantic attitude. In the third book of Rabelais[1] Panurge had exhausted the subject with a delight in the lesser fry of deities—"lutins, lamies, lemures," *etc.*—which must have pleased Milton, if ever he condescended to read the Frenchman.

21. In spite of the almost epic motif of the banishing of the pagan gods, *On the Morning of Christ's Nativity* is not an epic, nor even an epyllion. It sets out to be a pastoral poem, and Professor Rand is surely right in relating it to Virgil's "Messianic Eclogue," *Pollio.* There, in a pastoral setting, Milton found a prophecy of the birth of a child who was to restore the Golden Age to the Roman world. Medieval writers had identified that child with Jesus. While he did not make that mistake, he felt that Virgil's theme was akin to his own and perhaps had dreams of rivalling Virgil in English on his own ground. The two poems are alike in being timed at the birth of the babe of destiny and in looking forward to his marvellous life; but there the resemblance ends. Milton's images owe little and his rhythms nothing to Virgil.

22. The writing of his "Hymn" was a great experience for the young man barely twenty-one years old. His short account of it to his schoolboy friend, Charles Diodati, towards the end of the sixth elegy, is full of excitement and of the consciousness of power. He did not realize to how great a degree he had found not only his vocation as a poet in English, but also the very themes which were to be the inspiration of his later work—the magnificent fallen angels surrounded by the prestige of their names and cults in the ancient world, and the Christ, the Platonic champion of truth, who was to be drawn large in *Paradise Regained.* He was happy, too, in the invention of a stanza with an alternation of short with longer lines, ending in a Spenserian alexandrine, just suited to the gay but stately dance of his thought. Not unnaturally, he made the mistake of supposing that if one solemn day in the Christian year could evoke such music from him, another still more

---

[1]Chap. xxiv.

solemn would move him even more deeply. During Lent in
1630 he seems to have attempted *The Passion* and to have
suffered a disappointment when his imagination failed to
kindle. The poem opened with the same seven-lined stanza
of iambic pentameters with interlaced rhymes—full of the
luscious prettiness of Fletcher's *Christ's Victorie and Triumph*
—that he had used in the prelude to the "Hymn," but no
organ music followed. He laid the fragment aside and was
soon experimenting again with more congenial themes—with
Il Penseroso and *L'Allegro,* perhaps, or with *At a Solemn
Music* and *On Time,* and perhaps also, in the years before he
left Cambridge, with *Arcades.*

V. *ARCADES* AND *COMUS*

23. A convincing date for *Arcades* is hard to find. Its situation and appearance in the Cambridge manuscript make any
time from 1630 to 1633 possible. Its obvious points of kin-
ship to *Comus* incline me to put it late; but there is a point in
favour of placing it in 1630 in the occurrence in that year of
the seventieth birthday of the lady who was honoured—Alice
Spencer, the Countess Dowager of Derby. She was a distant
relative of the poet Edmund Spenser, and in his pastoral poem,
Colin Clouts Come Home Again, she appears as Amaryllis,
evidently the woman whom he most admired among the
nymphs attending upon the goddess Cynthia. Cynthia, or
Diana, was, of course, the virgin queen, Elizabeth. When
Spenser's poem was written in 1595 Alice Spencer was a
woman of thirty-five; and the recent death of her husband, the
Earl of Derby, better known as Lord Strange, allowed him to
describe her as

> freed from Cupids yoke by fate,
> Since which she doth new bands adventure dread.

Her dread did not prevent her from afterwards marrying Sir
Thomas Egerton, Lord Keeper of the Seal and later Lord
Chancellor. She was no stranger, then, to scenes like that

where Milton placed her with "some noble persons of her Family . . . in a pastoral habit" moving toward her with the song of recognition:

This this is she.

The words seem like an echo from Ben Jonson's *The Satyr*—the very similar entertainment for the welcome of Queen Anne to the grounds of Sir Robert Spencer at Althorpe in 1603. The lyrics in *Arcades* certainly owe much of their limpid beauty to Jonson's songs in his masques generally. They were sung in the open air, probably by young people, among whom may have been Lady Alice Egerton, who was to appear as the Lady in *Comus* in 1634. Then she was a girl not yet fifteen. If Milton was living at Horton at the time and had an acquaintance with the Egerton family on the estate at Harefield, less than a dozen miles away, he may have known several members of the chorus. Many of the singers must have been pupils of his friend, the musician, Henry Lawes, for he was long employed as music-master in the household of the Countess's stepson, Sir John Egerton, the Earl of Bridgewater. *Arcades* must have been written at Lawes' instigation. It is safe to assume that he appeared as the Genius of the Wood, singing of the heavenly sirens and the music of the spheres, for he was also the Attendant Spirit in *Comus*. He had a great reputation in such roles. Thinking of them and of his work as a composer, Robert Herrick mourned his death in 1662:

brave man! whose numbers have been hurled,
And no less praised than spread throughout the world.
Some have thee called Amphion, some of us
Named thee Terpander, or sweet Orpheus;
Some this, some that; but all in this agree,
Music had both her birth and death with thee.

24. It is Lawes to whom we owe *Comus*. He asked Milton to write the libretto of an entertainment for him to perform with Sir Thomas Egerton's children in honour of their father's

installation at Ludlow Castle as Lord President of Wales.
Lawes wrote the music of the songs and he was responsible
for the stage directions in the stage copy, which are those of
the first edition in 1637, and of its innumerable successors. In
1637 it was called simply *A Maske*. The name by which we
know it dates from the eighteenth century. Lawes was the
producer, and Milton was not present at the performance nor,
probably, at any rehearsals. For the actors—a girl hardly
fifteen and two much younger boys, her brothers—Lawes
mercifully cut several of the longer speeches. The audience
gathered in the great hall of the castle might have been a
little restive under the declamation of so many speeches
markedly longer than those in the masques which Ben Jonson
had furnished for the court of King James. It is safe to assume that they were not restive under what they heard and
that the verdict was something like Sir Henry Wotton's when
he read *Comus* complete in 1637; "ipsa mollities"—"sweetness
itself." Dr. Johnson's dictum of "inelegantly splendid and
tediously instructive" would have astonished Wotton, though
it may not surprise many of the readers of the present edition
of Milton's poems.

25. The audience at Ludlow was prepared for something
which would allegorize the triumph of Virtue over Vice.
Milton's seriousness may have been a little disturbing, but it
is a question whether there is anything really incompatible
with the principles of the court masque in his idealistic treatment of the theme which Jonson handled so differently in
Pleasure Reconciled to Virtue. Of course, Milton's public
had no difficulties with his pastoral background and supernatural atmosphere and half-allegorical characters. Those
"unrealities" were far more prominent, for example, in Beaumont's *Masque of the Gentlemen of Grayes Inne, and the
Inner Temple;* which John Milton, Sr., as a member of the
bar, may have seen at its first performance in 1615, as well as
in Jonson's *Pleasure Reconciled to Virtue* in 1613. In Beaumont's masque and in Jonson's *Neptune's Triumph* the
pageantry included the actual appearance of the "blue-hair'd

Deities" to which Milton's Attendant Spirit merely alludes. Indeed, the whole rout of major gods from Olympus might be expected to come frankly forward, as they did in Jonson's *The Penates;* and instead of Milton's lone nymph, Sabrina, there would have been nothing strange in the appearance of all the daughters of Oceanus, who actually lighted their father's path onto the great scene which Inigo Jones designed at Whitehall for Jonson's *Masque of Blacknesse.* Milton did not have to contend with the dubious collaboration of a royal architect holding an almost unlimited warrant on a royal treasury. Collaboration with a royal musician was another matter. It gave an opportunity for the development of the lyrics which Jonson would have envied. Milton was free—as Miss Welsford has pointed out—to write something larger than a typical masque—something between a masque and a play, like Shirley's *The Triumph of Beauty.* He could write speeches in a dramatic blank verse full of reminiscences of Shakespeare; and he could experiment with some of the devices of Greek tragedy—notably, the initial declaration by a presiding divinity. The Attendant Spirit's introduction of himself and of the situation has loose parallels in the opening soliloquy or address to the audience by Dionysus in the *Bacchae* and by Apollo in the *Alcestis* and by other deities in several other plays of Euripides. Milton's setting can hardly have been so magnificent as the splendid scenes erected for the masques at the Inns of Court and at Whitehall, but his poetry—like Shakespeare's—created its own scenery among "the perplex't paths" of the "drear Wood," where the Attendant Spirit finds Comus and his victims.

26. The scene as well as the plot has much in common with Spenser's world. The "drear Wood" is like the "wandring wood" where Una strayed into an enchanter's power with the Redcross Knight. The Lady falls into Comus' hands as Amoret does into those of the enchanter, Busyrane; and like Amoret she is disenchanted at the sword's point. Sabrina's part in the disenchanting has no counterpart in *The Faerie Queene;* but—like many other features of *Comus*—it more or

less resembles an incident of frequent occurrence in a wide range of romantic literature, such as the purification of lust's victims by the water from Clorin's well in Fletcher's *The Faithful Shepherdess* and the disenchanting of Burd Ellen with lustral water in the story of Childe Rowland. On the whole, however, although there is good ground for the claims which have been advanced for Peele's *Old Wives Tale* and for William Drury's *Alveredus* as influences upon *Comus,* the pervasive influence is Spenser's; for it was mainly from his "sage and serious Spenser" that Milton learned how to use the story of Circe's son.

27. A Circe figured in most of the famous romances of the Renaissance. In *The Faerie Queene* she is Acrasia. In Tasso's *Jerusalem Delivered* she is Armida. In Ariosto's *Orlando Furioso* and in Boiardo's *Orlando Innamorato* she is the enchantress Alcina. Always she is an embodiment, not of lust, but of intemperance or incontinence in the broadest and most philosophical sense. The story in the *Odyssey* of the transformation of Ulysses' men into swine had become an allegory—as Milton put it in his seventh prolusion—of the failure of the soul's "ethereal vigour." Then, he says, with a boy's idealism, "let it lay aside the human; surely it will become familiar with the Circean cup. Stooping, let it migrate to the beasts." By making Comus Circe's son he intended to invest him with all her charm. It was by no chance or blunder that Comus became the "delicate enchanter" whose loveliness delighted Sir Walter A. Raleigh. A strange failure to understand the spirit of the traditional allegory has prompted the protest that he is lovelier than he ought to be—as if the poet who made him more attractive than the jovial Comus of Ben Jonson's *Pleasure Reconciled to Virtue* had no right to treat him less tolerantly than Jonson did. If only to carry out his plot, Milton had to be stern with him; just as Spenser was stern with Acrasia, whose

> pleasant bowres and Pallace brave,
> *Guyon* broke downe, with rigour pittilesse.

28. It is, then, no accident or flaw in conception that the most moving speech in *Comus* is the appeal to the Lady not to be cruel

> to those dainty limbs which nature lent
> For gentle usage and soft delicacy.

To some readers its power has seemed to be related to some latent personal feeling. The analogy of the argument for the free enjoyment of Nature's "odours, fruits and flocks" with a parallel passage in *The Muses' Looking Glass*[1] suggested to Mr. John S. Smart that Milton had the dissolute poet "Randolph and his favourite doctrines and practice in view, and intended an answer or criticism—in other words, that Randolph is Comus and the Lady is Milton replying to him." Yet I hardly think that the enchanter spoke for Thomas Randolph, although his creator may have felt him as a symbol of all the Cambridge undergraduates whom he called "rough satyrs" in *Lycidas*. He is no mere abstraction, yet he can hardly be the portrait or the herald of any individual. The beauty of the scenes where he speaks springs from their perfect fusion of two traditional elements. One of them was the antimasque, which Jonson invented to give variety to his masques and to furnish a foil for the tableaux where Love triumphed, or some lovely abstraction, personified in some marvellously costumed magnate of the realm, rose serene above the scattered minions of darkness. Good examples are the dance of monsters or antics like the tarantella of witches in the *Masque of Queens,* or like the "Follies, which were twelve She-Fools," in *Love Freed from Folly*. Comus is the choragus of an antimasque and the reader, if he has never been fortunate enough to see Milton's entertainment presented, should think of him as such when he appears at the head of his "rout of Monsters." The second and no less important element which went to his creation was those very sentiments which, as we have seen, had been expressed in similar language in *The Muses' Looking Glass*. Randolph put them into the mouth of a character

---

[1] Act II, scene iii.

named Kolax, *i. e.,* the flatterer. Milton put them into the mouth of a most accomplished flatterer. For a very long time they had been in the mouths of flatterers. One of them was the Circe-like fairy Phaedria whom Spenser has lure the heady knight, Cymochles, to her island paradise. While he slept in her lap she sang to him about Nature's neglected wealth;

> The lilly, Ladie of the flowring field,
> The Flowre-deluce, her louely Paramoure,
> Bid thee to them thy fruitlesse labours yield,
> And soone leaue off this toylesome wearie stoure.

> *   *   *   *   *   *   *   *   *

> Why then dost thou, O man, that of them all
> Art Lord, and eke of nature Soueraine,
> Wilfully make thy selfe a wretched thrall,
> And wast thy ioyous houres in needlesse paine?[1]

Such lines as these give us a key to the depth of beauty in Comus' appeal to the Lady. His voice is the last on the popular side in a great, medieval debate which—as Paul Shorey pointed out, and as Milton may well have been aware—went back as far as Porphyry's book *On Abstinence.*[2]

29. Few readers disagree with Raleigh about Comus; "What a ravishing lyric strain he is master of!" And for condemning him they, like Raleigh, accuse Milton of having "that severe and self-centred ideal of life and character which is called Puritanism." In his treatment of Comus, as we have seen, Milton was less severe than Spenser was with Acrasia; and it may be added that he was immeasurably less of a Puritan than the Flemish Catholic, Erycius Puteanus, whose *De Luxu Conviviorum* (On the Orgy of the Boon Companions) is often mentioned as one of his "sources." Puteanus indulged in a very didactic, though also a very amusing and realistic vision of the old god of revelling, Comus, whose figure, sodden with feasting as Philostratus had drawn it long ago in his *Images,*

---

[1]*Faerie Queene,* II, vi, 16 (1–4) and 17 (1–4).
[2]*De Abstinentia.* I, 16–17.

was familiar to every educated European of the seventeenth century. In *Comus* Milton's Puritanism is one with his Platonism. The conflict between the good and the beautiful was resolved for him in the vision of the good as so actual as to be all but perceptible, "visibly," as the Lady thought that she saw "pure-ey'd Faith, white-handed Hope," and the "unblemished form of Chastity." Her language was not conventional or sentimental. When Milton wrote the lines, he was thinking of the sixth book of the *Republic,* where Plato reasons that Justice, and by implication all the virtues, are not mere negations of our positive impulses; but are vital entities such as the mind of an artist projects; and that even though they are its creatures, the human spirit can live under their control. The result of surrender to them Milton, like Spenser, would have called by the name of the virtue of Temperance, and he would have agreed with Plato that it is the great source of human happiness. In *The Faerie Queene,* Book III, Canto vi, Spenser tried to embody his Platonism in an elaborate version of the myth of Venus and Adonis—making the Celestial Aphrodite or Heavenly Venus a symbol of the positive virtue of chastity, and her garden, the garden of Adonis, a symbol of the empire of the creative love which uses but transcends the senses. In that garden Psyche lives with Cupid

> and hath him borne a chyld,
> *Pleasure,* that doth both gods and men aggrate.

It was of Spenser's garden that Milton thought when he wrote the Attendant Spirit's epilogue about "the gardens fair of Hesperus . . . Where young Adonis oft reposes," and where the entranced Celestial Cupid holds Psyche in his arms—Psyche, from whose

> fair unspotted side
> Two blissful twins are to be born,
> Youth and Joy, so Jove hath sworn.

To Lawes, who chose in the stage version to begin his performance with this song, and to Milton's public generally, we may presume that it was a more ravishing strain than that of which Comus was the master.

30. Professor Hanford has pointed out the relation of the Spirit's epilogue—where, "if Milton's classic taste prevents him from concluding with an allusion to the Lamb and his eternal bride, it is because there is no need"—to the allusion to the celestial marriage of the soul in the closing lines of *Epitaphium Damonis*. Recent criticism has pronounced the *Epitaph* "hyperbolical and morbid" and granted short shrift to the "mystical rapture" and "apocalyptic fury" of its ending. Because in heaven Diodati hears the song which St. John in the Apocalypse said could be learned only by those "which were not defiled with women," and because Milton alluded to that scripture in *At a Solemn Music,* it has been urged—too confidently, I believe—that at Horton the chastity of which he boasted in *Smectymnuus* was negative and morbid. He is supposed to have had a kind of faith in "the magical power of chastity"—a mixture of Stoic pleasure in the repression of the passions with a primitive savage's confidence in some supernatural force accruing from abstinence—or he is regarded as having paid the price of his self-regarding purity by emotional servitude to Christian dogmas and symbols which were alien to his nature. The sentence of morbidity is a hard penalty to make him pay for any exaggeration of which he may have been guilty in an entertainment whose whole tradition was for that kind of thing. No one should expect *Comus* to have the genial romantic atmosphere of *The Winter's Tale*. As a matter of fact, its ideal of chastity is not very far from that of *The Tempest*. Spenser's doctrine in the canto of which the Spirit's epilogue is a reminiscence is anything but negative. In *Smectymnuus,* which was written on the eve of his marriage, it is true that he says he did not "slumber over that place expressing such high rewards of ever accompanying the Lamb, with those celestial songs to others inapprehensible, but not to those who were not defiled with women"; but he concludes that "marriage must not be called a defilement." Allowance must be made for the circumstances in which these

passages were written, in *Comus* no less than in the *Epitaph*. In both the *Epitaph* and *Lycidas* he mourned a friend who had died unmarried and perhaps frustrated in his hope of marriage. From the time when Virgil deified the dead Caesar, every elegy inevitably ended with a vision of the departed in the life beyond life—either a deification or a canonization, or a deliberate fusion of the two, like Spenser's glimpse of a young girl whom he mourned, in the skies, "a goddesse now emong the saintes." Neither Diodati (Damon) nor King (Lycidas) could fail of that reward. There is no more compulsion to read a hint of morbidity into the "unexpressive nuptial Song" which they hear than there is for reading it into Lord Herbert of Cherbury's expectation, in his *Epitaph for Himself,* that

> his immortal soul should find above,
> With his Creator, peace, joy, faith and love.

VI. *LYCIDAS*

31. *Lycidas,* as every critic since Dr. Johnson has said, was not inspired by any very deep grief for Edward King. In spite of the pastoral picture of the life which Milton shared with him at Cambridge, "nursed upon the self-same hill," there cannot have been much intimacy between the two. King was the younger and he stayed at the University, while Milton went to Horton. As the older man, disappointed of a fellowship, while the younger had obtained one, it is possible that he showed real magnanimity in consenting to contribute to the proposed volume of elegies the poem to which the Cambridge manuscript testifies that he must have devoted many hours in the November of 1637. On the other hand, in *Epitaphium Damonis* he felt the grief which is often blamed for the artistic weakness of the poem. The friendship with Charles Diodati had begun at St. Paul's School. It had survived the separation when Diodati went to Oxford, and later to the neighbourhood of Bristol to live. Two of the Latin elegies and several of the Familiar Letters attest its warmth; and there is no mistaking the tone of the letter to the Floren-

tine nobleman, Carolo Diodati, nearly ten years after the
Italian *wanderjahr* had ended with the discovery that his
friend had died in his absence. The contrast between the
regret over King's death and his sorrow for Diodati must
have been very great. Yet it does not follow that the *Epitaph*
fails because the poet's emotions were out of control while
Lycidas succeeds because he had them well in hand. The
emotion in *Lycidas* is even more overwhelming than that in
the *Epitaph,* and it is of a more personal kind.

32. Formally, King's death was the subject; but not merely
King's death, for Milton added a note to say that the poem
foretold "the ruin of our corrupted Clergy, then in their
height." The famous digression, ending with the threat of
the "two-handed engine at the door," was no intrusion on the
original design. It is too central for that. Nor is it a merely
partisan outburst, for its real theme was the universal one of
the betrayal of their trust by the educated. Satire of the
clergy had long been a recognized feature of Renaissance
pastoral poetry. It went back to Clement Marot in France
and beyond him to the ecclesiastical satire of Boccaccio and
Petrarch. If it has the taint of partisanship about it in work
like Spenser's *Shepheardes Calendar* and *Mother Hubberds
Tale,* it is redeemed there by motives of real patriotism. So it
is, more clearly, in *Lycidas.* Milton placed it in a context
of mourning for death—not merely King's death, but that of
all noble youth—and invested it with tragic quality. England
is betrayed by her intellectuals and premature death snatches
away the saving remnant among them. In itself King's loss
seemed merely pathetic to Milton. When he speaks of it, as
he does in the fourth and fifth paragraphs, he falls back upon
the "pathetic fallacy" of the woods and caves and trees and
flowers mourning it, as they mourn in Theocritus' first idyl for
the death of Daphnis. Like Theocritus, he reproaches the
nymphs for allowing the accident to happen. And later, after
the "dread voice" has spoken, he returns in the seventh paragraph to King's pathetic death with another of those pastoral
conventions which Dr. Johnson called "easy, vulgar, and

therefore disgusting." It is the catalogue of flowers that strew the "laureate hearse," and it merges into the Miltonic vista of the Irish Sea and of Namancos and Bayona's hold on the far-off Spanish coast.

33. From another point of view, Milton himself is the subject of *Lycidas*. His allusion to "my destined urn" betrays his fear of the disappointment of death on the threshold of the career for which he had so carefully prepared. Perhaps in the closing lines of the poem there is an allusion to the coming Italian journey. The form of the elegy, with its irregular lines and free rhyming, so like an Italian canzone, suggests that in imagination Milton was already in Italy. But to go there in the flesh he must cross the Channel and make the dangerous Mediterranean voyage from Marseilles to Genoa which Sir Henry Wotton advised, and which he finally decided to avoid. Twice, perhaps four times, he must risk King's fate. With death perhaps imminent, he might well ask what it boots to live the life of "labour and intense study" which he pursued at Horton. That is his very personal question to answer in *Lycidas;* but his preoccupation with himself does not seem to throw the poem off its proper centre, as it does in *Epitaphium Damonis*. There he is importuned by memories of his successes in the academies of Florence and Rome. "What a man I was on the banks of the Arno," he cries to the ghost of his dead friend. The poem is full of recollections of aborted literary hopes and imperfect prospects of new epic work ahead. In *Epitaphium Damonis* these conflicts are not resolved, but in *Lycidas* Milton rose above them on the wings of his life-long conviction that

> Fame is no plant that grows on mortal soil.

In the Imaginary Conversation between Andrew Marvell and Bishop Parker, Landor must have been thinking of this passage when he made Marvell boast of Milton's services to England and to the world that they are "hardly yet begun; and no mortal man, no series of transitory generations, can repay them. God will not delegate this; no, not even to his angels."

The beauty of *Lycidas* is that it makes this hyperbolical praise seem inadequate, and even a little unfair to Milton in the mood in which he wrote the poem.

VII. THE PRESENT EDITION

34. For the facts about Milton's life between the composition of *Epitaphium Damonis* and that of *Paradise Regained* the reader may turn to Mr. Tillyard's critical study or to Mr. Alden Sampson's essay. In the present series of editions their treatment belongs to the introduction of a forthcoming volume of selections from the prose works. The record of those years is partly written in the later sonnets and there are some flashes of light upon them in the bitter verses from the controversial prose which are included here. The group of Psalms which were translated in 1648—to take the place of the standard version of Sternhold and Hopkins in the churches—and the later group, which Milton said that he undertook for spiritual and poetical discipline, have their value too. They reveal him as an enthusiastic reader of the Hebrew Bible, but indicate that his conceptions of its language were coloured by the Vulgate and also by the many versions of the Psalms done into English during his own century and the sixteenth. And they occasionally betray his sense of his own isolation and blindness, which comes out, for example, in the twist of the passage in Psalm vi, 7—"Mine eye is consumed because of grief"—into

> But cloud instead and ever-during dark
> Surrounds me.

35. Professor Grierson did a great service in his beautiful edition of Milton's poems in 1925 in arranging them for the first time as nearly as possible in chronological order. Of course, their chronology can never be fixed with perfect finality and already—as we have seen—there is reason for putting *L'Allegro* and *Il Penseroso* earlier than Professor Grierson did. Mr. Hanford and Mr. Tillyard have modified several other

tentative dates. Lately Mr. W. R. Parker has supported an
early date for the translation of the fifth ode of Horace, which
stands in a novel position in this volume. Personally, I have
always believed that it was a school or college exercise. The
evidence is not final and no editor can be dogmatic about
many of the chronological questions which arise about Milton's
work. If those who follow where Professor Grierson was the
pioneer sometimes differ from him and from one another, the
reader should be excited, not perturbed.

36. Professor Grierson's arrangement has its disadvantages.
The result is very unlike the little volume which Milton issued
in 1645 with *On the Morning of Christ's Nativity* leading and
A Maske (*Comus*) closing the file of English poems.
Although the spelling has been modernized—except for a few
words which it has seemed well to keep in the form in which
Milton used them—and although the punctuation has been
cautiously and conservatively modernized also, I have tried to
preserve all that I could of the original editions. Milton's
elisions, it is now well known, do not mean the absolute
omission of a syllable; but even readers who are new to his
poetry, if they like to read it aloud or hear it distinctly with the
inner ear, will understand how to interpret them and make
them help in interpreting the scansion.

37. The notes to this volume have been written *con amore,*
but they are intended for the reader to use or neglect as his
mood and need may suggest. Milton's poetry abounds with
passages like

> Dear son of Memory, great heir of fame;

which, as Mr. Belloc says, "wants unravelling and checks the
flow; thousands quote it who could not tell you what it
means." Many of these passages can easily be unravelled, and
an editor who undertakes the task need not necessarily be
one of those who, as Dr. Johnson said, "cannot bear to think
themselves ignorant of that which, at last, neither diligence
nor sagacity can discover." Milton was the most reminiscent of poets and I have tried to suggest the directions in

which his memory played—sometimes over ancient and sometimes over medieval and contemporary literature. If any of
his readers keeps a Homer and Virgil, and a copy of Hesiod's
Theogony and Ovid's *Metamorphoses* at hand—either in the
original Greek or Latin or in English translation—and sometimes wanders into the context of one of his allusions, his
ghost will not turn. In countless cases, however, he is his
own best commentator, and I have tried to remember that
wherever possible an editor's business is to let him speak for
himself.

38. In conclusion I should like to thank my colleague, Professor George R. Potter, and my friend, Professor Percy H.
Houston, for criticism by which the Introduction has profited.
I am deeply indebted also to my pupils, Mr. Maurice P. Cun-
ningham and Mr. Robert Orem, for their generous help in
checking over the manuscript and correcting the proof; and to
Mrs. J. M. D. Olmsted for suggestions about the rendering of
the most difficult passages in the Latin and Greek poems. My
greatest debt, however, is to Professor Allan H. Gilbert of
Duke University for his generous criticism of the notes and
introduction while they were passing through the press. The
knowledge and kindness of William Ellery Leonard are responsible for the changes in my treatment of some metrical
problems in the text and notes of the second printing.

A LIST OF THE ABBREVIATIONS USED IN THE BIBLIOGRAPHY AND IN THE NOTES TO THE SEVERAL POEMS

Abbott: *A Shakespearian Grammar,* by E. A. Abbott. London. 1909.

Aen.: Virgil's *Aeneid.*

Anatomy: Robert Burton's *Anatomy of Melancholy.*

Animadversions: Animadversions upon the Remonstrant's Defence against Smectymnuus.

Antiquities: Flavius Josephus' *Antiquities of the Jews.*

du Bartas: *The Divine Weekes* of Guillaume de Salluste, sieur du Bartas, translated by Joshua Sylvester. London. 1605.

C.D.: Milton's *De Doctrina Christiana,* in the translation of Bishop Sumner as revised in the edition of Milton's *Prose Works* in Bohn's Standard Library.

Conti: Natalis Comitis *Mythologiae.* Frankfurt, 1596.

Doctrine of Divorce: The Doctrine and Discipline of Divorce, etc. The second edition, 1644, is used.

Dunster: *Paradise Regained . . .* with Notes of Various Authors, by Charles Dunster. London. 1800.

F.Q.: Spenser's *Faerie Queene.*

Gilbert: *A Geographical Dictionary of Milton,* by Allan H. Gilbert. Yale University Press. 1919.

Il.: Homer's *Iliad.*

Inf.: Dante's *Inferno.*

J.D.: Torquato Tasso's *Jerusalem Delivered.* Quotations are from Edward Fairfax's translation, edited by L'Estrange, Dublin, 1726.

J.E.G.P.: Journal of English and Germanic Philology.

Jerram: *Paradise Regained . . .* Edited with an Introduction and Notes by C. S. Jerram. London. 1877.

Keightley: *The Poems of John Milton, with Notes*, by T. Keightley. London. 1859. 2 Vols.

L.Q.R.: London Quarterly Review.

Masson: *The Poetical Works of John Milton, with Memoir, Introductions, Notes, and an Essay on Milton's Versification.* Edited by David Masson. London. 1894. 3 Vols. (First published 1874.)

Met.: Ovid's *Metamorphoses.*

M.L.N.: Modern Language Notes.

M.L.R.: Modern Language Review.

Moody: *The Complete Poetical Works of John Milton.* Edited by William Vaughan Moody. Boston. 1899.

N.E.D.: New English Dictionary.

Newton: *The Complete Poetical Works of John Milton, with a Life of the Poet and Notes on his Works*, by Thomas Newton. London. 1749–52.

Od.: Homer's *Odyssey.*

O.F.: Ludovico Ariosto's *Orlando Furioso.*

Of Reformation: Of Reformation in England.

Percival: *Samson Agonistes . . .* Edited by H. M. Percival. London. 1916.

Pilgrimes: Purchas his Pilgrimes. London, 1625. Reprinted at Glasgow, 1905–7.

P.L.: Paradise Lost.

*P.M.L.A.: Publications of the Modern Language **Association** of America.*

P.R.: Paradise Regained.

P.Q.: Philological Quarterly.

P.W.: The *Prose Works* of Milton in the Bohn *Standard Library.* So far as possible references to Milton's prose are made by book and chapter.

S.A.: Samson Agonistes.

S.C.: Spenser's *Shepheardes Calendar.*

Smart: *The Sonnets of Milton, with an Introduction and Notes.* By John S. Smart. Glasgow. 1921.

S.P.: Studies in Philology.

Todd: *The Poetical Works of John Milton.* Edited by H. J.
  Todd. Fourth edition. London. 1842. 4 Vols. (First
  published, 1801.)

Travels: George Sandys' *Travels.* Seventh edition. London.
  1673. (First published, 1615.)

Warton: Thomas Warton's edition of *Poems upon Several
  Occasions, English, Italian, and Latin,* by John Milton, London, 1785.

Abbreviations of the books of the Bible are those used
in Alexander Cruden's *Complete Concordance to the Holy
Scriptures.*

BIBLIOGRAPHY

I. BIBLIOGRAPHIES AND BOOKS OF REFERENCE

Bradshaw, John, *A Concordance to the Poetical Works of John Milton*. London. 1894.

Cooper, Lane, *A Concordance to the Latin, Greek and Italian Poems of John Milton*. Halle. 1923.

Gilbert, Allan H., *A Geographical Dictionary of Milton*. Yale University Press. 1919.

Lockwood, Laura E., *Lexicon to the English Poetical Works of John Milton*. New York. 1907.

Osgood, Charles G., *The Classical Mythology of Milton's English Poems*. New York. 1900. Reprinted, Oxford. 1925.

Stevens, David H., *Reference Guide to Milton from 1800 to the Present Day*. University of Chicago Press. 1930.

Thompson, Elbert N. S., *John Milton: Topical Bibliography*. New Haven. 1916.

II. MODERN BIOGRAPHY, CRITICISM, AND STUDY OF MILTON'S MILIEU

Agar, H., *Milton and Plato*. Princeton University Press. 1931.

Bailey, John C., *Milton*. London and New York. 1915. "The Home University Library."

Baum, Paull F., "The New Milton." *Freeman*, V, 225–8.

Belloc, Hilaire, *Milton*. London and Philadelphia. 1935.

Valuable in spite of the perpetuation of some old errors of fact and the indulgence of many prejudices.

Birrell, Augustine, *Obiter Dicta*. Second Series. New York. 1891. "Milton," pp. 1–51.

Bridges, Robert, *Milton's Prosody: with a Chapter on Accentual Verse, and Notes.* Revised Edition. Oxford University Press. 1921.

Bush, Douglas, *Mythology and the Renaissance Tradition.* University of Minnesota Press. 1932.

The chapter on Milton is an indispensable supplement to the traditional annotation of his mythology.

Collins, John C., "Miltonic Myths and their Authors," in *Studies in Poetry and Criticism.* London. 1905.

Cory, Herbert E., *Spenser, the School of the Fletchers and Milton. University of California Publications, Modern Philology.* 1912.

Garnett, Richard, *Life of John Milton.* London. 1890 and 1900.

Grierson, H. J. C., "John Milton: The Man and the Poet," in *Cross Currents in English Literature of the XVIIth Century.* London. 1929.

"John Milton," in *The Criterion,* VIII, pp. 7–26 and 240–57.

Hanford, James H., "The Chronology of Milton's Private Studies," in *P.M.L.A.,* XXXVI, pp. 251–314.

"The Youth of Milton: An Interpretation of his Early Literary Development," in *Studies in Shakespeare, Milton and Donne. University of Michigan Publications. Language and Literature,* I, pp. 89–163.

One of the most valuable recent studies.

"Milton and the Return to Humanism," in *S.P.,* XVI, pp. 126–47.

"Creative Personality: the Case of John Milton," in *Johns Hopkins Alumni Magazine,* XV, pp. 328–52.

A Milton Handbook. New York. 1926.

Herford, Charles, "Dante and Milton," in *The Post-War Mind of Germany and Other European Studies.* Oxford. 1927.

Jenks, Tudor, *In the Days of Milton.* New York. 1905.

Sketches of Milton's England

Jones, Richard, "The Background of the 'Battle of the Books',"
   in *Washington University Studies, Humanistic Series,* VII,
   No. 2.

   Touches Milton's interest in science and "progress."

Langdon, Ida, *Milton's Theory of Poetry and Fine Art.*   Yale
   University Press.   1924.
Larson, Martin A., "Milton's Essential Relationship to Puritan-
   ism and Stoicism," in *P.Q.,* VI, pp. 201–20.
Leach, A. F., "Milton as Schoolboy and Schoolmaster," in *Pro-
   ceedings of the British Academy,* III, pp. 295–318.
Liljegren, S. B., "Miltonic Philosophy in the Light of Recent
   Research," in *Scandinavian Scientific Review,* II, pp. 114–23.
   Studies in Milton.   Lund.   1919.

   The most considerable attack upon Milton as a Stoic, Calvinist
   and Machiavellian.

Lockwood, Laura E., "Milton's Corrections to the Minor
   Poems," in *M.L.N.,* XXV, 201–5.
Macaulay, Rose, *Milton.*   "Great Lives."   London.   1934.
Mackail, J. W., *The Springs of Helicon.*   London.   1909.

   Milton's use of the classics.

Masson, David, *The Life of Milton.*   London, 1859–94.
   7 Vols., the first revised in 1881.

   Still the richest collection of facts about Milton's life and times.

Masterman, J. H. B., *The Age of Milton.*   London.   1897.

   A good survey of Milton's literary milieu.   Six editions, the last
   in 1911.

Parker, W. R., "Some Problems in the Chronology of Milton's
   Early Poems," in *The Review of English Studies,* XI, 276–83.
Pattison, Mark, *Milton.*   English Men of Letters Series.

   First published in 1879 and often reprinted.   An outstanding
   study.

Pommerich, F., *Miltons Verhältnis zu Torquato Tasso.* Halle. 1902.

Pompen, Fr. R., "Recent Theories about Milton's Personality," in *Neophilologus,* VII, 272–9.

Refutation of the theories represented by S. B. Liljegren.

Raleigh, Sir Walter A., *Milton.* New York & London. 1900.

Raymond, Dora N., *Oliver's Secretary.* New York. 1932.

Sampson, Alden, *Studies in Milton.* New York. 1913. "From *Lycidas* to *Paradise Lost,*" pp. 1–163, is the main essay.

Saurat, Denis, *Milton: Man and Thinker.* New York. 1925.

A frequently misleading but exciting and original analysis of Milton's thinking in the light of a few of its neglected sources.

Schirmer, Walter F., *Antike, Renaissance und Puritanismus.* Munich. 1933. Second Edition, enlarged.

English culture in the sixteenth and seventeenth centuries analysed with considerable reference to Milton.

Sherburn, George W., "The Early Popularity of Milton's Minor Poems," in *Modern Philology,* XVII, pp. 259–78, and 515–40.

Spaeth, Sigmund G., *Milton's Knowledge of Music.* Sohn, Weimar. 1913.

An interesting and scholarly treatment of a side of Milton about which modern criticism is still chaotic.

Stern, Alfred, *Milton und seine Zeit.* Leipsic. 1877–9. 2 Vols.

A standard work and valuable supplement to Masson.

Stoll, Elmer E., "Milton, Puritan of the Seventeenth Century," in *Poets and Playwrights.* University of Minnesota Press. 1930.

A fine contribution to the problem of Milton's Puritanism *vs* his Humanism and Romanticism.

Thompson, Elbert N. S., "Mysticism in Seventeenth-Century English Literature," in *S.P.,* XVIII, pp. 170–231.

Analysis of the mystical elements in Milton's work and of the reasons why he was not essentially a mystic.

Tillyard, E. M. W., *Milton*. London and New York. 1930.

A most illuminating general study of Milton.

Trent, William P., *John Milton: a Short Study of his Life and Works*. New York. 1899.

Wendell, Barrett, *The Temper of the Seventeenth Century in English Literature*. New York. 1904.

Willey, Basil, *The Seventeenth-Century Background*. London. 1934.

III. OUTSTANDING MODERN EDITIONS OF THE MINOR POEMS

The best available text of all Milton's poems, with complete variants, is to be found in *The Works of John Milton,* edited by Frank Allen Patterson and others, and published by the Columbia University Press in 1931 and following years.

Bridge, Sir Frederick, *The "Masque of Comus"—the Original Music by Henry Lawes and Other Contemporary Composers*. London. 1908.

MacKellar, Walter, *The Latin Poems of John Milton*. Yale University Press. 1930.

Pattison, Mark, *The Sonnets of John Milton*. "The Parchment Library." London. 1883.

Smart, John S., *The Sonnets of John Milton*. Glasgow. 1921.

Verity, A. W., *A Maske (Comus)*. Cambridge University Press. 1909 and 1921.

The best annotation of Milton is by Mr. Verity in "The Pitt Press Series," which includes *Arcades* and *Comus, Ode on the Morning of Christ's Nativity,* etc.; *L'Allegro, Il Penseroso* and *Lycidas*—eleven volumes in all, with *Paradise Lost* and *Samson Agonistes,* frequently revised and reissued since 1891.

Wright, W. A., *The Poetical Works of John Milton*. Cambridge. 1903.

Full variant readings and a modernized text.

IV. SPECIAL STUDIES OF INDIVIDUAL MINOR POEMS

A. The Latin Poems

Harrison, Thomas P., Jr., "The Latin Pastorals of Milton and Castiglione," in *P.M.L.A.,* L, pp. 480–93.

Mabley, A. H., "Milton's Latin Poems," in *Western Reserve University Bulletin,* II, pp. 49–72.

Rand, Edward K., "Milton in Rustication," in *S.P.,* XIX, pp. 109–35.

A great critical essay, surveying the Latin poems both as autobiography and as literature.

B. *On the Morning of Christ's Nativity*

Cook, Albert S., "Notes on Milton's *Ode on the Morning of Christ's Nativity,*" in the *Transactions of the Connecticut Academy of Arts and Sciences,* XV, pp. 307–68.

C. *L'Allegro* and *Il Penseroso*

Lowes, John L., "*L'Allegro* and the *Passionate Shepherd,*" in *M.L.R.,* VI, pp. 206–9.

Mutschmann, Heinrich, "Miltons Selbstdarstellung in *L'Allegro* und *Il Penseroso,*" in *Beiblatt zur Anglia,* XXXIV, pp. 338–42.

Dogmatic psycho-physical analysis of the poet.

Padelford, Frederick M., "An Unnoted Source of *L'Allegro,*" in *M.L.N.,* XXII, p. 200.

Tillyard, E. M. W., "Milton: *L'Allegro* and *Il Penseroso.*" The English Association Pamphlet No. 82. July, 1932.

Relates the poems to the first *Prolusion* and suggests a date of composition before Milton left Cambridge.

D. *Comus*

Anonymous, "The Music in *Comus*," in *Christ's College Magazine*, XXIII, pp. 64–80.

Axon, W. E. A., "Milton's *Comus* and Fletcher's *Faithful Shepherdess*," *Manchester Quarterly*, I, 285.

Brie, F., "Das Märchen von Childe Rowland und sein Nachleben," in *Palaestra*, CXLVIII, pp. 118–43.

Diekhoff, John S., "The Punctuation of *Comus*," in *P.M.L.A.*, LI, pp. 757–68.

Hall, E. A., "*Comus, Old Wives Tale* and Drury's *Alvredus*," in *Manly Anniversary Studies in Language and Literature*. Chicago University Press. 1923. Pp. 140–4.

Thaler, Alwin, "Milton in the Theatre," in *S.P.*, XVII, pp. 269–308.

> An exhaustive account of the stagings of *Comus*.

Welsford, Enid, *The Court Masque*. Cambridge University Press. 1927.

> Much valuable background and criticism of *Comus*.

E. *Lycidas*

Coffman, George R., "The Parable of the Good Shepherd, 'De Contemptu Mundi,' and 'Lycidas,'" in *ELH—A Journal of English Literary History*, III, pp. 101–13.

Hamilton, H. F., "The Sources of Milton's *Lycidas*," in *Sewanee Review*, XVII, pp. 235–40.

Hanford, James H., "The Pastoral Elegy and Milton's *Lycidas*," in *P.M.L.A.*, XXV, pp. 403–47.

> Still the best survey of the backgrounds of the Elegy in classical and Renaissance literature.

More, Paul Elmer, "How to Read *Lycidas*," in *The American Review*, VII, pp. 140–58.

Norlin, G., "The Conventions of the Pastoral Elegy," in *American Journal of Philology*, XXXII, pp. 294–312.

Ransom, John C., "A Poem Nearly Anonymous," in *The American Review,* I, pp. 179–203, and 444–67.

Sandys, Sir John E., "The Literary Sources of Milton's *Lycidas,*" reprinted from *Transactions of the Royal Society of Literature,* XXXII.

Tuckwell, W., *"Lycidas": a Monograph.* London. 1911.

Deals mainly with the Trinity manuscript.

F.   *Psalms*

Baldwin, Edward C., "Milton and the Psalms," in *Modern Philology,* XVII, pp. 457–63.

Studley, Marian H., "Milton and his Paraphrases of the Psalms," in *P.Q.,* IV, pp. 364–72.

G.   *Sonnets*

Hanford, James H., "The Arrangement and Dates of Milton's Sonnets," in *Modern Philology,* XVIII, pp. 475–83.

Stevens, David H., "The Order of Milton's Sonnets," in *Modern Philology,* XVII, pp. 25–33.

POEMS

OF
Mr. *John Milton*,

BOTH
ENGLISH and LATIN,
Compos'd at several times.

Printed by his true Copies.

The Songs were set in Musick by
Mr. HENRY LAWES Gentleman of
the KINGS Chappel, and one
of His MAIESTIES
Private Musick.

———*Baccare frontem*
Cingite, ne vati noceat mala lingua futuro,
Virgil, Eclog. 7.

Printed and publish'd according to
ORDER.

LONDON,
Printed by *Ruth Raworth* for *Humphrey Moseley*,
and are to be sold at the signe of the Princes
Arms in *S. Pauls* Church-yard. 1645.

THE STATIONER

TO THE READER.

It is not any private respect of gain, Gentle Reader, *for the slightest Pamphlet is nowadays more vendible than the Works of learnedest men; but it is the love I have to our own Language that hath made me diligent to collect, and set forth such* Pieces *both in Prose and Verse as may renew the wonted honour and esteem of our English tongue: and it's the worth of these both English and Latin* Poems, *not the flourish of any prefixed* encomions, *that can invite thee to buy them, though these are not without the highest Commendations and Applause of the learned'st* Academics, *both domestic and foreign: And amongst those of our own Country, the un-parallel'd attestation of that renowned Provost of* Eton, *Sir* Henry Wotton: *I know not thy palate how it relishes such dainties, nor how harmonious thy soul is; perhaps more trivial Airs may please thee better. But howsoever thy opinion is spent upon these, that encouragement I have already received from the most ingenious men in their clear and courteous entertainment of Mr.* Waller's *late choice Pieces, hath once more made me adventure into the World, present-ing it with these ever-green, and not-to-be-blasted Laurels. The Author's more peculiar excellency in these studies was too well known to conceal his Papers, or to keep me from attempting to solicit them from him. Let the event guide itself which way it will, I shall deserve of the age, by bring-ing into the Light as true a Birth, as the Muses have brought forth since our famous* Spenser *wrote; whose Poems in these English ones are as rarely imitated, as sweetly excell'd. Reader, if thou art Eagle-eyed to censure their worth, I am not fearful to expose them to thy exactest perusal.*

Thine to command

HUMPH. MOSELEY.

3

[The Preface to the Latin Poems 1645.]

HAEC quae sequuntur de Authore testimonia, tametsi ipse intelligebat non tam de se quam supra se esse dicta, eo quod praeclaro ingenio viri, nec non amici ita fere solent laudare, ut omnia suis potius virtutibus, quam veritati congruentia nimis cupide affingant, noluit tamen horum egregiam in se voluntatem non esse notam; Cum alii praesertim ut id faceret magnopere suaderent. Dum enim nimiae laudis invidiam totis ab se viribus amolitur, sibique quod plus aequo est non attributum esse mavult, judicium interim hominum cordatorum atque illustrium quin summo sibi honori ducat, negare non potest.

Joannes Baptista Mansus, Marchio Villensis Neapolitanus ad Joannem Miltonium Anglum.

Ut mens, forma, decor, facies, mos, si pietas sic,
    Non Anglus, verum hercle Angelus ipse fores.

Ad Joannem Miltonem Anglum triplici poeseos laurea coronandum Graeca *nimirum,* Latina, *atque* Hetrusca, *Epigramma Joannis Salsilli Romani.*

CEDE Meles, cedat depressa Mincius urna;
    Sebetus Tassum desinat usque loqui;
At Thamesis victor cunctis ferat altior undas
    Nam per te Milto par tribus unus erit.

Ad Joannem Miltonum.

GRAECIA Maeonidem, jactet sibi Roma Maronem,
    Anglia Miltonum jactat utrique parem.
                      Selvaggi.

Translation

ALTHOUGH the author understands very well that the following tributes express a partial rather than a just estimate of himself, inasmuch as men of eminent talents, who are one's friends besides, very often make their eager compliments correspond better with their own virtues than with the truth; nevertheless, he was unwilling that their extraordinary good will to him should not be known; especially since others have been very importunate with him to do so. For, while he is doing everything in his power to ward off the odium of excessive praise, and prefers that nothing more than is just should be attributed to him, yet he cannot deny that the esteem of judicious and famous men contributes highly to his honour.

*　　*　　*　　*　　*　　*

Giovanni Battista Manso, Marquis of Villa, a citizen of
Naples, to John Milton, Englishman.

If your mind, form, grace, features and manners were equalled by your piety, then, I swear, you would be no Angle, but a veritable angel.

To John Milton, Englishman, who deserves to be crowned
with the triple laurel of poesy; Greek, Latin and Italian:
an Epigram of Giovanni Salzilli of Rome.

Yield, Meles, and let Mincius yield with lowered urn; let Sebetus cease to vaunt forever its Tasso; but let the triumphant Thames exalt its waves above them all, for, thanks to you, Milton, the one river will become the equal of the three.

To John Milton.

Let Greece vaunt its Homer and let Rome vaunt its Virgil; England vaunts you, Milton, the peer of them both.

Selvaggi.

Al Signor Gio. Miltoni Nobile Inglese.

ODE

Ergimi all' Etra ò Clio
Perche di stelle intreccierò corona
Non più del Biondo Dio
La Fronde eterna in Pindo, e in Elicona,
Diensi a merto maggior, maggiori i fregi,   5
A' celeste virtù celesti pregi.

Non puo del tempo edace
Rimaner preda, eterno alto valore
Non puo l' oblio rapace
Furar dalle memorie eccelso onore,   10
Su l' arco di mia cetra un dardo forte
Virtù m' adatti, e ferirò la morte.

Del Ocean profondo
Cinta dagli ampi gorghi Anglia resiede
Separata dal mondo,   15
Però che il suo valor l' umano eccede:
Questa feconda sà produrre Eroi,
Ch' hanno a ragion del sovruman tra noi.

Alla virtù sbandita
Danno ne i petti lor fido ricetto,   20
Quella gli è sol gradita,
Perche in lei san trovar gioia, e diletto;
Ridillo tu Giovanni e mostra in tanto
Con tua vera virtù, vero il mio Canto.

Lungi dal Patrio lido   25
Spinse Zeusi l' industre ardente brama;
Ch' udio d' Helena il grido
Con aurea tromba rimbombar la fama,
E per poterla effigiare al paro
Dalle più belle Idee trasse il più raro.   30

To John Milton, English Gentleman.

LIFT me to the heavens, O Clio, so that I may plait a crown of stars rather than of the immortal foliage of the fair-haired god on Pindus and on Helicon. To greater desert greater ornaments are due, to celestial virtue, celestial honour.

Immortal and exalted heroism cannot become a prey to rapacious Time; devouring Oblivion cannot rob our memories of sublime glory. Let Virtue fit a strong arrow to the bow of my lyre and I shall transfix Death.

Girt about by the wide gulfs of the ocean, England sits divided from the world, and so its worth transcends the human. This fertile island produces heroes who, in comparison with us, possess something properly superhuman.

To exiled Virtue they give a secure retreat in their hearts; she alone is welcome to them because they understand how to find joy and delight in her. Repeat it, John, and show by your true virtue that truth is in my song.

An ardent purpose drove the diligent Zeuxis far from his native shore, for he heard the echo of Helen's glory reverberating on fame's golden trumpet; and, to make a corresponding portrait of her, he took what was most rare from the most lovely forms.

Cosi l' Ape Ingegnosa
Trae con industria il suo liquor pregiato
Dal giglio e dalla rosa,
E quanti vaghi fiori ornano il prato;
Formano un dolce suon diverse Chorde,   35
Fan varie voci melodia concorde.

Di bella gloria amante
Milton dal Ciel natío per varie parti
Le peregrine piante
Volgesti a ricercar scienze, ed arti;   40
Del Gallo regnator vedesti i Regni,
E dell' Italia ancor gl' Eroi piu degni.

Fabro quasi divino
Sol virtù rintracciando il tuo pensiero
Vide in ogni confino   45
Chi di nobil valor calca il sentiero;
L' ottimo dal miglior dopo sceglica
Per fabbricar d' ogni virtu l' Idea.

Quanti nacquero in Flora
O in lei del parlar Tosco appreser l' arte,   50
La cui memoria onora
Il mondo fatta eterna in dotte carte,
Volesti ricercar per tuo tesoro,
E parlasti con lor nell' opre loro.

Nell' altera Babelle   55
Per te il parlar confuse Giove in vano,
Che per varie favelle
Di se stessa trofeo cadde su'l piano:
Ch' Ode oltr' all Anglia il suo piu degno Idioma
Spagna, Francia, Toscana, e Grecia e Roma.   60

I piu profondi arcani
Ch' occulta la natura e in cielo e in terra
Ch' a Ingegni sovrumani
Troppo avara tal' hor gli chiude, e serra,
Chiaramente conosci, e giungi al fine   65
Della moral virtude al gran confine.

Thus the ingenious bee busily extracts its precious liquor from the lily and the rose and all delightful flowers that deck the meadow. Various strings make one sweet sound; various voices make a tuneful melody.

Milton, lover of fair glory, you have turned your wandering feet from your native sky to various regions in search of sciences and arts. You have seen the realms of the puissant Gaul and also the noblest heroes of Italy.

A craftsman almost divine, your thought, which has no other quest than virtue, has seen those in every land who tread nobly on the path of the good. It chose out the best from the better in order to create the ideal pattern of all the virtues.

Your desire has been to seek out for your treasury all those natives of Florence or pupils of hers in the art of speaking the Tuscan tongue whose memory the world honours by perpetuating it in learned books, and with those men you have conversed in their works.

For you, from whose lips not England only, but Spain, France, Tuscany, Greece, and Rome hear each her noblest idiom, it was in vain that Jove confused the speech of top-lofty Babel, which fell by diversity of tongues and became the monument of its own ruin on the plain.

You comprehend clearly the profoundest arcana which nature hides in heaven and earth and sometimes locks and bars too enviously even from superhuman intellects, and finally you reach the great frontier of moral virtue.

Non batta il Tempo l' ale,
Fermisi immoto, e in un ferminsi gl' anni,
Che di virtù immortale
Scorron di troppo ingiuriosi a i danni;   70
Che s' opre degne di Poema o storia
Furon gia, l' hai presenti alla memoria.

Dammi tua dolce Cetra
Se vuoi ch' io dica del tuo dolce canto,
Ch' inalzandoti all' Etra   75
Di farti huomo celeste ottiene il vanto,
Il Tamigi il dirà che gl' è concesso
Per te suo cigno pareggiar Permesso.

Io che in riva del Arno
Tento spiegar tuo merto alto, e preclaro   80
So che fatico indarno,
E ad ammirar, non a lodarlo imparo;
Freno dunque la lingua, e ascolto il core
Che ti prende a lodar con lo stupore.

Del sig. Antonio Francini gentilhuomo
            Fiorentino.

Let Time beat its wings no more! Let it halt, immobile; and let one final pause stop the years, which speed along all too injuriously and ruinously to immortal virtue. If ever there were deeds worthy of poetry or history, you have them present in your memory.

Give me your sweet lyre, if you wish me to speak of your sweet song, which exalts you to heaven and so may boast of deifying you. Thanks to you, its swan, the Thames shall announce itself the rival of the Permessus.

I, who on Arno's bank try to expound your exalted and pre-eminent merit, know that I labour in vain; and I learn to admire, not to praise it. So I bridle my tongue and listen to my heart, which undertakes to praise you with admiration.

By Antonio Francini, a Florentine gentleman.

JOANNI MILTONI

LONDINIENSI.

Juveni Patria, virtutibus eximio,

VIRO *qui multa peregrinatione, studio cuncta orbis terrarum loca perspexit, ut novus Ulysses omnia ubique ab omnibus apprehenderet.*

Polyglotto, in cujus ore linguae jam deperditae sic reviviscunt, ut idiomata omnia sint in ejus laudibus infacunda; Et jure ea percallet ut admirationes & plausus populorum ab propria sapientia excitatos, intelligat.

Illi, cujus animi dotes corporisque, sensus ad admirationem commovent, & per ipsam motum cuique auferunt; cujus opera ad plausus hortantur, sed venustate vocem laudatoribus adimunt.

Cui in Memoria totus Orbis: In intellectu Sapientia: in voluntate ardor gloriae: in ore Eloquentia: Harmonicos celestium Sphaerarum sonitus Astronomia Duce audienti; Characteres mirabilium naturae per quos Dei magnitudo describitur magistra Philosophia legenti; Antiquitatum latebras, vetustatis excidia, eruditionis ambages comite assidua autorum Lectione.

Exquirenti, restauranti, percurrenti.

At cur nitor in arduum?

Illi in cujus virtutibus evulgandis ora Famae non sufficiant, nec hominum stupor in laudandis satis est, Reverentiae & amoris ergo hoc ejus meritis debitum admirationis tributum offert Carolus Datus Patricius Florentinus.

Tanto homini servus, tantae virtutis amator.

To John Milton of London,

A youth distinguished by his fatherland and his rare qualities.

To A man who, in his travels, has surveyed many places and, in his studies, has examined all the regions of the whole world, that he might, like another Ulysses, learn all things from all men.

To the polyglot, in whose mouth languages that are dead recover such life that all idioms are inadequate for his praise; and who is so accurately versed in them all that he comprehends the utterances of admiration and applause evoked among the nations by the wisdom which he alone possesses.

To him whose endowments of mind and body arouse the senses to admiration and by that very admiration deprive every man of the faculty of motion; whose performances prompt men to applause, yet by their charm strike those who applaud dumb.

To one in whose memory the universal world reposes; in whose mind, wisdom; in whose affections, the passion for glory; in whose mouth, eloquence; who with the guidance of Astronomy hears the harmonious music of the celestial spheres; who, with Philosophy as his instructress, reads deeply into the significance of the marvels of nature by which the greatness of God is portrayed; who, with the constant study of good authors to friend him, investigates the mysteries of past ages, restores the ravages of time, and ranges through all the by-paths of erudition.

But why do I struggle up the steeps?

To him, for the proclamation of whose merits the tongues of Rumour would not suffice, nor for their praise the speechless admiration of men; to him, in reverence and affection, this tribute of admiration due to his excellence is offered by Charles Dati, a Florentine Patrician,

> Humble servant to so great a man and
> lover of such eminent merit.

A PARAPHRASE ON *PSALM* 114

This and the following *Psalm* were done by the Author at
fifteen years old.

WHEN the blest seed of *Terah's* faithful Son,
After long toil their liberty had won,
And past from *Pharian* fields to *Canaan* Land,
Led by the strength of the Almighty's hand,
Jehovah's wonders were in *Israel* shown,   5
His praise and glory was in *Israel* known.
That saw the troubl'd Sea, and shivering fled,
And sought to hide his froth-becurled head
Low in the earth; *Jordan's* clear streams recoil,
As a faint host that hath receiv'd the foil.   10
The high, huge-bellied Mountains skip like Rams
Amongst their Ewes, the little Hills like Lambs.
Why fled the Ocean?   And why skipt the Mountains?
Why turned *Jordan* toward his Crystal Fountains?
Shake earth, and at the presence be aghast   15
Of him that ever was, and aye shall last,
That glassy floods from rugged rocks can crush,
And make soft rills from fiery flint-stones gush.

                                                        (1624)

---

1. Milton altered the reading of his original—which calls the Children of Israel "the house of Jacob"—for the sake of the allusion to
Abraham's faith in God. Although his father, *Terah* (Gen. xi, 27)
was an idolater, "by faith Abraham, when he was called to go out into
a place which he should after receive for an inheritance, obeyed."
(Heb. xi, 8.)   *P.L.* XII, 151–2, recurs to
              "This Patriarch blest,
        Whom *faithful Abraham* due time shall call."

3. *Pharian,* belonging to Pharaoh, *i.e.* Egyptian.   The epithet is noted
by the *N.E.D.* in Sylvester's line,
        "The Ephesian Temple and high Pharian Tower."
                        (*The Divine Weekes,* I, i, 500.)
Mr. Hanford refers it to Buchanan's "fields of Pharaoh" ("arva Phari")
in his Latin version of this Psalm.   Its background, like that of epithets such as "froth-becurled" (l. 8) and "huge-bellied" (l. 11), should
be sought in the technique of the wide-spread practice of paraphrasing
Scripture, and especially the Psalms, in the classical as well as the modern languages, of which Milton's own translation of this Psalm into
Greek verse was another instance.   See p. 272.

10. *foil,* defeat in battle.

PSALM 136

LET us with a gladsome mind
Praise the Lord, for he is kind,
  For his mercies aye endure,
  Ever faithful, ever sure.

refrain — based on original idea enforced; God's perpetual mercy.

pron. - ae (when expletive ae)

Let us blaze his Name abroad,   5
For of gods he is the God;
  For, &c.

O let us his praises tell, *addition*
That doth the wrathful tyrants quell.   10
  For, &c.

That with his miracles doth make
Amazed Heav'n and Earth to shake. *addition*
  For, &c.   15

That by his wisdom did create
The painted Heav'ns so full of state.
  For his, &c.   *weak adv.*   20

That did the solid Earth ordain
To rise above the wat'ry plain.
  For his, &c.

too many dids (padding)

That by his all-commanding might,   25
Did fill the new-made world with light.
  For his, &c.

And caus'd the Golden-tressed Sun,
All the day long his course to run.   30
  For his, &c.

Sylv. 29. *Golden-tressed* may be a reminiscence of "auricomum solem" in Buchanan's version of this Psalm, or it may have been written with a characteristically Miltonic side-glance at the use of that epithet for Apollo in the Greek paeans. It has nothing in the Scripture to justify it, nor have *horned* (l. 33) and *thunder-clasping* (l. 37). The whole of line 10 is an addition, due perhaps to Buchanan. See the note to l. 3 in *Psalm 114.*

└ based on Sylvester

The horned Moon to shine by night,
Amongst her spangled sisters bright.
    For his, &c.   35

He with his thunder-clasping hand,
Smote the first-born of *Egypt* Land.
    For his, &c.   40

And in despite of *Pharaoh* fell,
He brought from thence his *Israel*.
    For, &c.

The ruddy waves he cleft in twain,   45
Of the *Erythraean* main.
    For, &c.

The floods stood still like Walls of Glass,
While the Hebrew Bands did pass.
    For, &c.   50

But full soon they did devour
The Tawny King with all his power.
    For, &c.   55

His chosen people he did bless
In the wasteful Wilderness.
    For, &c.   60

In bloody battle he brought down
Kings of prowess and renown.
    For, &c.

---

46. Sylvester's influence emerges again in this reference to the Red Sea by its Greek name.

49. Compare Sylvester's description of the scene when the marching file of Israelites
         "on each side is flanked all along
      With Wals of Crystall, beautiful and strong, . . .
      Two Wals of Glasse, built with a word alone."
            (*The Divine Weekes,* 171, lc.)
Sylvester's language emerged again in *P.L.* XII, 197.

He foil'd bold *Seon* and his host,   65
That rul'd the *Amorrean* Coast.
    For, &c.

And large-limb'd *Og* he did subdue,
With all his over-hardy crew.   70
    For, &c.

And to his Servant *Israel,*
He gave their Land therein to dwell.
    For, &c.   75

He hath with a piteous eye
Beheld us in our misery.
    For, &c.   80

And freed us from the slavery
Of the invading enemy.
    For, &c.

All living creatures he doth feed,   85
And with full hand supplies their need.
    For, &c.

Let us therefore warble forth
His mighty Majesty and worth.   90
    For, &c.

That his mansion hath on high
Above the reach of mortal eye.
    For his mercies aye endure,   95
    Ever faithful, ever sure.

                                        (1624)

_____

65-69. In *P.L.* I, 406-11, there is an allusion in like vein to the defeat of the Amorite king, Seon or Sihon; and Og reappears among the
giants of old in *S.A.* 1080.

VERSES FROM THE COMMONPLACE BOOK

CARMINA ELEGIACA

Surge, age, surge!   Leves, iam convenit, excute somnos!
   Lux oritur; tepidi fulcra relinque tori.
Iam canit excubitor gallus, praenuncius ales
   Solis, et invigilans ad sua quemque vocat.
Flammiger Eois Titan caput exerit undis   5
   Et spargit nitidum laeta per arva iubar.
Daulias argutum modulatur ab ilice carmen
   Edit et excultos mitis alauda modos.
Iam rosa fragrantes spirat silvestris odores;
   Iam redolent violae luxuriatque seges.   10
Ecce novo campos Zephyritis gramine vestit
   Fertilis, et vitreo rore madescit humus.
Segnes invenias molli vix talia lecto,
   Cum premat imbellis lumina fessa sopor.
Illic languentes abrumpunt somnia somnos   15
   Et turbant animum tristia multa tuum.
Illic tabifici generantur semina morbi.
   Qui pote torpentem posse valere virum?
Surge, age, surge!   Leves, iam convenit, excute somnos!
   Lux oritur; tepidi fulcra relinque tori.   20

                        (1624?)

---

   5. *Titan*, the son of Hyperion who in Ovid (*e.g. Met.* I, 10, II, 118, and VI, 438) often represents the sun. Compare Spenser's allusion to him as "Hyperions fierie childe" (*Muiopotmos*, 51) and his description of the dawn, when
> "Titan, playing on the eastern streames,
> Gan cleare the deawy ayre with springing light."
>
>   (*F.Q.* II, iii, 1, 3–4.)

   7. *Daulias:* Daulis, in Phocis, was the scene of Ovid's story (*Met.* VI, 668–74) of Procne's wrongs by her husband, Tereus, and of his pursuit of her and her sister, Philomela, which ended in his transformation into a hoopoe and theirs into a swallow and nightingale respectively.

   11. *Zephyr,* the "herald of Venus," seems to have had a daughter only in Milton's imagination. Compare *L'Allegro*, 19.

ELEGIAC VERSES

Arise, haste, arise! Now that the time is right, shake off gentle slumbers. The light is springing up; leave the posts of your languid couch. Now sings the sentinel cock, the harbinger bird of the sun, alert to call every man to his task. Flaming Titan[5] lifts his head above the eastern waves and scatters his shining radiance over the happy fields. The Daulian[7] modulates her thrilling song from the oak-tree and the gentle lark pours out her skilful notes. Now the wild rose is breathing its fragrant perfumes; now the scent of violets is sweet and the corn is flourishing. Look, the bounteous daughter of Zephyr[11] is clothing the fields with new verdure and the turf is moist with dew like beads of glass. Lazy one, you will hardly find such delights in your soft bed, when relaxing slumber weighs on your tired eyes. There dreams break in upon your dull sleep and many griefs disturb your spirit. There the seeds of a consuming illness are bred. What strength can a sluggard enjoy?

Arise, haste, arise! Now that the time is right, shake off gentle slumbers. The light is springing up; leave the posts of your languid couch.

[The following verses have no caption in the Commonplace
                        Book.]

> Ignavus satrapam dedecet inclytum
> Somnus qui populo multifido praeest.
> Dum Dauni veteris filius armiger
> Stratus purpureo p . . . buit . . .
> Audax Eurialus Nisus et impiger   5
> Invasere cati nocte sub horrida
> Torpentes Rutilos castraque Volscia:
> Hinc caedes oritur clamor et absonus.

SLOTHFUL sleep is disgraceful to a famous governor who presides over the hosts of a people. While the warrior son of old Daunus[3] lay prone[4] on his purple couch, bold Euryalus and keen Nisus cunningly attacked the sleeping Rutilians and the Volscian camp in the dreadful night.[5] Hence slaughter arose and a hideous outcry.

---

3. *Dauni . . . filius,* Turnus, the leader of the Volscian, Rutilian and other native Italian tribes with which Aeneas had to contend for the possession of Italy.

4. The mutilated verb is evidently *procubuit.* For the noun *strato* and, with better reason, *toro,* have been proposed.

5. The story of the raid upon the Rutilian and Volscian camp by Aeneas' followers, Nisus and Euryalus, is told in the *Aeneid,* IX, 176–449.

Anno Aetatis 17 *years old*

ON THE DEATH OF A FAIR INFANT DYING OF A COUGH

I

O FAIREST flower no sooner blown but blasted,
Soft silken Primrose fading timelessly,
Summer's chief honour if thou hadst out-lasted
Bleak winter's force that made thy blossom dry;
For he being amorous on that lovely dye   5
That did thy cheek envermeil, thought to kiss
But kill'd alas, and then bewail'd his fatal bliss.

II

For since grim Aquilo his charioteer
By boist'rous rape th' Athenian damsel got,
He thought it toucht his Deity full near, *elevated*   10
If likewise he some fair one wedded not,
Thereby to wipe away th' infamous blot,
   Of long-uncoupled bed, and childless eld,
Which 'mongst the wanton gods a foul reproach was held.

III

So mounting up in icy-pearled car,   15
Through middle empire of the freezing air

---

1. The *flower,* Milton's niece, was the infant daughter of his sister Anne, who married Edward Phillips on November 27, 1623. The child's death may have occurred as late as the winter of 1625–6, for Milton dated his poem as written when he was seventeen.

1–2. Perhaps the commonplace is one of the first evidences of Shakespeare's influence on Milton. Compare:
> "Sweet rose, fair flower, untimely pluck'd, soon vaded,
> Pluck'd in the bud, and vaded in the spring!"
>   (*The Passionate Pilgrim,* x, 1–2.)

6. *envermeil*—colour with vermilion.

8–9. *Aquilo,* the north wind, who Ovid says (*Met.* VI, 682–713) resolved to make his wooing of the Athenian princess, Orithyia, in keeping with his own boisterous nature and snatched her away over the mountains in storm and darkness. Compare *To Salzilli,* 11.

16. Compare "the middle Region of thick Air" in *P.R.* II, 117, and the note.

He wander'd long, till thee he spy'd from far,
There ended was his quest, there ceast his care.
Down he descended from his Snow-soft chair,
But all unwares with his cold-kind embrace   *sonorous*
Unhous'd thy Virgin Soul from her fair biding place.   20 *quality*

IV

Yet art thou not inglorious in thy fate;   *effect - soaring,*
For so *Apollo,* with unweeting hand   *elevating*
Whilom did slay his dearly-loved mate,
Young *Hyacinth* born on *Eurotas'* strand,   25
Young *Hyacinth* the pride of *Spartan* land,
   But then transform'd him to a purple flower;
Alack, that so to change thee winter had no power.

V

Yet can I not persuade me thou art dead
Or that thy corse corrupts in earth's dark womb,   30
Or that thy beauties lie in wormy bed,   *gd. poetic*
Hid from the world in a low-delved tomb;   *fervor*
Could Heav'n for pity thee so strictly doom?
   Oh no! for something in thy face did shine
Above mortality that show'd thou wast divine.   35

VI

Resolve me then oh Soul most surely blest   *cf. Lycidas*
(If so it be that thou these plaints dost hear)

23–27. Compare the allusion to the myth of Hyacinth in *Lycidas,* 106, and the note there.

29–31. This lyric faith in immortality, which finds expression again in *Lycidas* and *Il Penseroso,* owes something to "metaphysical" invocations of death like George Herbert's,
            "But since our Saviour's death did put some bloud
                     Into thy face,
            Thou art grown fair and full of grace,
         Much in request, much sought for, as a good."
                     (*The Temple,* "Death," stanza 4.)
Here the language stems from the verse in Ps. xvi, 10, which St. Peter interpreted (Acts ii, 27) as referring to Christ; "For thou wilt not leave my soul in hell; neither wilt thou suffer thine Holy One to see corruption."

Tell me bright Spirit where'er thou hoverest
Whether above that high first-moving Sphere
Or in the Elysian fields (if such there were.)   40
   Oh say me true if thou wert mortal wight
And why from us so quickly thou didst take thy flight.

VII

Wert thou some Star which from the ruin'd roof
Of shak't Olympus by mischance didst fall;
Which careful Jove in nature's true behoof   45
Took up, and in fit place did reinstall?
Or did of late earth's Sons besiege the wall
   Of sheeny Heav'n, and thou some goddess fled
Amongst us here below to hide thy nectar'd head.

VIII

Or wert thou that just Maid who once before   50
Forsook the hated earth, O tell me sooth,

38–40. Compare the guesses about the spirit of Plato in *Il Penseroso*, 88–92, and about the spirit of Lycidas in the elegy, 174–181.

39. *that high first-moving Sphere,* the outermost of the spheres in the Alphonsine astronomy. It was called the "first mover" because it was regarded as imparting motion to the spheres of the fixed stars and the planets. Compare *Arcades*, 63–73, and *Nativity Hymn*, 75 and 125–130, and their notes.

40. Fond as he was of the thought of pagan paradises like the Elysian fields, Milton often checked himself with the reminder that they were unreal. Compare *P.R.* II, 358–360.

44. *shak't,* shaken. Like many other "weak" past participles which have since disappeared, "shaked" was used alternatively with the "strong" form.

45. *true behoof,* true interest. Compare Satan's promise to the devils to bring "no mean recompense" to their "behoof." (*P.L.* II, 981–982.)

47–48. Again in *P.L.* I, 197–200, Milton merged the myth of the Titans, who Hesiod says (*Theogony,* 134 and 207–10) were the sons of Earth and Heaven, with the myth of the giants who attacked the gods on Mt. Olympus.

50–51. The *just Maid* is Astraea, the goddess of justice, the Greek myth of whose flight from earth to heaven after the end of the Age of Gold was fused with the Christian conception of her as the
"Most sacred vertue . . of all the rest,
Resembling God in his imperiall might."
(F.Q. V, Prologue, 10, 1–2.)

And cam'st again to visit us once more?
Or wert thou Mercy that sweet smiling Youth?
Or that crown'd Matron, sage white-robed Truth?
   Or any other of that heav'nly brood   55
Let down in cloudy throne to do the world some good?

IX

Or wert thou of the golden-winged host,
Who having clad thyself in human weed,
To earth from thy prefixed seat didst post,
And after short abode fly back with speed,   60
As if to show what creatures Heav'n doth breed,
   Thereby to set the hearts of men on fire
To scorn the sordid world, and unto Heav'n aspire?

X

But oh! why didst thou not stay here below
To bless us with thy heav'n-lov'd innocence,   65
To slake his wrath whom sin hath made our foe
To turn Swift-rushing black perdition hence,
Or drive away the slaughtering pestilence,
   To stand 'twixt us and our deserved smart?
But thou canst best perform that office where thou art.   70

XI

Then thou the mother of so sweet a child
Her false imagin'd loss cease to lament,
And wisely learn to curb thy sorrows wild;
Think what a present thou to God hast sent,
And render him with patience what he lent;
   This if thou do, he will an off-spring give   75
That till the world's last-end shall make thy name to live.

(1625–6)

Tillyard: should self-assurance of tone; commanding nature

---

53. *Mercy* is the not altogether satisfactory conjecture of most editors to complete this defective line. Compare *Nativity Hymn*, 141–144.

57. Compare the "golden wing" of the "Cherub Contemplation" in *Il Penseroso*, 52 and 54.

58. Compare the "pure Ambrosial weeds" which the Attendant Spirit in *Comus*, 16, lays aside when he descends to earth.

68. In the summer preceding the child's death the plague had raged in London with extraordinary violence.

ELEGIA PRIMA

Ad Carolum Diodatum

Tandem, care, tuae mihi pervenere tabellae,
  Pertulit et voces nuntia charta tuas;
Pertulit occidua Devae Cestrensis ab ora
  Vergivium prono qua petit amne salum.
Multum, crede, iuvat terras aluisse remotas   5
  Pectus amans nostri, tamque fidele caput,
Quodque mihi lepidum tellus longinqua sodalem
  Debet, at unde brevi reddere iussa velit.
Me tenet urbs reflua quam Thamesis alluit unda,
  Meque nec invitum patria dulcis habet.   10
Iam nec arundiferum mihi cura revisere Camum,
  Nec dudum vetiti me laris angit amor.
Nuda nec arva placent, umbrasque negantia molles.
  Quam male Phoebicolis convenit ille locus!
Nec duri libet usque minas perferre magistri,   15
  Caeteraque ingenio non subeunda meo.
Si sit hoc exilium, patrios adiise penates,
  Et vacuum curis otia grata sequi,
Non ego vel profugi nomen sortemve recuso,
  Laetus et exilii conditione fruor.   20
O utinam vates nunquam graviora tulisset
  Ille Tomitano flebilis exul agro;

---

1. In the Lent Term of 1626, when the rustication described in this Elegy occurred, Milton was in his second year at Cambridge. In the preceding December Diodati had taken his degree at Oxford and gone to the neighbourhood of Chester, where he seems to have practiced medicine. In 1637 Milton addressed him there in a Familiar Letter, dated September 2.

3. Chester lies on the east bank of the Dee. Compare *Lycidas,* 55, and *Vacation Exercise,* 98, notes.

4. *Vergivium . . . salum.* The Vergivian salt is the Irish Sea.

9. The only things certain about Milton's rustication from Cambridge are that it arose from a difference between him and his tutor, Chappell, and that after a short absence he returned and was assigned to another tutor, whose name was Tovey.

ELEGY I

To Charles Diodati[1]

AT LAST, dear friend, your letter has come to me and its news-laden pages have brought me your words—brought them from the western bank of the Dee beside Chester,[3] where with precipitate current it seeks the Irish Sea.[4] There is great delight, believe me, in the fact that remote regions have bred a heart that is loving and a head so devoted to me, that I have a claim for a charming comrade upon a distant land, which is willing soon to return him to me at my bidding.

I am in the city which the Thames washes with its tidal waters and I am willingly detained in my dear native place.[9] At present I feel no concern about returning to the sedgy Cam and I am troubled by no nostalgia for my forbidden quarters there.[11] The bare fields, so niggardly of pleasant shade, have no charm for me. How wretchedly suited that place is to the worshippers of Phoebus![14] It is disgusting to be constantly subjected to the threats of a rough tutor and to other indignities which my spirit cannot endure. But if this be exile, to have returned to the paternal home and to be carefree to enjoy a delightful leisure, then I have no objection to the name or to the lot of a fugitive and I am glad to take advantage of my banishment. Ah! Would that the bard who was a pitiful exile in the land of Tomis[22] had never had to bear anything worse! Then he would have

---

11. Compare the allusion to the Cam in *Lycidas,* 103–4, note.

14. Milton's coinage, *Phoebicolis,* worshippers of Phoebus Apollo, *i.e.* poets, should be compared with his many allusions to Apollo by his Homeric epithet, Phoebus, *i.e.* bright or shining one. The name was traditionally given to Apollo as the inspirer of song. Compare *Manso,* 38.

21–22. The bard is Ovid, whose influence on Milton's Elegies was far greater than that of any other Roman poet. In the year 8 A.D. Augustus banished him irrevocably to the city of Tomis on the north-

Non tunc Ionio quicquam cessisset Homero,
    Neve foret victo laus tibi prima, Maro.
Tempora nam licet hic placidis dare libera Musis,   25
    Et totum rapiunt me, mea vita, libri.
Excipit hinc fessum sinuosi pompa theatri,
    Et vocat ad plausus garrula scena suos.
Seu catus auditur senior, seu prodigus haeres,
    Seu procus, aut posita casside miles adest,   30
Sive decennali foecundus lite patronus
    Detonat inculto barbara verba foro;
Saepe vafer gnato succurrit servus amanti,
    Et nasum rigidi fallit ubique Patris;
Saepe novos illic virgo mirata calores   35
    Quid sit amor nescit, dum quoque nescit, amat.
Sive cruentatum furiosa Tragoedia sceptrum
    Quassat, et effusis crinibus ora rotat.
Et dolet, et specto, iuvat et spectasse dolendo.
    Interdum et larcrymis dulcis amaror inest: 40
Seu puer infelix indelibata reliquit
    Gaudia, et abrupto flendus amore cadit;
Seu ferus e tenebris iterat Styga criminis ultor,
    Conscia funereo pectora torre movens;
Seu maeret Pelopeia domus, seu nobilis Ili,   45
    Aut luit incestos aula Creontis avos.

---

west shore of the Black Sea. As Mr. James Goode suggests, Sannazaro's
allusion (*Elegies*, 1725, p. 74) to "that exiled man on Tomitan soil"
shows that Milton's reference was a part of the tradition of the Latin
elegists of the Renaissance.

23. For Homer's traditional Ionian origin see *Manso*, 22, note.

24. *Maro*, Virgil's family name, was as familiar to Milton's contemporaries as the name *Virgilius*, by which we know him best.

27. *sinuosi*: perhaps there is a reminiscence of Ovid's *curvis theatris*
(*Art of Love*, I, 89)—curved or circular theatres—or of Propertius'
allusion (IV, i, 15) to the *sinuosa vela* or awnings used to protect the
audience against the sun. The characters in the following account of
Milton's theatrical interests, with the single exception of the lawyer, all
come from Latin comedy and Milton seems to have visualized a Roman
rather than a London theatre.

31–32. Warton seems to have been right in recognizing an allusion
here to George Ruggle's *Ignoramus*, which was twice played at Cambridge before King James and ran into five editions in the seventeenth
century.

yielded nothing to Ionian Homer[23] and you, O Maro,[24] would have been conquered and stripped of your prime honours.

Here my hours are free to be dedicated to the quiet Muses; and my books, which are my life, quite carry me away. When I am tired, the magnificence of the arched theatre[27] diverts me and the chattering actors invite me to applaud them. Sometimes the speaker is a shrewd old man, sometimes he is the wastrel heir, and sometimes the wooer. Or the soldier lays aside his helmet and appears, or the barrister who has fattened on a ten-year suit volleys his barbarous verbiage at an illiterate court-room.[31] Often a wily slave comes to the rescue of a love-struck son and seems ubiquitous as he dupes the stiff-necked father under his very nose. And often the virgin, who is surprised by the strange fire within her and has no idea what love is, falls in love without knowing what she does.

Or Tragedy, with streaming hair and rolling eyes, tosses her blood-stained sceptre in her frenzy.[37] The sight is painful, but still I watch and find pleasure in watching and suffering, and sometimes there is a sweet pain even in tears: at times when an unhappy youth must leave his joys untasted and is torn away from his love to perish lamentably; or when the stern avenger of crime returns from the shades across the Styx and his fatal torch perturbs hearts that are conscious of guilt; or when the house of Pelops or of noble Ilus is stricken with grief;[45] or the palace of Creon expiates the incest of its sires.[46]

37–38. Milton seems to have had Greek and Senecan rather than Elizabethan tragedy in mind here as well as in *Il Penseroso*, 97–8. Warton compared Ovid's picture (*Amores*, III, i, 11–3) of "violent Tragedy, moving with mighty strides, her brow gloomy under her locks, and her robe (*palla*) thrown down and a royal sceptre brandished in her left hand."

45. Compare "Pelops' line" in *Il Penseroso*, 99, note. *Ilus* was the founder of Troy, which was called Ilium after him. Milton had plays like Euripides' *Troades* in mind.

46. *Creon* was king of Thebes. Compare *Il Penseroso*, 99, note.

Sed neque sub tecto semper nec in urbe latemus,
   Irrita nec nobis tempora veris eunt.
Nos quoque lucus habet vicina consitus ulmo,
   Atque suburbani nobilis umbra loci.   50
Saepius hic, blandas spirantia sidera flammas,
   Virgineos videas praeteriisse choros.
Ah quoties dignae stupui miracula formae
   Quae possit senium vel reparare Iovis!
Ah quoties vidi superantia lumina gemmas,   55
   Atque faces quotquot volvit uterque polus;
Collaque bis vivi Pelopis quae brachia vincant,
   Quaeque fluit puro nectare tincta via,
Et decus eximium frontis, tremulosque capillos,
   Aurea quae fallax retia tendit Amor;   60
Pellacesque genas, ad quas hyacinthina sordet
   Purpura, et ipse tui floris, Adoni, rubor!
Cedite laudatae toties Heroïdes olim,
   Et quaecunque vagum cepit amica Iovem.
Cedite Achaemeniae turrita fronte puellae,   65
   Et quot Susa colunt, Memnoniamque Ninon;
Vos etiam Danaae fasces submittite Nymphae,
   Et vos Iliacae, Romuleaeque nurus,
Nec Pompeianas Tarpeia Musa columnas
   Iactet, et Ausoniis plena theatra stolis.   70

---

56. *polus:* compare the note on the word in *To his Father,* 34.

57. "When Pelops had been cut to pieces by his own father's hand,
they say, the gods joined his members together again, when they had
all been found, except that which was between the neck and the upper
arm. A piece of ivory was substituted for the missing part and so
Pelops was made whole again." (Ovid, *Met.* VI, 407–11.)

58. Compare the allusion to the Milky Way in *On the Death of the
Bishop of Ely,* 60.

60. *Amor.* Cupid; Ovid's wanton boy with irresistible arrows, not
the cosmic Cupid of *Damon's Epitaph,* 191.

62. Compare the allusion to Adonis' death in *Comus,* 999, note.
From his blood—according to Ovid's story (*Met.* X, 735–9)—Venus
caused the anemone to grow.

63. *Heroïdes,* demigoddesses or heroines. There is some allusion to
the women who figure in Ovid's collection of epistles called the
Heroïdes.

64. In Ovid's *Metamorphoses* Milton was familiar with Jove's intrigues
with Latona, Europa, Alcmena and Semele and with countless nymphs
and mortal women.

But I am not always hiding indoors nor even in the city, and the spring does not pass without some profit to me. I also am a visitor in the grove where the elms stand close together and in the magnificent shade of a place just beyond the city's confines. Here, like stars that breathe out soft flames, you may see groups of maidens go dancing past. Ah, how many times have I been struck dumb by the miraculous grace of a form which might make decrepit Jove young again! Ah, how many times have I seen eyes which outshine jewels and all the stars that wheel about either pole,[56] necks which excel the arms of Pelops the twice-living[57] and the Way[58] that flows tinctured with pure nectar, and a brow of surpassing loveliness, and waving tresses which were golden nets flung by Cupid, the deceiver![60] How often have I seen seductive cheeks beside which the purple of the hyacinth and even the blush of your flower, Adonis, turn pale.[62] Give way, ye Heroïdes[63] so much praised in olden times, and every mistress who made inconstant Jove her captive.[64] Give way, you Achaemenian[65] damsels with the turrets on your brows, and you, whose home is Susa or Memnonian Nineveh,[66] and you Danaid[67] maidens also, and you women of Troy and of Rome,[68] make your submission. Let not the Tarpeian Muse boast of Pompey's colonnade[69] or of the theatres crowded with Ausonian[70] robes. The prime honour

---

65. *Achaemenian*, Persian. The founder of the great Persian dynasty of kings was Achæmenes.

66. It was not Nineveh, but Susa ("Shushan, the palace," the Persian capital of Nehemiah, i, 1), that was founded by Tithonus, the father of Memnon. In *P.L.* X, 308, Milton correctly refers to Xerxes' "Memnonian Palace high."

67. The adjective derived from the name of Danaus, the mythical founder of the kingdom of Argos, was applied to the Greeks generally.

68. For the derivation of *Iliacae*—Trojan—see the note on l. 45 above.

Romuleae—Roman—is derived from the name of the traditional founder of Rome, Romulus.

69. Pompey's porch or colonnade, built in 55 B.C. in the Campus Martius, was a fashionable Roman promenade.

The *Tarpeian Muse* is Ovid, who lived on the Capitoline hill near the Tarpeian rock.

70. *Ausonia* was an ancient name for Italy.

Gloria Virginibus debetur prima Britannis;
   Extera, sat tibi sit, foemina, posse sequi.
Tuque urbs Dardaniis, Londinum, structa colonis,
   Turrigerum late conspicienda caput,
Tu nimium felix intra tua moenia claudis   75
   Quicquid formosi pendulus orbis habet.
Non tibi tot caelo scintillant astra sereno,
   Endymioneae turba ministra deae,
Quot tibi conspicuae formaque auroque puellae
   Per medias radiant turba videnda vias.   80
Creditur huc geminis venisse invecta columbis
   Alma pharetrigero milite cincta Venus,
Huic Cnidon, et riguas Simoentis flumine valles,
   Huic Paphon, et roseam posthabitura Cypron.
Ast ego, dum pueri sinit indulgentia caeci,   85
   Moenia quam subito linquere fausta paro;
Et vitare procul malefidae infamia Circes
   Atria, divini Molyos usus ope.
Stat quoque iuncosas Cami remeare paludes,
   Atque iterum raucae murmur adire Scholae.   90
Interea fidi parvum cape munus amici,
   Paucaque in alternos verba coacta modos.

                            (1625–6)

---

73. *Dardanian, i.e.* Trojan, is derived from the name of Dardanus, the son of Jove and Electra, one of the mythical founders of Troy. Compare *Damon's Epitaph,* 162, note.

74. *Turrigerum . . . caput:* compare the "Tower'd Cities" of *L'Allegro,* 117. Both phrases are a reminiscence of Virgil's *turrigeraeque urbes (Aen.* X, 253). Compare *Arcades,* 21, note.

76. Here and again when he pictured "This pendant world" in *P.L.* II, 1052, and "The pendulous round Earth" in *P.L.* IV, 1000, Milton remembered Ovid's account of the world as pendant in mid-air:
        "Nec circumfuso pendebat in aere tellus
          Ponderibus librata suis."
            (*Met.* I, 12–3.)

77–80. Milton remembered Ovid's congratulation of Rome on possessing more maidens than the sky has stars. (*Art of Love,* I, 59.)

78. *Endymion,* "whom the poets fayne to have bene so beloved of Phoebe, sc. the moone, that he was by her kept a sleepe in a cave by the space of xxx yeares, for to enjoye his companye." (Gloss to Spenser's *July,* 63.)

81–84. *Alma . . . Venus* stems from Lucretius' invocation of the goddess at the opening of the *De rerum natura,* a passage familiar

is due to the virgins of Britain; be content, foreign women, to follow after. And you, London, the city built by Dardanian[73] colonists and now widely conspicuous with towered head,[74] yours is the excessive happiness of bounding within your walls whatever beauty the pendant world[76] possesses. The ministrant hosts of Endymion's[78] goddess, the stars that shine down upon you in the calm sky, are fewer than the radiant host in your streets—maidens whose forms and golden ornaments dazzle the eye.[77] Venus, the giver of life (it is believed) has come hither, drawn by her twin doves and escorted by her quiver-bearing soldiery, and she will prefer[84] this city to Cnidus[81] and to the valleys that are watered by the river Simois,[83] and to Paphos and rosy Cyprus.

But for my part—while the blind boy's indulgence permits it—I am preparing the speediest possible departure from this city of delights—preparing, with the help of divine moly,[87] to secure the safety of distance from the infamous halls of the deceiver, Circe. It is decided also that I am to go back to the reedy fens of the Cam and return again to the hum of the noisy school. Meanwhile, accept this small tribute of a loyal friend and these few words that have been forced into alternating measures.[92]

---

through many imitations, such as Spenser's paraphrase (*F.Q.* IV, x, 44). Spenser set the example of describing Venus as preferring new haunts to her traditional homes:

> "Whether in Paphos, or Cythaeron hill,
> Or . . . Gnidus."
> (*F.Q.* III, vi, 39, 4–8.)

83. The river *Simois* is included because it rises on Mount Ida, where Paris awarded the famous apple to Venus.

84. *posthabitura:* see the note on *posthabita* in *To Rouse,* 65.

87–88. Compare the note on the use of moly (a kind of herb) by the shepherd boy (by whom, as Professor Hanford seems to me rightly to suggest, Milton may have meant himself) in *Comus,* 636, to escape the enchantments of Circe's son, Comus.

92. *alternos . . . modos,* alternating measures, the alternate hexameter and pentameter of the elegiac couplet.

ELEGIA SECUNDA

Anno Aetatis 17

<small>IN OBITUM PRAECONIS ACADEMICI CANTABRIGIENSIS</small>

TE, QUI conspicuus baculo fulgente solebas
    Palladium toties ore ciere gregem,
Ultima praeconum praeconem te quoque saeva
    Mors rapit, officio nec favet ipsa suo.
Candidiora licet fuerint tibi tempora plumis   5
    Sub quibus accipimus delituisse Iovem,
O dignus tamen Haemonio iuvenescere succo,
    Dignus in Aesonios vivere posse dies,
Dignus quem Stygiis medica revocaret ab undis
    Arte Coronides, saepe rogante dea.   10
Tu si iussus eras acies accire togatas,
    Et celer a Phoebo nuntius ire tuo,
Talis in Iliaca stabat Cyllenius aula
    Alipes, aetherea missus ab arce Patris;
Talis et Eurybates ante ora furentis Achillei   15
    Rettulit Atridae iussa severa ducis.

1–3. The beadles or criers—for the English word "beadle" and the Latin "praeco" both mean a crier or herald—acted an extensive ceremonial rôle in the life of Milton's Cambridge. The University still possesses the silver gilt maces which were given to the three Esquire Beadles in 1626, the year of the death of Richard Ridding, the Senior Beadle, for whom this Elegy was written.

2. Milton calls the students the Palladian band or the followers of the goddess of wisdom, Athene. Compare *To Rouse*, 62, note.

5. At his death, Ridding was an old man, for he had been in office thirty years.

5–6. The poets had long made a proverb of the whiteness of Jove's plumes when he was

> "turnd into a snowy swan,
> To win faire Leda to his lovely trade."
>   (*F.Q.* III, xi, 32, 1–2.)

7–8. Ovid tells the story (*Met.* VII, 264) of Medea's rejuvenation of old Aeson by dissecting him and reuniting his limbs after boiling them in a brew of "Haemonian roots." Haemonia was an ancient name of Thrace, the land of magic. Compare *Manso*, 75.

9–10. *Coronides*, Aesculapius, the god of healing. He was the son of Coronis, the story of whose unfaithful love for his father, Apollo,

ELEGY II

At Age 17

<small>On the Death of the Beadle of Cambridge University</small>

You, who were so often conspicuous with your glittering mace[1] when your voice assembled the Palladian[2] host—beadle though you were—you have become the prey of the last of beadles, Death, who shows no favour even to her own profession. Though your brows were whiter than the plumes in which we are told that Jove was disguised,[5] you were none the less worthy to have your youth restored by the drugs of Haemonia[7] and to be endued with the power to live to an Aeonian old age. You deserved that, at the repeated prayer of some goddess, Coronides[9] should use his healing art to recall you from the Stygian waves. If you were bidden by your Apollo[12] to go—a swift messenger—and convene the files of gownsmen, you were like wing-footed Cyllenius[13] when he was dispatched from the heavenly citadel of his father and stood in the palace at Ilium. You were like Eurybates[15] when he delivered the stern orders of his chief, Atrides, in the presence of the angry Achilles.

Ovid tells (*Met.* II, 542–6 and 596–611). Milton knew Virgil's allusion to the restoration of Hippolytus to life by the drugs of Aesculapius and the devotion of Diana—a tale which Spenser retold (*F.Q.* I, v, 37, 7–9) and imitated (*ibid.* stanzas 41–4).

12. *Phoebo . . . tuo:* your Phoebus, *i.e.* the Vice-Chancellor.

13. *Cyllenius* was an epithet of Hermes (Mercury) going back to the Homeric Hymn to Hermes (1–2), which says that he was born on the Arcadian mountain, Cyllene.

15–16. *Eurybates,* one of the "heralds and bold retainers" of Agamemnon, the son of Atreus (*Il.* I, 320–33), who took their master's demand for Briseis to Achilles.

Magna sepulchrorum regina, satelles Averni,
    Saeva nimis Musis, Palladi saeva nimis,
Quin illos rapias qui pondus inutile terrae?
    Turba quidem est telis ista petenda tuis.   20
Vestibus hunc igitur pullis, Academia, luge,
    Et madeant lacrimis nigra feretra tuis.
Fundat et ipsa modos querebunda Elegeia tristes,
    Personet et totis naenia moesta scholis.

(1626)

---

17. Lake Avernus, near Naples, was one of the reputed entrances to Hades and its name came to signify hell itself. Milton's phrase, *satelles Averni,* was applied by Horace (*Odes,* II, xviii, 34) to Charon, but Milton's conception anticipates that of Death at Hell's gates in *P.L.* X, 268, scenting his "prey innumerable" on earth.

Great queen of sepulchres, accomplice of Avernus[17]—too terrible to the Muses and too terrible to Pallas—why do you not make your prey of those who are useless burdens of the earth?   That is the rabble which ought to be made the target of your darts.

Therefore grieve for this man, O Academe, in robes of black, and make his dark hearse wet with your tears.[22]   Let wailing Elegy herself pour out her sad dirge and fill all the schools with its sound.

---

22. In these *tears* and in the "tears of perfect moan" of the *Epitaph on the Marchioness of Winchester,* 55, and the "melodious tear" of *Lycidas,* 14, editors see a conventional allusion to the old practice of fastening mourning verses to the pall.

ELEGIA TERTIA

Anno Aetatis 17

In obitum Praesulis Wintoniensis

Moestus eram, et tacitus nullo comitante, sedebam.
  Haerebantque animo tristia plura meo,
Protinus en subiit funestae cladis imago
  Fecit in Angliaco quam Libitina solo;
Dum procerum ingressa est splendentes marmore turres   5
  Dira sepulchrali Mors metuenda face,
Pulsavitque auro gravidos et iaspide muros,
  Nec metuit satrapum sternere falce greges.
Tunc memini clarique ducis, fratrisque verendi,
  Intempestivis ossa cremata rogis;   10
Et memini Heroum quos vidit ad aethera raptos,
  Flevit et amissos Belgia tota duces.
At te praecipue luxi, dignissime praesul,
  Wintoniaeque olim gloria magna tuae;
Delicui fletu, et tristi sic ore querebar: 15
  "Mors fera, Tartareo diva secunda Iovi,
Nonne satis quod silva tuas persentiat iras,
  Et quod in herbosos ius tibi detur agros,
Quodque afflata tuo marcescant lilia tabo,
  Et crocus, et pulchrae Cypridi sacra rosa?   20
Nec sinis ut semper fluvio contermina quercus
  Miretur lapsus praetereuntis aquae;

3–8. The plague was extraordinarily severe throughout England in
1625 and 1626.

4. *Libitina,* an ancient Italian goddess of corpses whose name was
poetically used to mean death.

6. *Mors:* compare the use of the name in *Elegy* II, 4, and the characterization also.

7. Probably a reminiscence of Horace's "pale Death" that smites both
the cottages of the poor and the towers of kings:
  "Pallida Mors aequo pulsat pede pauperum tabernas
            Regumque turris."
            (*Odes* I, iv, 13–4.)

9. Editors identify the *duke* with Count Ernest of Mansfield and his
brother-in-arms, Christian, Duke of Brunswick, both of whom died
fighting on the Protestant side in the Thirty Years' War in 1626.

ELEGY III

At Age 17

ON THE DEATH OF THE BISHOP OF WINCHESTER

I WAS grief-stricken, and without any companion I was sitting in silence. Many sorrows were besetting my spirit,
when, lo, suddenly there arose a vision of the baneful destruction[3] which Libitina[4] wrought upon English soil when
dire Death[6]—terrible with his sepulchral torch—entered the
bright, marble palaces of the patricians, attacked the walls
that are weighted with jasper and gold, and presumed to
mow down hosts of princes with his scythe.[7] Then I remembered that glorious duke and his brother,[9] whose bones
were burned on untimely pyres; and I remembered the heroes
whom Belgia saw rapt into the skies—the lost leaders whom
the whole nation mourned. But my greatest grief was for
you, most worthy Bishop, and in time past the noble ornament of your Winchester.[14] I melted in tears and complained in this sad language.

"O fell Death, goddess second to Tartarean Jove,[16] are you
not satisfied that the forest suffers your fury, that power is
given to you over the herb-bearing fields and that the lilies,
the crocuses and the rose, that is sacred to the beautiful
Cypris,[20] wither when touched by your poisonous breath?
And you do not permit the oak on the river-bank to watch

---

14. Milton expressed the general feeling of his contemporaries about
Lancelot Andrewes (1555–1626). He had won universal love and respect as Master of Pembroke Hall, Cambridge (1595–1605), as a
preacher at Court and at Westminster, where he was Dean, as the
King's Almoner (or official dispenser of charity), and as Bishop successively of Chichester, Ely and Winchester.

16. *Tartareo . . . Iovi,* Pluto, the brother of Jove. Compare the
"nether Jove" of *Comus,* 20, note.

20. *Cypridi:* Cypris was one of the earliest names of Aphrodite
(Venus), because she was supposed to have risen from the sea near
Cyprus and had her principal temples there. See *Elegies* V, 60, and VII,
ᴄ and 48.

Et tibi succumbit liquido quae plurima caelo
  Evehitur pennis, quamlibet augur, avis,
Et quae mille nigris errant animalia silvis,   25
  Et quod alunt mutum Proteos antra pecus.
Invida, tanta tibi cum sit concessa potestas,
  Quid iuvat humana tingere caede manus?
Nobileque in pectus certas acuisse sagittas,
  Semideamque animam sede fugasse sua?"   30
Talia dum lacrymans alto sub pectore volvo,
  Roscidus occiduis Hesperus exit aquis,
Et Tartessiaco submerserat aequore currum
  Phoebus, ab eöo littore mensus iter.
Nec mora, membra cavo posui refovenda cubili,   35
  Condiderant oculos noxque soporque meos,
Cum mihi visus eram lato spatiarier agro.
  Heu! nequit ingenium visa referre meum.
Illic punicea radiabant omnia luce,
  Ut matutino cum iuga sole rubent,   40
Ac veluti cum pandit opes Thaumantia proles
  Vestitu nituit multicolore solum;
Non dea tam variis ornavit floribus hortos
  Alcinoi Zephyro Chloris amata levi.
Flumina vernantes lambunt argentea campos,   45
  Ditior Hesperio flavet arena Tago.

---

26. The *herd of Proteos*, the seals. See *Damon's Epitaph*, 99, note.

32. *Hesperus*, the evening star. Ovid uses the epithet *roscidus*—
dewy or dew-bringing—of it (*Fasti*, II, 314). Compare "roscida luna"
in *Damon's Epitaph*, 140, and also
                    "*Hesperus*, whose Office is to bring
                    Twilight upon the Earth."
                              (*P.L.* IX, 49–50.)

33. *Tartessiaco . . . aequore*: the ancient Tartessus, now El Rocadillo,
gave its name to the seas that wash the Atlantic coast of Spain. Ovid
speaks of the setting sun bathing the Spanish shores ("Tartessia litora,"
Met. XIV, 416).

34. *Phoebus* Apollo, who was often imagined as a sun-god by the
Greeks, was identified by the Roman poets with the other Greek sun-
god, Helios, the charioteer. See *Comus*, 95, note.

41. *Thaumantia proles*: Iris, goddess of the rainbow, who, Hesiod
says (*Theogony*, 265–6), was the daughter of Thaumas and Electra.

the flow of the ebbing water forever. And all the countless birds that are borne through the liquid sky on their pinions —in spite of their gift of prophecy—succumb to you, and so do the myriad wild creatures that stray in the dark forests and the dumb herd[26] which the caves of Proteus nourish. Envious one, when such vast power has been granted you, what pleasure is there in staining your hands with human slaughter, in sharpening your unerring darts against a noble breast, and driving a spirit that is half-divine from its habitation?"

While I was weeping and entertaining such meditations in my heart, the dewy Hesperus[32] rose out of the western sea and Phoebus[34]—after measuring his course from the Orient —had sunk his chariot in the Spanish ocean.[33] Not delaying, I sought rest for my limbs in the depths of my bed, and night and sleep had fast closed my eyes, when I seemed to be walking in a broad field—but, alas! my faculties cannot report what I saw. There all things were radiant with rosy light, like mountain-crests flushing in the morning sunshine. The earth was brilliant in a garb of many colours, as it is when the child of Thaumas[41] scatters her wealth abroad. Chloris,[44] the goddess beloved by delicate Zephyr, did not deck the gardens of Alcinous with such various flowers. Silver rivers washed the green fields and their sands gleamed with greater wealth than Hesperian Tagus.[46] Through the

---

44. *Chloris* (in Latin, Flora), Ovid says (*Fasti,* 195–398), was wooed by the west wind, Zephyr.

Again in *P.L.* V, 340–1, and IX, 441, Milton compared Paradise with Homer's gardens of Alcinous (*Od.* VI, 292–4).

46. The *Tagus,* which flows into the Atlantic at Lisbon, as Ovid (*Met.* II, 251) and several other Roman writers testify, was famous for its golden sand.

Serpit odoriferas per opes levis aura Favoni,
    Aura sub innumeris humida nata rosis.
Talis in extremis terrae Gangetidis oris
    Luciferi regis fingitur esse domus.   50
Ipse racemiferis dum densas vitibus umbras
    Et pellucentes miror ubique locos,
Ecce mihi subito praesul Wintonius astat,
    Sidereum nitido fulsit in ore iubar;
Vestis ad auratos defluxit candida talos;   55
    Infula divinum cinxerat alba caput.
Dumque senex tali incedit venerandus amictu,
    Intremuit laeto florea terra sono.
Agmina gemmatis plaudunt caelestia pennis;
    Pura triumphali personat aethra tuba.   60
Quisque novum amplexu comitem cantuque salutat,
    Hosque aliquis placido misit ab ore sonos:
"Nate, veni, et patrii felix cape gaudia regni;
    Semper abhinc duro, nate, labore vaca."
Dixit, et aligerae tetigerunt nablia turmae;   65
    At mihi cum tenebris aurea pulsa quies;
Flebam turbatos Cephaleia pellice somnos.
    Talia contingant somnia saepe mihi!

                                                    (1626)

47–48. *Favonius* was the Roman equivalent of the Greek Zephyr,
which Homer (*Od.* IV, 567) describes as blowing through the Elysian
Fields.   Compare *P.L.* IV, 329.

49. Compare the use of the *Ganges* to suggest the most distant east
in *P.L.* IX, 82.

50. *Lucifer*, the "light-bringer," is not the morning star of *Nativity
Hymn*, 74, nor the Satan of *P.L.*, but the sun himself. Claudian
(*Against Rufinus*, II, 336–7) describes him by that name, rising over
Mount Haemus and urging his chariot onward.   Here Milton may have
thought of Ovid's description of the palace of Phoebus (*Met.* II, 1–18),
which lay beyond India (*Met.* I, 778–9).

51–52. In the description of the sun's gardens with which Claudian
ended *On Stilicho's Consulship*, II, the god gathers fragrant flowers to
deck his steeds.

59. Keightley was probably right in saying that Milton thought of the
applause of the happy spirits in Virgil's Elysium:
          "Pars pedibus plaudunt choreas et carmina dicunt."
                      (*Aen.* VI, 644.)

61. Compare *Damon's Epitaph*, 215–19, and *Lycidas*, 178–81.

perfumed opulence stole the light breath of Faunus[47]—the dewy breath that is born beneath myriad roses. Such a place, on the most distant shores of the land of the Ganges,[49] do men imagine the home of the monarch, Lucifer,[50] to be. While I was looking with admiration at the shining landscape all around and at the shady retreats under the clustering vines,[51] lo, suddenly Winchester's bishop stood before me and a starry light shone in his glorious face. A robe of shining white fell flowing down to his golden sandals and a white fillet encircled his divine head. And while the reverend old man, arrayed in this way, walked forward, the flowery earth was vibrant with joyous sound. The heavenly host applauded[59] with their jewelled wings and the clear air of heaven rang with the triumphal trumpet. Everyone saluted his new companion with an embrace and a song,[61] and one of them uttered these words from his serene lips:

"Come, my son, and joyously enter into the delights of your father's kingdom; and rest here from your labours forever."[63]

He spoke, and the winged hosts touched their harps.[65] But my golden rest was banished with the night and I wept for the slumber that was disturbed by the mistress of Cephalus.[67] May dreams like these often befall me![68]

---

63. Compare Revelation xiv, 13: "And I heard a voice from heaven, . . . 'Blessed are the dead which die in the Lord. . . . Yea, saith the Spirit, that they may rest from their labours.'"

65. Compare the "voice of harpers harping with their harps," which St. John heard in heaven (Rev. xiv, 2).

67. *Cepheleia pellice,* the mistress of Cephalus, Aurora, the dawn, who carried him away—as Ovid makes him tell the story (*Met.* VII, 700–8)—quite against his will, from Procris, the wife whom he loved.

68. Perhaps, as Professor Rand suggests, the closing wish is a bold adaptation of Ovid's prayer for the return of a golden day with Corinna:

"Proveniant medii sic mihi saepe dies!"
(*Amores*, I, v. 26.)

IN OBITUM PRAESULIS ELIENSIS

Anno Aetatis 17

Adhuc madentes rore squalebant genae,
　　Et sicca nondum lumina
Adhuc liquentis imbre turgebant salis,
　　Quem nuper effudi pius,
Dum moesta caro iusta persolvi rogo   5
　　Wintoniensis praesulis,
Cum centilinguis Fama (proh! semper mali
　　Cladisque vera nuntia)
Spargit per urbes divitis Britanniae,
　　Populosque Neptuno satos,   10
Cessisse morti et ferreis sororibus,
　　Te, generis humani decus,
Qui rex sacrorum illa fuisti in insula
　　Quae nomen Anguillae tenet.
Tunc inquietum pectus ira protinus   15
　　Ebulliebat fervida,
Tumulis potentem saepe devovens deam:
　　Nec vota Naso in Ibida
Concepit alto diriora pectore;
　　Graiusque vates parcius   20
Turpem Lycambis execratus est dolum,
　　Sponsamque Neobulen suam.
At ecce! diras ipse dum fundo graves,
　　Et imprecor neci necem,
Audisse tales videor attonitus sonos   25
　　Leni, sub aura, flamine:
"Caecos furores pone; pone vitream
　　Bilemque et irritas minas.

---

6. Winchester's bishop, Lancelot Andrewes, the subject of *Elegy III*.

10. For the tradition that Britain was called after Neptune's son, Albion, see *On the Fifth of November,* 28–30, note.

11. The "iron" or implacable sisters are the Fates.

13–14. Literally, the name Ely means "eel-island."

18. When he went into exile Ovid attacked an unidentified enemy in a satire which he called *Ibis,* or *The Crane.*

20–22. The Greek poet, Archilochus of Paros, who is said to have

ON THE DEATH OF THE BISHOP OF ELY

At Age 17

MY CHEEKS were still drenched and stained with tears and my eyes, not yet dry, were still swollen with the rain of salt water which but now my reverent affection poured out as I paid my debt of sorrow to the bier of Winchester's beloved bishop,[6] when hundred-tongued Fame—alas! always the true messenger of evil and disaster—spreads through the cities of affluent Britain and the people who are descended from Neptune[10] the news that you—the ornament of mankind, who were the prince of the saints in the island called Ely[13]— had yielded to death and the implacable sisters.[11] Suddenly then my disquieted breast surged with hot anger and frequent imprecations upon the goddess who is powerful in the grave. Ovid, in the depths of his heart, conceived no worse curses against Ibis,[18] and the Greek poet was more restrained in his abuse of the shameful deceit of Lycambes and Neobule, his betrothed.[20] But behold, while I am pouring out these grievous curses and calling down death upon death[24]—astonished—I seem to hear these sounds in the gently moving air:

"Leave your blind anger, leave your madness and furious curses.[27] Why do you offer rash violence to deities which

been inspired to the writing of his great satires by the refusal of his fellow citizen, Lycambes, to allow his daughter, Neobule, to keep her promise to marry the poet.

24. Perhaps the play on "death" is due to passages like Hosea xiii, 14: "O death, I will be thy plagues; O grave, I will be thy destruction." The Vulgate reads: "ero mors tua, o mors."

27–28. *vitream bilem,* "glassy bile." Madness or melancholy was related to the black bile, but Burton (*Anatomy,* I, i, 3, 1) would not risk an opinion as to which "be a cause or an effect, a disease, or symptom." Galen, as MacKellar points out, attributed madness to a peculiar, glittering condition of the black bile, to which Horace referred (*Satires* II, iii, 141) when he called the homicidal fury of Orestes a kind of bondage to the "shining bile" (splendida bilis). Persius, in a similar passage, called it "glassy bile" (vitrea bilis). Compare the Preface to *S.A.,* l. 2, note.

Quid temere violas non nocenda numina,
   Subitoque ad iras percita?   30
Non est, ut arbitraris elusus miser,
   Mors atra Noctis filia,
Erebove patre creta, sive Erinnye,
   Vastove nata sub Chao:
Ast illa, caelo missa stellato, Dei   35
   Messes ubique colligit;
Animasque mole carnea reconditas
   In lucem et auras evocat,
Ut cum fugaces excitant Horae diem,
   Themidos Iovisque filiae;   40
Et sempiterni ducit ad vultus patris,
   At iusta raptat impios
Sub regna furvi luctuosa Tartari
   Sedesque subterraneas.
Hanc ut vocantem laetus audivi cito   45
   Foedum reliqui carcerem,
Volatilesque faustus inter milites
   Ad astra sublimis feror,
Vates ut olim raptus ad caelum senex,
   Auriga currus ignei.   50
Non me Boötis terruere lucidi
   Sarraca tarda frigore, aut
Formidolosi Scorpionis brachia,
   Non ensis, Orion, tuus.

31–34. Compare *On the Fifth of November,* 141–50, note.

33. Usually the Furies are thought of as a group of three or more earth-born monsters, avengers of crime, but Homer sometimes mentioned a single Fury. (*E.g., Il.* XIX, 87, and *Od.* XV, 234.)

34. The personification of Chaos goes back to Hesiod's statement that, "First Chaos was born, and then the broad-bosom'd Earth, the safe seat of all things for ever." (*Theogony,* 116.) Here it is hard to tell whether Chaos is regarded as a place or a deity. In *P.L.* II, 891, ff. the two conceptions are distinguished and combined.

37. The thought is essentially Christian, but Milton was familiar with Platonic passages like that in the *Phaedo,* 64a, where Socrates explains that a philosopher, when he is to die, has good ground to hope for greater blessings beyond the grave than he enjoys in this life. *On the religious memory of Mrs. Catherine Thomason,* l. 4, expresses the same thought in definitely Christian form.

cannot be harmed and are swift to anger? Contrary to your notion, O deluded wretch, Death is not the dark daughter of Night,[31] nor of Erebus nor of Erynis;[33] nor was she born in the gulf of Chaos.[34] But she is sent from the starry sky to reap God's harvest everywhere.[37] As the flying Hours, the daughters of Justice and Jove,[39] arouse the day, so she summons into the light and air the spirits which are buried under the weight of flesh, and she leads them into the presence of the eternal Father; but because she is just she sweeps the wicked away to the realms of grief in dark Tartarus, to the infernal abodes. I was glad when I heard her calling and eagerly I left my sordid prison. Among the winged warriors[47] I was carried aloft, clear to the stars, like the venerable prophet of old, charioteer of a fiery chariot, who was caught up to heaven.[49] I was not terrified either by the wain of bright Boötes,[51] slow-moving with the cold, nor by the claws of the frightful Scorpion,[53] nor by your sword, O Orion.

39–40. Hesiod made the Hours the daughters of Zeus and Themis, or Justice; but they appear first as followers of the sun god in Ovid's *Metamorphoses*, II, 26 and 118. Compare *O Nightingale*, 4, and *Comus*, 986, notes.

47. Compare the "winged Warriors" of *Upon the Circumcision*, 1, and the "wing'd Warrior" of *P.L.* IV, 576.

49–50. Compare the allusion to Elijah's translation to heaven in *P.R.* II, 16–7, note.

51–52. *Boötes*, "the ploughman," is the constellation containing Arcturus. The ancients thought of the Great Bear as "the ploughman's wain," which moves around the celestial pole more slowly than any other conspicuous group of stars. Here Milton remembered Juvenal's allusion to the proverbial "cold wain of lazy Boötes." (Frigida circumagunt pigri serraca Boötae.—*Satires*, V, 23.)

53–58. Milton must have been familiar with Cicero's account of the flight of Scipio's soul (in *The Dream of Scipio*) through the starry heavens and perhaps he already knew Dante's *Paradise*, with its record of the poet's ascent to the highest heaven. He was certainly familiar with less serious celestial journeys like Chaucer's in *The House of Fame*, Book II, and Phaeton's ride as Ovid described it (*Met.* II, 195–7), beset by the terrible Scorpion stretching his winding tail and arms across the sky.

Praetervolavi fulgidi solis globum,   55
    Longeque sub pedibus deam
Vidi triformem, dum coercebat suos
    Fraenis dracones aureis.
Erraticorum siderum per ordines,
    Per lacteas vehor plagas,   60
Velocitatem saepe miratus novam,
    Donec nitentes ad fores
Ventum est Olympi, et regiam Crystallinam, et
    Stratum smaragdis Atrium.
Sed hic tacebo, nam quis effari queat   65
    Oriundus humano patre
Amoentitates illius loci?   Mihi
    Sat est in aeternum frui."

                                                        (1626)

_____

57. When he referred to the moon's "countenance triform" in *P.L.*
III, 730, Milton considered primarily its three phases, but here he
thought of the three divinities in one—Luna, Diana and Proserpina or
Hecate—of Virgil's line,
        "Tergeminamque Hecaten, tria virginis ora Dianae."
                    (*Aen.* IV, 511.)

I flew beyond the globe of the glittering sun and far below my feet I saw the triform goddess[57] controlling her dragons[58] with reins of gold. Through the ranks of the planets and the Milky Way I was borne, wondering often at my strange speed, until I reached the shining portals of Olympus, the palace of crystal and the beryl-paved courts.[63] But here I fall silent, for who that is begotten of a mortal father can tell the delights of that place? For me it is enough to enjoy them forever."

---

58. Ancient writers never describe the moon's car as drawn by steeds any fiercer than the snow-white hinds of Claudian's description in *Stilicho's Consulship*, III, 285–91, or the bulls of his *Rape of Proserpine*, III, 403. Later tradition assigned her the "Dragon yoke" of *Il Penseroso*, 59. Compare *Comus*, 131, note.

63. Compare the "Crystal wall of Heav'n" in *P.L.* VI, 860, and heaven's "Frontispiece of Diamond and Gold" in III, 506. In the background is St. John's description of the new Jerusalem shining "like a jasper stone, clear as crystal" (Rev. xxi, 11). Milton merges the abode of the gods on Olympus with the Christian heaven and there is a suggestion here of Ovid's approach to the glittering doors of the palace of the sun. (*Met.* II, 1–7.)

IN OBITUM PROCANCELLARII MEDICI

Anno Aetatis 16 [*17*]

Parere fati discite legibus
Manusque Parcae iam date supplices,
   Qui pendulum telluris orbem
     Iapeti colitis nepotes.
Vos si relicto mors vaga Taenaro   5
Semel vocarit flebilis, heu! morae
   Tentantur incassum dolique;
     Per tenebras Stygis ire certum est.
Si destinatam pellere dextera
Mortem valeret, non ferus Hercules   10
   Nessi venenatus cruore
     Aemathia iacuisset Oeta;
Nec fraude turpi Palladis invidae
Vidisset occisum Ilion Hectora, aut
   Quem larva Pelidis peremit   15
     Ense Locro, Iove lacrymante.
Si triste fatum verba Hecateia
Fugare possint, Telegoni parens
   Vixisset infamis, potentique
     Aegiali soror usa virga.   20
Numenque trinum fallere si queant
Artes medentum, ignotaque gramina,
   Non gnarus herbarum Machaon
     Eurypyli cecidisset hasta;
Laesisset et nec te, Philyreie,   25
   Sagitta echidnae perlita sanguine;

---

4. Iapetus, who Hesiod (*Theogony,* 507–15) says was the father of Prometheus and Epimetheus, was identified by a tradition which Milton followed in *P.L.* I, 508, with the Japhet of Genesis x, 2, the son of Noah.

5. *Taenaro.* See *Elegy V,* 66, note.

10–12. Compare the allusion to the vengeance of the centaur, Nessus, upon Hercules in *P.L.* II, 542, note.

15–16. Milton thought of Homer's description of Sarpedon as he lay, like an oak felled by foresters or like a bull slain by a lion, under the walls of Troy when Patroclus slew him. (*Il.* XVI, 477–91.)

18. Compare the allusion to Circe in *Comus,* 253, and the note. Tradition made her the mother of Telegon by Ulysses.

ON THE DEATH OF THE VICE-CHANCELLOR,
A PHYSICIAN

At Age 16 [*17*]

LEARN obedience to the laws of destiny and lift suppliant hands to the Goddess of Fate, you descendants of Iapetus[4] who inhabit the pendulous orb of the earth. If Death, the grievous rover from Tartarus,[5] once summons you, alas! it is vain to try delays and tricks. The journey through the shadows of the Styx is inevitable. If the human arm had power to repel fated death, the poisonous blood of Nessus would not have laid the untamable Hercules low on Thessalian Oeta;[10] nor would Troy have seen Hector slain by the shameful deceit of vengeful Athene, nor Sarpedon killed[15]—though Jove shed tears—by the Locrian disguised in Achilles' armour. If the spells of Hecate could banish sad fate, Circe[18] would have lived on in her infamy and Medea would have survived to use her potent wand.[19] If the arts of the physicians and mysterious herbs had power to deceive the triple deity, Machaon,[23] with his knowledge of medicinal plants, would not have succumbed to the wound of Eurypylus' spear; nor would the arrow smeared with serpent's blood have stricken you, O son of Philyra;[25] nor would you have been smitten

---

19–20. The child Aegialeus, or Absyrtus, was Medea's brother, whose limbs Apollodorus (*Bibliotheca*, I, 112–3) describes her as throwing into the sea so as to divert her father, Æetes, in his pursuit of her when she fled in the *Argo* with Jason.

23–24. Homer calls Machaon a healer among the Greeks before Troy (*Il.* XI, 514). His death is described by Quintus Smyrnaeus as coming from the hands of Eurypylus. (*The Fall of Troy,* VI, 391–428.)

25–26. Though the centaur, Chiron, the son of the nymph, Philyra, was immortal and was the tutor of the god of healing, Aesculapius, whom his father, Apollo, cut from the womb of his mother, Coronis, he was destined to beg his death from the Fates as a cure for the wounds of Hercules' poisoned arrows. (Ovid, *Met.* II, 596–654.) Aesculapius was killed by Zeus, as Milton goes on to say that the Vice-Chancellor was by Persephone, because his medical skill saved too many lives.

Nec tela te fulmenque avitum,
    Caese puer genitricis alvo.
Tuque O alumno major Apolline,
Gentis togatae cui regimen datum,   30
    Frondosa quem nunc Cirrha luget,
        Et mediis Helicon in undis,
Iam praefuisses Palladio gregi
Laetus superstes, nec sine gloria;
    Nec puppe lustrasses Charontis   35
        Horribiles barathri recessus.
At fila rupit Persephone tua
Irata cum te viderit artibus
    Succoque pollenti tot atris
        Faucibus eripuisse mortis.   40
Colende praeses, membra precor tua
Molli quiescant cespite, et ex tuo
    Crescant rosae calthaeque busto,
        Purpureoque hyacinthus ore.
Sit mite de te iudicium Aeaci,   45
Subrideatque Aetnaea Proserpina,
    Interque felices perennis
        Elysio spatiere campo.

(1626)

---

29. Dr. John Gostlin, who became Regius Professor of Medicine at
Cambridge in 1623 and was elected Vice-Chancellor for the second
time in 1625, died on October 21, 1626.

The line is difficult, but the reading is justified by both early editions.
There is nothing really impossible in making Apollo the pupil of Dr.
Gostlin, for the extravagant compliment would harmonize with the
spirit of the poem.

with the bolts and thunder of your grandsire, O boy cut from your mother's womb.

And you—who are greater than your pupil, Apollo,[29] to whom the government of our gowned society was given, and whom leafy Cirrha[31] mourns and Helicon in the midst of its streams—you would be the happy and glorious leader of the flock of Athena[33] instead of traversing the frightful depths of hell in Charon's boat. But Persephone broke the thread of your life,[37] angered because she saw you snatching so many victims from the black jaws of death by your arts and powerful potions.

Reverend Chancellor, may your limbs find rest in the soft turf, I pray, and from your grave may roses and marigolds and the purple-lipped hyacinth spring. May the judgement of Aeacus upon you be gentle, and may Sicilian Proserpina smile! May you walk forever among the blessed in Elysium!

31. Cirrha was a port associated with Apollo and situated not far from his shrine at Delphi. Here it represents Cambridge, as Mount Parnassus and the springs which the Muses haunted represent the learned world generally.

33. Again in the Second Elegy, 2, the University community at Cambridge is called "the flock of Athene" or "the Palladian host."

37. Milton gives the Queen of Hell, Persephone, the power to slit the thread of human life which was usually attributed to Atropos, the third of the goddesses of Fate. Compare *Lycidas,* 75, note.

IN QUINTUM NOVEMBRIS

Anno Aetatis 17

Iam pius extrema veniens Iacobus ab arcto
Teucrigenas populos, lateque patentia regna
Albionum tenuit, iamque inviolabile foedus
Sceptra Caledoniis coniunxerat Anglica Scotis:
Pacificusque novo, felix divesque, sedebat   5
In solio, occultique doli securus et hostis:
Cum ferus ignifluo regnans Acheronte tyrannus,
Eumenidum pater, aethereo vagus exul Olympo,
Forte per immensum terrarum erraverat orbem,
Dinumerans sceleris socios, vernasque fideles,   10
Participes regni post funera moesta futuros.
Hic tempestates medio ciet aere diras;
Illic unanimes odium struit inter amicos.
Armat et invictas in mutua viscera gentes,
Regnaque olivifera vertit florentia pace;   15
Et quoscunque videt purae virtutis amantes,
Hos cupit adiicere imperio, fraudumque magister
Tentat inaccessum sceleri corrumpere pectus,
Insidiasque locat tacitas, cassesque latentes
Tendit, ut incautos rapiat, ceu Caspia Tigris   20
Insequitur trepidam deserta per avia praedam
Nocte sub illuni, et somno nictantibus astris.
Talibus infestat populos Summanus et urbes,
Cinctus caeruleae fumanti turbine flammae.
Iamque fluentisonis albentia rupibus arva   25
Apparent, et terra Deo dilecta marino,

---

2. Milton shared the contemporary interest in "Trojan Brute," whose colonization of England Spenser described at length in *The Faerie Queene* (II, x, 9 and III, ix, 46–51). The legend goes back to Geoffrey of Monmouth, who represents Brutus as a grandson of Aeneas.

7. *Acheron,* "the stream of woe," was one of the four rivers of hell. Like *Phlegethon* in l. 74 and like Acheron in *Comus,* 604, it stands for hell itself.

8. Perhaps Milton remembered that Virgil (*Aen.* VII, 327) made Pluto the father of the Eumenides or Furies, the avengers of crime. Here there is a suggestion of Christian tradition like that which made Satan, the exile from heaven, the father of Sin and Death in *P.L.* II, 747–89.

ON THE FIFTH OF NOVEMBER

At Age 17

Now the devout James, coming from the remote north, assumed the lordship of the Troy-born race[2] and of the wide-spreading realms of the English, and now an inviolable league had united the English and the Scottish sceptres. The establisher of peace was seated on his new throne, fortunate and affluent, with no suspicion of a secret conspiracy or of a foe, when the cruel tyrant who governs the fiery streams of Acheron,[7] the father of the Eumenides,[8] the wandering outcast from the celestial Olympus, chanced to range through the vast circle of the earth, counting the companions of his wickedness, his faithful slaves, who are destined after their miserable deaths to take their share in his kingdom.

Here he stirs up wild tempests in mid air;[12] there he instigates hatred among loyal friends. He arms unconquerable nations for a death-struggle together and overturns kingdoms which are flourishing under the olive of peace. Whatever lovers of pure virtue he can find, he seeks to add to his empire and—master of guile that he is—he tries to corrupt even the heart that is locked against sin. He lays silent plots and stretches unseen nets to capture the unwary, like the Caspian[20] tigress pursuing her trembling prey through trackless deserts at night in the moonless darkness when the stars are drowsily glimmering. With horrors like his does Summanus,[23] girdled with a smoking tornado of lightning flame, beset peoples and cities. And now he sees the white fields and wave-beaten cliffs of the favourite land of the sea-god,

---

12. Compare the demon-haunted middle air in *P.R.*, especially Book II, 117, and its note.

20. Compare the note on *Caucasus* in *P.R.* III, 318.

23. Summanus, an ancient god of lightning at midnight, was identified with Pluto by Ovid. (*Fasti*, VI, 731.)

Cui nomen dederat quondam Neptunia proles,
Amphitryoniaden qui non dubitavit atrocem,
Aequore tranato, furiali poscere bello,
Ante expugnatae crudelia saecula Troiae.   30
　　At simul hanc, opibusque et festa pace beatam,
Aspicit, et pingues donis Cerealibus agros,
Quodque magis doluit, venerantem numina veri
Sancta Dei populum, tandem suspiria rupit
Tartareos ignes et luridum olentia sulphur.   35
Qualia Trinacria trux ab Iove clausus in Aetna
Efflat tabifico monstrosus ab ore Typhoeus.
Ignescunt oculi, stridetque adamantinus ordo
Dentis, ut armorum fragor, ictaque cuspide cuspis;
Atque "Pererrato solum hoc lacrymabile mundo   40
Inveni," dixit, "gens haec mihi sola rebellis,
Contemtrixque iugi, nostraque potentior arte.
Illa tamen, mea si quicquam tentamina possunt,
Non feret hoc impune diu, non ibit inulta."
Hactenus; et piceis liquido natat aere pennis;   45
Qua volat, adversi praecursant agmine venti,
Densantur nubes, et crebra tonitrua fulgent.
　　Iamque pruinosas velox superaverat alpes,
Et tenet Ausoniae fines.　A parte sinistra
Nimbifer Apenninus erat, priscique Sabini;   50
Dextra veneficiis infamis Etruria,　nec non
Te furtiva, Tibris, Thetidi videt oscula dantem;
Hinc Mavortigenae consistit in arce Quirini.

28–30. "Albion, a giant son of Neptune, who called the island after his own name," Milton wrote in the *History of Britain* (*P.W.* V, 166), "ruled it forty-four years.　Till at length passing over into Gaul, in aid of his brother Lestrygon, against whom Hercules was hasting out of Spain into Italy, he was there slain in fight."

32. Compare "a field of Ceres ripe for harvest."　*P.L.* IV, 980–1.

36–37. Milton was familiar with Ovid's account (*Met.* V, 346–58) of the entire island of Sicily as resting on the body of the Titan, Typhoeus, whose struggles explain its volcanoes and earthquakes.

38. Compare Satan's "Eyes That Sparkling blaz'd" in *P.L.* I, 193–4.

48. The line reflects Lucan's picture of Caesar surmounting the frozen Alps on his way to the Rubicon and Rome:
　　　　"Iam gelidas Caesar cursu superaverat Alpes."
　　　　(On the Civil War, Book I, 183.)

the land to which Neptune's son long ago gave his name,[28] he who was bold enough to cross the sea and challenge Hercules to a dire combat before the dreadful times of the conquest of Troy.

As soon as he catches sight of this land in its enjoyment of the blessings of wealth and festal peace, with its fields rich in the gifts of Ceres[32] and—what irked him worse—a people worshipping the sacred deity of the true God, he broke into sighs that were redolent of lurid sulphur and the fires of Tartarus. Such sighs the horrid and monstrous Typhoeus, whom Jove imprisoned under Sicilian Aetna,[36] emits from his consuming mouth. His eyes flash[38] and his adamantine array of teeth grinds like the clash of arms and the blow of spear against spear. "After wandering throughout the whole world," says he, "I find this my only grief, this nation alone rebellious against me, contemptuous of my yoke and stronger than my art. Yet if my efforts avail at all, they shall not go on so with impunity, they shall not continue unpunished." That much he said and oared away on pitch-black wings through the liquid air. Wherever he flies warring winds run before him; clouds mass up and thunderbolts flash incessantly.

Now his speed had carried him beyond the frosty Alps[48] and he reaches the borders of Italy. To his left was the cloud-wrapped Apennine chain, the home of the ancient Sabines; to his right, Etruria, infamous for its magic potions; and not far away he sees the furtive kisses which you are giving to the sea, O Tiber.[52] Thence he came to rest on the citadel of Quirinus, the son of Mars. The dusk of evening

---

52. In later Roman poetry the name of the sea-nymph, Thetis, often stood for the sea itself. Here the god of the river Tiber is imagined as kissing Thetis because his stream falls gently through its delta into the Mediterranean.

Reddiderant dubiam iam sera crepuscula lucem,
Cum circumgreditur totam Tricoronifer urbem,   55
Panificosque Deos portat, scapulisque virorum
Evehitur; praeeunt submisso poplite reges,
Et mendicantum series longissima fratrum;
Cereaque in manibus gestant funalia caeci,
Cimmeriis nati in tenebris vitamque trahentes.   60
Templa dein multis subeunt lucentia taedis—
Vesper erat sacer iste Petro—fremitusque canentum
Saepe tholos implet vacuos, et inane locorum.
Qualiter exululat Bromius, Bromiique caterva,
Orgia cantantes in Echionio Aracyntho,   65
Dum tremit attonitus vitreis Asopus in undis,
Et procul ipse cava responsat rupe Cithaeron.
   His igitur tandem solenni more peractis,
Nox senis amplexus Erebi taciturna reliquit,
Praecipitesque impellit equos stimulante flagello,   70
Captum oculis Typhlonta, Melanchaetemque ferocem,
Atque Acherontaeo prognatam parte Siopen
Torpidam, et hirsutis horrentem Phrica capillis.
   Interea regum domitor, Phlegetontius haeres,
Ingreditur thalamos—neque enim secretus adulter   75
Producit steriles molli sine pellice noctes;
At vix compositos somnus claudebat ocellos
Cum niger umbrarum dominus, rectorque silentum

---

60. Compare *Cimmerian* in *L'Allegro*, 10, and its note.

62. The feast of St. Peter is celebrated on June twenty-eighth.

65. Mount Aracynthus lies on the Attic frontier of Boeotia. Echion was one of the Theban heroes who sprang from the dragon's teeth sown by Cadmus.

66. The Asopus is a tributary of the Euripus, with its source on Mount Cithaeron.

67. Mount Cithaeron, which separates Boeotia and Megara from Attica, Ovid says (*Met*. III, 702) was the scene of the first celebration of the rites of Bacchus.

69. Compare the "eldest Night" of *P.L.* II, 894. Hesiod describes Night as the daughter of Chaos (*Theogony*, 123-4) and as ancestress, with her brother Erebus, of all created things.

had already made the light uncertain, when the wearer of the Triple Crown, borne on men's shoulders, makes a circuit of the whole city, carrying with him his gods made of bread. Kings went before him with bended knee and the vast procession of mendicant brothers. They carried wax candles in their hands—those men who are born and lead their lives in Cimmerian darkness.[60] Then they enter the temples that gleam with many a torch (it was the eve sacred to St. Peter[62]) and the cry of the chanters often fills the hollow domes and void spaces. Such are the shrieks of Bacchus and the followers of Bacchus when they chant their orgies on Theban Aracynthus,[65] while astonished Asopus[66] shudders under his glassy waves and in the distance Cithaeron[67] itself gives back the sound from its hollow cliff.

When at last these rites had been performed with solemn pomp, Night[69] silently left the embraces of old Erebus to drive her swift coursers with the goading whip; blind Typhlos, cross-grained Melanchaetes, torpid Siope born of an infernal sire, and Phrix with his shaggy, rough hair.[70]

Meanwhile the tamer of kings, and heir of hell[74] enters his chamber (for the secret adulterer passes no barren nights without a gentle concubine); but sleep was hardly quieting and closing his eyes when the dark lord of shadows, the ruler

---

70–73. Milton imagined Night as Virgil described her:
  "Et Nox atra polum bigis subvecta tenebat."
              (*Aen.* V, 721.)
"Her twyfold Teme, of which," Spenser said (*F.Q.* I, v, 28) two were "blacke as pitch, And two were brown," had no traditional names. Milton's epithets indicate the original Greek significance of the names which he gave to the horses, except in the case of Melanchaetes, the "black-haired." Perhaps he remembered the names which Claudian invented for the horses of Pluto's chariot in the *Rape of Proserpine* (I, 284–6); Orphnaeus, Aethon, Nycteus and Alastor.

74. Phlegethon, "the flaming," was one of the rivers of hell. Compare the note on l. 7 above.

Praedatorque hominum, falsa sub imagine tectus,
Astitit. Assumptis micuerunt tempora canis;   80
Barba sinus promissa tegit; cineracea longo
Syrmate verrit humum vestis; pendetque cucullus
Vertice de raso; et, ne quicquam desit ad artes,
Cannabeo lumbos constrinxit fune salaces,
Tarda fenestratis figens vestigia calceis.   85
Talis, uti fama est, vasta Franciscus eremo
Tetra vagabatur solus per lustra ferarum,
Silvestrique tulit genti pia verba salutis
Impius, atque lupos domuit, Libycosque leones.
  Subdolus at tali Serpens velatus amictu   90
Solvit in has fallax ora execrantia voces:
  "Dormis, nate?   Etiamne tuos sopor opprimit artus?
Immemor O fidei, pecorumque oblite tuorum!
Dum cathedram, venerande, tuam diademaque triplex
Ridet Hyperboreo gens barbara nata sub axe,   95
Dumque pharetrati spernunt tua iura Britanni.
Surge, age! surge piger, Latius quem Caesar adorat,
Cui reserata patet convexi ianua caeli.
Turgentes animos et fastus frange procaces,
Sacrilegique sciant tua quid maledictio possit,   100
Et quid Apostolicae possit custodia clavis;
Et memor Hesperiae disiectam ulciscere classem,
Mersaque Iberorum lato vexilla profundo,

80–89. Warton first compared Satan's disguise here with that in
which he approached Christ in *P.R.* I, 314–20, and noticed also that
the picture has close analogues in Buchanan's satires of the Franciscans,
"Franciscannus" (*Buchani Poemata,* 1687, p. 261) and the "Somnium"
(*ibid,* p. 293).

86–89. It seems likely that St. Francis, the founder of the Franciscan
Order, is intended, for his sermons to the birds and his conversion of
the wolf of Agobio were familiar and Milton may have been well
enough acquainted with his legend to know of the African journey
which *The Little Flowers* (IX, vi) record. Warton referred to an old
print of St. Francis Xavier taming lions in the desert; but, though Milton's "Libyan lions" may have been merely conventional, they fit
St. Francis of Assisi better than the Jesuit missionary to the Indies.

90–91. Here as well as in the picture of Satan "collecting all his
Serpent wiles" in *P.R.* III, 5, Milton followed the biblical conception of
him as "that old serpent." (Rev. xii, 9 and xx, 2.)

92. So Aeneas dreamed that Mercury saluted him with the words,
"Goddess-born." (*Aen.* IV, 560.)

of the speechless dead, who preys upon men, stood beside him, covered with a false shape. His temples shone under the disguise of grey hairs; a long beard covered his breast; his ash-coloured robe trailed with a long train on the ground; a hood dangled from his shaven crown; and—to make his wiles complete—his lustful loins are bound with a hempen rope and his slow feet are thrust into laced sandals.[80]   In such a guise, the story goes, Francis used to wander in the expanse of the desert, alone among the hideous haunts of wild beasts; and, though he was impious himself, he bore the pious word of salvation to the woodland folk, and tamed the wolves and the Libyan lions.[86]

Dressed in such a garb the Deceiver, the Serpent,[90] lyingly shaped his execrable lips to these words;

"Do you sleep, my son?[92]   Does slumber weigh down your limbs?   O, heedless of the faith and neglectful of your flocks! While a savage nation born under the northern sky[95] mocks your throne and your triple crown and while the archer-English[96] insult your rights, O venerable one. Up and act![97]   Up from this indolence, you whom the Roman Emperor venerates and for whom the locked gate of the vault of heaven lies open; break their insolent spirit and upstart pride, and let the sacrilegious know the force of your malediction and the power of your control of the Apostolic key. Remember to avenge the scattered Hesperian fleet,[102] the Iberian standards swallowed by the sea's depths, and the

---

95. *Hyperboreo* means hardly more than "northern," although Milton may have remembered that Diodorus Siculus (2, 47) located the Hyperborean land in the sea "opposite Gaul."

96. The "quivered-" or "archer-English" is an allusion to the reputation for skill with the long bow which was won in the Hundred Years' War and which Roger Ascham wrote his *Toxophilus* to try to help maintain.

97. The summons, "Up and act," parallels a divine call to Aeneas in a vision. (*Aen.* III, 169.)

102. Hesperia rarely meant Spain in classical Latin, *e.g.* Horace, *Odes,* I, xxxvi, 4. The reference is to the Spanish Armada.

Sanctorumque cruci tot corpora fixa probrosae,
Thermodoontea nuper regnante puella.   105
At tu si tenero mavis torpescere lecto,
Crescentesque negas hosti contundere vires,
Tyrrhenum implebit numeroso milite Pontum,
Signaque Aventino ponet fulgentia colle.
Relliquias veterum franget, flammisque cremabit,   110
Sacraque calcabit pedibus tua colla profanis,
Cuius gaudebant soleis dare basia reges.
Nec tamen hunc bellis et aperto Marte lacesses;
Irritus ille labor; tu callidus utere fraude.
Quaelibet haereticis disponere retia fas est.   115
Iamque ad consilium extremis rex magnus ab oris
Patricios vocat, et procerum de stirpe creatos,
Grandaevosque patres trabea canisque verendos;
Hos tu membratim poteris conspergere in auras,
Atque dare in cineres, nitrati pulveris igne   120
Aedibus iniecto, qua convenere, sub imis.
Protinus ipse igitur quoscunque habet Anglia fidos
Propositi factique mone. quisquamne tuorum
Audebit summi non iussa facessere Papae?
Perculsosque metu subito, casuque stupentes,   125
Invadat vel Gallus atrox, vel saevus Iberus.
Saecula sic illic tandem Mariana redibunt,
Tuque in belligeros iterum dominaberis Anglos.
Et, nequid timeas, divos divasque secundas
Accipe, quotque tuis celebrantur numina fastis."   130
    Dixit, et adscitos ponens malefidus amictus
Fugit ad infandam, regnum illaetabile, Lethen.

104–105. Several Jesuit missionaries suffered martyrdom under Elizabeth.

105. The river Thermodon (the modern Thermeh) in Pontus was
famous for the Amazons who were supposed to live on its banks. Milton was familiar with many compliments to Elizabeth like that which
Spenser paid her when he called her greater than the Amazonian
queen, the "bold Penthesilee." (F.Q. III, iv, 2, 5.)

108. The Greeks called that part of the Mediterranean which washes
the west coast of Italy the Tyrrhene Sea. Compare Comus, 49.

109. The summit of the Aventine is one of the most conspicuous
landmarks in modern Rome.

116–118. The representatives in the House of Commons, the heredi-
tary peers and the bishops in the House of Lords seem to be intended

bodies of so many saints shamefully hung on gallows[104] during the recent reign of the Amazonian virgin.[105] If you prefer to lie languid in your soft bed and refuse to crush the growing strength of the foe, he will soon fill the Tyrrhene Sea[108] with a numerous host and plant his glittering standards on the Aventine hill.[109] He will destroy and burn with fire what remains of the ancients and with profane feet he will trample upon your neck—you, whose shoes kings were once glad to kiss. Yet you must not attack him with open war. To do so would be lost labour. Rather be shrewd enough to use treachery. It is lawful to spread nets of any kind for heretics. Just now the great king is summoning the patricians[116] from distant places to council, summoning men sprung from distinguished stock and the venerable old fathers, gowned and grey-haired. You have it in your power to scatter their dismembered bodies through the air, to burn them to cinders, by exploding nitrous powder under the halls where they will assemble. Immediately therefore give notice to whatever faithful there are in England of the deed proposed. Will any of your people dare neglect the commands of the sovereign Pope? Then let the fierce Gaul or savage Spaniard attack them instantly, while they are panic-stricken and stupefied by the catastrophe. So at last the Marian[127] epoch will return to that land and you will rule again over the warlike English. And—so that you may fear nothing— accept the fact that the gods and goddesses are favourable,[130] as many deities as are honoured in your feast days."

So the deceiver spoke and, doffing his disguise, fled to Lethe,[132] the unspeakable and joyless kingdom.

---

by the patricians, the men sprung from distinguished stock and the fathers respectively.

127. There is a pun in "Mariana," for the word occurs in Florus' *Epitome* (3, 12, 11 and 4, 2, 2), where it refers to the fury of the soldiers of Marius in the long civil war with Sulla.

130. The gods and goddesses are the saints of the Church.

132. In *P.L.* II, 583, Milton makes *"Lethe* the River of Oblivion" one of the infernal rivers.

Iam rosea Eoas pandens Tithonia portas
Vestit inauratas redeunti lumine terras;
Maestaque adhuc nigri deplorans funera nati   135
Irrigat ambrosiis montana cacumina guttis;
Cum somnos pepulit stellatae ianitor aulae
Nocturnos visus et somnia grata revolvens.
   Est locus aeterna septus caligine noctis,
Vasta ruinosi quondam fundamina tecti,   140
Nunc torvi spelunca Phoni, Prodotaeque bilinguis,
Effera quos uno peperit Discordia partu.
Hic inter caementa iacent praeruptaque saxa
Ossa inhumata virum, et traiecta cadavera ferro;
Hic Dolus intortis semper sedet ater ocellis,   145
Iurgiaque, et stimulis armata Calumnia fauces,
Et Furor, atque viae moriendi mille, videntur,
Et Timor, exanguisque locum circumvolat Horror,
Perpetuoque leves per muta silentia Manes
Exululant, tellus et sanguine conscia stagnat.   150
Ipsi etiam pavidi latitant penetralibus antri
Et Phonos et Prodotes, nulloque sequente per antrum,
Antrum horrens, scopulosum, atrum feralibus umbris,
Diffugiunt sontes, et retro lumina vortunt.
Hos pugiles Romae per saecula longa fideles   155
Evocat antistes Babylonius, atque ita fatur:
   "Finibus occiduis circumfusum incolit aequor
Gens exosa mihi, prudens natura negavit
Indignam penitus nostro coniungere mundo.

---

133. In making this transition with the picture of Dawn Milton followed an epic device which goes back to Homer's opening of the
fifth book of the *Odyssey:* "Now Dawn rose from her bed, from the
side of the lordly Tithonus, to bear light to the immortals and to mortal
men." Compare *P.L.* V, 1–2, and VI, 12–5, and *Elegy V*, 49, note.

135. *Memnon*—the son of the Dawn, Aurora, and of Tithonus, whose
slaying by Achilles is mentioned in the *Odyssey*, XI, 521. Compare
Il Penseroso, 18, and the note.

137. Because he has the keys of heaven, Milton called the Pope the
door-keeper of the skies.

141–150. Milton found models in Hesiod's list of the children of
Night—Death, Distress, the Fates, the Eumenides, Murders and Quarrels, Anarchy, Disaster and many more—and in countless similar
catalogues of which perhaps the most influential was Phineas Fletcher's

Now rosy Dawn,[133] throwing open the eastern gates, dresses the gilded world with returning light, and grieving for the sad death of her swarthy son[135] she sprinkles the mountain-tops with ambrosial tears. Then the keeper of the starry vault[137] banished slumber, turning over his nocturnal visions and delightful dreams.

There is a place wrapped eternally in the darkness of night, once the vast foundation of a structure now ruinous which has become the den of brutal Murder and double-tongued Treason, twins whom savage Discord bore. Here amid rubble and shattered rock lie the unburied bones of men and corpses pierced by steel; here forever sits dark Guile with eyes distorted, and Contentions and Calumny with her fang-armed jaws, and Fury and a thousand ways of dying and Fear are seen.[141] Pale Horror wings about the place and unsubstantial ghosts shriek perpetually through the mute silences.[149] The conscious earth[150] rots with blood. Murder and Treason themselves shudder in the inmost depths of the cavern and, though no one pursues them, through the cave—a horrid cave with outcropping rocks and dark with deathly shadows—the guilty pair flee away with many a backward glance. The Babylonian high priest[156] summons these defenders of Rome which have been faithful to her for centuries, and thus he speaks:

"A race that is odious to me lives on the western verge of the world amid the surrounding ocean. Prudent Nature has cut that unworthy people off from our continent. Thither,

account of the companions of Sin at Hell's gate—Despair, Sickness, Languor, Fear, Fright, Horror, Grief and Pangs. (*Apollyonists*, I, 15–6.)

149. *muta silentia*, "mute silences," is a reminiscence of Ovid's "mute silences of the night" (*Met.* VII, 184) which left its trace also in *Il Penseroso*, 55.

150. So Ovid speaks (*Met.* II, 438) of the "conscious forest" which knew of Jove's love-thefts. Compare the description of the devils laying their plots "under conscious Night" in *P.L.* VI, 521.

156. The Babylonian high priest is the Pope. Compare the allusion to Rome as Babylon in *Avenge, O Lord, thy slaughter'd Saints*, 14.

Illuc, sic iubeo, celeri contendite gressu,   160
Tartareoque leves difflentur pulvere in auras
Et rex et pariter satrapae, scelerata propago,
Et quotquot fidei caluere cupidine verae
Consilii socios adhibete, operisque ministros."
Finierat, rigidi cupide paruere gemelli.   165
    Interea longo flectens curvamine caelos
Despicit aetherea dominus qui fulgurat arce,
Vanaque perversae ridet conamina turbae,
Atque sui causam populi volet ipse tueri.
    Esse ferunt spatium, qua distat ab Aside terra   170
Fertilis Europe, et spectat Mareotidas undas;
Hic turris posita est Titanidos ardua Famae,
Aerea, lata, sonans, rutilis vicinior astris
Quam superimpositum vel Athos vel Pelion Ossae.
Mille fores aditusque patent, totidemque fenestrae,   175
Amplaque per tenues translucent atria muros.
Excitat hic varios plebs agglomerata susurros;
Qualiter instrepitant circum mulctralia bombis
Agmina muscarum, aut texto per ovilia iunco,
Dum Canis aestivum caeli petit ardua culmen.   180
Ipsa quidem summa sedet ultrix matris in arce,

---

161. So in the papal council in Phineas Fletcher's *Locustae* (*Poems*, ed. by Grosart, Vol. II, p. 44) the Jesuit, inspired by the fiend, Aequivocus, proposes the destruction of the English Parliament with "Stygian powder" and imagines the spectacle:
        "juvat semusta virorum
    Membra, omnesque supra volitantes aethere Reges
    Cernere."

166. Compare *Comus,* 1015: "Where the bow'd welkin slow doth bend." Milton had Ovid's "wide curve of the heavens" (*Met.* II, 130, and VI, 64) in mind, and perhaps also, as Todd suggested, Psalm xviii, 9: "He bowed the heavens also."

168. Psalm ii, 4—"He that sitteth in the heavens shall laugh; the Lord shall have them in derision."—is echoed again in *P.L.* II, 731, V, 737, and VIII, 78.

171. Lake Mareotis lies west of the Nile, not far from Alexandria. Here it represents Africa, for Milton made the house of Fame equidistant from Europe, Asia and Africa. So Ovid described it, vaguely centred amid the three continents of the world and commanding an outlook everywhere. (*Met.* XII, 39–40.)

172. Fame, or Rumour, Virgil said (*Aen.* IV, 178–180) was the

for so I command, you are to go with all speed; you are to bring all who are fired with love for the true faith into the plot and make them the tools of its execution. Let the king and his nobles together, the whole wicked race, be blown into thin air by Tartarean powder."[161] He ended and the cruel twins were eager in their obedience.

Meanwhile the Lord, who turns the heavens in their wide revolution[166] and hurls the lightning from his skyey citadel, laughs[168] at the vain undertakings of the degenerate mob and is willing to take upon himself the defence of his people's cause.

There is a place situated, men say, with its aspect toward Lake Mareotis,[171] in the gulf between fertile Europe and Asia. Here is the lofty tower of Titanean Fame[172]—a brazen structure, broad, noise-haunted, and closer to the glowing stars than Athos or Pelion, piled upon Ossa.[174] A thousand doors and entrances and no fewer windows are open wide and the courts within shine through the unsubstantial walls. Here a crush of people start various whispers. So swarms of flies buzz and hum about the milk-pails or in the wattled sheepfolds,[178] when in summer the Dog Star climbs aloft to the summit of the skies. Fame herself, the avenger of her mother, sits atop of her citadel and raises her

---

youngest of the Titans. Milton's description of her draws almost all its details alternately from those of Virgil and Ovid.

174. When the Titans rebelled against the gods, Homer said in a famous passage (*Od.* XI, 312-5), they tried to overwhelm Mount Olympus by burying it under Mounts Ossa and Pelion. Both mountains are in Thessaly, while Athos is a peak at the end of the most easterly promontory of Chalcidice in Macedon.

178-179. The simile is Homeric. Compare its use in *P.R.* IV, 15-7, and the note there.

Auribus innumeris cinctum caput eminet olli,
Queis sonitum exiguum trahit, atque levissima captat
Murmura, ab extremis patuli confinibus orbis.
Nec tot, Aristoride, servator inique iuvencae   185
Isidos, immite volvebas lumina vultu,
Lumina non unquam tacito nutantia somno,
Lumina subiectas late spectantia terras.
Istis illa solet loca luce carentia saepe
Perlustrare, etiam radianti impervia soli.   190
Millenisque loquax auditaque visaque linguis
Cuïlibet effundit temeraria; veraque mendax
Nunc minuit, modo confictis sermonibus auget.
  Sed tamen a nostro meruisti carmine laudes,
Fama, bonum quo non aliud veracius ullum,   195
Nobis digna cani, nec te memorasse pigebit
Carmine tam longo. Servati scilicet Angli
Officiis, vaga diva, tuis tibi reddimus aequa.
Te Deus, aeternos motu qui temperat ignes,
Fulmine praemisso, alloquitur, terraque tremente: 200
  "Fama, siles? an te latet impia Papistarum
Coniurata cohors in meque meosque Britannos,
Et nova sceptrigero caedes meditata Iacobo?"
  Nec plura, illa statim sensit mandata Tonantis,
Et, satis ante fugax, stridentes induit alas   205
Induit et variis exilia corpora plumis;
Dextra tubam gestat Temesaeo ex aere sonoram.
Nec mora, iam pennis cedentes remigat auras,
Atque parum est cursu celeres praevertere nubes;
Iam ventos, iam solis equos, post terga reliquit.   210

182–184. Milton thought of Virgil's monstrous Titaness, with eyes
as numberless as her tongues, sleeplessly ranging through the world
in the darkness of night. (*Aen.* IV, 180–5.)

185–188. Ovid calls the hundred-eyed Argus the son of Arestor
(*Met.* I, 624) when he describes Juno's delivery of Io to Argus for safe-
keeping, after Jove had transformed her into a heifer in a vain attempt
to hide his liaison with her. Renaissance mythographers generally (*e.g.*
Natale Conti, *Mythology*, VIII, xviii) identified Io with the Egyptian
goddess Isis.

191. So Ovid described "tattling Fame" (Fama loquax—*Met.* IX, 137)
spreading rumours which proved fatal to Hercules.

207. Temesa, an ancient Calabrian city, was first mentioned for its
copper mines in the *Odyssey*, I, 184.

head, which is girt about with innumerable ears,[182] so as to catch the faintest sound and seize the lightest murmur from the uttermost ends of the wide world. You, O Argus, spiteful guardian of the heifer, Io, had not so many eyes in your cruel face, eyes never winking in silent sleep, eyes gazing abroad over the lands below.[185] With them it is Fame's habit to pry into dark places where the sun's rays never penetrate. With a thousand tongues the blab recklessly pours out what she has heard and seen to any auditor,[191] and lyingly she pares down the truth or enlarges it with fabrications.

Nevertheless, O Fame, you deserved the praise of our song, for one good deed than which there was never any more genuine. You deserve that I should sing about you and I shall never regret this commemoration of you at such length in my song. Because we English plainly owe our safety to your good offices, O vagrant goddess, we render you a just return. God, who controls the eternal fires in their motion, hurled his thunderbolt and, while the earth still trembled, he said to you:

"Fame, are you silent? Or have you no inkling of the impious band of Papists conspiring against me and my English, nor of the novel kind of murder designed against sceptrebearing James?"

He said no more, but she instantly responded to the Thunderer's command and—swift though she was before—she assumes strident wings and covers her slender body with parti-coloured feathers, and in her right hand she takes a trumpet of Temesan brass.[207] She makes no delay, but on her wings goes oaring[208] through the yielding air. Not content to outstrip the swift clouds in her flight, she passes now the winds and now the horses of the sun. First, in her usual

---

208. The "oarage of wings" is a Latinism which occurs again in *P.L.* V, 269–70, and II, 841–2. Perhaps Milton thought here of Virgil's picture of Mercury—Volat ille per aera magnum Remigio alarum. (*Aen.* I, 300–1.)

Et primo Angliacas, solito de more, per urbes
Ambiguas voces incertaque murmura spargit,
Mox arguta dolos et detestabile vulgat
Proditionis opus, nec non facta horrida dictu
Authoresque addit sceleris, nec garrula caecis   215
Insidiis loca structa silet.   Stupuere relatis,
Et pariter iuvenes, pariter tremuere puellae,
Effoetique senes pariter, tantaeque ruinae
Sensus ad aetatem subito penetraverat omnem.
Attamen interea populi miserescit ab alto   220
Aethereus Pater, et crudelibus obstitit ausis
Papicolum.   Capti poenas raptantur ad acres;
At pia thura Deo et grati solvuntur honores;
Compita laeta focis genialibus omnia fumant;
Turba choros iuvenilis agit: Quintoque Novembris   225
Nulla dies toto occurrit celebratior anno.

(1626)

way, she scatters ambiguous rumours and uncertain whispers through the English cities. Presently, grown clear-voiced, she publishes the plots and the detestable work of treason—not merely the deeds which are abominable to utter, but also the authors of the crime; nor does her garrulity make a secret of the places prepared for the treacherous attempt. Men are aghast at what is reported. Youths and maidens and weak old men alike tremble, and folk of all ages are reached by the sense of so great ruin impending. But meanwhile the heavenly Father takes pity on his people from on high and thwarts the outrages which the Papists have dared. They are seized and dragged to painful punishments. Pious incense and grateful honours are paid to God. The joyous streets are all lurid with genial bonfires. In throngs youth goes dancing. Throughout the whole year there shall be no day more celebrated than the fifth of November.

[EPIGRAMMATA]

IN PRODITIONEM BOMBARDICAM

Cum simul in regem nuper satrapasque Britannos
    Ausus es infandum, perfide Fauxe, nefas,
Fallor? an et mitis voluisti ex parte videri,
    Et pensare mala cum pietate scelus?
Scilicet hos alti missurus ad atria caeli,   5
    Sulphureo curru flammivolisque rotis;
Qualiter ille, feris caput inviolabile Parcis,
    Liquit Iordanios turbine raptus agros.

---

2. By the arrest of Guy Fawkes as he stood guard over the explosives which were to have restored Roman Catholic liberties in England by the destruction of King James and his Parliament on November fifth, 1605, the "Gunpowder Plot" was frustrated. Celebration of the event is still a popular holiday in England and Milton's epigrams were written for its anniversaries when he was at St. Paul's School or in Cambridge.

3. *Fallor? an:* see *Elegy V,* 5, note.

EPIGRAMS

ON THE GUNPOWDER PLOT

PERFIDIOUS FAWKES,[2] when you attempted your recent un-speakable outrage against the King and the English nobles—do I misjudge,[3] or did you wish to seem merciful in one way and to atone for your crime with a kind of wicked piety? You were going, obviously, to send them to the courts of high heaven in a sulphurous chariot with wheels of whirling fire[7]— as he whose head proved inviolable by the fell Parcae was rapt away in a whirlwind, leaving the banks of the Jordan behind him.[8]

---

7. *ille,* Elijah. See *P.R.* II, 16–17, note.
Parcis, the Fates. Here and seemingly in *Lycidas,* 75, Milton thought of them as representing Death itself. Compare *On the Death of the Vice-Chancellor,* 21; *Manso,* 19; *To his Father,* 29; and *Arcades,* 65.

8. II Kings ii, 7, describes Elijah's escape from the fate of death by translation to heaven in a fiery chariot from the banks of the river Jordan.

IN EANDEM

SICCINE tentasti caelo donasse Iäcobum,
   Quae septemgemino Bellua monte lates?
Ni meliora tuum poterit dare munera numen,
   Parce, precor, donis insidiosa tuis.
Ille quidem sine te consortia serus adivit   5
   Astra, nec inferni pulveris usus ope.
Sic potius foedos in caelum pelle cucullos,
   Et quot habet brutos Roma profana Deos;
Namque hac aut alia nisi quemque adiuveris arte,
   Crede mihi, caeli vix bene scandet iter.   10

---

2. *Bellua:* the beast is that which St. John describes (Rev. xiii, 1) as
rising "out of the sea, having seven heads and ten horns . . . and
upon his heads the name of blasphemy." Like Spenser, and like Protestant writers generally, Milton identified it with Rome. "This beast,"
wrote Bishop Bale (*Select Works,* p. 496), "is the great Antichrist . . .
or beastly body of the devil, comprehending in him popes, patriarchs,
cardinals," *etc.*

ON THE SAME

WAS this the kind of attempt that you made to bestow
heaven upon James, you beast[2] in ambush on the Seven Hills?
Unless your divinity has better gifts in its power, O weaver of
plots, I implore you to spare your largess.   Without your
help, it is true, and without the aid of your infernal gunpowder, the King has gone at a ripe old age[5] to be with his
kindred, the stars.

Blow your detestable cowls, rather, up to the skies,[7] and
all the idol gods that profane Rome contains; for, unless you
help them in this way or in some other, believe me, not one
of them will climb very prosperously on the path to heaven.

---

5. The line dates the epigram as later than the death of James I
on March twenty-seventh, 1625.   In the autumn of that year Milton was
a freshman at Cambridge.

7-8. Compare the Paradise of Fools in *P.L.* III, 476-97.

IN EANDEM

Purgatorem animae derisit Iäcobus ignem,
   Et sine quo superum non adeunda domus.
Frenduit hoc trina monstrum Latiale corona,
   Movit et horrificum cornua dena minax.
Et "Nec inultus," ait, "temnes mea sacra Britanne;   5
   Supplicium spreta religione dabis
Et, si stelligeras unquam penetraveris arces,
   Non nisi per flammas triste patebit iter."
O quam funesto cecinisti proxima vero,
   Verbaque ponderibus vix caritura suis!   10
Nam prope Tartareo sublime rotatus ab igne
   Ibat ad aethereas, umbra perusta, plagas.

---

1. Mr. MacKellar quotes from *A Premonition to All Most Mightie Monarches* (*Political Works of James I*, edited by McIlwain, p. 125):
"As for Purgatorie and all the trash depending thereupon, it is not worth the talking of; Bellarmine cannot finde any ground for it in all the Scriptures. Onely I would pray him to tell me; if that faire greene meadow, that is in Purgatorie, have a brooke running thorow it; that in case I come there, I may have hawking upon it."

ON THE SAME

JAMES made a jest of the purgatorial fire[1] without which there is no way for the soul to reach the heavenly mansions. At that the Latin monster[3] with its triple crown gnashed its teeth and wagged its ten horns with menace horrid:

"Englishman," it cried, "you shall not despise my sanctities with impunity; you shall pay a forfeit for the insult to religion. And if ever you attain the starry citadels, the only way open to you will be the sad one through fire."

How close your vaticinations came to the grim truth and how little your utterances lacked of fulfilment!   For he did—almost—go to the celestial shores, a cindery ghost, whirled aloft by Tartarean[11] fire.

---

3. *monstrum:* compare *Bellua* in the preceding Epigram, 2.

trina . . . corona, triple crown.   See the Sonnet *On the Late Massacre in Piedmont,* 12, note.

11. *Tartareo,* Tartarean, infernal.   See *Elegy III,* 16, note.

IN EANDEM

Quem modo Roma suis devoverat impia diris,
    Et Styge damnarat, Taenarioque sinu,
Hunc, vice mutata, iam tollere gestit ad astra,
    Et cupit ad superos evehere usque Deos.

(1626?)

---

1. Milton meant to say that James I was under the formal interdict of the Pope.

2. *Taenarioque sinu:* see *Elegy V, 66,* note.

ON THE SAME

HIM whom impious Rome had consigned to her curses[1] and condemned to the Styx and the Taenarian gulf,[2] him—quite contrarily—she sets about to lift to the stars and wishes to hoist among the celestial gods.

IN INVENTOREM BOMBARDAE

Iapetionidem laudavit caeca vetustas,
  Qui tulit aetheream solis ab axe facem;
At mihi maior erit qui lurida creditur arma
  Et trifidum fulmen surripuisse Iovi.

(1626?)

---

1. *Iapetionidem:* the son of Iapetus.   See *On the Death of the Vice-Chancellor,* 4.   The story of the theft of fire in a hollow reed from the sun by the "resourceful and wily" Prometheus is told by Hesiod (*Theogony,* 565–9).

3–4. In *P.L.* VI, 503–4, artillery is called the invention of
       "Some one intent on mischief, or inspir'd
       With dev'lish machination."
Traditionally, cannon had been attributed to the diabolic inspiration, which Rabelais (III, viii) blamed for them, but opinion was shifting

ON THE INVENTOR OF GUNPOWDER

THE ancients in their blindness paid honour to the son of Iapetus,[1] who brought down the celestial fire from the chariot of the sun; but in my eyes he will be a greater man[3] who is credited with having stolen his flaming weapons and three-forked thunderbolt from Jove.[4]

---

toward Cowley's view that, "for above a thousand years together nothing almost of ornament or advantage was added to the uses of human society, except only guns and printing." (Preface to *A Proposition for the Advancement of Experimental Philosophy,* 1661.) Compare *P.L.* VI, 607, note.

    4. Warton compared *P.L.* VI, 490–1:
> "they shall fear we have disarm'd
> The Thunderer of his only dreaded bolt."

ELEGIA QUARTA

Anno Aetatis 18

Ad Thomam Iunium,[1]

PRAECEPTOREM SUUM, APUD MERCATORES ANGLICOS HAMBURGAE
AGENTES PASTORIS MUNERE FUNGENTEM

Curre per immensum subito, mea littera, pontum;
   I, pete Teutonicos laeve per aequor agros;
Segnes rumpe moras, et nil, precor, obstet eunti,
   Et festinantis nil remoretur iter.
Ipse ego Sicanio fraenantem carcere ventos   5
   Aeolon, et virides sollicitabo Deos,
Caeruleamque suis comitatam Dorida Nymphis,
   Ut tibi dent placidam per sua regna viam.
At tu, si poteris, celeres tibi sume iugales,
   Vecta quibus Colchis fugit ab ore viri;   10
Aut queis Triptolemus Scythicas devenit in oras,
   Gratus Eleusina missus ab urbe puer.
Atque, ubi Germanas flavere videbis arenas,
   Ditis ad Hamburgae moenia flecte gradum,

---

[1]Thomas Young (1588–1665) was a Scot, an M.A. of St. Andrews in 1606, who came to London early enough to be Milton's tutor for some time before he entered St. Paul's School in 1620. By 1622 Young was in Hamburg. In 1628 he was appointed to the living of Stowmarket, Suffolk, which he held until his death. In 1641 he was the principal contributor to *An Answer to a Book Entitled "An Humble Remonstrance"* (*i.e.* Bishop Hall's defence of Episcopacy), which was signed, by a combination of the initials of its five authors, "Smectymnuus." In its defence Milton wrote *Animadversions upon the Remonstrant's Defence against Smectymnuus* and *An Apology for Smectymnuus.*

3. *Segnes rumpe moras* is Virgil's phrase (*Georgics,* III, 42–3).

5–6. Milton is indebted to a line,
        "Aeolon Hippoteden, cohibentem carcere ventos,"
                (*Met.* XIV, 224),
in Ovid's retelling of Homer's story (*Od.* X, 1–22) of Aeolus, son of Hippotas, who kept the winds locked up in a cavern on an island, which was later identified with Lipara, off the coast of Sicily, or Sicania, as it was earlier called. Compare *Lycidas,* 96.

6. *virides . . . Deos* is an Ovidian phrase (*Tristia,* I, ii, 59) for the sea-gods. Compare "the blue-hair'd deities" of *Comus,* 29.

ELEGY IV

At Age 18

To Thomas Young,[1]

His Tutor, Performing the Duties of a Pastor among the English Merchants Resident in Hamburg

Swiftly, my letter, dart across the boundless ocean; go, and over the smooth sea seek Teutonic lands. Shake off slothful delays[3] and let nothing, I implore, stand in the way of your dispatch or interfere with the speed of your journey. I myself will offer prayers to the glaucous deities[6] and to Aeolus, who bridles the waves in his Sicanian cave,[5] and to caerulian Doris, escorted by her nymphs,[7] to give you a quiet journey through their kingdoms. Obtain for yourself, if you can, the swift team by which the Colchian[10] was borne away in her flight from the face of her husband, or that by which the boy, Triptolemus,[11] reached the bounds of Scythia, when he was sent, a welcome messenger, from the Eleusinian city. But when you see the sands of Germany shining yellow, turn your steps toward the walls of opulent Hamburg, which is said to derive its name from Hama, who, they say, was slain by a

---

7. The nymphs are the daughters of Doris,
      "All goodly damzels, deckt with long greene haire,
      Whom of their sire *Nereides* men call,
      All which the Oceans daughter to him bare
      The gray eyde *Doris:* all which fifty are."
              (*F.Q.* IV, xi, 48, 2–5.)
Milton's ultimate source was Hesiod's *Theogony*, 240–64, but he was indebted to a later tradition for the idea that the Nereids befriended sailors. Compare *Lycidas*, 99 and *Comus*, 835–8, notes.

10. The *Colchian* is Medea, whose flight in a car drawn by winged dragons after she had murdered their children in the palace of her husband, Jason, Milton remembered in Euripides' *Medea* (1314–6).

11. Ovid (*Met.* V, 643–50) tells how Ceres sent Triptolemus in her chariot from Eleusis in Attica to sow the world with wheat, as far as Scythia. Later (*Tristia*, III, viii, 1–4) he wished for the chariot of Triptolemus to carry him back from Thrace to Rome.

Dicitur occiso quae ducere nomen ab Hama,   15
    Cimbrica quem fertur clava dedisse neci.
Vivit ibi antiquae clarus pietatis honore
    Praesul, Christicolas pascere doctus oves;
Ille quidem est animae plusquam pars altera nostrae;
    Dimidio vitae vivere cogor ego.   20
Hei mihi, quot pelagi, quot montes interiecti,
    Me faciunt alia parte carere mei!
Carior ille mihi quam tu, doctissime Graium,
    Cliniadi, pronepos qui Telamonis erat;
Quamque Stagirites generoso magnus alumno,   25
    Quem peperit Lybico Chaonis alma Iovi.
Qualis Amyntorides, qualis Philyrëius Heros
    Myrmidonum regi, talis et ille mihi.
Primus ego Aonios illo praeeunte recessus
    Lustrabam, et bifidi sacra vireta iugi,   30
Pieriosque hausi latices, Clioque favente
    Castalio sparsi laeta ter ora mero.
Flammeus at signum ter viderat arietis Aethon
    Induxitque auro lanea terga novo,
Bisque novo terram sparsisti, Chlori, senilem   35
    Gramine, bisque tuas abstulit Auster opes;
Necdum eius licuit mihi lumina pascere vultu,
    Aut linguae dulces aure bibisse sonos.

15–16. Warton traced the name of Hamburg to "Hama, a puissant Saxon champion, who was killed on the spot where that city stands, by Starchater, a Danish giant. The *Cimbrica clava* is the club of the Dane."

19. Bacon (*Essays,* XXVII) called it "a sparing speech of the ancients, to say, *that a friend is another himself,*" for, he added, "a friend is far more than himself."

20. Wishing Virgil good luck on a voyage, Horace (*Odes,* I, iii, 8) called him *animae dimidium meae*—"the half of my soul."

22–23. *Cliniades,* Alcibiades, the son of Clinias. In Plato's *Alcibiades* (120d) he boasts to Socrates of his descent from Eurysaces, the grandson of Telamon. For the characterization of Socrates see *P.R.* IV, 274–6.

25. The *Stagirite,* Aristotle, who was born in the Macedonian seaport of Stagira. As a boy of about thirteen, Alexander the Great became his pupil.

26. *Chaonia*—Epirus. Olympias, Alexander's mother, was an Epirote princess. For the story of his paternity see *P.L.* IX, 508–9, and *P.R.* III, 84, notes.

Cimbrian club.[15]   There a pastor lives, who is illustrious for
his honour of the primitive faith and well instructed how to
feed the sheep that love Christ.   Truly, that man is more[19]
than the other half of my soul[20] and without him I am com-
pelled to live a life which is but the half of itself.   Dearer is
that man to me than you were, O wisest of the Greeks, to
Cliniades,[22] who traced his ancestry back to Telamon—dearer
than was the great Stagirite[25] to his magnanimous pupil, whom
the bountiful daughter of Chaonia bore to Libyan Jove.[26]
What the son of Amyntor[27] and what Philyra's heroic son
were to the Myrmidons' king, such is this man to me.   Under
his guidance I first visited the Aonian retreats and the sacred
lawns of the twin-peaked mountain.[30]   I drank the Pierian[31]
waters and by the favour of Clio I thrice wet my blessed lips
with Castalian wine.   Three times has fiery Aethon[33] looked
upon the sign of the Ram and gilded his woolly back afresh
with gold; and twice, Chloris,[35] have you sown the old earth
with new herbage, and twice, Auster,[36] you have swept her
riches away; and not yet have my eyes been allowed to feast
on his face or my ears to drink in the sweet sounds of his
tongue.

---

27. The *son of Amyntor* was Phoenix, who, Apollodorus says (*Library*,
III, iii, 8), was one of Achilles' tutors.

Phylireius—Chiron, the son of the nymph, Philyra. See *Manso*, 60,
note.

30. The twin peaks of the mountain of the Muses, Parnassus, were
in Aonia, between Attica and Boeotia, and the Castalian spring at its
foot was sacred to them.

31. It was on *Mount Pierus* in Macedonia that Hesiod's account
(*Theogony*, 52–79) represents the Muses as having been born by
Mnemosyne (Memory) to Zeus. *Clio*, the Muse of History, is first in
Hesiod's list.

33. *Aethon* is one of the four horses of the sun's chariot which Ovid
names (*Met.* II, 153–5). Milton means that the sun has entered the
zodiacal sign of the Ram three times since Young's departure. Evidently, Young left England in the winter, probably of 1624–5.

35. *Chloris*. See the note on *Elegy III*, 44.

36. *Auster*. See the note on the south wind in *Damon's Epitaph*,
60.

Vade igitur, cursuque Eurum praeverte sonorum;
  Quam sit opus monitis res docet, ipsa vides.   40
Invenies dulci cum coniuge forte sedentem,
  Mulcentem gremio pignora cara suo;
Forsitan aut veterum praelarga volumina Patrum
  Versantem, aut veri Biblia sacra Dei,
Caelestive animas saturantem rore tenellas,   45
  Grande salutiferae religionis opus.
Utque solet, multam sit dicere cura salutem,
  Dicere quam decuit, si modo adesset, herum.
Haec quoque, paulum oculos in humum defixa modestos,
  Verba verecundo sis memor ore loqui.   50
"Haec tibi, si teneris vacat inter praelia Musis,
  Mittit ab Angliaco littore fida manus.
Accipe sinceram, quamvis sit sera, salutem;
  Fiat et hoc ipso gratior illa tibi.
Sera quidem, sed vera fuit, quam casta recepit   55
  Icaris a lento Penelopeia viro.
Ast ego quid volui manifestum tollere crimen,
  Ipse quod ex omni parte levare nequit?
Arguitur tardus merito, noxamque fatetur,
  Et pudet officium deseruisse suum.   60
Tu modo da veniam fasso, veniamque roganti;
  Crimina diminui quae patuere solent.
Non ferus in pavidos rictus diducit hiantes,
  Vulnifico pronos nec rapit ungue leo.
Saepe sarissiferi crudelia pectora Thracis   65
  Supplicis ad moestas delicuere preces;
Extensaeque manus avertunt fulminis ictus,
  Placat et iratos hostia parva Deos.

-----

39. *Eurus.* See the note on *Damon's Epitaph,* 60.

43. *Patrum*—of the Fathers, *i.e.,* the Greek and Latin Fathers who left the Church its body of patristic writings.

46. *salutiferae*—salvation-bearing, *i.e.,* bringing "all the joyes of Life Eternall," which Hobbes (*Leviathan,* III, xxxviii, 245) said were "comprehended . . . under the name of *Salvation.*"

51. In 1626 the Protestant allies in the Thirty Years' War, under Christian IV of Denmark, were defeated by the Imperialists, under Tilly, at Lutter. The seat of war shifted to lower Saxony and for some time Hamburg was in danger of a siege.

Be off, then, and speed on your way faster than shrieking Eurus.[39] How necessary is my urging the situation itself suggests and you yourself perceive. Perhaps you will find him sitting with his sweet wife, fondling the dear pledges of their love on his lap, or perhaps turning over the mighty volumes of the old Fathers[43] or the Holy Scriptures of the true God, or watering tender souls with the dew of heaven— which is the grand affair of healing religion.[46] As the custom is, be careful to give him generous greeting and to speak as it would become your master to do, if only he were present; and remember to fix your eyes for a little while modestly upon the ground and to speak these words with reverent lips.

"These verses—if there is leisure for the delicate Muses in the midst of the fighting[51]—a devoted hand sends to you from English shores. Even though it be late, accept this sincere greeting and may it be the more welcome to you on that very account. Late, indeed, but loyal was the greeting which the daughter of Icarius, Penelope,[56] received from her long-delaying husband. But why should I wish to deny a manifest fault, which the delinquent himself is utterly unable to mitigate? He is justly accused of being dilatory and confesses the crime and is ashamed of his neglect of his duty. Only grant me forgiveness, because I confess my fault and ask for absolution; for offences acknowledged are half wiped out. No wild beast opens its maw upon victims that tremble nor does the lion do violence with his rending paw to those who are prostrate.[64] The cruel hearts of Thracian spearmen have often melted at a suppliant's sad appeals. Outstretched hands avert the stroke of the thunder-bolt and even a small sacrifice pacifies the gods when they are angry.

---

56. Milton thought of the opening scene in the *Odyssey*, XXIII, when Penelope is painfully convinced that Ulysses has indeed returned from Troy.

64. The experience of the sleeping Oliver with the lion in *As You Like It*, IV, iii, 119–20, showed that it is
"The royal disposition of that beast
To prey on nothing that doth seem as dead."

Iamque diu scripsisse tibi fuit impetus illi,
    Neve moras ultra ducere passus Amor;   70
Nam vaga Fama refert—heu nuntia vera malorum!
    In tibi finitimis bella tumere locis,
Teque tuamque urbem truculento milite cingi,
    Et iam Saxonicos arma parasse duces.
Te circum late campos populatur Enyo,   75
    Et sata carne virum iam cruor arva rigat.
Germanisque suum concessit Thracia Martem;
    Illuc Odrysios Mars pater egit equos.
Perpetuoque comans iam deflorescit oliva;
    Fugit et aerisonam Diva perosa tubam,   80
Fugit, io! terris, et iam non ultima virgo
    Creditur ad superas iusta volasse domos.
Te tamen interea belli circumsonat horror,
    Vivis et ignoto solus inopsque solo;
Et, tibi quam patrii non exhibuere penates,   85
    Sede peregrina quaeris egenus opem.
Patria, dura parens, et saxis saevior albis
    Spumea quae pulsat littoris unda tui,
Siccine te decet innocuos exponere foetus,
    Siccine in externam ferrea cogis humum,   90
Et sinis ut terris quaerant alimenta remotis
    Quos tibi prospiciens miserat ipse Deus,
Et qui laeta ferunt de caelo nuntia, quique
    Quae via post cineres ducat ad astra docent?
Digna quidem Stygiis quae vivas clausa tenebris,   95
    Aeternaque animae digna perire fame!

---

71. Compare the characterization of *Fame*, or *Rumour*, in *On the
Fifth of November*, 191–5.

74. The Elector of Saxony, John George I, was luke-warm in his
opposition to the Imperialists, but six of the sons of Duke John of
Saxe-Weimar, including Dukes Bernard, William and Frederick, were
their determined opponents. Hamburg desired only to remain neutral
and unmolested.

75. Homer's *Enyo*, the goddess of war, "the devastator of cities"
(*Il*. V, 333), came, like Mars and Bellona, to be a synonym for war.

77. Conti's chapter on Mars points out that Thrace was his traditional home (*Od*. VIII, 361), and that his worship was a Thracian
institution.

"He has long felt the impulse to write to you and now Love would not endure any further delay, for vagrant Rumour[71]—alas, the veracious reporter of disasters—says that in regions bordering upon you wars are ready to burst out, that you and your city are beset by insolent troops, and that the Saxon leaders[74] have already prepared their munitions of war. All around you Enyo[75] is laying waste the fields and blood is watering the ground which has been sown with human flesh. Thrace has given up Mars to the Germans[77] and father Mars has driven his Odrysian[78] horses into their territories. The ever-flourishing olive-tree is withering and the goddess who hates the brazen blare of the trumpet has fled—look, fled from the earth[81]—and it is believed that the just virgin was not the last to fly for refuge to the heavenly mansions. Nevertheless, you live resourceless and alone on that strange soil, where the horror of war echoes all around you; and on alien soil you seek in your poverty for the livelihood which your native country withholds. O Fatherland, hard parent, more cruel than the white cliffs that are battered by the frothing waves of your coast, does it become you thus to expose your innocent offspring; do you drive them away thus with iron implacability to foreign soil and do you allow men to seek their subsistence in strange lands whom God himself in his providence has sent to you—men who bring glad tidings from heaven and teach the way which leads beyond the grave to the stars? Indeed, you deserve to live shut up in Stygian darkness and to perish by undying hunger of the soul. In

---

78. *Odrysia*—an ancient name for Thrace.

81–82. Ovid's (*Met.* I, 141–50) was the classical version of the story that, after the Iron Age had followed the Ages of Gold, Silver and Bronze, the goddess of Justice, Astraea,

"loathing lenger here to space
Mongst wicked men, in whom no truth she found,
Return'd to heaven, whence she deriv'd her race."
(*F.Q.* V, i, 11, 2–5.)

In the fourth *Prolusion* Milton questioned "that Ovidian story; whether . . . Astraea was the last of the goddesses to leave the earth; for," he said, "I suspect that Peace and Truth would not have abandoned even hostile mortals many ages after her."

Haud aliter vates terrae Thesbitidis olim
  Pressit inassueto devia tesqua pede,
Desertasque Arabum salebras, dum regis Achabi
  Effugit atque tuas, Sidoni, dira, manus.   100
Talis et, horrisono laceratus membra flagello,
  Paulus ab Aemathia pellitur urbe Cilix;
Piscosaeque ipsum Gergessae civis Iesum
  Finibus ingratus iussit abire suis.
At tu sume animos, nec spes cadat anxia curis,   105
  Nec tua concutiat decolor ossa metus.
Sis etenim quamvis fulgentibus obsitus armis,
  Intententque tibi millia tela necem,
At nullis vel inerme latus violabitur armis,
  Deque tuo cuspis nulla cruore bibet.   110
Namque eris ipse Dei radiante sub aegide tutus;
  Ille tibi custos, et pugil ille tibi;
Ille Sionaeae qui tot sub moenibus arcis
  Assyrios fudit nocte silente viros;
Inque fugam vertit quos in Samaritidas oras   115
  Misit ab antiquis prisca Damascus agris;
Terruit et densas pavido cum rege cohortes,
  Aere dum vacuo buccina clara sonat,
Cornea pulvereum dum verberat ungula campum,
  Currus arenosam dum quatit actus humum,   120

97–100. Compare the allusions to Elijah in *P.R.* I, 353, and II, 19 and 277, and the notes there.

100. The Sidonian woman is Jezebel, "the daughter of Ethbaal, king of the Zidonians" (I Kings xvi, 31), King Ahab's queen, who threatened Elijah's life (I Kings xix, 2) and obliged him to become a fugitive in the desert.

102. When the Apostle Paul, often called Saul of Tarsus (which was a Cilician city), visited Philippi in Macedonia he was publicly scourged (Acts xvi, 22–3). Emathia was an ancient name for Macedonia. Compare *Emathian* in the Sonnet *When the assault was intended,* 10, and in *P.R.* III, 290.

103–104. When Jesus healed a man possessed by a legion of devils near Gergessa, on the Sea of Galilee, and allowed them to destroy a herd of swine, the Gergesenes "besought him that he would depart out of their coasts." (Mat. viii, 34.)

109–111. In the background are passages like Psalm xci, 4–5; "his truth shall be thy shield and buckler. Thou shalt not be afraid for the terror by night, nor for the arrow that flieth by day."

just this way the Tishbite[97] prophet long ago walked the by-
ways of the desert with unaccustomed steps and trod the
rough sands of Arabia when he fled from the hands of King
Ahab and from your hands also, O vindictive Sidonian
woman.[100]   In this way Cilician Paul was driven out of the
Emathian city with his flesh bleeding from the hissing
scourge;[102] and the ungrateful citizenry of fishy Gergessa[103]
bade Jesus himself to depart from their coasts.

"But take heart and do not let your anxious hope yield to
your embarrassments nor pale fear strike palsy to your bones.
Even though you are beset by flashing arms and though a
thousand shafts threaten you with death, your unarmed breast
shall not be violated by any weapon and no spear shall drink
of your blood.[109]   For you shall be secure under the radiant
aegis of God.[111]   He will be your guardian and he will be
your champion—He, who wiped out so many Assyrian
soldiers[112] in a silent night under the walls of Zion, who
turned to flight the men whom ancient Damascus sent from
her venerable fields into the coasts of Samaria,[115] and smote
their massed cohorts and their trembling king with terror
when the loud trumpet sounded in the empty air, and the
horny hoof beat the dusty plain,[119] and the hard-driven chariot
shook the sandy earth, and the neigh of horses plunging into

---

111. Both Jove and Minerva had shields of superlative powers, the
first of which (*Il.* V, 738) was that of putting all attacking enemies to
rout.

112-113. When Sennacherib attacked Jerusalem, "it came to pass that
night, that the angel of the Lord . . . smote in the camp of the
Assyrians an hundred fourscore and five thousand."   (II Kings xix, 35.)

115-122. When Ben Hadad of Damascus attacked Samaria, "the
Lord . . . made the host of the Syrians to hear a noise of chariots,
and a noise of horses, even the noise of a great host . . . Wherefore
they arose and fled in the twilight, and left . . . the camp as it was."
(II Kings vii, 6–7.)

119. The onomatopoeia imitates Virgil's famous line;
      "Quadrupedante putrem sonitu quatit ungula campum."
                                        (*Aen.* VIII, 596.)

Auditurque hinnitus equorum ad bella ruentum,
  Et strepitus ferri, murmuraque alta virum.
Et tu (quod superest miseris) sperare memento,
  Et tua magnanimo pectore vince mala.
Nec dubites quandoque frui melioribus annis,   125
  Atque iterum patrios posse videre lares."

(1627)

battle was heard, and the din of steel weapons and the deep roar of the voices of men.

"And for your part—because hope is the right of the unhappy—remember to hope, and let your magnanimous heart triumph over your misfortunes. Do not doubt that some time you will enjoy better years and be able once more to see your native home."

ELEGIA SEPTIMA

Anno Aetatis undevigesimo

NONDUM blanda tuas leges, Amathusia, noram,
    Et Paphio vacuum pectus ab igne fuit.
Saepe cupidineas, puerilia tela, sagittas,
    Atque tuum sprevi maxime numen, Amor.
"Tu puer imbelles," dixi, "transfige columbas,   5
    Conveniunt tenero mollia bella duci.
Aut de passeribus tumidos age, parve, triumphos;
    Haec sunt militiae digna trophaea tuae.
In genus humanum quid inania dirigis arma?
    Non valet in fortes ista pharetra viros."   10
Non tulit hoc Cyprius—neque enim Deus ullus ad iras
    Promptior—et duplici iam ferus igne calet.
Ver erat, et summae radians per culmina villae
    Attulerat primam lux tibi, Maie, diem;
At mihi adhuc refugam quaerebant lumina noctem,   15
    Nec matutinum sustinuere iubar.
Astat Amor lecto, pictis Amor impiger alis;
    Prodidit astantem mota pharetra Deum;
Prodidit et facies, et dulce minantis ocelli,
    Et quicquid puero dignum et Amore fuit.   20
Talis in aeterno iuvenis Sigeius Olympo
    Miscet amatori pocula plena Iovi;

---

1. Venus was called *Amathusia* because one of her most famous temples in Cyprus was at Amathus.

2. *Paphio*. See *Elegy V, 60*, note.

4. *Amor*. See *Elegy I, 60*, note.

11. *Cyprius*. Milton gives Cupid his mother's title. See *Elegy III, 20*, and line 48 below.

16. The line is sometimes taken as evidence that Milton was already suffering from weak eyes.

18. So, in *The Cheat of Cupid; or the Ungentle Guest*, which is based upon *Anacreonta* 34 (3) 23, Herrick recognized Cupid standing in the dark beside his bed:
    "I saw he had a bow,
        And wings too, which did shiver;
    And looking down below,
        I spied he had a quiver."

ELEGY VII

At Age 19

O CHARMING Amathusia,[1] I did not yet know your laws and
my breast was free from Paphian[2] fire.   Often I poured scorn
on the arrows of Cupid as childish weapons, and upon thy
divinity particularly, O Love.[4]

"Boy," I said, "go shoot the unwarlike doves; gentle combats suit a tender champion; or else, little one, go keep your
boasted triumphs over the sparrows.   Why do you aim your
contemptible weapons at mankind?   Against strong men that
quiver of yours has no power."

The Cyprian[11] would not bear the insult—for no deity is
swifter to anger—and the vengeful boy burned with double
heat.

It was spring, and the light pouring over the roof-tops of
the town had brought your first day, O May.   But my eyes
still craved the retreating night and could not endure the
radiance of dawn.[16]   Then Love stood beside my bed,[18] Love
the indefatigable with his painted wings.   The swaying
quiver betrayed the god as he stood; his features and his
sweetly menacing eyes betrayed him and so did all else beseeming the boy who is Love.   So the Sigeian youth appeared
when he mixed the flowing cups for amorous Jove on everlasting Olympus;[21] and so Hylas, the son of Theomadas, who

---

21. *iuvenis Sigeius*—the "Phrygian Ganymede" for whose love Jove
assumed the form of an eagle and "stole away the Trojan boy, who
even now," Ovid says (*Met.* X, 155–61), "mingles the nectar and
serves the cups to Jove."   Sigeius is the name of a town and promontory near ancient Troy.

Aut, qui formosas pellexit ad oscula nymphas,
  Thiodamantaeus Naiade raptus Hylas.
Addideratque iras, sed et has decuisse putares;   25
  Addideratque truces, nec sine felle minas.
Et "Miser exemplo sapuisses tutius," inquit;
  "Nunc mea quid possit dextera testis eris.
Inter et expertos vires numerabere nostras,
  Et faciam vero per tua damna fidem.   30
Ipse ego, si nescis, strato Pythone superbum
  Edomui Phoebum, cessit et ille mihi;
Et, quoties meminit Peneidos, ipse fatetur
  Certius et gravius tela nocere mea.
Me nequit adductum curvare peritius arcum,   35
  Qui post terga solet vincere, Parthus eques.
Cydoniusque mihi cedit venator, et ille
  Inscius uxori qui necis author erat.
Est etiam nobis ingens quoque victus Orion,
  Herculeaeque manus, Herculeusque comes.   40
Iupiter ipse licet sua fulmina torqueat in me,
  Haerebunt lateri spicula nostra Iovis.
Caetera quae dubitas melius mea tela docebunt,
  Et tua non leviter corda petenda mihi.

23–24. Compare *P.R.* II, 353, note.

31–36. Ovid described (*Met.* I, 38–9) the monstrous snake, Python, as half covering a mountain. Apollo killed it with his darts, but then, in his pride, flouted Cupid's archery. One of Cupid's arrows instantly inspired him with love for Daphne, the daughter of Peneus, and another inspired her with hate for him. The frontispiece of Cowley's *The Mistress* showed Apollo victorious over Python but vanquished by Cupid.

36. After Crassus' defeat in 53 B.C. by the Parthian cavalry, who shot backward with terrible effect, Parthian archery became proverbial.

37. *Cydonius . . . venator.* Cydon was a port on the north coast of Crete, famous for its archers. Virgil (*Aen.* XII, 858–9.) mentions them together with the Parthians.

38. *Inscius etc.*—Cephalus, to whose separation from his wife, Procris, Milton alludes in *Elegy III,* 67, later killed her with a dart thrown at what he supposed was a wild beast in a covert where she was hiding. (Ovid, *Met.* VII, 840–4.)

39. *Orion*—the mighty hunter who was raised to the skies with his dogs, and who had ill-starred passions for Diana and for Merope, the wife of the Chian chieftain, Oenopian.

40. Ovid (*Met.* IX, 127–8) describes Hercules sending an arrow to

lured the lovely nymphs to his kisses and was carried off by a
Naiad.[28] He was wrathful, but you would have thought
his wrath becoming to him; and he poured out cruel threats,
full of gall.

"Wretch," he said, "you might more safely have learned
wisdom from the experience of others; but now you yourself
shall be a witness to the power of my right hand. You shall
be counted among those who have felt my strength and by
your agony, truly, I shall establish the truth. You may not
be aware that it was I—I my very self—who tamed Phoebus
in all his pride after he had slain the Python,[31] and that he
yielded to me. As often as he remembers the daughter of
Peneus, he confesses that my arrows harm more certainly
and more gravely than his own. The Parthian horseman,[36]
who makes victory out of retreat, cannot draw the taut bow
more skilfully than I. The Cydonian hunter[37] yields to me and
he who was the unwitting author of his own wife's death.[38]
Gigantic Orion[39] was a victim of mine and so were strong-
handed Hercules and the companion of Hercules.[40] And
though Jove himself hurls his thunderbolts at me, my darts
shall first pierce the side of Jove.[41] Whatever other doubts
you have shall be resolved by my shafts and by your own
heart, at which I must aim no gentle stroke. Fool! Neither

---

the heart of the Centaur, Nessus, who was running away with his wife,
Deianira. Among Hercules' companions the only famous archer was
Philoctetes, but of him no love affair is recorded. Perhaps Jason, the
lover of Medea and Creusa, is meant, for Hercules was his companion
on the Argonautic expedition.

41–42. Cupid, with a quiver of arrows hanging to his back, catch-
ing and breaking the thunderbolts of Jove, was a familiar "emblem."
In *Andreae Alciati Emblemata* (Patavij, 1661, no. 108) he is pictured
so at the head of a translation of an epigram from the Greek Anthology, Book IV, on the power of the winged god to break the
winged thunderbolt. On the following pages Alciati cited countless
stories of Cupid's triumphs over Jove.

Nec te, stulte, tuae poterunt defendere Musae,   45
    Nec tibi Phoebaeus porriget anguis opem.”
Dixit, et, aurato quatiens mucrone sagittam,
    Evolat in tepidos Cypridos ille sinus.
At mihi risuro tonuit ferus ore minaci,
    Et mihi de puero non metus ullus erat.   50
Et modo qua nostri spatiantur in urbe Quirites,
    Et modo villarum proxima rura placent.
Turba frequens, facieque simillima turba dearum,
    Splendida per medias itque reditque vias.
Auctaque luce dies gemino fulgore coruscat.   55
    Fallor? an et radios hinc quoque Phoebus habet?
Haec ego non fugi spectacula grata severus,
    Impetus et quo me fert iuvenilis agor.
Lumina luminibus male providus obvia misi,
    Neve oculos potui continuisse meos.   60
Unam forte aliis supereminuisse notabam;
    Principium nostri lux erat illa mali.
Sic Venus optaret mortalibus ipsa videri,
    Sic regina Deum conspicienda fuit.
Hanc memor obiecit nobis malus ille Cupido,   65
    Solus et hos nobis texuit ante dolos.
Nec procul ipse vafer latuit, multaeque sagittae,
    Et facis a tergo grande pependit onus.
Nec mora; nunc ciliis haesit, nunc virginis ori,
    Insilit hinc labiis, insidet inde genis;   70
Et quascunque agilis partes iaculator oberrat,
    Hei mihi! mille locis pectus inerme ferit.

---

    45. The Muses stand for Milton's poetical efforts, like the "thankless
Muse" of *Lycidas,* 66.

    46. *Phoebaeus . . . anguis.* By the serpent of Apollo Milton meant
Apollo's son, Aesculapius, who inherited his father's healing art. Ovid
described (*Met.* XV, 626–744) his voyage in the form of a serpent
from his shrine in Epidaurus to Rome. Like Spenser, Milton remembered the commonplace that love is a disease
        "Which to recure no skill of leaches art
        Mote . . . availe."
            (*F.Q.* VI, x, 31, 4–5.)
    55. Compare Drayton:
        "Who list to praise the dayes delicious lyght,
        Let him compare it to her heauenly eye,
        The sun-beames to the lustre of her sight."
            (*Ideas Mirrour,* XLVIII, 1–3.)

will your Muses[45] be able to protect you nor will the serpent
of Apollo[46] afford you any help."

Thus he spoke, and, shaking the arrow with the point of
gold, he flew away to the warm breast of Cypris. But I was
inclined to laugh at the threats that the angry fellow thundered
at me and I had not the least fear of the boy.

Sometimes parts of the town where our citizens walk abroad
and sometimes the suburban fields offer me their pleasures.
Groups of radiant girls with divinely lovely faces come and
go along the walks. When they add their glory, the day
shines with double splendour.[55] Am I deceived,[56] or is it
from them also that Phoebus has his rays? I did not turn
puritanically away from the pleasant sights, but was carried where the impulse of youth led me. Heedlessly I sent
my glances to encounter theirs and lost all control of my eyes.
Then, by chance, I caught sight of one who was supreme
above all the rest; her radiance was the beginning of my
disaster. In such a guise Venus herself might choose to appear to mortals. Glorious to look upon, like her, must the
queen of the gods have been.[64] She was thrown in my way
by the grudge-harbouring rascal, Cupid; he alone has woven
these snares in my path. Not far away the rogue was hiding
with his store of arrows[67] and his mighty torch burdening his
back. Without delay he fixed himself now on the maiden's
eyelids, now on her mouth; then sped away between her lips
or perched on her cheek; and wherever the agile dart-thrower
strayed—alas for me—he struck my defenceless breast in a

---

56. *Fallor?* See *Elegy V*, 5, note.

64. *regina Deum*—the queen of the gods, Hera or Juno. Compare
Arcades, 23.

67. *multae sagittae*—many arrows. Compare *Elegy I*, 60, note, and
lines 41–2 above.

Protinus insoliti subierunt corda furores;
    Uror amans intus, flammaque totus eram.
Interea misero quae iam mihi sola placebat   75
    Ablata est, oculis non reditura meis.
Ast ego progredior tacite querebundus, et excors,
    Et dubius volui saepe referre pedem.
Findor; et haec remanet, sequitur pars altera votum,
    Raptaque tam subito gaudia flere iuvat.   80
Sic dolet amissum proles Iunonia caelum,
    Inter Lemniacos praecipitata focos.
Talis et abreptum solem respexit ad Orcum
    Vectus ab attonitis Amphiaraus equis.
Quid faciam infelix, et luctu victus?   Amores   85
    Nec licet inceptos ponere, neve sequi.
O utinam spectare semel mihi detur amatos
    Vultus, et coram tristia verba loqui!
Forsitan et duro non est adamante creata,
    Forte nec ad nostras surdeat illa preces.   90
Crede mihi, nullus sic infeliciter arsit;
    Ponar in exemplo primus et unus ego.
Parce, precor, teneri cum sis Deus ales amoris;
    Pugnent officio nec tua facta tuo.
Iam tuus O certe est mihi formidabilis arcus,   95
    Nate dea, iaculis nec minus igne potens;
Et tua fumabunt nostris altaria donis,
    Solus et in superis tu mihi summus eris.

81–82. *proles Iunonia*—Vulcan (Hephaestus), the son of Juno (Hera). Homer says (*Il.* I, 588–95) that he was thrown down from heaven among the humble cottages of the isle of Lemnos by his father, Jove (Zeus). Compare *P.L.* I, 740–5, and *Nature is not subject to Old Age,* 23–4.

83–84. *Amphiaraus* was struck by Jove's thunderbolt and swept through the opening earth to Hades for joining the expedition of the Seven against Thebes, when he knew, as a seer and prophet, that it was impious and ill-omened. Milton, like Dante (*Inferno* XX, 29–36) was moved by the dramatic references to the story in Ovid (*Met.* IX, 406–7) and Statius (*Thebaide* VII, 818–23 and VIII, 8–12).
Orcum—the infernal world.

89. Compare Helena's cry, "You draw me, you hard-hearted adamant." (*Midsummer Night's Dream* II, i, 192.)

thousand places. In an instant unfamiliar passions assailed my heart. Inwardly I was consumed by love and was all on fire.

While I suffered, she who alone could give me happiness was borne away, never to return to my eyes again. Distressed and dispirited, I went on my way, often questioning whether I should not turn my steps backward. I am rent asunder; one part of me stays here, but the other follows after my desire. There was pleasure in weeping for delights so suddenly snatched away. Such was the grief of the child of Juno[81] for his lost heaven when he was hurled down among the hearths of Lemnos; such was the grief of Amphiaraus[83] when he looked his last upon the sun as he was swept away to Hades by his thunder-driven horses. Unhappy and grief-stricken as I was, what should I do? I can neither dismiss nor pursue my incipient love. O, would that it might be given me once to look into those beloved features and to tell her the story of my pain face to face. Perhaps she is not made of hard adamant;[89] perhaps she would not be deaf to my prayers. Believe me! No one ever suffered such misery in the fire of love. I may be rated the first and unique example. Spare me, I pray, since you are the winged god of tender love. Do not let your deeds conflict with your duty. Now, O child of the goddess, with your darts no less powerful than fire, your bow is beyond all doubt dreadful to me. Your altars shall smoke with my sacrifices, and, as far as I am concerned, you shall be sole and supreme among the gods. Take away

Deme meos tandem, verum nec deme, furores;
   Nescio cur, miser est suaviter omnis amans.   100
Tu modo da facilis, posthaec mea siqua futura est,
   Cuspis amaturos figat ut una duos.

Haec ego mente olim laeva, studioque supino,
   Nequitiae posui vana trophaea meae.
Scilicet abreptum sic me malus impulit error,
   Indocilisque aetas prava magistra fuit;
Donec Socraticos umbrosa Academia rivos   5
   Praebuit, admissum dedocuitque iugum.
Protinus, extinctis ex illo tempore flammis,
   Cincta rigent multo pectora nostra gelu;
Unde suis frigus metuit puer ipse Sagittis,
   Et Diomedeam vim timet ipsa Venus.   10

(1627-8)

101–102. The conceit goes back to the epigram of Rufinus in the
Palatine Anthology V, 97.

1. *Haec*—these, *i.e.,* verses. The reference seems to me particularly
to the last of the Elegies, from which this "retractation" is separated
in the volume of 1645 by only a fine line across the page.

madness, then! But rather, do not take it away. I cannot tell why, but every lover's misery is sweet. Only be gracious enough to grant, if any maiden is ever to be mine, that a single dart shall transfix the destined lovers.[101]

These[1] are the monuments to my wantonness that with a perverse spirit and a trifling purpose I once erected. Obviously, mischievous error led me astray and my undisciplined youth was a vicious teacher until the shady Academy[5] offered its Socratic streams and taught me how to escape from the yoke to which I had submitted. From that hour those flames were extinct and thenceforward my breast has been rigid under a thick case of ice, of which the boy himself fears the frost for his arrows, and Venus herself is afraid of my Diomedean strength.[10]

5–6. *umbrosa Academia*—the shady Academy, *i.e.* of Plato. Compare *P.R.* IV, 244. Masson and Mr. MacKellar are doubtless right in interpreting this passage in the light of Milton's statement in *An Apology for Smectymnuus* (*P.W.* III, 119) that "from the laureate fraternity of poets, riper years and the ceaseless round of study and reading led me to the shady spaces of philosophy, but chiefly to the divine volumes of Plato."

10. Milton thought of Homer's account of Aphrodite mingling in the battle before Troy and screaming with pain when Diomedes wounded her. (*Il.* V, 335–43.)

NATURAM NON PATI SENIUM

Heu quam perpetuis erroribus acta fatiscit
Avia mens hominum, tenebrisque immersa profundis
Oedipodioniam volvit sub pectore noctem!
Quae vesana suis metiri facta deorum
Audet, et incisas leges adamante perenni   5
Assimilare suis, nulloque solubile saeclo
Consilium fati perituris alligat horis.
   Ergone marcescet sulcantibus obsita rugis
Naturae facies, et rerum publica mater
Omniparum contracta uterum, sterilescet ab aevo?   10
Et se fassa senem male certis passibus ibit
Sidereum tremebunda caput?   Num tetra vetustas
Annorumque aeterna fames, squalorque situsque,
Sidera vexabunt?   An et insatiabile Tempus
Esuriet Caelum, rapietque in viscera patrem?   15
Heu, potuitne suas imprudens Iupiter arces
Hoc contra munisse nefas, et Temporis isto
Exemisse malo, gyrosque dedisse perennes?
Ergo erit ut quandoque, sono dilapsa tremendo,
Convexi tabulata ruant, atque obvius ictu   20
Stridat uterque polus, superaque ut Olympius aula
Decidat, horribilisque retecta Gorgone Pallas;
Qualis in Aegaeam proles Iunonia Lemnon

---

1. Milton evidently sympathized with the ideas expressed in this poem, although a letter to Alexander Gill, dated July 2, 1628, which must refer either to it or—less probably—to *On the Platonic Idea,* explains that it was written for a candidate who had to defend its thesis publicly in qualifying for the M.A., but did not care to write the verses on his subject which custom required.

The errors in question arose from the medieval belief which is discussed in the Introduction, § 12–§ 14.

3. Compare the reproach of Samson beginning with the words, "Dungeon of thyself," in *S.A.* 156–67. Oedipus, by his voluntary blindness, is a better symbol than Samson of the wilful darkness of the soul.

4–7. The lines are a bold adaptation of Isaiah lv, 8; "For my thoughts are not your thoughts, neither are your ways my ways, saith the Lord."

9. Compare "Earth all-bearing Mother" in *P.L.* V, 338.   Hesiod described (*Theogony,* 117–53) Earth as next born after Chaos and as

THAT NATURE IS NOT SUBJECT TO OLD AGE

ALAS! how persistent are the errors by which the wandering mind of man is pursued and overwearied,[1] and how profound is the darkness of the Oedipean night in his breast![3] His insane mind dare make its own acts the measure of those of the gods[4] and compare its own laws to those that are written upon eternal adamant; and it binds the eternally immutable plan of fate to the perishing hours.

Shall the face of Nature, then, be overspread with wrinkles and shall the common mother[9] contract her all-generating womb and become sterile? Shall she confess herself old and move with uncertain steps, her starry head a-trembling? Shall the stars be vexed by foul old age and the undying hunger of the years, and by squalor and mould? Shall insatiable Time devour the heavens and gorge the vitals of his own father?[14] Alas! could not Jupiter, the improvident, fortify his citadels against this outrage and make them immune from the harm of time? Could he not endue them with perpetual revolutions? Some day, then, it will come to pass that the vaulted floor of heaven, collapsing with a mighty uproar, will fall and both poles will rattle with the impact, while Olympian Jove drops down from his celestial hall, and with him Pallas Athene, spreading horror from her exposed Gorgon shield.[22] So the child of Juno[23] fell upon Aegean Lemnos, where he was tossed down from the sacred

the mother of Heaven and the mountains, of Time, Hyperion and many of the elder gods and of the giants that first peopled the world.

14–15. Hesiod described Cronos (who was later, mistakenly, identified with Chronos, Time) as the son of Earth and Heaven and the devourer of his children until his son, Zeus, mastered him. (*Theogony*, 453–96.)

22. Ovid's (*Met.* IV, 773–803) is the most familiar version of the myth of the Gorgon, Medusa, whose snaky locks and dreadful eyes had power to turn the beholder to stone, but the story that Athene wore the severed head upon her shield goes back to the *Il.* V, 741.

23. *proles Iunonia*, "the child of Juno"—Hephaestus. Compare *Elegy VII*, 81, note.

Deturbata sacro cecidit de limine caeli.
Tu quoque, Phoebe, tui casus imitabere nati   25
Praecipiti curru, subitaque ferere ruina
Pronus, et extincta fumabit lampade Nereus
Et dabit attonito feralia sibila ponto.
Tunc etiam aerei divulsis sedibus Haemi
Dissultabit apex, imoque allisa barathro   30
Terrebunt Stygium deiecta Ceraunia Ditem,
In superos quibus usus erat, fraternaque bella.
     At pater omnipotens, fundatis fortius astris,
Consuluit rerum summae, certoque peregit
Pondere fatorum lances, atque ordine summo   35
Singula perpetuum iussit servare tenorem.
Volvitur hinc lapsu mundi rota prima diurno,
Raptat et ambitos socia vertigine caelos.
Tardior haud solito Saturnus, et acer ut olim
Fulmineum rutilat cristata casside Mavors.   40
Floridus aeternum Phoebus iuvenile coruscat,
Nec fovet effoetas loca per declivia terras
Devexo temone Deus; sed semper, amica
Luce potens, eadem currit per signa rotarum.

25–28. Compare the allusion to Apollo's son, Phaeton, in *Elegy V*, 92.

27. *Nereus*, whom Hesiod called the oldest of the children of Ocean
(*Theogony*, 233–6), came to stand for the sea itself. Compare
Spenser's picture of a ship sunk
              "Within the gulfe of greedie *Nereus*."
                    (*The Visions of Bellay*, xiii, 11.)

29. *Haemus*—a range of mountains in Thrace.

31. The *Ceraunian Mountains* lie on the coast of ancient Epirus.
Stygian Dis—Hades or Pluto.

31–32. There is a vague allusion to the war of the gods against the
Titans which Hesiod records (*Theogony*, 617–735), or to their war
against the giants which Homer mentions (*Od.* XI, 304–19), in both
of which their foes attacked Olympus by piling up the Thracian hills
against it.

33–34. MacKellar compares the scene in the attack of the rebel
angels when
                    "all Heav'n
      Had gone to wrack, with ruin overspread,
      Had not th'Almighty Father where he sits

threshold of heaven.   And you also, Phoebus Apollo,[25] shall
share the fate of your son in your precipitate chariot and be
swept down in sudden ruin; and at the quenching of your
light Nereus[27] shall send up jets of steam and dreadful hisses
from his astonished waters.   Then the rending of the foundations of lofty Haemus[29] shall shatter its summit and the
Ceraunian Mountains,[31] which Stygian Dis once used against
the gods in fratricidal conflicts,[32] shall be cast down to terrify
him in the lowest depth of the abyss.[33]

But by founding the stars more strongly the omnipotent
Father has taken thought for the universe.   He has fixed the
scales of fate with sure balance and commanded every individual thing in the cosmos to hold to its course forever.
Therefore the Prime Wheel[37] of the universe turns in daily
rotation and transmits its movement to its enclosed spheres.
Saturn is no slower than his wont and Mars, as fierce as he
was of old, darts lightning from his crested helmet.   Phoebus[41] shines with the ruddy beauty of eternal youth.   He
does not drive his team down descending slopes to warm
exhausted lands, but, strong in his friendly light, he pursues
his course forever through the same signs of the Zodiac.

Shrin'd in his Sanctuary of Heav'n secure,
Consulting on the sum of things, foreseen
This tumult."
            (*P.L.* VI, 669–74.)
Compare also the warning to Satan, when

"Th'Eternal to prevent such horrid fray
Hung forth in Heav'n his golden Scales, yet seen
Betwixt *Astraea* and the *Scorpion* sign,
Wherein all things created first he weigh'd,
The pendulous round Earth with balanc't Air
In counterpoise."
            (*P.L.* IV, 996–1001.)

37. *rota prima,* "the Prime Wheel"—the *primum mobile* or outermost sphere of the universe, which medieval astronomers imagined revolving daily from east to west and imparting its motion to the
enclosed spheres of the stars and planets.

41. *Phoebus,* "the bright," Homer's epithet for Apollo, came to be
used later to designate Apollo as the sun god.

Surgit odoratis pariter formosus ab Indis   45
Aethereum pecus albenti qui cogit Olympo,
Mane vocans, et serus agens in pascua caeli,
Temporis et gemino dispertit regna colore.
Fulget, obitque vices alterno Delia cornu,
Caeruleumque ignem paribus complectitur ulnis.   50
Nec variant elementa fidem, solitoque fragore
Lurida perculsas iaculantur fulmina rupes.
Nec per inane furit leviori murmure Corus,
Stringit et armiferos aequali horrore Gelonos
Trux Aquilo, spiratque hiemem, nimbosque volutat.   55
Utque solet, Siculi diverberat ima Pelori
Rex maris, et rauca circumstrepit aequora concha
Oceani tubicen, nec vasta mole minorem
Aegaeona ferunt dorso Balearica cete.
Sed neque, Terra, tibi saecli vigor ille vetusti   60
Priscus abest; servatque suum Narcissus odorem;
Et puer ille suum tenet, et puer ille, decorem,
Phoebe tuusque et Cypri tuus, nec ditior olim
Terra datum sceleri celavit montibus aurum

45–48. The beautiful planet is Venus, who appears as Lucifer or the
morning star and also as the evening star, Hesperus.   Compare *Nativity
Hymn,* 74, and *P.L.* IV, 605–9.

46. The Greeks, as Varro pointed out (*On the Latin Language* VII,
20), began the practice of calling the heavens Olympus.

49. *Delia* was an epithet of Diana because she was born on the
island of Delos.   Later Greek and Roman writers identified Artemis,
or Diana, with the moon goddess.

51. Todd compared Claudian's lines in a description of the strife of
the elements:
  "Paene reluctatis iterum pugnantia rebus rupissent elementa fidem."
              (*Rape of Proserpine* I, 42–3.)

53. *Corus*—the northwest wind.

55. *Aquilo*—the northeast wind.   Compare *On the Death of a
Fair Infant,* 8.

56. *Pelorus*—the northeastern promontory of Sicily.   In *P.L.* I,
232–3, Milton mentions it together with "thund'ring Aetna."

57. *Rex maris,* the sea king, is Neptune.   Compare *Comus,* 18–23,
note.

58. The trumpeter is Triton.   Compare *Comus,* 873, and *Lycidas,*
89, and Spenser's
              "Triton blowing loud his wreathed horne."
              (*Colin Clouts Come Home Again,* 245.)

Equally beautiful, the planet[45] which drives in the heavenly[46] flock through the sky at dawn and at evening drives them out into the pastures of heaven, rises out of the perfumed Indies and divides the kingdoms of time with its two-fold radiance. Delia[49] still shines and wanes with alternating horns and holds her heavenly effulgence in undiminished arms. The elements do not vary from their faith and with their accustomed uproar the lightning-bolts strike and shatter the rocks.[51] Corus[53] goes raging with no gentler voice through the void and the ferocious Aquilo[55] torments the armed Scythians with undiminished chill as he breathes out winter and sweeps the clouds along. In his accustomed style the sea king[57] smites the foundations of Sicilian Pelorus[56] and the trumpeter[58] of the ocean still blows his hoarse conch throughout the seas. The Balearic whales[59] bear upon their backs an Aegaeon of no less vast bulk. Nor has the pristine vigour of your earliest time forsaken you, O Earth. Narcissus[61] still preserves his fragrance. Your beloved youth, O Phoebus,[62] and yours, O Cypris,[63] still keep their beauty; nor did the earth in times past conceal beneath the mountains a greater wealth of the gold which her bad conscience knows is to be the root of evil, nor hide more gems beneath the seas.[65]

58–59. Milton remembered Ovid's picture of Hesiod's hundred-armed giant, *Aegaeon* (*Theogony*, 147), among the gods of the sea, clasping the vast backs of whales in his strong arms. (*Met.* II, 9–10.)

61. The name of the flower is capitalized in allusion to Ovid's story of its origin in the metamorphosis of the youth, Narcissus. (*Met.* III, 509–10.)

62. Compare the allusion to Apollo's favourite, Hyacinth, in *Lycidas*, 106, note, and the allusion to Venus' favourite, Adonis, in *Comus*, 999, note. From Adonis' blood, Ovid says (*Met.* X, 735–9), Venus created the anemone.

63. *Cypris*—Aphrodite or Venus. The name derives from the island sacred to her, Cyprus.

63–65. In *P.L.* I, 685–8, Milton reverted to this thought, which was a commonplace when Ovid described the degenerate men of the Age of Brass as violating the soil for the precious metals which incite to crimes. (*Met.* I, 137–42.)

Conscia, vel sub aquis gemmas. Sic denique in aevum   65
Ibit cunctarum series iustissima rerum,
Donec flamma orbem populabitur ultima, late
Circumplexa polos et vasti culmina caeli
Ingentique rogo flagrabit machina mundi.

(June, 1628)

67–69. Milton thought of the prophecy in II Peter iii, 10, of "the
day of the Lord," when "the elements shall melt with fervent heat; the
earth also and the works that are therein shall be burned up." In *C.D.*
I, xxxiii, he looked forward to "the destruction of this present un-

Thus, in a word, the righteous sequence of all things shall go on perpetually, until the final fire shall destroy the world, enveloping the poles and summits of vast heaven, while the fabric of the universe consumes in a mighty funeral pyre.[67]

---

clean and polluted world itself, namely, *its final conflagration,"* and he closed the eleventh book of *P.L.* with the hope of the day when fire shall

> "purge all things new,
> Both Heav'n and Earth, wherein the just shall dwell."

Anno Aetatis 19. *At a Vacation Exercise in the College,
part* Latin*, part* English. *The* Latin *speeches ended, the*
English *thus began.*

HAIL native Language, that by sinews weak
Didst move my first endeavouring tongue to speak,
And mad'st imperfect words with childish trips,
Half unpronounc't, slide through my infant lips,
Driving dumb silence from the portal door,   5
Where he had mutely sat two years before:
Here I salute thee and thy pardon ask,
That now I use thee in my latter task:
Small loss it is that thence can come unto thee,
I know my tongue but little Grace can do thee: 10
Thou needst not be ambitious to be first,
Believe me, I have thither packt the worst:
And, if it happen as I did forecast,
The daintiest dishes shall be serv'd up last.
I pray thee then deny me not thy aid   15
For this same small neglect that I have made:

1. This appeal to English was Milton's justification of his abandon-
ment of the Latin in which, up to this point, he had written the sixth
of the *Prolusiones Oratoriae,* or Academic Exercises, of which these
verses are a part. At the end of the Easter term, in July, 1628, he
was chosen the "Father" or leader of a group of students who were
to amuse their classmates and tutors with a traditional entertainment
at the beginning of the long vacation. In the Latin he did his best
to be amusing according to the taste of his audience, but improved the
opportunity to turn the tables upon the men who were responsible
for his nickname of the "Lady of Christ's." Characteristically, also, he
amused himself with the scholastic logic which was still a part of the
routine at Cambridge—although this was usual in such skits as he was
writing—and he chose for his theme the proposition: "That occasional
indulgence in sportive activities is not inconsistent with philosophic
studies." He appeared as the Aristotelian principle of *Ens,* or Absolute Being, and his ten "sons" impersonated the ten Aristotelian categories of Substance and its nine accidents or aspects, Quantity, Quality,
Relation, Place, Time, Posture, Possession or Having, Action and
Passion.

8. *latter*—later, *i.e.,* present.

But haste thee straight to do me once a Pleasure,
And from thy wardrope bring thy chiefest treasure;
Not those new fangled toys, and trimming slight
Which takes our late fantastics with delight,   20
But cull those richest Robes, and gay'st attire
Which deepest Spirits, and choicest Wits desire:
I have some naked thoughts that rove about
And loudly knock to have their passage out;
And weary of their place do only stay   25
Till thou hast deck't them in thy best array;
That so they may without suspect or fears
Fly swiftly to this fair Assembly's ears.
Yet I had rather, if I were to choose,
Thy service in some graver subject use,   30
Such as may make thee search thy coffers round,
Before thou clothe my fancy in fit sound:
Such where the deep transported mind may soar
Above the wheeling poles, and at Heav'n's door
Look in, and see each blissful Deity   35
How he before the thunderous throne doth lie,
Listening to what unshorn *Apollo* sings

---

18. As in *Lycidas,* 47, Milton wrote the frequent, seventeenth century form "wardrope" for *wardrobe.*

19. *toys*—trifles. Compare *Il Penseroso,* 4.

20. *takes*—captivates, pleases. Compare *Nativity Hymn,* 98, note.
The *fantastics* may be identified in a secondary way with Donne and the Metaphysicals generally; but Mr. R. C. Browne is surely right in identifying them primarily with the students whom Milton described in the first Prolusion as "priding themselves on a certain over-boiling, and truly laughable foam of words; from which, if you strip the rags that they have borrowed from new-fangled authors, how much barer than any nail would you behold them."

22. *Spirits* is usually equivalent to a monosyllable in Milton's verse. Spenser used the form "spright" and the form "spirt" is found in seventeenth century prose.

27. *suspect*—suspicion.

31. *coffers*—chests, *i.e.,* wardrobes. Compare line 18.

33. Imitating a Latin usage, Milton wrote *deep* to mean "high."

37. Apollo's classical epithet, *unshorn,* goes back through Horace's Ode (I, xxi, 2) in his honour to Pindar (*Pythian Odes,* 3, 14) and Homer. (*Il.* XX, 39.)

To th' touch of golden wires, while *Hebe* brings
Immortal Nectar to her Kingly Sire:
Then passing through the Spheres of watchful fire,   40
And misty Regions of wide air next under,
And hills of Snow and lofts of piled Thunder,
May tell at length how green-ey'd *Neptune* raves,
In Heav'n's defiance mustering all his waves;
Then sing of secret things that came to pass   45
When Beldam Nature in her cradle was;
And last of Kings and Queens and *Heroes* old,
Such as the wise *Demodocus* once told
In solemn Songs at King *Alcinous'* feast,
While sad *Ulysses'* soul and all the rest   50
Are held with his melodious harmony
In willing chains, and sweet captivity.
But fie, my wand'ring Muse, how thou dost stray!
Expectance calls thee now another way,
Thou know'st it must be now thy only bent   55
To keep in compass of thy Predicament:

---

38. *Hebe*—the cupbearer of the gods and herself the goddess of
youth. Compare *L'Allegro*, 29.

39. *Immortal*—immortality-conferring.   Compare the "immortal
streams" of heaven in the Sonnet *On Mrs. Catherine Thomason*, 14. In
P.L. V, 633-7, the "rubied Nectar" of the Olympian gods becomes the
drink of angels who "Quaff immortality."

40. Milton called the planets *watchful fires* perhaps because he was
familiar with Plato's idea that, "by the design of God, the sun and
moon and the five other stars which bear the name of 'planets' came
into existence for determining and watching over the numbers of
time." (*Timaeus*, 38c.)

41–42. Below the spheres of the planets and the region of fire,
which "Ptolemaic" astronomers imagined as just beneath the sphere of
the moon, was the region of air, to which Milton referred in *On the
Death of a Fair Infant*, 16, and *P.R.* II, 117. Below that was the
watery region of clouds and ocean which was Neptune's realm. Compare the note on Neptune in *Comus*, 18.

46. *Beldam*—grandmother.

48–50. Milton thought of Homer's story of Ulysses' tears as he listened to the bard, Demodocus, at the table of King Alcinoüs. (*Od*.
VIII, 521.)

56. In the technical language of scholastic logic the predicaments
corresponded to the Aristotelian categories. Compare the note on line
1 above.

Then quick about thy purpos'd business come,
That to the next I may resign my Room.

Then Ens *is represented as Father of the Predicaments his*
ten Sons, whereof the Eldest stood for Substance *with his*
Canons, which Ens *thus speaking, explains.*

Good luck befriend thee Son; for at thy birth
The Fairy Ladies danc't upon the hearth;   60
Thy drowsy Nurse hath sworn she did them spy
Come tripping to the Room where thou didst lie;
And sweetly singing round about thy Bed
Strew all their blessings on thy sleeping Head.
She heard them give thee this, that thou should'st still   65
From eyes of mortals walk invisible;
Yet there is something that doth force my fear,
For once it was my dismal hap to hear
A *Sibyl* old, bow-bent with crooked age,
That far events full wisely could presage,   70
And in time's long and dark Prospective Glass
Fore-saw what future days should bring to pass!
Your son, said she, (nor can you it prevent)
Shall subject be to many an Accident.
O'er all his Brethren he shall Reign as King,   75
Yet every one shall make him underling,
And those that cannot live from him asunder

---

65. *still*—forever, always.

66. Because the school logic described Substance as absolutely un-
knowable except in terms of its "accidents," Milton could pretend
that a fairy godmother gave it the gift of invisibility in its cradle.

69. *Sibyl*—not one of the nine prophetesses of antiquity but some
wise old woman like Othello's
        "sibyl, that had number'd in the world
    The sun to course two hundred compasses."
                (III, iv, 69–70.)

71. *Prospective Glass*—a magic glass for looking into future or distant events. *N.E.D.* compares Greene's *Friar Bacon,* V, 110; "In a
glasse prospectiue I will shew/Whats done this day in merry Fresing-
field."

74–78. The thought plays about the literal meaning of the word
"substance"—what "stands beneath" or "underlies" other things.

Ungratefully shall strive to keep him under;
In worth and excellence he shall out-go them,
Yet being above them, he shall be below them;   80
From others he shall stand in need of nothing,
Yet on his Brothers shall depend for Clothing.
To find a Foe it shall not be his hap,
And peace shall lull him in her flow'ry lap;
Yet shall he live in strife, and at his door   85
Devouring war shall never cease to roar;
Yea it shall be his natural property
To harbour those that are at enmity.
What power, what force, what mighty spell, if not
Your learned hands, can loose this Gordian knot?   90

The next Quantity *and* Quality, *spake in Prose, then* Relation
was call'd by his Name.

Rivers, arise; whether thou be the Son
Of utmost *Tweed,* or *Ouse,* or gulfy *Dun,*
Or *Trent,* who like some earth-born Giant spreads
His thirty Arms along the indented Meads,
Or sullen *Mole* that runneth underneath,   95
Or *Severn* swift, guilty of maiden's death,
Or Rocky *Avon,* or of Sedgy *Lee,*

85–86. Milton was thinking of the controversies over the Doctrine of Transubstantiation—the doctrine that "After Consecration there is no longer the substance of Bread, but that the Bread is transubstantiated, and turned into the substance of Christ's Body." Christopher Cartwright's definition (1651), quoted by the *N.E.D.*

87–88. Some of the predicaments, such as action and passion, are inconsistent with each other.

90. The knot which the Phrygian king Gordius tied, and which no one could loosen until Alexander the Great cut it with his sword, had been proverbial for two thousand years.

91. The part of the predicament *Relation* was taken by either George or Nizell Rivers, the sons of Sir John Rivers, who were freshmen at Christ's College.

92–100. The passage looks back to the great catalogues of English rivers in Drayton's *Polyolbion* and Spenser's account of the marriage of the Thames and the Medway in *The Faerie Queene,* IV, xi, 24–39.

96. For the *Maiden's death* see the note on Sabrina in *Comus,* 826.

Or Coaly *Tyne,* or ancient hallowed *Dee,*
Or *Humber* loud that keeps the *Scythian's* Name,
Or *Medway* smooth, or Royal Tow'red *Thame.*   100

The rest was Prose.

(July, 1628)

―――――――

98. The Dee, Spenser says (*F.Q.* IV, xi, 39), "Britons long ygone Did call divine." Changes in its course and flow were supposed to make it possible to divine the national future. Compare *Lycidas,* 55, note.

DE IDEA PLATONICA QUEMADMODUM
ARISTOTELES INTELLEXIT

DICITE, sacrorum praesides nemorum deae,
Tuque O noveni perbeata numinis
Memoria mater, quaeque in immenso procul
Antro recumbis otiosa Aeternitas,
Monumenta servans, et ratas leges Iovis,   5
Caelique fastos atque ephemeridas Deum
Quis ille primus cuius ex imagine
Natura solers finxit humanum genus,
Aeternus, incorruptus, aequaevus polo,
Unusque et universus, exemplar Dei?   10
Haud ille, Palladis gemellus innubae,
Interna proles insidet menti Iovis.
Sed quamlibet natura sit communior,
Tamen seorsus extat ad morem unius,
Et, mira, certo stringitur spatio loci.   15
Seu sempiternus ille siderum comes
Caeli pererrat ordines decemplicis,
Citimumve terris incolit Lunae globum.

1–3. The goddesses seem to be the nine Muses, whose chapter in
Conti's *Mythology* (VII, xv) describes them as crowned with flowers
and leaves and mentions several woodlands and mountains dedicated
to them. The first chapter of Geoffrey Linocre's *Musarum libellus* in-
terprets Hesiod's account (*Theogony*, 53–4) of them as the daughters
of Zeus and Mnemosyne, or Memory, as an allegory of the Platonic
doctrine that all knowledge is memory or—in Christian terms—innate
ideas implanted by God.

7–10. Finally this description rests upon Claudian's account (*On
Stilicho's Consulship*, 11, 424–40) of a mysterious old man who controls the events of time from a cave "somewhere beyond the range of
human minds and hardly approachable by the gods"; but it was Boccaccio, in the opening chapter of the *Genealogy of the Gods,* who gave
to Claudian's old man the name of Eternity.

In the background are Platonic passages such as the discussion in
the *Republic* (X, 596b–597d) of the Eternal ideas or divinely established patterns upon which all things were supposed to be moulded,

ON THE PLATONIC IDEA AS UNDERSTOOD BY
ARISTOTLE

REVEAL,[1] you goddesses who preside over the sacred groves, and you too, O happy mother of the nine-fold deity, and you, Eternity, far away where you lie at ease in some vast cave, guarding the records and the immutable decrees of Jove and the calendars of heaven and the day-books of the gods, reveal who was that first being[7]—eternal, incorruptible, unique yet universal, coeval with the heavens and made in the image of God—in whose likeness skilful Nature has moulded the human race. Certainly he does not lurk, a twin of the virgin Athene, unborn in the brain of Jove.[11] But, though all men have a share in his nature, yet—strange as it may be—he exists by himself as an individual apart and is limited by his own definite bounds in space. Or is he a comrade of the eternal stars who goes wandering through the ten-fold spheres of heaven or inhabits the neighbour of this world, the moon?[18] Or perhaps he sits torpidly beside the stream

---

but the archetypal man is a Neo-Platonic conception and may owe something to the Hermetic Books (*e.g., Poimander* I, 12–4) and to Kabbalistic interpretations of the story in Genesis i, 27, of the creation of man in the image of God. In his college exercises Milton is sometimes ironical with "Aristotle, the envious and perpetual calumniator of Pythagoras and Plato" (Second *Prolusion*), and here he satirizes the unimaginative objections to the doctrine of ideas in Aristotle's *Metaphysics*. Even the study of natural science seemed to him to confirm the Platonic doctrine. "For who can contemplate and examine attentively the ideal forms of things, human and divine," he asked in the seventh *Prolusion,* "unless he has a mind saturated and perfected by knowledge?" Compare the Introduction, § 13.

11–12. In his chapter on Athene (IV, v) Conti treated the myth that she was born, adult and fully armed, from the brain of Zeus as the most rational of the stories of her origin, taking the ground that it is an allegory representing the mind as the seat of memory and wisdom.

18. In the Ptolemaic astronomy the moon's was the lowest or nearest to the earth of the celestial spheres.

Sive inter animas corpus adituras sedens
Obliviosas torpet ad Lethes aquas;   20
Sive in remota forte terrarum plaga
Incedit ingens hominis archetypus gigas,
Et diis tremendus erigit celsum caput,
Atlante maior portitore siderum.
Non, cui profundum caecitas lumen dedit,   25
Dircaeus augur vidit hunc alto sinu;
Non hunc silenti nocte Pleiones nepos
Vatum sagaci praepes ostendit choro;
Non hunc sacerdos novit Assyrius, licet
Longos vetusti commemoret atavos Nini,   30
Priscumque Belon, inclytumque Osiridem.
Non ille trino gloriosus nomine
Ter magnus Hermes (ut sit arcani sciens)
Talem reliquit Isidis cultoribus.
At tu perenne ruris Academi decus   35
(Haec monstra si tu primus induxti scholis)
Iam iam poetas, urbis exules tuae,
Revocabis, ipse fabulator maximus,
Aut institutor ipse migrabis foras.

(1628 ?)

---

20. Milton thought of Virgil's Pythagorean passage where Anchises
explains the doctrine of metempsychosis to Aeneas—how all spirits
drink the oblivion-bringing waters of Lethe after death and suffer
various purifications before rebirth is possible. (*Aen.* VI, 713–51.)

24. The giant Atlas, whom Hesiod describes as supporting wide
heaven with head and arms (*Theogony,* 507–20), was related to Mount
Atlas in north Africa, to which Milton compares Satan in *P.L.* IV,
985–9.

26. The Dircean, or Theban, seer is Tiresias, whose mother, Conti
says (IV, v), somewhat oversimplifying the story in Callimachus' *Hymn
for the Bath of Pallas,* persuaded Athene to give him spiritual illumination and the gift of prophecy in exchange for the loss of his eyes.
Compare *P.L.* III, 36.

27. The grandchild of Pleione was Hermes, or Mercury, whose
mother, Maia, was one of the Pleiades and the daughter of the sea-
nymph, Pleione. In the *Heroides* (xvi, 62) Milton found him called
the grandchild of Pleione and he might remember the allusion to his
genealogy also in Ovid's *Metamorphoses.* (I, 667–70.)

29. Warton identified the Assyrian priest with the legendary Phoenician sage, Sanchuniathon; but who he really was is doubtful. Perhaps
Milton vaguely individualized a figure among those learned orientals

of Lethe among the spirits waiting to re-enter the body.[20]
Or perhaps the human archetype is a huge giant, a tremendous figure in some remote region of the earth who
lifts his head higher than the star-bearer, Atlas,[24] to terrify
the gods. Even in the depths of the soul of the Dircean[26]
seer, to whom blindness brought a profound illumination,
no vision of him appeared. Never in the silent night was
any revelation of him made to the wise company of the
prophets by the swift grandchild[27] of Pleione. This being
was unknown to the Assyrian priest,[29] though he was
familiar with the long line of the progenitors of old Ninus
and with primeval Belus[31] and with renowned Osiris. Not
even thrice-great Hermes,[33] glorious for his triple name, in
spite of all his esoteric knowledge, left any such tradition to
the worshippers of Isis.[34]

But you, the eternal glory of the Academy[35] that was set
among the fields—if you were the first who brought these
absurdities into the schools—must surely now call home again
those exiles from your city, the poets,[37] for you are the supreme
fabler yourself. Either that, or, even though you are the
founder, you shall go into exile yourself.

———————

to whom Herodotus referred (I, 1) as authorities for his account (i, 7)
of the half-mythical Assyrian king, Ninus, the husband of Semiramis.

31. The Assyrian god, Bel, is identified with the Canaanitish deity, Baal.
Compare *Nativity Hymn*, 197, note. *P.L.* I, 720, mentions Bel as Belus.

33–34. Compare the allusion to "thrice great *Hermes*" in *Il Penseroso*, 88, note.

34. The worshippers of Isis are the Egyptians. Compare the allusion
to her in *Nativity Hymn*, 212, note.

35. Plato's Academy lay in the open country about a mile to the
northwest of Athens.

35–39. In spite of Plato's exclusion of the poets from his ideal state
on the ground that their imitations of reality were false and demoral-
izing (*Republic* VIII, 568b, and X, 595 and 607), apologists for poetry
in the Renaissance were never tired of pointing out, like Sir Philip
Sidney, that "in the body of his work, though the inside and strength
were Philosophy, the skinne as it were, and beautie depended most of
Poetrie. . . Besides, his . . . enterlacing meere tales, as Giges Ring, and
others, which who knoweth not to be flowers of Poetrie did never
walke into *Apollos* Garden." (*Elizabethan Critical Essays,* ed. by
G. Smith, I, p. 152.)

THE FIFTH ODE OF HORACE. LIB. I

Quis multa gracilis te puer in Rosa, *Rend'red almost word for word without Rhyme according to the Latin Measure, as near as the Language will permit.*

WHAT slender Youth bedew'd with liquid odours
Courts thee on Roses in some pleasant Cave,
    Pyrrha? for whom bind'st thou
    In wreaths thy golden Hair,
Plain in thy neatness?   O, how oft shall he   5
On Faith and changed Gods complain, and Seas
    Rough with black winds and storms
    Unwonted shall admire,
Who now enjoys thee credulous, all Gold;
Who always vacant, always amiable   10
    Hopes thee; of flattering gales
    Unmindful.   Hapless they
To whom thou untried seem'st fair.   Me in my vow'd
Picture the sacred wall declares t' have hung
    My dank and dropping weeds   15
    To the stern God of Sea.

                     (1628–9?)

AD PYRRHAM. ODE V

Horatius ex Pyrrhae illecebris tanquam è naufragio enataverat,
cuius amore irretitos, affirmat esse miseros.[1]

> Quis multa gracilis te puer in rosa
> Perfusus liquidis urget odoribus,
>   Grato, *Pyrrha,* sub antro?
>   Cui flavam religas comam,
>
> Simplex munditie? Heu quoties fidem
> Mutatosque deos flebit, et aspera
>   Nigris aequora ventis
>   Emirabitur insolens,
>
> Qui nunc te fruitur credulus aurea:
> Qui semper vacuam, semper amabilem
>   Sperat, nescius aurae
>   Fallacis. Miseri, quibus
>
> Intentata nites. Me tabula sacer
> Votiva paries indicat uvida
>   Suspendisse potenti
>   Vestimenta maris Deo.

---

[1]Milton subjoined the Latin text to his translation.

ELEGIA QUINTA

Anno Aetatis 20

In Adventum Veris

In se perpetuo Tempus revolubile gyro
    Iam revocat Zephyros, vere tepente, novos.
Induiturque brevem Tellus reparata iuventam,
    Iamque soluta gelu dulce virescit humus.
Fallor? an et nobis redeunt in carmina vires,   5
    Ingeniumque mihi munere veris adest?
Munere veris adest, iterumque vigescit ab illo—
    Quis putet?—atque aliquod iam sibi poscit opus.
Castalis ante oculos, bifidumque cacumen oberrat,
    Et mihi Pyrenen somnia nocte ferunt;   10
Concitaque arcano fervent mihi pectora motu,
    Et furor, et sonitus me sacer intus agit.
Delius ipse venit—video Peneide lauro
    Implicatos crines—Delius ipse venit.
Iam mihi mens liquidi raptatur in ardua caeli,   15
    Perque vagas nubes corpore liber eo.
Perque umbras, perque antra feror, penetralia vatum;
    Et mihi fana patent interiora Deum.
Intuiturque animus toto quid agatur Olympo,
    Nec fugiunt oculos Tartara caeca meos.   20
Quid tam grande sonat distento spiritus ore?
    Quid parit haec rabies, quid sacer iste furor?

---

3. *Tellus*—Earth. Gaia, the equivalent Greek deity, is called in the Homeric *Hymn to Gaia* the wife of Heaven and the mother of all things. In Rome Tellus stood for the earth in all its genial aspects.

5. *Fallor? an;* a frequent device in Latin Poetry (*e.g.*, Ovid, *Amores* III, i, 34), which Milton used in *Comus*, 221–3. Compare *Elegy VII*, 56.

6–8. In his *Life* Phillips quoted his uncle as saying that when he wrote *P.L.* "his vein never happily flowed but from the autumnal equinox to the vernal, . . . and whatever he attempted [at other times] was never to his satisfaction, though he courted his fancy never so much."

8. *poscit opus*—asks for employment. Professor Rand suggests a daring reminiscence of Ovid's *Amores* III, vii, 68.

ELEGY V

At Age 20

ON THE COMING OF SPRING

Now, in the growing warmth of the spring, Time—as it turns in its perpetual cycle—is calling back the Zephyrs afresh. Earth,[3] with her strength renewed, is donning her brief youth and the frost-free soil is putting forth its sweet greenness. Am I deluded?[5]   Or are my powers of song returning?   And is my inspiration with me again by grace of the spring?[6]   By the spring's grace it is with me and—who would guess such a thing?—it is already clamouring for some employment.[8] Castaly[9] and the riven peak float before my eyes and by night I am beside Pirene[10] in my dreams.   My breast is aflame with the excitement of its mysterious impulse and I am driven on by the madness and the divine sounds within me.   The Delian[13] himself is approaching—I see the locks that are braided with Daphne's laurel[13]—the Delian himself comes. Already my mind is being borne up into the sheer liquid heights of the sky and, quit of the body, I go through the wandering clouds.   I am carried through shadows and grottoes, the secret haunts of the poets; and the innermost shrines of the gods are open to me.   My spirit surveys all that is done on Olympus[19] and the unseen infernal world is not impervious to my eyes.   What mighty song is my soul pouring from its full throat?   What is to be the offspring of this madness and

---

9. *Castalis.* See *Elegy IV,* 30 and 31, notes.

10. *Pyrenen.* See *To John Rouse,* 36, and *Elegy IV,* 31.

13. *Peneide lauro*—with the laurel of the daughter of Peneus. See *Comus,* 661, and *Elegy VII,* 31–6.

13–14. *Delius* was an epithet of Apollo from his birthplace, Delos. Compare *Delia* in *Nature is not Subject to Old Age,* 49.

19. By *Olympus* Milton means simply the home of the gods, either on the summit of Mount Olympus in Thessaly or in the heavens. In *On the Death of a Fair Infant,* 44, and *Nature is not Subject to Old Age,* 46, the word means simply the sky.

Ver mihi, quod dedit ingenium, cantabitur illo;
    Profuerint isto reddita dona modo.
Iam, Philomela, tuos foliis adoperta novellis   25
    Instituis modulos, dum silet omne nemus.
Urbe ego, tu silva, simul incipiamus utrique,
    Et simul adventum veris uterque canat.
Veris, io! rediere vices; celebremus honores
    Veris, et hoc subeat Musa perennis opus.   30
Iam sol, Aethiopas fugiens Tithoniaque arva,
    Flectit ad Arctoas aurea lora plagas.
Est breve noctis iter, brevis est mora noctis opacae;
    Horrida cum tenebris exulat illa suis.
Iamque Lycaonius plaustrum caeleste Boötes   35
    Non longa sequitur fessus ut ante via,
Nunc etiam solitas circum Iovis atria toto
    Excubias agitant sidera rara polo,
Nam dolus et caedes, et vis cum nocte recessit,
    Neve Giganteum Dii timuere scelus.   40
Forte aliquis scopuli recubans in vertice pastor,
    Roscida cum primo sole rubescit humus,
"Hac," ait, "hac certe caruisti nocte puella,
    Phoebe, tua, celeres quae retineret equos."
Laeta suas repetit silvas, pharetramque resumit   45
    Cynthia, Luciferas ut videt alta rotas,
Et tenues ponens radios gaudere videtur
    Officium fieri tam breve fratris ope.

---

25. *Philomel*—the nightingale. See *Il Penseroso, 56*, note, and compare the Sonnet, *O Nightingale.*

30. In 1673 Milton substituted *perennis* for *quotannis.* The long syllable *quo-* was one of the false quantities with which Salmasius twitted Milton in the *Responsio.*

31. *Aethiopas*—the Ethiopians. The connotation is like that of "the Ethiop Line" of *P.L.* IV, 282, where the equator is meant. Anciently the Ethiopians were supposed to occupy all equatorial Africa.

Tithonia arva—the east. See the note on l. 49 below.

35. *Boötes.* Compare *On the Death of the Bishop of Ely, 51*, note.

40. The *giants,*
      "whom the Fables name of monstrous size,
    Titanian, or *Earth-born,* that warr'd on *Jove.*"
          (*P.L.* I, 197–8.)

this sacred ecstasy? The spring shall be the song of the in-spiration that it has given to me, and so she may profit by her gift's return.

Already, Philomela,[25] you are beginning your trills in your covert among the budding leaves, while all the woods guard their silence. I in the city and you in the forest, let us both begin together and let us both together sing the advent of the spring. Ho, for the change of spring is returning. Let us celebrate the honours of the spring and let the Muse take up the task that she perennially[30] assumes. Now the sun, in full flight from the Ethiopians[31] and the fields of Tithonus,[31] is turning his golden reins toward northern lands. Brief is the journey and brief the tarrying of gloomy night; the frightful night is an exile with its shadows. Lycaonian Boötes[35] no longer plods wearily—as of yore—over a long course after the heavenly wain; now even the stars are but few as they keep their accustomed watch about the courts of Jove throughout the whole sky, for fraud, murder and violence vanish with the night and the gods have no fear of outrage by the giants.[40] Some shepherd, perhaps, as he lies on the top of a crag, says, while the dewy earth reddens under the first rays of the sun:

"Last night,[43] surely, O Phoebus,[44] last night you were un-provided with a fair bed-fellow who would delay your swift coursers."

Delighted, Cynthia[46] returns to her forests and resumes her quiver, when from on high she sees the wheels of Lucifer; and, laying aside her delicate rays, she seems to be happy that by her brother's help her own task is cut short.

43–44. Compare Randolph's shepherds in the *Amyntas:*
    Alexis. "I much wonder the Sunne so soone can rise!"
    Damon. "Did he lay his head in faire *Laurinda's* lap,
            We should have but short daies."
    Alexis. "No summer, *Damon*." (Act IV, scene iv.)

44. *Phoebe.* See *Elegy III,* 34, note.

46. *Cynthia*—the moon, personified as the huntress goddess, Diana. Compare *Nativity Hymn,* 103, and *Il Penseroso,* 59, note.

"Desere," Phoebus ait, "thalamos, Aurora, seniles;
    Quid iuvat effoeto procubuisse toro?   50
Te manet Aeolides viridi venator in herba;
    Surge; tuos ignes altus Hymettus habet."
Flava verecundo dea crimen in ore fatetur,
    Et matutinos ocius urget equos.
Exuit invisam Tellus rediviva senectam,   55
    Et cupit amplexus, Phoebe, subire tuos.
Et cupit, et digna est; quid enim formosius illa,
    Pandit ut omniferos luxuriosa sinus,
Atque Arabum spirat messes, et ab ore venusto
    Mitia cum Paphiis fundit amoma rosis?   60
Ecce, coronatur sacro frons ardua luco,
    Cingit ut Idaeam pinea turris Opim;
Et vario madidos intexit flore capillos,
    Floribus et visa est posse placere suis,
Floribus effusos ut erat redimita capillos,   65
    Taenario placuit diva Sicana Deo.
Aspice, Phoebe; tibi faciles hortantur amores,
    Mellitasque movent flamina verna preces;
Cinnamea Zephyrus leve plaudit odorifer ala,
    Blanditiasque tibi ferre videntur aves.   70

---

49. The story that Aurora's mortal husband, Tithonus, was granted
immortality without immortal youth goes back to the Homeric Hymn
to Aphrodite, 218–38.   At sunrise
        "faire *Aurora* rising hastily,
     Doth by her blushing tell, that she did lye
     All night in old *Tithonus* frozen bed,
     Whereof she seemes ashamed inwardly."
               (*F.Q.* III, iii, 20, 4–7.)

51. *Aeolides,* the son of Aeolus, Cephalus.   See *Elegy III,* 67, note.

52. *tuos ignes*—your fires, *i.e.* the object of your passion.   So Virgil's Menalcas speaks of his minion as "meus ignis, Amyntas."   (*Eclogue
III,* 66.)

55–56. So Pontano describes the vernal earth longing for the sun as
a woman longs for her husband:
      "Ac veluti virgo, absenti cum sola marito
      Suspirat sterilem lecto traducere vitam
      Illius expectans complexus anxia caros,
      Ergo, ubi Sol imo victor convertit ab Austro,
      Tum gravidos aperitque sinus et caeca relaxat
      Spiramenta, novas veniat qua succus in herbas,
      Et tandem complexa suum laetatur Adonim."
            (*Urania* I, 500–6.)

"Leave the couch of an old man, O Aurora,"[49] is the cry of Phoebus; "what pleasure is there in the bed of impotence? On the green lawns the hunter, Aeolides,[51] is waiting for you. Up! the heights of Hymettus are in possession of your fires."[52]

With blushing face the bright goddess acknowledges her guilt and urges the horses of the dawn to greater speed.

The reviving earth throws off her hated old age and craves thy embraces, O Phoebus.[55] She craves them and she is worthy of them; for what is lovelier than she as she voluptuously bares her fertile breast and breathes the perfume of Arabian harvests and pours sweet spices and the scent of Paphian[60] roses from her lovely lips? Behold, her towering brow is girdled with a sacred grove as Idaean Ops[62] is turreted with pines. She twines her dewy hair with various bloom and with her flowers seems powerful to charm, as the Sicanian goddess with the flowers plaited in her flowing hair was charming to the Taenarian god.[66] Look Phoebus, facile loves are calling to you and the winds of spring carry honied appeals. Perfume-bearing Zephyr[69] gently fans his cinnamon-scented wings and the birds seem to carry their blandishments

---

60. The most celebrated of the temples of Aphrodite (Venus) in the island of Cyprus was at Paphos.

62. *Ops*, the Italian goddess of fertility, seems to be identified with "the tow'red Cybele" of *Arcades*, 21.

66. *Taenario . . . Deo*—to the Taenarian god, *i.e.* Pluto. Taenarus was the name of a promontory on what is now known as the peninsula of Mattapan, in ancient Laconia, where Dis (Pluto) had a temple in a cave which was supposed to be an entrance to the infernal regions. *diva Sicana*—the Sicilian goddess, *i.e.* Proserpina, who
          "gath'ring flow'rs,
     Herself a fairer Flow'r, by gloomy *Dis*
     Was gather'd."
               (*P.L.* IV, 269–71.)

69. *Zephyrus*. See *Elegy III*, 43–4, note.

Nec sine dote tuos temeraria quaerit amores
   Terra, nec optatos poscit egena toros;
Alma salutiferum medicos tibi gramen in usus
   Praebet, et hinc titulos adiuvat ipsa tuos.
Quod si te pretium, si te fulgentia tangunt   75
   Munera—muneribus saepe coemptus Amor—
Illa tibi ostentat quascunque sub aequore vasto,
   Et superiniectis montibus, abdit opes.
Ah, quoties, cum tu clivoso fessus Olympo
   In vespertinas praecipitaris aquas,   80
"Cur te," inquit, "cursu languentem Phoebe diurno
   Hesperiis recipit Caerula mater aquis?
Quid tibi cum Tethy? quid cum Tartesside lympha?
   Dia quid immundo perluis ora salo?
Frigora, Phoebe, mea melius captabis in umbra.   85
   Huc ades; ardentes imbue rore comas.
Mollior egelida veniet tibi somnus in herba.
   Huc ades, et gremio lumina pone meo.
Quaque iaces circum mulcebit lene susurrans
   Aura per humentes corpora fusa rosas.   90
Nec me, crede mihi, terrent Semeleia fata,
   Nec Phaetonteo fumidus axis equo.
Cum tu, Phoebe, tuo sapientius uteris igni,
   Huc ades, et gremio lumina pone meo."
Sic Tellus lasciva suos suspirat amores;   95
   Matris in exemplum caetera turba ruunt.
Nunc etenim toto currit vagus orbe Cupido,
   Languentesque fovet solis ab igne faces.
Insonuere novis lethalia cornua nervis,
   Triste micant ferro tela corusca novo.   100

---

74. Milton thought of invocations of Apollo as a healer, like that in the first chorus of the *Agamemnon* of Aeschylus.

77–78. Compare *Comus*, 732–6, note.

79. *Olympo.* See the note on l. 19 above.

83. *Tethys.* See *Comus*, 870, note.

91. *Semele*, who bore Bacchus to Jove, was persuaded by Juno to ask him to appear to her in all his divine glory, but "her mortal body could not bear that celestial violence and she was consumed by that marriage gift." (Ovid, *Met.* III, 308–9.)

to you. The earth is not so bold as to beg for your love without offering a dowry in return and she makes no pauper's appeal for the nuptials that she desires. In her bounty she provides you with health-giving herbs for healing and so she adds to your titles of honour.[74] If a bribe and if glittering gifts have power over you—and love is often bought with gifts—she spreads before you all the wealth in the vast ocean[77] and under the mass of the mountains. Ah, how often, when, wearied from the steep of heaven,[79] you would plunge into the western sea, she cries:

"Why, O Phoebus, should the blue mother receive you into the Hesperian waves when you are fainting from your daily course? What have you to do with Tethys?[83] What have you to do with Tartessian streams? Why do you bathe your divine face in the unclean salt water? You will find coolness much better, Phoebus, in my shadow. Come hither and steep your glowing locks in dew. A gentler sleep will be yours in the cool grass. Come hither and lay your glories in my lap. Where you lie a gently murmuring breeze will soothe our bodies on their couch of humid roses. I have no fear, believe me, of a fate like that of Semele,[91] nor of the axle that smoked when Phaeton was the driver of the horses.[92] When you shall have put your fire to wiser use, come hither and lay your glories in my lap."[93]

Thus the wanton earth breathes out her passion, and her thronging children follow hard after her example. Now wandering Cupid runs at large throughout the whole world and kindles his dying torch in the flame of the sun. The lethal horns of his bow are resonant with new strings, and his gleaming shafts, tipped with new steel, are ominously glittering.

---

92. Ovid tells the story (*Met.* II, 19–328) of Apollo's unwilling consent that his son, Phaeton, should drive the sun's chariot for a day and of the wild drive which followed, when heaven and earth were threatened with destruction until Jove finally struck Phaeton dead with a thunder-bolt. Compare *To his Father,* 38 and 97–100.

93. In Ovid's story (*Met.* III, 272–300) the earth protests against the unwise use to which the sun's fires are being put by Phaeton

Iamque vel invictam tentat superasse Dianam,
   Quaeque sedet sacro Vesta pudica foco.
Ipsa senescentem reparat Venus annua formam,
   Atque iterum tepido creditur orta mari.
Marmoreas iuvenes clamant Hymenaee per urbes;   105
   Litus io Hymen et cava saxa sonant.
Cultior ille venit, tunicaque decentior apta;
   Puniceum redolet vestis odora crocum.
Egrediturque frequens ad amoeni gaudia veris
   Virgineos auro cincta puella sinus.   110
Votum est cuique suum; votum est tamen omnibus unum,
   Ut sibi quem cupiat det Cytherea virum.
Nunc quoque septena modulatur arundine pastor,
   Et sua quae iungat carmina Phyllis habet.
Navita nocturno placat sua sidera cantu,   115
   Delphinasque leves ad vada summa vocat.
Iupiter ipse alto cum coniuge ludit Olympo,
   Convocat et famulos ad sua festa Deos.
Nunc etiam Satyri, cum sera crepuscula surgunt,
   Pervolitant celeri florea rura choro,   120
Sylvanusque sua Cyparissi fronde revinctus,
   Semicaperque Deus, semideusque caper.
Quaeque sub arboribus Dryades latuere vetustis
   Per iuga, per solos expatiantur agros.
Per sata luxuriat fruticetaque Maenalius Pan;   125
   Vix Cybele mater, vix sibi tuta Ceres;

---

101. The story that Artemis (Diana) obtained the gift of eternal chastity from Zeus goes back to Callimachus' *Hymn to Artemis*, 5. Compare *Comus*, 441–5.

102. *Vesta*. See *Il Penseroso*, 23–4, note.

104. The myth of the birth of Venus from the sea was the subject of one of the most famous ancient paintings, by Apelles, and of a no less famous picture by Botticelli.

105–108. *Io Hymen Hymenaee* is the choral cry in Catullus' beautiful epithalamium for Malius Torquatus (LXI). Hymen was the Greek divinity of marriage. See *P.L.* XI, 591, and *L'Allegro*, 125–6, note.

114. *Phyllis*. Compare *L'Allegro*, 86, note.

116. For the fancy about the dolphins see *To his Father*, 60, note.

121. *Sylvanus*. See *Il Penseroso*, 134, and *Comus*, 268, note.

122. Milton seems to confuse Sylvanus with the satyrs, as he did in *P.R.* II, 191. The description fits Pan rather than Sylvanus, and it

And now he attempts the conquest of even the unconquerable Diana[101] and of the chaste Vesta,[102] whose seat is the sacred hearth. Venus herself is making her annual renewal of her aging form and appears to have sprung afresh out of the warm sea.[104] Through marble cities the youths are chanting *Hymenaee;*[105] the shores and the caverns echo with the cry, *Io, Hymen.* And Hymen appears in festal attire, properly robed in a becoming tunic, and his fragrant vestment diffuses the perfume of the purple crocus. Many a damsel with her virgin breast girdled with gold goes forth to the pleasures of the lovely spring. Each one has her own prayer and the prayer of each is the same—that Cytherea will give her the man of her desire.

Now also the shepherd is making music on his pipe of reeds and Phyllis[114] has her songs which she adds to his. With his chant by night the sailor wins the favour of his stars and calls up the fleet dolphins to the surface of the waves.[116] On the heights of Olympus Jove himself sports with his spouse and invites even the gods that serve in his household to his feast. And now, as the late shadows thicken, even the satyrs go darting through the flowery fields in swift bands, and Sylvanus[121] also, crowned with cypress leaves, the god who is half goat and the goat who is half god.[122] The Dryads who have been in hiding under the ancient trees are ranging over the mountains and through the lonely fields. Maenalian[125] Pan takes his wanton pleasure in the sown fields and the copses. There[126] mother Cybele is hardly safe from him and

---

is applied to Pan by Sannazaro in a line which, as Mr. James Goode points out, coincides with this one. (See Sannazaro's *Elegiae,* Paris, 1725, p. 92.)

125. *Maenalus* was the name of a range of mountains in Arcadia, sacred to Pan.

126. Keightley's suggestion of *ibi* for *sibi* in the editions of 1645 and 1673 seems inevitable.

Cybele. See *Arcades,* 21, note.

Ceres was goddess of agriculture. See *Elegy IV,* 11, and *To his Father,* 48, notes.

Atque aliquam cupidus praedatur Oreada Faunus,
  Consulit in trepidos dum sibi Nympha pedes,
Iamque latet, latitansque cupit male tecta videri,
  Et fugit, et fugiens pervelit ipsa capi.   130
Dii quoque non dubitant caelo praeponere silvas,
  Et sua quisque sibi numina lucus habet.
Et sua quisque diu sibi numina lucus habeto,
  Nec vos arborea, dii, precor, ite domo.
Te referant miseris te, Iupiter, aurea terris   135
  Saecla! quid ad nimbos aspera tela redis?
Tu saltem lente rapidos age, Phoebe, iugales
  Qua potes, et sensim tempora veris eant;
Brumaque productas tarde ferat hispida noctes,
  Ingruat et nostro serior umbra polo!   140

(1628 ?)

---

127. *Faunus.* See *To Salzilli*, 27-8, note.

135-136. Milton thought of the myth that after the Golden Age, one
by one, the gods abandoned the earth. See *Elegy IV*, 81-2, note.

Ceres herself is hardly safe. The lustful Faunus[127] seeks to make some Oread his victim. The nymph takes to her trembling heels for safety. And now she hides but as she does so her hope is to be seen in her poor covert. She darts away, but, though she runs, she hopes to be overtaken. The gods do not hesitate to prefer our woods to their heaven and every grove possesses its own deities.

And long may every grove possess its deities! And my prayer to you, O gods, is not to desert your forest home.[135] Let the Age of Gold restore you, Jupiter, to a wretched world. Why return your terrible missiles to the clouds? At least, O Phoebus, drive your swift coursers as moderately as you can and let the spring-tide pass slowly. Let the foul winter be long in bringing back its endless nights and let the shadows be later than their wont in attacking our pole.

SONG

On May Morning

Now the bright morning Star, Day's harbinger,
Comes dancing from the East, and leads with her
The Flow'ry *May,* who from her green lap throws
The yellow Cowslip, and the pale Primrose.
   Hail bounteous *May* that dost inspire   5
   Mirth and youth and warm desire!
   Woods and Groves are of thy dressing,
   Hill and Dale doth boast thy blessing.
Thus we salute thee with our early Song,
And welcome thee, and wish thee long.   10

(1628 ?)

1–4. Perhaps Milton thought of the traditional identification of the *morning Star,* Lucifer, with Venus, for whom the famous induction to Lucretius' *De rerum natura* (I, 7–8) describes the earth as bringing forth sweet flowers. His miniature poem has a suggestion of the mysterious beauty of Botticelli's *Spring,* although its substance is simply the beauty of the English meadows, which

         "brought sweetly forth
   The freckled cowslip, burnet, and green clover."
         (*Henry V,* V, ii, 47–8.)

O NIGHTINGALE!

O Nightingale, that on yon bloomy Spray
  Warbl'st at eve, when all the Woods are still,
  Thou with fresh hope the Lover's heart dost fill,
  While the jolly hours lead on propitious *May*
Thy liquid notes that close the eye of Day,   5
  First heard before the shallow Cuckoo's bill,
  Portend success in love; O, if *Jove's* will
  Have linkt that amorous power to thy soft lay,
Now timely sing, ere the rude Bird of Hate
  Foretell my hopeless doom in some Grove nigh: 10
  As thou from year to year hast sung too late
For my relief; yet hadst no reason why,
  Whether the Muse, or Love call thee his mate,
  Both them I serve, and of their train am I.

                               (1628 ?)

1–2. This sonnet perhaps marks Milton's first mastery of the classical, medieval and Renaissance Italian elements which his mature art was to blend. Its opening recalls some of the sonnets of Giovanni Della Casa and Giacomo Cenci and its first line might serve as a word-for-word translation of a similar invocation of the nightingale by Cardinal Bembo.

2. Compare lines 25–6 in the *Fifth Elegy.*

4. The *jolly hours,* whose meaning for the Renaissance is best conveyed by Guido Reni's picture of them following the chariot of the sun, go back to the earliest Greek poetry, as for example in the description of them in an Orphic Hymn (2, 13) as "born in the springtime, happy and rich in flowers."

5–7. In the background is a medieval convention which Milton may have met in Sir Thomas Clanvowe's *The Cuckoo and the Nightingale,* a poem which, like Milton's contemporaries, he would attribute to Chaucer. It is a debate about love between its champion, the nightingale, and its ignorant enemy, the cuckoo, whom the poet overheard in a dream one night when he lay long awake and
               "thoghte how lovers had a tokeninge,
    And among hem it was a comune tale,
    That it were good to here the nightingale
    Rather than the lewde cukkow singe."
                (Stanza X.)

DONNA LEGGIADRA

Donna leggiadra il cui bel nome onora
  L'erbosa val di Reno, e il nobil varco,
  Ben è colui d' ogni valore scarco
  Qual tuo spirto gentil non innamora,
Che dolcemente mostrasi di fuora,   5
  De' suoi atti soavi giamai parco,
  E i don', che son d' amor saette ed arco,
  Là onde l' alta tua virtù s' infiora.
Quando tu vaga parli, o lieta canti
  Che mover possa duro alpestre legno,   10
  Guardi ciascun agli occhi, ed agli orecchi
L' entrata, chi di te si trova indegno;
  Grazia sola di sù gli vaglia, innanti
  Che'l disio amoroso al cuor s' invecchi.

(1628 ?)

1–4. The lady, as Mr. J. S. Smart showed, must have been called
Aemilia, for that name is the solution of the riddle which Milton set
by referring to the river Reno and the famous ford, *i.e.* the ford of
the Rubicon. The two rivers were conspicuous on contemporary maps
of the province of Aemilia. Of the lady we know only what the
Italian poems tell us. They were written, as the second and third of
them plainly imply, when Milton was in England, and probably as
early as 1628; and they lend no support to the theory that they were
composed during Milton's visit to Bologna and the valley of the Reno
in 1639.

BEAUTIFUL LADY

GENTLE and beautiful lady,[1] whose fair name honours the verdant valley of Reno and the glorious ford, surely he is a man void of all worth who is not inspired with love by your gracious spirit. Sweetly it expresses itself in the bounty of fair looks and the gifts which are the arrows and the bow of Love,[7] there where your high virtue wears its garland.

When you speak in your beauty and sing in your happiness, so that the tough trees on the mountains might respond,[10] let every man who finds himself unworthy of you ward well the approaches to the eye and ear. Grace from above alone can avail him to prevent the desire of a lover from becoming fixed immovably in his heart.

7–8. Countless Italian, French and English examples might be cited of the "Platonism" which identifies a woman's glances with the weapons of Cupid and also with the heavenly virtue that rains down upon men as "influence" from the starry skies. So Spenser:

> "More then most faire, full of the living fire
> Kindled above unto the Maker neere:
> No eies, but joyes, in which al powers conspire,
> That to the world naught else be counted deare:
> Thrugh your bright beams doth not the blinded guest
> Shoot out his darts to base affections wound."
> (*Amoretti*, viii, 1–6.)

Compare *L'Allegro*, 121–3.

10. One of Ovid's most famous passages catalogues the trees (*Met.* X, 90–105) which gathered around Orpheus to listen to his music,

> "In *Rhodope*, where Woods and Rocks had Ears
> To rapture."
> (*P.L.* VII, 35–6.)

QUAL IN COLLE ASPRO

QUAL in colle aspro, al imbrunir di sera,
   L' avezza giovinetta pastorella
   Va bagnando l' erbetta strana e bella
   Che mal si spande a disusata spera
Fuor di sua natia alma primavera,   5
   Così Amor meco insù la lingua snella
   Desta il fior nuovo di strania favella,
   Mentre io di te, vezzosamente altera,
Canto, dal mio buon popol non inteso,
   E'l bel Tamigi cangio col bel Arno.   10
   Amor lo volse, ed io a l' altrui peso
Seppi ch' Amor cosa mai volse indarno.
   Deh! foss' il mio cuor lento e'l duro seno
   A chi pianta dal ciel si buon terreno.

(1628 ?)

AS ON A RUGGED MOUNTAIN . . .

As, ON a rugged mountain when twilight is darkening, the young shepherd girl, familiar with the spot, waters a strange and lovely little plant which spreads its leaves feebly in the alien clime, remote from its fostering, native springtime; so on my prompt tongue Love calls forth the novel flower of a foreign speech, when I sing of you, graciously proud lady,[9] and change the fair Thames for the fair Arno[10]—not understood by my own good countrymen. Love willed it, and at the cost of others I know that Love never willed anything in vain.

Ah, that my dull heart and hard breast might be as good a soil for Him who plants from heaven.

---

9. See the preceding sonnet, 1–4, note.

10. To change the Thames for the Arno means simply to exchange English for the Tuscan, or pure Italian, spoken in Florence on the banks of the Arno. Compare the use of Thames in *Manso,* 32, to signify English literature in contrast with Italian.

CANZONE

Ridonsi donne e giovani amorosi,
M' accostandosi attorno, e perchè scrivi,
Perchè tu scrivi in lingua ignota e strana
Verseggiando d'amor, e come t'osi?
Dinne, se la tua speme sia mai vana,   5
E de' pensieri lo miglior t' arrivi.
Così mi van burlando; altri rivi,
Altri lidi t' aspettan, ed altre onde
Nelle cui verdi sponde
Spuntati ad or, ad or a la tua chioma   10
L'immortal guiderdon d'eterne frondi.
Perchè alle spalle tue soverchia soma?
  Canzon dirotti, e tu per me rispondi:
Dice mia Donna, e'l suo dir è il mio cuore
Questa è lingua di cui si vanta Amore.   15

(1628 ?)

CANZONE

Amorous young men and maidens press about me, jesting: "Why write—why do you write in a language unknown and strange, versifying of love, and how do you dare? Speak, if your hope is ever to prove not vain and if the best of your desires is to come to pass."

And thus they make sport of me; "Other rivers, other shores and other waters are waiting for you, on whose green banks now, even now, an immortal guerdon of undying leaves is putting forth its shoots to crown your locks. Why the superfluous burden on your shoulders?"

Canzone,[13] I will tell you, and you shall answer for me. My lady, whose words are my very heart, says, "This is the language of which Love makes his boast."

---

13. Although Barnabe Barnes familiarized Englishmen with the *canzone* in *Parthenophil and Parthenophe,* and although Petrarch and many other Italians had used it hardly less than the sonnet, it never became common in England. The stanzas in Spenser's *Prothalamion* and *Epithalamion* were developed from it. In the orthodox *canzone* the rhyme-scheme—which Milton treated with characteristic freedom— was as exacting as that of the sonnet, but some variation was allowed in the number of verses. A *canzone* ended with an envoy, called the *commiato,* in which the poet often addressed his poem, as Milton does here and as Spenser did in the last stanza of the *Epithalamion.*

DIODATI, E TE 'L DIRÒ

DIODATI, e te 'l dirò con maraviglia,
   Quel ritroso io ch' Amor spreggiar solea
   E de' suoi lacci spesso mi ridea
   Gia caddi, ov' uom dabben talor s' impiglia.
Nè treccie d' oro nè guancia vermiglia   5
   M' abbaglian sì, ma sotto nuova idea
   Pellegrina bellezza che 'l cuor bea,
   Portamenti alti onesti, e nelle ciglia
Quel sereno fulgor d' amabil nero,
   Parole adorne di lingua più d' una,   10
   E 'l cantar che di mezzo l' emispero
Traviar ben può la faticosa Luna,
   E degli occhi suoi avventa si gran fuoco
   Che l' incerar gli orecchi mi fia poco.

                                        (1628 ?)

1–4. The lover's proud inexperience may be quite as conventional in inspiration as it may be autobiographical. The "love at first sight" to which Milton confesses in *Elegy VII* has the same prelude.

5–6. *idea*. The word is used less in its genuinely Platonic sense than in the Petrarchan way which Drayton reduced to an absurdity in *Ideas Mirrour*. Because she was "vertues right Idea" (*Amour* xix, 9), or pattern, the lady to whom he gave the name was a hardly incarnate creature,

> "That yet the world unworthy neuer knew;
>   Whose pure *Idea* neuer tongue exprest."
>   (*Amour* xxxix, 12–3.)

DIODATI . . .

Diodati—and I will say it to you with amazement—that obstinate I, who used to pour contempt upon Love and often mocked his snares, have fallen where a good man sometimes entangles himself.[1] No tresses of gold nor vermeil cheeks have dazzled me so, but an alien beauty under a new pattern,[5] which rejoices my heart—a manner nobly decorous, and in her eyes that quiet radiance of lovely black, speech that is adorned with more than one language, and a gift of song which might draw the labouring moon[12] from its course in mid-sky. And so potent a fire flashes from her eyes that it would be of little avail to me to seal up my ears.[14]

6–7. The lines seem like a retractation of the praise of Englishwomen as the loveliest in the world in *Elegy I*, 71–2. The following description of the lady may owe something to Petrarch's sonnet ccxiii.

12. Again in *P.L.* II, 665, Milton used Virgil's term (*Georgics*, II, 478), "labouring moon." He was indebted to Virgil (*Eclogue* VIII, 69) also for the conception of the moon as lured from its course by the song of a mortal—though Virgil's songs are the charms (*carmina*) of enchantresses.

14. A glance at the story of Ulysses' escape from the Sirens by stopping his ears with wax against their song. Compare *Comus*, 253–9, note.

PER CERTO I BEI VOSTR' OCCHI

PER certo i bei vostr' occhi, Donna mia,
   Esser non può che non sian lo mio sole,
   Si mi percuoton forte, come ei suole
Per l' arene di Libia chi s' invia,
Mentre un caldo vapor (nè sentì pria)   5
   Da quel lato si spinge ove mi duole,
   Che forse amanti nelle lor parole
   Chiaman sospir; io non so che si sia:
Parte rinchiusa, e turbida si cela
   Scossomi il petto, e poi n' uscendo poco   10
   Quivi d' attorno o s' agghiaccia, o s' ingiela;
Ma quanto agli occhi giunge a trovar loco
   Tutte le notti a me suol far piovose
   Finchè mia Alba rivien colma di rose.

                            (1628 ?)

1–4. Compare the turn given to this most time-worn Petrarchan conceit in *Elegy VII*, 56–7.

IN TRUTH, YOUR FAIR EYES . . .

IN TRUTH, your fair eyes, my lady, cannot but be my sun,[1]
for they beat upon me as powerfully as the sun beats upon
one who pursues his way through the sands of Libya. Meanwhile an ardent vapour,[5] such as I never felt before, presses
up from that side[6] where my pain lies. Perhaps lovers in their
language call it a sigh; I do not know what it may be. A
turbulent part hidden in the confinement of my breast makes
it heave and, a little escaping, it then turns frosty and con-
geals. But the part of it which comes to find a place in my
eyes makes all my nights rainy, until my Dawn returns, sur-
charged with roses.

5–11. Like many an earlier sonneteer, Milton felt that
      "These sorrowing sighes, the smoakes of mine annoy;
      These teares, which heate of sacred flame distils;
      Are these due tributes that my faith dooth pay
      Vnto the tyrant."
          (Samuel Daniel, *Delia,* Sonnet xxi, 1–4.)
  6. *Da quel lato*—from that side, *i.e.,* the side of the heart.

GIOVANE PIANO, E SEMPLICETTO AMANTE

GIOVANE piano, e semplicetto amante,
  Poichè fuggir me stesso in dubbio sono,
  Madonna a voi del mio cuor l' umil dono
  Farò divoto; io certo a prove tante
L' ebbi fedele, intrepido, costante,   5
  Di pensieri leggiadro, accorto, e buono.
  Quando rugge il gran mondo, e scocca il tuono,
  S' arma di se, e d' intero diamante,
Tanto del forse, e d' invidia sicuro,
  Di timori, e speranze al popol use,   10
  Quanto d' ingegno, e d' alto valor vago,
E di cetra sonora, e delle muse:
  Sol troverete in tal parte men duro
  Ove Amor mise l' insanabil ago.

(1628 ?)

---

2. It is hard to tell whether the poet is doubtful *how* or *whether* to flee from himself. The former idea was a familiar convention, which editors trace back to Petrarch, but the latter is more consistent with the Stoic ideal in terms of which Milton proceeded to draw his own portrait.

5–10. In the background is the Stoic doctrine that, "It is a true marke of a vulgar basenesse, for a man to expect neither good nor harme from himselfe, but all from externall euents. Contrariwise, the true note of a Philosopher, is to repose all his expectation, vpon himselfe alone." (John Healey's translation of *Epictetus his Manuell,* edition of 1616, p. 91.)

YOUNG, GENTLE AND CANDID LOVER . . .

YOUNG, gentle and candid lover that I am, because I am doubtful, my lady, how[2] to fly from myself, I shall make the humble gift of my heart in devotion to you. In countless ordeals I have proved it faithful, courageous and constant, and in its thoughts gracious, courteous and good.[5] When the world is in an uproar and the thunder crashes, it arms itself from within itself with perfect adamant[7]—as secure against fortune, envy, and the fears and hopes of ordinary men as it is keen in its desire for the mind's gifts, high courage, and the sounding lyre, and the Muses. Only at a single point will you find it less unyielding—the point where Love's dart has pierced incurably.

7–8. Far in the background is Horace's account (*Odes,* III, iii) of the just man invulnerable amid the ruin of the world and the worst that Fate can do, which many a Christian poet had lightly baptized, as Campion did in *The Man of Life Upright:*

> "He only can behold
> With unaffrighted eyes
> The horrors of the deep
> And terrors of the skies.

> "Thus scorning all the cares
> That fate or fortune brings,
> He makes the heaven his book,
> His wisdom heavenly things."

ON THE MORNING OF CHRIST'S NATIVITY

I

This is the Month, and this the happy morn
Wherein the Son of Heav'n's eternal King,
Of wedded Maid, and Virgin Mother born,
Our great redemption from above did bring;
For so the holy sages once did sing,
　　That he our deadly forfeit should release,   5
And with his Father work us a perpetual peace.

II

That glorious Form, that Light unsufferable,
And that far-beaming blaze of Majesty,
Wherewith he wont at Heav'n's high Council-Table,   10
To sit the midst of Trinal Unity,
He laid aside; and here with us to be,
　　Forsook the Courts of everlasting Day,
And chose with us a darksome House of mortal Clay.

---

3. The doctrine of Christ's virgin birth often enters into Milton's
great epics, not challenged even by Satan when he salutes Jesus as
　　　　　　　"Son of David, Virgin-born!
　　　　　For Son of God to me is yet in doubt."
　　　　　　　　　(*P.R.* IV, 500–1.)

5–7. *the holy sages*—the Hebrew prophets, of whom Milton speaks
in *P.L.* XII, 243–4, as singing "the times of great Messiah."

6. *deadly forfeit*—the "penalty of death" which the angel Michael
explains to Adam that his disobedience to the Law of God in Eden has
brought upon his descendants. (*P.L.* XII, 396–410. Compare IX,
1003.)
　　release—remit.

10–12. Perhaps Milton had been struck by Phineas Fletcher's concep-
tion of God, at the moment when the first man was to be created
(Gen. i, 26), as "That Trine-one with himself in council" sitting.
(*The Purple Island*, I, Stanza 44.)

10. *wont*—was wont. Compare *S.A.* 1487, note.

11. *midst; i.e.,* between God the Father and the Holy Spirit, Christ's
position in artistic representations of the doctrine of the Trinity.

13. Compare *P.L.* V, 645–6, and VI, 4–15.

III

Say Heav'nly Muse, shall not thy sacred vein   15
Afford a present to the Infant God?
Hast thou no verse, no hymn, or solemn strain,
To welcome him to this his new abode,
Now while the Heav'n by the Sun's team untrod,
    Hath took no print of the approaching light,   20
And all the spangled host keep watch in squadrons bright?

IV

See how from far upon the Eastern road   *learned = magi (Wizard)*
The Star-led <u>Wizard</u>s haste with odours sweet:
O run, prevent them with thy humble ode,
And lay it lowly at his blessed feet;   25
Have thou the honour first, thy Lord to greet,
    And join thy voice unto the Angel Quire,
From out his secret Altar toucht with hallow'd fire.

---

15. Compare the invocations of the *Heav'nly Muse,* Urania, in *P.L.* I, 6–7, and VII, 1.

19. Compare "the gilded Car of Day" in *Comus,* 95, note.

21. The Hebrew belief that "the host of heaven worshippeth thee" (*i.e.,* God—Neh. ix, 6) fuses later with the Platonic conception of the spheres as animate and making a divine harmony.

23. *Wizards*—the "wise men from the east" (Mat. ii, 1) who were led to Jerusalem by a miraculous star and brought presents of gold and myrrh and the perfume, frankincense, to the young Jesus. Spenser called them
> "those Ægyptian wisards old,
> Which in star-read were wont have best insight."
> (*F.Q.* V, Prologue, 8, 1–2.)

28. Milton thought of the coal from the altar which a seraph laid on the prophet Isaiah's lips. (Isa. vi, 6.)

THE HYMN

[handwritten: 5 parts]

[handwritten in margin: 1. peaceful circumstances of nativity]

I

It was the Winter wild, *a*
While the Heav'n-born child, *a*   30
   All meanly wrapt in the rude manger lies; *b*
Nature in awe to him *c*
Had dofft her gaudy trim, *c*
   With her great Master so to sympathize: *b*
It was no season then for her *d*   35
To wanton with the Sun, her lusty Paramour. *d*

II

Only with speeches fair
She woos the gentle Air
   To hide her guilty front with innocent Snow,
And on her naked shame,   40
Pollute with sinful blame,
   The Saintly Veil of Maiden white to throw,
Confounded, that her Maker's eyes
Should look so near upon her foul deformities.

29–31. Professor A. S. Cook compared Mantuan's description of a
northern European winter as extending even to the Arabian desert at
Christ's nativity (*Opera*, Ed. 1513, I, 70 a, b), but Milton may have
thought simply of the popular tradition of the old song that
        "On Christmas nyght, whan it was cold,
        Owr lady lay amonge bestes bolde."

36. Again in *Elegy V*, 95, Milton refers to the immemorial idea that
the earth is the sun's mistress, or "Leman," as Spenser said in a passage (*F.Q.* I, i, 6, 7) which goes back to Virgil (*Georgics*, II, 325–6)
and Lucretius. (*De rerum natura*, I, 251.) Compare the note on
Elegy V, 55–6.

41. *Pollute*—polluted. The form is based on the Latin passive participle and was felt as such.

42. The far-flung symbolism of white raiment is rooted extensively
in the Bible. Perhaps Milton thought of the angel's advice to the
Laodiceans in Revelation iii, 18; "I counsel thee to buy . . . white raiment . . . that the shame of thy nakedness do not appear."

visual

III

delicacy of tableau

& sounds

But he her fears to cease,
Sent down the meek-ey'd Peace;   45
   She crown'd with Olive green, came softly sliding
Down through the turning sphere,

consonants
fluid &
soft

His ready Harbinger,
   With Turtle wing the amorous clouds dividing,   50
And waving wide her myrtle wand,
She strikes a universal Peace through Sea and Land.

IV   *becomes simpler in style*

No War, or Battle's sound
Was heard the World around,
   The idle spear and shield were high up hung;   55
The hooked Chariot stood
Unstain'd with hostile blood;
   The Trumpet spake not to the armed throng,
And Kings sat still with awful eye,
As if they surely knew their sovran Lord was by.   60

---

45. *cease*—make cease, allay.

46. *Peace* corresponds roughly to Ben Jonson's description of Irene or Peace, who was the "principal person" in his *Entertainments at the Coronation of James I;* but with her olive crown and myrtle wand she answers even better to the details of a typical, allegorical print such as that by Galle.

Ptolemaic 7 concentric spheres

48. *the turning sphere*—"the visible Diurnal Sphere" of *P.L.* VII, 22, which means the whole globe of the stars turning daily about the earth.

50. *Turtle wing; i.e.,* the wings of a dove, with all their traditional symbolism.

amorous: i.e., in love with her beauty. Cowley uses the same classical conceit in *Bathing iii,* in *The Mistress;*
     "The amorous Waves would fain about her stay."

53–54. Many Fathers of the Church appealed to the seven-year peace throughout the Roman Empire at the time when Christ was born as proof that His birth could occur only after the fulfilment of Isaiah's prophecy that "nation shall not lift up sword against nation, neither shall they learn war any more." Popularly it was believed—as Lyly said in *Euphues* (Arber Ed. p. 456)—that "Christ would not be borne, vntill there were peace throughout the whole worlde."

56. *hooked*—armed with hooks projecting from the hubs.

59. *awful*—full of awe, reverent.

V

But peaceful was the night
Wherein the Prince of light
   His reign of peace upon the earth began:
The Winds, with wonder whist,
Smoothly the waters kiss't,
   Whispering new joys to the mild Ocean,   65
Who now hath quite forgot to rave,
While Birds of Calm sit brooding on the charmed wave.

VI

The Stars with deep amaze
Stand fixt in steadfast gaze,
   Bending one way their precious influence,   70
And will not take their flight,
For all the morning light,
   Or *Lucifer* that often warn'd them thence;

---

61. The *peaceful . . . night* was also a tradition and found poignant
expression in Herbert's *Christmas* sonnet:
     "O Thou, Whose glorious yet contracted light,
       Wrapt in Night's mantle, stole into a manger."

64. *whist*—stilled, hushed.

68. *Birds of Calm*—the halcyons of Greek tradition, at whose nesting
time, "which happeneth about the brumal solstice," as Sir Thomas
Browne says (*Pseudodoxia*, III, x), "it hath been observed even unto
a proverb, that the Sea is calm, and the winds do cease, till the young
ones are excluded."

69. *amaze*—amazement, wonder. Compare *P.R.* II, 38, and *S.A.* 1645.

71. Medieval astrologers believed in the effluence of an ethereal
"liquid" from the stars, which
               "with kindly heat
   Of various influence foment and warm,
   Temper or nourish, or in part shed down
   Thir stellar virtue on all kinds that grow
   On Earth."
            (*P.L.* IV, 668–72.)

73. *For all the morning light*—in spite of the light of morning.

74. *Lucifer* may mean the morning star, Venus, or the sun itself, as
it does in *Elegy III*, 50, and *Elegy V*, 46.

But in their glimmering Orbs did glow,   75
Until their Lord himself bespake, and bid them go.

VII

And though the shady gloom
Had given day her room,
   The Sun himself withheld his wonted speed,
And hid his head for shame,   80
As his inferior flame,
   The new enlight'n'd world no more should need;
He saw a greater Sun appear
Than his bright Throne, or burning Axletree could bear.

(2) apparition or song of angels

VIII

The Shepherds on the Lawn,   *hav identified witeth*   85
Or ere the point of dawn,   *christ*
   Sat simply chatting in a rustic row;
Full little thought they than,

---

75. *Orbs,* in "Ptolemaic" terminology, meant the hollow, concentric "spheres" with the earth at their centre in which the planets and the fixed stars were supposed to move. Here the meaning is uncertain, for the orbs were regarded as invisible. Compare line 47 above.

76. *bespake*—spoke. Compare *Lycidas,* 112, and *P.R.* I, 43.

bid—bade. So in *P.L.* VIII, 518–9,
        "the amorous Bird of Night
    Sung Spousal, and bid haste the Ev'ning Star."

80. In the background are biblical conceptions such as St. John's description of Christ as "the light of men" (i, 4) and metaphors like Malachi's vision of "the Sun of righteousness" rising "with healing in his wings." (Mal. iv, 2.) A long Christian tradition lay behind lines like George Herbert's in *Miserie:*
    "The sunne holds down his head for shame,
    Dead with eclipses, when we speak of Thee."

84. Compare *Comus,* 95–101, note.

85. *Lawn*—grassland or pasture.

86. *Or ere*—before.

88. *than*—then. The words were variant forms, neither of which had become exclusively established.

That the mighty *Pan*
   Was kindly come to live with them below;   90
Perhaps their loves, or else their sheep,
Was all that did their silly thoughts so busy keep.

IX

When such music sweet
Their hearts and ears did greet,
   As never was by mortal finger strook,   95
Divinely-warbled voice
Answering the stringed noise,
   As all their souls in blissful rapture took:
The Air such pleasure loth to lose,
With thousand echoes still prolongs each heav'nly close.   100

X

Nature that heard such sound
Beneath the hollow round
   Of *Cynthia's* seat, the Airy region thrilling,
Now was almost won
To think her part was done,   105
   And that her reign had here its last fulfilling;

---

89. The Greek god Pan, whom Virgil called "the guardian of flocks" (*Georgics*, I, 17) and who appeared with mysterious, cosmic aspects in the Orphic Hymn to Pan, was early associated with Christ as a divine shepherd. In Renaissance pastoral poetry Pan was very often identified with Christ, "which," as the glosse to Spenser's *Maye* explains, "calleth himselfe the greate and good shepherd. The name is most rightly . . . applyed to him, for Pan signifieth all, or omnipotent, which is onely the Lord Jesus."

95. *strook* is more common than "struck" in Milton.

97. Compare the "melodious noise" of *At a Solemn Music,* 18.

98. *took*—captivated. Compare *Comus,* 256 and 558.

100. *close*—cadence.

102–103. *the hollow round Of Cynthia's seat*—the orb or sphere of the moon. Compare lines 75 above, 130 below, note, and *Comus,* 131, note.

103. The *Airy region* may be a reminiscence of Virgil's phrase in describing the flight of swans (*Aen.* I, 394). It definitely means the upper air, as "Region" does in *P.L.* VII, 425. Compare *P.R.* II, 117, and *P.L.* I, 516.

She knew such harmony alone
Could hold all Heav'n and Earth in happier union.

XI

At last surrounds their sight
A Globe of circular light,   110
   That with long beams the shame-fac't night array'd,
The helmed Cherubim
And sworded Seraphim
   Are seen in glittering ranks with wings display'd,
Harping in loud and solemn quire,   115
With unexpressive notes to Heav'n's new-born Heir.

XII

Such Music (as 'tis said)
Before was never made,
   But when of old the sons of morning sung,
While the Creator Great   120
His constellations set,
   And the well-balanc't world on hinges hung,
And cast the dark foundations deep,
And bid the welt'ring waves their oozy channel keep.

107–108. The thought seems to be that the music of the spheres (compare *Arcades*, 63–9), which was a part of nature and was supposed to keep the frame of the universe together, was excelled by the songs of the angels, which Nature realized might, if they continued, bind the cosmos together into a happier union than she maintained with the harmony of the spheres.

110. Compare the "Globe of fiery Seraphim" in *P.L.* II, 512.

112–113. *Cherubim . . . Seraphim;* plural forms. For their places in the heavenly hierarchy see the notes on *Il Penseroso*, 52–4, and *S.A.* 672.

116. *unexpressive*—inexpressible. Compare *Lycidas*, 176.

117–119. The allusion is to Job's question about the universe; "Whereupon are the foundations thereof fastened? or who laid the corner stone thereof, When the morning stars sang together, and all the sons of God shouted for joy?" (Job xxxviii, 6–7.)

122. Perhaps, like *P.L.* VII, 242—"And Earth self-balanc't on her Centre hung"—this stems from Job xxvi, 7: "He . . . hangeth the earth upon nothing."
   hinges; compare the picture in *Arcades*, 63–9, note.

XIII

Ring out ye Crystal spheres,   125
Once bless our human ears,
   (If ye have power to touch our senses so)
And let your silver chime
Move in melodious time;
   And let the Bass of Heav'n's deep Organ blow;   130
And with your ninefold harmony
Make up full consort to th'Angelic symphony.

XIV

3. promise + reality of golden age

For if such holy Song
Enwrap our fancy long,
   Time will run back, and fetch the age of gold,   135
And speckl'd vanity
Will sicken soon and die,
   And leprous sin will melt from earthly mould,
And Hell itself will pass away,
And leave her dolorous mansions to the peering day.   140

XV

Yea, Truth and Justice then
Will down return to men,

125–127. Milton's idea is as old as Pythagoras and it was as contemporary as Lorenzo's teaching of Jessica that every orb
         "in his motion like an angel sings,
      Still quiring to the young-eyed cherubins;
      Such harmony is in immortal souls,
      But whilst this muddy vesture of decay
      Doth grossly close it in, we cannot hear it."
         (*Merchant of Venice*, V, i, 61–5.)

130. In the harmony of the spheres the bass was sometimes assigned
to the outermost sphere, that of Saturn, and sometimes to the innermost, that of the Moon.

133–138. Perhaps Milton thought of Hesiod's account of the Golden
Age, when the earth was filled with men so glorious that Zeus changed
them into immortal, ministering spirits. (*Works and Days*, 111–126.)
Here, as often in the Bible, *Vanity* stands for all the sins to which "the
creature was made subject" (Rom. viii, 20), and from which Milton
says that the angels' song might redeem human nature so that men
could hear "the heavenly tune, which none can hear Of human
mould." (*Arcades*, 72–3.)

141–146. The lines are built upon Psalm lxxxv, 10–1; "Mercy and

Th'enamel'd *Arras* of the Rain-bow wearing,
And Mercy set between,
Thron'd in Celestial sheen,   145
  With radiant feet the tissued clouds down steering,
And Heav'n as at some festival,
Will open wide the Gates of her high Palace Hall.

XVI

But wisest Fate says no,
This must not yet be so,   150
  The Babe lies yet in smiling Infancy,
That on the bitter cross
Must redeem our loss;
  So both himself and us to glorify:
Yet first to those ychain'd in sleep,   155
The wakeful trump of doom must thunder through the deep,

---

truth are met together; righteousness and peace have kissed each other.
Truth shall spring out of the earth and righteousness shall look down
from heaven." The *enamel'd Arras,* or painted drapery, suggests the
allegorical figures in contemporary masques as well as the angel in
Revelation x, 1—"clothed with a cloud, and a rainbow was upon his
head."

143–144. In 1673 Milton changed the reading of these lines to:
        "Orb'd in a Rainbow; and like glories wearing
    Mercy will sit between."

147–148. The scene suggests Plato's allegory of the house of the
gods, whither "they go to a feast and a banquet, mounting steeply to
the vault of heaven." (*Phaedrus,* 247b.)

153. *loss*—ruin. *P.L.* III. 305–8, describes Christ as leaving "highest
bliss Equal to God . . . to save A World from utter loss."

155. *ychain'd,* like *yclep'd* in *L'Allegro,* 12, keeps the Old English
prefix ge-, reduced to y-, which survived sporadically in many of
Chaucer's past participles. Milton added it here, as he did mistakenly to a present participle in the *Epitaph on Shakespeare,* 4, because, as the glosse to Spenser's *April* explains, "Y is a poetical addition."

sleep has its biblical sense of "death," from which many "that sleep
in the dust of the earth shall awake." (Dan. xii, 2.)

156. *wakeful*—awakening. Compare *awful* in 59.

XVII

With such a horrid clang
As on mount *Sinai* rang
   While the red fire, and smould'ring clouds out brake:
The aged Earth aghast   160
With terror of that blast,
   Shall from the surface to the centre shake,
When at the world's last session,
The dreadful Judge in middle Air shall spread his throne.

XVIII

And then at last our bliss   165
Full and perfect is,
   But now begins; for from this happy day
Th'old Dragon under ground,
In straiter limits bound,
   Not half so far casts his usurped sway,   170
And wrath to see his Kingdom fail,
Swinges the scaly Horror of his folded tail.

XIX

The Oracles are dumb,
No voice or hideous hum

157–159. When Moses ascended the mountain to receive the Ten Commandments, "there were thunders and lightnings . . . and the voice of the trumpet exceeding loud." (Ex. xix, 16.) In *P.L.* XI, 74–6, Milton suggested that the "Trumpet, heard in *Oreb*" may be destined "perhaps once more To sound at general Doom."

164. Milton remembered Christ's prophecy of the Day of Doom, when "they shall see the Son of man coming in the clouds of heaven with power and great glory." (Mat. xxiv, 30.)

168. "And the great dragon was cast out, that old serpent, called the Devil, and Satan, which deceiveth the whole world: he was cast out into the earth." (Rev. xii, 9.)

173. Like Spenser, Milton was interested in Plutarch's "booke of the ceasing of oracles" which many Christian writers had interpreted as a pagan testimony to the fact that Satan's "kingdome at that time was by Christ conquered . . . for at that time . . . all oracles surceased, and enchaunted spirits, that were wont to delude the people, thenceforth held theyr peace." Spenser's glosse to *Maye*. Compare *P.R.* I, 454–64, note.

174–220. Countless details in this survey of the flight of the pagan

Runs through the arched roof in words deceiving.   175
Apollo from his shrine
Can no more divine,
    With hollow shriek the steep of *Delphos* leaving.
No nightly trance, or breathed spell,
Inspires the pale-ey'd Priest from the prophetic cell.   18c

[handwritten marginalia]

XX

The lonely mountains o'er,
And the resounding shore,
    A voice of weeping heard, and loud lament;
From haunted spring and dale
Edg'd with poplar pale,   185
    The parting Genius is with sighing sent;
With flow'r-inwov'n tresses torn
The Nymphs in twilight shade of tangled thickets mourn.

XXI

In consecrated Earth,
And on the holy Hearth,   190
    The *Lars,* and *Lemures* moan with midnight plaint;
In Urns and Altars round,
A drear and dying sound
    Affrights the *Flamens* at their service quaint;
And the chill Marble seems to sweat,   195
While each peculiar power forgoes his wonted seat.

---

gods—as Professor Cook's notes indicate—may be indebted to the *Apotheosis* (lines 435–89) of Prudentius or to the *Parthenicae* (III, i) of Mantuan. See the Introduction §20.

178. *Delphos*—Delphi, Apollo's famous oracle, which lay high on the precipitous upper slopes of Mt. Parnassus.

186. *Genius*—local divinity. Compare *Lycidas,* 184, and *Arcades,* 44–60.

191. *Lars*—tutelary gods of cities or of houses and families.
Lemures—ghosts or spirits of the dead. Both terms come from ancient Roman religion.

194. *Flamens*—priests serving any particular Roman deity.
quaint—ingenious or elaborate. Compare *S.A.* 1303.

195. Many ancient writers, like Virgil in the *Georgics,* I, 480, mention the sweating of ivory and bronze statues in the temples of the gods as portents of dire events to come.

XXII

Peor and *Baalim*
Forsake their Temples dim,
  With that twice-batter'd god of *Palestine,*
And mooned *Ashtaroth,*   200
Heav'n's Queen and Mother both,
  Now sits not girt with Tapers' holy shine,
The Libyc *Hammon* shrinks his horn,
In vain the *Tyrian* Maids their wounded *Thammuz* mourn.

XXIII

And Sullen *Moloch,* fled,   205
Hath left in shadows dread

---

197. Baal was the supreme god of the Canaanites, but countless inferior Baals or *Baalim* (the Hebrew plural) were worshipped in various places, of which the most famous was the mountain, Peor, "that looketh toward the wilderness" (Num. xxiii, 28), where he had a great shrine as Baal-Peor.

199. The *twice-batter'd god* is Dagon, to punish whose Philistine worshippers his image at Ashdod was twice miraculously broken, so that "only the stump of Dagon was left to him." (I Sam. v, 4. Compare *P.L.* I, 457–66, and *S.A.* 13, note.)

200–201. *Ashtaroth* is really a plural of *Ashtoreth,*
              "whom the *Phœnicians* call'd
    Astarte, Queen of Heav'n, with crescent Horns."
              (*P.L.* I, 438–9.)
She was a fertility goddess, identified with the moon as Baal was with the sun, and the crescent moon was one of her symbols.

203. *Libyc Hammon*—the mysterious Egyptian deity, Ammon, who was represented as a ram with mighty horns, and had his chief shrine far in the Libyan desert to the west of Memphis.

204. *Thammuz* or Tammuz was the lover of Ashtoreth and the Tyrian (*i.e.,* Phœnician) women had an annual ceremony of mourning for him as a symbol of the beauty of summer slain by the boar, winter. The Greeks adopted him as Adonis. Compare *P.L.* I, 446–57, and *Elegy I,* 52.

205–209. King Josiah's decree against any man's making "his son or his daughter to pass through the fire to Molech" (II Kings xxiii, 10) suggests the kind of worship given to the "Idoll of brasse, hauing the head of a Calfe, the rest of a kingly figure, with armes, extended to receive the miserable sacrifice," which is described in Sandys' *Travels* (Ed. of 1637, p. 186), where a point is made of the din of cymbals kept up to drown the cries of the children. Compare *P.L.* I, 392.

His burning Idol all of blackest hue;
In vain with Cymbals' ring
They call the grisly king,
   In dismal dance about the furnace blue;   210
The brutish gods of *Nile* as fast,
Isis and *Orus,* and the Dog *Anubis* haste.

XXIV

Nor is *Osiris* seen
In *Memphian* Grove or Green,
   Trampling the unshow'r'd Grass with lowings loud: 215
Nor can he be at rest
Within his sacred chest,
   Naught but profoundest Hell can be his shroud:
In vain with Timbrel'd Anthems dark
The sable-stoled Sorcerers bear his worshipt Ark.   220

XXV

He feels from *Juda's* Land
The dreaded Infant's hand,

---

211. Compare the "wand'ring Gods disguis'd in brutish forms Rather than human" with which Milton reproached "Fanatic Egypt" in *P.L.* I, 480–2.

212. *Isis,* the sister and wife of Osiris and the mother of Horus, was usually represented by the Egyptians with the disc of the sun and a cow's horns on her head.

Orus or Horus was a sun god, and his figure had a hawk's head. Anubis was the god shown with a jackal's head in Egyptian art, conducting the souls of the dead to Osiris for judgement. The Greeks identified him with Hermes and the Romans with Mercury. Compare *Il Penseroso,* 88, and *One the Platonic Idea,* 31–4.

213–217. Osiris, the creator, the god of the Nile, whose shrine was at Memphis, was supposed to be incarnate in the sacred Bulls of Memphis, which were known as Apis.

215. *unshow'r'd* refers to the rainless Egyptian climate.

218. Compare *shroud* in *Comus,* 147, note.

219–220. Herodotus describes the priests of Osiris carrying his "image, placed in a small wooden temple, gilded all over," on a four-wheeled carriage, from one building in his sacred enclosure to another (Book II, Cap. 63.)

220. *sable-stoled*—black-robed.

The rays of *Bethlehem* blind his dusky eyn;
Nor all the gods beside,
Longer dare abide,   225
  Nor *Typhon* huge ending in snaky twine:
Our Babe, to show his Godhead true,
Can in his swaddling bands control the damned crew.

                                XXVI

So when the Sun in bed,
Curtain'd with cloudy red,   230
  Pillows his chin upon an Orient wave,
The flocking shadows pale
Troop to th'infernal jail;
  Each fetter'd Ghost slips to his several grave,
And the yellow-skirted *Fays*   235
Fly after the Night-steeds, leaving their Moon-lov'd maze.

                                XXVII

5. conclusion

But see! the Virgin blest,
Hath laid her Babe to rest.

223. *eyn*, the all but obsolete plural of "eye," is used for its rhyme.

226–228. Milton was thinking, probably, not of the Egyptian *Typhon*, the monstrous deity of evil whom Osiris overthrew, but of the Greek Typhon, whom Zeus or Hercules, or both together vanquished. Apollodorus describes him as a monstrous serpent below the waist and above it a man so tall that his head sometimes touched the stars. (*Bibliotheca*, 1, 6, 3. Compare *P.L.* II, 539.)

229–231. With this much-criticized conceit compare Marvell's in *Upon Appleton House*, 661–4:

               "The sun himself of her aware,
                 Seems to descend with greater care,
                 And, lest she see him go to bed,
                 In blushing clouds conceals his head."

231. *Orient*—oriental, eastern.

232–236. Compare Puck's warning in *Midsummer-Night's Dream*, III, ii, 379–82:

               "night's swift dragons cut the clouds full fast,
                 And yonder shines Aurora's harbinger,
                 At whose approach, ghosts, wandering here and there,
                 Troop home to churchyards;" *etc.*

Compare also *Comus*, 434, *L'Allegro*, 114, note.

236. *Moon-lov'd maze*—the forests, where Diana loved to hunt. Compare *Comus*, 131, note.

Time is our tedious Song should here have ending;
Heav'n's youngest teemed Star   240
Hath fixt her polisht Car,
   Her sleeping Lord with Handmaid Lamp attending:
And all about the Courtly Stable,
Bright-harness'd Angels sit in order serviceable.

                                        (Dec. 1629)

───────────

240. *youngest teemed*—newest born. The star of the Wise Men is
the most recent recruit to the heavenly host, and now the moment has
arrived when it "came and stood over where the young child was."
(Mat. ii, 9.)

243. *Courtly,* because it is a king's residence.

244. *Bright-harness'd*—clad in bright armour.

ELEGIA SEXTA

Ad Carolum Diodatum, Ruri Commorantem

(Qui cum idibus Decemb. scripsisset, et sua carmina excusari
postulasset si solito minus essent bona, quod inter lautitias quibus
erat ab amicis exceptus haud satis felicem operam Musis dare se
posse affirmabat, hunc habuit responsum.)

Mitto tibi sanam non pleno ventre salutem,
   Qua tu distento forte carere potes.
At tua quid nostram prolectat Musa camenam,
   Nec sinit optatas posse sequi tenebras?
Carmine scire velis quam te redamemque colamque.   5
   Crede mihi, vix hoc carmine scire queas,
Nam neque noster amor modulis includitur artis,
   Nec venit ad claudos integer ipse pedes.
Quam bene solennes epulas, hilaremque Decembrim
   Festaque caelifugam quae coluere Deum,   10
Deliciasque refers, hiberni gaudia ruris,
   Haustaque per lepidos Gallica musta focos.
Quid quereris refugam vino dapibusque poesin?
   Carmen amat Bacchum, Carmina Bacchus amat.
Nec puduit Phoebum virides gestasse corymbos,   15
   Atque hederam lauro praeposuisse suae.

---

3. *Musa camenam*. The words, in this case, both mean poetic inspiration. *Camena* was the native Italian equivalent of the Greek word
"Muse."

8. *claudos . . . pedes*. The term *clauda carmina* was used (*e.g.*, by
Ovid, *Tristia*, III, i, 11) to mean elegy, for it suggested the alternating
elegiac hexameter and pentameter. Compare *To Salzilli*, i, note.

9. *hilaremque Decembrim*. Milton thought of the figure which was
familiar in both painting and poetry,
          "the chill December:
    Yet he, through merry feasting which he made,
    And great bonfires, did not the cold remember;
    His Saviours birth his mind so much did glad."
          (*F.Q.* VII, vii, 41, 1–4.)

10. *caelifugam*—heaven-forsaking—appears to be Milton's coinage.

14. Bacchus, Conti said (V, xiii, p. 506), was traditionally associated
with the Muses because "the heat of wine awakens genius and strong
potations make men fluent, bold and mighty." A Rabelaisian Eliza-

ELEGY VI

To Charles Diodati When He Was Visiting in the Country

(Who, when he wrote on the thirteenth of December, begging that his verses might be excused if they were not so good as usual, pled that, in the magnificence of his reception by his friends, he was not able to cultivate the Muses very prosperously. He had this answer:—)

On an empty stomach I send you a wish for the good health of which you, with a full one, may perhaps feel the lack. But why does your Muse[3] provoke mine, instead of permitting her to seek the obscurity that she craves? You would like to be informed by a song how I return your love and how fond I am of you. Believe me, you can hardly learn it from this song, for my love is not confined by narrow metres and it is too sound to use the lame feet of elegy.[8]

How well you report the splendid feasts and the hilarious December[9]—the festivals which do honour to the heaven-forsaking[10] God—the sports and pleasures of winter in the country and the French vintages quaffed beside merry fires. But why do you complain that poetry is a fugitive from wine and feasting? Song loves Bacchus[14] and Bacchus loves songs. Phoebus was not ashamed to wear the green garland of ivy[15] and to prefer its leaves to his own laurel.[16] On the Aonian

bethan, John Eliot, in his *Fruits* urged that "Aeschylus (if you giue credit to Plutarchus in his bankets) did drinke composing, did compose drinking."

15. *corymbos*—clusters of ivy-leaves. Compare the "ivy-crowned Bacchus" of *L'Allegro*, 16, and "his clust'ring locks With Ivy berries wreath'd" in *Comus*, 54–5.

16. Compare the note on Apollo's ivy in *Elegy V*, 13.

Saepius Aoniis clamavit collibus Euoe
   Mista Thyoneo turba novena choro.
Naso Corallaeis mala carmina misit ab agris;
   Non illic epulae, non sata vitis erat.   20
Quid nisi vina, rosasque racemiferumque Lyaeum
   Cantavit brevibus Teia Musa modis?
Pindaricosque inflat numeros Teumesius Euan,
   Et redolet sumptum pagina quaeque merum;
Dum gravis everso currus crepat axe supinus,   25
   Et volat Eleo pulvere fuscus eques.
Quadrimoque madens Lyricen Romanus Iaccho
   Dulce canit Glyceran, flavicomamque Chloen.
Iam quoque lauta tibi generoso mensa paratu
   Mentis alit vires ingeniumque fovet.   30
Massica foecundam despumant pocula venam,
   Fundis et ex ipso condita metra cado.
Addimus his artes, fusumque per intima Phoebum
   Corda; favent uni Bacchus, Apollo, Ceres.
Scilicet haud mirum tam dulcia carmina per te   35
   Numine composito tres peperisse Deos.
Nunc quoque Thressa tibi caelato barbitos auro
   Insonat arguta molliter icta manu;
Auditurque chelys suspensa tapetia circum,
   Virgineos tremula quae regat arte pedes.   40
Illa tuas saltem teneant spectacula Musas,
   Et revocent quantum crapula pellit iners.

---

17. For the *Aonian hills* and their relation to the Muses see *Elegy IV*, 30, note.

   Euoe, the traditional cry of the Bacchantes, was the source of the name *Euan* (see l. 23 below) for Bacchus.

18. Bacchus is called *Thyoneus* because his mother, Semele, was known as Thyone after Zeus had translated her to heaven.

19. *Naso*—Ovid, whose full name was Publius Ovidius Naso. For his banishment see *Elegy I*, 22, note. The *Coralli* were a barbarous tribe on the Danube of whom he complained in the *Epistles from Pontus*, IV, viii, 80–3. The *Epistles* and *Tristia* both mention the dearth of vines, good wine and good cheer in Pontus.

21. *Lyaeum*—Bacchus. See *To his Father*, 43, note.

22. *Teia Musa*—The allusion here is to Anacreon, who was a native of Teios in Ionia.

   brevibus . . . modis—short measures. The Anacreontics which were written by Anacreon and his imitators, both Greek and Latin, were typically short lyrics on erotic and convivial themes.

hills[17] the chorus of the Nine has often mingled with the rout of Thyoneus[18] and raised the cry, *Euoe*. Naso[19] sent bad verses from the Corallian fields because there were no banquets in that land and the vine had not been planted. O what but wine and roses and Lyaeus[21] wreathed with clusters did the Teian Poet sing in his short measures?[22] Teumesian Euan inspires the Pindaric Odes[23] and their every page is redolent of the consumed wine; as he paints the crash of the heavy chariot overturned by a shattered axle, and the rush of the horseman, all blackened with the Elean dust. In his potations of four-year-old wine the Roman lyrist[27] sang of Glycera and of golden-haired Chloe.[28] In your case also the sumptuous board with its generous provision gives strength to your mind and fire to your genius. Your Massic cups foam with creative impulse and you decant the store of your verses out of the wine-jar itself. To all this we add the arts and Apollo's presence in your secret heart. In your single self the favour of Bacchus, Apollo,[33] and Ceres is united. No wonder, then, if the three gods by their combined potency should have brought forth such sweet songs through you!

Now also for you the Thracian lyre,[37] inlaid with gold and gently touched by a skilled hand, is sounding; and in tapestried halls you have the music of the harp that rules the dancing feet of maidens by its rhythmic art. At least, let these scenes hold the attention of your Muse and recall what-

---

23. *Pindaricos . . . numeros*. The Odes of Pindar, many of which celebrated the victors in the chariot races in the Olympian Games, which were held in Elis.

Teumesius Euan—Teumesian Bacchus. Teumesus was a town in Boeotia from which the whole country derived one of its names. Bacchus was supposed to have been born in Thebes, the Boeotian capital.

27. *Lyricen Romanus*—Horace. *Iaccho,* one of the cult names of Bacchus, is used like *Lyaeo* in *To his Father,* 43, to mean "wine."

28. Glycera and Chloe both appear in several of Horace's *Odes* and once (III, ix, 19) Chloe is called "flava"—blond or golden-haired.

33–34. Apollo is mentioned as the god of poetry who conspires with the goddess of good cheer, Ceres, and with Bacchus to inspire Diodati.

37. *Thressa . . . barbitos*. The lyre is called Thracian because it belonged to Orpheus, the "Thracian Bard" of *P.L.* VII, 34. Compare *Lycidas,* 63, note.

Crede mihi, dum psallit ebur, comitataque plectrum
    Implet odoratos festa chorea tholos,
Percipies tacitum per pectora serpere Phoebum,   45
    Quale repentinus permeat ossa calor;
Perque puellares oculos digitumque sonantem
    Irruet in totos lapsa Thalia sinus.
Namque Elegia levis multorum cura deorum est,
    Et vocat ad numeros quemlibet illa suos;   50
Liber adest elegis, Eratoque, Ceresque, Venusque,
    Et cum purpurea matre tenellus Amor.
Talibus inde licent convivia larga poetis,
    Saepius et veteri commaduisse mero.
At qui bella refert, et adulto sub Iove caelum,   55
    Heroasque pios, semideosque duces,
Et nunc sancta canit superum consulta deorum,
    Nunc latrata fero regna profunda cane,
Ille quidem parce, Samii pro more magistri,
    Vivat, et innocuos praebeat herba cibos.   60
Stet prope fagineo pellucida lympha catillo,
    Sobriaque e puro pocula fonte bibat.
Additur huic scelerisque vacans et casta iuventus,
    Et rigidi mores, et sine labe manus.
Qualis veste nitens sacra, et lustralibus undis,   65
    Surgis ad infensos augur iture Deos.
Hoc ritu vixisse ferunt post rapta sagacem
    Lumina Tiresian, Ogygiumque Linon,
Et lare devoto profugum Calchanta, senemque
    Orpheon edomitis sola per antra feris.   70

---

48. *Thalia,* who later became the Muse of Comedy, was first known as the patroness of rural sports and social pleasures.

51. *Liber* was an ancient Italian god who presided over vines and agriculture and who became identified with Bacchus.
Erato—the Muse of erotic and lyric poetry.

55. *adulto sub Iove* is, perhaps, an allusion to the settled reign of Jove on Olympus after his violent youth, when he usurped the power of his father, Saturn, and fought against the remaining Titans to defend his throne.

55–56. Compare *Il Penseroso,* 45–8.

58. The dog is Cerberus, the three-headed guardian of Hades.

59–60. *Samii . . . magistri*—Pythagoras, whom Ovid introduces (*Met.* XV, 60) as "a Samian by birth." The following passage is famous for

ever power dull dissipation drives away. Believe me, when the ivory key is played and the festive throng dances through the perfumed halls to the sound of the lute, you will feel the silent approach of Phoebus in your breast like a sudden heat that permeates to the marrow; and through a maiden's eyes and music-making fingers Thalia[48] will glide into full possession of your breast.

For many of the gods patronize the gay elegy and she calls whom she will to her measures. Liber and Erato,[51] Ceres and Venus are at hand to help her, and beside his rosy mother is the stripling Cupid. For such poets, then, grand banquets are allowable and frequent potations of old wine. But he whose theme is wars and heaven under Jupiter in his prime,[55] and pious heroes and chieftains half-divine, and he who sings now of the sacred counsels of the gods on high, and now of the infernal realms where the fierce dog[58] howls, let him live sparingly, like the Samian teacher;[59] and let herbs furnish his innocent diet. Let the purest water stand beside him in a bowl of beech and let him drink sober draughts from the pure spring. Beyond this, his youth must be innocent of crime and chaste, his conduct irreproachable and his hands stainless. His character should be like yours, O Priest, when, glorious with sacred vestments and lustral water, you arise to go into the presence of the angry deities.

By this rule it is said that the wise Tiresias[67] lived after the loss of his eyes, and Ogygian[68] Linus, and Calchas[69] when he was a fugitive from his doomed home, and Orpheus in his old age, when he tamed the wild beasts among the lonely caves.

---

its account of the Pythagorean teaching about the origins of the universe and the Pythagorean belief that the consumption of all meats is "impious."

67–68. *sagacem . . . Tiresian.* See *On the Platonic Idea*, 25–6, and *P.L.* III, 36, notes.

68. *Ogygium*—Theban. Ogygia was an ancient name for Thebes.

69. *Calchanta.* Calchas was the most famous soothsayer in the Greek expedition against Troy. His association with Tiresias may be due to the coupling of their names by Cicero in *On the Nature of the Gods,* II, iii, 7.

Sic dapis exiguus, sic rivi potor Homerus
    Dulichium vexit per freta longa virum
Et per monstrificam Perseiae Phoebados aulam,
    Et vada foemineis insidiosa sonis,
Perque tuas, rex ime, domos, ubi sanguine nigro   75
    Dicitur umbrarum detinuisse greges.
Diis etenim sacer est vates, divumque sacerdos,
    Spirat et occultum pectus et ora Iovem.
At tu si quid agam scitabere (si modo saltem
    Esse putas tanti noscere siquid agam)—   80
Paciferum canimus caelesti semine regem,
    Faustaque sacratis saecula pacta libris;
Vagitumque Dei, et stabulantem paupere tecto
    Qui suprema suo cum patre regna colit;
Stelliparumque polum, modulantesque aethere turmas, 85
    Et subito elisos ad sua fana Deos.
Dona quidem dedimus Christi natalibus illa;
    Illa sub auroram lux mihi prima tulit.
Te quoque pressa manent patriis meditata cicutis;
    Tu mihi, cui recitem, iudicis instar eris.   90

                                 (Dec. 1629)

---

71. In Boccaccio's defence of the poets (*Genealogy of the Gods*, XIV, xix) the familiar tradition of Homer's blindness and wandering is developed into an account of an almost Christian hermit living a life of deprivation among rough crags and mountains, where he composed his poems. Milton was interested in the *Odyssey* here because, as Chapman said in the Epistle Dedicatory of his translation, the word "man" in its first line symbolized the triumph of manliness, or wisdom, over passion.

72. *Dulichium . . . virum*—the Dulichian man, *i.e.*, Ulysses, who was lord of the tiny (and now unknown) island of Dulichium, near Ithaca.

73. *Circe*. See *Comus*, 50–3, and 253–9, and *Elegy I*, 87, notes.

74. *vada foemineis insidiosa sonis*. Homer's story of Ulysses' escape from the Sirens is told in the *Odyssey*, XII, 165–200.

So Homer, the spare eater and the water-drinker,[71] carried the Dulichian hero[72] through vast stretches of ocean, through the monster-making palace of the daughter of Phoebus and Perseis,[73] through the seas made treacherous by the songs of the Sirens,[74] and through your mansions, O infernal King, where he is said to have constrained the hosts of shades by means of a libation of dark blood.[75]   For truly, the bard is sacred to the gods and is their priest.   His hidden heart and his lips alike breathe out Jove.

But if you will known what I am doing (if only you think it of any importance to know whether I am doing anything)— I am singing the heaven-descended King,[81] the bringer of peace, and the blessed times promised in the sacred books— the infant cries of our God and his stabling under a mean roof who, with his Father, governs the realms above.   I am singing the starry sky[85] and the hosts that sang high in air, and the gods that were suddenly destroyed in their own shrines.

These are my gifts for the birthday of Christ—gifts which the first light of its dawn brought to me.   Also some simple strains that have been meditated on my native pipes are await- ing you; and you, when I recite them to you, shall be my judge.

---

75. Milton thought of the scene (*Od.* XI, 34–9) when the shadowy dead gathered around Ulysses as he poured a libation of the black blood of sheep.

81–90. The lines refer to the *Nativity Hymn* as the poem which has been composed *patriis . . . cicutis, i.e.,* in English, and fix the date of the Elegy at about Christmas, 1629.

85. *polum.* See *Elegy I,* 56, note.

THE PASSION

I

Ere-while of Music and Ethereal mirth,
Wherewith the stage of Air and Earth did ring,
And joyous news of heav'nly Infant's birth,
My muse with Angels did divide to sing;
But headlong joy is ever on the wing,   5
    In Wintry solstice like the short'n'd light
Soon swallow'd up in dark and long out-living night.

II

For now to sorrow must I tune my song,
And set my Harp to notes of saddest woe,
Which on our dearest Lord did seize ere long,   10
Dangers, and snares, and wrongs, and worse than so,
Which he for us did freely undergo:
    Most perfect *Hero,* tried in heaviest plight
Of labours huge and hard, too hard for human wight.

III

He sovran Priest, stooping his regal head   15
That dropt with odorous oil down his fair eyes,
Poor fleshly Tabernacle entered,
His starry front low-rooft beneath the skies;
O what a Mask was there, what a disguise!
    Yet more; the stroke of death he must abide,   20
Then lies him meekly down fast by his Brethren's side.

---

1. *Ethereal*—heavenly, *i.e.,* belonging to the angels. Compare the
"ethereal People" of *P.L.* X, 27, and the "Ethereal Powers" of *P.R.* I,
163, note.

4. *divide* was a musical term nearly equivalent to "descant." A
division was "a variation on or accompaniment to a plain song."
(*N.E.D.*)

13–14. For the allusion to Hercules which is implicit here see the
Introduction to *P.R.* and *S.A.* §3.

14. *wight*—creature.

15. Milton thought of Christ as St. Paul described him, setting aside
his divinity "to be made like unto his brethren, that he might be a
merciful and faithful High Priest . . . to make reconciliation for the

IV

These latter scenes confine my roving verse,
To this Horizon is my *Phoebus* bound;
His Godlike acts and his temptations fierce,
And former sufferings other where are found;   25
Loud o'er the rest *Cremona's* Trump doth sound;
   Me softer airs befit, and softer strings
Of Lute or Viol still, more apt for mournful things.

V

Befriend me night, best Patroness of grief,
Over the Pole thy thickest mantle throw,   30
And work my flatter'd fancy to belief,
That Heav'n and Earth are colour'd with my woe;
My sorrows are too dark for day to know:
   The leaves should all be black whereon I write,
And letters where my tears have washt, a wannish white.   35

VI

See, see the Chariot and those rushing wheels
That whirl'd the Prophet up at *Chebar* flood;
My spirit some transporting *Cherub* feels,
To bear me where the Towers of *Salem* stood,
Once glorious Towers, now sunk in guiltless blood;   40
   There doth my soul in holy vision sit,
In pensive trance, and anguish, and ecstatic fit.

---

sins of the people." (Heb. ii, 17.) When he was consecrated, the Jewish High Priest was anointed with sacred oil.

23. Because Phoebus Apollo was the god of poetry, Milton speaks of him as he does of his Muse in line 4, meaning his poetic impulse.

26. *Cremona's Trump*—the *Christias* or epic poem on the life of Christ by Marco Girolamo Vida, who was a native of Cremona. See the Introduction, §5.

28. *still*—gentle. Compare *Il Penseroso,* 127.

30. Compare "the dusky Pole" of *Comus,* 99, and the "starry Pole" of *P.L.* IV, 724.

36–37. Ezekiel's vision of the marvellous living creatures whose appearance "was as it were a wheel in the middle of a wheel" (Ezek. i, 16) was "by the river of Chebar" (Ezek. i, 1), a name which perhaps meant the Euphrates to Milton and certainly stood for some Babylonian stream.

39. *Salem*—Jerusalem, which represents the home of sacred poetry.

VII

Mine eye hath found that sad Sepulchral rock
That was the Casket of Heav'n's richest store,
And here though grief my feeble hands up-lock,   45
Yet on the soft'ned Quarry would I score
My plaining verse as lively as before;
 For sure so well instructed are my tears,
That they would fitly fall in order'd Characters.

VIII

Or should I thence hurried on viewless wing,   50
Take up a weeping on the Mountains wild,
The gentle neighbourhood of grove and spring
Would soon unbosom all thir Echoes mild,
And I (for grief is easily beguil'd)
 Might think th'infection of my sorrows loud   55
Had got a race of mourners on some pregnant cloud.

This Subject the Author finding to be above the years
he had, when he wrote it, and nothing satisfied
with what was begun, left it unfinisht.

          (1630)

---

43. *that sad Sepulchral rock*—the new tomb where Joseph of Arima-
thea laid the body of Jesus.

48–49. Contrast Richard Crashaw's treatment of this conceit in *Upon
the Death of a Gentleman:*
  "Eyes are vocal, tears have tongues,
   And there be words not made with lungs;
   Sententious showers, O, let them fall,
   Their cadence is rhetorical."

50. *viewless*—invisible. Compare *Comus*, 92.

51. The extravagance is partly due to Jeremiah ix, 10; "For the
mountains will I take up a weeping and a wailing, and for the habita-
tions of the wilderness a lamentation."

ON SHAKESPEARE.

WHAT needs my *Shakespeare* for his honour'd Bones
The labour of an age in piled Stones,
Or that his hallow'd reliques should be hid
Under a Star-ypointing *Pyramid?*
Dear son of memory, great heir of Fame,   5
What need'st thou such weak witness of thy name?
Thou in our wonder and astonishment
Hast built thyself a live-long Monument.
For whilst to th'shame of slow-endeavouring art,
Thy easy numbers flow, and that each heart   10

1–4. In the Second Folio (1632) these lines appeared with the title, *An Epitaph on the Admirable Dramatic Poet, W. Shakespear.* When they were written, Milton evidently thought of them as an inscription for a monument of some kind. His dubious date, 1630, suggests that the poem may have been written some time before it was first published, perhaps with the expectation that the Stratford or some other monument would be reproduced instead of the Droeshout portrait, which is the actual frontispiece.

4. For the y- prefix in *-ypointing* see the note on *ychain'd* in *Nativity Hymn,* 155.

5. As the *son of memory,* Shakespeare becomes the brother of the Muses themselves, for Hesiod says (*Theogony,* 53–9) that Mnymosyne, or Memory, bore them to Zeus and that their hearts are free from care because they are dedicated to song.

7–8. Browne's line—
        "No grave befits him but the hearts of men."
                (*Britannia's Pastorals,* I, v, 186.)
—is only one of many parallels to Milton's fancy, but no other poet ever developed the conceit so boldly and poetically as he went on to do.

9–10. Perhaps Milton contrasted his own self-critical habits of work with the "excellent phantasy, brave notions, and gentle expressions, wherein" Jonson complained in *Timber* that Shakespeare "flowed" with too much "facility." Certainly here, as in *L'Allegro,* 134–5, he thought of Shakespeare as "fancy's child."

10. *numbers*—verses.
In 1645 *heart* supplanted *part,* which appeared in 1632, probably not as a misprint, but because Milton meant to say that Shakespeare moved every part or faculty of the spirit.

Hath from the leaves of thy unvalu'd Book
Those Delphic lines with deep impression took,
Then thou our fancy of itself bereaving,
Dost make us Marble with too much conceiving;
And so Sepulcher'd in such pomp dost lie,   15
That Kings for such a Tomb would wish to die.

(1630)

---

11. *unvalu'd*—invaluable, precious. Mr. Garrod compares Chapman's
postscript to his translation of the *Iliad:*

> "In which, repaid
> With thine own value, go, unvalued book,
> Live and be loved."

12. The meaning of *Delphic* is hardly "oracular," but rather, "inspired by Apollo" and therefore authentically poetical. Carew used
the word in the same way when he said that Donne possessed

> "the fire
> That fills with spirit and heat the Delphic choir."

(*An Elegy upon the Death of Doctor Donne, Dean of Paul's.*)
Compare the note on *Nativity Hymn,* 178.

14. *Dost make us Marble:* compare *Il Penseroso,* 42, note.

ON THE UNIVERSITY CARRIER

Who sicken'd in the time of his vacancy, being forbid to go
to *London,* by reason of the Plague.

HERE lies old *Hobson,* Death hath broke his girt,
And here, alas, hath laid him in the dirt,
Or else the ways being foul, twenty to one,
He's here stuck in a slough, and overthrown.
'Twas such a shifter, that if truth were known,   5
Death was half glad when he had got him down;
For he had any time this ten years full,
Dodg'd with him, betwixt *Cambridge* and the Bull.
And surely, Death could never have prevail'd,
Had not his weekly course of carriage fail'd;   10
But lately finding him so long at home,
And thinking now his journey's end was come,
And that he had ta'en up his latest Inn,
In the kind office of a Chamberlin
Show'd him his room where he must lodge that night, 15
Pull'd off his Boots, and took away the light:
If any ask for him, it shall be said,
Hobson has sup't, and 's newly gone to bed.

(1631)

---

1. Thomas Hobson had been carrier or coach-driver between Cambridge and the Bull Inn, in Bishopsgate Street, from 1564 until the
spring of 1630, when his weekly trips to London were stopped on
account of the plague there. He was a figure among the undergraduates because, beside his service as carrier, he owned what is
supposed to have been the first livery stable in England. His clients
are said to have had what came to be known as "Hobson's choice"
among his mounts because he insisted that the horse nearest the door
should always be the first to go out. Hobson died on New Year's
Day, 1631, in his eighty-seventh year.

girt was a frequent variant form of "girth."

5. *shifter*—dodger, evader.

13. *ta'en up his latest Inn*—taken quarters in the last inn that he was
to visit.

14. *Chamberlin*—a man-servant about an inn, such as appears in
Shakespeare's *Henry IV,* Part I, II, i, 52–106.

ANOTHER ON THE SAME

Here lieth one who did most truly prove
That he could never die while he could move,
So hung his destiny never to rot
While he might still jog on and keep his trot,
Made of sphere-metal, never to decay   5
Until his revolution was at stay.
Time numbers motion, yet (without a crime
'Gainst old truth) motion number'd out his time;
And like an Engine mov'd with wheel and weight,
His principles being ceast, he ended straight.   10
Rest that gives all men life, gave him his death,
And too much breathing put him out of breath;
Nor were it contradiction to affirm
Too long vacation hasten'd on his term.
Merely to drive the time away he sick'n'd,   15
Fainted, and died, nor would with Ale be quick'n'd;
Nay, quoth he, on his swooning bed out-stretch'd,
If I may not carry, sure I'll ne'er be fetch'd,
But vow, though the cross Doctors all stood hearers,
For one Carrier put down to make six bearers.   20
Ease was his chief disease, and to judge right,
He died for heaviness that his Cart went light.
His leisure told him that his time was come,
And lack of load made his life burdensome,
That even to his last breath (there be that say't)   25

5–6. *sphere-metal*—the heavenly substance or "Ethereal Mould" of which God is described (*P.L.* VII, 353–6) as framing the "Celestial Bodies." Milton's "conceit" rests upon the Aristotelian doctrine that the heavenly substance is indestructible. (*De Coelo*, I, iii.)

7–8. Here the "conceit" depends upon the very familiar doctrine of Aristotle (*De Coelo*, I, 9) that time is the measure of motion.

10. *principles*—motive forces. The word is used punningly, for it could apply both to the motive power of a machine and to the faculties of the body. We still speak vaguely of a "life principle."

14. The play is on the vacations and terms or "semesters" of the University.

22. *heaviness; i.e.,* "the dumpishe heavinesse, that proceedeth of Melancholy." (Barnabe Googe's terms, quoted by the *N.E.D.*)

As he were prest to death, he cry'd, more weight;
But had his doings lasted as they were,
He had been an immortal Carrier.
Obedient to the Moon he spent his date
In course reciprocal, and had his fate   30
Linkt to the mutual flowing of the Seas,
Yet (strange to think) his wain was his increase:
His Letters are deliver'd all and gone,
Only remains this superscription.

(1631)

_____

26. The victims of the old punishment of gradual pressing to death
must often have asked for more weight to hasten the inevitable.

29. *date*—time, *i.e.,* allotted life-time.

32. *wain*—a wagon—puns with "wane," a diminishing. We still
say that the moon is "on the wane."

AN EPITAPH ON THE MARCHIONESS OF
WINCHESTER

THIS rich Marble doth inter
The honour'd Wife of *Winchester,*
A Viscount's daughter, an Earl's heir,
Besides what her virtues fair
Added to her noble birth,   5
More than she could own from Earth.
Summers three times eight save one
She had told; alas too soon,
After so short time of breath,
To house with darkness, and with death.   10
Yet had the number of her days
Been as complete as was her praise,
Nature and fate had had no strife
In giving limit to her life.
Her high birth, and her graces sweet,   15
Quickly found a lover meet;
The Virgin quire for her request
The God that sits at marriage feast;
He at their invoking came
But with a scarce-well-lighted flame;   20
And in his Garland as he stood,
Ye might discern a Cypress bud.

2–3. Jane Savage was the daughter of Thomas, Viscount of Rock-
Savage, and through her mother she was the heir of Lord Darcy, Earl
of Rivers. Her husband, John Paulet, was the fifth Marquis of Winchester. Whether Milton had any acquaintance with her family at the
time of her death in April, 1631, is doubtful, but some of her relatives
may have been among his friends at Cambridge. Or he may have
written this Epitaph simply as an exercise in the vein of Ben Jonson's
formal elegy upon her.

18–22. *The God*—Hymen. Perhaps in some masque entertainment
at the lady's wedding the God of Marriage appeared, dressed in the
traditional saffron robe in which Ovid (*Met.* X, 1) described him at
the marriage of Orpheus and Eurydice, where he failed to bring a
lucky omen and his torch sputtered out in spite of all his efforts to
keep it blazing.

22. *Cypress* was a traditional funeral decoration. Compare Spenser's
Daphnaida, 528–9:
> "When as my hearse shall happen to your sightes,
> Vouchsafe to deck the same with Cyparesse."

Once had the early Matrons run
To greet her of a lovely son,
And now with second hope she goes,   25
And calls *Lucina* to her throes;
But whether by mischance or blame
Atropos for *Lucina* came,
And with remorseless cruelty,
Spoil'd at once both fruit and tree: 30
The hapless Babe before his birth
Had burial, yet not laid in earth,
And the languisht Mother's Womb
Was not long a living Tomb.
So have I seen some tender slip   35
Sav'd with care from Winter's nip,
The pride of her carnation train,
Pluck't up by some unheedy swain,
Who only thought to crop the flow'r
New shot up from vernal show'r;   40
But the fair blossom hangs the head
Side-ways as on a dying bed,
And those Pearls of dew she wears,
Prove to be presaging tears
Which the sad morn had let fall   45
On her hast'ning funeral.
Gentle Lady, may thy grave
Peace and quiet ever have:
After this thy travail sore
Sweet rest seize thee evermore,   50

24. The son was Charles, afterward first Duke of Bolton.

26. *Lucina,* the Roman goddess of childbirth. The mother in *Cymbeline* (V, iv, 43–4) complains that Lucina
> "lent not me her aid,
> But took me in my throes."

28. *Atropos,* the "inflexible," was the Fate who cut the threads of human lives. Compare *Arcades,* 63–9, note, and *Lycidas,* 75–6, note.

36–37. Compare the image in *S.A.* 1576–7.

46. *funeral*—death. Spenser describes a servant who, deeming his master dead,
> "Fled fast away, to tell his funerall
> Vnto his brother."
>   (*F.Q.* II, v, 25, 8–9.)

50. *seize*—possess.

That to give the world increase,
Short'ned hast thy own life's lease;
Here besides the sorrowing
That thy noble House doth bring,
Here be tears of perfect moan   55
Wept for thee in *Helicon,*
And some Flowers and some Bays
For thy Hearse to strew the ways,
Sent thee from the banks of *Came,*
Devoted to thy virtuous name;   60
Whilst thou, bright Saint, high sitt'st in glory,
Next her much like to thee in story,
That fair *Syrian* Shepherdess,
Who after years of barrenness
The highly favour'd *Joseph* bore   65
To him that serv'd for her before,
And at her next birth, much like thee,
Through pangs fled to felicity,
Far within the bosom bright
Of blazing Majesty and Light;   70
There with thee, new welcome Saint,
Like fortunes may her soul acquaint,
With thee there clad in radiant sheen,
No Marchioness, but now a Queen.

                                                        (1631)

---

55. Compare *Lycidas,* 14.   Tears was a name given to the mourning
verses which it was customary to pin to the biers of the dead at funerals.

56. *Helicon*—the mountain range in Boeotia which was sacred to the
Muses.

59. *Came*—the river Cam, standing here for Cambridge.   Compare
Camus, reverend Sire, in *Lycidas,* 103.

63–68. The *Syrian Shepherdess* is Rachel, who first enters the Bible
story "with her father's sheep, for she kept them." (Gen. xxix, 9.)
Jacob served her father, Laban, fourteen years for her and only after
long disappointment she bore him Joseph, whom he loved "more than
all his children." (Gen. xxxvii, 3.)   She died in giving birth to Benjamin.   (Gen. xxxv. 18.)

HOW SOON HATH TIME . . .

How soon hath Time, the subtle thief of youth,
   Stol'n on his wing my three and twentieth year!
   My hasting days fly on with full career,
   But my late spring no bud or blossom shew'th.
Perhaps my semblance might deceive the truth,   5
   That I to manhood am arriv'd so near,
   And inward ripeness doth much less appear,
   That some more timely-happy spirits endu'th.
Yet be it less or more, or soon or slow,
   It shall be still in strictest measure ev'n   10
   To that same lot, however mean, or high,
Toward which Time leads me, and the will of Heav'n;
   All is, if I have grace to use it so,
   As ever in my great task-Master's eye.

                              (1631 or 1632)

1–2. Milton's twenty-third birthday fell on December ninth, 1631, in the winter before he took his degree of M.A. and left the University. A few months later, seemingly, or not long after his residence at Horton had begun, he enclosed a copy of this sonnet to a friend who, he said, had accused him of "too much love of learning" and of dreaming away his "years in the arms of studious retirement." His reply is; "Lastly, the love of learning, as it is the pursuit of something good, it would sooner follow the more excellent and supreme good known and presented, and so be quickly diverted from the empty and fantastic chase of shadows . . . to the solid good flowing from due and timely obedience to that command in the Gospel set out by the terrible seising of him that hid the talent." Compare the Sonnet, *When I consider* . . . 3, note, and the Introduction, §3.

10. *still*—always, forever.

13–14. The pledge of the four preceding lines is transformed into an assertion of "due and timely obedience" to the Gospel command to labour.

L'ALLEGRO

Hᴇɴᴄᴇ loathed Melancholy
 Of *Cerberus* and blackest midnight born,
In *Stygian* Cave forlorn
 'Mongst horrid shapes, and shrieks, and sights unholy,
Find out some uncouth cell,   5
 Where brooding darkness spreads his jealous wings,
And the night-Raven sings;
 There under *Ebon* shades, and low-brow'd Rocks,
As ragged as thy Locks,
 In dark *Cimmerian* desert ever dwell.   10
But come thou Goddess fair and free,
In Heav'n yclep'd *Euphrosyne,*
And by men, heart-easing Mirth,
Whom lovely *Venus* at a birth
With two sister Graces more   15

1–4. Virgil describes the den of the three-headed dog, Cerberus, on the dark shores of the Styx where other monsters, "countless and various" (*Aen.* VI, 418), guard the rivers of Hades; but here the immediate background was the allegorical embroidery upon Virgil of mythographers like Natale Conti, who made Cerberus a symbol of death itself. So in this humorous invocation, which may parody *On the Fifth of November* (60 and 139–54), with its "Cimmerian darkness" and its monsters, Melancholy needs no classical justification for appearing as the daughter of Cerberus and Midnight.

5. *uncouth*—unfamiliar, solitary, desolate.

7. Whatever bird it be, the *night-Raven,* as Spenser tells us, belonged to the realm of "elvish ghosts" and "gastly owles." (*June,* 23–4.)

8–10. So Ovid described (*Met.* XI, 592–6) the cave of the slumber-god, Morpheus, lying under a mountain in the land of the Cimmerians, which Homer placed (*Od.* XI, 14–8) in a sunless region of perpetual clouds on the far confines of the ocean.

9. *ragged* and also the related "rugged" were used in both of the former's connexions here. Compare the biblical "ragged rocks" (Is. ii, 21) and Fairfax's lines:
   "His feltred Locks, that on his Bosome fell,
    On rugged Mountains Briers and Thorns resemble."
       (*J.D. IV,* 7, 5–6.)

12. *yclep'd*—called. For the prefix see *Nativity Hymn,* 155, note.

12–16. Among the classical genealogies of the Graces—Euphrosyne (mirth), Aglaia (festive beauty) and Thalia (festive joy or the bloom of life)—Milton first followed Servius' account of them as the children

To Ivy-crowned *Bacchus* bore;
Or whether (as some Sager sing)
The frolic Wind that breathes the Spring,
Zephyr with *Aurora* playing,
As he met her once a-Maying,   20
There on Beds of Violets blue,
And fresh-blown Roses washt in dew,
Fill'd her with thee a daughter fair,
So buxom, blithe, and debonair.
Haste thee nymph, and bring with thee   25
Jest and youthful Jollity,
Quips and Cranks, and wanton Wiles,
Nods, and Becks, and Wreathed Smiles,
Such as hang on *Hebe's* cheek,
And love to live in dimple sleek;   30
Sport that wrinkled Care derides,
And Laughter holding both his sides.
Come, and trip it as ye go
On the light fantastic toe,
And in thy right hand lead with thee,   35
The Mountain Nymph, sweet Liberty;
And if I give thee honour due,
Mirth, admit me of thy crew

---

of Venus and Bacchus (commentary on *Aen.* I, 724) and then he invented his own wiser myth of the west wind, *Zephyr,* and the dawn,
Aurora, as the parents of Euphrosyne.

18. *breathes*—exhales. Compare Aquilo, the north wind, "breathing"
winter in *Nature is Immune to Old Age,* 55.

24. *buxom*—lively, merry.
debonair—courteous, pleasant.
Mr. G. C. Moore Smith compares Randolph's lines in *Aristippus:*
        "A bowl of good wine is wondrous good cheer
            To make one blithe, buxom and debonair."

27. *Quips:* Lyly called a quip "a short saying of a sharpe wit, with a
bitter sense in a sweet word." (*Alexander and Campaspe,* III, i, 30–1.)
Cranks—humorous turns of speech.

28. *Becks*—bows, curtseys.

29. *Hebe,* in Greek, signified both Youth personified and the goddess
cupbearer of Zeus, who appears in the *Vacation Exercise,* 38, bringing
"immortal Nectar."

31–32. Compare the derision of Rigour, Advice, "Strict Age, and
sour Severity" in *Comus,* 108–9.

38. *of thy crew*—to membership in thy crew.

To live with her, and live with thee,
In unreproved pleasures free;   40
To hear the Lark begin his flight,
And singing startle the dull night,
From his watch-tow'r in the skies,
Till the dappled dawn doth rise;
Then to come in spite of sorrow,   45
And at my window bid good morrow,
Through the Sweet-Briar, or the Vine,
Or the twisted Eglantine;
While the Cock with lively din,
Scatters the rear of darkness thin,   50
And to the stack, or the Barn door,
Stoutly struts his Dames before;
Oft list'ning how the Hounds and horn
Cheerly rouse the slumb'ring morn,
From the side of some Hoar Hill,   55
Through the high wood echoing shrill;
Some time walking not unseen
By Hedge-row Elms, on Hillocks green,
Right against the Eastern gate,

---

40. *unreproved*—unreprovable. Compare the note on *uninchanted* in *Comus*, 395.

45. *in spite of sorrow*—in despite or contempt of sorrow.

46–48. Is it the dawn, the lark, or the poet who says good morning? And to whom? It seems to me that the poet is as plainly the subject of "to come . . . And . . . bid" as he is of "To live" (39), "To hear" (41), and "list'ning" (53); but Mr. Verity makes a strong plea for the lark on the strength of Sylvester's *Du Bartas* (Grosart's ed. I, 49):

> "But cheerful Birds, chirping him sweet good-morrows,
> With Nature's Musick do beguile his sorrows."

55. The *N.E.D.* defines *Hoar* in this line as meaning "grey from absence of foliage," but it is likely that in this description of a spring landscape Milton was thinking of effects of foliage like that which Shakespeare intended when he mentioned the willow as a tree
> "That shows his hoar leaves in the glassy stream."
> (*Hamlet*, IV, vii, 168.)

57. *not unseen*—not avoiding being seen. Contrast *Il Penseroso*, 65.

59. Compare Shakespeare's "eastern gate, all fiery-red," which
> "Opening on Neptune with fair blessed beams,
> Turns into yellow gold his salt green streams."
> (*Midsummer Night's Dream*, III, ii, 391–3.)

Where the great Sun begins his state,   60
Rob'd in flames, and Amber light,
The clouds in thousand Liveries dight;
While the Plowman near at hand,
Whistles o'er the Furrow'd Land,
And the Milkmaid singeth blithe,   65
And the Mower whets his scythe,
And every Shepherd tells his tale
Under the Hawthorn in the dale.
Straight mine eye hath caught new pleasures
Whilst the Lantskip round it measures,   70
Russet Lawns and Fallows Gray,
Where the nibbling flocks do stray;
Mountains on whose barren breast
The labouring clouds do often rest;
Meadows trim with Daisies pied,   75
Shallow Brooks, and Rivers wide.
Towers and Battlements it sees
Bosom'd high in tufted Trees,
Where perhaps some beauty lies,

---

60. *state*—stately procession.

62. *Liveries*—gorgeous costumes. Compare the verb in *Comus*, 455.

67. The *N.E.D.* seems to be right in interpreting *tells his tale* as meaning, "tells his story," for the expression does not occur in any other sense earlier than the nineteenth century. The traditional interpretation of "counts his tale" or tally of sheep is tempting beside such a line as Dryden's
      "Once she takes the tale of all the lambs."
      (Translation of Virgil's Pastorals, III, 51.)

70. *Lantskip* was an accepted form of "landscape" and Milton used it regularly. Compare *P.L.* II, 491.

71. *russet*—reddish brown or grey, like the homespun cloth called russet. Compare Shakespeare's "morn in russet mantle clad." (*Hamlet*, I, i, 166.)

75. *pied*—variegated, spotted. The phrase was very common. Compare Shakespeare's song beginning:
      "When daisies pied and violets blue
    *   *   *   *   *   *
      Do paint the meadows with delight,—"
      (*Love's Labour's Lost*, V, ii, 882-5.)

78. *Bosom'd*—embraced, hidden.
Compare *tufted grove* in *Comus*, 225.

The Cynosure of neighbouring eyes.   80
Hard by, a Cottage chimney smokes,
From betwixt two aged Oaks,
Where *Corydon* and *Thyrsis* met,
Are at their savoury dinner set
Of Herbs, and other Country Messes,   85
Which the neat-handed *Phyllis* dresses;
And then in haste her Bow'r she leaves,
With *Thestylis* to bind the Sheaves;
Or if the earlier season lead
To the tann'd Haycock in the Mead.   90
Sometimes with secure delight
The up-land Hamlets will invite,
When the merry Bells ring round,
And the jocund rebecks sound
To many a youth, and many a maid,   95
Dancing in the Chequer'd shade;
And young and old come forth to play
On a Sunshine Holiday,
Till the live-long day-light fail;
Then to the Spicy Nut-brown Ale,   100
With stories told of many a feat,
How *Faery Mab* the junkets eat;

---

80. *Cynosure*—focus, object of attention. For the origin and poetic
value of the word compare *Comus*, 342, note.

83. Milton found the names of his two rustics used over and over
again by most of the poets in the pastoral tradition since Theocritus, in
whose first and fourth Idyls respectively they first appear.

86–88. *Phyllis* is a common name in the Greek Anthology and Milton remembered it in Virgil's *Eclogues*, V, as well as in many an English pastoral. *Thestylis* is a slave girl in Theocritus' second Idyl.

87. *Bow'r* probably has its primitive meaning of "cottage" rather
than the more familiar one of "chamber," as in *Comus*, 45.

91. *secure*—careless. The word keeps the force of the Latin phrase
from which it is derived—"free from care."

94. *rebecks*—primitive fiddles, with three strings.

102.   "This is that very Mab
        That plats the manes of horses in the night,
        And bakes the elf-locks in foul sluttish hairs."
                    (*Romeo and Juliet*, I, iv, 88–90.)
So ends Mercutio's account of Oberon's queen, the same Mab who

She was pincht and pull'd, she said,
And he, by Friar's Lanthorn led,
Tells how the drudging *Goblin* sweat   105
To earn his Cream-bowl duly set,
When in one night, ere glimpse of morn,
His shadowy Flail hath thresh'd the Corn
That ten day-labourers could not end;
Then lies him down the Lubber Fiend,   110
And, stretch'd out all the Chimney's length,
Basks at the fire his hairy strength;
And Crop-full out of doors he flings,
Ere the first Cock his Matin rings.
Thus done the Tales, to bed they creep,   115
By whispering Winds soon lull'd asleep.

———————

sent Drayton's fairies to
> "make our girls their sluttery rue
> By pinching them both black and blue,
> And put a penny in their shoe,
>   The house for cleanly sweeping."
>   (*Nymphidia*, 65–8.)

104. *Friar's Lanthorn*—the will-o'-the-wisp.

105. *the drudging Goblin*—Robin Goodfellow or Hobgoblin, to both of which names Shakespeare's fairy makes Puck own when it accuses him of misleading "night-wanderers, laughing at their harm," while yet he is a willing household drudge for his friends.
> "Those that Hobgoblin call you and sweet Puck,
> You do their work, and they shall have good luck."
>   (*Midsummer Night's Dream*, II, i, 39–41.)

106. In "superstitious times," Burton says (*Anatomy*, I, ii, 1, 2), it was believed that "*Hobgoblins* and *Robin Goodfellows* . . . would . . . grind corn for a mess of milk, cut wood, or do any manner of drudgery work."

110. *the Lubber Fiend;* so Shakespeare's fairy calls Puck "thou lob of spirits." (*Midsummer Night's Dream*, II, 1, 16.) "Lob" and "lubber" are distinct words, but their meanings have long been associated.

111. *Chimney* has its original, but obsolete, meaning of "fire-place."

114. *matin*—song. At the cock's
> "warning,
> Whether in sea or fire, in earth or air,
> The extravagant and erring spirit hies
> To his confine."
>   (*Hamlet*, I, i, 152–5.)

Tow'red Cities please us then,
And the busy hum of men,
Where throngs of Knights and Barons bold,
In weeds of Peace high triumphs hold,   120
With store of Ladies, whose bright eyes
Rain influence, and judge the prize
Of Wit, or Arms, while both contend
To win her Grace, whom all commend.
There let *Hymen* oft appear   125
In Saffron robe, with Taper clear,
And pomp, and feast, and revelry,
With mask, and antique Pageantry—
Such sights as youthful Poets dream
On Summer eves by haunted stream.   130
Then to the well-trod stage anon,
If *Jonson's* learned Sock be on,

117–120. Perhaps in contrast to the real pleasures which he described here Milton thought of the imaginary entertainment in Burton's *Abstract of Melancholy:*

> "Methinks I hear, methinks I see,
> Sweet musick, wondrous melody,
> Towns, Palaces, and Cities fine;
> Here now, then there; the world is mine.
> Rare beauties, gallant Ladies shine."

120. *weeds*—dress, garments.   Compare *Comus,* 16 and 84.

triumphs—splendid festivals.   Compare the title of Bacon's *Essay XXXVII,* "Of Masques and Triumphs."

122. Milton thought of the ladies' eyes as being metaphorically stars, which could rain or shed their rays of influence, like the real stars in the *Nativity Hymn,* 71.   Compare the Italian sonnet, *Bright Lady,* 7–8.

125. *Hymen,* the god of marriage, suggests the splendid masques in which he was the presiding deity and of which so many were given to celebrate great weddings. In Jonson's *Masque of Hymen* he appeared "in a saffron-coloured robe, . . . in his right hand a torch of pine-tree."

127. *revelry* stood to Milton for theatrical entertainments like those which it was the business of the Master of the Revels to arrange at Court.

131. *well-trod* seems to be a compliment to the acting.

132. *Sock:* the light shoe, called a sock, which Greek comic actors wore, came to stand for comedy itself. Milton was thinking of Ben Jonson's famous comedies, to the making of which a great deal of rather self-conscious learning contributed.

Or sweetest *Shakespeare,* fancy's child,
Warble his native Wood-notes wild.
And ever against eating Cares,   135
Lap me in soft *Lydian* Airs,
Married to immortal verse,
Such as the meeting soul may pierce
In notes, with many a winding bout
Of linked sweetness long drawn out,   140
With wanton heed, and giddy cunning,
The melting voice through mazes running;
Untwisting all the chains that tie
The hidden soul of harmony;
That *Orpheus'* self may heave his head   145
From golden slumber on a bed
Of heapt *Elysian* flow'rs, and hear
Such strains as would have won the ear
Of *Pluto,* to have quite set free
His half-regain'd *Eurydice.*   150
These delights if thou canst give,
Mirth, with thee I mean to live.

(1631 ?)

────────

133–134. By *fancy* Milton meant the imagination or creative faculty.
It was on the poet's fancy that he insisted in the Epitaph *On Shakespeare,* thinking probably of the fluent poetry in passages like those
from *The Tempest* and *A Midsummer Night's Dream* which have been
quoted in these notes.

135. *eating Cares* is paralleled in *On the Death of Damon,* 46, where
the Latin varies a famous phrase of Horace for the cares which Bacchus
dissipates. (*Odes* II, xi, 18.)

136. Milton hardly sympathized with Plato's condemnation of Lydian
music and in *Areopagitica* he scoffed at the notion that, "No music
must be heard, no song be set or sung, but what is grave and Doric."
(*P.W.* II, 73. Compare *S.A.* 662, note.)

143–144. Compare *P.R.* IV, 254–7. The personification of Harmony rests upon the doctrine that the human soul is a kind of
harmony.

145–150. On their wedding day, Orpheus lost his wife, Eurydice, and,
when he followed her to Hades, his music drew tears even from the
Furies and won the consent of Proserpina, Pluto's queen in the under-
world, that he should take back his wife. But the consent, Ovid
explains (*Met.* X, 50–63), was limited by the impossible condition that
he should not once look back at her as he led her up into the sunlight.

IL PENSEROSO

HENCE vain deluding joys,
  The brood of folly without father bred,
How little you bested,
  Or fill the fixed mind with all your toys;
Dwell in some idle brain,   5
  And fancies fond with gaudy shapes possess,
As thick and numberless
  As the gay motes that people the Sun-Beams,
Or likest hovering dreams,
  The fickle Pensioners of *Morpheus'* train.   10
But hail thou Goddess, sage and holy,
Hail divinest Melancholy,
Whose Saintly visage is too bright
To hit the Sense of human sight;
And therefore to our weaker view,   15
O'erlaid with black, staid Wisdom's hue.
Black, but such as in esteem,

1–2. Many superficial parallels are quoted, from the pious denuncia-
tion of "false Pleasures, momentary Joyes" and "illuding Toyes" in the
first scene (lines 331–2) of Sylvester's *Tragedie of Henry the Great* to
the Passionate Mad-Man's ditty in Fletcher's (?) *The Nice Valour* (III,
iii):

> "Hence all you vain Delights,
>   As short as are the nights,
>   Wherein you spend your folly,
> There's nought in this life sweet,
> If man were wise to see't,
>   But only melancholy,
>   O, sweetest melancholy."

3. *bested*—avail, profit.

5–6. Here, as in *L'Allegro*, 133, "fancy" means imagination and Milton thought of the diseased imagination of the traditional melancholy
man, whom Spenser represented as sitting in a chamber

> "dispainted all within,
> With sundry colours, in the which were writ
> Infinite shapes of things dispersed thin;

> —   —   —   —   —

> Such as in idle fantasies doe flit:

> —   —   —   —   —

> Deuices, dreams, opinions vnsound."
>   (*F.Q.* II, ix, l,1–li, 7.)

Prince *Memnon's* sister might beseem,
Or that Starr'd *Ethiop* Queen that strove
To set her beauty's praise above   20
The Sea Nymphs, and their powers offended.
Yet thou art higher far descended;
Thee bright-hair'd *Vesta* long of yore,
To solitary *Saturn* bore;
His daughter she (in *Saturn's* reign,   25
Such mixture was not held a stain).
Oft in glimmering Bow'rs and glades
He met her, and in secret shades
Of woody *Ida's* inmost grove,
While yet there was no fear of *Jove*.   30

18. The Ethiopian prince, Memnon, whom Ulysses called the hand-somest of men (*Od.* XI, 521), had, according to Dictys Cretensis (*Ephemeris Belli Trojani*, VI), a sister, Hemera, whose devotion to him seems to have given rise to the medieval idea that she was his wife. Milton, although he calls her Memnon's sister, may have been influenced by Lydgate's picture of her as his wife, appearing from the skies at his tomb years after they both had died. She comes,

> "Downe descendynge fro the fyrmament
> Full many man beynge there present,
> Clade in a mantell ful celestyall
> And of hir porte passyngly royall."
> (*Troy Book*, V.)

19. The *Starr'd Ethiop Queen* is Cassiopeia, who, as Hyginus ex-plained in his work on astronomy, 2, 10, was transformed into the familiar constellation as a punishment for boasting that *her daughter,* Andromeda, was more beautiful than the Nereids. Milton lets it ap-pear that her boast was about herself.

23–24. Though she was one of the younger gods and, like Jove, a child of Saturn, Vesta stood apart as the patroness of purity. Milton made her the mother of Melancholy simply because in classic myth she never had any romantic adventures, while in Platonic allegory she appeared as enthroned forever in the heavenly house which can never be attained by any being with the least taint of impurity. (*Phaedrus,* 247a–b.)

25–30. Milton thought of the myth of the Golden Age when Saturn reigned on Mt. Ida in Crete, where Jove was born and later overthrew his father; but Saturn's share in this fanciful genealogy is due in part to Neo-Platonic interpretations of him as "the collective angelic mind" or embodiment of all contemplative spirits, and also to the astrological notion that all melancholic persons were born under

> "ill disposed skyes,
> When oblique *Saturne* sate in the house of agonyes."
> (*F.Q.* II, ix, lii, 8–9.)

Come pensive Nun, devout and pure,
Sober, steadfast, and demure,
All in a robe of darkest grain,
Flowing with majestic train,
And sable stole of *Cypress* Lawn,   35
Over thy decent shoulders drawn.
Come, but keep thy wonted state,
With ev'n step, and musing gait,
And looks commercing with the skies,
Thy rapt soul sitting in thine eyes: 40
There held in holy passion still,
Forget thyself to Marble, till
With a sad Leaden downward cast,
Thou fix them on the earth as fast.
And join with thee calm Peace and Quiet,   45
Spare Fast, that oft with gods doth diet,
And hears the Muses in a ring
Aye round about *Jove's* Altar sing.
And add to these retired Leisure,
That in trim Gardens takes his pleasure;   50
But first, and chiefest, with thee bring
Him that yon soars on golden wing,
Guiding the fiery-wheeled throne,
The Cherub Contemplation;

33. *grain*—colour.

35. *stole*—a long robe.
Cypress Lawn—"A transparent material resembling . . . crape; when black, much used for habiliments of mourning." (*N.E.D.*)

36. *decent*—comely, beautiful.

37. *state*—stateliness. *N.E.D.* compares Fuller: "True, there is a state sometimes in decent plainnesse."

40. Compare *rapt* in *Comus*, 794, note.

42. Mr. Garrod parallels Thomas Tomkins' *Albumazor* (I, iv, 3–4); "*Wonder* for me, admire and be *astonished*, Marvel thyself to marble." Compare *On Shakespeare*, 13.

43. *sad*—serious. Compare *Comus*, 189. *Leaden;* compare *Damon's Epitaph*, 80.

47–48. Compare *Lycidas*, 15–6, note.

52–54. Ezekiel x, is the basis of this imagery, which was to take ampler form in the "Cherubic shapes" that convoy the "Chariot of Paternal deity" in *P.L.* VI, 750–3; but the thought reflects the medieval classification of the angels into nine orders, of which the highest was

And the mute Silence hist along,   55
'Less *Philomel* will deign a Song,
In her sweetest, saddest plight,
Smoothing the rugged brow of night.
While *Cynthia* checks her Dragon yoke,
Gently o'er th' accustom'd Oak;   60
Sweet Bird that shunn'st the noise of folly,
Most musical, most melancholy!
Thee Chantress oft the Woods among,
I woo to hear thy even-Song;
And missing thee, I walk unseen   65
On the dry smooth-shaven Green,
To behold the wand'ring Moon,
Riding near her highest noon,
Like one that had been led astray
Through the Heav'n's wide pathless way;   70
And oft, as if her head she bow'd,
Stooping through a fleecy cloud,
Oft on a Plat of rising ground,
I hear the far-off *Curfew* sound,
Over some wide-water'd shore,   75
Swinging slow with sullen roar;
Or if the Air will not permit,
Some still removed place will fit,
Where glowing Embers through the room
Teach light to counterfeit a gloom,   80
Far from all resort of mirth,
Save the Cricket on the hearth,
Or the Bellman's drowsy charm,

_____

that of the seraphim and the second that of the cherubim, whose
Hebrew name signifies "the fulness of knowledge" and who were
supposed to live in contemplation of God. Compare *Upon the Circumcision*, 1, note, and the Introduction, § 11.

56. *Philomel,* the Greek name for the nightingale, would suggest its
etymology—"lover of song"—to Milton.

58. *rugged*—wrinkled. Compare *P.R.* II, 164.

59. *Cynthia*—Diana, the goddess of the moon. Compare the note
on *Comus*, 131.

65. Compare *not unseen* in *L'Allegro*, 57.

83. A *Bellman* was a night-watchman who cried the hours.
charm is used with the Latin meaning of "a song." Compare *S.A.*
934.

To bless the doors from nightly harm:
Or let my Lamp at midnight hour,   85
Be seen in some high lonely Tow'r,
Where I may oft out-watch the *Bear,*
With thrice great *Hermes,* or unsphere
The spirit of *Plato* to unfold
What Worlds, or what vast Regions hold   90
The immortal mind that hath forsook
Her mansion in this fleshly nook:
And of those *Dæmons* that are found
In fire, air, flood, or under ground,
Whose power hath a true consent   95
With Planet, or with Element.
Sometime let Gorgeous Tragedy
In Scepter'd Pall come sweeping by,

---

84. Compare Chaucer:
      "Jhesu Crist and seinte Benedight,
        Blesse this hous from every wikked wight."
          (*The Miller's Tale,* I (A) 3483–4.)
nightly; i.e., occurring at night.

87. Outwatching the constellation of the Great Bear, which never sets, can have but one meaning.

88. Hermes Trismegistus, the Egyptian god Thoth who was identified with the Greek Hermes, was once believed to be the author of a body of forty-two esoteric books which actually were written by Alexandrian authors in the third and fourth centuries A.D., and had a great influence for two centuries after the appearance of the Latin translation of Marsilio Ficino at Paris in 1494. Bacon explained that the "triplicity, which in great veneration was ascribed to the ancient Hermes" consisted in "the power and fortune of a king, the knowledge and illumination of a priest, and the learning and universality of a philosopher." (Dedication of *The Advancement of Learning.*) Compare *On the Platonic Idea,* 33.

88–92. For the thought and the reference to Plato see the note on *Comus,* 1–3.

93–96. In one of the Hermetic books, the *Definitions of Asclepias to King Amon* (13), Milton may have read that each of the four elements of which the universe is composed has its own "choir of daemons," to each of which has been allotted authority over things upon the earth; but he need have gone no further than Burton's "Digression of Spirits" (*Anatomy,* I, ii, 1, 2) for the theory that the evil daemons "can work no farther than the four elements" and are commonly classified as fiery, aerial, terrestrial and watery, beside subterranean devils and "those Fairies, Satyrs, Nymphs, &c." Compare *P.R.* II, 122–4, note.

98. *Pall*—a splendid robe of any kind. Compare *Elegy I,* 37–8, note.

Presenting *Thebes,* or *Pelop's* line,
Or the tale of *Troy* divine,   100
Or what (though rare) of later age,
Ennobled hath the Buskin'd stage.
But, O sad Virgin, that thy power
Might raise *Musaeus* from his bower,
Or bid the soul of *Orpheus* sing   105
Such notes as, warbled to the string,
Drew Iron tears down *Pluto's* cheek,
And made Hell grant what Love did seek.
Or call up him that left half told
The story of *Cambuscan* bold,   110
Of *Camball,* and of *Algarsife,*
And who had *Canace* to wife,
That own'd the virtuous Ring and Glass,
And of the wond'rous Horse of Brass,
On which the *Tartar* King did ride;   115
And if aught else great Bards beside
In sage and solemn tunes have sung,
Of Tourneys and of Trophies hung,
Of Forests, and inchantments drear,
Where more is meant than meets the ear.   120

99–100. A review of the Greek tragic themes. *Thebes* suggests
Aeschylus' *Seven against Thebes* and Sophocles' *Oedipus the King;*
Pelops' descendants included Agamemnon, Orestes Iphigenia and
Electra; and the *Tale of Troy* might include Euripidean tragedies such
as *The Trojan Dames, Andromache* and *Hecuba.*

102. *Buskin'd stage*—the tragic stage. Because Greek tragic actors
wore a high boot or buskin, the buskin became the emblem of tragedy.
Compare the note on *Sock* in *L'Allegro,* 132.

104. Perhaps Milton remembered Virgil's picture of the heroes and
priests and bards in the laurel groves of Elysium with "Musaeus foremost of all" (*Aen.* VI, 656–68), for he was already an almost vanished
figure of myth when Virgil wrote.

105–108. Compare the note on *L'Allegro,* 145–50.

109–115. In *The Squire's Tale* Chaucer *left half-told* the story of the
"Tartre Cambyuskan" and his three children, Algarsyf, Cambalo, and
Canacee, whose unknown lover gave her a marvellous mirror and ring
and offered her father the *wond'rous Horse of Brass.*

118–120. Milton looked at the whole field of medieval romance
which he was to survey in a very different spirit in *P.L.* VII, 34–42.
Perhaps in stressing the allegorical value of the romances he had in

Thus night oft see me in thy pale career,
Till civil-suited Morn appear,
Not trickt and frounc't as she was wont
With the Attic Boy to hunt,
But Kerchieft in a comely Cloud,   125
While rocking Winds are Piping loud,
Or usher'd with a shower still,
When the gust hath blown his fill,
Ending on the rustling Leaves,
With minute drops from off the Eaves.   130
And when the Sun begins to fling
His flaring beams, me Goddess bring
To arched walks of twilight groves,
And shadows brown that *Sylvan* loves
Of Pine or monumental Oak,   135
Where the rude Axe with heaved stroke
Was never heard the Nymphs to daunt,
Or fright them from their hallow'd haunt.
There in close covert by some Brook,
Where no profaner eye may look,   140
Hide me from Day's garish eye,
While the Bee with Honied thigh,
That at her flow'ry work doth sing,
And the Waters murmuring
With such consort as they keep,   145
Entice the dewy-feather'd Sleep;

---

mind particularly the enchanted forest of error in the first canto of *The
Faerie Queene.* Compare *Comus,* 37–9, note.

122. *civil-suited*—soberly dressed.

123. *frounc't*—with hair frizzed or curled.

124. Compare the use made of Ovid's story of the love of Aurora
for Cephalus, *"the Attic Boy,"* in *Elegy III,* 67.

127. *still*—gentle, making a soft sound.

128. *his* had not yet been supplanted by the modern "its."

130. *minute drops*—drops falling at minute intervals.

134. *brown*—dark. Compare the note on *P.R.* II, 293.
Perhaps Milton thought of the ancient forest shrine of Sylvanus
which Virgil mentions. *Aen.* VIII, 597–9. Compare *Comus,* 268.

141. *garish;* compare Shakespeare's "pay no worship to the garish
sun." *Romeo and Juliet,* III, ii, 25.

145. *consort*—harmony.

And let some strange mysterious dream
Wave at his Wings in Airy stream,
Of lively portraiture display'd,
Softly on my eye-lids laid.   150
And as I wake, sweet music breathe
Above, about, or underneath,
Sent by some spirit to mortals good,
Or th'unseen Genius of the Wood.
But let my due feet never fail   155
To walk the studious Cloister's pale,
And love the high embowed Roof,
With antic Pillars massy proof,
And storied Windows richly dight,
Casting a dim religious light.   160
There let the pealing Organ blow
To the full voic'd Quire below,
In Service high and Anthems clear,
As may with sweetness, through mine ear,
Dissolve me into extasies,   165
And bring all Heav'n before mine eyes,
And may at last my weary age
Find out the peaceful hermitage,
The Hairy Gown and Mossy Cell,

147–150. The thought seems to be a wish that a dream may come
floating (waving) on the wings of sleep, displaying a series of vivid
images. Compare the speech of Night in Jonson's *Vision of Delight:*
    "Break, Phant'sie, from thy cave of cloud,
        And spread thy purple wings;
    Now all thy figures are allowed,
        And various shapes of things;
    Create of airy forms a stream," etc.

153–154. Compare the Attendant Spirit in *Comus* (1–3, note) and the
Genius into which Milton dreamed of Lycidas being transformed.
(*Lycidas,* 183.)

157. *embowed*—arched.

158. *antic*—decorated with antic or quaint carving.

proof; the thought seems to be that by their massiveness the pillars
are proof against destruction.

159. *storied Windows*—windows decorated with scenes from sacred
story in the stained glass.

166. Compare the *Vacation Exercise,* 33–35.

Where I may sit and rightly spell   170
Of every Star that Heav'n doth shew,
And every Herb that sips the dew;
Till old experience do attain
To somthing like Prophetic strain.
These pleasures *Melancholy* give,   175
And I with thee will choose to live.

                                        (1631 ?)

---

170. *spell*—consider, speculate.

170–174. Il Penseroso finally learns that
                    "Nothing hath got so farre
        But Man hath caught and kept it as his prey;
            His eyes dismount the highest starre;
            He is in little all the sphere;
        Herbs gladly cure our flesh, because that they
            Finde their acquaintance there."
                    (George Herbert's *Man*, 19–24.)

ON TIME

Fly envious *Time,* till thou run out thy race,
Call on the lazy leaden-stepping hours,
Whose speed is but the heavy Plummet's pace;
And glut thyself with what thy womb devours,
Which is no more than what is false and vain,   5
And merely mortal dross;
So little is our loss,
So little is thy gain.
For when as each thing bad thou hast entomb'd,
And, last of all, thy greedy self consum'd,   10
Then long Eternity shall greet our bliss
With an individual kiss;
And Joy shall overtake us as a flood,
When everything that is sincerely good
And perfectly divine,   15
With Truth, and Peace, and Love, shall ever shine
About the supreme Throne
Of him, t'whose happy-making sight alone,
When once our heav'nly-guided soul shall climb,
Then all this Earthy grossness quit,   20
Attir'd with Stars, we shall for ever sit,

---

3. An allusion to the plummet or weight which moved the works
was appropriate in a poem which, as the manuscript sub-title suggests,
was intended "to be set on a clock case."

4–8. These closing lines of the first movement of the poem lead
through commonplace ideas, like those of "cormorant devouring Time"
(*Love's Labour's Lost,* I, i, 4) and of time "that makes and unfolds
error" (*Winter's Tale,* IV, i, 2), to the Christian hope of immortality,
when "this corruptible must put on incorruption." (I Cor. xv, 53.)

12. *Individual*—undividable. The kiss symbolizes the union of the
"individual Soul For ever happy" (*P.L.* VI, 610–1) to God.

16. Compare *Nativity Hymn,* 141–4.

18. In *happy-making sight* Milton anglicized the theological term,
Beatific Vision—the vision of God to which Dante devoted the final
canto of the *Paradiso.* The angels, he said in *P.L.* III, 61–2, from
God's "sight receiv'd Beatitude past utterance."

20. *quit*—abandoned, discarded.

Triumphing over Death, and Chance, and thee
  O Time.

(1631–3)

---

22. Ben Jonson ended his Elegy on the *Lady Jane Pawlet, Marchioness
of Winton,* by describing the Christian soul which rises
"above Death and Sin,
  And sure of Heaven, rides triumphing in."

Compare the Introduction, § 30.

UPON THE CIRCUMCISION

YE FLAMING Powers, and winged Warriors bright,
That erst with Music, and triumphant song
First heard by happy watchful Shepherds' ear,
So sweetly sung your Joy the Clouds along
Through the soft silence of the list'ning night,   5
Now mourn; and, if sad share with us to bear
Your fiery essence can distill no tear,
Burn in your sighs, and borrow
Seas wept from our deep sorrow:
He, who with all Heav'n's heraldry whilere   10
Enter'd the world, now bleeds to give us ease;
Alas, how soon our sin
   Sore doth begin
     His Infancy to seize!
O more exceeding love or law more just?   15
Just law indeed, but more exceeding love!
For we by rightful doom remediless

---

1. The *Powers* were the sixth among the nine traditional orders of angels. (Compare *Il Penseroso,* 52–4, and *S.A.* 672, notes.) They are *flaming* because Milton always thought of the heavenly beings as made of "Ethereal mould" (*P.L.* II, 139), *i.e.,* of the ether or fiery quintessence of which medieval philosophers learned from Aristotle to suppose that the heavens were composed. And he had the authority of the Psalms civ, 4, for regarding the angels as "a flaming fire."

2. *erst*—formerly, *i.e.,* at Christ's nativity.

7–8. The thought, which seems like a "conceit" of Crashaw's best mintage, reappears in Milton's account of the reception of the news of Adam's sin in heaven:
     ". . . dim sadness did not spare
     That time Celestial visages, yet mixt
     With pity, violated not thir bliss."
       (*P.L.* X, 23–5.)

15–16. The antithesis of Law with Love recurs in Michael's prophecy of Christ satisfying "high Justice":
     "The Law of God exact he shall fulfil
     Both by obedience and by love, though love
     Alone fulfil the Law."
       (*P.L.* XII, 401–4.)

17. *doom*—judgement. "I submit," Adam says in his soliloquy in *P.L.* X, 769, after judgement has been pronounced on him from God for his sin, "his doom is fair."

Were lost in death, till he that dwelt above
High thron'd in secret bliss, for us frail dust
Emptied his glory, ev'n to nakedness;   20
And that great Cov'nant which we still transgress
Entirely satisfi'd,
And the full wrath beside
Of vengeful Justice bore for our excess,
And seals obedience first with wounding smart   25
This day; but Oh! ere long
Huge pangs and strong
　　　Will pierce more near his heart.

                                              (1632–3)

————————

20. Milton thought of St. Paul's conception of Christ, "Who, being in
the form of God, . . . took upon him the form of a servant, and
was made in the likeness of men." (Phil. ii, 6–7.)

21. The *Cov'nant* is the Law of Moses as found in the legal books of
the Old Testament.

still—constantly, continually.　Compare Satan "roving still About the
world." (*P.R.* I, 33–4.)

AT A SOLEMN MUSIC

BLEST pair of *Sirens,* pledges of Heav'n's joy,
Sphere-born harmonious Sisters, Voice, and Verse,
Wed your divine sounds, and mixt power employ
Dead things with inbreath'd sense able to pierce,
And to our high-rais'd phantasy present   5
That undisturbed Song of pure concent,
Aye sung before the sapphire-colour'd throne
To him that sits thereon,
With Saintly shout, and solemn Jubilee,
Where the bright Seraphim in burning row   10
Their loud up-lifted Angel-trumpets blow,
And the Cherubic host in thousand quires
Touch their immortal Harps of golden wires,
With those just Spirits that wear victorious Palms,
Hymns devout and holy Psalms   15
Singing everlastingly;
That we on Earth with undiscording voice
May rightly answer that melodious noise;

1. Compare the note on the "celestial Sirens" of *Arcades, 63.*

5. *phantasy*—imagination.

6. *concent*—harmony—is the certainly preferable reading in the 1673 edition for *content* in the edition of 1645.

7–8. Milton thought of the seraphs in Ezekiel's vision, over whose "heads was the likeness of a throne, as the appearance of a sapphire stone; and upon the likeness of the throne was the likeness as the appearance of a man above upon it." (Ezek. i, 26.)

12–13. Compare Milton's description of the angelic symphony before the throne of God at the creation, when
    "All sounds on Fret by String or Golden Wire
    Temper'd soft Tunings."
                (*P.L.* VII, 597–8.)

14. The *just Spirits* are the souls of Christians with "palms in their hands," as St. John saw them (Rev. vii, 9); and their song is the "new song before the throne," which St. John said (Rev. xiv, 3–4) could be learned only by those "which were not defiled with women." What follows fuses Christian mysticism with the Pythagorean belief that the music of the spheres can be reproduced on earth. "Some learned men," of whom Pythagoras was the chief, Cicero says in *The Dream of Scipio,* "by imitating this harmony with strings and vocal melodies, have opened a way for their return" to heaven. Compare *Arcades, 63,* and *Nativity Hymn, 107–8,* notes.

As once we did, till disproportion'd sin
Jarr'd against nature's chime, and with harsh din   20
Broke the fair music that all creatures made
To their great Lord, whose love their motion swav'd
In perfect Diapason, whilst they stood
In first obedience, and their state of good.
O may we soon again renew that Song,   25
And keep in tune with Heav'n, till God ere long
To his celestial consort us unite,
To live with him, and sing in endless morn of light.

                                        (1632-3)

19–24. So in the second *Prolusion* Milton spoke of men's wickedness
as the "reason why we hear so little of this harmony" and added that,
"if we possessed hearts so pure, so spotless, so snowy, as once upon a
time Pythagoras had, then indeed would our ears be made to resound
and to be entirely filled with that most delectable music of the revolving stars." The thought was familiar in Cardinal Bembo's prayer at the
close of Castiglione's *Book of the Courtier:* "Make us to . . . heare the
heavenly harmony so tunable, that no discorde of passion take place
any more in us." (Hoby's translation.)
Compare the treatment of "Sin, that first distemper'd all things," in
P.L. XI, 55–6.   •

23. *Diapason* is used in the double sense of "the concord of the octave"
and of "spiritual harmony." The *N.E.D.* compares Burton's *Anatomy*
"A true correspondence, perfect mity, a diapason of vows and wishes"
between friends.

27. *consort*—band of musicians. Compare George Herbert's *The
Temple, Employment* vi, "Lord place me in thy consort; give one strain
To my poor reed."

ARCADES

Part of an Entertainment presented to the Countess Dowager
of *Derby* at *Harefield,* by some Noble persons of her Family,
who appear on the Scene in pastoral habit, moving toward
the seat of State, with this Song.

1. Song

Look Nymphs, and Shepherds look,
What sudden blaze of majesty
Is that which we from hence descry,
Too divine to be mistook:
   This, this is she   5
To whom our vows and wishes bend,
Here our solemn search hath end.

Fame that her high worth to raise,
Seem'd erst so lavish and profuse,
We may justly now accuse   10
Of detraction from her praise,

---

1. The *Nymphs and Shepherds*—the Arcades—are natives of *Arcady*
(l. 28) or Arcadia, the ancient Greek state in central Peloponnesus
within which lay the rivers *Alpheus* (l. 30) and *Ladon* (l. 97) and
the mountains *Cyllene* (l. 98), *Erymanthus* (l. 100) and *Maenalus* (l.
102). Theocritus and Virgil did not connect their Eclogues with this
region, but Ovid laid the story of Pan's unsuccessful courtship of the
nymph Syrinx (l. 106, compare *Met.* I, 689) there and it was there also
that he placed (*Met.* II, 405) Jove's wooing of one of Diana's nymphs,
a figure with bow and javelin to whose family Milton's *silver-buskin'd
Nymphs* (l. 33) belong. "Gilden buskins," like those which Spenser
gave to Belphoebe (*F.Q.* II, iii, 27, 3), were a conventional part of the
dress of huntress nymphs in "Arcadia," but the idealization of Arcadia
itself was the greatest of such pastoral conventions in the poetry of the
Renaissance—going back through the *Arcadia* of Sir Philip Sidney to
that of Sannazaro.

2–5. For the Countess Dowager of Derby and Milton's mode of introducing her see the Introduction §23.

4. *mistook*—mistaken.

6. *vows* has its Latin meaning of "prayer" or "desire."

8. *Fame* is thought of vaguely as the goddess to whom Milton refers more definitely in *S.A.* 971. Compare the note there.

9. *erst*—before the present moment, until now.

Less than half we find exprest,
Envy bid conceal the rest.

Mark what radiant state she spreads,
In circle round her shining throne,   15
Shooting her beams like silver threads.
This, this is she alone,
    Sitting like a Goddess bright,
    In the centre of her light.

Might she the wise *Latona* be,   20
Or the tow'red *Cybele,*
Mother of a hunderd gods;
Juno dares not give her odds;

---

14. *state*—any "imposing display, such as befits persons of rank."
(*N.E.D.*) Here the word means the canopy and the illumination around
the Countess' seat, as it does in *P.L.* X, 445–7, where Satan's
            "high Throne, which under state
            Of richest texture spread, at th'upper end
            Was plac't in regal lustre."

20. As she sits in state with her children around her, Milton suggests that the Countess is like the mother of Apollo and Diana, *Latona.*
Latona is *wise,* perhaps because her myth was sometimes interpreted
(*e.g.,* by Conti, IX, vi) to mean that she was the source of the harmony
of soul which men learn from Apollo, god both of the sun and of
music, which banishes discord from life.

21–22. In the chapter preceding that on Latona Conti recalled that
Cybele (otherwise called Rhea) was one of the eldest goddesses, often
called the mother of gods and men, and that she appears in Virgil's
Aeneid (X, 252–3) wearing a turreted crown because she first taught
men to build fortified cities, and again (VI, 789) as the mother of a
hundred gods. There are countless echoes of these Virgilian passages in
Renaissance literature; *e.g.,* Spenser's picture of
            "Old Cybele, arayd with pompous pride,
            Wearing a diademe embattild wide
            With hundred turrets."
                    (*F.Q.* IV, xi, 28, 4–7.)

23. *Juno,* the first of the goddesses because she was Jove's wife, dares
not set aside the advantage of her divinity in order to compete on
equal terms with the Countess's beauty. Compare George Wither's
hope that with the help of his verses his lady's fame may,
            "without respect of odds,
            Vie renown with demi-gods."
                    (*Fair Virtue,* London, 1818, p. 22.)

Who had thought this clime had held
A deity so unparallel'd?   25

As they come forward, the Genius of the Wood appears, and
turning toward them, speaks.

Genius. Stay gentle Swains, for though in this disguise,
I see bright honour sparkle through your eyes.
Of famous *Arcady* ye are, and sprung
Of that renowned flood, so often sung,
Divine *Alpheus,* who by secret sluice,   30
Stole under Seas to meet his *Arethuse;*
And ye the breathing Roses of the Wood,
Fair silver-buskin'd Nymphs as great and good,
I know this quest of yours and free intent
Was all in honour and devotion meant   35
To the great Mistress of yon princely shrine,
Whom with low reverence I adore as mine,
And with all helpful service will comply
To further this night's glad solemnity;
And lead ye where ye may more near behold   40

---

24. *clime*—region. In *P.L.* IX, 45, there is a more interesting reference to the belief that northern Europe was too cold for men to develop to their best.

26. The ideas in the Genius' account of himself in lines 44–60 are developed from the Roman conception (explained in Servius' commentary on Virgil's *Georgics,* I, 302) that a nature-divinity, called the genius of the place, was attached to every locality. In *Il Penseroso* (l. 154) Milton fancied an "unseen Genius of the Wood" rousing him with music in his ideal, forest retreat; while for his use of the Genius here he had the example of many masques, such as Jonson's *The Satyr,* where wood-gods take a leading part in the entertainment.

26–27. The masquers would all belong to the Countess's own family or to other noble houses no less honourable.

29–31. Nestor's story of the sacrifice of a bull to the river-god Alpheus in the *Iliad* (XI, 725–8) is the first of countless tributes to the river in ancient poetry. Ovid (*Met.* V, 574–641) makes the nymph, Arethusa, tell the story of her pursuit by the god, of her transformation into a stream by Diana, and of her escape in that form under the Adriatic Sea to Sicily, only to be overtaken there by the pursuing waters of the Alpheus.

32. *breathing* may mean either "living" (*i.e.,* human) or "fragrant," "exhaling perfume."

39. *solemnity* has the Latin meaning of "a festival." Compare the "conceal'd Solemnity" of the revellers in *Comus,* 142.

W at shallow-searching *Fame* hath left untold;
W ich I full oft amidst these shades alone
Have sat to wonder at, and gaze upon:
For know by lot from *Jove* I am the pow'r
Of this fair Wood, and live in Oak'n bow'r,   45
To nurse the Saplings tall, and curl the grove
With Ringlets quaint, and wanton windings wove.
And all my Plants I save from nightly ill,
Of noisome winds, and blasting vapours chill;
And from the Boughs brush off the evil dew,   50
And heal the harms of thwarting thunder blue,
Or what the cross dire-looking Planet smites,
Or hurtful Worm with canker'd venom bites.
When Ev'ning gray doth rise, I fetch my round
Over the mount, and all this hallow'd ground,   55
And early ere the odorous breath of morn
Awakes the slumb'ring leaves, or tassell'd horn
Shakes the high thicket, haste I all about,
Number my ranks, and visit every sprout

------

44. *by lot*—by the allotment of Jove. Compare the same phrase in *Comus*, 20.

47. *quaint* keeps its primitive meaning of "cunningly made" or "ingenious."
Wove—woven. *mistook* in l. 4 above is another case of the use of a preterite form for a past participle to secure a rhyme. The two forms were not always so definitely distinguished as they now are.

51. *thwarting thunder blue*—blue lightning, either zigzagging across the sky or striking diagonally across or athwart the trees. Compare "the cross blue lightning" in *Julius Caesar* (I, ii, 50–1) which "seem'd to open The breast of heaven."

52. The *dire-looking Planet* is Saturn, whose oblique rays are described as falling like a dart in *Epitaphium Damonis*, 79–80. With the idea of a planet smiting compare Marcellus' reference in *Hamlet* (I, i, 161) to the "wholesome" nights at Christmas time, when "no planets strike."

53. *canker'd*—infectious. Compare Titania's dispatch of her fairies "to kill cankers (*i.e.,* cankerworms) in the musk-rose buds." (*A Midsummer Night's Dream*, II, ii, 3.)

54. *fetch*—take (a walk, run, leap). *N.E.D.* compares William Lithgow's *Travels* (v, 205); "I would often fetch a walke, to stretch my legs."

57–58. Compare *L'Allegro*, 53–4.

59. As in *P.L.* IV, 140, *ranks* refers to masses of trees. The Genius counts them as a general would his troops.

With puissant words and murmurs made to bless;   60
But else in deep of night, when drowsiness
Hath lockt up mortal sense, then listen I
To the celestial *Sirens'* harmony,
That sit upon the nine enfolded Spheres
And sing to those that hold the vital shears   65
And turn the Adamantine spindle round,
On which the fate of gods and men is wound.
Such sweet compulsion doth in music lie,
To lull the daughters of *Necessity,*
And keep unsteady Nature to her law,   70
And the low world in measur'd motion draw

---

60. *puissant words*—words of magic power. *murmurs*—charms.
Compare Comus' "baneful cup, With many murmurs mixt." (*Comus,*
525–6.)

62. *mortal sense*—the senses or consciousness of men.

63–69. The *celestial Sirens* are described in the vision of Er, at the
close of Plato's *Republic,* as sitting on the eight spheres of the planets,
each "uttering her voice in one monotone, but all of them being
eight, composed one harmony." The entire vision of the Genius is
based upon that of Er, whom Plato describes in the life beyond life as
having seen "the distaff of Necessity, by which all the revolutions of
the universe are maintained, whose spindle and point were both of
adamant." Plato goes on to describe the distaff as driven right through
the spheres which were supposed to support and move each of the
seven planets, and through the eighth sphere, that of the fixed stars,
comparing them to boxes inside one another. The distaff spins on the
knees of Necessity, turning the eight spheres and the sirens with them.
"At equal distances," Plato adds, three other personages are enthroned
round about, the daughters of Necessity, the Fates, Lachesis, Clotho
and Atropos, vested in white and with crowns on their heads. They
sing to the harmony of the Sirens, Lachesis singing of the past, Clotho
of the present and Atropos of the future." (*Republic,* 616–617.)
Strictly speaking, only Atropos held the shears which cut the
threads of life which her sisters spun and drew out. Compare *At a
Solemn Music,* 14, note.

70–72. Compare Sir Thomas Browne's suggestion that "thus far we
may maintain the musick of the Sphears: for those well-ordered motions, and regular paces, though they give no sound unto the ear, yet to
the understanding they strike a note most full of harmony . . . There
is something in it of Divinity more than the ear discovers: it is an
Hieroglyphical and shadowed lesson of the whole World, and creatures
of God; such a melody to the ear, as the whole World well understood,
would afford the understanding." (*Religio Medici,* II, 9.)
Compare *Nativity Hymn,* 125–132, *At a Solemn Music,* and *To his
Father,* 35–7.

After the heavenly tune, which none can hear
Of human mould with gross unpurged ear;
And yet such music worthiest were to blaze
The peerless height of her immortal praise,   75
Whose lustre leads us, and for her most fit,
If my inferior hand or voice could hit
Inimitable sounds; yet as we go,
Whate'er the skill of lesser gods can show,
I will assay, her worth to celebrate,   80
And so attend ye toward her glittering state;
Where ye may all that are of noble stem
Approach, and kiss her sacred vesture's hem.

2. Song

O'er the smooth enamell'd green
Where no print of step hath been,   85
    Follow me as I sing,
    And touch the warbled string.
Under the shady roof
Of branching Elm Star-proof,
    Follow me;   90
I will bring you where she sits
Clad in splendor as befits
    Her deity.
Such a rural Queen
All *Arcadia* hath not seen.   95

---

73. *mould*—substance.   Compare "the mortal mixture of Earth's mould" in *Comus,* 243.

74. *blaze*—publish, proclaim. Compare Mark I, 45: "he . . . began to publish it much, and to blaze abroad the matter."

80. *assay*—essay, try, test. Compare *P.R.* I, 143, note.

82. *stem*—line, stock, family.

84. *enamell'd* seems intended to intensify the impression of absolutely unbroken smoothness in the lawn, but in *Lycidas* (l. 139) it refers to flowers spangling the turf, and in *P.L.* (IV, 149) the foliage and fruit of trees appear "with gay enamell'd colours mixt."

89. *Star-proof*—"Not perceable with power of any starr," as Spenser described a summer forest in *F.Q.* I, i, 7, 6.

3. Song

Nymphs and Shepherds dance no more
  By sandy *Ladon's* Lillied banks.
On old *Lycæus* or *Cyllene* hoar,
  Trip no more in twilight ranks,
Though *Erymanth* your loss deplore,   100
  A better soil shall give ye thanks.
From the stony *Mænalus,*
Bring your Flocks, and live with us.
Here ye shall have greater grace,
To serve the Lady of this place.   105
    Though *Syrinx* your *Pan's* mistress were,
    Yet *Syrinx* well might wait on her.
        Such a rural Queen
    All *Arcadia* hath not seen.

(1633 ?)

---

97. *Ladon;* see the note on l. 1.

98. *Lycæus* is mentioned by Theocritus (I, 123) as one of the haunts of the supreme wood-god, Pan. Like Erymanthus, it is a mountain in Arcadia.

102. Virgil's invocation of Pan, the guardian of flocks, in *Georgics,* I, 16–17, associates him with both mounts Lycaeus and Maenalus.

106. For the story of Pan and Syrinx see the note on l. 1. Pan and "His paramour, the Syrinx bright," are the gods whom Fletcher's shepherds invoke in *The Faithful Shepherdess.*

A MASK

Presented at Ludlow Castle
1634:
on Michaelmas Night, Before the Right Honourable
John, Earl of Bridgewater, Viscount Brackley, Lord
President of Wales, and One of His Majesty's Most
Honourable Privy Council.

Eheu quid volui misero mihi! floribus austrum Perditus . . .

(The title-page of the first (1637) edition of the then anonymous masque which we know as *Comus* read as above, and
the volume carried the following dedication by Henry Lawes.)

To the Right Honourable John, Lord Viscount Brackley,
Son and heir-apparent to the Earl of *Bridgewater, &c.*

My Lord,
        This Poem, *which receiv'd its first occasion of Birth
from your Self, and others of your Noble Family, and much
honour from your own Person in the performance, now returns again to make a final Dedication of itself to you. Although not openly acknowledg'd by the Author, yet it is a
legitimate off-spring, so lovely, and so much desired, that the
often Copying of it hath tir'd my Pen to give my several friends
satisfaction, and brought me to a necessity of producing it to
the public view; and now to offer it up in all rightful devotion
to those fair Hopes, and rare Endowments of your much-
promising Youth, which give a full assurance, to all that know
you, of a future excellence. Live sweet Lord to be the honour
of your Name, and receive this as your own, from the hands of
him, who hath by many favours been long oblig'd to your most
honour'd Parents, and as in this representation your attendant*
Thyrsis, *so now in all real expression*

Your faithful, and most
humble Servant
H. Lawes.

The Copy of a Letter writt'n by SIR HENRY WOTTON, to the Author, upon the following Poem.[1]

From the College, this 13. of April, 1638.

SIR,

It was a special favour, when you lately bestowed upon me here the first taste of your acquaintance, though no longer than to make me know that I wanted more time to value it, and to enjoy it rightly; and in truth, if I could then have imagined your farther stay in these parts, which I understood afterwards by Mr. *H.,* I would have been bold (in our vulgar phrase) to mend my draught (for you left me with an extreme thirst) and to have begged your conversation again, jointly with your said learned Friend, at a poor meal or two, that we might have banded together some good Authors of the ancient time: Among which, I observed you to have been familiar.

Since your going, you have charg'd me with new Obligations, both for a very kind Letter from you dated the sixth of this Month, and for a dainty piece of entertainment which came therewith. Wherein I should much commend the Tragical part if the Lyrical did not ravish me with a certain Doric delicacy in your Songs and Odes, whereunto I must plainly confess to have seen yet nothing parallel in our Language: *Ipsa mollities.* But I must not omit to tell you, that I now only owe you thanks for intimating unto me (how modestly soever) the true Artificer. For the work itself I had view'd some good while before, with singular delight, having receiv'd it from our common Friend Mr. *R.* in the very close of the late *R's* Poems, Printed at *Oxford,* whereunto it was added (as I now suppose) that the Accessory might help out the Principal, according to the Art of *Stationers,* and to leave the Reader *Con la bocca dolce.*

Now Sir, concerning your travels, wherein I may challenge a little more privilege of Discourse with you; I suppose you

---

[1] Omitted in 1673.

will not blanch *Paris* in your way; therefore I have been bold
to trouble you with a few lines to Mr. *M. B.* whom you shall
easily find attending the young Lord *S.* as his Governor, and
you may surely receive from him good directions for the shap-
ing of your farther journey into *Italy,* where he did reside by
my choice some time for the King, after mine own recess from
Venice.

I should think that your best Line will be through the
whole length of *France* to *Marseilles,* and thence by Sea to
Genoa, whence the passage into *Tuscany* is as Diurnal as a
Gravesend Barge: I hasten, as you do, to *Florence* or *Siena,* the
rather to tell you a short story from the interest you have
given me in your safety.

At *Siena* I was tabled in the House of one *Alberto Scipioni,*
an old Roman Courtier in dangerous times, having been
Steward to the *Duca di Pagliano,* who with all his Family
were strangled, save this only man that escap'd by foresight
of the Tempest: With him I had often much chat of those
affairs; Into which he took pleasure to look back from his
Native Harbour; and at my departure toward *Rome* (which
had been the centre of his experience) I had won confidence
enough to beg his advice, how I might carry myself securely
there, without offence of others, or of mine own conscience.
Signor Arrigo mio (says he) "I pensieri stretti, ed il viso
sciolto" will go safely over the whole World: Of which *Delphian* Oracle (for so I have found it) your judgement doth
need no commentary; and therefore (Sir) I will commit you
with it to the best of all securities, God's dear love, remaining
              Your Friend as much at command
                        as any of longer date,
                                  Henry Wotton.

Postscript.

Sir, *I have expressly sent this my Foot-boy to prevent your
departure without some acknowledgement from me of the re-
ceipt of your obliging Letter, having myself through some
business, I know not how, neglected the ordinary conveyance.*

In any part where shall understand you fixed, I shall be glad
and diligent to entertain you with Home-Novelties; even for
some fomentation of our friendship, too soon interrupted in
the Cradle.

THE PERSONS

The attendant Spirit, afterwards in the habit of *Thyrsis*.
Comus with his crew.
The Lady.
First Brother.
Second Brother.
Sabrina, the Nymph.

The chief persons which presented, were
The Lord *Brackley*.
Mr. *Thomas Egerton*, his Brother.
The Lady *Alice Egerton*.

The first Scene discovers a wild Wood.

The attendant Spirit descends or enters.

BEFORE the starry threshold of *Jove's* Court
My mansion is, where those immortal shapes
Of bright aerial Spirits live inspher'd

1–3. *mansion*—home. In contrast to the opening of *Comus* in the
Cambridge manuscript, where the Spirit comes from the "Hesperian
gardens" to which he returns in line 982 below, this may be an
allusion to the many mansions promised by Christ (John xiv, 2) to his
disciples. In the manuscript the Spirit is called a daemon, for Renaissance Neo-Platonists identified good angels with the daemons which
Hesiod said (*Works and Days*, 109–23) were the souls of men of the
Golden Age who are now the unseen guardians of all who deserve the
protection of Zeus. Plato imagined such daemons as at home in the
vague heavens of the myth of Er, to which *Arcades* (63–9) refers, and
which were in Milton's mind when he dreamt of unsphering
       "The spirit of *Plato* to unfold
       What Worlds, or what vast Regions hold
       The immortal mind that hath forsook
       Her mansion in this fleshly nook."
(*Il Penseroso*, 89–92. Compare *P.L.* III, 461–2, and *To Leonora*, 1,
                         note.)

In Regions mild of calm and serene Air,
Above the smoke and stir of this dim spot,   5
Which men call Earth, and with low-thoughted care
Confin'd and pester'd in this pin-fold here,
Strive to keep up a frail and Feverish being,
Unmindful of the crown that Virtue gives
After this mortal change, to her true Servants   10
Amongst the enthron'd gods on Sainted seats.
Yet some there be that by due steps aspire
To lay their just hands on that Golden Key
That opes the Palace of Eternity:
To such my errand is, and but for such,   15
I would not soil these pure Ambrosial weeds
With the rank vapours of this Sin-worn mould.
    But to my task. *Neptune,* besides the sway
Of every salt Flood, and each ebbing Stream,
Took in by lot 'twixt high and nether *Jove,*   20

---

4. Perhaps there is a reminiscence of the home of the gods, where
no storm ever blows and the landscape smiles in perpetual glory, as
Homer describes it in a passage (*Od.* VI, 42–5) which Lucretius paraphrased in *De rerum natura,* III, 18–22. Compare *P.L.* II, 867.

5. Perhaps Milton thought of London, for the line is an echo of
Horace's invitation of Maecenas away from the "smoke and luxury and
noise of Rome." (*Odes,* III, xxix, 12.)

7. *pester'd*—embarrassed, clogged. *pinfold*—pound (for animals).

9. The Wisdom of Solomon (iv, 2) says that virtue "weareth a
crown, . . . having gotten the victory, striving for undefiled rewards."

11. *Sainted seats*—seats of saints, such as those which St. John describes "about the throne" of God; "and upon the seats . . . elders
sitting, clothed in white raiment; and they had on their heads crowns
of gold." (Rev. iv, 4.)

16. *ambrosial*—heavenly. Compare the note on l. 840.
weeds—garments.

17. *mould*—(human) substance. In *P.L.* IV, 360, Satan contrasts
the fallen angels, who are made of heavenly substance, with men,
"Creatures of other mould, earth-born."

18–23. In the *Iliad,* XV, 190–3, when Zeus asserts the right to control him, Poseidon (in Latin, Neptune) retorts that he and Zeus and
Hades (Milton's *nether Jove;* in Latin, Pluto) are brothers among whom
the universe has been divided by equal lots; the hoary sea falling to
him, the wide sky to Zeus, and the murky darkness of the under-
world to Hades.

Imperial rule of all the Sea-girt Isles
That like to rich and various gems inlay
The unadorned bosom of the Deep;
Which he to grace his tributary gods
By course commits to several government,   25
And gives them leave to wear their Sapphire crowns,
And wield their little tridents; but this Isle,
The greatest and the best of all the main,
He quarters to his blue-hair'd deities;
And all this tract that fronts the falling Sun   30
A noble Peer of mickle trust and power
Has in his charge, with temper'd awe to guide
An old and haughty Nation proud in Arms:
Where his fair off-spring nurs't in Princely lore,
Are coming to attend their Father's state,   35
And new-entrusted Sceptre. But their way
Lies through the perplex't paths of this drear Wood,
The nodding horror of whose shady brows

21–23. The thought is like John of Gaunt's description of England as
"This precious stone set in the silver sea."
(*Richard II*, II, i, 46.)

24–29. Milton was familiar with Spenser's grand catalogue of over
two hundred sea and river gods who follow "great Neptune with his
three-forkt mace" (*F.Q.* IV, xi, 11, 1) and among whom Albion and
the English river deities are prominent. Such deities actually figured
in masques like Jonson's *Neptune's Triumph* and Beaumont and
Fletcher's *Masque of the Inner Temple and Gray's Inn*. In the latter
four Naiads appeared "with blueish tresses on their heads." Compare
Elegy IV, 6, note.

29. *quarters to*—divides among.

30–31. *this tract*—Wales and the bordering counties which were
under the "presidency" of the Earl of Bridgewater.
mickle trust—great fidelity.

33. There was a double compliment to the Welsh in this allusion to
them by a phrase which translates Virgil's description of the Roman
(whose descendants the Welsh believed themselves to be) as a natio
"proud in arms." (*Aen.* I, 21.)

35. *state*—official position.

37–39. The wood with its *perplex't* (*i.e.,* tangled) *paths* is symbolic,
like Spenser's wood of error which puzzled Redcross and Una because
it had
"So many pathes, so many turnings seene,
That which of them to take, in diverse doubt they been."
(*F.Q.* I, i, 10, 8–9.)

Threats the forlorn and wand'ring Passenger;
And here their tender age might suffer peril,   40
But that by quick command from Soveran *Jove*
I was dispatcht for their defence, and guard;
And listen why, for I will tell ye now
What never yet was heard in Tale or Song
From old or modern Bard, in Hall or Bow'r.   45
      Bacchus that first from out the purple Grape
Crusht the sweet poison of mis-used Wine,
After the *Tuscan* Mariners transform'd,
Coasting the *Tyrrhene* shore, as the winds listed,
On *Circe's* Island fell.   (Who knows not *Circe*   50
The daughter of the Sun?   Whose charmed Cup
Whoever tasted, lost his upright shape,
And downward fell into a groveling Swine.)
This Nymph that gaz'd upon his clust'ring locks,
With Ivy berries wreath'd, and his blithe youth,   55

---

41. The spelling *Soveran,* a form which Milton preferred, is based on the Italian word *sovrano.*

43. *ye* was frequently used as object of a verb.   Compare *S.A.,* 1453.

44–45. Many romances open with this boast; *e.g., Horned Seyfried* in the Nibelung Cycle:

> "Herein ye find a noble lay
> Of Horny Seyfried's might;
> 'Tis Hildebrand's, and I assay
> No man has heard its like."

Compare *P.L.* I, 16.

45. *Hall*—the great banquet room of a castle.
Bow'r—the ladies' apartment in a castle.
The phrase was a cliché when Chaucer wrote of Chauntecleer's mistress that,

> "Ful sooty was hire bour and eek hir halle."
> (*Canterbury Tales,* 8444.)

46–49. The Homeric Hymn to Bacchus is the ultimate source of the story that the god transformed the ship of some Tuscan (Italian) pirates who kidnapped him into an arbour of vines. Ovid (*Met.* III, 670–686) added that his captors themselves were turned into dolphins.

48. For the construction of this line compare the note on *S.A.* 1294.

50. *Circe's Island,* Aeaea, as Homer called it in the *Odyssey* X, 135, was supposed to lie near the Circean promontory in the Tyrrhenian sea, off the southwest coast of Italy.

50–54. *Circe:* see *Elegy VI,* 73, note.

Had by him, ere he parted thence, a Son
Much like his Father, but his Mother more,
Whom therefore she brought up, and *Comus* nam'd:
Who, ripe and frolic of his full grown age,
Roving the *Celtic* and *Iberian* fields,   60
At last betakes him to this ominous Wood,
And in thick shelter of black shades imbow'r'd,
Excels his Mother at her mighty Art,
Off'ring to every weary Traveller
His orient liquor in a Crystal Glass,   65
To quench the drouth of *Phœbus,* which as they taste
(For most do taste through fond intemperate thirst)
Soon as the Potion works, their human count'nance,
Th' express resemblance of the gods, is chang'd
Into some brutish form of Wolf, or Bear,   70
Or Ounce, or Tiger, Hog, or bearded Goat,
All other parts remaining as they were.
And they, so perfect is their misery,
Not once perceive their foul disfigurement,
But boast themselves more comely than before   75
And all their friends and native home forget
To roll with pleasure in a sensual sty.

---

55. Bacchus' crown of ivy berries (compare *L'Allegro,* 16) was traditional as far back as Pindar (Fragment 75 [45]).

58. *Comus:* see the Introduction, §27–§29.

60. *Celtic*—French. *Iberian*—Spanish.

65. *orient*—bright. In *P.L.* I, 546, Milton mentions the "Orient Colours" of banners. The meaning arose from the fact that eastern or orient pearls were the most brilliant.

66. *the drouth of Phoebus*—the thirst caused by the sun, of which Phoebus Apollo was the god.

67. *fond*—foolish; *i.e.,* not in its nature but in its effect.

69. The idea that "God created man in his own image, in the image of God created he him" (Gen. i, 27), is echoed repeatedly in *P.L.* (IV, 292, 567, etc.)

71. *Ounce*—any member of the lynx family.

72–77. Homer describes Ulysses' men as changed into swine by Circe, who "mixed drugs with their food to make them utterly forget their own country" (*Od.* X, 237–40); but Milton, influenced perhaps by Ariosto's account of Alcina's victims (*O.F.* VI, 61–2), represents Comus's rout as human from the head downward. In Browne's *Inner Temple Masque* Circe appeared followed by "Two with harts'

Therefore when any favour'd of high *Jove*
Chances to pass through this advent'rous glade,
Swift as the Sparkle of a glancing Star,   80
I shoot from Heav'n to give him safe convoy,
As now I do: But first I must put off
These my sky robes spun out of *Iris'* Woof,
And take the Weeds and likeness of a Swain,
That to the service of this house belongs,   85
Who with his soft Pipe and smooth-dittied Song
Well knows to still the wild winds when they roar,
And hush the waving Woods, nor of less faith,
And in this office of his Mountain watch
Likeliest, and nearest to the present aid   90
Of this occasion.   But I hear the tread
Of hateful steps, I must be viewless now.

Comus *enters with a Charming Rod in one hand, his Glass in
the other; with him a rout of Monsters, headed like sundry*

heads and bodies, . . . two like wolves, . . . two like baboons,
[and] Grillus (of whom Plutarch writes . . .) in the shape of a hog."
Plutarch's dialogue, *Whether the Beasts Enjoy the Use of Wisdom,*
which influenced Machiavelli's *Golden Ass* and the once famous *Circe*
of Giambattista Gelli, treats Circe's beasts as pleased with their condition rather than pathetically human and unhappy, as they seem in
the *Odyssey.*

80–82. Milton used the figure in *P.L.* IV, 555–7, to describe the
descent of the angel
        "*Uriel,* gliding through the Even
        On a Sun-beam, swift as a shooting Star
        In *Autumn* thwarts the night."

83. In *P.L.* XI, 244, to suggest the glorious colours worn by the
angel Michael, Milton said that the rainbow goddess, Iris, "had
dipt the woof."

86–88. Again in 494–6 Milton paid a compliment to Henry Lawes.
The implied comparison of him here to Orpheus is no more extravagant than Herrick's question in the epigram *To Mr. Henry Lawes,* "tell
me, canst thou be Less than Apollo?"

87. *knows to*—understands how to. Compare another instance of
this Latinism in *Lycidas,* 10–11.

88. *nor of less faith*—no less trustworthy, *i.e.,* than he is admired as
a musician.

90. *Likeliest*—best fitted. N.E.D. cites the Acts of Philip and Mary;
"Suche as were most able and lykelyest to serve well."

92. *viewless*—invisible. Compare *The Passion,* 50.

sorts of wild Beasts, but otherwise like Men and Women, their
Apparel glistering. They come in making a riotous and un-
ruly noise, with Torches in their hands.

Comus. The Star that bids the Shepherd fold,
Now the top of Heav'n doth hold,
And the gilded Car of Day   95
His glowing Axle doth allay
In the steep *Atlantic* stream,
And the slope Sun his upward beam
Shoots against the dusky Pole,
Pacing toward the other goal   100
Of his Chamber in the East.
Meanwhile welcome Joy, and Feast,
Midnight shout and revelry,
Tipsy dance and Jollity.
Braid your Locks with rosy Twine   105
Dropping odours, dropping Wine.
Rigour now is gone to bed,
And Advice with scrupulous head,

93–94. So Spenser thought of Venus or Hesperus as "the folding
star" because when it "rises" the shepherd,
        "Gathering his straying flocke, does homeward fare;"
                    (*Virgils Gnat,* 319.)
and he suggested that a certain night was dark and late because
            "Now the golden *Hesperus*
      Was mounted high in top of heauen sheene."
                    (*F.Q.* III, iv, 51, 6–7.)

95–101. The Greek conception of the sun as "sitting exalted in a
golden chariot and dividing his path through the starry heavens" (as
Euripides described it, *Phoenician Damsels,* 1–2), and as cooling its
glowing wheels in the western ocean at evening, reached Milton through
many channels—among them St. Jerome's commentary on Ecclesiastes
i, 5: "The sun also ariseth, and the sun goeth down, and hasteth to
his place where he arose."

102–105. The comic effect in this antimasque in contrast with that in
Browne's *Inner Temple Masque,* is lost in pure poetry which owes much
to familiar Horatian odes, such as Horace's invitation to Maecenas to
come and enjoy the chaplets of flowers and the perfumes for his hair
that await him at the Sabine farm. (*Odes,* III, xxix, 1–5.)

107–109. Compare the abstractions in *Nativity Hymn,* 136, 141 and
144 and in *L'Allegro,* 26–32. Such personifications were a part of the
tradition of the Morality plays and of the Court masque and they

Strict Age, and sour Severity,
With their grave Saws in slumber lie.   110
We that are of purer fire
Imitate the Starry Quire,
Who in their nightly watchful Spheres,
Lead in swift round the Months and Years.
The Sounds and Seas with all their finny drove   115
Now to the Moon in wavering Morrice move,
And on the Tawny Sands and Shelves
Trip the pert Fairies and the dapper Elves;
By dimpled Brook, and Fountain brim,
The Wood-Nymphs deckt with Daisies trim,   120
Their merry wakes and pastimes keep:
What hath night to do with sleep?
Night hath better sweets to prove,
Venus now wakes, and wak'ns Love.
Come let us our rites begin,   125
'Tis only day-light that makes Sin,
Which these dun shades will ne'er report.

---

were at home even in pastoral poetry like Browne's *Britannia's Pastorals,*
where (I, v) figures like Riot and Remembrance play vague parts.

110. *Saws*—sayings, maxims. Compare Jaques' justice,
     "Full of wise saws and modern instances."
                    (*As You Like It,* II, vii, 156.)

111. The Attendant Spirit has referred (l. 17) to the earthy "mould"
of which men are made. The hierarchy of spirits, as an interesting
passage in *P.L.* II, 139–142, suggests, was regarded as being made of
fire of various degrees of refinement.

113. Compare the "Spheres of watchful fire" in *Vacation Exercise,* 40,
and the references to the music and dances of the spheres in *Nativity
Ode,* 117–132, and *P.L.* V, 178 and 620–7.

114. There is an allusion to the creation of the "lights in the firmament" in Genesis i, 14, which were to "be for signs, and for seasons,
and for days, and years."

116. *Morrice*—any grotesque dance by people in fancy dress. *N.E.D.*
cites John Fryer's *New Account of East India and Persia,* 23; "A Chorus
of Porpoises had taken the sea in their Dance; which Morris once over,
the Seas were quiet."

118. *pert*—brisk, sprightly. Compare *Midsummer Night's Dream,* I,
i, 13; "Awake the pert and nimble spirit of mirth."

121. Originally a wake was a religious festival lasting through the
night.

Hail Goddess of Nocturnal sport,
Dark veil'd *Cotytto,* t' whom the secret flame
Of mid-night Torches burns; mysterious Dame   130
That ne'er art call'd, but when the Dragon womb
Of Stygian darkness spets her thickest gloom,
And makes one blot of all the air,
Stay thy cloudy Ebon chair,
Wherein thou rid'st with *Hecat',* and befriend   135
Us thy vow'd Priests, till utmost end
Of all thy dues be done, and none left out,
Ere the blabbing Eastern scout,
The nice Morn on th' *Indian* steep,
From her cabin'd loop-hole peep,   140
And to the tell-tale Sun descry
Our conceal'd Solemnity.
Come, knit hands, and beat the ground,
In a light fantastic round.

128–130. In his condemnation of Rome as more skilful in oriental
vices than the East itself Juvenal (*Satire* ii, 91–2) attacked the orgies
of the Thracian goddess, Cotytto. Her obscene rites at midnight were
burlesqued by Horace. (*Epode* xvi, 56–7.) Perhaps Milton alludes to
Horace in 535.

131. Perhaps in *Dragon womb* there is an allusion like that in the
prayer of Iachimo to the "dragons of the night" (*Cymbeline,* II, ii, 48)
to cover him with darkness. Dragons seem to have composed "triple
Hecate's team" (*Midsummer Night's Dream,* V, 373). For Hecate's
three-fold nature as the Moon or Cynthia, Diana or Artemis, and
Proserpina, who was uncertainly identified with Hecate, see *On the
death of the Bishop of Ely,* 57 and 58, notes.

132. *Stygian darkness*—darkness like that around the Styx, the river
of hell.

spets—spits. The form was obsolescent when Milton wrote.

134. *ebon*—black like ebony.

135. *Hecate* was familiar to Milton in many classical invocations like
the terrible appeals to her which Ovid put into Medea's mouth (*Met.*
VII, 94, 194), and he knew her also as the "Mistress" of the witches
and the "close contriver of all harms" in *Macbeth,* III, v, 10.

140. "Peep" was constantly used in this sense. *N.E.D.* cites Good-
wyne's *Blanchardyn,* ii, I ij; "When the day began to peepe, they
tooke their horses and rode to Tormaday."

142. *Solemnity;* compare *Arcades,* 39, note.

144. Compare the "fantastic toe" of *L'Allegro,* 34, and the shep-

The Measure.

Break off, break off, I feel the different pace,   145
Of some chaste footing near about this ground.
Run to your shrouds, within these Brakes and Trees;
Our number may affright: Some Virgin sure
(For so I can distinguish by mine Art)
Benighted in these Woods. Now to my charms,   150
And to my wily trains; I shall ere long
Be well stock't with as fair a herd as graz'd
About my Mother *Circe*. Thus I hurl
My dazzling Spells into the spongy air,
Of power to cheat the eye with blear illusion,   155
And give it false presentments, lest the place
And my quaint habits breed astonishment,
And put the Damsel to suspicious flight,
Which must not be, for that's against my course.
I under fair pretence of friendly ends,   160
And well plac't words of glozing courtesy,
Baited with reasons not unplausible,
Wind me into the easy-hearted man,

----

herds' song in *The Faithful Shepherdess*, I, ii, 32–5:
> "And arm in arm
> Tread we softly in a round,
>   Whilst the hollow neighbouring ground
>   Fills the music with her sound."

The Measure which was actually danced, as the name implied, was probably rather formal.

147. "Shroud" is used similarly in *Nativity Ode*, 218. Compare the verb in l. 316, below.

151. *trains;* compare "venereal trains" (*i.e.,* lures) in *S.A.* 533.

154. In the Cambridge MS "powder'd" in the place of *dazzling* suggests that something bright like confetti may have been thrown. *spongy*—absorbing.

155. *blear*—misty, confusing.

156. *false presentments*—misleading representations, illusions.

157. *quaint habits*—strange dress. Compare "quaint" in *Nativity Ode*, 194, and *S.A.* 1303.

160. *ends*—objects, purposes.

161. *glozing*—insinuating, flattering.

163. *Wind me*—insinuate myself—Compare *Coriolanus*, III, iii, 64; "To winde Yourselfe into a power tyranicall."

And hug him into snares. When once her eye
Hath met the virtue of this Magic dust,   165
I shall appear some harmless Villager
Whom thrift keeps up about his Country gear;
But here she comes, I fairly step aside,
And hearken, if I may her business hear.

The Lady enters.

    Lady. This way the noise was, if mine ear be true, 170
My best guide now; methought it was the sound
Of Riot and ill manag'd Merriment,
Such as the jocund Flute or gamesome Pipe
Stirs up among the loose unletter'd Hinds,
When for their teeming Flocks and granges full   175
In wanton dance they praise the bounteous *Pan,*
And thank the gods amiss. I should be loath
To meet the rudeness and swill'd insolence
Of such late Wassailers; yet O where else
Shall I inform my unacquainted feet   180
In the blind mazes of this tangl'd Wood?
My Brothers, when they saw me wearied out

---

165. *virtue*—power.

167. *gear*—tasks, occupations. Properly the word means a kit of tools for any purpose or equipment of any kind.

168. *fairly*—gently, quietly.

174. *Hinds*—farm-servants, field labourers.

175. *teeming*—multiplying, bearing young.
granges—barns.

176. Compare the note on Pan in *Arcades,* 106. "Pan, the shep-heards god" (*Calendar,* April, 5), as Spenser often called him, commonly represented the Christian God in pastoral poetry rather than the classical nature deity whom it would be natural for the peasants to worship with revelry.

178. *swill'd*—glutted with drink, *N.E.D.* cites Elyot's *Appotus;* "welle . . . swilled with drynke, almost drunke."

179. *Wassailers*—drinkers of wassail, a traditional old English spiced ale. Compare Herrick's *The Country Life:*
> "Thy wakes, thy quintals, here thou hast,
> Thy Maypoles too with garlands graced,
> Thy morris-dance, thy Whitsun-ale,
> Thy shearing feast, which never fail,
> Thy harvest home, thy wassail bowl."

180. *inform*—guide, teach. Compare *S.A.* 335.

With this long way, resolving here to lodge
Under the spreading favour of these Pines,
Stept as they said to the next Thicket side   185
To bring me Berries, or such cooling fruit
As the kind hospitable Woods provide.
They left me then, when the gray-hooded Ev'n
Like a sad Votarist in Palmer's weed
Rose from the hindmost wheels of *Phœbus'* wain.   190
But where they are, and why they came not back,
Is now the labour of my thoughts; 'tis likeliest
They had engag'd their wand'ring steps too far,
And envious darkness, ere they could return,
Had stole them from me; else O thievish Night   195
Why shouldst thou, but for some felonious end,
In thy dark lantern thus close up the Stars,
That nature hung in Heav'n, and fill'd their Lamps
With everlasting oil, to give due light
To the misled and lonely Traveller?   200
This is the place, as well as I may guess,
Whence ev'n now the tumult of loud Mirth
Was rife and perfet in my list'ning ear,
Yet nought but single darkness do I find.
What might this be?   A thousand fantasies   205

---

189. *sad Votarist*—solemn pilgrim. A votarist was a religious person
under any kind of vow, but a palmer was a pilgrim who carried a bit
of palm as evidence that he had been to the Holy Land. Compare
the morning "with Pilgrim steps in amice grey." (*P.R.* IV, 427.)

198–199. The figure was very familiar. Compare Fairfax's Tasso IX,
10, 5; "when Heav'ns small Candles next shall shine." And Banquo's
"There's Husbandry in Heaven, Their Candles are all out." (*Macbeth*,
II, i, 10–11.)

203. *perfet*—perfectly distinct.

204. *single*—absolute, total.

205–209. Fletcher refers to similar popular superstitions when he
makes Clorin say:
        "No goblin, wood-god, fairy, elf, or fiend,
         Satyr, or other power that haunts these groves,
         Shall hurt my body, or by vain illusion
         Draw me to wander after idle fires;
         Or voices calling me in dead of night,
         To make me follow, and so tole me on,
         Through mire and standing pools, to find my ruin."
(*The Faithful Shepherdess*, I, i, 114–20. Compare *P.L.* I, 781–7.)

Begin to throng into my memory
Of calling shapes, and beck'ning shadows dire,
And airy tongues, that syllable men's names
On Sands and Shores and desert Wildernesses.
These thoughts may startle well, but not astound   210
The virtuous mind, that ever walks attended
By a strong siding champion Conscience.——
O welcome pure-ey'd Faith, white-handed Hope,
Thou hov'ring Angel girt with golden wings,
And thou unblemish't form of Chastity,   215
I see ye visibly, and now believe
That he, the Súpreme good, t' whom all things ill
Are but as slavish officers of vengeance,
Would send a glist'ring Guardian, if need were,
To keep my life and honour unassail'd.   220
Was I deceiv'd, or did a sable cloud
Turn forth her silver lining on the night?
I did not err, there does a sable cloud
Turn forth her silver lining on the night,
And casts a gleam over this tufted Grove.   225
I cannot hallow to my Brothers, but
Such noise as I can make to be heard farthest
I'll venture, for my new enliv'n'd spirits
Prompt me; and they perhaps are not far off.

212–220. There is a suggestion of the Christian virtues of Faith and
Hope as they appeared in allegorical paintings and in masques, but
Milton put Chastity in the place of the third Theological Virtue of
Charity or Love because he thought of that virtue in Platonic terms, as
the love of the Supreme Good which chastens all inferior passions. It
is almost visible to the Lady because he thought, like Bacon (*Advancement,* II, xviii, 3), " 'that virtue, if she could be seen, would move
great love and affection'; so seeing that she cannot be showed to the
sense by corporal shape, the next degree is to show her to the
imagination in lively representation."

221–223. See *Elegy V,* 5, note.

SONG

Sweet Echo, sweetest Nymph that liv'st unseen   230
        Within thy airy shell
    By slow Meander's margent green,
And in the violet embroider'd vale
    Where the love-lorn Nightingale
Nightly to thee her sad Song mourneth well.   235
Canst thou not tell me of a gentle Pair
        That likest thy Narcissus are?
         O if thou have
      Hid them in some flow'ry Cave,
      Tell me but where   240
  Sweet Queen of Parley, Daughter of the Sphere,
So mayst thou be translated to the skies,
And give resounding grace to all Heav'n's Harmonies.

    Comus. Can any mortal mixture of Earth's mould
Breathe such Divine enchanting ravishment?   245
Sure somthing holy lodges in that breast,
And with these raptures moves the vocal air
To testify his hidd'n residence;
How sweetly did they float upon the wings
Of silence, through the empty-vaulted night,   250
At every fall smoothing the Raven down
Of darkness till it smil'd: I have oft heard

230–243. Songs in which Echo answered, as in Jonson's *Masque of Queens* and Browne's *Inner Temple Masque,* were common; but this lyric springs out of memories of myths like that which made Echo a mountain nymph in love with Narcissus (*Met.* III, 351–401) and of glimpses of her in the Greek Anthology (*Anth. Pal.* 9, 825) as a water nymph. Her haunts were everywhere, from the river Meander in Phrygia to the valleys of the nightingales below Pindar's "violet-crowned Athens." (Frag. 75 [45].) She is the *Daughter of the Sphere* perhaps because—as Thomas Warton suggested—her *airy shell* is the overarching sky.

244–8. The thought is explained by *To Leonora Singing,* where Milton suggested that the voice was that of an angel in the singer's breast or of God himself mysteriously speaking through her.

250–251. Compare the imagery in *L'Allegro,* 6–7.

My mother *Circe* with the Sirens three,
Amid'st the flow'ry-kirtl'd *Naiades,*
Culling their Potent herbs and baleful drugs,   255
Who as they sung, would take the prison'd soul,
And lap it in *Elysium; Scylla* wept,
And chid her barking waves into attention,
And fell *Charybdis* murmur'd soft applause:
Yet they in pleasing slumber lull'd the sense,   260
And in sweet madness robb'd it of itself,
But such a sacred and home-felt delight,
Such sober certainty of waking bliss,
I never heard till now. I'll speak to her
And she shall be my Queen. Hail foreign wonder, 265
Whom certain these rough shades did never breed,
Unless the Goddess that in rural shrine
Dwell'st here with *Pan,* or *Silvan,* by blest Song
Forbidding every bleak unkindly Fog
To touch the prosperous growth of this tall Wood.   270
     Lady. Nay gentle Shepherd, ill is lost that praise
That is addrest to unattending Ears;
Not any boast of skill, but extreme shift
How to regain my sever'd company
Compell'd me to awake the courteous Echo   275
To give me answer from her mossy Couch.

253–259. Influenced, perhaps, by the *Inner Temple Masque* and re-
membering Ovid's picture of Circe gathering flowers with the Nereids
(*Met.* XIV, 264–270), Milton brought the water nymphs, the Naiades,
together here with Circe and the Sirens, whose songs lured seamen to
death. (*Od.* XII, 39–46, and 166–200.) The Sirens' rocks were near
the Sicilian straits where the whirlpool, Charybdis, confronts the surf-
beaten rocks into which Circe was fabled to have transformed the
nymph, Scylla. (*Met.* XIV, 8–74.) Her "barking waves" go back to
Homer. (*Od.* XII, 85.)

265–267. Warton traced this bit of "classical gallantry" to the
Odyssey (VI, 149) where Ulysses greets Nausicaa as lady or goddess.
Pastoral drama has countless parallels, *e.g.,* Ferdinand's greeting to
Miranda:

> "Most sure, the goddess
> On whom these airs attend!"
> (*Tempest,* I, ii, 420–421.)

268. Here Pan is simply a wood-god, like Sylvanus, with whom
Virgil linked him. (*Eclogues,* X, 24–26.)

273. *boast of skill*—wish to display skill.

Comus. What chance, good Lady, hath bereft you thus?
Lady. Dim darkness and this leavy Labyrinth.
Comus. Could that divide you from near-ushering guides?
Lady. They left me weary on a grassy turf.   280
Comus. By falsehood, or discourtesy, or why?
Lady. To seek i'th' valley some cool friendly Spring.
Comus. And left your fair side all unguarded, Lady?
Lady. They were but twain, and purpos'd quick return.
Comus. Perhaps fore-stalling night prevented them.   285
Lady. How easy my misfortune is to hit!
Comus. Imports their loss, beside the present need?
Lady. No less than if I should my brothers lose.
Comus. Were they of manly prime, or youthful bloom?
. .*Lady.* As smooth as *Hebe*'s their unrazor'd lips.   290
  Comus. Two such I saw, what time the labour'd Ox
In his loose traces from the furrow came,
And the swink't hedger at his Supper sat;
I saw them under a green mantling vine
That crawls along the side of yon small hill,   295
Plucking ripe clusters from the tender shoots;
Their port was more than human, as they stood;
I took it for a faëry vision
Of some gay creatures of the element

277–290. Milton was experimenting with the device of alternate
lines of question and answer, known as stichomythia in Greek tragedy,
which often gave curious excitement to encounters between strangers,
as it does in many of the scenes in Sophocles' *Oedipus at Colonus.*

289. In *P.L.* XI, 245–6, Michael is described as "prime In Manhood
where Youth ended."

290. The epithet *unrazor'd* seems like a reminiscence of Virgil's
contrast of the beardless Euryalus with his older friend, Nisus. (*Aen.*
IX, 181.)

291–292. Virgil made the unyoking of oxen a warning of approaching sunset (*Eclogues,* II, 66–7) and in Homer's language (*Il.* XVI, 779)
the "unyoking of oxen" meant evening.

293. *swink't*—hard-worked, tired.

297. *port*—bearing, deportment. Todd compared the situation with
that in Euripides' *Iphigeneia in Tauris* (260–273), when a herdman tells
Iphigeneia that at his first view of her ship-wrecked brother, Orestes,
and Pylades he took them for gods.

299. *element*—the air. For the belief about the spirit-inhabitants of
the air compare *P.R.* II, 122–4, note, and *Il Penseroso,* 93–6.

That in the colours of the Rainbow live   300
And play i'th' plighted clouds.   I was awe-strook,
And as I past, I worship; if those you seek
It were a journey like the path to Heav'n,
To help you find them.
    Lady.   Gentle villager,
What readiest way would bring me to that place?   305
    Comus. Due west it rises from this shrubby point.
    Lady. To find out that, good Shepherd, I suppose,
In such a scant allowance of Star-light,
Would overtask the best Land-Pilot's art,
Without the sure guess of well-practis'd feet.   310
    Comus. I know each lane and every alley green,
Dingle or bushy dell of this wild Wood,
And every bosky bourn from side to side,
My daily walks and ancient neighbourhood,
And if your stray attendance be yet lodg'd,   315
Or shroud within these limits, I shall know
Ere morrow wake, or the low-roosted lark
From her thatch't pallet rouse; if otherwise,
I can conduct you, Lady, to a low
But loyal cottage, where you may be safe   320
Till further quest.
    Lady.   Shepherd, I take thy word,
And trust thy honest offer'd courtesy,

---

  301. *plighted*—interwoven or folded.

  312. *Dingle*—a cleft between hills.

  313. *bosky bourn*—a stream overhung by shrubbery. *Bosk* is a dialectal variant of *bush*.

  316. *shroud*—take shelter.   Compare the noun in 147.

  317. *morrow*—morning.

  318. *thatch't pallet*—bed or nest of straw.

  322–326. Milton is less confident than Spenser that,
        "Of Court, it seemes, men Courtesie doe call,
         For that it there most useth to abound."
                (*F.Q.* VI, I, i, 1–2.)
Perhaps he remembered that in the *Orlando Furioso* (XIV, 62) Mandricardo and Doralice were glad to discover that
         "courtesie oftimes in simple bowres
      Is found as great as in the stately towres."
         (Harington's translation.)
The commonplace goes back to Aeschylus' *Agamemnon*, 772–3.

Which oft is sooner found in lowly sheds
With smoky rafters, than in tap'stry Halls
And Courts of Princes, where it first was nam'd,   325
And yet is most pretended: In a place
Less warranted than this, or less secure
I cannot be, that I should fear to change it.
Eye me blest Providence, and square my trial
To my proportion'd strength.   Shepherd lead on.—   330

The Two Brothers.

Elder Brother. Unmuffle ye faint stars, and thou fair Moon
That wont'st to love the traveller's benison,
Stoop thy pale visage through an amber cloud,
And disinherit *Chaos,* that reigns here
In double night of darkness and of shades;   335
Or if your influence be quite damm'd up
With black usurping mists, some gentle taper,
Though a rush Candle from the wicker hole
Of some clay habitation, visit us
With thy long levell'd rule of streaming light,   340
And thou shalt be our star of *Arcady,*
Or *Tyrian* Cynosure.

---

324. *tap'stry Halls*—halls hung with tapestries.

327. *warranted*—protected, secure.

331. *Unmuffle:* compare Romeo's speech; "Muffle me, night, awhile."
(*Romeo and Juliet,* V, iii, 21.)

332. *wont'st*—art accustomed.   Compare *S.A.* 1487, note.

benison—blessing.   So Spenser said of the moon shining unexpectedly through the clouds—
                "Of the poore traueller, that went astray,
                  With thousand blessings she is heried."
                              (*F.Q.,* III, i, 43, 5–6.)

333. Compare *Il Penseroso,* 71–2.

334. *disinherit*—dispossess.   Milton thought of the traditional association of "Night And Chaos, Ancestors of Nature."   (*P.L.* II, 894–5.)

335. Compare the thought of night and the forest double-shading the
desert in *P.R.* I, 500.

336. Compare the "precious influence" of the stars in *Nativity Ode,*
71.

341–342. *Tyrian Cynosure*—the pole star by which the Phoenician
sailors steered.   Milton remembered Ovid's story (*Met.* II, 401–507) of

Second Brother. Or if our eyes
Be barr'd that happiness, might we but hear
The folded flocks penn'd in their wattled cotes,
Or sound of pastoral reed with oaten stops,   345
Or whistle from the Lodge, or village cock
Count the night watches to his feathery Dames,
'Twould be some solace yet, some little cheering
In this close dungeon of innumerous boughs.
But O that hapless virgin, our lost sister,   350
Where may she wander now, whither betake her
From the chill dew, amongst rude burrs and thistles?
Perhaps some cold bank is her bolster now
Or 'gainst the rugged bark of some broad Elm
Leans her unpillow'd head fraught with sad fears.   355
What if in wild amazement and affright,
Or while we speak, within the direful grasp
Of Savage hunger, or of Savage heat?
    Elder Brother. Peace brother, be not over-exquisite
To cast the fashion of uncertain evils;   360
For grant they be so, while they rest unknown,
What need a man forestall his date of grief,
And run to meet what he would most avoid?
Or if they be but false alarms of Fear,

---

the Arcadian princess, Callisto, whose fate it was, after bearing a son,
Arcas, to Jove, to be set in the heavens as the Great Bear, while Arcas
became the Little Bear, the tip of whose tail is the North Star.

    344. *wattled cotes*—sheepfolds made of upright stakes with twigs
twisted over them. Both words were popular, yet the phrase was
poetical, like the "hurdl'd Cotes" of *P.L.* IV, 186.

    345. The traditional shepherd's instrument in English pastoral poetry
was the "oaten pype" of Colin Clout in Spenser's *Shepheardes Calendar,*
72.

    349. *innumerous*—innumerable.

    355. *fraught*—freighted, filled.

    359. *exquisite*—curious, anxious.

    360. *cast the fashion*—forecast or anticipate the nature. *N.E.D.* cites
E. F.'s *History of Edward II,* 126, "With a world of melancholy
thought, he casts the danger."

    361. *grant they be so*—even if it be granted that they are as you
imagine them.

    362. *forestall*—anticipate.

How bitter is such self-delusion?   365
I do not think my sister so to seek,
Or so unprincipl'd in virtue's book,
And the sweet peace that goodness bosoms ever,
As that the single want of light and noise
(Not being in danger, as I trust she is not)   370
Could stir the constant mood of her calm thoughts,
And put them into mis-becoming plight.
Virtue could see to do what virtue would
By her own radiant light, though Sun and Moon
Were in the flat Sea sunk.   And Wisdom's self   375
Oft seeks to sweet retired Solitude,
Where with her best nurse Contemplation
She plumes her feathers, and lets grow her wings
That in the various bustle of resort
Were all to-ruffl'd, and somtimes impair'd.   380
He that has light within his own clear breast
May sit i'th' centre, and enjoy bright day,

---

365. Pronounce *delusi-ön*. This was the usual pronunciation of the ending and it is illustrated in *Contemplation* in l. 377 and *condition* in l. 685.

366. *to seek*—at a loss. *N.E.D.* cites Lassels' *Voyage to Italy*, II (1670), 317, "Lest they should grow idle and have their strength to seek when the war should break out."

367. *unprincipl'd*—untaught in the principles.

368. *bosoms*—keeps in its breast. Compare Norfolk's advice to Buckingham; "Bosom up my counsel." (*Henry VIII*, I, i, 112.)

369. *single*—mere.

373–375. Compare the Redcross Knight's maxim to encourage Una in the wood of error:
    "Vertue giues her selfe light, through darkenesse for to wade."
                    (*F.Q.* I, i, 12, 9.)

375. *the flat Sea;* compare "the level brine" of *Lycidas*, 98.

376. *seeks to*—resorts to.

377. Compare *Contemplation* in *Il Penseroso*, 54, and the notes on lines 212–220 and 365 above.

379. *resort*—assembly, meeting of people.

380. *to-ruffl'd*—ruffled up, bedraggled.

381. So Milton prayed the "Celestial light" to "shine inward" in *P.L.* III, 51–2, and made Samson deplore the loss of "inward light." (*S.A.*, 162.)

382. *centre*—the earth, the depths of the soil which Milton says are "ransack'd" for metals. (*P.L.* I, 686.)

But he that hides a dark soul and foul thoughts
Benighted walks under the mid-day Sun;
Himself is his own dungeon.
    Second Brother.   'Tis most true   385
That musing meditation most affects
The Pensive secrecy of desert cell,
Far from the cheerful haunt of men and herds,
And sits as safe as in a Senate house;
For who would rob a Hermit of his Weeds,   390
His few Books, or his Beads, or Maple Dish,
Or do his gray hairs any violence?
But beauty, like the fair Hesperian Tree
Laden with blooming gold, had need the guard
Of dragon watch with unenchanted eye,   395
To save her blossoms, and defend her fruit
From the rash hand of bold Incontinence.
You may as well spread out the unsunn'd heaps
Of Miser's treasure by an out-law's den,
And tell me it is safe, as bid me hope   400
Danger will wink on Opportunity,

---

385. The thought was a great commonplace, embodied again in Milton's picture of Satan as unable to escape from the "Hell within him" (*P.L.* IV, 20) and in the Chorus's reproach to Samson:
> "Thou art become (O worst imprisonment!)
> The Dungeon of thyself."
>   (*S.A.* 155–6.)

386. *affects,* loves, feels an affection for.

391. The *Beads* of the rosary were a part of the traditional picture of the hermit,
> "Silly old man, that liues in hidden cell,
> Bidding his beades all day for his trespas."
>   (*F.Q.* I, i, 30, 6–7.)

393–395. In lines 981–3 below Milton returns to the Golden Tree in the Gardens of the Hesperides which was watched by a dragon so terrible that only Hercules could conquer it.
unenchanted—unenchantable. This use of the perfect participle is a Greek and Latin practice. Compare "unblemished" in l. 215.

398. *unsunn'd*—unseen by the sun, hidden.

401. Ulysses uses *Opportunity* with great effect in this sense when he jeers at women of Cressida's kind as
> "sluttish spoils of opportunity
> And daughters of the game."
>   (*Troilus and Cressida,* IV, v, 62–3.)

And let a single helpless maiden pass
Uninjured in this wild surrounding waste.
Of night, or loneliness it recks me not,
I fear the dread events that dog them both,   405
Lest some ill-greeting touch attempt the person
Of our unowned sister.
   Elder Brother.   I do not, brother,
Infer as if I thought my sister's state
Secure without all doubt or controversy:
Yet where an equal poise of hope and fear   410
Does arbitrate th'event, my nature is
That I incline to hope, rather than fear,
And gladly banish squint suspicion.
My sister is not so defenceless left
As you imagine, she has a hidden strength   415
Which you remember not.
   Second Brother.   What hidden strength,
Unless the strength of Heav'n, if you mean that?
   Elder Brother. I mean that too, but yet a hidden strength
Which if Heav'n gave it, may be term'd her own:
'Tis chastity, my brother, chastity: 420
She that has that, is clad in complete steel,
And like a quiver'd Nymph with Arrows keen

---

404. *it recks me not*—it makes no difference to me whether. Compare *Lycidas,* 122 for another impersonal use of the verb and *P.L.* II, 50, for the more usual, personal use; "of God, or Hell, or worse He reck'd not."

407. *unowned*—unaccompanied, unprotected.

408. *Infer*—mean, intend to speak as if, *etc.*

409. *without all*—beyond any.

411. *arbitrate th'event*—determine the outcome.

413. The adjective *squint* commonly meant "suspicious" or "envious," as it does in Spenser's *Shepheardes Calendar,* August, 129:
      "Herdgrome, I fear me thou have a squint eye."

421. Perhaps Milton thought of the steel-clad championess of chastity, Britomart, in *The Faerie Queene;* but his conception, as Todd suggested, may owe something to passages in the Fathers of the Church such as St. Ambrose's account of virginity as walled about with a rampart and guarded by a fence of divine protection. (*D. Ambrosii Opera,* Paris, 1586, Vol. III, p. 1046.)

422. *a quiver'd Nymph*—a nymph whose quiver of arrows marked her as a follower of "the huntress Dian" (l. 441), all whose attendants

May trace huge Forests and unharbour'd Heaths,
Infamous Hills and sandy perilous wilds,
Where through the sacred rays of Chastity, 425
No savage fierce, Bandit, or mountaineer
Will dare to soil her Virgin purity:
Yea there, where very desolation dwells,
By grots and caverns shagg'd with horrid shades,
She may pass on with unblench't majesty, 430
Be it not done in pride or in presumption.
Some say no evil thing that walks by night
In fog or fire, by lake or moorish fen,
Blue meagre Hag, or stubborn unlaid ghost,
That breaks his magic chains at *curfew* time, 435
No goblin or swart Faëry of the mine,

were bound to chastity. Editors compare Phineas Fletcher's embodiment of virgin chastity, the

> "warlike maid,
> Parthenia, all in steel and gilded arms."
> (*The Purple Island*, X, 27, 1–2.)

423. *trace*—travel through. Compare *P.R.* II, 109.
unharbour'd—lacking harbours, offering no shelter.

424. *Infamous* has the Latin meaning of "ill-famed."

426. *mountaineer* had lawless and monstrous connotations. Gonzalo in *The Tempest* (III, iii, 45–7) remembered stories that
> "there were mountaineers
> Dew-lapp'd like bulls, whose throats had hanging at 'em
> Wallets of flesh."

428. *very*—absolute. Compare *P.R.* IV, 12.

429. *horrid* keeps the Latin meaning of "bristling" or "rough" as applied to undergrowth. Compare *P.R.* I, 296, and *P.L.* IX, 185: "in horrid Shade or dismal Den."

430. *unblench'd*—undismayed. *N.E.D.* cites Fletcher's *False One*, IV, iv; "Art thou so poor to blench at what thou has done?"

433. *fire: i.e.,* the will-o'-the-wisp, Jack-o'-lantern or fatuous fire. Compare 205–9, note.

434. A hag was any "evil spirit . . . in female form." (*N.E.D.*) Macbeth's "black and midnight hags" were identified by Burton (*Anatomy*, I, ii, i, 2) with water-devils, and Milton may have thought of his *meagre Hag* as a bluish fog-form. Or perhaps he had in mind the "flame of fyre that shyneth by night" which Palgrave said was popularly called a "Hagge." (*L'esclarcissement de la langue Francoyse*, 228–32, quoted by *N.E.D.*) Ghosts could walk only after curfew.

436. Compare the daemons of underground in *Il Penseroso*, 93–4. A wide-spread folk-belief imagined some earth-spirits as living in mines

Hath hurtful power o'er true virginity.
Do ye believe me yet, or shall I call
Antiquity from the old Schools of *Greece*
To testify the arms of Chastity?   440
Hence had the huntress *Dian* her dread bow,
Fair silver-shafted Queen for ever chaste,
Wherewith she tam'd the brinded lioness
And spotted mountain pard, but set at nought
The frivolous bolt of *Cupid;* gods and men   445
Fear'd her stern frown, and she was queen o' th' Woods.
What was that snaky-headed *Gorgon* shield
That wise *Minerva* wore, unconquer'd Virgin,
Wherewith she freez'd her foes to congeal'd stone
But rigid looks of Chaste austerity,   450
And noble grace that dash't brute violence
With sudden adoration, and blank awe?
So dear to Heav'n is Saintly chastity,
That when a soul is found sincerely so,
A thousand liveried Angels lackey her,   455
Driving far off each thing of sin and guilt,
And in clear dream and solemn vision

---

and stained from smelting ore, like the fiends which Guyon saw at their
furnaces in Mammon's delve,

> "Deformed creatures, horrible in sight."
> (*F.Q.* II, vii, 35, 7.)

441–446. Milton's allegory was then very familiar, for Conti's chapter
on Diana (*Mythologiae*, III, xviii) explains that the myths of the
huntress-virgin are symbols of the value of field-sports in taming and
"sublimating" passion.

444. *pard*, panther or mountain "lion."

447–452. The traditional figure of Minerva, carrying the Gorgon's
head as she is described in the *Iliad* V, 738–41, is explained by Conti
(*Mythologiae*, IV, v) as symbolizing the dread which she strikes into
her lustful enemies, "not one of whom dare arise when she wears the
frightful Gorgon's head with its serpent-hair on her breast."

449. *freez'd*—froze. There was much uncertainty in the use of
regular *vs.* irregular preterite forms of many verbs.

452. *blank*—helpless. Compare the verb in *S.A.* 471.

455. The picture is that of a nobleman followed by his retainers
dressed in the gorgeous uniforms or liveries which were once common
sights in London.

457. Bacon quoted from "the Hebrew rabbins—'Your young men
shall see visions, and your old men shall dream dreams'" to prove

Tell her of things that no gross ear can hear,
Till oft converse with heav'nly habitants
Begin to cast a beam on th'outward shape,   460
The unpolluted temple of the mind,
And turns it by degrees to the soul's essence,
Till all be made immortal: but when lust
By unchaste looks, loose gestures, and foul talk,
But most by lewd and lavish act of sin,   465
Lets in defilement to the inward parts,
The soul grows clotted by contagion,
Imbodies, and imbrutes, till she quite lose
The divine property of her first being.
Such are those thick and gloomy shadows damp   470
Oft seen in Charnel vaults, and Sepulchres,
Lingering, and sitting by a new made grave,

that the object of education should be to secure such "apparitions of
God." (*Advancement,* I, iii, 3.) Compare *P.L.* xii, 611.

459–463. In *P.L.* V, 469–504, Raphael explains the laws of matter to
Adam as ground for hope that perhaps human
        "bodies may at last turn all to Spirit,
    Improv'd by tract of time, and wing'd ascend Ethereal."

461–463. The thought is Platonic, but Milton remembered St. Paul's
words; "Know ye not that ye are the temple of God, and that the
Spirit of God dwelleth in you?" Compare the advice given to Imo-
gene; "keep unshak'd That temple, thy fair mind." (*Cymbeline,* II, i,
60–1.)

466. There is a glance at Psalm li, 6; "Behold, thou desirest truth in
the inward parts."

468. Compare Satan's protest, when he enters the serpent in order
to tempt Eve, that he is
            "constrain'd
    Into a Beast, and mixt with bestial slime
    This essence to incarnate and imbrute."
            (*P.L.* IX, 164–6.)

469. *property*—quality, nature.

470. *gloomy shadows damp* is Milton's recollection of Plato's phrase
(*Phaedo,* 81d) in a passage where Socrates argues for the soul's immortality on the ground that noble spirits welcome the release from
the body and its passions which death brings; while the souls of the
wicked are dragged back after death to this visible world by their fear
of the invisible and their load of fleshly lusts, and are seen haunting their
tombs. Plato's thought, with emphasis on the *contagion* of the body
as evil in itself, was echoed by Lactantius (*Divine Institutes,* VII, xx,
§8–9) and by other Christian writers, who may have influenced Milton's
impression of Plato's famous passage.

As loath to leave the body that it lov'd,
And link't itself by carnal sensual'ty
To a degenerate and degraded state.   475
   Second Brother. How charming is divine Philosophy!
Not harsh and crabbed as dull fools suppose,
But musical as is *Apollo's* lute,
And a perpetual feast of nectar'd sweets,
Where no crude surfeit reigns.
   Elder Brother. List, list, I hear   480
Some far off hallow break the silent Air.
   Second Brother. Methought so too; what should it be?
   Elder Brother.   For certain
Either some one like us night-founder'd here,
Or else some neighbour Wood-man, or at worst,
Some roving Robber calling to his fellows.   485
   Second Brother. Heav'n keep my sister! Again again and
     near,
Best draw, and stand upon our guard.
   Elder Brother.   I'll hallow;
If he be friendly he comes well, if not,
Defence is a good cause, and Heav'n be for us.

    The attendant Spirit habited like a Shepherd.

That hallow I should know, what are you? speak;   490
Come not too near, you fall on iron stakes else.
   Spirit. What voice is that? my young Lord? speak again.
   Second Brother. O brother, 'tis my father's Shepherd sure.

   476–480. The conventionality of the younger brother's answer is
illustrated by the first canto of Henry More's *Platonicall Song of the
Soul* (1647), where—as Todd pointed out—"crabbed" and "sour"
doctrines are contrasted with the philosophy of "divinest Plato," which
     "fires the nobler heart with spotlesse love,
     And sadder minds with Nectar drops doth chear."
               (Stanza 18.)
   480. *crude*—indigestible or undigested.
   483. *night-founder'd*—overwhelmed by the night. Compare the
"night-founder'd Skiff" of *P.L.* I, 204.
   486–487. In the performance the shout would be heard again, coming closer, while the brothers draw their swords.
   491. *iron stakes—i.e.,* their swords.

Elder Brother. Thyrsis? Whose artful strains have oft de-
lay'd
The huddling brook to hear his madrigal,   495
And sweeten'd every muskrose of the dale.
How cam'st thou here good Swain? hath any ram
Slipt from the fold, or young Kid lost his dam,
Or straggling wether the pent flock forsook?
How couldst thou find this dark sequester'd nook?   500
   Spirit. O my lov'd master's heir, and his next joy,
I came not here on such a trivial toy
As a stray'd Ewe, or to pursue the stealth
Of pilfering Wolf; not all the fleecy wealth
That doth enrich these Downs, is worth a thought   505
To this my errand, and the care it brought.
But O my Virgin Lady, where is she?
How chance she is not in your company?
   Elder Brother. To tell thee sadly, Shepherd, without blame,
Or our neglect, we lost her as we came.   510
   Spirit. Ay me unhappy! then my fears are true.
   Elder Brother. What fears good *Thyrsis?* Prithee briefly
show.
   Spirit. I'll tell ye; 'tis not vain or fabulous,
(Though so esteem'd by shallow ignorance)
What the sage Poets taught by th' heav'nly Muse   515
Storied of old in high immortal verse

---

494. *Thyrsis* is the name given to the first shepherd mentioned in
Theocritus' *Idyls.* For the compliment to Lawes in these lines compare the note on 86–8.

495. A *madrigal* was a love-song often written in parts for several
voices, but its original Italian associations were with pastoral poetry.
Masson suggested that the rhymed dialogue (495–512) bears the
stamp of the heroic couplet in which English pastoral poetry had
usually been written.

huddling—pressing, crowding, *i.e.,* to hear.

501. *his next joy* is the Spirit's way of addressing the Second Brother.

502. *toy*—trifle, insignificant matter.

506. *to*—in comparison to.

508. *How chance*—how does it happen that, *etc.*

509. *sadly*—seriously. Compare *Romeo and Juliet,* I, i, 191; "Tell me
in sadness, who is that you love."

without blame—without our being blameworthy.

515–519. Homer, with whom the myth of the fire-spouting Chimaera

Of dire *Chimeras* and enchanted Isles,
And rifted Rocks whose entrance leads to hell,
For such there be, but unbelief is blind.
   Within the navel of this hideous Wood,   520
Immur'd in cypress shades, a Sorcerer dwells,
Of *Bacchus* and of *Circe* born, great *Comus,*
Deep skill'd in all his mother's witcheries,
And here to every thirsty wanderer,
By sly enticement gives his baneful cup,   525
With many murmurs mixt, whose pleasing poison
The visage quite transforms of him that drinks,
And the inglorious likeness of a beast
Fixes instead, unmoulding reason's mintage
Chará̈cter'd in the face; this have I learnt   530
Tending my flocks hard by i'th' hilly crofts,
That brow this bottom glade, whence night by night
He and his monstrous rout are heard to howl
Like stabl'd wolves, or tigers at their prey,

---

begins (*ll.* VI, 179), and all the poets down to Spenser, who was the last who
                  "counselled,
   To shunne *Rocke of Reproch,* and it as death to dred,"
              (*F.Q.* II, xii, 9, 9.)
were in Milton's mind. In the invocation to the *heav'nly Muse,* Urania, in *P.L.* VII, 1–20, he referred to the myth of Bellerophon, who killed the Chimaera, with the same sense of the value of the story that transpires here.

   520. *navel*—centre. Todd paralleled this Greek use of the word from Michael Drayton's *Polyolbion,* Song xxxiii, 147–8:
     "Up tow'rds the navell then of England from her flanke,
      Which Lincolnshire we call."

   526. *murmurs*—incantations muttered while the drink was being mixed. Compare *S.A.* 934–5.

   529. *mintage*—stamp.

   530. *Chará̈cter'd*—impressed or engraved. Compare *Two Gentlemen of Verona,* II, vii, 3–4, where Julia calls Lucetta
        "the table wherein all my thoughts
        Are visibly character'd and engrav'd."

   531. *crofts*—small, enclosed farms or tilled fields.

   532. *brow*—overlook. *bottom glade*—glade in a valley.

   533. *monstrous rout*—mob or crowd of monsters.

   534. If "stabl'd" has the force that it does in *P.L.* XI, 752, *stabl'd*

Doing abhorred rites to *Hecate*   535
In their obscured haunts of inmost bow'rs.
Yet have they many baits and guileful spells
To inveigle and invite th'unwary sense
Of them that pass unweeting by the way.
This evening late, by then the chewing flocks   540
Had ta'en their supper on the savoury Herb
Of Knot-grass dew-besprent, and were in fold,
I sat me down to watch upon a bank
With Ivy canopied, and interwove
With flaunting Honey-suckle, and began,   545
Wrapt in a pleasing fit of melancholy,
To meditate my rural minstrelsy,
Till fancy had her fill; but ere a close
The wonted roar was up amidst the Woods,
And fill'd the Air with barbarous dissonance,   550
At which I ceas't, and listen'd them a while,
Till an unusual stop of sudden silence
Gave respite to the drowsy-flighted steeds

---

wolves means "wolves in their lairs." Perhaps the meaning, however, is, "wolves in the stables or sheepfolds."

535. *abhorred*—abominable. Compare the note on *unenchanted* in 395, and the note on 128–130 above.

539. *unweeting*—unwitting, uninformed.

546. *melancholy;* not sadness but the mood invoked in *Il Penseroso*, 12.

547. Compare *meditate* in *Lycidas*, 66. Thyrsis means that he improvised a tune on his pipe. The language is that of Virgil's Eclogue, 1, 2.

548. *ere a close*—before a close (probably a cadence or conclusion of the musical theme) was reached.

549. *wonted*—accustomed.

551. *listen'd*—listened to. Originally the verb was transitive, as it is in Macbeth's confession (II, ii, 29); "List'ning their feare, I could not say Amen."

553. *drowsy-flighted* is the reading of the Cambridge MS, while all the original editions have *drowsie frighted.* So Browne describes the "pitchy curtains" about "Night's chariot"—

> "All-drowsie night, . . . in a car of jet,
> By steeds of iron-gray . . . . . .
> . . . . . . drawne through the skye."
> (*Britannia's Pastorals*, Book II, Song I.)

That draw the litter of close-curtain'd sleep;
At last a soft and solemn breathing sound   555
Rose like a steam of rich distill'd Perfumes,
And stole upon the Air, that even Silence
Was took ere she was ware, and wish't she might
Deny her nature, and be never more,
Still to be so displac't.   I was all ear,   560
And took in strains that might create a soul
Under the ribs of Death; but O ere long
Too well I did perceive it was the voice
Of my most honour'd Lady, your dear sister.
Amaz'd I stood, harrow'd with grief and fear,   565
And O poor hapless Nightingale, thought I,
How sweet thou sing'st, how near the deadly snare!
Then down the Lawns I ran with headlong haste
Through paths and turnings oft'n trod by day,
Till guided by mine ear I found the place   570
Where that damn'd wizard hid in sly disguise
(For so by certain signs I knew) had met
Already, ere my best speed could prevent,
The aidless innocent Lady his wish't prey,
Who gently ask't if he had seen such two,   575
Supposing him some neighbour villager;
Longer I durst not stay, but soon I guess'd
Ye were the two she meant; with that I sprung
Into swift flight, till I had found you here,
But further know I not.
        Second Brother.   O night and shades,   580

---

554. *litter*—a chariot built so that the traveller could lie down.
With *close-curtain'd sleep* compare Macbeth's "Curtain'd sleepe."
(*Macbeth*, II, i, 64.)

555–556. Todd quoted Bacon's remark in the Essay *Of Gardens* that
"the breath of flowers is far sweeter in the air (where it comes and
goes like the warbling of music) than in the hand."

557–558. Compare *Il Penseroso*, 56–7.

560. *Still to be so displac't: i.e.,* provided that she might always be
supplanted by such music.

562. Allegorical pictures of skeletons were very familiar in books
like Quarles's *Emblems,* where (Book V, No. viii) Milton may have
seen such a figure with a pendant poem morbidly preaching chastity.

568. *Lawns*—grassy, open lanes in the forest.

How are ye join'd with hell in triple knot
Against th'unarmed weakness of one Virgin
Alone, and helpless!   Is this the confidence
You gave me Brother?
   Elder Brother.   Yes, and keep it still,
Lean on it safely, not a period   585
Shall be unsaid for me: against the threats
Of malice or of sorcery, or that power
Which erring men call Chance, this I hold firm;
Virtue may be assail'd, but never hurt,
Surpris'd by unjust force, but not enthrall'd,   590
Yea even that which mischief meant most harm
Shall in the happy trial prove most glory.
But evil on itself shall back recoil,
And mix no more with goodness, when at last
Gather'd like scum, and settl'd to itself,   595
It shall be in eternal restless change
Self-fed and self-consum'd; if this fail,
The pillar'd firmament is rott'nness,
And earth's base built on stubble.   But come, let's on.
Against th' opposing will and arm of Heav'n   600
May never this just sword be lifted up,
But for that damn'd magician, let him be girt
With all the grisly legions that troop
Under the sooty flag of *Acheron,*

---

585. *period*—sentence.

586. *for me*—for my part, by my judgement.

591. *i.e.,* the very thing which mischievous men meant should do most harm.

592. *happy trial*—trial whose outcome proves fortunate.

593–597. So in *P.L.* XI, 50–3, Milton explains that by the Law of Nature
     "Those pure immortal Elements that know
      No gross, no unharmonious mixture foul,
      Eject him (*i.e.,* Adam) tainted now, and purge him off
      As a distemper."

598. Compare "the pillar'd frame of Heaven" in *P.R.* IV, 455 and note.

604. *Acheron* was one of the four rivers of Hades (all of which figure together in *P.L.* II, 577–80), but here it represents hell itself.

Harpies and *Hydras,* or all the monstrous forms   605
'Twixt *Africa* and *Inde,* I'll find him out,
And force him to restore his purchase back,
Or drag him by the curls, to a foul death,
Curs'd as his life.

    Spirit. Alas good vent'rous youth,
I love thy courage yet, and bold Emprise,   610
But here thy sword can do thee little stead;
Far other arms, and other weapons must
Be those that quell the might of hellish charms.
He with his bare wand can unthread thy joints,
And crumble all thy sinews.

    Elder Brother.   . Why, prethee Shepherd, 615
How durst thou then thyself approach so near
As to make this relation?

    Spirit.   Care and utmost shifts
How to secure the Lady from surprisal,
Brought to my mind a certain Shepherd Lad
Of small regard to see to, yet well skill'd   620
In every virtuous plant and healing herb
That spreads her verdant leaf to th'morning ray.
He lov'd me well, and oft would beg me sing,
Which when I did, he on the tender grass
Would sit, and hearken even to extasy,   625

---

605. *Harpies* (compare *P.R.* II, 403, note) and *Hydras,* like the "*Gorgons* and Hydras, and *Chimeras* dire" of *P.L.* II, 628, stand for "all monstrous, all prodigious things."

606. *Inde,* India, stands for the far east as Africa does for the west, since Mt. Atlas, opposite Gibraltar, represented the extreme western landmark for the ancient world.

607. *purchase*—prey, captive. Originally the word meant the chase of wild animals.

611. *stead*—advantage, service.

614. *bare*—mere.

615. *prethee*—prithee, a very common contraction of "I pray thee." Compare 512.

617. *relation*—report.

620. *to see to*—to look at.

621. *virtuous*—rich in healing quality, like Friar Lawrence's
                "precious-juiced flowers . . . .
            Many for many virtues excellent."
            (*Romeo and Juliet,* II, iii, 8 and 13.)

And in requital ope his leathern scrip,
And show me simples of a thousand names,
Telling their strange and vigorous faculties;
Amongst the rest a small unsightly root,
But of divine effect, he cull'd me out;   630
The leaf was darkish, and had prickles on it,
But in another Country, as he said,
Bore a bright golden flow'r, but not in this soil:
Unknown, and like esteem'd, and the dull swain
Treads on it daily with his clouted shoon,   635
And yet more med'cinal is it than that *Moly*
That *Hermes* once to wise *Ulysses* gave;
He call'd it *Haemony,* and gave it me,
And bade me keep it as of sovran use
'Gainst all enchantments, mildew blast, or damp,   640
Or ghastly furies' apparitïon;
I purs't it up, but little reck'ning made,
Till now that this extremity compell'd,
But now I find it true; for by this means
I knew the foul enchanter though disguis'd,   645

---

626. *scrip*—bag.

627. *simples*—medically useful plants, so called because they were classed with the simple remedies.

634. *like esteem'd; i.e.,* unknown and so unvalued.

635. *clouted*—patched, or studded with iron clouts.

636–638. *Moly* was the herb given to Ulysses by Hermes (*Od.* X, 287) to immunize him against Circe's charms. Thereby said Roger Ascham (*English Works,* Ed. Wright, p. 226), "the Diuine Poete *Homer* ment couertly . . . that loue of honestie, and hatred of ill, which *Dauid* more plainly doth call the feare of God." Traditionally it symbolized temperance, and in *Elegy I,* 88, Milton said that it was his antidote against the Circean charms of London. By calling it *Haemony,* a word derived from Haemonia, an ancient name for Thrace, the land of magic, he suggested Socrates' story (in Plato's *Charmides,* 157) of the charm of a Thracian physician who wrought magical cures because he understood that the body's health depends upon the soul.

639. *sovran*—superlatively efficacious. Hotspur was told that
        "the sovereign'st thing on earth
    Was parmeceti for an inward bruise."
            (*Henry IV,* Part I, I, iii, 57–8.)

640. The "foul fiend Flibbertigebbet," says Edgar in *Lear* III, iv, 118–22, "mildews the white wheat, and hurts the poor creature of earth."

641. *Furies'* has the vague meaning of Hag in 435 above.

Enter'd the very lime-twigs of his spells,
And yet came off: if you have this about you
(As I will give you when we go) you may
Boldly assault the necromancer's hall;
Where if he be, with dauntless hardihood   650
And brandish't blade rush on him, break his glass,
And shed the luscious liquor on the ground,
But seize his wand; though he and his curst crew
Fierce sign of battle make, and menace high,
Or like the sons of *Vulcan* vomit smoke,   655
Yet will they soon retire, if he but shrink.
    Elder Brother. Thyrsis lead on apace, I'll follow thee,
And some good angel bear a shield before us.

*The Scene changes to a stately Palace, set out with all manner of
deliciousness; soft Music, Tables spread with all dainties.*
Comus *appears with his rabble, and the Lady set in an enchanted Chair, to whom he offers his Glass, which she puts by,
and goes about to rise.*

    Comus. Nay Lady, sit; if I but wave this wand,
Your nerves are all chain'd up in Alabaster,   660

---

646. The figure is that of a bird flying safely among twigs smeared
with bird-lime.

650–651. So Mercury (*Od.* X, 294–5) tells Ulysses to draw his sword
and spring to attack Circe on the instant when she smites him with her
long wand.

651–652. Spenser's Knight of Temperance, Guyon, when he met the
tempter Agdistes in the Circean Bower of Bliss,
        "his idle curtesie defide,
    And ouerthrew his bowle disdainfully,"
          (*F.Q.* II, xii, 49, 7–8.)
and a second such cup
        "to ground did violently cast
    That all in peeces it was broken fond,
    And with the liquor stained all the lond."
          (Ibid. 57, 3–5.)

655. The *sons of Vulcan:* the god of fire, whose forge was under Mt.
Aetna, was the father or master of the "Fiery Spirits" which Burton
(*Anatomy*, I, ii, 1, 2) describes as supposed to keep "their residence in
that *Hecla*, a mountain in *Iceland*, *Aetna*, in Sicily, *Lipari, Vesuvius, &c."*

658. The "irony" in this prayer which is fulfilled before it is made
suggests the influence of Greek drama.

660. *nerves*—sinews. Compare *S.A.* 1646.

And you a statue; or as *Daphne* was,
Root-bound, that fled *Apollo*.
   Lady. Fool, do not boast,
Thou canst not touch the freedom of my mind
With all thy charms, although this corporal rind
Thou hast immanacl'd, while Heav'n sees good.   665
   Comus. Why are you vext, Lady? why do you frown?
Here dwell no frowns, nor anger, from these gates
Sorrow flies far: See, here be all the pleasures
That fancy can beget on youthful thoughts,
When the fresh blood grows lively, and returns   670
Brisk as the *April* buds in Primrose-season.
And first behold this cordial Julep here,
That flames and dances in his crystal bounds
With spirits of balm and fragrant Syrops mixt.
Not that *Nepenthes* which the wife of *Thone*   675
In *Egypt* gave to *Jove*-born *Helena*
Is of such power to stir up joy as this,
To life so friendly, or so cool to thirst.
Why should you be so cruel to yourself,
And to those dainty limbs which nature lent   680
For gentle usage and soft delicacy?
But you invert the cov'nants of her trust,
And harshly deal like an ill borrower

661–662. When Daphne, the daughter of Peneus, was caught by her
lover, Apollo, Ovid says (*Met.* I, 547–52) that she was changed in his
arms into a laurel, her arms turning into branches and her feet into
roots where she stood.   Compare *Elegy V,* 13.

664. *corporal rind; i.e.,* the body thought of as the husk of the soul.

670. *returns*—resumes the lively circulation of spring after winter.

675–676. On their way home from Troy Homer says (*Od.* IV, 220–
29) that Menelaus and Zeus-born Helen were entertained by an Egyptian
named Thone at a banquet where Polydamna, his wife, mixed a marvellous drug called nepenthes with the wine to banish all sorrow.

679–681. Comus's appeal is a tissue of distortions of the wisdom of
the wise.   His approach, like Shakespeare's in Sonnet I, 8—
     "Thyself thy foe, to thy sweet self too cruel"—
may carry a reminiscence of Proverbs xi, 17; "The merciful man doeth
good to his own soul: but he that is cruel troubleth his own flesh."

682–686. Compare Shakespeare's Sonnet IV, 3–4:
     "Nature's bequest gives nothing, but doth lend,
     And being frank, she lends to those are free."

With that which you receiv'd on other terms,
Scorning the unexempt condition   685
By which all mortal frailty must subsist,
Refreshment after toil, ease after pain,
That have been tir'd all day without repast,
And timely rest have wanted; but, fair Virgin,
This will restore all soon.
    Lady.   'Twill not, false traitor,   690
'Twill not restore the truth and honesty
That thou hast banish't from thy tongue with lies.
Was this the cottage, and the safe abode
Thou told'st me of?   What grim aspects are these,
These ugly-headed Monsters?   Mercy guard me!   695
Hence with thy brew'd enchantments, foul deceiver;
Hast thou betray'd my credulous innocence
With visor'd falsehood and base forgery,
And wouldst thou seek again to trap me here
With lickerish baits fit to ensnare a brute?   700
Were it a draught for *Juno* when she banquets,
I would not taste thy treasonous offer; none
But such as are good men can give good things,
And that which is not good, is not delicious
To a well-govern'd and wise appetite.   705
    Comus. O foolishness of men! that lend their ears
To those budge doctors of the *Stoic* Fur,

---

685. *unexempt condition*—condition from which none is exempt.

698. *visor'd*—masked.
forgery—deception. In *P.L.* IV, 800–3, Satan sitting "close at the ear of *Eve*," tried to
                         "forge
    Illusions as he list, Phantasms and Dreams."

700. *lickerish*—delicious, tempting.

701. Milton seems to have thought of the scene in the *Iliad* I, 584, when Hephaestus appeased Hera's (Juno's) wrath in the presence of all the other gods by offering her a glorious cup of nectar.

707. *budge* was one of the kinds of fur regularly used on doctoral hoods when Milton was a student at Cambridge and it evidently had unpleasant connotations. For his attitude both toward the scholastic spirit and toward Stoicism see the Introduction to *Paradise Regained*, §7.

And fetch their precepts from the *Cynic* Tub,
Praising the lean and sallow Abstinence.
Wherefore did Nature pour her bounties forth   710
With such a full and unwithdrawing hand,
Covering the earth with odours, fruits, and flocks,
Thronging the Seas with spawn innumerable,
But all to please and sate the curious taste?
And set to work millions of spinning Worms,   715
That in their green shops weave the smooth-hair'd silk
To deck her Sons; and that no corner might
Be vacant of her plenty, in her own loins
She hutch't th'all-worshipt ore and precious gems
To store her children with. If all the world   720
Should in a pet of temperance feed on Pulse,
Drink the clear stream, and nothing wear but Frieze,
Th'all-giver would be unthank't, would be unprais'd,
Not half his riches known, and yet despis'd,
And we should serve him as a grudging master,   725
As a penurious niggard of his wealth,
And live like Nature's bastards, not her sons,
Who would be quite surcharg'd with her own weight,
And strangl'd with her waste fertility;
Th'earth cumber'd, and the wing'd air dark't with plumes, 730
The herds would over-multitude their Lords,
The Sea o'erfraught would swell, and th'unsought diamonds
Would so emblaze the forehead of the Deep,
And so bestud with Stars, that they below

---

708. The Cynic philosopher, Diogenes, was famous for living in a tub in Athens to express his contempt for the amenities of civilization.

719. *hutch'd*—locked away, shut up.

721. *pet*—fit.

722. *Frieze*—coarse woolen cloth.

723-724. The recurrence of this idea in *P.L.* V, 318–20, lends colour to Professor Shorey's suggestion that it was part of a tradition going back to Porphyry's work *On Abstinence,* I, 16–7, where a critic of vegetarianism argues that, if the doctrine prevailed, the rivers would be choked with fish and the land overrun by animals.

732-736. Milton's variant of 733—"Would so bestud the centre with their starlight"—indicates that *Deep* means the earth, as it does in

Would grow inur'd to light, and come at last   735
To gaze upon the Sun with shameless brows.
List Lady, be not coy, and be not cosen'd
With that same vaunted name Virginity;
Beauty is nature's coin, must not be hoarded,
But must be current, and the good thereof   740
Consists in mutual and partak'n bliss,
Unsavoury in th'enjoyment of itself.
If you let slip time, like a neglected rose
It withers on the stalk with languish't head.
Beauty is nature's brag, and must be shown   745
In courts, at feasts, and high solemnities

P.L. VI, 482, where Satan argues of certain substances in the ground
that, when

> "toucht
> With Heav'n's ray, and temper'd, they shoot forth
> So beauteous, op'ning to the ambient light."

Again in *P.L.* III, 609–612, Milton refers to the belief that the sun's
rays continually produce gold and gems out of the base material in the
ground. Here his thought seems to be that, if the precious metals were
not mined, the face of the earth would soon be luminous like a star
and the earth-spirits who inhabit its depths would learn to face the
sunshine. Compare *That Nature is not subject to Old Age,* 65–6.

735. *inur'd*—accustomed. Compare *P.R.* II, 102, and IV, 139.

737–755. These lines are not found in the Bridgewater MS. and
therefore were not spoken when *Comus* was presented.

737. *coy*—shy, reserved. *cosen'd*—deluded, duped.

738. Compare the witch Armida's appeal in Tasso:
> "O Fools who Youth possess, yet scorn the same,
> A precious, but a short-abiding Treasure,
> Vertue it self is but an Idle Name."
> (*J.D.* XIV, 63, 1–3. Fairfax's translation.)

739–742. The classic expression of this commonplace is in Shakespeare's first seventeen Sonnets, notably the sixth:
> "Then let not winter's ragged hand deface
> In thee thy summer, ere thou be distill'd:
> Make sweet some vial; treasure thou some place
> With beauty's treasure, ere it be self-kill'd.
> That use is not forbidden usury,
> Which happies those that pay the willing loan."

743–744. Theseus makes use of the commonplace with Hermia;
> "But earthlier happy is the rose distill'd,
> Than that which withering on the virgin thorn
> Grows, lives, and dies in single blessedness."
> (*Midsummer Night's Dream,* I, i, 76–8.)

Where most may wonder at the workmanship;
It is for homely features to keep home,
They had their name thence; coarse complexiöns
And cheeks of sorry grain will serve to ply   750
The sampler, and to tease the huswife's wool.
What need a vermeil-tinctur'd lip for that,
Love-darting eyes, or tresses like the Morn?
There was another meaning in these gifts,
Think what, and be advis'd; you are but young yet.   755
    Lady. I had not thought to have unlockt my lips
In this unhallow'd air, but that this Juggler
Would think to charm my judgement, as mine eyes,
Obtruding false rules prankt in reason's garb.
I hate when vice can bolt her arguments,   760
And virtue has no tongue to check her pride:
Impostor, do not charge most innocent nature,
As if she would her children should be riotous
With her abundance; she good cateress
Means her provision only to the good   765
That live according to her sober laws,
And holy dictate of spare Temperance:
If every just man that now pines with want
Had but a moderate and beseeming share
Of that which lewdly-pamper'd Luxury   770
Now heaps upon some few with vast excess,
Nature's full blessings would be well dispens't
In unsuperfluous even proportion,
And she no whit encumber'd with her store,
And then the giver would be better thank't,   775
His praise due paid, for swinish gluttony
Ne'er looks to Heav'n amidst his gorgeous feast,

---

750. *grain*—colour.

751. *tease*—comb.

752. *vermeil-tinctur'd*—vermilion.

760. *bolt;* the metaphor is from bolting flour and the meaning is illustrated in Lambarde's *Perambulation of* Kent; "Neither may *I* boult out
the whole Etymologie . . . of every Townes name."   (*N.E.D.*)

766–778. The thought was a part of the Christian condemnation of
gluttony as far back as Dio Chrysostom's Oration 30, where the prodigal and incontinent are accused of seeing and hearing nothing above
them while they eat like swine in the pen.   In *King Lear,* IV, i, 68–72,

But with besotted base ingratitude
Crams, and blasphemes his feeder.   Shall I go on?
Or have I said enough?   To him that dares   780
Arm his profane tongue with contemptuous words
Against the Sun-clad power of Chastity
Fain would I something say, yet to what end?
Thou hast nor Ear nor Soul to apprehend
The sublime notion, and high mystery   785
That must be utter'd to unfold the sage
And serious doctrine of Virginity,
And thou art worthy that thou shouldst not know
More happiness than this thy present lot.
Enjoy your dear Wit and gay Rhetoric   790
That hath so well been taught her dazzling fence,
Thou art not fit to hear thyself convinc't;
Yet should I try, the uncontrolléd worth
Of this pure cause would kindle my rapt spirits
To such a flame of sacred vehemence,   795
That dumb things would be mov'd to sympathize,
And the brute Earth would lend her nerves, and shake,

-----

the same charge is brought against "the superfluous and lust-dieted
man . . . that will not see Because he does not feel. . . .
                    So distribution should undo excess,
                    And each man have enough."

779. *Shall I go on, etc.,* as far as "more strongly" in 806 are not
found in the Bridgewater MS.

785. *mystery* is used in its religious sense of a doctrine revealed
supernaturally, like St. Paul's great "mystery of godliness, God was
manifest in the flesh." (I Tim. iii, 16.) Milton is thinking of mysteries
such as Socrates says that he learned from Diotima about love (*Symposium,* 201d–212b) as well as of "the doctrine of Holy Scripture unfolding those chaste and high mysteries . . . that the body is for the
Lord, and the Lord for the body." (*An Apology for Smectymnuus, P.W.*
III, 122.)

791. *fence*—art of fencing or debating.

793. *uncontrolléd*—uncontrollable. Compare *Unenchanted* in 395,
note.

794. *rapt*—transported. Compare the word in *P.R.* II, 40, note.

797. *brute Earth* translates Horace's phrase (*Odes,* I, xxxiv, 9) where
he describes the earth as shaken by a thunderbolt so marvellous that it
shook his scepticism about the gods.
nerves; compare 660, note.

Till all thy magic structures rear'd so high,
Were shatter'd into heaps o'er thy false head.

    Comus. She fables not, I feel that I do fear   800
Her words set off by some superior power;
And though not mortal, yet a cold shudd'ring dew
Dips me all o'er, as when the wrath of *Jove*
Speaks thunder, and the chains of *Erebus*
To some of *Saturn's* crew. I must dissemble,   805
And try her yet more strongly.   Come, no more,
This is mere moral babble, and direct
Against the canon laws of our foundation;
I must not suffer this, yet 'tis but the lees
And settlings of a melancholy blood;   810
But this will cure all straight, one sip of this
Will bathe the drooping spirits in delight
Beyond the bliss of dreams. Be wise, and taste.—

*The Brothers rush in with Swords drawn, wrest his Glass out of
his hand, and break it against the ground; his rout make sign
of resistance, but are all driven in; The attendant Spirit comes
in.*

    Spirit. What, have you let the false enchanter scape?
O ye mistook, ye should have snatcht his wand   815
And bound him fast; without his rod revers't,
And backward mutters of dissevering power,

---

    800. *fables not*—does not talk idly or falsely. Compare *P.R.* IV, 295.

    803. *the wrath of Jove;* a Latinism for wrathful Jove.

    804–805. By another classical figure of speech, called zeugma, *Speaks*
is used in two senses; (1) utters thunder and (2) pronounces the sentence of bondage under Mt. Erebus upon the Titans who rebelled with
Saturn and were overthrown by Jove's thunderbolts.

    810. Compare the discussion of *melancholy* in the third note on
Milton's Preface to *S.A.*

    811. Armida's cup is so potent that
    "One Sup thereof the Drinker's Heart doth bring
      To sudden Joy, whence Laughter vain doth rise,
        Nor that strange Merriment once stops or stayes,
        Till with his Laughters End, he end his Dayes."
      (*J.D.* XIV, 74, 5–8. Fairfax's translation.)

    816–817. So Ovid (*Met.* XIV, 300–1) says that Circe's charms were
annulled with her rod reversed and her formula of words said back-

We cannot free the Lady that sits here
In stony fetters fixt, and motionless;
Yet stay, be not disturb'd, now I bethink me,   820
Some other means I have which may be us'd,
Which once of *Meliboeus* old I learnt
The soothest Shepherd that ere pip't on plains.
   There is a gentle Nymph not far from hence,
That with moist curb sways the smooth Severn stream,   825
Sabrina is her name, a Virgin pure;
Whilom she was the daughter of *Locrine,*
That had the Sceptre from his father *Brute.*
She, guiltless damsel, flying the mad pursuit
Of her enraged stepdam *Guendolen,*   830
Commended her fair innocence to the flood
That stay'd her flight with his cross-flowing course.
The water Nymphs that in the bottom play'd,

------

ward; and so Milton remembered that the charms of the enchanter
Busyrane in *The Faerie Queene* III, xii, 36, and of many another wizard
and witch, were undone when they were reversed.

822. In giving the name of one of the two shepherds, Meliboeus and
Tityrus, in Virgil's First Eclogue to his "shepherd" Milton intended a
reference to Spenser, just as Spenser regularly used the other name to
refer to Chaucer. Milton's version of the myth of Sabrina is so sketchy
that it might be derived from any of its treatments by sixteenth century
writers such as Drayton in the Sixth Song of *Polyolbion,* or Spenser in
The Faerie Queene, II, x, 14–9, or Thomas Sackville in *The Mirrour
for Magistrates,* or the author of the old play of *Locrine,* as well as
from that of Geoffrey of Monmouth (who is sometimes identified with
Meliboeus) in his *History of the Kings of Britain.*

823. *soothest*—truest, most trustworthy.

825. *curb*—the chain placed under the bit for controlling an unruly
horse.

    sways—governs, controls.

825–834. Sabrina was the Roman name (given in Tacitus' *Annals,*
12, 31) for the river Severn which rises in Montgomeryshire in Wales
and flows through Shropshire, Worcestershire and Gloucestershire into
the Bristol Channel. In Geoffrey's version of the story of the nymph
Sabrina both she and her mother, for whose unlawful love King Locrine
deserted his wife, Guendolen (whom Milton calls her *stepdam*), are
thrown into the Severn together. Because Sabrina is to be a symbol of
purity and was also a favourite figure in local Welsh tradition, Milton
says nothing at all about her guilty mother, but lays stress on her
descent from Brutus, the mythical grandson of Aeneas whom Geoffrey
says colonized England and founded the line of British kings. In *The*

Held up their pearled wrists and took her in,
Bearing her straight to aged *Nereus'* Hall,   835
Who piteous of her woes, rear'd her lank head,
And gave her to his daughters to imbathe
In nectar'd lavers strew'd with Asphodil,
And through the porch and inlet of each sense
Dropt in Ambrosial Oils till she reviv'd   840
And underwent a quick immortal change,
Made Goddess of the River; still she retains
Her maid'n gentleness, and oft at Eve
Visits the herds along the twilight meadows,
Helping all urchin blasts, and ill luck signs   845
That the shrewd meddling Elf delights to make,
Which she with precious vial'd liquors heals.
For which the Shepherds at their festivals
Carol her goodness loud in rustic lays,
And throw sweet garland wreaths into her stream   850

History of Britain (Book I, *P.W.* V, pp. 173–4) Milton's version of the
story agrees with Geoffrey's.

835–838. Milton was familiar with Spenser's use of the myth of
Nereus, Homer's "Ancient One of the Sea" (*Il.* XVIII, 141), and his
fifty daughters, the Nereids, who are described in *The Faerie Queene,*
III, iv, 40–44, as taking a wounded mortal to a submarine chamber
where they treat his wounds with

"soueraine Balme, and Nectar good,
Good both for earthly med'cine, and for heauenly food."
(Stanza 40, 8–9.)

Compare *Elegy IV,* 7, note.

838. *Asphodil,* which covered the meadows where Ulysses found the
immortal spirits of the great dead (*Od.* XI, 538), was traditionally a
flower of immortality. Asphodel belongs to the lily family and the
white variety or "King's Spear covers large tracts . . . in Apulia."
(*N.E.D.*)

839. *porch;* compare *Hamlet,* I, v, 61–4; "thy uncle . . . in the
porches of my ears did pour . . . leperous distilment."

840. Ambrosia, the food of the gods, was supposed to confer immortality. Compare *P.R.* IV, 589–90.

845. *urchin* was a common name for the hedgehog, but mischievous
fairies like those described in *L'Allegro,* 102–14, were supposed to take
its form. Caliban, fearing Prospero's "spirits," says,

"But they'll nor pinch,
Fright me with urchin-shows, pitch me i' the mire,
Nor lead me, like a firebrand, in the dark
Out of my way, unless he bid 'em."
(*Tempest,* II, ii, 4–7.)

Of pansies, pinks, and gaudy Daffadils.
And, as the old Swain said, she can unlock
The clasping charm and thaw the numbing spell,
If she be right invok't in warbled Song,
For maid'nhood she loves, and will be swift   855
To aid a Virgin, such as was herself,
In hard besetting need.   This will I try
And add the power of some adjuring verse.

SONG

Sabrina fair
*   Listen where thou art sitting*   860
Under the glassy, cool, translucent wave,
*   In twisted braids of Lilies knitting*
The loose train of thy amber-dropping hair;
*   Listen for dear honour's sake,*
*   Goddess of the silver lake,*   865
*   Listen and save.*

Listen and appear to us
In name of great *Oceanus,*
By the earth-shaking *Neptune's* mace,
And *Tethys'* grave majestic pace,   870
By hoary *Nereus'* wrinkled look,

---

852. *the old Swain*—Meliboeus.

863. *amber-dropping;* Milton wrote that
        "the river of Bliss through midst of Heav'n
    Rolls o'er *Elysian* Flow'rs her Amber stream."
             (*P.L.* III, 358–59.)

  868. Editors note that many of the epithets of the sea-gods have classical justification.   *Ocean* is called "the great" in the list of deities which opens Hesiod's *Theogony* (20) and in the *Iliad*, XXI, 195, it is from the great strength of deep-flowing Ocean that all rivers come.

  869. Poseidon (Neptune) is regularly called the "Earthshaker" in Homer.

  mace, i.e., his trident.

  870. *Tethys,* the wife of Oceanus, Hesiod says (*Theogony*, 337–70) was the mother of the rivers and of countless divine children.

  871. To Virgil (*Georgic* IV, 392) *Nereus* was "most aged."   Compare 835.

And the *Carpathian* wizard's hook,
By scaly *Triton's* winding shell,
And old sooth-saying *Glaucus'* spell,
By *Leucothea's* lovely hands,   875
And her son that rules the strands,
By *Thetis'* tinsel-slipper'd feet,
And the Songs of *Sirens* sweet,
By dead *Parthenope's* dear tomb,
And fair *Ligea's* golden comb,   880
Wherewith she sits on diamond rocks
Sleeking her soft alluring locks,
By all the *Nymphs* that nightly dance
Upon thy streams with wily glance,
Rise, rise, and heave thy rosy head   885
From thy coral-pav'n bed,

---

872. The *Carpathian wizard* is the Old Man of the Sea, Proteus, who, Virgil says (*Georgics* IV, 433), haunted the Carpathian Sea between Crete and Rhodes. He carries a sheep-hook because Homer described him (*Od.* IV, 411–3) as counting his sea-calves and lying down among them like a shepherd.

873. *Triton,* the merman god whose body terminated in the tail of a fish, appears in Ovid's *Metamorphoses,* I, 330–5, as the herald of the sea, announcing Neptune's decrees with his conch shell. Compare *Lycidas,* 89.

874. Milton remembered the appearance of "Glaucus, that wise southsayes understood," in similar romantic catalogues of sea-gods in Spenser (*F.Q.* IV, xi, 13, 3) and Virgil. (*Aen.* V, 823.)

875–876. Homer (*Od.* V, 331–8) says that Ulysses was befriended by "Ino of the fair ankles, Leucothea, who in time past was a maiden of mortal speech, but now in the depths of the salt sea she had obtained a share of the honour of the gods." The name *Leucothea* means "the white goddess" and Roman writers identified her with the goddess of the dawn, Matuta, and even with Aurora (Lucretius, *De rerum natura,* V, 656), whose epithet of "rosy-fingered" Milton may have adapted for her here. Compare *P.L.* XI, 135. Her son, Melicertes, was changed into a sea-god and so he *rules the strands.*

877. *Thetis,* one of the Nereids and the mother of Achilles, often is called the "silver-footed" in the *Iliad.*

879. *Parthenope* was a siren whose tomb, Strabo says (i, 23, 26) was supposed to lie near Naples, and from whom the city took its ancient name.

880. *Ligea* is a name given to one of Homer's sirens by the commentator, Eustathius.

885. *heave*—lift. Compare *L'Allegro,* 145.

And bridle in thy headlong wave,
Till thou our summons answer'd have.
                              Listen and save.

Sabrina rises, attended by water-Nymphs, and sings.

   By the rushy-fringed bank,   890
Where grows the Willow and the Osier dank,
   My sliding Chariot stays,
Thick set with Agate and the azurn sheen
Of Turkis blue and Em'rald green
   That in the channel strays,   895
Whilst from off the waters fleet
Thus I set my printless feet
O'er the Cowslip's Velvet head,
   That bends not as I tread;
Gentle swain at thy request   900
   I am here.

   Spirit. Goddess dear
We implore thy powerful hand
To undo the charmed band
Of true Virgin here distrest,   905
Through the force and through the wile
Of unblest enchanter vile.

---

892. Warton recalled Drayton's "wasteful luxuriance of fancy" in describing Sabrina "as a Queene miraculously fair," who
     "Is absolutely plac'd in her imperial Chair,
       Of crystal richly wrought, that gloriously did shine."
          (*Polyolbion,* Song V, 1-2.)

893. *azurn*—azure.

894. *Turkis*—turquoise.

897. *printless*—leaving no trace. Prospero summons the
     "elves of hills, brooks, standing lakes, and groves,
     And ye that on the sands with printless foot
     Do chase the ebbing Neptune."
          (*Tempest,* V, i, 33-5.)

907. *unblest*—excluded from the blessing of God's grace, or *damn'd,*
as he is called in 571.

Sabrina. Shepherd 'tis my office best
To help ensnared chastity;
Brightest Lady look on me, 910
Thus I sprinkle on thy breast
Drops that from my fountain pure
I have kept of precious cure,
Thrice upon thy finger's tip,
Thrice upon thy rubied lip; 915
Next this marble venom'd seat
Smear'd with gums of glutinous heat
I touch with chaste palms moist and cold.
Now the spell hath lost his hold;
And I must haste ere morning hour 920
To wait in *Amphitrite's* bow'r.

Sabrina descends, and the Lady rises out of her seat.

Spirit. Virgin, daughter of *Locrine*
Sprung of old *Anchises'* line,
May thy brimmed waves for this
Their full tribute never miss 925
From a thousand petty rills,
That tumble down the snowy hills:

911–913. The scene vaguely resembles that in *The Faithful Shep-
herdess*, where Amarillis presides over a "holy well" which
"Hath power to change the form of any creature,"
and whose water avails to heal the wounded Amoret while the God
of the River chants:
"If thou be'st a virgin pure,
I can give a present cure:
Take a drop into thy wound,
From my watery locks, more round
Than orient pearl, and far more pure,
Than unchaste flesh may endure."
(III, i, 380–5.)

914–915. This detail is found in the account of the disenchantment
of Burd (maiden) Ellen in the story of Childe Rowland.

921. *Amphitrite* was Neptune's wife.

923. *Anchises* was the father of Aeneas, whom Geoffrey made the
great grandfather of Locrine. Compare 825–34, note.

Summer drouth, or singed air
Never scorch thy tresses fair,
Nor wet *October's* torrent flood   930
Thy molten crystal fill with mud;
May thy billows roll ashore
The beryl and the golden ore,
May thy lofty head be crown'd
With many a tower and terrace round,   935
And here and there thy banks upon
With Groves of myrrh, and cinnamon.

Come Lady, while Heaven lends us grace,
Let us fly this cursed place,
Lest the Sorcerer us entice   940
With some other new device.
Not a waste or needless sound
Till we come to holier ground.
I shall be your faithful guide
Through this gloomy covert wide,   945
And not many furlongs thence
Is your Father's residence,
Where this night are met in state
Many a friend to gratulate
His wish't presence, and beside   950

---

928. *singed*—burned, torrid with summer heat.

928–937. Editors refer to other blessings pronounced on streams, such as Marina's in Browne's *Britannia's Pastorals:*

> "May first,"
> (Quoth Marine) "swaines give lambs to thee;
> And may thy floud have seignorie
> Of all flouds else. . . . . .
> . . . . Let no man dare
> To spoil thy fish, make locke or ware,
> But on thy margent still let dwell
> Those flowers which have the sweetest smell.
> And let the dust upon thy strand
> Become like Tagus' golden sand.
> Let as much good betide to thee,
> As thou hast favour shew'd to me."
> (Book I, Song ii.)

942. *waste*—idle, unnecessary.

949. *gratulate*—welcome. Compare *P.R.* IV, 438.

All the Swains that there abide,
With Jigs and rural dance resort.
We shall catch them at their sport,
And our sudden coming there
Will double all their mirth and cheer;   955
Come let us haste, the Stars grow high,
But night sits monarch yet in the mid sky.

The Scene changes, presenting Ludlow *Town and the President's
Castle, then come in Country-Dancers, after them the attendant
Spirit, with the two Brothers and the Lady.*

SONG

Spirit. Back Shepherds, back, enough your play,
Till next Sun-shine holiday;
Here be without duck or nod   960
Other trippings to be trod
Of lighter toes, and such Court guise
As Mercury *did first devise*
With the mincing Dryades
On the Lawns and on the Leas.   965

This second Song presents them to their father and mother.

Noble Lord, and Lady bright,
I have brought ye new delight,
Here behold so goodly grown
Three fair branches of your own.
Heav'n hath timely tri'd their youth,   970

---

960. *duck*—a jerky curtsy or bow. The meaning is that no peasants'
dances must interfere with the courtly dancing by the Earl of Bridgewater's guests which is to follow the presentation of *Comus.*

963–964. As early as the *Homeric Hymn to Hermes* the god was a
leader of the dancing nymphs. Jonson's nymphs in *Pan's Anniversary*
(*Masques,* ed. by H. Morley, p. 336) sing of
        "the best of leaders, Pan,
    That leads the Naiads and the Dryads forth;
    And to their dances more than Hermes can."

964. *mincing*—dancing with delicate steps.

970. *timely*—early.

Their faith, their patience, and their truth,
And sent them here through hard assays
With a crown of deathless Praise,
 To triumph in victorious dance
O'er sensual Folly, and Intemperance.   975

 The dances ended, the Spirit Epilogizes.

 Spirit. To the Ocean now I fly,
And those happy climes that lie
Where day never shuts his eye,
Up in the broad fields of the sky:
There I suck the liquid air   980
All amidst the Gardens fair
Of *Hesperus,* and his daughters three
That sing about the golden tree:
Along the crisped shades and bow'rs
Revels the spruce and jocund Spring,   985
The Graces and the rosy-bosom'd Hours,
Thither all their bounties bring,
That there eternal Summer dwells,
And West winds with musky wing

---

972. *assays*—trials, ordeals. Compare *P.R.* I, 264.

976–983. The mood and rhythm are obviously those of Ariel's song,
     "Where the bee sucks, there suck I."
                         (*Tempest,* V, i, 87–94.)
The Spirit is returning to that vaguely located mansion from which
he has come. Compare ll. 1–3, note. The tree is *golden* only because it is "Laden with blooming gold," as Milton described it in 393.

984. *crisped:* N.E.D. compares "the crisped yew" in Herrick's *Ceremonies for Candlemas Eve.*"

985. *spruce*—brisk, lively.

986. The pastoral poetry of the Renaissance is filled with visions of
the Graces,
            "the daughters of sky-ruling Jove,
         By him begot of faire Euronyme,"
                      (*F.Q.* VI, x, 22, 1–2.)
dancing in fields of more than earthly beauty such as Spenser described and Botticelli painted. All of them go back to the Homeric
Hymn to Pythian Apollo (16–19), where "the fair-tressed Graces, and
the wise Hours, and Harmony, and Hebe, and Venus, the daughter of
Jove, dance, holding one another's hands by the wrist."

989. *West winds etc.,* zephyrs loaded with perfume.

About the cedarn alleys fling   990
Nard, and *Cassia's* balmy smells.
Iris there with humid bow,
Waters the odorous banks that blow
Flowers of more mingled hue
Than her purfl'd scarf can shew,   995
And drenches with *Elysian* dew
(List mortals, if your ears be true)
Beds of *Hyacinth* and Roses
Where young *Adonis* oft reposes,
Waxing well of his deep wound   1000
In slumber soft, and on the ground
Sadly sits th' *Assyrian* Queen;
But far above in spangled sheen
Celestial *Cupid* her fam'd son advanc't,
Holds his dear *Psyche* sweet intranc't   1005

---

990. *cedarn*—lined with cedar trees.

991. *Nard*—spikenard. Compare the earthly paradise in *P.L.* V, 293–4, with its

> "flow'ring Odours, Cassia, Nard and Balm;
> A Wilderness of sweets."

992. *Iris*—the goddess of the rainbow.

993. *blow*—cause to blossom.

995. *purfl'd*—variegated, decorated.

996. *Elysian*—"heavenly." Literally, the word refers to the land of the blessed dead which Homer placed (*Od.* IV, 561–4) on the verge of the western ocean.

997. Compare the charge that Comus has no ear for mystery, 784.

999–1002. Milton thought of the story of Venus, whom he called *th' Assyrian Queen* because the Assyrians were "the first men to revere the Celestial Aphrodite" (Pausanias, I, 14, 6), and of Adonis, her lover whose death while boar-hunting she mourns, as the allegory of the immortality of love which Spenser embodied in his description of the Garden of Adonis:

> "There yet, some say, in secret he does ly,
> Lapped in flowres and pretious spycery,
> By her hid from the world, and from the skill
> Of *Stygian* Gods, which doe her loue enuy;
> But she her selfe, when euer that she will,
> Possesseth him, and of his sweetnesse takes her fill."
>   (*F.Q.* III, vi, 46, 4–9.)

1004–1011. The story of Cupid's much-thwarted love for Psyche was told by Apuleius (*Metamorphoses,* 4, 28–36, 24), who says that when

After her wand'ring labours long,
Till free consent the gods among
Make her his eternal Bride,
And from her fair unspotted side
Two blissful twins are to be born,   1010
Youth and Joy; so *Jove* hath sworn.
   But now my task is smoothly done,
I can fly, or I can run
Quickly to the green earth's end,
Where the bow'd welkin slow doth bend,   1015
And from thence can soar as soon
To the corners of the Moon.
   Mortals that would follow me,
Love virtue, she alone is free,
She can teach ye how to climb   1020

---

at last the gods in full council had given the lovers to each other
Psyche bore the child Pleasure to Cupid. Spenser made

> "*Pleasure,* that doth both both gods and men aggrate,
>   *Pleasure,* the daughter of *Cupid* and *Psyche* late,"
>   (*F.Q.* III, vi, 50, 8–9.)

a symbol of idealized love, and Milton, with similar motives, put the
twins Youth and Joy in her place. Compare *Damon's Epitaph,* 193–7,
note.

1012–1017. Again there are echoes of Ariel's song and perhaps of the
Satyr's final offer of his services to Clorin in *The Faithful Shepherdess,*
V, v:

>   "Shall I stray
>   In the middle air, and stay
>   The sailing rack, or nimbly take
>   Hold by the moon, and gently make
>   Suit to the pale queen of night
>   For a beam to give thee light?"

1015. *welkin*—sky. The line alludes to the gradual bending of the
sky down to the horizon.

1018–1023. Comparison is inevitable with the summons of Mercury
to the masquers at the close of Jonson's *Pleasure Reconciled to Virtue*
to return to their mountain peak and to the pursuit of Virtue, who

>   "though a stranger here on earth,
>   In heaven she hath her right of birth.
>
>   There, there is Virtue's seat:
>   Strive to keep her your own;
>   'Tis only she can make you great,
>   Though place here make you known."

Higher than the Sphery chime;
Or if Virtue feeble were,
Heav'n itself would stoop to her.

THE END.

1021. *Sphery chime*—the music of the spheres, which plays a con-spicuous part in *Arcades,* 63–9.

1023. Spenser's pervasive presence in *Comus* is finally confessed, as Professor Hanford suggests, by this reminiscence of his comment upon Florimel's rescue from the lustful fisherman:

"See how the heauens of voluntary grace,
And soueraine fauour towards chastity,
Doe succour send to her distressed cace:
So much high God doth innocence embrace."
(*F.Q.* III, viii, 39, 2–5).

PSALM 114

Ἰσραὴλ ὅτε παῖδες, ὅτ' ἀγλαὰ φῦλ' Ἰακώβου
Αἰγύπτιον λίπε δῆμον, ἀπεχθέα, βαρβαρόφωνον,
Δὴ τότε μοῦνον ἔην ὅσιον γένος υἷες Ἰούδα.
Ἐν δὲ θεὸς λαοῖσι μέγα κρείων βασίλευεν.
Εἶδε, καὶ ἐντροπάδην φύγαδ' ἐρρώησε θάλασσα,   5
Κύματι εἰλυμένη ῥοθίῳ, ὁ δ' ἄρ' ἐστυφελίχθη
Ἱρὸς Ἰορδάνης ποτὶ ἀργυροειδέα πηγήν.
Ἐκ δ' ὄρεα σκαρθμοῖσιν ἀπειρέσια κλονέοντο,
Ὡς κριοὶ σφριγόωντες ἐϋτραφερῷ ἐν ἀλωῇ.
Βαιότεραι δ' ἅμα πᾶσαι ἀνασκίρτησαν ἐρίπναι,   10
Οἷα παραὶ σύριγγι φίγη ὑπὸ μητέρι ἄρνες.
Τίπτε σύ γ' αἰνὰ θάλασσα πέλωρ φυγάδ' ἐρρώησας,
Κύματι εἰλυμένη ῥοθίῳ; τί δ' ἄρ' ἐστυφελίχθης
Ἱρὸς Ἰορδάνη ποτὶ ἀργυροειδέα πηγήν;
Τίπτ' ὄρεα σκαρθμοῖσιν ἀπειρέσια κλονέεσθε   15
Ὡς κριοὶ σφριγόωντες ἐϋτραφερῷ ἐν ἀλωῇ;
Βαιότεραι τί δ' ἄρ' ὔμμες ἀνασκιρτησατ' ἐρίπναι,
Οἷα παραὶ σύριγγι φίλη ὑπὸ μητέρι ἄρνες,
Σείεο, γαῖα, τρέουσα θεὸν μεγάλ' ἐκτυπέοντα,
Γαῖα, θεὸν τρείουσ' ὕπατον σέβας Ἰσσακίδαο   20
Ὅς τε καὶ ἐκ σπιλάδων ποταμοὺς χέε μορμύροντας
Κρήνην τ' ἀέναον πέτρης ἀπὸ δακρυοέσσης.

(1634)

PSALM 114

WHEN the children of Israel, when the glorious tribes of Jacob left the land of Egypt—a land abhorred and barbarous in speech—then, in truth, the only holy race was the sons of Judah, and among those tribes God reigned in mighty power. The sea saw it and, reverently rolling back its roaring waves, it gave comfort to the fugitive. The sacred Jordan was thrust back upon its silver sources. The huge mountains flung themselves about with mighty leaps like lusty rams in a flourishing garden. All the little hills skipped like lambs dancing to the music of the syrinx about their dear mother.

Why, O dreadful and monstrous sea, didst thou give comfort to the fugitive, rolling back thy roaring waves? Why wast thou, sacred Jordan, thrust back upon thy silver fountains? Why did the huge mountains fling themselves about with mighty leaps like lusty rams in a flourishing garden? Why did you, O little hills, skip like lambs dancing to the music of the syrinx about their dear mother?

Shake, O earth, and fear the Lord who does mighty things; O earth, fear the Lord, the high and holy One of the seed of Isaac, who poured roaring rivers out of the crags and a perennial fountain out of the trickling rock.

AD PATREM

Nunc mea Pierios cupiam per pectora fontes
Irriguas torquere vias, totumque per ora
Volvere laxatum gemino de vertice rivum;
Ut, tenues oblita sonos, audacibus alis
Surgat in officium venerandi Musa parentis.   5
Hoc utcunque tibi gratum, pater optime, carmen
Exiguum meditatur opus, nec novimus ipsi
Aptius a nobis quae possint munera donis
Respondere tuis, quamvis nec maxima possint
Respondere tuis, nedum ut par gratia donis   10
Esse queat vacuis quae redditur arida verbis.
Sed tamen haec nostros ostendit pagina census,
Et quod habemus opum charta numeravimus ista,
Quae mihi sunt nullae, nisi quas dedit aurea Clio
Quas mihi semoto somni peperere sub antro,   15
Et nemoris laureta sacri, Parnassides umbrae.
    Nec tu vatis opus divinum despice carmen,
Quo nihil aethereos ortus, et semina caeli,
Nil magis humanam commendat origine mentem,
Sancta Promethea retinens vestigia flammae.   20
Carmen amant superi, tremebundaque Tartara carmen
Ima ciere valet, divosque ligare profundos,
Et triplici duros Manes adamante coercet.
Carmine seposti retegunt arcana futuri
Phoebades, et tremulae pallentes ora Sibyllae;   25

1–3. Compare the allusion to *Parnassus* in *Elegy IV*, 30–1, note.

4. *tenues . . . sonos,* "trivial songs." Some of the Latin poems,
such as *Elegy* V, are likely to have been in Milton's mind.

4–5. Compare the invocation of the Muse to aid the
                    "advent'rous Song,
            That with no middle flight intends to soar
                Above th' *Aonian* Mount,"
in *P.L.* I, 13–5.

5. Compare the use of *Muse* to mean poetic inspiration in *Vacation
Exercise*, 53, and *Lycidas*, 133.

14. If Milton meant anything in particular by referring to Clio, the
Muse of history, it was the glory that he hoped to win for himself and
his country by writing poetry based on the heroic past of England.

TO HIS FATHER

Now I wish that the Pierian[1] fountains would send their waters flooding through my breast and make my lips the channel for the whole stream that pours from the twin peaks, so that my Muse[5]—her trivial songs[4] forgotten—might rise on bold wings to do honour to my revered father. The song that she is meditating is a poor attempt, dearest father, and not at all certain to please you. Yet I do not know what gifts of mine could more aptly repay yours—though my greatest gifts could never repay yours, for they cannot be equalled by any barren gratitude of futile words. On this page, however, you have an account of my means and whatever wealth I possess I have reckoned up on this paper, for I have nothing except what golden Clio[14] has given and what has been the fruit of dreams in a remote cavern and of the laurel groves of the sacred wood and of the shadows of Parnassus.

You should not despise the poet's task, divine song, which preserves some spark of Promethean fire[20] and is the unrivalled glory of the heaven-born human mind and an evidence of our ethereal origin and celestial descent. The gods on high love song and song has power to move the frightful depths of Tartarus and to bind the gods below and control the implacable shades with triple adamant. By song Apollo's priestesses[25]

---

20. The story that Prometheus brought down fire from heaven to men was interpreted by Conti (*Mythology,* IV, vi), on the authority of Theophrastus, as meaning that he first gave men "cognizance of philosophy and divine matters."

25. *Phoebades*—priestesses of Apollo, especially at Delphi, where the answers of the oracle were usually made in verse.

tremulae . . . Sibyllae: Milton may have thought particularly of the Cumaean Sibyl, whose prophecies Aeneas called "songs" (*carmina, Aen.* VI, 74) and whose changing colour and excitement when she made her prophecy to him (*Aen.* VI, 46–9) were familiar to every schoolboy.

Carmina sacrificus sollennes pangit ad aras,
Aurea seu sternit motantem cornua taurum,
Seu cum fata sagax fumantibus abdita fibris
Consulit, et tepidis Parcam scrutatur in extis.
Nos etiam, patrium tunc cum repetemus Olympum,   30
Aeternaeque morae stabunt immobilis aevi,
Ibimus auratis per caeli templa coronis,
Dulcia suaviloquo sociantes carmina plectro,
Astra quibus geminique poli convexa sonabunt.
Spiritus et rapidos qui circinat igneus orbes   35
Nunc quoque sidereis intercinit ipse choreis
Immortale melos et inenarrabile carmen;
Torrida dum rutilus compescit sibila serpens,
Demissoque ferox gladio mansuescit Orion,
Stellarum nec sentit onus Maurusius Atlas.   40
Carmina regales epulas ornare solebant,
Cum nondum luxus, vastaeque immensa vorago
Nota gulae, et modico spumabat coena Lyaeo.
Tum de more sedens festa ad convivia vates,
Aesculea intonsos redimitus ab arbore crines,   45
Heroumque actus imitandaque gesta canebat,
Et chaos, et positi late fundamina mundi,

---

27. The ancient custom of gilding the horns of sacrificial bulls goes
back as far as Homer's account of Nestor's sacrifice, with its solemn
prayer to Athene and a final felling of the victim by a single blow of
the axe. (*Od.* III, 435–50.) In ancient Rome the forecasting of the
future from the entrails of sacrificed animals was a prominent feature
of official religion.

30–33. Milton remembered St. John's account of the heavenly elders
who are crowned with gold (Rev. iv, 4) and of the "voice of harpers
harping with their harps" (Rev. xiv, 2). Compare the description of
"Olympus" in Christian terms in *On the death of the Bishop of Ely,*
63, note.

34. Compare the "starry Pole" of *P.L.* IV, 724, where "pole" is used,
as Virgil used it (*Aen.* III, 586), to mean the sky itself.

35–37. Perhaps Milton remembered Virgil's allusion (*Aen.* VI, 724–7)
to the Pythagorean doctrine that heaven and earth are animated by a
spirit which is interfused through all their parts. Compare Milton's
allusions to the Pythagorean doctrine of the music of the spheres in
Arcades, 70–3, *Nativity Hymn,* 125–32, note, and in *At a Solemn Music.*

37. With the quintessentially Miltonic phrase, *inenarrabile carmen,*
compare the "unexpressive Nuptial Song" of *Lycidas,* 176.

38. Milton thought of Ovid's account of Phaeton riding the chariot

and the trembling Sibyl, with blanched features, lay bare the
mysteries of the far-away future. Songs are composed by the
sacrificing priest at the altar, both when he smites the bull
that tosses its gilded horns[27] and when his acute eye consults
the secrets of destiny in the steaming flesh and reads fate in
the warm entrails. When we return to our native Olympus
and the everlasting ages of immutable eternity are established,
we shall walk, crowned with gold,[30] through the temples of
the skies and with the harp's soft accompaniment we shall
sing sweet songs to which the stars shall echo and the vault
of heaven from pole to pole.[34] Even now the fiery spirit[35]
who flies through the swift spheres is singing his immortal
melody and unutterable[37] song in harmony with the starry
choruses. Meanwhile the shining Serpent restrains his burning hisses,[38] fierce Orion[39] grows gentle and drops his sword,
and Mauretanian Atlas[40] no longer feels the load of the stars.

Songs were the usual ornaments of royal tables in the times
before luxury and the bottomless appetite of gluttony were
known, when Lyaeus[43] sparkled at the banquet in temperate
cups. Then the custom was that the bard should sit at the
festal banquet, wearing a garland of oak leaves on his unshorn
locks, and should sing of the deeds and emulable achievements
of heroes, and of chaos and of the broad foundations on which

---

of the sun, when he was threatened by the Serpent (the constellation
which winds between the two celestial bears) and by all the other
formidable constellations in the sky. (*Met.* II, 173–5.)

39. See the note on Orion in *On the death of the Bishop of Ely,* 54.

40. See the note on Atlas in *On the Platonic Idea,* 24.

43. *Lyaeus,* "the releaser," was one of Bacchus' epithets. Classical
tradition used both names as synonyms for "wine." *N.E.D.* quotes
Marston's *Antonio's Revenge,* V, iv, "Let Lyeus flote in burnisht gob-
blets."

43–48. Milton thought of Iopas' song about the heavenly bodies and
the origin of the human race at the banquet of Dido and Aeneas (*Aen.*
I, 740–55) and perhaps of Apollo's song to the lyre at the banquet of
the gods in the *Iliad,* I, 603–4.

Reptantesque Deos, et alentes numina glandes,
Et nondum Aetnaeo quaesitum fulmen ab antro.
Denique quid vocis modulamen inane iuvabit   50
Verborum sensusque vacans, numerique loquacis?
Silvestres decet iste choros, non Orphea, cantus,
Qui tenuit fluvios, et quercubus addidit aures,
Carmine, non cithara, simulacraque functa canendo
Compulit in lacrymas; habet has a carmine laudes.   55
     Nec tu perge, precor, sacras contemnere Musas,
Nec vanas inopesque puta, quarum ipse peritus
Munere mille sonos numeros componis ad aptos,
Millibus et vocem modulis variare canoram
Doctus, Arionii merito sis nominis haeres.   60
Nunc tibi quid mirum si me genuisse poetam
Contigerit, caro si tam prope sanguine iuncti
Cognatas artes studiumque affine sequamur?
Ipse volens Phoebus se dispertire duobus,
Altera dona mihi, dedit altera dona parenti,   65
Dividuumque Deum genitorque puerque tenemus.
     Tu tamen ut simules teneras odisse Camenas,
Non odisse reor. Neque enim, pater, ire iubebas
Qua via lata patet, qua pronior area lucri,
Certaque condendi fulget spes aurea nummi;   70
Nec rapis ad leges, male custoditaque gentis
Iura, nec insulsis damnas clamoribus aures.
Sed magis excultam cupiens ditescere mentem,

---

48. The deities who loitered through the forests in search of acorns
seem to be the primitive Titans, before they learned the art of agriculture from Ceres, as Apollonius of Rhodes says that they did.
(*Argonautica, IV,* 982.)

49. Jove's thunderbolts were forged by the Cyclops under Mount
Aetna, where Virgil describes them at work in *Georgic* IV, 170–3.

50–51. There is no inconsistency between these lines and the invocation of Voice and Verse as "sphere-born, harmonious Sisters" in *At a
Solemn Music,* 1–2, for in both cases Milton was expressing his attachment to the traditional conception of the two arts as vitally related to
each other.

52. Compare the allusions to Orpheus in *L'Allegro,* 145–50, and
Il Penseroso, 105–8, notes.

58–60. Of the musical gifts and interests of John Milton, Sr., his songs
in *The Triumphs of Oriana* (1601) and his tunes, *Norwich* and *York,*
in Ravenscroft's *Whole Book of Psalms* (1621), are convincing evidence.

the earth rests, of the deities who once went creeping about in
search of their acorn-food,[48] and of the thunderbolt not yet
sought out of the depths of Aetna.[49]   And now, to sum it all
up, what pleasure is there in the inane modulation of the voice
without words and meaning and rhythmic eloquence?[50]
Such music is good enough for the forest choirs, but not for
Orpheus,[52] who by his song—not by his cithara—restrained
rivers and gave ears to the oaks, and by his singing stirred the
ghosts of the dead to tears.   That fame he owes to his song.

Do not persist, I beg of you, in your contempt for the sacred
Muses, and do not think them futile and worthless whose gift
has taught you to harmonize a thousand sounds to fit numbers,[58] and given you skill to vary the voice of the singer with
countless modulations, so that you are deservedly the heir of
Arion's[60] name.   Now, since it is my lot to have been born a
poet, why does it seem strange to you that we, who are so
closely united by blood, should pursue sister arts and kindred
interests?   Phoebus himself,[64] wishing to part himself between us two, gave some gifts to me and others to my father;
and, father and son, we share the possession of the divided
god.

You may pretend to hate the delicate Muses,[67] but I do not
believe in your hatred.   For you would not bid me go where
the broad way lies wide open, where the field of lucre is easier
and the golden hope of amassing money is glittering and
sure; neither do you force me into the law and the evil ad-
ministration of the national statutes.   You do not condemn
my ears to noisy impertinence.   But rather, because you wish
to enrich the mind which you have carefully cultivated, you

---

60. Arion was a lyric poet of Methymna, in Lesbos, famous for
Herodotus' story (I, 23–4) of his rescue from drowning by the dolphins
that he charmed with his song to his own accompaniment on the lyre.

64. Compare the allusions to Phoebus Apollo as god of music in *At
a Vacation Exercise*, 37, *Comus*, 478, *On Shakespeare*, 12, and *Mansus*, 2.

67. *Camenas;* compare the note on *Camenam* in *Elegy VI*, 3.

Me procul urbano strepitu, secessibus altis
Abductum, Aoniae iucunda per otia ripae,   75
Phoebaeo lateri comitem sinis ire beatum.
    Officium cari taceo commune parentis;
Me poscunt maiora. Tuo, pater optime, sumptu
Cum mihi Romuleae patuit facundia linguae,
Et Latii veneres, et quae Iovis ora decebant   80
Grandia magniloquis elata vocabula Graiis,
Addere suasisti quos iactat Gallia flores,
Et quam degeneri novus Italus ore loquelam
Fundit, Barbaricos testatus voce tumultus
Quaeque Palaestinus loquitur mysteria vates.   85
Denique quicquid habet caelum, subiectaque caelo
Terra parens, terraeque et caelo interfluus aer,
Quicquid et unda tegit, pontique agitabile marmor,
Per te nosse licet, per te, si nosse libebit.
Dimotaque venit spectanda scientia nube,   90
Nudaque conspicuos inclinat ad oscula vultus,
Ni fugisse velim, ni sit libasse molestum.
    I nunc, confer opes, quisquis malesanus avitas
Austriaci gazas Perüanaque regna praeoptas.
Quae potuit maiora pater tribuisse, vel ipse   95
Iupiter, excepto, donasset ut omnia, caelo?
Non potiora dedit, quamvis et tuta fuissent,
Publica qui iuveni commisit lumina nato,
Atque Hyperionios currus, et fraena diei,

---

75. *Aonia,* the name of a plain in Boeotia, standing for the country
itself. Here Milton was thinking of "th' Aonian Mount," *i.e.* Helicon,
the haunt of the Muses, to which he refers in *P.L.* I, 15. Compare
Elegies IV, 29, and *VI,* 17, and *On the Marchioness of Winchester,* 56.

78–85. In *The Reason of Church Government* Milton confirms what
is said here by writing, "I must say . . . that . . . I had for my
first years, by the ceaseless diligence and care of my father, (whom
God recompense!) been exercised to the tongues, and some sciences,
as my age would suffer, by sundry masters and teachers, both at home
and at the schools." (*P.W.* II, 477.)

79. In the Renaissance Romulus was treated as the progenitor of all
the Romans—
            "Great *Romulus* the Grandsyre of them all,"
                        (*F.Q.* I, v, 49, 5.)
as Spenser called him.

lead me far away from the uproar of cities into these high
retreats of delightful leisure beside the Aonian[75] stream, and
you permit me to walk there by Phoebus' side, his blessed
companion.

I will not mention a father's usual generosities, for greater
things have a claim on me. It was at your expense,[78]
dear father, after I had got the mastery of the language of
Romulus[79] and the graces of Latin, and acquired the lofty
speech of the magniloquent Greeks, which is fit for the lips of
Jove himself, that you persuaded me to add the flowers which
France boasts and the eloquence which the modern Italian
pours from his degenerate mouth—testifying by his accent to
the barbarian wars—and the mysteries uttered by the Palestinian prophet.[85]   And finally, all that heaven contains and
earth, our mother, beneath the sky, and the air that flows between earth and heaven, and whatever the waters and the
trembling surface of the sea cover, your kindness gives me the
means to know, if I care for the knowledge that your kindness
offers.   From the opening cloud science appears and, naked,
she bends her face to my kisses, unless I should wish to run
away or unless I should find her enjoyment irksome.

Go now, gather riches,[93] whoever you are whose morbid
preference is for the ancient treasures of Austria and the
lucre of Peru.   What greater gift could come from a father,
or from Jove himself if he had given everything, with the
single exception of heaven?   He who gave to his young son
the common light,[98] the chariot of Hyperion[99] and the reins
of day and the aureole radiating a flood of glory (even assum-

---

85. The mysteries of the Palestinian prophet stand for the Old Testament Scriptures.

93. Warton compared Ovid's ironical advice to amass wealth,
        "I nunc, Sisyphias, improbe, confer opes!"
                (*Heroides,* xii, 204.)

98. The *common lights* (*Publica . . . lumina*) are an echo of Phaeton's address of his father, Apollo, as "O lux inmensi publica mundi."
(*Met.* II, 35.   Compare the note on 38 above.)

99. Hesiod first made Hyperion the father of the sun god (*Theogony,*

Et circum undantem radiata luce tiaram.   100
Ergo ego iam doctae pars quamlibet ima catervae
Victricis hederas inter laurosque sedebo,
Iamque nec obscurus populo miscebor inerti,
Vitabuntque oculos vestigia nostra profanos.
Este procul vigiles curae, procul este querelae,   105
Invidiaeque acies transverso tortilis hirquo,
Saeva nec anguiferos extende, Calumnia, rictus;
In me triste nihil, foedissima turba, potestis,
Nec vestri sum iuris ego; securaque tutus
Pectora vipereo gradiar sublimis ab ictu.   110
    At tibi, care pater, postquam non aequa merenti
Posse referre datur, nec dona rependere factis,
Sit memorasse satis, repetitaque munera grato
Percensere animo, fidaeque reponere menti.
    Et vos, O nostri, iuvenilia carmina, lusus,   115
Si modo perpetuos sperare audebitis annos,
Et domini superesse rogo, lucemque tueri,
Nec spisso rapient oblivia nigra sub Orco,
Forsitan has laudes, decantatumque parentis
Nomen, ad exemplum, sero servabitis aevo.   120

                                                (1636-7)

_____

371-4), but later classical tradition justified his identification with the
sun himself. Compare Spenser in his paraphrase of Virgil's *Culex:*
        "*Hyperion* throwing foorth his beames full hott,
         Into the highest top of heaven gan clime,
         And the world parting by an equall lott,
         Did shed his whirling flames on either side."
                    (*Virgils Gnat*, 156-9.)

    101-104. The thought, though it is characteristic of Milton and looks
forward to his hope for "fit audience . . . though few" in *P.L.* VII,
31, was probably an echo of Horace's boast that his poetry would distinguish him from the mob. (*Odes*, I, i, 29-34.) The spirit of the
entire passage is conventional. Compare Spenser:
        "But such as neither of themselves can sing,
         Nor yet are sung of others for reward,
         Die in obscure oblivion," *etc.*
                    (*The Ruines of Time*, 344-6.)

    105-107. Again the attitude is conventional. Compare the young
Spenser's saying that
        "The vaunted verse a vacant head demaundes,
         Ne wont with crabbed Care the Muses dwell:
         Unwisely weaves, that takes two webbes in hand."
                    (*October*, 100-2.)

ing that those gifts were harmless) bestowed no grander gifts. Therefore, however humble my present place in the company of learned men, I shall sit with the ivy and laurel of a victor.[101] I shall no longer mingle unknown with the dull rabble and my walk shall be far from the sight of profane eyes. Begone,[105] sleepless cares and complaints, and the twisted glance of envy with goatish leer.[106] Malevolent Calumny, open not your dragon gorge. You have no power to harm me, O detestable band; and I am not under your jurisdiction. I shall walk with heart secure, lifted high above your viper stroke.

But to you, dear father, since no requital equal to your desert and no deeds equal to your gifts are within my power, let it suffice that with a grateful mind I remember and tell over your constant kindnesses, and lay them up in a loyal heart.

And you, my juvenile verses and amusements, if only you dare hope for immortality[111] and a life and a glimpse of the light beyond your master's funeral pyre, and if dark oblivion does not sweep you down into the throngs of Orcus,[118] perhaps you will preserve this eulogy and the name of the father whom my song honours as an example to remote ages.

----

106. The allusion is to the "evil eye" of envy and the twisted syntax, as MacKellar points out, seems to owe something to Virgil's "transversa tuentibus hircis," in *Eclogue* III, 8.

111–120. Milton's faith in the power of his verse to confer immortality is more modest than Horace's in the famous Ode (III, xxx) which begins, "I have raised a monument more enduring than brass."

118. *Orcus*—the abode of the dead.

LYCIDAS

In this Monody the Author bewails a learned Friend, unfortunately drown'd in his Passage from *Chester* on the *Irish* Seas, 1637.
And by occasion foretells the ruin of our corrupted Clergy then in
their height.

YET once more, O ye Laurels, and once more
Ye Myrtles brown, with Ivy never sere,
I come to pluck your Berries harsh and crude,
And with forc'd fingers rude,
Shatter your leaves before the mellowing year.   5
Bitter constraint, and sad occasion dear,
Compels me to disturb your season due:
For *Lycidas* is dead, dead ere his prime,
Young *Lycidas,* and hath not left his peer:
Who would not sing for *Lycidas*? he knew   10

1–2. In the invocation of the laurel, with which poets since Pindar
were traditionally supposed to be crowned, and of its kindred myrtle,
and of the ivy, with which Horace in his first Ode prayed that his
learned brows might some day be bound, there is an indication that
Milton's real theme is to be his own poetic aspirations.

2. *brown*—dusky, dark. Compare "the alleys brown" of *P.R.* II, 293.

2. *sere*—dry, withered.

3–5. *crude*—unripe. Milton was thinking of his own "late spring"
as an artist and of the want of "inward ripeness" which disturbed him
in the Sonnet *On his being arrived at the Age of Twenty-three.*

6. *dear* has the obsolete meaning, "of intimate concern," "personally costly." So Shakespeare spoke of himself as "made lame by
fortune's dearest spite." (Sonnet xxxvii, 3.)

7. *Compels* is singular because its two subjects fuse into one conception. Compare Shakespeare's "Plenty and Peace breeds cowards."
(*Cymbeline,* III, vi, 21.)

8–9. Spenser, in his "pastoral elegie" for Sir Philip Sidney, who died
in his thirty-second year, when he was seven years older than King,
used similar repetition with its stress on youth:
"Young *Astrophel* the pride of shepheards praise,
    Young *Astrophel,* the rusticke lasses love."
                    (*Astrophel,* 7–8.)

10. The line translates Virgil's question, "Who would refuse songs
for Gallus?" (*Eclogues,* X, 3.)

10–11. *he knew . . . to sing,* i.e., he understood singing, is a
Latin idiom. King's music seems to have been limited to a few
mediocre Latin poems.

Himself to sing, and build the lofty rhyme.
He must not float upon his wat'ry bier
Unwept, and welter to the parching wind,
Without the meed of some melodious tear.
   Begin then, Sisters of the sacred well,   15
That from beneath the seat of *Jove* doth spring,
Begin, and somewhat loudly sweep the string.
Hence with denial vain, and coy excuse,
So may some gentle Muse
With lucky words favour my destin'd Urn,   20
And as he passes turn,
And bid fair peace be to my sable shroud.
For we were nurst upon the self-same hill,
Fed the same flock, by fountain, shade, and rill.
   Together both, ere the high Lawns appear'd   25

---

11. Milton may have thought of Horace's compliment to Florus on his skill in "building lovely verses" (*Epistles*, I, iii, 24) and perhaps also of Aristophanes' praise of Aeschylus (*Frogs*, 1004) for his "towering language."

14. Compare the Heliconian "tears of perfect moan" in *An Epitaph on the Marchioness of Winchester*, l. 55.

15. The line brings back the refrain with which Thyrsis begins his lament for Daphnis in Theocritus' first Idyl and the similar refrain in Moschus' *Lament for Bion;* "Begin ye Sicilian Muses, begin the dirge."

15–16. Here and in *Il Penseroso*, 47–8, Milton thought of Hesiod's induction to the *Theogony*, which chants the Muses, "queens of Mount Helicon," who dance about the fountain Aganippe and the altar of Zeus. In the second *Prolusion* he found a symbol of the divine harmony of the universe in the story—which "has prevailed from the very beginning of things . . . . . about the Muses dancing day and night about the altar of Jove."

19–22. "So (*i.e.*, on condition that I lament Lycidas) may some gentle poet favour my memory by writing something felicitous" is Milton's thought, which, like his syntax, was moulded by Virgil's invocation of his Muse to mourn for Gallus. (*Eclogues* X, 4–5.)

23–24. In Castiglione's Latin elegy, *Alcon*, he describes himself as living with his friend from childhood, bearing heat and cold and day and night with him; but in Milton's use of the convention there is little more than recognition that both he and King were alumni of the same nursing mother, Cambridge.

25. *high Lawns*—grassy uplands. Milton's setting is really a conventional Italian landscape rather than the drenched plains which surround Cambridge.

Under the opening eye-lids of the morn,
We drove afield, and both together heard
What time the Gray-fly winds her sultry horn,
Batt'ning our flocks with the fresh dews of night,
Oft till the Star that rose, at Ev'ning, bright   30
Toward Heav'n's descent had slop'd his westering wheel.
Meanwhile the Rural ditties were not mute,
Temper'd to th'Oaten Flute;
Rough *Satyrs* danc'd, and *Fauns* with clov'n heel,
From the glad sound would not be absent long,   35
And old *Damaetas* lov'd to hear our song.
    But O the heavy change, now thou art gone,
Now thou art gone, and never must return!
Thee Shepherd, thee the Woods, and desert Caves,
With wild Thyme and the gadding Vine o'ergrown,   40
And all their echoes mourn.
The Willows and the Hazel Copses green
Shall now no more be seen,
Fanning their joyous Leaves to thy soft lays.
As killing as the Canker to the Rose,   45

---

26. Perhaps there is a trace of the marginal reading in Job iii, 9—
"the eyelids of the morning"—both here and in *Comus*, 978. Henry
More used Milton's phrase here in *Psychozoia*, Canto I, stanza 24.

28. *winds*—blows.
sultry refers to the noon-day heat when the "horn" is heard.

29. *Batt'ning*—fattening.

30–31. Compare *Comus*, 93, *rose*—appeared in the zenith.

33. Compare *Comus*, 345, note.

34. So Virgil says that the Wood-gods and wild beasts came thronging
to hear the song of Old Silenus. (*Eclogues*, VI, 27.)

36. *Damaetas* must have meant some figure of Milton's undergraduate
days, perhaps someone who had actually had the name of the character in
Virgil's third *Eclogue* attached to him. Miss Nicolson suggests Joseph
Mede, the greatest of the Cambridge tutors in Milton's time.

39–41. The "pathetic fallacy" goes back to Theocritus' first *Idyl*, but
there it is the flocks and even the wild animals that grieve for Daphnis.
In the *Lament for Bion* the spirits of the fountains grieve and "Echo in
the rocks laments that thou art silent, and no more she mimics thy
voice." (Lang's translation of Moschus' *Idyl*, III.)

44. The trees flutter their leaves with pleasure, as Virgil says that the
oaks did when Silenus sang.

45. *Canker;* compare *Arcades*, 53, note.

Or Taint-worm to the weanling Herds that graze,
Or Frost to Flowers, that their gay wardrobe wear,
When first the White-thorn blows,
Such, *Lycidas,* thy loss to Shepherd's ear.
    Where were ye Nymphs when the remorseless deep   50
Clos'd o'er the head of your lov'd *Lycidas?*
For neither were ye playing on the steep,
Where your old *Bards,* the famous *Druids,* lie,
Nor on the shaggy top of *Mona* high,
Nor yet where *Deva* spreads her wizard stream: 55
Ay me, I fondly dream!
Had ye been there—for what could that have done?

---

46. The *Taint-worm,* which Thomas Tusser's *Hundreth pointes of good husbandry* says "lurks where ox should eat," was supposed to be deadly to cattle.

47. *wardrobe* was written by Milton in the not unusual seventeenth century form, "wardrop."

48. *White-thorn*—hawthorn.

50. So Thyrsis begins his lament in Theocritus' first *Idyl* by asking: "Where were ye, O where were ye, Nymphs, when Daphnis was languishing? Beside the Peneus in beautiful Tempe or on the slopes of Pindus? For surely you were not near the great stream of the river Anapus nor on the look-out crest of Aetna nor by the sacred water of Acis." Virgil's lament for Gallus makes a similar, but less poignant and circumstantial appeal to the Naiades. (*Eclogues,* X, 9–12.)

52–53. Warton was probably right in identifying *the steep* with the mountain Kerig-y-Druidion in Denbigh, the ancient burying-place of the Druids. In the opening paragraph of *The History of Britain* Milton betrays his enthusiasm over "the *British Druids,* who taught those of *Gaul,*" and were masters of Greek and "inquisitive into the highest" things, especially into "the Knowledge of Times and Ages." Compare *Manso,* 41–3.

54. *Mona*—the Isle of Anglesea, a centre of Druid activity.

55. *Deva*—the river Dee, which forms part of the boundary between England and Wales and falls into the Irish Sea northwest of Chester, is called *wizard* because, as Drayton explained, it was
                "an ominous flood,
  That changing of his foards, the future ill or good
  Of either country told, of either's war or peace,
  The sickness or the health, the dearth or the increase."
             (*Polyolbion,* Song X, 205–8.)

56. *I fondly dream etc.*—*i.e.,* it is idle to dream that ye might have been there.

What could the Muse herself that *Orpheus* bore,
The Muse herself, for her enchanting son
Whom Universal nature did lament,   60
When by the rout that made the hideous roar,
His gory visage down the stream was sent,
Down the swift *Hebrus* to the *Lesbian* shore?
    Alas!   What boots it with uncessant care
To tend the homely slighted Shepherd's trade,   65
And strictly meditate the thankless Muse?
Were it not better done as others use,
To sport with *Amaryllis* in the shade,
Or with the tangles of *Neaera's* hair?
Fame is the spur that the clear spirit doth raise   70
(That last infirmity of Noble mind)
To scorn delights, and live laborious days;
But the fair Guerdon when we hope to find,
And think to burst out into sudden blaze,
Comes the blind *Fury* with th'abhorred shears,   75

---

58. *the Muse*—Calliope, the muse of epic poetry, or Polyhymnia, the muse of hymns to the gods.

60–63. Milton remembered Ovid's description of "the huge uproar of Berecyntian flutes, mixed with discordant horns, the drums, the breast-beatings and howlings" of the Thracian women, devotees of Bacchus, who found Orpheus with the beasts and trees and rocks about him, enchanted by his song, and tore him limb from limb, sending his head adrift down the Hebrus to float at last across the Aegean sea to Lesbos. (*Met.* XI, 1–60.) In *P.L.* VII, 32–5, he reverted to the myth, but identified himself with Orpheus.

64. *boots*—profits. Compare S.A. 560, note.

65–69. "To meditate the Muse" is Virgil's phrase (*Eclogues,* 1, 2) for the poet's task, and Virgil's Amaryllis (*Eclogues,* II, 14–5) might serve as a symbol for the inspiration of the erotic poets whom Milton condemned. The names of both nymphs were traditional and Milton may have had a poem of George Buchanan entitled *Naera* in mind.

67. *as others use*—as other poets are accustomed to do. Compare *use* in 136 below.

70. Compare *Comus,* 381; "He that has light within his own clear breast."

71. A famous passage in Tacitus' *Histories,* IV, v, praises Helvidius Priscus for dedicating his youth to strenuous study and excuses his ambition on the ground that "the passion for glory is the last from which even wise men free themselves."

75–76. *the blind Fury*—Atropos, the Fate whose duty it was to cut the threads of men's lives after her sisters had spun them out. See

And slits the thin-spun life.   But not the praise,
Phoebus repli'd, and touch'd my trembling ears;
Fame is no plant that grows on mortal soil,
Nor in the glistering foil
Set off to th'world, nor in broad rumour lies,   80
But lives and spreads aloft by those pure eyes
And perfect witness of all judging *Jove;*
As he pronounces lastly on each deed,
Of so much fame in Heav'n expect thy meed.

   O Fountain *Arethuse,* and thou honour'd 'flood,   85
Smooth-sliding *Mincius,* crown'd with vocal reeds,
That strain I heard was of a higher mood: *forced figure*
But now my Oat proceeds,
And listens to the Herald of the Sea
That came in *Neptune's* plea.   90
He ask'd the Waves, and ask'd the Felon winds,

Arcades, 63–9, note. Milton called her *blind* because she works indiscriminately, like the goddess Fortune. He called her a Fury, perhaps thinking of Prometheus' saying that those who guide the helm of Necessity are the "Fates triple-formed, the Furies unforgetting." (Aeschylus' *Prometheus,* 516.)

77. *Phoebus*—Apollo, god of poetic inspiration, who Virgil says (*Eclogues* VI, 3–4) plucked his ears, warning him against hasty ambitions.

79. *glistering foil*—the glittering setting of a gem. Fuller speaks of false diamonds as deceptive even to a good jeweller when "set with a good foil." (*Worthies,* I, 300 [1840].)

80. *broad rumour*—widespread fame or reputation.

81–84. These essentially Christian lines have been compared with Lactantius' promise that, although it may suffer in this world, virtue is sure of an eternal reward with God as its judge (*Divine Institutes,* V, xviii, §9); and they might be compared with St. Thomas Aquinas' faith in the beatific vision as the heavenly reward of those who are not blinded by earthly prizes. (*Summa contra Gentiles,* III, lxiii, §5.)

85–87. By invoking the Sicilian fountain Arethusa, to which Theocritus made Thyrsis appeal (*Idyl* I, 117), and the river Mincius which Virgil describes in its course across the Lombard plains to join the Po as moving between banks sheltered by delicate reeds (*Eclogues,* VII, 12–3), Milton returns from the "higher mood" of the preceding lines to the level of pastoral poetry. Compare the note on *mood, S.A.* 662.

88. *Oat*—oaten pipe, song. Compare *Comus,* 345, note.

89. *Herald of the Sea*—Compare the note on Triton as the herald of Neptune in *Comus,* 873.

90. *in Neptune's plea*—for Neptune's defence, *i.e.,* against the charge that he was responsible for the drowning of Lycidas in his realm.

What hard mishap hath doom'd this gentle swain?
And question'd every gust of rugged wings
That blows from off each beaked Promontory.
They knew not of his story,   95
And sage *Hippotades* their answer brings,
That not a blast was from his dungeon stray'd,
The Air was calm, and on the level brine,
Sleek *Panope* with all her sisters play'd.
It was that fatal and perfidious Bark   100
Built in 'th'eclipse, and rigg'd with curses dark,
That sunk so low that sacred head of thine.
   Next *Camus,* reverend Sire, went footing slow,
His Mantle hairy, and his Bonnet sedge, *sea wicks*
Inwrought with figures dim, and on the edge   105
Like to that sanguine flower inscrib'd with woe.
Ah! Who hath reft (quoth he) my dearest pledge?

[marginal handwritten notes: "imply something iron into ship", "no real Consolation"]

96. *Hippotades*—Aeolus, the son of Hippotas and god of the winds,
is called sage, perhaps because Diodorus Siculus says that he invented sails and taught the art of predicting storms. (*Historical
Library,* 5, 7.) Compare *Elegy IV,* 5–6, note.

99. *Panope* is mentioned in the *Aeneid* V, 240, as if she were the
greatest of the Nereids and one of the gods who have "the empire of
the sea." Compare *Comus,* 837, note, and *Elegy IV,* 7.

100. Here (and perhaps elsewhere in *Lycidas*) there may be a reminiscence of Propertius' *Elegies,* III, 7. Mr. F. R. B. Godolphin compares
Propertius' doomed voyagers in the line (100) ". . . portabat sanctos
alveus ille viros." (*Elegies,* IV, vi, 16.)

101. Milton suggests that the ship was doomed because a curse was
laid on it when it was first built or because an eclipse shed its "dis-
astrous twilight" (*P.L.* I, 597) on the construction.

103. *Camus,* the river god of the Cam, represents the ancient University of Cambridge. Milton makes him as mysterious and venerable
as Virgil did the river god of the Tiber, the "Father Tiber" to whom
Aeneas prays. (*Aen.* VIII, 72.)

105. The *figures dim* may refer to the markings on the ripening
sedge-leaves or to symbolical embroidery of some kind on the mantle.

106. The *sanguine flower* is the "inscribed hyacinth" of Theocritus
(*Idyl* X, 28), which Ovid explains was created by Apollo from the
blood of the youth, Hyacinth, whom he killed by accident when they
were throwing the discus together. "And not satisfied with this,
Apollo inscribed his grieving words upon the leaves, AI AI, characters
of mourning." (*Met.* X, 214–6.)

107. *pledge*—a child, considered as "a hostage given to fortune."
(*N.E.D.*)

Last came, and last did go,
The Pilot of the *Galilean* lake.
Two massy Keys he bore of metals twain,   110
(The Golden opes, the Iron shuts amain).
He shook his Mitred locks, and stern bespake:
How well could I have spar'd for thee, young swain,
Enough of such as for their bellies' sake,
Creep and intrude and climb into the fold?   115
Of other care they little reck'ning make,
Than how to scramble at the shearers' feast,
And shove away the worthy bidden guest.
Blind mouths! that scarce themselves know how to hold
A Sheep-hook, or have learn'd aught else the least   120

109–112. *The Pilot*—St. Peter, in whose ship Jesus preached to the crowd beside the Sea of Galilee (Luke v, 2–4) and to whom Jesus promised (Mat. xvi, 19) to give "the keys of the kingdom of heaven." He comes wearing a mitre as the first bishop of the universal Church, for King was preparing to become a clergyman. By a symbolism like that which represents God as ruling Heaven with a golden sceptre and Hell with a sceptre of iron in *P.L.* II, 327–8, Milton imagined St. Peter's keys as made of gold and iron so as respectively to open and shut Heaven's gates.

114–115. Milton remembered Jesus' ideal of the good shepherd who "giveth his life for the sheep" and his parable of the thief who "entereth not by the door into the sheep-fold, but climbeth up some other way." (John x, 11 and 1.) Satire of the corrupt clergy which stemmed from this passage went back in English pastoral poetry through *The Shepheardes Calendar*—May, July and September eclogues —to John Skelton's charge that:

> Laye men say indede
> How they take no hede
> Theyr sely shepe to fede,
> But plucke away and pull
> The fleces of theyr wull,
> Vnethes they leue a locke
> Of wull amonges theyr flocke.
> (*Colin Clout*, 75–81.)

117. *the shearers' feast*—Compare *Comus*, 179, note.

119. *Blind mouths*—the spiritually blind pastors whose sermons Milton said were "huddled up at the odd hours of a whole lazy week," while they often rambled "from benefice to benefice, like ravenous wolves seeking where they may devour the biggest." (*Tenure of Kings*, *P.W.* II, 36.)

120. As a matter-of-course in his prose Milton used the sheep-hook as an emblem of a clergyman's responsibility, and threatened the clergy who could "reject the pastorly rod and sheep-hook of Christ"

That to the faithful Herdman's art belongs!
What recks it them?   What need they?   They are sped;
And when they list, their lean and flashy songs
Grate on their scrannel Pipes of wretched straw.
The hungry Sheep look up, and are not fed,   125
But swoln with wind, and the rank mist they draw,
Rot inwardly, and foul contagion spread:
Besides what the grim Wolf with privy paw
Daily devours apace, and nothing said;
But that two-handed engine at the door   130
Stands ready to smite once, and smite no more.
    Return *Alpheus,* the dread voice is past,
That shrunk thy streams; Return *Sicilian* Muse,
And call the Vales, and bid them hither cast

with "the iron sceptre of his anger." (*Of Reformation in England, P.W.*
II, 412.)

    122. *What recks it them?*—Of what importance is it to them?   For
the impersonal verb see *Comus,* 404, note.
    They are sped—they have prospered (*i.e.,* are in secure positions).

    123. *flashy*—tasteless, vapid. "Distilled books," said Bacon, "are
flashy things." (*Of Studies.*)

    124. *scrannel*—thin, feeble. The racy word is Milton's parallel to a
jibe of one of Virgil's shepherds at another whose strident pipe had
been heard too often in the market-place. (*Eclogues,* III, 27.)

    126. *rank*—poisonous.

    128–131. The *grim Wolf* may refer both to the Roman Catholics and
to the partisans of the reactionary Archbishop Laud. Of the countless interpretations of the *two-handed engine* which have been proposed none is demonstrable, but the two hands may represent the
two Houses of Parliament. The engine seems like a symbol of its
power to establish true liberty, like the "wholesome and preventive
Shears" which Milton foresaw the Long Parliament using against "the
New Forcers of Conscience." (*On the New Forcers etc.,* l. 15.)

    132–133. To make a transition like that at line 85 Milton invokes the
river Alpheus, whose god loved Arethusa and mingled his streams
with hers. Compare *Arcades,* 30, note.

    134–135. Milton's justification here is found in passages in earlier
pastoral elegies, like Spenser's fancy that grief for Dido could
                    "undoe Dame Natures kindly course;
        The faded lockes fall from the loftie oke,
        The flouds do gaspe, for dryed is theyr sourse,
        And flouds of teares flowe in theyr stead perforse.
              The mantled meadows mourne,
              Theyr sondry colours tourne."
(November Eclogue, 124–9. Compare ll. 39–41 above, note.)

Their Bells and Flowrets of a thousand hues.   135
Ye valleys low where the mild whispers use
Of shades and wanton winds and gushing brooks,   *flowers*
On whose fresh lap the swart Star sparely looks,   *escape*
Throw hither all your quaint enamell'd eyes,
That on the green turf suck the honied showers,   140
And purple all the ground with vernal flowers.
Bring the rathe Primrose that forsaken dies,
The tufted Crow-toe, and pale Jessamine,
The white Pink, and the Pansy freakt with jet,
The glowing Violet,   145
The Musk-rose, and the well attir'd Woodbine,
With Cowslips wan that hang the pensive head,
And every flower that sad embroidery wears:
Bid *Amaranthus* all his beauty shed,

---

135. *Bells*—flowers.

138. *the swart Star*—Sirius, whose rising in the late summer brings
heats which burn the landscape swart or dark.

139. *quaint*—fantastic. Compare the use in *Arcades,* 47.

enamell'd; so Milton spoke of the "gay enamell'd colours mixt" of
the "Blossoms and Fruits . . . of golden hue" against their background of foliage in Eden. (*P.L.* IV, 147–8.)

141. *purple*—stain with purple or brilliant colour, as Milton described the celestial pavement, "Impurpl'd with Celestial Roses." (*P.L.*
III, 363.)

142. *rathe*—early. Milton's first draft for *forsaken* was "unwedded."
In the first *Prolusion* he speaks of the languishing flowers as "almost
surrendering themselves to the sun and secretly asking that he wipe
away with his kisses their tears, which his absences had caused." So
George Wither made the primrose the sun's lover, who
                    "droops and mourns,
          Bedew'd, as 'twere, with tears till he returns."

143. *Crow-toe*—probably the hyacinth, although the name is popularly given in England to various species of buttercup. (*N.E.D.*)

144. *freakt*—mottled, speckled.

146. *attir'd* may imply comparison with a woman's hat, for the word
was used, as Palsgrave explained (195/2), to mean something appropriate for a gentlewoman's head.

149. *Amaranthus,* "the unfading flower" in St. Peter's "crown of glory
that fadeth not away" (I Peter v, 4), seems always to have been for
Milton
                    "a Flow'r which once
          In Paradise, fast by the Tree of Life
          Began to bloom."
                    (*P.L.* III, 353–5.)

And Daffadillies fill their cups with tears,　　　　　　　150
To strew the Laureate Hearse where *Lycid* lies.
For so to interpose a little ease,
Let our frail thoughts dally with false surmise.
Ay me! Whilst thee the shores, and sounding Seas
Wash far away, where'er thy bones are hurl'd,　　　　　155
Whether beyond the stormy *Hebrides,*
Where thou perhaps under the whelming tide
Visit'st the bottom of the monstrous world;
Or whether thou to our moist vows denied,
Sleep'st by the fable of *Bellerus* old,　　　　　　　　160
Where the great vision of the guarded Mount
Looks toward *Namancos* and *Bayona's* hold;

---

151. *Hearse*—bier. Compare *An Epitaph on the Marchioness of Winchester,* 22 and 55, notes.

152. Perhaps Milton was familiar with the "flower passage" in Castiglione's *Alcon.* Like Milton's, it is justified as "a solace for our grief."

155. *Hebrides*—the large island group west of Scotland.

158. *the monstrous world*—the world of sea-monsters. Compare the "monstrous rout" in *Comus,* 533.

159. *moist vows*—tearful prayers. Compare the use of "vows" in *Arcades,* 6.

160. The phrasing of *by the fable of Bellerus (i.e.,* by fabulous Bellerus) should be compared with *the dreaded name of Demogorgon (i.e.,* dreadful Demogorgon) in *P.L.* II, 964–5.
　Bellerium was the Roman name for Land's End, supposedly for Bellerus, a companion of the legendary Corineus for whom Giraldus Cambrensis (*Description of Wales, Historical Works,* ed. by Wright, 1863, p. 479) says that Cornwall was named. In Milton's manuscript *Corineus* is deleted in favour of *Bellerus,* and in *Manso,* 46, there is an allusion to him. Here he may have been influenced by Ludowick Brisket's Elegy for Sir Philip Sidney, where Corineus appears, "cursing oft the fates that this mishap had bred." (*The Mourning Muse of Thestylis,* 31.)

162. Nemancos is a region near the Spanish coast just east of Cape Finisterre, which was represented in Ojea's map of Galicia (first published by Ortelius in 1606) as so picturesquely mountainous that Milton could readily imagine a landmark there to correspond with St. Michael's Mount. Ojea was responsible for the misspelling, *Namancos,* which was perpetuated by Mercator's and many other popular atlases.
　Bayona was a famous Spanish stronghold with a fortification on a steep promontory about fifty miles south of Cape Finisterre.

Look homeward Angel now, and melt with ruth:
And, O ye *Dolphins,* waft the hapless youth.
   Weep no more, woeful Shepherds weep no more,   165
For *Lycidas* your sorrow is not dead,
Sunk though he be beneath the wat'ry floor,
So sinks the day-star in the Ocean bed,
And yet anon repairs his drooping head,
And tricks his beams, and with new spangled Ore, 170
Flames in the forehead of the morning sky:
So *Lycidas,* sunk low, but mounted high,
Through the dear might of him that walk'd the waves,
Where other groves, and other streams along,

---

163. If the thought in lines 161–2 is parenthetical, the *Angel* is Lycidas; but the play on *Looks—Look* suggests that Michael is meant.

   ruth—pity.

164. In the background is the story of the poet, Arion, whom a crew of pirates cast adrift; but his song

                "unto him drew
    The eares and hearts of all that goodly crew,
    That even yet the dolphin, which him bore
    Through the Ægæan seas from pirates vew,
    Stood still by him astonisht at his lore,
And all the raging seas for joy forgot to rore."
                (*F.Q.* IV, xi, 23, 4–9.)

   waft—to convey safely by water. (*N.E.D.*) Compare, "Away with her, and waft her hence to France." (*III Henry VI,* V, vi, 41.)

165. This form of transition to the final movement of the elegy was a tradition which went back to the corresponding line in Theocritus' first *Idyl;* "Stay, O Muses, stay your pastoral songs."

166. *your sorrow*—the cause of your sorrow.

168. The *day-star* is probably the sun, the "diurnal star" of *P.L.* X, 1069, rather than the morning star.

170. *tricks*—dresses gorgeously. Compare *Il Penseroso,* 123.

171. The ancient conception of the sun sinking into the ocean at night in order to rise more glorious in the morning appears again in *Comus,* 95–101.

173. *him that walk'd the waves*—Christ, whom "the disciples saw . . . walking on the sea." (Mat. xiv, 26.)

174–176. Milton thought of the marriage song of the Lamb in Revelation, xix, and of "the living fountains of waters" (Rev. vii, 17) and "the tree of life" (Rev. xxii, 2) beside which he later described "the Spirits elect" binding "thir resplendent locks inwreath'd with beams." (*P.L.* III, 361. Compare the *Third Elegy,* 40–68, and *Damon's Epitaph,* 198–219.)

With *Nectar* pure his oozy Locks he laves,   175
And hears the unexpressive nuptial Song,
In the blest Kingdoms meek of joy and love.
There entertain him all the Saints above,
In solemn troops, and sweet Societies
That sing, and singing in their glory move,   180
And wipe the tears for ever from his eyes.
Now *Lycidas* the Shepherds weep no more;
Henceforth thou art the Genius of the shore,
In thy large recompense, and shalt be good
To all that wander in that perilous flood.   185
 Thus sang the uncouth Swain to th'Oaks and rills,
While the still morn went out with Sandals gray.
He touch't the tender stops of various Quills,
With eager thought warbling his *Doric* lay:
And now the Sun had stretch't out all the hills,   190
And now was dropt into the Western bay;

176. *unexpressive*—inexpressible, indescribable. Compare the closing allusion to the "marriage supper of the Lamb" (Rev. xix, 9) in *Epitaphium Damonis*, 216–7.

181. An echo of the promise that "God shall wipe away all tears from their eyes." (Rev. vii, 17 and xxi, 4.)

183–185. King becomes a *Genius* or local god of the Irish Sea, who will be "good" to voyagers there. So Virgil imagined Julius Caesar as deified and begged him (*Eclogues*, V, 56–65) to look down from above the stars and be "good" to his countrymen. In countless pastoral elegies the pagan motif had been christianized, and perhaps most strikingly by Sannazaro in his Latin piscatory eclogues (I), where he mourned for a friend who had been drowned at sea and begged him to look down from the sacred societies on high to be kind to poor travellers and fishermen. Compare *Damon's Epitaph*, 207–8.

186. *uncouth*—unknown or unlearned and rude. In either sense, the word is an apologetic allusion to the writer.

187. Compare the "Pilgrim steps" and "amice gray" of morning in *P.R.* IV, 427.

188. *Quills*—hollow stems of reeds in Pan's pipes.

189. Because Theocritus, Bion, and Moschus wrote in the Doric Greek of Sicily, *Doric* became the conventional term for pastoral poetry.

190. Milton remembered the allusion to the lengthening shadows from the mountain-tops which closes Virgil's first *Eclogue*.

At last he rose, and twitch't his Mantle blue:
Tomorrow to fresh Woods, and Pastures new.

(Nov. 1637)

---

192. *twitch't: i.e.,* threw the mantle on.

193. The line is little more than the poet's leave-taking of his song—
like Virgil's leave-taking of his lament for Gallus in closing *Eclogue X,*
but it may bear interpretation as a solemn farewell to pastoral poetry,
or to England (*i.e.,* for Italy), or to scenes which too poignantly recall
the poet's happiness with Lycidas.

*see Paul E. More: "How
To Read Lycidas"
not too valid*

AD LEONORAM ROMAE CANENTEM

Angelus unicuique suus—sic credite, gentes—
　Obtigit aethereis ales ab ordinibus.
Quid mirum, Leonora, tibi si gloria maior?
　Nam tua praesentem vox sonat ipsa Deum.
Aut Deus, aut vacui certe mens tertia caeli,　　　　　　5
　Per tua secreto guttura serpit agens;
Serpit agens, facilisque docet mortalia corda
　Sensim immortali assuescere posse sono.
Quod, si cuncta quidem Deus est, per cunctaque fusus,
　In te una loquitur, caetera mutus habet.　　　　　10

(1638–9)

1–2. The Attendant Spirit in *Comus* is Milton's best expression of the belief in guardian spirits. "Socrates had his *Daemonium saturnium & igneum*," said Burton (*Anatomy*, I, ii, 1, 2), "*Plotinus* his; and we Christians our assisting Angel."

3. Masson (*Life of Milton*, 1881, Vol. I, p. 803) suggests that it was during his first Roman visit, in October and November, 1638, at an entertainment in the palace of Cardinal Barberini, that Milton heard the famous Neapolitan singer, Leonora Baroni. In 1639 a volume of tributes to her, by many hands and in several languages, was published in Rome: *Applausi Poetici alle Glorie della Signora Leonora Baroni*.

5. Is this an allusion to I John v, 7: "For there are three that bear record in heaven, the Father, the Word, and the Holy Ghost"?

TO LEONORA SINGING IN ROME

Over everyone—so let the nations believe—his own particular angel[1] from out the heavenly hierarchies spreads protecting
wings.   What wonder, Leonora,[3] if a greater glory be yours?
For the music of your voice itself bespeaks the presence of
God.   Either God, or certainly some third mind[5] from the
untenanted skies, is moving mysteriously in your throat—
mysteriously moving and graciously teaching mortal hearts
how they may gradually become accustomed to immortal
tones.   If God is all things and permeates all things,[9] in you
alone he speaks and possesses all His other creatures in silence.

9–10. Keightley properly compared Virgil's conception of the universe
as moved by an omnipresent intelligence:
". . . . totamque infusa per artus
Mens agitat molem, et toto se corpore miscet";
(*Aen.* VI, 726–7.)
for it was constantly cited by Italian Neo-Platonists in proof of
pantheistic theories like those of Giordano Bruno, who cited the lines
in *De la causa, Principio e Uno*. (*Opere Italiane*, Ed. by Gentile, 1925,
I, p. 179.)

AD EANDEM

Altera Torquatum cepit Leonora Poetam,
  Cuius ab insano cessit amore furens.
Ah miser ille tuo quanto felicius aevo
  Perditus, et propter te, Leonora, foret!
Et te Pieria sensisset voce canentem   5
  Aurea maternae fila movere lyrae!
Quamvis Dircaeo torsisset lumina Pentheo
  Saevior, aut totus desipuisset iners,
Tu tamen errantes caeca vertigine sensus
  Voce eadem poteras composuisse tua;   10
Et poteras, aegro spirans sub corde quietem,
  Flexanimo cantu restituisse sibi.

                                                      (1638–9)

_____

  1. The insanity of Torquato Tasso (1544–95), from which he suffered intermittently during the last twenty years of his career, was due
to many causes—among them his difficulties with the critics of the
Jerusalem Delivered. His attachment to Leonora d'Este, the sister of
his patron, Alfonso, the Duke of Ferrara, has played a larger part in
the literature about him than it did in his life.

TO THE SAME

ANOTHER Leonora made a captive of the poet, Torquato, who, for passionate love of her, went mad.[1] Ah, unhappy man, how much more blessedly he might have been brought to ruin in your times and for your sake, Leonora. He would have heard you singing with Pierian voice as you touched the strings of your mother's harp.[6] Although he had rolled his eyes more dreadfully than that Dircean Pentheus,[7] and raved until he was insensible, your voice could still have composed his straying wits in their blind confusion. And, breathing peace into his diseased breast with your heart-stirring song, you might have restored him to himself.

---

6. Leonora's mother, Adriana Baroni, was a musician.

7. *Dircaeo*—Theban. See *On the Platonic Idea*, 26, note.

Pentheo—Pentheus, the king of Thebes who was torn to pieces by the celebrants of the orgies of Bacchus—among them (according to Euripides' *Bacchae*, 916–28), his own mother, Agave.

AD EANDEM

CREDULA quid liquidam Sirena, Neapoli, iactas,
   Claraque Parthenopes fana Acheloiados,
Littoreamque tua defunctam Naiada ripa
   Corpora Chalcidico sacra dedisse rogo?
Illa quidem vivitque, et amoena Tibridis unda   5
   Mutavit rauci murmura Pausilipi.
Illic, Romulidum studiis ornata secundis,
   Atque homines cantu detinet atque Deos.

(1638–9)

1–3. *Parthenope.* See *Comus,* 253 and 879, notes.
4. *Chalcidico.* See *Damon's Epitaph,* 182, note.

TO THE SAME

Why, credulous Naples, do you boast of your liquid-voiced Siren and of the famous shrine of the daughter of Achelous, Parthenope,[1] the Naiad of the shore, that, when she perished on your coast, her body was consecrated on a Chalcidian[4] pyre? In truth, she lives and has exchanged the confusion of noisy Pausilipus[6] for the smooth waves of the Tiber. There she is honoured by the cordial applause of the sons of Romulus and lays the spell of her song upon both men and gods.

———

6. *Pausilipi*—Pausilipum, a mountain between Naples and Puteoli, penetrated by a tunnel through which passed much of the traffic of the metropolis.

AD SALSILLUM

Poetam Romanum, Aegrotantem, Scazontes

O Musa gressum quae volens trahis claudum,
Vulcanioque tarda gaudes incessu,
Nec sentis illud in loco minus gratum
Quam cum decentes flava Dëiope suras
Alternat aureum ante Iunonis lectum,   5
Adesdum, et haec s'is verba pauca Salsillo
Refer, camena nostra cui tantum es cordi,
Quamque ille magnis praetulit immerito divis.
Haec ergo alumnus ille Londini Milto
Diebus hisce qui suum linquens nidum   10
Polique tractum, (pessimus ubi ventorum,
Insanientis impotensque pulmonis,
Pernix anhela sub Iove exercet flabra)
Venit feraces Itali soli ad glebas,
Visum superba cognitas urbes fama,   15
Virosque, doctaeque indolem iuventutis,
Tibi optat idem hic fausta multa, Salsille,
Habitumque fesso corpori penitus sanum;
Cui nunc profunda bilis infestat renes,
Praecordiisque fixa damnosum spirat.   20

---

1. Compare the use of "Muse" to mean the poetic impulse or inspiration in *To his Father,* 5, note.
  To the Greeks, who invented the scazontic, or "limping" metre, the name corresponded with the effect of using a final spondee in the iambic line and allowing occasional variations from the iambic base in any position. Milton's Latin models seldom varied irregularly from the iambic pattern, and never in the position before the final spondee, but he did not feel himself bound by their example.

2. *Vulcan,* or Hephaestus, Homer's "limping god" (*Il.* I, 607), appears under the name Mulciber in *P.L.* I, 739–46, where Milton repeats Homer's story (*Il.* I, 588–95) of his fall from Heaven upon the island of Lemnos.

4. Virgil made Juno herself declare that *Dëiope* was the loveliest of all her nymphs. (*Aen.* I, 72.)

6. The forgotten Roman poet, Giovanni Salzilli, was identified by Masson (*Poetical Works,* ed. by Masson, 1893, I, 105) as the contributor of eleven sonnets and several other poems to the *Poesie de' Signori*

TO SALZILLI

A Roman Poet, when He Was Ill

O my Muse[1]—fond as you are of moving with a halting step and pleased as you are with a gait like Vulcan's,[2] which seems to you, when it is in the right place, no less charming than the graceful ankles of blond Dëiope[4] dancing before the golden couch of Juno—come, if you please, and carry these few words to Salzilli,[6] who likes my Muse[7] so cordially that, quite undeservedly, he ranks me above great and divine poets.[8] For you, then, Salzilli, these are the wishes of that London-bred Milton who recently left his nest and his own quarter of the sky[9]—where the worst of the winds[11] in its headlong flight, with its lungs uncontrollably raging, rolls its panting gusts beneath the heavens[13]—and came to the genial soil of Italy to see its cities, which their proud fame has made familiar, and its men and its talented and cultured youth; that same Milton, Salzilli, wishes you many blessings and a healthy constitution for your exhausted body, whose reins are deeply infected with the bile[18] which spreads bane from its seat in your vitals.

Accademici Fantastici (*Poems by Members of the Academy of Fantastics*) to Cardinal Cesarini in 1637.

7. Compare the note on *Camenam* in *Elegy VI*, 3.

8. In his epigram of compliment to Milton, which appears among the commendatory verses prefixed to the volume of 1645, Salzilli ranked him above Homer, Virgil and Tasso. See page 4 above.

9–16. Compare stanzas 7 to 9 of Francini's Italian ode among the commendatory verses in the volume of 1645. See page 8 above.

11. The "worst of the winds" is Aquilo (whose Greek name was "Boreas"), the north wind which appears as Winter's charioteer in *Fair Infant*, 8. The epithet "impotens," which Milton found in Horace's *Odes* (III, xxx, 3), expressed the impotence of the wind to control its own violence.

13. Milton was familiar with many instances, such as Horace's "sub Iove frigido" ("under the cold sky," *Odes*, I, i, 25), where Roman writers used "Jupiter" as a name for the sky. "Zeus" and "Jupiter" both go back to the root *div* or *diu*, which means "the bright sky."

18–20. Compare the allusion to melancholy, or black bile, in Milton's preface to *S.A.* and the note there.

Nec id pepercit impia quod tu Romano
Tam cultus ore Lesbium condis melos.
O dulce divum munus, O Salus, Hebes
Germana! Tuque Phoebe, morborum terror,
Pythone caeso, sive tu magis Paean   25
Libenter audis, hic tuus sacerdos est.
Querceta Fauni, vosque rore vinoso
Colles benigni, mitis Evandri sedes,
Siquid salubre vallibus frondet vestris,
Levamen aegro ferte certatim vati.   30
Sic ille caris redditus rursum Musis
Vicina dulci prata mulcebit cantu.
Ipse inter atros emirabitur lucos
Numa, ubi beatum degit otium aeternum,
Suam reclivis semper Aegeriam spectans.   35
Tumidusque et ipse Tibris, hinc delinitus,
Spei favebit annuae colonorum;
Nec in sepulchris ibit obsessum reges,
Nimium sinistro laxus irruens loro;
Sed fraena melius temperabit undarum,   40
Adusque curvi salsa regna Portumni.

                                              (1638–9)

---

22. Alcaeus and Sappho, both natives of Lesbos, were the greatest
lyric poets of ancient Greece.

23–24. The name of Hebe, whom Hesiod called (*Theogony*, 950–5)
the daughter of Zeus and Hera and the heavenly bride of Heracles,
and who became for later writers the goddess of youth, was merely
the Greek word for "youth," personified. The Latin word for health,
salus, was also personified and the goddess, Salus, had her temple on
the Quirinal hill in Rome.

25. Homer mentions (*Il.* V, 401, 899, etc.) *Paean* as the physician
of the gods, but as early as the *Agamemnon* (146) of Aeschylus the
name had become an epithet of Apollo when he was thought of as
the god of healing. Compare the allusion to *Python* in *Elegy VII*, 31.

26. MacKellar compares Aeschylus' *Agamemnon*, 160–62, the passage which Blackie translates thus:
                    "Jove, or what other name
        The god that reigns supreme delights to claim,
        Him I invoke."

27. As the father of the first king of Latium, Latinus, whom Virgil
pictures as consulting his oracle beside the Tiber, was the protecting
deity of the countryside, whose sacrifices Horace describes (*Odes*, I,
iv, 11–2). The wood-god *Faunus* typifies the plains and hills which

Although you have taught your Roman mouth to produce elegant Lesbian melody,[22] the accursed thing has shown you no mercy.

O sweet gift of the gods, O Health, sister of Hebe![23] And you too, O Phoebus—or Paean,[25] if you prefer to be called by that name[26]—you who by virtue of your destruction of Python became the terror of diseases—this man is your priest. Oakgroves of Faunus,[27] and you hills that are generous with the liquor of the grape, and you seats of the gentle Evander,[28] if any health-giving plant burgeons in your valleys, let all of you contend to be the first to bring alleviation to the suffering Bard. Thus restored again to his dear Muses he will gladden the neighbouring meadows with his sweet song. Numa[34] himself will marvel, under the dark groves where he lies forever entertaining the leisure of eternity in the contemplation of his Egeria. The swelling Tiber[36] himself, calmed by the song, will bless the annual hopes of the farmers. He will not run wild and uncontrolled, with his left rein lax,[39] to overwhelm kings in their sepulchres, but he will more effectively control his waves as far as the salt realms of curving Portumnus.[41]

---

surround Rome. Compare *Elegy V,* 127, *Damon's Epitaph,* 32, and *Comus,* 268.

28. Milton thought of the scene (*Aen.* VIII, 51–65) where *Evander* welcomes Aeneas to Italy and recounts his own settlement in the country and his building of a lofty city, Pallanteum, beside the Tiber.

34–35. *Numa,* the second of the legendary kings of Rome, Livy says (I, 19), established himself by pretending to hold nightly interviews with the goddess, Egeria, who taught him to institute various religious rites and to work out a calendar by interpreting the heavenly bodies. Ovid's less sceptical account (*Met.* XV, 482–92) of the goddess justifies the poetical faith in *"Aegerie,* that *Numa* tought" which Milton met in *The Faerie Queene* (II, x, 42, 8).

36–41. The "swelling Tiber" was traditional. Milton may have thought of Horace's description of the river in spate. (*Odes,* I, ii, 13–20.)

39. The Tiber's left bank was especially subject to floods.

41. The name of the god of harbours, *Portumnus,* Cicero explains (*On the Nature of the Gods,* II, xxvi), was derived from the word for a port, *portus.* Milton may have thought of his temple on the curving shore of the Tiber.

MANSUS

Ioannes Baptista Mansus, Marchio Villensis, vir ingenii laude,
tum literarum studio, nec non et bellica virtute apud Italos clarus
in primis est.   Ad quem Torquati Tassi dialogus extat de Ami-
citia scriptus; erat enim Tassi amicissimus; ab quo etiam inter
Campaniae principes celebratur, in illo poemate cui titulus *Geru-
salemme conquistata, lib. 20:*

> Fra cavalier magnanimi e cortesi
> Risplende il Manso.

Is authorem Neapoli commorantem summa benevolentia prose-
cutus est, multaque ei detulit humanitatis officia.   Ad hunc
itaque hospes ille antequam ab ea urbe discederet, ut ne in-
gratum se ostenderet, hoc carmen misit.

HAEC quoque, Manse, tuae meditantur carmina laudi
Pierides; tibi, Manse, choro notissime Phoebi,
Quandoquidem ille alium haud aequo est dignatus honore,
Post Galli cineres, et Maecenatis Etrusci.
Tu quoque, si nostrae tantum valet aura Camenae,   5
Victrices hederas inter laurosque sedebis.
   Te pridem magno felix concordia Tasso
Iunxit, et aeternis inscripsit nomina chartis.
Mox tibi dulciloquum non inscia Musa Marinum
Tradidit; ille tuum dici se gaudet alumnum,   10

---

1. Manso's patronage of countless Italian poets had brought him
many literary tributes before Milton sent him "these verses."   In the
Second Defence Milton recalled his introduction to "John Baptista
Manso, Marquis of Villa, a nobleman of distinguished rank and
authority, to whom Torquato Tasso, the illustrious poet, inscribed
his book on friendship."   (*P.W.* I, 256.)   Compare the note on 70–2,
below.

2. *Pierides*—the Muses, whom Hesiod describes (*Theogony*, 53–5) as
born in Pieria, a region lying between Mt. Olympus and the southeastern shore of Macedonia.

3–4. Cornelius Gallus, who was himself the first great Roman elegist,
was the friend of Virgil to whom the tenth *Eclogue* was dedicated.   In
Eclogue VI, 64–6, he is described as walking by the banks of the
Permessus on Mt. Helicon and being saluted by Apollo's choir (*i.e.,*
the Muses).   Here Milton borrowed Virgil's phrase to mean the poets.

MANSO

John Baptista Manso, Marquis of Villa, is one of the first men in Italy alike for the renown of his intellect and his literary pursuits and no less for his martial prowess. There is extant a dialogue on Friendship which Torquato Tasso wrote to him; for he was in the highest degree friendly to Tasso, by whom he is honoured among the Campanian princes in the poem entitled *Jerusalem Conquered,* Book 20:

> Among magnanimous and courteous cavaliers
> Manso is resplendent.

This gentleman honoured the present author with supreme kindness during his stay in Naples and showed him many courteous attentions. Accordingly, before leaving the city, the visitor, in order not to seem ungrateful, sent him this poem.

THESE verses[1] also, Manso, the Pierides[2] are meditating in your praise—in yours, Manso of the wide acquaintance among the choir of Phoebus, for since the death of Gallus[3] and Etruscan Maecenas[4] the god has granted to hardly any one else honours equal to yours. If my Muse has breath sufficient, you too shall sit among the victorious ivy and laurels.[6]

You were once bound to the great Tasso[7] by a happy friendship which has written your names in an everlasting record. Not long afterward the Muse, not ill-advised, entrusted to you the sweet-tongued Marini,[9] who took pleasure in being called your foster-child when he sang his voluminous song of the

---

4. *Maecenas,* the great patron of letters under Augustus, is addressed in the opening line of Horace's *Odes* as the descendant of Rome's early kings, several of whom were Etruscans. Propertius saluted him (*Elegies,* 3, 9, 1) as sprung "from the Etruscan blood of kings."

6. Compare *To his Father,* 102.

7–8. Manso's claim that he had shown hospitality to Tasso has been challenged, but there is no reason to doubt that during the three visits which the poet made to Naples in his old age, in 1588, 1592, and 1594, he lived in Manso's villa and perhaps even finished the *Jerusalem Conquered* there.

9. *Marini* (1569–1625) published the *Adone,* a poem of some 40,000 lines, on the Venus and Adonis story, in 1623.

Dum canit Assyrios divum prolixus amores,
Mollis et Ausonias stupefecit carmine nymphas.
Ille itidem moriens tibi soli debita vates
Ossa, tibi soli supremaque vota reliquit.
Nec manes pietas tua cara fefellit amici;   15
Vidimus arridentem operoso ex aere poetam.
Nec satis hoc visum est in utrumque, et nec pia cessant
Officia in tumulo; cupis integros rapere Orco,
Qua potes, atque avidas Parcarum eludere leges:
Amborum genus, et varia sub sorte peractam   20
Describis vitam, moresque, et dona Minervae;
Aemulus illius Mycalen qui natus ad altam
Rettulit Aeolii vitam facundus Homeri.
Ergo ego te, Clius et magni nomine Phoebi,
Manse pater, iubeo longum salvere per aevum,   25
Missus Hyperboreo iuvenis peregrinus ab axe.
Nec tu longinquam bonus aspernabere Musam,
Quae nuper, gelida vix enutrita sub Arcto,
Imprudens Italas ausa est volitare per urbes.
Nos etiam in nostro modulantes flumine cygnos   30
Credimus obscuras noctis sensisse per umbras,
Qua Thamesis late puris argenteus urnis

---

11. Renaissance mythography stressed the eastern origin of Adonis.
Conti's chapter on him (V, xvi) first identifies him as the son of the
Assyrian king, Thias, and later cites the account in Lucian's *Syrian
Goddess* (6–8) of the annual mourning for him beside the river Adonis,
which turns red during the freshets, supposedly with blood from the
god's wound by the boar on Mt. Lebanon. His "annual wound in
Lebanon," Milton wrote in *P.L.* I, 447–9,
                    "allur'd
        The *Syrian* Damsels to lament his fate
        In amorous ditties all a Summer's day."
Compare the note on *Comus*, 999.

12. *Ausonia* was an ancient name of Italy.

18. *Orco*—the infernal world.

19. See the allusion to the Fates in the first epigram *On the Gunpowder Plot,* 7, note.

21. Milton's word here is our only evidence that Manso wrote a
life of Marini. His authorship of the life of Tasso has been challenged,
but there is little doubt that he really wrote the biography which appeared first, in part, in 1620.
Minerva's gifts are intellectual endowments.

loves of the Assyrian gods[11] and laid the soft spell of his song
upon the Italian[12] maidens. So, at his death, the poet paid
his obligation by leaving his remains in your care and entrust-
ing his last wishes to you alone. And your affectionate devotion has not disappointed your friend's spirit, for we have
seen him smiling down from his carved bronze. But you
were not content to do merely this much for either poet, and
your loving fidelity did not end at the tomb. As far as lies
within your power, you labour to snatch them uninjured out
of Orcus[18] and to cheat the voracious laws of the Fates.[19]
So you write the family history of both,[21] the varying fortunes
through which their lives were lived, their traits, and their
gifts from Minerva. You are the rival of that eloquent man,
the son of lofty Mycale, who recounted the life of Aeolian
Homer.[22] Therefore, father Manso, in the name of Clio[24]
and of great Phoebus, I, a young pilgrim sent from Hyperborean[26] skies, wish you health and long life. You, who are
so good, will not despise an alien Muse, which, though poorly
nourished under the frozen Bear,[28] has recently presumed to
make her rash flight through the cities of Italy.[29] I believe
that in the dim shadows of night I too have heard the swans
singing on our river, where the silvery Thames with pure urns

---

22–23. Although modern scholarship discredits the tradition that
Herodotus wrote the life of Homer which Milton had in mind here,
it was of Herodotus that he was thinking, and of his birthplace, Mycale,
whose "lofty crests" on the coast of Asia Minor figure in the *Iliad*, II,
869. Most of the cities which claimed to be Homer's birthplace were
in Asia Minor.

24. Compare the allusion to *Clio* in *To his Father*, 14, note, and that
to *Phoebus* in the same poem, 64, note.

26. Compare *Hyperboreo . . . sub axe* in *On the Fifth of November*, 95.

28. A "cold Climate," as Milton remembered in *P.L.* IX, 44–5, was
traditionally supposed to dull the mind. In *Areopagitica* he hopes that
his "natural endowments" are "haply not the worst for two and
fifty degrees of northern latitude." (*P.W.* II, 53.)

29. Milton was thinking of other poems, like that to Salzilli in
Rome, with which he had challenged attention in Italy.

Oceani glaucos perfundit gurgite crines.
Quin et in has quondam pervenit Tityrus oras.

   Sed neque nos genus incultum, nec inutile Phoebo,   35
Qua plaga septeno mundi sulcata Trione
Brumalem patitur longa sub nocte Boöten.
Nos etiam colimus Phoebum, nos munera Phoebo,
Flaventes spicas, et lutea mala canistris,
Halantemque crocum (perhibet nisi vana vetustas)   40
Misimus, et lectas Druidum de gente choreas.
Gens Druides antiqua, sacris operata deorum,
Heroum laudes imitandaque gesta canebant.
Hinc quoties festo cingunt altaria cantu
Delo in herbosa Graiae de more puellae   45
Carminibus laetis memorant Corineïda Loxo,
Fatidicamque Upin, cum flavicoma Hecaërge,
Nuda Caledonio variatas pectora fuco.

   Fortunate senex! ergo quacunque per orbem
Torquati decus et nomen celebrabitur ingens,   50
Claraque perpetui succrescet fama Marini,
Tu quoque in ora frequens venies plausumque virorum,
Et parili carpes iter immortale volatu.
Dicetur tum sponte tuos habitasse penates
Cynthius, et famulas venisse ad limina Musas.   55

---

34. Milton must have been familiar with the references to Chaucer as *Tityrus* in Spenser's *Shepheardes Calendar—February*, 92, *June*, 81, and *December*, 4.

36. *Triones*—the ploughing oxen—was an early name for the constellation of the Great Bear, which was imagined as a plough with seven oxen. Martial spoke of the Triones as "Hyperborean." (*Epigrams*, 9, 46, 1.)

37. Compare *Boötes* in *On the death of the Bishop of Ely*, 51, note.

41–43. John Selden's *Notes upon Drayton's Polyolbion* (*Opera Omnia*, 1726, III, 1785–6), as Warton noticed, identified the Druid god of healing, Belinus, with Apollo. Both here and in *Lycidas*, 53, Milton thought of the Druids as "bards," in accordance with a tradition going back to Caesar's statement (*Gallic War*, VI, 14) that they were reputed to have their memories stored with many verses.

46. The patronymic *Corineïda* is formed from the name of the ancient British hero, Corineus. Compare the note on *Lycidas*, 160.

46–48. Milton fused Herodotus' story (IV, 35) of two Hyperborean virgins, Arge and Opis, who in a dim past carried tribute to Delos and were honoured there in a hymn which became popular among all the Ionian Greeks, with the account in Callimachus' Hymn to Delos (291–

spreads her green locks wide in the swell of the ocean. And Tityrus[34] also long ago made his way to these shores.

Yet we, who in the long nights endure the wintry Boötes[37] in that zone of the world which is furrowed by the seven-fold Wain,[36] are no uncultivated race, profitless to Phoebus. We also worship Phoebus and—unless antiquity asserts vain things —we sent him gifts, golden ears of grain, baskets of yellow apples, the fragrant crocus and chosen bands of the stock of the Druids. The ancient race of the Druids, experienced in the cult of the gods, used to sing the praises of heroes[41] and their emulable acts. So, as often as the Greek maidens observe their custom of encircling the altars in grassy Delos with a festal chant, their happy songs commemorate Corinedian[46] Loxo and Prophetic Upis,[47] with golden-haired Hecaërge— damsels whose naked breasts were coloured with Caledonian woad.

Fortunate old man![49] For wherever the glory and the mighty name of Torquato shall be celebrated through all the world and wherever the glorious reputation of the immortal Marini shall spread, your name and fame also shall constantly be in men's mouths,[52] and with flight no less swift than theirs you shall mount the way of immortality. It shall be said that of his own free will Apollo[55] dwelt in your house and that the Muses were familiar attendants at your doors. Unwillingly that same Apollo came, when he was an exile from

---

4) of Oupis, Loxo and Hecaërge, maidens from the remote north who came with a chosen band of youths bearing offerings of first-fruits to Delos.

49. The line adapts Virgil's
       "Fortunate senex! ergo tua rura manebunt."
("Fortunate old man! for your farms shall remain secure." *Eclogue* I, 46.)

52. See the Introduction, §6.

54. *penates;* compare *Elegy I,* 17, note.

55. Apollo's poetical name of Cynthius is derived from Mt. Cynthus on the island of Delos, where the Homeric Hymn to Apollo (l. 26) fixes his birth.

At non sponte domum tamen idem, et regis adivit
Rura Pharetiadae caelo fugitivus Apollo;
Ille licet magnum Alciden susceperat hospes;
Tantum, ubi clamosos placuit vitare bubulcos,
Nobile mansueti cessit Chironis in antrum,   60
Irriguos inter saltus frondosaque tecta
Peneium prope rivum.   Ibi saepe sub ilice nigra,
Ad citharae strepitum, blanda prece victus amici,
Exilii duros lenibat voce labores.

Tum neque ripa suo, barathro nec fixa sub imo   65
Saxa stetere loco; nutat Trachinia rupes,
Nec sentit solitas, immania pondera, silvas;
Emotaeque suis properant de collibus orni,
Mulcenturque novo maculosi carmine lynces.

   Diis dilecte senex, te Iupiter aequus oportet   70
Nascentem, et miti lustrarit lumine Phoebus,
Atlantisque nepos; neque enim nisi carus ab ortu
Diis superis poterit magno favisse poetae.
Hinc longaeva tibi lento sub flore senectus
Vernat, et Aesonios lucratur vivida fusos,   75
Nondum deciduos servans tibi frontis honores,
Ingeniumque vigens, et adultum mentis acumen.
O mihi si mea sors talem concedat amicum
Phoebaeos decorasse viros qui tam bene norit,

56–69. The story of Apollo's banishment from heaven and of his
year of service as herdsman to Admetus, the king of Pherae in Thessaly
and son of Pheres, goes back as far as Pindar's *Pythian Odes* (IX, 112–4).

58. Milton admired the account in the *Alcestis* of Euripides of the
visit of Hercules to Admetus' house and of his hospitable welcome
there on the day when the queen, Alcestis, died. According to the
myth, however, Hercules' visit was later than Apollo's.

For Hercules' patronymic name, Alcides, see the note on *P.R.* IV, 565.

60. Chiron, of whom Homer spoke as "the most righteous of the
centaurs" and as the guardian of Achilles (*Il.* XI, 830–1), was famous
also as the guardian of Hercules, Jason, and Jason's son, Medeius, and
because (according to Ovid, *Met.* II, 630), Apollo entrusted his own
son, Aesculapius, to his care.

61–62. Perhaps there is a reminiscence of Ovid's description (*Met.* I,
567–73) of the course of the Peneus through the groves in the vale of
Tempe, in Thessaly, to the Aegean Sea.

66. Mt. Oeta, between Thessaly and Aetolia, was called the
"Trachinian cliff" because the town of Trachis was situated there.

heaven,[56] to the farmstead of Admetus, although Admetus had been host to the great Alcides.[58]   When he wished to get away from the clamorous ploughmen, he retreated to the renowned cave of the gentle Chiron[60] among the moist woodland pastures and verdurous shades beside the river Peneus.[61] There, under the dark ilex, persuaded by his friend's soft entreaty, he would lighten the hard labours of exile by singing to the accompaniment of the cithara.   Then neither the banks nor the rocks fixed in the lowest depths of the chasm stood fast in their places; the Trachinian cliff[66] swayed and no longer felt the vast weight of its familiar forests; the trees were moved and hastened down from their hills and the spotted lynxes became gentle at the unfamiliar song.[68]

Old man, beloved of the gods![70]   At your birth Jupiter must have been favourable, Phoebus, and the grandson of Atlas[72] must have shed their gentle light upon you, for no one, unless from his birth he were dear to the gods, could have befriended a great poet.   Therefore your old age is green with lingering bloom and, still robust, amasses the spindles of Aeson[75]—preserving the honours of your brow unfallen, your spirit strong and the power of your mind at its height.   O, if my lot might but bestow such a friend upon me, a friend who understands how to honour the devotees of Phoebus—if ever

---

68. Milton may have thought of Ovid's great catalogue (*Met.* X, 87–106) of the trees which crowded to hear Orpheus singing to his lyre, or of the singers, Damon and Alphesiboeus, whose song, Virgil said (*Eclogue* VIII, 1–5), quieted the lynxes and made rivers turn backward in their courses to listen.

70–72. For thirty years before Milton's visit, says Angelo Borzelli in *Giovan Battista Manso* (Naples, 1916, p. 101), Manso had received countless poetical tributes which compared him to Jove, Apollo and Mars.

72. The *grandson of Atlas* is Mercury. See *On the Platonic Idea*, 27, note.

75. The spindles are those of the Fates (see the note on *Lycidas*, 75–6).

Aeson, the father of Jason, as Ovid tells the story (*Met.* VII, 251–93), was delivered by Medea's enchantments from forty years of his burden of age.

Si quando indigenas revocabo in carmina reges,   80
Arturumque etiam sub terris bella moventem,
Aut dicam invictae sociali foedere mensae
Magnanimos Heroas, et—O modo spiritus adsit—
Frangam Saxonicas Britonum sub Marte phalanges!
Tandem ubi non tacitae permensus tempora vitae,   85
Annorumque satur, cineri sua iura relinquam,
Ille mihi lecto madidis astaret ocellis,
Astanti sat erit si dicam, 'Sim tibi curae.'
Ille meos artus, liventi morte solutos,
Curaret parva componi molliter urna.   90
Forsitan et nostros ducat de marmore vultus,
Nectens aut Paphia myrti aut Parnasside lauri
Fronde comas, at ego secura pace quiescam.
Tum quoque, si qua fides, si praemia certa bonorum,
Ipse ego, caelicolum semotus in aethera divum,   95
Quo labor et mens pura vehunt atque ignea virtus,
Secreti haec aliqua mundi de parte videbo,
Quantum fata sinunt, et tota mente serenum
Ridens purpureo suffundar lumine vultus,
Et simul aethereo plaudam mihi laetus Olympo.   100

                                                     (1639)

———————

80. Out of ninety-nine possible subjects jotted down in the Cambridge manuscript as suggestions for the epic poem which Milton
dreamed of writing, twenty-eight were subjects in British history. Milton was familiar with the tradition that Arthur was alive in the other
world and would return to rule over the Britons—a tradition which he
perhaps knew in the closing pages of the *Bruts* of Wace and Layamon
or in Malory's *Morte d'Arthur,* XXI, vii. His dream was to bring
Arthur to life in a great poem, as Spenser had done in *The Faerie
Queene.*

82. *mensae:* the famous Round Table.

84. Even in Latin prose "Mars" was often used by metonymy to
mean the shock of war. Livy (3, 62, 9) describes the shock of two
battle-lines, "where Mars was most furious."

91. See the Introduction, §6.

92. The *myrtle,* which, like the laurel, was used in the wreaths of
victors, was sacred to Venus, one of whose favourite shrines was at
the city of *Paphos* in Cypress.

92. See the note on *Parnassus* in *Elegy IV,* 30.

96. See the Introduction, §6.

100. Compare the use of *Olympus* in *On the death of the Bishop of
Ely,* 63.

I shall summon back our native kings into our songs,[80] and
Arthur, waging his wars beneath the earth, or if ever I shall
proclaim the magnanimous heroes of the table[82] which their
mutual fidelity made invincible, and (if only the spirit be with
me) shall shatter the Saxon phalanxes under the British
Mars![84]   And at last, after I shall have lived through the span
of no silent career, and when, full of years, I shall pay to the
ashes their due, that friend would stand with tears in his eyes
beside my bed. I should be content if I might say to him as
he stood there, "Take me into your care."   He would see to
it that, when livid death had relaxed them, my limbs were
gently bestowed in a little urn. Perhaps he might even cause
my features to take form in marble and wreathe my locks with
Paphian myrtle[92] and Parnassian laurel.[92] So I should rest in
perfect peace. Then, if there be such a thing as faith and
assured rewards of the righteous, I myself, far remote in the
ethereal homes of the gods who dwell in heaven, whither
labour and a pure mind and ardent virtue lead,[96] shall look
down upon these events—as much as the fates permit—from
some part of that mysterious world, and with a serene spirit
and a face suffused with smiles and rosy light, I shall congratulate myself on ethereal Olympus.[100]

EPITAPHIUM DAMONIS

ARGUMENTUM

(Thyrsis et Damon, eiusdem viciniae Pastores, eadem studia sequuti a pueritia amici erant, ut qui plurimum. Thyrsis animi causa profectus peregre de obitu Damonis nuntium accepit. Domum postea reversus, et rem ita esse comperto, se, suamque solitudinem hoc carmine deplorat. Damonis autem sub persona hic intelligitur Carolus Diodatus ex urbe Etruriae Luca paterno genere oriundus, caetera Anglus; ingenio, doctrina, clarissimisque caeteris virtutibus, dum viveret, iuvenis egregius.)

HIMERIDES NYMPHAE—nam vos et Daphnin et Hylan,
Et plorata diu meministis fata Bionis—
Dicite Sicelicum Thamesina per oppida carmen:
Quas miser effudit voces, quae murmura Thyrsis,
Et quibus assiduis exercuit antra querelis   5
Fluminaque, fontesque vagos, nemorumque recessus,
Dum sibi praereptum queritur Damona, neque altam
Luctibus exemit noctem, loca sola pererrans.
Et iam bis viridi surgebat culmus arista,
Et totidem flavas numerabant horrea messes,   10
Ex quo summa dies tulerat Damona sub umbras,
Nec dum aderat Thyrsis; pastorem scilicet illum
Dulcis amor Musae Tusca retinebat in urbe.
Ast ubi mens expleta domum pecorisque relicti
Cura vocat, simul assueta seditque sub ulmo,   15
Tum vero amissum, tum denique, sentit amicum,
Coepit et immensum sic exonerare dolorem:

1–2. The northern of the two rivers in Sicily which were called Himera (the modern Fiume Grande) figures twice in Theocritus' *Idyls* (v, 124, and vii, 75). Milton's invocation of its Muses, like his appeal to the "Sicilian Muse" of pastoral poetry in *Lycidas,* 133, means that he looked back to such models as Theocritus' *Lament for Daphnis* (*Idyl* I) and Moschus' *Epitaph of Bion* (*Idyl* III). Compare the notes on lines 4 and 18 below.

1. *Hylas.* See *P.R.* II, 353, note.

4. *Thyrsis,* by whose name Milton refers to himself, is the mourning shepherd in Theocritus' *Lament for Daphnis.*

DAMON'S EPITAPH

ARGUMENT

(Thyrsis and Damon, shepherds of the same neighbourhood, from childhood had pursued the same interests and were most affectionate friends. While studying abroad, Thyrsis received the report of Damon's death. When, later, he returned home and found that it was so, he bewailed himself and his loneliness in this song. Now Damon represents Charles Diodati, who through his father was descended from the Tuscan city of Lucca, but in all else was an Englishman—a youth who, while he lived, was outstanding for genius, learning, and every other splendid virtue.)

NYMPHS OF HIMERA[1]—for you remember Daphnis and Hylas and the long-lamented destiny of Bion—utter your Sicilian song through the cities of the Thames. Sing the moans and sighs that the wretched Thyrsis[4] poured out, his ceaseless complaints that importuned the caves and rivers, the vagrant streams and the depths of the groves, when he mourned the cutting off of Damon and went wandering through solitary places, even in the latest hours of the night never sparing his groans. And now twice[9] the stalk with its green ear had grown up and twice the yellow harvest had been numbered into the barns since his last day had swept Damon to the shades below, and still Thyrsis was absent, for love of the sweet Muse detained that shepherd in the Tuscan city.[13] But when he had filled his mind full and the care of the flock that he had left behind him recalled him to his home, and when he sat down under the accustomed elm, then truly, then at last, he felt the loss of his friend, and he began to pour out his tremendous sorrow in words like these:

9–11. Spring and harvest time have twice come and gone since Charles Diodati's death in August, 1638.

13. The Tuscan city is Florence, where Milton's second sojourn detained him during March and April, 1639.

"Ite domum impasti, domino iam non vacat, agni.
Hei mihi! quae terris, quae dicam numina caelo,
Postquam te immiti rapuerunt funere, Damon;   20
Sicine nos linquis, tua sic sine nomine virtus
Ibit, et obscuris numero sociabitur umbris?
At non ille animas virga qui dividit aurea
Ista velit, dignumque tui te ducat in agmen,
Ignavumque procul pecus arceat omne silentum.   25
    "Ite domum impasti, domino iam non vacat, agni.
Quicquid erit, certe, nisi me lupus ante videbit,
Indeplorato non comminuere sepulchro,
Constabitque tuus tibi honos, longumque vigebit
Inter pastores. Illi tibi vota secundo   30
Solvere post Daphnin, post Daphnin dicere laudes
Gaudebunt, dum rura Pales, dum Faunus amabit—
Si quid id est, priscamque fidem coluisse, piumque,
Palladiasque artes, sociumque habuisse canorum.
    "Ite domum impasti, domino iam non vacat, agni.   35
Haec tibi certa manent, tibi erunt haec praemia, Damon.
At mihi quid tandem fiet modo? quis mihi fidus
Haerebit lateri comes, ut tu saepe solebas
Frigoribus duris, et per loca foeta pruinis,

---

18. Similar refrains are used to give unity and variety in Bion's
Epitaph of Adonis and Moschus' *Epitaph of Bion*. In Theocritus'
Lament for Daphnis there are sixteen repetitions (with one variation)
of the refrain,
        "Begin, dear Muses, begin your pastoral songs."
Milton's line is an adaptation of Virgil's
        "Ite domum pasti, siquis pudor, ite iuvenci."
                    (*Eclogues* VII, 44.)
"Away home, if you have any shame, away, full-fed bullocks."

23. Milton thought of Virgil's account of Mercury, which Dryden
rendered:
        "But first he grasps within his awful hand
        The mark of sov'reign pow'r, his magic wand:
        With this he draws the ghosts from hollow graves;
        With this he drives them down the Stygian waves;
        With this he seals in sleep the wakeful sight,
        And eyes, though clos'd in death, restores to light."
                    (*Aen.* IV, 242–5.)

27. The Romans believed that if a wolf saw a man before the man
saw him, the man became dumb. So Virgil explained the loss of his
voice by the sorcerer, Moeris, on the ground that the wolves had
seen him. (*Eclogues*, IX, 53–4.)

'Go home unfed, for your master has no time for you, my lambs.[18]   Ah me! what deities shall I profess in earth or heaven, now that they have torn you mercilessly away in death, O Damon?   And do you leave us in this way and shall your virtue go down without a name to be numbered with the company of the unknown dead?   But he who divides the souls with his golden wand would not wish this,[23] for he would lead you into a company worthy of you and would warn off the whole brutal herd of the silent dead.

"Go home unfed, for your master has no time for you, my lambs.   Whatever befalls, Damon, you may be sure—unless a wolf first sets eyes upon me[27]—that you shall not turn to dust in the sepulchre unmourned.[28]   Your fame shall abide and long be held in esteem among the shepherds.   To you, next after Daphnis, it shall be their delight to pay their vows,[30] and to sing praises of you next after Daphnis, as long as Pales[32] and Faunus shall love the fields—if there be any profit in having cultivated the ancient faith and piety and the Palladian[34] arts, and in having possessed a comrade who was a poet.

"Go home unfed, for your master has no time for you, my lambs.   For you these rewards are certainly in store and you shall certainly possess them, Damon.   But what at last is to become of me?   What faithful companion will stay by my side as you always did when the cold was cruel and the frost thick on the ground, and when the herbs were dying of thirst under

---

28. Compare *Manso*, 17-8, and *Lycidas*, 14.

30-32. Editors compare the lines in Virgil's *Eclogue* V, 76-80, which Dryden rendered:
> "While savage boars delight in shady woods,
> And finny fish inhabit in the floods—
> While bees on thyme, and locusts feed on dew—
> Thy grateful swains these honours shall renew.
> Such honours as we pay to pow'rs divine,
> To Bacchus and to Ceres, shall be thine."

32. The goddess *Pales*, whom Milton made Eve outrival in loveliness (*P.L.* IX, 393), was a protectress of the flocks.   For *Faunus* see the note on *To Salzilli*, 27.

34. The *Palladian arts* are the arts protected by Pallas Athene.

Aut rapido sub sole, siti morientibus herbis,   40
Sive opus in magnos fuit eminus ire leones,
Aut avidos terrere lupos praesepibus altis?
Quis fando sopire diem cantuque solebit?
   "Ite domum impasti, domino iam non vacat, agni.
Pectora cui credam? quis me lenire docebit   45
Mordaces curas, quis longam fallere noctem
Dulcibus alloquiis, grato cum sibilat igni
Molle pirum, et nucibus strepitat focus, at malus auster
Miscet cuncta foris, et desuper intonat ulmo.
   "Ite domum impasti, domino iam non vacat, agni.   50
Aut aestate, dies medio dum vertitur axe,
Cum Pan aesculea somnum capit abditus umbra
Et repetunt sub aquis sibi nota sedilia nymphae,
Pastoresque latent, stertit sub saepe colonus,
Quis mihi blanditiasque tuas, quis tum mihi risus   55
Cecropiosque sales referet, cultosque lepores?
   "Ite domum impasti, domino iam non vacat, agni.
At iam solus agros, iam pascua solus oberro,
Sicubi ramosae densantur vallibus umbrae,
Hic serum expecto; supra caput imber et Eurus   60
Triste sonant, fractaeque agitata crepuscula silvae.
   "Ite domum impasti, domino iam non vacat, agni.
Heu! quam culta mihi prius arva procacibus herbis
Involvuntur, et ipsa situ seges alta fatiscit!
Innuba neglecto marcescit et uva racemo,   65
Nec myrteta iuvant; ovium quoque taedet, at illae

---

45. Milton's entire correspondence with Diodati (in *Elegies I* and *VI*
and in the two *Familiar Letters*) bore out the tradition that, "A principal fruit of friendship is the ease and discharge of the fulness and
swellings of the heart, which passions of all kinds do cause and in-
duce." (Bacon, *Essays,* xxvii.)

45–49. The spirit and letter here are both indebted to Horace's
Epode xiii, with its contrast of song and wine and the confidences of
friends within to the uproar of winter outside. Compare the Sonnets
To Mr. Lawrence and the first *To Cyriack Skinner.*

52–53. The picture of the still heat of noon is a relic of Theocritus'
Sicily and Pan's noonday rest, as Warton suggested, recalls the goat-
herd's warning against waking the sleeping Pan as he rests from the
chase at noon. (*Idyl* I, 15–7.) Compare *Arcades,* 1, note.

56. "All life's charm and its greatest pleasures and rest from its

a consuming sun—whether the work were to chase the lions to close quarters or to frighten the hungry wolves away from the high sheepfolds? Who now is to beguile my days with conversation and song?

"Go home unfed, for your master has no time for you, my lambs. To whom shall I confide my heart? Who will teach me to alleviate my mordant cares and shorten the long night with delightful conversation while the ripe pear simmers before the grateful fire and nuts burst on the hearth, when the wicked southwind makes general confusion outside and thunders in the peak of the elm tree?[45]

"Go home unfed, for your master has no time for you, my lambs. Or in summer, when the day is at the turn of high noon, and Pan is asleep and out of sight in the shade of the oak,[52] and the nymphs go back to their familiar haunts beneath the waters, and the shepherds hide themselves, and the ploughman snores under the hedge, who then will bring back to me your mirth and Cecropian salt,[56] your culture and humour?

"Go home unfed, for your master has no time for you, my lambs. Alone now I stray through the fields, alone through the pastures, wherever the branches make dense shadows in the valleys, there I wait for the evening. Over my head the rain and the southeast wind make their sad sound in the restless twilight of the wind-swept trees.

"Go home unfed, for your master has no time for you, my lambs. Alas, how entangled with insolent weeds are my once well cultivated fields! The tall grain itself is tumid with mould. The unwedded grapes[65] are shrivelled on their neglected vine and the myrtle groves have no loveliness. My

---

labours," Pliny explained (31, 7, 41), were called its salt, and Martial refers (3, 20, 9) to Attic salt as proverbial for witty conversation.

Cecropian—Attic—is derived from the name of the legendary founder of Athens, Cecrops.

65. Because vines were traditionally "wedded" to trees, Horace could speak playfully of trees which lacked their vines as "celibate" (Odes, II, xv, 4) or "widowed" (Odes, IV, v, 30). Compare P.L. V, 215-9.

Moerent, inque suum convertunt ora magistrum.
    "Ite domum impasti, domino iam non vacat, agni.
Tityrus ad corylos vocat, Alphesiboeus ad ornos,
Ad salices Aegon, ad flumina pulcher Amyntas: 70
'Hic gelidi fontes, hic illita gramina musco,
Hic Zephyri, hic placidas interstrepit arbutus undas.'
Ista canunt surdo, frutices ego nactus abibam.
    "Ite domum impasti, domino iam non vacat, agni.
Mopsus ad haec, nam me redeuntem forte notarat,   75
Et callebat avium linguas et sidera Mopsus:
'Thyrsi, quid hoc?' dixit, 'quae te coquit improba bilis?
Aut te perdit amor, aut te male fascinat astrum.
Saturni grave saepe fuit pastoribus astrum,
Intimaque obliquo figit praecordia plumbo.'   80
    "Ite domum impasti, domino iam non vacat, agni.
Mirantur nymphae, et 'Quid te, Thyrsi, futurum est?
Quid tibi vis?' aiunt: 'non haec solet esse iuventae
Nubila frons, oculique truces, vultusque severi;
Illa choros, lususque leves, et semper amorem   85
Iure petit; bis ille miser qui serus amavit.'
    "Ite domum impasti, domino iam non vacat, agni.
Venit Hyas, Dryopeque, et filia Baucidis Aegle,

69–70. *Tityrus, Aegon* and *Amyntas* are all names found in Theocritus' *Idyls. Alphesiboeus,* "the bringer of oxen," is also of Greek
origin. They stand for the friends of Thyrsis and may, of course, have
stood for some once recognizable individuals.

71. See the Introduction, §6.

75–76. Mopsus, who is first mentioned in Hesiod's *Buckler,* 181, and
whom Virgil (*Aen.* 359–61) called a master of the lore of the stars
and the birds and of many other divine mysteries, had his counterpart
in the "Mopso, who understands the speech of birds" in Tasso's
Aminta and the burlesque seer, Mopsus, of Randolph's *Amyntas.*

77. Compare Milton's use of *bile* in *To Salzilli,* 19, and in his preface
to *S.A.,* note.

79–80. Saturn's remoteness and sluggish motion made astrologers
attribute a malign influence to the planet. In Chaucer's *Knight's Tale*
Saturn confesses to many evils wrought by his influence, among them
"the maladyes colde" (l. 2467) and the "pestilence" (l. 2469); and
Spenser's melancholy man, Phantastes, looked as if he had been born
        "When oblique *Saturne* sate in the house of agonyes."
                        (*F.Q.* II, ix, 52–9.)
In Alchemy Saturn was the technical name for lead. Compare *Il Penseroso,* 43.

sheep also are disgusting and mope and turn their gaze upon their master.

"Go home unfed, for your master has no time for you, my lambs. Tityrus[69] is calling me to the hazels, Alphesiboeus to the ash-trees, Aegon to the willows, and comely Amyntas to the rivers. 'Here are cool springs, here are lawns soft with moss, here are zephyrs, and here the arbutus and the quiet streams whisper together.'[71] They sing to deaf ears, for I slip away into the thickets and am gone.

"Go home unfed, for your master has no time for you, my lambs. The next was Mopsus[75]—Mopsus who had skill in the language of the birds and the stars—for he had chanced to notice my return: 'What now, Thyrsis?' he said, 'what excess of bile[77] ails you? Either you are pining away with love or you are banefully influenced by some star. Saturn's star has often been malignant to shepherds and his slanting, leaden shot strikes to the innermost vitals.'[79]

"Go home unfed, for your master has no time for you, my lambs. The nymphs are astonished and cry, 'What is to become of you, Thyrsis? What do you wish? The brow of youth is not usually clouded, nor its eyes severe, nor its aspect stern. Youth's lawful pursuits are dances and frivolous sports and love always. Twice miserable is the man who loves late.'[86]

"Go home unfed, for your master has no time for you, my lambs. Hyas[88] and Dryope came, and Aegle, the daughter of Baucis—Aegle accomplished in music and skilled with the

---

86. The epigram is obviously traditional. Jerram quoted from Guarini's Il Pastor Fido, I, i, a saying which may be translated thus:
"If your hairs are grey,
    When first love troubles,
        The misery doubles."

88. All the names of the girls are Greek, but all are to be found in Ovid's Metamorphoses. Baucis and her husband, Philemon, were the old couple whom Ovid describes (Met. VIII, 630–724) as entertaining Jupiter and Mercury unawares. According to the myth, she had no children, but her name—as Persius' use of it (Satires, iv, 21) proves—might mean simply an old woman.

Docta modos, citharaeque sciens, sed perdita fastu;
Venit Idumanii Chloris vicina fluenti.   90
Nil me blanditiae, nil me solantia verba,
Nil me, si quid adest, movet, aut spes ulla futuri.
    "Ite domum impasti, domino iam non vacat, agni.
Hei mihi! quam similes ludunt per prata iuvenci,
Omnes unanimi secum sibi lege sodales,   95
Nec magis hunc alio quisquam secernit amicum
De grege; sic densi veniunt ad pabula thoes,
Inque vicem hirsuti paribus iunguntur onagri;
Lex eadem pelagi, deserto in littore Proteus
Agmina phocarum numerat, vilisque volucrum   100
Passer habet semper quicum sit, et omnia circum
Farra libens volitet, sero sua tecta revisens;
Quem si fors letho obiecit, seu milvus adunco
Fata tulit rostro, seu stravit arundine fossor,
Protinus ille alium socio petit inde volatu.   105
Nos durum genus, et diris exercita fatis
Gens, homines, aliena animis, et pectore discors,
Vix sibi quisque parem de millibus invenit unum,
Aut, si sors dederit tandem non aspera votis,
Illum inopina dies, qua non speraveris hora   110
Surripit, aeternum linquens in saecula damnum.
    "Ite domum impasti, domino iam non vacat, agni.
Heu! quis me ignotas traxit vagus error in oras
Ire per aëreas rupes, Alpemque nivosam?
Ecquid erat tanti Romam vidisse sepultam?   115
Quamvis illa foret, qualem dum viseret olim,
Tityrus ipse suas et oves et rura reliquit,
Ut te tam dulci possem caruisse sodale,

---

89. The line is based upon Horace's account of "Thracian Chloe" as
"Dulcis docta modos et citharae sciens," in the famous "Lovers'
quarrel." (*Odes,* III, ix, 9–10.)

90. The *Idumanum aestuarium* was identified by Camden (*Britain,*
1607, II, 45) with Blackwater Bay in Essex. A real person seems to be
lurking behind Chloris, but no editor has identified her.

99–100. The earliest appearance of Proteus, the "Shepherd of the
sea," as Spenser called him (*F.Q.* III, viii, 30, 1), is Homer's picture
of him counting his "flock" of seals as a shepherd would his sheep.
(*Od.* IV, 411–3.) Compare *Elegy* III, 26, and *P.L.* III, 604.

106. The phrasing derives from Virgil's allusion to the repeopling

harp, but ruined by pride[89]—and Chloris, the neighbour of
the Idumenian river,[90] came also. No flattery and no words
of comfort move me, nor does anything that is present nor any
hope of the future.

"Go home unfed, for your master has no time for you, my
lambs. How like one another are the steers at play in the
meadows, all mutually companions together, because, under
the law which gives them one mind together in common, not
one singles out another from the herd as a friend. So the
wolves come to their food in packs and the rough-coated wild
asses mate together by turns. The law of the sea is the same,
where Proteus[99] counts his hosts of seals on the deserted shore.
Even that pariah of birds, the sparrow, always has a fellow to
play with and flits gaily about to every shock of grain, returning late to his own roof. Yet if death has chanced to carry off
his fellow, or the kite's hooked beak has brought his doom, or
the peasant's arrow has struck him down, the bird incon-
tinently seeks out another to share his flight. But we men are
a painful race,[106] a stock tormented by cruel fate, with minds
mutually alienated and hearts discordant. A man can hardly
find a comrade for himself in a thousand; or, if one is granted
to us by a fate at last not unkind to our prayers, a day and
hour when we apprehend nothing snatches him away, leaving
an eternal loss to all the years.

"Go home unfed, for your master has no time for you, my
lambs. Alas! what wandering fancy carried me across the
skyey cliffs of the snow-bound Alps to unknown shores? Was
it of such importance to have seen buried Rome, even though
it were what it was when long ago Tityrus[117] left his sheep
and his fields to see it, that I should suffer separation from so

---

of the earth after Deucalion's flood by the stones which turned into
men:

> "Unde nati homines, durum genus."
> (*Georgics* I, 63.)
> ("Whence were born men, the hard race.")

117. *Tityrus*, here, as in *Manso*, 34, refers to Chaucer, neither of whose
Italian journeys, however, appears to have included Rome.

Possem tot maria alta, tot interponere montes,
Tot silvas, tot saxa tibi, fluviosque sonantes?   120
Ah! certe extremum licuisset tangere dextram,
Et bene compositos placide morientis ocellos,
Et dixisse, 'Vale! nostri memor ibis ad astra.'
    "Ite domum impasti, domino iam non vacat, agni.
Quamquam etiam vestri nunquam meminisse pigebit,   125
Pastores Tusci, Musis operata iuventus,
Hic Charis, atque Lepos; et Tuscus tu quoque Damon,
Antiqua genus unde petis Lucumonis ab urbe.
O ego quantus eram, gelidi cum stratus ad Arni
Murmura, populeumque nemus, qua mollior herba,   130
Carpere nunc violas, nunc summas carpere myrtos,
Et potui Lycidae certantem audire Menalcam!
Ipse etiam tentare ausus sum, nec puto multum
Displicui, nam sunt et apud me munera vestra,
Fiscellae, calathique, et cerea vincla cicutae.   135
Quin et nostra suas docuerunt nomina fagos
Et Datis et Francinus, erant et vocibus ambo
Et studiis noti, Lydorum sanguinis ambo.
    "Ite domum impasti, domino iam non vacat, agni.
Haec mihi tum laeto dictabat roscida luna,   140
Dum solus teneros claudebam cratibus haedos.
Ah! quoties dixi, cum te cinis ater habebat,
'Nunc canit, aut lepori nunc tendit retia Damon

---

119. Compare *Elegy IV*, 21–2.

121–122. So Castiglione's Alcon, who is mourning in Rome for the
childhood friend who has died in his absence, cries out that he might
have held his dying friend's hand and given him a final kiss. (*Alcon*,
84–6.)

128. *Lucumo* was an Etruscan title for princes and priests which was
misunderstood by Livy (I, 34) as the personal name of Tarquinius
Priscus (of whom Milton thought as the founder of Lucca) before he
left Tarquinii to seek his fortune in Rome.

129. The beautiful upper valley of the Arno, the *Valdarno* of *P.L.*
I, 290, became familiar to Milton during his visits to Florence in 1638
and 1639. In a letter written September 10, 1638, and addressed to
Benedetto Buonmattai, he speaks of "visiting with delight the stream
of the Arno, and the hills of Faesolae." (*P.W.* III, p. 497.)

132. *Menalcas* and *Lycidas* are both names of shepherds in Theocritus' *Idyls*. In *Idyl* VII Menalcas is a competitor in such a contest
of song with another shepherd as Milton imagines here, but here the

sweet a friend or be able to put so many deep seas,[119] so many
mountains, so many forests and cliffs and roaring rivers between us? Ah! had I not gone, surely I might have touched
his right hand at the last and closed his eyes as he lay peace-
fully dying,[121] and have said, 'Farewell! remember me in your
flight to the stars.'

"Go home unfed, for your master has no time for you, my
lambs. Though I shall never weary of your memory, Tuscan
shepherds, youths in the service of the Muses, yet here was
grace and here was gentleness; you also, Damon, were a
Tuscan, tracing your lineage from the ancient city of Lucca.[128]
Ah, what a man was I when I lay beside cool, murmuring
Arno,[129] where the soft grass grows by the poplar grove, and
I could pluck the violets and the myrtle shoots and listen to
Menalcas competing with Lycidas.[132] And I myself even
dared to compete, and I think that I did not much displease,
for your prizes[133] are still in my possession, the baskets of
reeds and osiers and the pipes with fastenings of wax. Even
their beech-trees learned my name from Dati and Francini,
men who were both famous for their song and their learning,
and both were of Lydian blood.[138]

"Go home unfed, for your master has no time for you, my
lambs. These things the dewy moon would say to me, when
happy and solitary, I would be shutting the tender kids in the
wattled folds.

"Ah! how often would I say, when already dark ashes possessed you, 'Now Damon is singing or stretching his nets for

---

contest represents the poetical duels which he witnessed in the Gaddian
Academy in Florence.

133–137. The gifts represent books or copies of verses like the Ode
by Antonio Francini which Milton placed at the head of his Latin
poems in the edition of 1645. In a letter to Carlo Dati, dated April
21, 1647, he recalls "the memory of those times, when . . . with you,
I tasted bliss without alloy." (*P.W.* III, p. 501.)

138. Virgil's belief that "long ago the Lydian race, glorious in war,
settled the Etruscan hills" (*Aen.* VIII, 479–80), goes back to Herodotus
(*1*, 74).

Vimina nunc texit varios sibi quod sit in usus;'
Et quae tum facile sperabam mente futura   145
Arripui voto levis, et praesentia finxi.
'Heus bone! numquid agis? nisi te quid forte retardat,
Imus, et arguta paulum recubamus in umbra,
Aut ad aquas Colni, aut ubi iugera Cassibelauni?
Tu mihi percurres medicos, tua gramina, succos,   150
Helleborumque, humilesque crocos, foliumque hyacinthi,
Quasque habet ista palus herbas, artesque medentum.'
    "Ah! pereant herbae, pereant artesque medentum,
Gramina, postquam ipsi nil profecere magistro!
Ipse etiam—nam nescio quid mihi grande sonabat   155
Fistula—ab undecima iam lux est altera nocte—
Et tum forte novis admoram labra cicutis,
Dissiluere tamen, rupta compage, nec ultra
Ferre graves potuere sonos; dubito quoque ne sim
Turgidulus, tamen et referam; vos cedite, silvae.   160
    "Ite domum impasti, domino iam non vacat, agni.
Ipse ego Dardanias Rutupina per aequora puppes
Dicam, et Pandrasidos regnum vetus Inogeniae,
Brennumque Arviragumque duces, priscumque Belinum,

---

144. Editors refer to the closing warning to Corydon in Virgil's
Eclogue II, 71–2, to mind the ordinary needs of life and work at his
weaving of willow twigs.
    "Quin tu aliquid saltem potius, quorum indiget usus,
        Viminibus mollique paras dextere iunco?"

149. The river *Colne* flows near Horton. *Cassibelauni* is interpreted
by Gilbert (p. 76) as signifying "the neighborhood of Horton, Buckinghamshire, for the realm of Cassivaleunus lay north of the Thames, and
included that county." Cassivellaunus was a British leader whose conquest cost Caesar serious effort. (See the *Gallic War*, V, xi.)

150–152. At Cambridge Diodati took medical training.

153–154. Compare *On the Death of the Vice-Chancellor*, 22.

155–160. Milton's grief for Diodati, as the broken exclamations are
intended to suggest, prevents him from prosecuting the poetical ambitions which we know from *Manso*, 80–4, that he cherished in Italy.

160. The dismissal of the forests is a conventional farewell to pastoral
poetry. So Virgil's Gallus takes leave of Arcadianism (*Eclogue* X, 63)
with the words, "concedite silvae." In the next paragraph Milton
turns to an epic theme.

162. Milton may have thought of opening his British epic with a
picture of the Dardanian (*i.e.*, Trojan) fleet, under Brutus (see *Comus*,

the hare or weaving osiers for his various objects.'[144]   And all
that my careless mind hoped for the future I snatched from
the mere wish and imagined it to be a present reality. 'Ho,
good friend, have you any work in hand? If, by good luck,
nothing prevents, let us go and lie for a little while in the
murmurous shade, either by the waters of Colne[149] or in the
country of Cassivellaunus. You shall run over all your
healing balms and herbs,[150] your hellebore, humble crocus,
and leaf of the hyacinth—all the simples that the meadow
holds—and the arts of the physicians.'

   "Ah! let the herbs and simples perish, let all the arts of
the doctors perish, since they are worthless to their master.[153]
And myself[155]—for I do not know what grand song my pipe
was sounding—it is now eleven nights and a day—perhaps I
was setting my lips to new pipes, but their fastenings snapped
and they fell asunder and could carry the grave notes no
further. I am afraid that I am vain, yet I will relate it. Give
way, then, O forest.[160]

   "Go home unfed, for your master has no time for you, my
lambs. I, for my part, am resolved to tell the story of the
Dardanian ships[162] in the Rutupian sea and of the ancient kingdom of Inogene,[163] the daughter of Pandrasus, and of the
chiefs, Brennus and Arviragus, and of old Belinus,[164] and of

---

828, note), approaching the English coast. *Rutupina,* to which Lucan
refers (*Pharsalia,* VI, 67), as one of the great colonial cities of the
Roman Empire, was identified by Camden, in his account of Kent, with
Richborow.

   163. *Inogene*—whom Spenser called "Inogene of Italy" (*F.Q.* II, x,
13, 5) and the wife of "Trojan Brute"—is represented by Geoffrey of
Monmouth as having been won by Brutus in a struggle with her
father, Pandracos, a king of Greece.

   164. *"Brennus* and *Belinus,* kings of Britany,"* as Spenser recalled
(*F.Q.* II, x, 40), were supposed to have "ransackt Greece," beside con-
quering France and Germany. Brennus is identified with the Gallic
leader who sacked Rome in 390 B.C.

   Arvirago was supposed to have led the Britons bravely against the
legions of Claudius:
      "Was neuer king more highly magnifide,
         Nor dred of *Romanes,* then was *Aruirage.*"
                              (*F.Q.* II, x, 52, 1–2.)

Et tandem Armoricos Britonum sub lege colonos;   165
Tum gravidam Arturo fatali fraude Iogernen,
Mendaces vultus, assumptaque Gorloïs arma,
Merlini dolus.   O, mihi tum si vita supersit,
Tu procul annosa pendebis, fistula, pinu
Multum oblita mihi, aut patriis mutata camenis   170
Brittonicum strides! Quid enim? omnia non licet uni,
Non sperasse uni licet omnia.   Mi satis ampla
Merces, et mihi grande decus—sim ignotus in aevum
Tum licet, externo penitusque inglorius orbi—
Si me flava comas legat Usa, et potor Alauni,   175
Vorticibusque frequens Abra, et nemus omne Treantae,
Et Thamesis meus ante omnes, et fusca metallis
Tamara, et extremis me discant Orcades undis.
    "Ite domum impasti, domino iam non vacat, agni.
Haec tibi servabam lenta sub cortice lauri.   180
Haec, et plura simul; tum quae mihi pocula Mansus,
Mansus, Chalcidicae non ultima gloria ripae,
Bina dedit, mirum artis opus, mirandus et ipse,
Et circum gemino caelaverat argumento.
In medio rubri maris unda, et odoriferum ver,   185

---

165. In the *History of Britain* (*P.W.* V, p. 251) Milton tells the story of the establishment of a colony of British veterans by Constantine the Great in what is now Brittany.

166–168. Milton intended to retell the story of King Uther Pendragon's deception of Igraine, the wife of Gorlois, Duke of Cornwall, when the King, disguised like her husband, "by the means of Merlin," (as Malory has it in *Morte d'Arthur*, I, ii) lay with the Duchess and begot Arthur.

169. *fistula,* as Professor Rand insists, must mean pastoral poetry, which Milton intends to abandon, in Latin at least.

172–178. In the Second Book of *The Reason of Church Government* (*P.W.* II, 478) Milton recorded the resolve "to fix all the industry and art I could unite to the adorning of my native tongue, . . . to be an interpreter and relater of the best and sagest things among mine own citizens throughout this island in the mother dialect."

175. The Ouse flows through the counties of Oxford, Buckingham, Bedford, Huntington, Cambridge, and Norfolk into the Wash. Compare *Vacation Exercise,* 92.
    According to Camden, the Alne in Northumberland and the united Stour and Avon in Hampshire both bore the Latin name of *Alaunus.*

178. Gilbert quotes Camden (i, 7) as saying that the Tamar, be-

the Armorican settlers who came at last under British law.[165]
Then I shall tell of Igraine pregnant with Arthur by fatal
deception,[166] the counterfeiting of Gorlois' features and arms
by Merlin's treachery. And then, O my pipe,[169] if life is
granted me, you shall be left dangling on some old pine tree
far away and quite forgotten by me; or else, quite changed,
you shall shrill forth a British theme to your native Muses.[172]
What then? One man cannot do everything nor so much as
hope to do everything. I shall have ample reward and think
my glory great—though I may be forever unknown and inglorious throughout all the outside world—if only blond-
haired Ouse[175] reads me and he who drinks from the Alne
and the Humber with its many whirlpools, and every forest
by the Trent, and before them all my Thames, and the
Tamora,[178] which minerals discolour, and if the Orkneys in
their distant seas will learn my song.

"Go home unfed, for your master has no time for you, my
lambs. These things I was keeping for you in the tough-barked
laurel.[180] These and more also—and in addition the two
cups[181] which Manso gave me—Manso, who is not the least
glory of the Chalcidian shore.[182] They are a marvellous work
of art, and he is a marvellous man. Around them goes an
engraving with a double motif.[185] In the middle are the

tween Devon and Cornwall, "passes at the bottom of a range of very
high mountains . . . anciently rich in mines."

180. Some editors believe that Milton was cherishing his poetic
purposes like valuables in a box of laurel bark, but may it not mean
that the songs which he dreamed of singing were like those which
Virgil says that Apollo taught to his sacred laurel (*Eclogue,* VI, 83)?

181. Instead of two real cups, Mr. M. De Filippis suggests that
Manso gave Milton two volumes of his poems corresponding in subject with the decorations on the cups. One of them would be his
Poesie nomiche (Venice, 1635) which contained his translation of the
poem on the Phoenix which is attributed to Lactantius. See the note
on ll. 133-7 above and on *S.A.* 1699.

182. Like Virgil (*Aen.* VI, 17) Milton calls the Neapolitan coast the
Chalcidian shore. The advent of the Greek colonists from Chalcis in
Euboea, in 326 B.C., is dramatically recorded by Livy (VIII, 22).

185-197. Elaborate descriptions of such carvings on cups run through
pastoral literature from Theocritus' account of the relief showing a

Littora longa Arabum, et sudantes balsama silvae;
Has inter Phoenix, divina avis, unica terris,
Caeruleum fulgens diversicoloribus alis,
Auroram vitreis surgentem respicit undis.
Parte alia polus omnipatens, et magnus Olympus.   190
Quis putet? hic quoque Amor, pictaeque in nube pharetrae,
Arma corusca, faces, et spicula tincta pyropo;
Nec tenues animas, pectusque ignobile vulgi,
Hinc ferit; at, circum flammantia lumina torquens,
Semper in erectum spargit sua tela per orbes   195
Impiger, et pronos nunquam collimat ad ictus.
Hinc mentes ardere sacrae, formaeque deorum.
      "Tu quoque in his—nec me fallit spes lubrica, Damon—
Tu quoque in his certe es; nam quo tua dulcis abiret
Sanctaque simplicitas, nam quo tua candida virtus?   200
Nec te Lethaeo fas quaesivisse sub orco,
Nec tibi conveniunt lacrymae, nec flebimus ultra.
Ite procul, lacrymae; purum colit aethera Damon,
Aethera purus habet, pluvium pede reppulit arcum;
Heroumque animas inter, divosque perennes,   205
Aethereos haurit latices et gaudia potat
Ore Sacro.   Quin tu, caeli post iura recepta,
Dexter ades, placidusque fave, quicunque vocaris,

---

boy weaving a basket while a fox steals his lunch, which ornamented
a prize cup, to Spenser's portrayal of the decorated "mazer" in *August*,
26–35.

186. Compare the allusion to "*Araby* the blest" and its perfumed
seas in *P.L.* IV, 159–165.

187–189. Of the many possible ancient "sources" for this description
of the brilliant colours of the Phoenix, that in the *De ave Phoenici*
(125–44), which is attributed to Lactantius, is perhaps the closest in
letter and spirit to Milton's.   But see *S.A.* 1699, note.

189. Compare the note on the goddess of the dawn, Eos or Aurora,
in *On the Fifth of November*, 133.

190. *Olympus*—the heavens.   Compare *Nature is not subject to Old
Age*, 46; *To his Father*, 30; and *Manso*, 100.

193–197. Milton's Cupid is akin to the Heavenly Eros which Plato
distinguished from the Popular Eros (*Symposium*, 180c, ff.) and to
Hesiod's Eros (*Theogony*, 120–2), the deity who masters the mind and
the wise will in the breasts of gods and men.   From such conceptions
—and especially from the Orphic picture of Eros as a winged deity

waves of the Red Sea, the perfumed springtime, the far-
stretching shores of Arabia,[186] and the groves that distil
balsam. Among those trees the Phoenix,[187] the divine bird
which is unique on earth, gleams cerulean with parti-coloured
wings, and watches Aurora[189] rise over the glassy waters.   In
another part are the widespreading sky and mighty Olympus.[190]
Who would suppose such a thing?   Here is Cupid[193] also, his
quiver painted against a cloud, his gleaming arms, his torches
and his darts of bronze tincture, the colour of flame.   From
that height he does not wound frivolous spirits or the ignoble
hearts of the rabble, but—looking around him with flaming
eyes—he tirelessly scatters his darts aloft through the spheres
and never points his shots downward.   That is why the minds
of the elect and the essences of the gods themselves are en-
kindled.

"You also are among them—for no uncertain hope deceives
me—certainly you also are among them; for where else should
your sweet and holy simplicity have gone?   Where else your
unsullied virtue?   It would be sinful to look to find you in
Lethean Orcus.[201]   Tears for you are an impertinence and I
do not shed them any more. Be gone, my tears! Damon
dwells in the pure aether, the aether which he is pure enough
to possess, and his foot spurns the rainbow.   Among the souls
of heroes and the immortal gods he drinks the draughts of
heaven and quaffs its joys with his sacred lips. And now,
since you have received the privileges of heaven, assist and
gently favour me, however you may be called;[207] whether you

floating on the tenuous air and creating both gods and men—the Neo-
Platonism of the Renaissance evolved Spenser's celestial Cupid, the
                "Victor of Gods, subduer of mankind,"
                    (*An Hymne in Honour of Love*, 45.)
and the
                "Lord of truth and loialtie,
        Lifting himselfe out of the lowly dust
        On golden plumes up to the purest skie."
                    (*Ibid.* 176–8.)
Compare *Comus*, 1004–11, note, and the Introduction, §6.
  201. Compare *Lethe* in *On the Fifth of November*, 132, note.
  207–208. Compare *Lycidas*, 183–5, note.

Seu tu noster eris Damon, sive aequior audis
Diodatus, quo te divino nomine cuncti   210
Caelicolae norint, silvisque vocabere Damon.
Quod tibi purpureus pudor, et sine labe iuventus
Grata fuit, quod nulla tori libata voluptas,
En! etiam tibi virginei servantur honores!
Ipse, caput nitidum cinctus rutilante corona,   215
Laetaque frondentis gestans umbracula palmae,
Aeternum perages immortales hymenaeos,
Cantus ubi, choreisque furit lyra mista beatis,
Festa Sionaeo bacchantur et Orgia Thyrso." (1640)

---

210. *Diodatus,* like the Greek name, Theodore, means "God-given."

212. Editors trace the phrase *purpureus pudor* to Ovid's *Amores,* I,
iii, 14. Milton was thinking of modesty or shame like that which
Plato said (*Phaedrus,* 254a) restrains the soul from incontinence, or
like that which was called by St. Bernard "the sister of Continence,"
and by St. Ambrose, "the friend of Pudicity."

215. Milton was moved by St. John's heavenly vision of those "which
were not defiled with women; for they are virgins" (Rev. xiv, 4), and
he must have been familiar with the medieval tradition which gave
to virgins a crown of lilies like that brought by an angel to St. Cecilia
before her martyrdom in Chaucer's *Second Nun's Tale,* 220–3.

216–217. Compare St. John's vision of the heavenly host before the
throne "with palms in their hands" (Rev. vii, 9) and of "the marriage
of the Lamb" (Rev. xix, 7). Compare *Lycidas,* 176–7, note.

219. The thyrsus was the vine-wreathed wand carried by Bacchic
revellers. By comparing the joys of heaven to their orgies Milton—to
whom Bacchus was a symbol of all human passions in excess (as he
was to Bacon in *The Wisdom of the Ancients*)—meant to say that in
the life to come the passions of this life would be intensified and
chastened into ecstasy.

are to be known as our Damon or would rather be Diodati, by which divine name[210] the inhabitants of heaven will know you, while in the forests you will keep the name of Damon. Because you loved the blush of modesty[212] and a stainless youth and because you did not taste the delight of the marriage-bed, lo! the rewards of virginity are reserved for you. Your glorious head shall be bound with a shining crown[215] and with shadowing fronds of joyous palms in your hands[216] you shall enact your part eternally in the immortal marriage where song and the sound of the lyre are mingled in ecstasy with blessed dances, and where the festal orgies rage under the heavenly thyrsus."[219]

TRANSLATIONS FROM *OF REFORMATION TOUCH-ING CHURCH DISCIPLINE IN ENGLAND.*

Ah, *Constantine,* of how much ill was Cause,
Not thy Conversion, but those rich Domains
That the first wealthy *Pope* receiv'd of thee.
                    (Dante, *Inferno,* xix, 115–7.)

Founded in chaste and humble Poverty,
'Gainst them that rais'd thee dost thou lift thy Horn,
Impudent Whore, where hast thou plac'd thy Hope?
In thy Adulterers, or thy ill got wealth?
Another *Constantine* comes not in haste.
                    (Petrarch, *Sonnet* 138. [108.])

And to be short, at last his guide him brings
Into a goodly Valley, where he sees
A mighty Mass of Things, strangely confus'd,
Things that on Earth were lost, or were abus'd.[1]
                    (Ariosto, *Orlando Furioso,*
                         Canto xxxiv, stanza 73.)

Then past he to a flow'ry Mountain green,
Which once smelt sweet, now stinks as odiously;
This was that Gift (if you the Truth will have)
That *Constantine* to good *Sylvestro* gave.[2]
                    (*Orlando Furioso,* xxxiv, 80.)
                                        (1641)

---

[1]The lines correspond word for word with Harington's translation, except that Harington has "But" for "And" in the first line.

[2]These lines seem to be quite independent of Harington.

TRANSLATION FROM *THE REASON OF CHURCH GOVERNMENT URGED AGAINST PRELATY*. BOOK I, CAP. V.

When I die, let the Earth be roll'd in Flames.
(Attributed to Tiberius.)

(1641)

TRANSLATIONS FROM *AN APOLOGY FOR SMECTYMNUUS*

—laughing to teach the Truth
What hinders?   As some teachers give to Boys
Junkets and Knacks, that they may learn apace.
(Horace, *Satires,* I, i, 25–7.)

—Jesting decides great Things
Stronglier, and better oft than earnest can.
(Horace, *Satires,* I, x, 14–5.)

'Tis you that say it, not I: you do the Deeds,
And your ungodly Deeds find me the Words.
(Sophocles, *Electra,* 624–5.)

(1642)

WHEN THE ASSAULT WAS INTENDED TO THE CITY[1]

CAPTAIN or Colonel, or Knight in Arms,
    Whose chance on these defenceless doors may seize,
    If ever deed of honour did thee please,
    Guard them, and him within protect from harms;
He can requite thee, for he knows the charms   5
    That call Fame on such gentle acts as these,
    And he can spread thy Name o'er Lands and Seas,
    Whatever clime the Sun's bright circle warms.
Lift not thy spear against the Muse's Bow'r:
    The great *Emathian* Conqueror bid spare   10
    The house of *Pindarus,* when Temple and Tow'r
Went to the ground; And the repeated air
    Of sad *Electra's* Poet had the pow'r
    To save th' *Athenian* Walls from ruin bare.

(1642)

---

[1]The Cambridge manuscript entitles this sonnet, *When the assault was intended to the city,* or alternatively, *On his door when the city expected an assault.* Milton wrote it about the thirteenth of November, 1642, when the Royalists, fresh from their partial victory at Edgehill on October twenty-third, reached London fully resolved to take the city, but were turned back by the unexpectedly large force brought against them by the Earl of Essex at Turnham Green.

1. *Colonel* has three syllables, for in the seventeenth century it had not much altered from its original, French form.

10. The *Emathian* is Alexander the Great of Macedon. Again in *P.R.* III, 290, there is an allusion to Macedon by its ancient name of Emathia. Here Milton refers to Alexander's punishment of the Boeotian capital, Thebes, for its revolt in 335 B.C., when—according to a dubious but popular tradition—the only house which he spared was the ancient home of the poet, Pindar. (Pliny tells the story, *Natural History,* VII, 19.)

12. *the repeated air*—the repetition of the air. For the Latin construction compare *S.A.* 1294, note.

13. In his Life of the Spartan general, Lysander, who conquered Athens in 404 B.C., Plutarch says that the officers who decided the city's fate would have destroyed it outright, if one of them had not dissuaded the rest by singing the first chorus in Euripides' *Electra,* which begins:

      "Electra, Agamemnon's child, I come
        Unto thy desert home."

LADY THAT IN THE PRIME

LADY, that in the prime of earliest youth
   Wisely hast shunn'd the broad way and the green,
   And with those few art eminently seen,
   That labour up the Hill of Heav'nly Truth,
The better part with *Mary,* and with *Ruth,*   5
   Chosen thou hast; and they that overween,
   And at thy growing virtues fret their spleen,
   No anger find in thee, but pity and ruth.
Thy care is fixt and zealously attends
   To fill thy odorous Lamp with deeds of light,   10
   And Hope that reaps not shame.   Therefore be sure
Thou, when the Bridegroom with his feastful friends
   Passes to bliss at the mid-hour of night,
   Hast gain'd thy entrance, Virgin wise and pure.

                         (1642–5)

---

1. Until positive evidence comes to light, little is to be gained by speculation about the *Lady's* identity.   Smart's assumption that she was "a girl . . . still very young" who had made Milton her confidant about her social difficulties among people who found her prudish, is certainly preferable to the conjecture that she was the Miss Davis whom he had some thought of marrying in 1644.

2–4. Milton thought of Christ's saying that "broad is the way that leadeth to destruction" (Mat. vii, 13), and probably also of one of Holbein's endlessly reproduced illustrations of the Table of Cebes, where young people play on the lawns among temptations at the foot of a rugged mountain while men and women climb a rocky path to the citadel of true felicity and are crowned by a king, who—in spite of the pagan origin of the Table—seems to be the Christian God himself. Compare *P.R.* II, 217, note.

5. *Mary,* whom Jesus praised for having "chosen that good part, which shall not be taken away from her" (Luke x, 42), and *Ruth,* who preferred to give up her home in Moab for the sake of her Hebrew mother-in-law, Naomi, were traditional exemplars of Christian womanhood.   (See Ruth i, 14.)

8. *ruth*—pity. Milton had the example of Italian poetry and of many earlier English poets for rhyming words of the same sound and of different meanings.

10–14. Milton thought of the parable of the ten virgins, of whom only five were wise enough to fill their lamps with oil and be ready to go to the marriage feast when, "at midnight, there was a cry made, Behold, the bridegroom cometh; go ye out to meet him." (**Mat.** xxv, 6.)

TRANSLATION PREFIXED TO *AREOPAGITICA*

This is true Liberty, when freeborn Men,
Having to advise the Public, may speak free:
Which he who can, and will, deserves high praise:
Who neither can nor will may hold his Peace.
What can be juster in a State than this?
                    (Euripides, *Suppliants,* 438–42.)

                                        (1644)

TRANSLATION IN *TETRACHORDON*

Whom do we count a good man, whom but he
Who keeps the laws and statutes of the Senate,
Who judges in great suits and controversies,
Whose witness and opinion wins the cause?
But his own house, and the whole neighbourhood
See his foul inside through his whited skin.
                    (Horace, *Epistles,* I, xvi, 40.)

                                        (1645)

TO THE LADY MARGARET LEY

DAUGHTER to that good Earl, once President
    Of *England's* Council, and her Treasury,
    Who liv'd in both, unstained with gold or fee,
    And left them both, more in himself content,
Till the sad breaking of that Parliament   5
    Broke him, as that dishonest victory
    At *Chaeronéa,* fatal to liberty,
    Kill'd with report that Old man eloquent;
Though later born than to have known the days
    Wherein your Father flourisht, yet by you,   10
    Madam, methinks I see him living yet;
So well your words his noble virtues praise,
    That all both judge you to relate them true,
    And to possess them, Honour'd *Margaret.*

                            (1644–5)

---

1. After Mary Powell left him in 1642, Milton's nephew, Phillips, says that he, being "now as it were a single man again, made it his chief diversion now and then in an evening, to visit the Lady Margaret Lee, daughter to the — Lee, Earl of Marlborough. . . . This lady being a woman of great wit and ingenuity had a particular honor for him, and took much delight in his company, as likewise her husband Captain Hobson, a very accomplished gentleman."

The *good Earl* was Sir James Ley, who became Lord Chief Justice in 1622, and successively Lord High Treasurer and Lord President of the Council under Charles I, who created him Earl of Marlborough.

5–6. The Earl died on March 14, 1629, four days after the dissolution of Parliament which marked the first violent and open breach between its leaders and the King. Presumably, his sympathies were with Charles, for most of his family later sided with the Royalists, although his oldest daughter married the Parliamentary Captain, John Hobson, in December, 1641.

6. *dishonest* has the Latin meaning of "disgraceful" or "shameful."

7. At Chaeronea, in eastern Boeotia, in 338 B.C., Philip of Macedon crushed the united armies of Thebes and Athens and permanently ended the independence of both cities.

8. The *Old man eloquent*—Isocrates, the Athenian orator, who was ninety-eight years old when the battle occurred. A questionable tradition says that within four days, and while the slain were being buried, he starved himself to death.

*Philosophus ad regem quendam qui eum ignotum & insontem
inter reos forte captum inscius damnaverat* τὴν ἐπὶ θανάτῳ
πορευόμενος, *haec subito misit.*

'Ω ἄνα εἰ ὀλέσῃς με τ ὸν ἔννομον, οὐδέ τιν' ἀνδρῶν
Δεινὸν ὅλως δράσαντα, σοφώτατον ἴσθι κάρηνον
Ῥηϊδίως ἀφέλοιο, τὸδ' ὕστερον αὖθι νοήσεις,
Μαψ αὔτως δ' ἀρ' ἔπειτα χρόνῳ μάλα πολλὸν ὀδύρῃ,
Τοιόνδ' ἐκ πόλεως περιώνυμον ἄλκαρ ὀλέσσας.

(1645?)

IN EFFIGIEI EIUS SCULPTOREM.[1]

'Αμαθεῖ γεγράφθαι χειρὶ τήνδε μὲν εἰκόνα
Φαίης τάχ' ἄν, πρὸς εἶδος αὐτοφυὲς βλέπων'
Τὸν δ' ἐκτυπωτ ὸν οὐκ ἐπιγνόντες, φίλοι,
Γελᾶτε φαύλου δυσμίμημα ζωγράφου.

(1645)

---

[1]Humorous lines placed by Milton below the engraving of himself
which served as a frontispiece to the edition of 1645. It is so bad a
likeness that its only interest is bibliographical.

This message was suddenly sent to a king by a philos-
opher who was on the way to his death because the
ruler had unwittingly condemned him—unrecognized
and innocent—when he happened to be seized among
some robbers.

O King, if you make an end of me, an observer of the laws
and a doer of absolutely no harm to any man, you must know
that you would find it easy to destroy one of the wisest of
heads, but later you will sorrow vainly and grievously because
you have done away with so famous a protection of the city.

ON THE ENGRAVER OF HIS LIKENESS

Looking at the form of its original, you might say, mayhap,
that this likeness had been drawn by a tyro's hand; but,
friends, since you do not recognize what is modelled here,
have a laugh at a caricature by a good-for-nothing artist.

TO MY FRIEND, MR. HENRY LAWES

HARRY, whose tuneful and well measur'd Song
  First taught our English Music how to span
  Words with just note and accent, not to scan
  With *Midas'* Ears, committing short and long,
Thy worth and skill exempts thee from the throng,   5
  With praise enough for Envy to look wan;
  To after age thou shalt be writ the man
  That with smooth air couldst humour best our tongue.
Thou honour'st Verse, and Verse must lend her wing
  To honour thee, the Priest of *Phoebus'* Quire   10
  That tun'st thir happiest lines in Hymn, or Story.
Dante shall give Fame leave to set thee higher
  Than his *Casella,* whom he woo'd to sing,
  Met in the milder shades of Purgatory.

(1646)

---

1. Milton's admiration for Lawes emerges in the opening song which is given to him in the part of the Attendant Spirit in *Comus.* (See also lines 86–8, note.) Although his devotion to the Royalist cause was confessed in the Dedication of his *Choice Psalms* to Charles I in 1648 and in 1653 by his *Airs and Dialogues*—in which the verses set to music represent the poetry of all the better known "Cavalier Lyrists"—Milton's friendship for him did not suffer. In the Cambridge manuscript this sonnet is dated February 9, 1646 and it may have been written then in the expectation that the *Airs* would soon appear. It was first published among the poetic tributes to Lawes in the *Choice Psalms* in 1648, with the present title.

4. The famous ass's ears of King Midas, Ovid relates, were given to him because he preferred Pan's music to Apollo's. (*Met.* XI, 153–79.)
committing has the rare meaning (which contains a reminiscence of the term for pitting gladiators against each other in the Roman arena) of "putting into a state of hostility or incongruity." (*N.E.D.*)

11. The *Story,* as a marginal note in the *Choice Psalms* points out, was William Cartwright's poem, the *Complaint of Ariadne,* which Lawes set to music.

13–14. Milton thought of Dante's greeting, "My Casella," to the friend whom he met on the threshold of Purgatory, of his vain attempt to embrace the shade, and of his joy in finding that Casella could still charm him with the song of love which he remembered as having long ago brought unfailing consolation to his famished spirit. (*Purgatory,* II, 76–119.)

14. *milder, i.e.,* than those of hell.

I DID BUT PROMPT THE AGE

I DID but prompt the age to quit their clogs
   By the known rules of ancient liberty,
   When straight a barbarous noise environs me
   Of Owls and Cuckoos, Asses, Apes and Dogs.
As when those Hinds that were transform'd to Frogs   5
   Rail'd at *Latona's* twin-born progeny
   Which after held the Sun and Moon in fee.
   But this is got by casting Pearl to Hogs,

1–2. The *known rules of ancient liberty* to which Milton appealed in his divorce tracts were drawn mainly from the Mosaic law and from other records of early Hebrew practice about marriage and divorce in the Old Testament.

4. All the beasts mentioned had rich traditions of bad character, such for example as the shallowness or lewdness of the cuckoo which figures in the sonnet *O Nightingale,* or the owl's barbarity as it appears in the thirteenth-century *Owl and the Nightingale,* or the dog's vociferous impudence as it was embodied in Spenser's slanderous Blatant Beast, the off-spring of Cerberus, the dog of hell.

5–7. Ovid tells the story of the Lycian peasants who wantonly refused to let Latona drink of their lake when she came to them, weary after a long journey with the infant Apollo and Diana, the destined deities of the sun and moon, in her arms. At her prayer, the children's father, Jove, turned her tormentors into frogs. (*Met.* VI, 317–81.)

7. *fee, i.e.,* fee-simple, absolute possession.

That bawl for freedom in their senseless mood,
   And still revolt when truth would set them free.   10
   Licence they mean when they cry liberty;
For who loves that, must first be wise and good;
   But from that mark how far they rove we see
   For all this waste of wealth, and loss of blood.

(1646?)

---

11. The distinction between liberty and licence goes back to some famous episodes in Roman history. Livy was perhaps the first to make the distinction, when he described the licentiousness of the young nobles who refused to support the better elements in Republican Rome against the tyranny of Appius Claudius and the other Decemvirs. (*History of Rome,* III, 37.)

12. Compare Michael's explanation to Adam that since his
           "original lapse, true Liberty
     Is lost, which always with right Reason dwells
     Twinn'd."
           (*P.L.* XII, 83–5.)

ON THE NEW FORCERS OF CONSCIENCE UNDER THE LONG PARLIAMENT

Because you have thrown off your Prelate Lord,
    And with stiff Vows renounc'd his Liturgy
    To seize the widow'd whore Plurality
    From them whose sin ye envied, not abhorr'd,
Dare ye for this adjure the Civil Sword   5
    To force our Consciences that Christ set free,
    And ride us with a classic Hierarchy
    Taught ye by mere *A. S.* and *Rotherford?*
Men whose Life, Learning, Faith and pure intent
    Would have been held in high esteem with *Paul*   10
    Must now be nam'd and printed Heretics
    By shallow *Edwards* and Scotch what d'ye call:
    But we do hope to find out all your tricks,

1–4. On July first, 1643, shortly after the abolition of the episcopate in the English Church by the Long Parliament, the Westminster Assembly began the deliberations "for the settling of the liturgy and the government of the Church of England," which lasted until February 22, 1649. There was a heavy majority of Presbyterians, and those "great rebukers of non-residence," as Milton called them again in his *History of Britain* (III), "were not ashamed to be seen quickly pluralists and non-residents themselves, to a fearful condemnation doubtless by their own mouths." (*P.W.* V, p. 238.)

7. Classis was a usual name for the presbyteries or governing bodies under Presbyterianism. Samuel Butler made the zealously Independent Ralpho opine that

> "*Bear-baiting* may be made out
> In Gospel-times, as lawful as is
> *Provincial,* or *Parochial Classis.*
> (*Hudibras,* I, i, 837–9.)

8. *A.S.* was Adam Stewart, a Scottish divine who was in London as an active pamphleteer against the Independents during the first year of the sessions of the Westminster Assembly, although he was not one of its members.

9–10. Milton referred to the leaders of the small minority of Independents, with whom he sympathized and who were destined, thanks to Cromwell's support, to triumph in the end. Thomas Goodwin, whose pamphlets in defence of religious freedom anticipated the essential points in *Areopagitica,* was the most conspicuous.

12. Thomas Edwards deserved the charge of *shallow* by his *Antapologia,* which was written in reply to the collaborative *Apologetical*

Your plots and packing worse than those of *Trent*,
                    That so the Parliament   15
May with their wholesome and preventive Shears
Clip your Phylacteries, though baulk your Ears,
                    And succour our just Fears,
When they shall read this clearly in your charge:
New Presbyter is but *Old Priest* writ Large.   20

(1646?)

Narration in which Goodwin and several other Independents stated the case for religious freedom.

Robert Baillie, the most outspoken and bitter of the Scottish members of the Westminster Assembly, appears to be *Scotch what d'ye call.*

14. The Council of Trent, which met irregularly from 1545 to 1563, was famous for its intrigues and compromises.

15. This and the two normal lines which follow it constitute the first of the sonnet's two tails. Italian practice permitted satirical sonneteers to add indefinite numbers of such "tails" to the normal fourteen lines.

17. *Phylacteries,* little parchments containing fragments of the Mosaic law which were worn conspicuously by pious Jews, were made a by-word for hypocrisy by Jesus' charge that the Pharisees made "broad their phylacteries." (Mat. xxiii, 5.)

baulk—stop short of, *i.e.,* do not clip the ears. Milton's eye was on William Prynne, the Presbyterian pamphleteer who actually lost his ears in 1633 for publishing *Histriomastix*. In the manuscript the line originally ran:

            "Clip ye as close as marginal P———'s ears."

20. *Presbyter* and *Priest* are originally derived from the same Greek word, but the latter came into English through French and Latin very early, while the former was a learned invention of the close of the sixteenth century.

In 1644 (June or July) William Walwyn had written in the *Compassionate Samaritane* (pp. 16–7) that, "Some say the tyrannie over conscience that was exercised by the Bishops, is like to be continued by the Presbiters: that the oppressours are only changed, but the oppression not likely to be removed."

ON THE RELIGIOUS MEMORY OF
MRS. CATHARINE THOMASON, MY CHRISTIAN
FRIEND,
DECEASED DECEMBER, 1646[1]

WHEN Faith and Love which parted from thee never,
    Had ripen'd thy just soul to dwell with God,
    Meekly thou didst resign this earthy load
Of Death, call'd Life; which us from Life doth sever.
Thy Works and Alms and all thy good Endeavour   5
    Stay'd not behind, nor in the grave were trod;
    But, as Faith pointed with her golden rod,
Follow'd thee up to joy and bliss for ever.
Love led them on, and Faith who knew them best
    Thy hand-maids, clad them o'er with purple beams   10
    And azure wings, that up they flew so drest,
And spake the truth of thee in glorious Themes
    Before the Judge, who thenceforth bid thee rest
    And drink thy fill of pure immortal streams.

(1646)

---

[1]From George Thomason's will, which was written about the time of his death in 1666, Smart drew evidence of Thomason's lasting affection for his wife, whom he had mourned for twenty years as a widower. Milton's conventional sonnet may have been a tribute as much to Thomason's affection for her as to the lady herself. The friendship of the two men in the years previous to her death is attested by Milton's signature as the donor of several of his prose pamphlets, which form a part of Thomason's great collection of Civil War tracts, which is now in the British Museum.

4. Compare Sir Thomas Browne in *Religio Medici*, I, 38; "When I take a full view and circle of my self, without this reasonable moderator, . . . Death, I do conceive my self the miserablest person extant; were there not another life that I hope for, all the vanities of this World should not intreat a moment's breath from me." Compare *On the death of the Bishop of Ely*, 37, note.

6. "Blessed are the dead which die in the Lord from henceforth: Yea, saith the Spirit, that they may rest from their labours; and their works do follow them." (Rev. xiv, 13.)

11–13. So the prayers of Adam and Eve, "clad With incense, where the Golden Altar fum'd, . . . came in sight Before the Father's Throne." (*P.L.* XI, 17–20.)

14. *immortal*—immortality-conferring. Milton thought of the "pure river of water of life, clear as crystal, proceeding out of the throne of God and of the Lamb." (Rev. xxii, 1.)

AD IOANNEM ROUSIUM

Oxoniensis Academiae Bibliothecarium

(De libro Poematum amisso, quem ille sibi denuo mitti pos-
tulabat, ut cum aliis nostris in Bibliotheca Publica reponeret, Ode.)

Strophe 1

Gemelle cultu simplici gaudens liber,
Fronde licet gemina,
Munditieque nitens non operosa
Quam manus attulit
Iuvenilis olim   5
Sedula, tamen haud nimii Poetae;
Dum vagus Ausonias nunc per umbras,
Nunc Britannica per vireta lusit,
Insons populi, barbitoque devius
Indulsit patrio, mox itidem pectine Daunio   10
Longinquum intonuit melos
Vicinis, et humum vix tetigit pede.

Antistrophe

Quis te, parve liber, quis te fratribus
Subduxit reliquis dolo,
Cum tu missus ab urbe,   15
Docto iugiter obsecrante amico,
Illustre tendebas iter
Thamesis ad incunabula
Caerulei patris,
Fontes ubi limpidi   20
Aonidum, thyasusque sacer,
Orbi notus per immensos

---

1. This poem was first published in 1673. The stolen book was the
volume of poems published in 1645, a copy of which Milton had sent
to Rouse together with a volume containing the eleven prose pamphlets
which he had published up to that date. The replacement copy of the
poems is still in the Bodleian with the manuscript of this ode where
Milton placed it, between the English and Latin poems.

TO JOHN ROUSE

Librarian of Oxford University

(An ode on a volume of my poems which was lost and another copy of which he requested so that he might place it in the
public library with the rest of my books.)

Twin-membered book[1] rejoicing in a single cover, yet with
a double leaf,[2] and shining with unlaboured elegance which a
hand once young imparted—a careful hand, but hardly that
of one who was too much a poet—while he played, foot-loose,
now in the forest-shades of Ausonia[7] and now on the lawns
of England, and, following his own devious ways aloof from
the people, he trifled with his native lute or chanted some
exotic strain with a Daunian[10] quill to his neighbours—his
foot scarcely touching the ground.

Who was it, little book, who furtively purloined you from
your remaining brothers, when, in response to my learned
friend's importunity, you had been dispatched from the town
and were going on the glorious journey to the nursery of the
Thames[18]—blue father Thames—where the limpid fountains
of the Muses[21] are found and also that consecrated band,
which has been famous through the world while vast ages

---

2. *fronde*—either the title pages under which the Latin and English
poems were separately paginated or the double crown deserved by the
collections of poems in the two languages.

7. *Ausonia*—an ancient name for Italy.

7-12. Compare Milton's statement in *The Second Defence:* "I thought
it base to be travelling for amusement abroad, while my fellow-citizens
were fighting for liberty at home." (*P.W.* I, p. 256.)

10. *Daunia* was the ancient name of the modern province of Puglia
in southeastern Italy. Here it stands by metonymy for the whole
country.

18. Milton refers to Oxford as the birthplace of the Thames because
it lies on the river Isis, not far above that river's confluence with the
Thames, where the Thames proper begins.

21. *Aonidum*—the Aonides or Muses, whose traditional home was
Mount Helicon in Aonia. Compare *To his Father,* 75, note.

Temporum lapsus redeunte caelo,
Celeberque futurus in aevum?

Strophe   2

Modo quis deus, aut editus deo,   25
Pristinam gentis miseratus indolem—
Si satis noxas luimus priores,
Mollique luxu degener otium—
Tollat nefandos civium tumultus,
Almaque revocet studia sanctus,   30
Et relegatas sine sede Musas
Iam paene totis finibus Angligenum,
Immundasque volucres
Unguibus imminentes
Figat Apollinea pharetra,   35
Phineamque abigat pestem procul amne Pegaseo?

Antistrophe

Quin tu, libelle, nuntii licet mala
Fide, vel oscitantia,
Semel erraveris agmine fratrum,
Seu quis te teneat specus,   40
Seu qua te latebra, forsan unde vili
Callo tereris institoris insulsi,
Laetare felix; en! iterum tibi
Spes nova fulget posse profundam
Fugere Lethen, vehique Superam   45
In Iovis aulam remige penna:

Strophe 3

Nam te Rousius sui
Optat peculi, numeroque iusto
Sibi pollicitum queritur abesse,
Rogatque venias ille, cuius inclyta   50
Sunt data virum monumenta curae;

---

29. Milton was writing in the fourth year of the Civil War.
31–33. As the headquarters of Charles I's forces for about three

have rolled under the revolving heaven, and which is destined to be glorious forever?

What god or what god-begotten man will take pity on the ancient character of our race—if we have sufficiently atoned for our earlier offenses and the degenerate idleness of our effeminate luxury—and will sweep away these accursed tumults among the citizens?[29] What deity will summon our fostering studies home[31] and recall the Muses who have been left with hardly a retreat anywhere in all the confines of England? Who will use the arrows of Apollo to transfix the foul birds[33] whose claws menace us,[35] and will drive the pest of Phineas far away from Pegasus' river?[36]

But, my little book—even though, thanks to a messenger's dishonesty or drowsiness, you have wandered from the company of your brothers—whether some den or some dive imprisons you now, where perhaps you are scraped by the dirty, calloused hand of an illiterate dealer—still you may rejoice, for you are fortunate. Lo, again a new hope shines that you may avoid the depths of Lethe and be carried on oaring wing to the courts of Jupiter on high.

For Rouse—to whose keeping are entrusted the glorious monuments of heroes[51]—covets you as part of his treasure,

---

years, before it surrendered to Lord Fairfax in June, 1646, Oxford had almost completely lost its academic character.

33-36. Milton thought of the Harpies as Virgil described them (*Aen.* III, 225-41), monstrous birds that defiled everything which they could not devour, and of a story (stemming from Apollonius of Rhodes, *Argonautica,* II, 195-228) that they had once been sent by Zeus to punish the prophet, Phineas, for the abuse of his powers.

35. See the note on Apollo's destruction of the Python in *Elegy VII,* 31-2.

36. Milton called the Thames the river of Pegasus not merely because he thought of the more famous fountain of Pirene, near Corinth, which was associated with the winged horse, but also because his flight to heaven with Bellerophon (Compare *P.L.* VII, 18) was regarded (*e.g.,* by Conti, IX, iv) as a symbol of the human mind in quest of astronomical knowledge and of the control of nature generally.

51. Compare the description in *Areopagitica* of a good book as "the precious life-blood of a master-spirit, embalmed and treasured up on purpose to a life beyond life." (*P.W.* II, p. 55.)

Teque adytis etiam sacris
Voluit reponi, quibus et ipse praesidet
Aeternorum operum custos fidelis,
Quaestorque gazae nobilioris   55
Quam cui praefuit Ion,
Clarus Erechtheides,
Opulenta dei per templa parentis,
Fulvosque tripodas, donaque Delphica,
Ion Actaea genitus Creusa.   60

Antistrophe

Ergo tu visere lucos
Musarum ibis amoenos
Diamque Phoebi rursus ibis in domum
Oxonia quam valle colit,
Delo posthabita,   65
Bifidoque Parnassi iugo.
Ibis honestus,
Postquam egregiam tu quoque sortem
Nactus abis, dextri prece sollicitatus amici.
Illic legeris inter alta nomina   70
Authorum, Graiae simul et Latinae
Antiqua gentis lumina et verum decus.

Epodos

Vos tandem haud vacui mei labores,
Quicquid hoc sterile fudit ingenium.
Iam sero placidam sperare iubeo   75
Perfunctam invidia requiem, sedesque beatas
Quas bonus Hermes
Et tutela dabit solers Roüsi,
Quo neque lingua procax vulgi penetrabit, atque longe
Turba legentum prava facesset;   80
At ultimi nepotes,

---

55. *gazae.* See the note on *gazas* in *To his Father,* 94, note.

56–60. Milton thought of the atmosphere of charmed magnificence
thrown around Apollo's Delphian temple in the first act of Euripides'

complains that you are missing from the just number promised, and requests that you may come to him. He has desired that you may be placed in those sacred sanctuaries where he himself presides, a faithful warden of immortal works and a custodian of wealth[55] nobler than the gilt tripods and Delphic offerings which were committed in the rich temple of his divine father to Ion,[56] the glorious descendant of Apollo—Ion who was born of Actaean Creusa.

So you shall go to see the delightful groves of the Muses[62] and again you shall go to the divine home of Phoebus, which he inhabits in Oxford's valley in preference to Delos[65] and the riven[66] peak of Parnassus. You shall go with honour, since you are departing assured of a splendid destiny and are invited by a propitious friend. There you shall be read among the sublime names of authors who were the ancient lights and the true glory of the Greek and Latin race.

You then, my labours[73]—whatever my sterile brain has produced—have hardly been in vain. Now at last I bid you look forward to quiet rest, after you have outlived envy, in the blessed retreats provided by kind Hermes[77] and the alert protection of Rouse, where the insolent noise of the crowd never shall enter and the vulgar mob of readers shall forever be excluded.[79] But our distant descendants and a more sensitive

---

Ion. The hero, who is Apollo's son, begotten by violence on Creusa, the daughter of Erechtheus, king of Athens, has been secretly reared to be the custodian of his father's temple. Creusa is called *Actaean* because Acte was an ancient name of Attica.

62. So, at Cambridge, in the sixth *Prolusion,* Milton humorously imagined "that all Helicon, and whatsoever shrines of the Muses there are in addition, have poured forth all their foster children for the purposes of taking part in the exercises."

65. See the note on *Delo* in *Manso,* 45.

66. *Bifidoque Parnassi iugo.* See *Elegy IV,* 30, note.

73. By *labores* Milton intended, probably, to refer to the controversial pamphlets which he had presented to the Bodleian as well as to the poems in the volume which he was sending to Rouse.

77. *Hermes.* See *On the Platonic Idea,* 32–4, note.

79–80. Compare Milton's promise to himself of no vulgar fame in *To his Father,* 103–4.

Et cordatior aetas
Iudicia rebus aequiora forsitan
Adhibebit integro sinu.
Tum livore sepulto,   85
Si quid meremur sana posteritas sciet
Roüsio favente.

(Ode tribus constat Strophis, totidemque Antistrophis, una
demum epodo clausis; quas, tametsi omnes nec versuum numero,
nec certis ubique colis exacte respondeant, ita tamen secuimus,
commode legendi potius, quam ad antiquos concinendi modos
rationem spectantes.   Alioquin hoc genus rectius fortasse dici
monostrophicum debuerat.   Metra partim sunt   κατὰ σχέσιν,
partim ἀπολελυμένα.[1] Phaleucia quae sunt, spondaeum tertio
loco bis admittunt, quod idem in secundo loco Catullus ad libitum
fecit.)   (Jan. 23, 1647)

[1]Compare the use of the same term in Milton's Preface to *S.A.*

age will perhaps render a more nearly just judgement of things out of its unprejudiced heart. Then, when envy has been buried, a sane posterity will know what my deserts are—thanks to Rouse.

(The ode consists of three strophes and the same number of antistrophes, concluding with an epode. Although these units do not perfectly correspond in their number of verses or in divisions which are strictly parallel, nevertheless I have divided them in this way with a view rather to convenience in reading than to conformity with the ancient rules of versification. In other respects a poem of this kind should perhaps more correctly be called monostrophic. The metres are in part regularly patterned and in part free. There are two Phaleucian[1] verses which admit a spondee in the third foot, a practice which Catullus freely followed in the second foot.)

---

[1]The Phaleucian line consisted of a spondee, a dactyl, and three trochees:

$$-\ -\ /\ -\ \smile\ \smile\ /\ -\ \smile\ /\ -\ \smile\ /\ -\ \smile.$$

Milton reasoned badly, as Landor protested, in appealing to Catullus to justify his liberties with his verse. He really meant to declare his purpose to experiment with his metre as freely as he had experimented with his scazons in *To Salzilli.*

ON THE DETRACTION WHICH FOLLOWED UPON MY WRITING CERTAIN TREATISES

A Book was writ of late call'd *Tetrachordon;*
  And wov'n close, both matter, form and style;
  The Subject new: it walk'd the Town a while,
  Numb'ring good intellects; now seldom por'd on.
Cries the stall-reader, bless us! what a word on   5
  A title page is this! and some in file
  Stand spelling false, while one might walk to Mile-
  End Green.   Why is it harder, Sirs, than Gordon,
Colkitto, or Macdonnel, or Galasp?
  Those rugged names to our like mouths grow sleek   10
  That would have made *Quintilian* stare and gasp.
Thy age, like ours, O Soul of Sir *John Cheke,*
  Hated not Learning worse than Toad or Asp,
  When thou taught'st *Cambridge,* and King *Edward* Greek.
                                                (1647?)

1–6. In spite of the confusion which the title of Milton's third divorce tract caused, the term *tetrachord*—a half-octave or scale-series of four notes—was familiar, at least to musicians. He knew that the three modes or scales of Greek music had all been limited to tetrachords and his title expressed his feeling that he had wrought genuine harmony within the metaphorical tetrachord of four great biblical passages on divorce—in Genesis, Deuteronomy, St. Matthew's Gospel and I Corinthians respectively. Casual readers, dipping into his book in the shops, may have been puzzled; but such readers, as he knew from one of Martial's Epigrams (xi, 1), had been fair targets for satire even in ancient Rome.

7. *spelling false*—misreading, misinterpreting.

8–10. Instead of *rugged* Milton originally wrote *barbarian,* for he assumed that his readers would sympathize with the condemnation of foreign names and words in Quintilian's *Institutes,* that "easy and delightful book of education" (*P.W.* III, p. 468) which he thought should be the foundation of a boy's training in Latin. He chose his names for their roughness rather than for their politics. *Colkitto* was a lieutenant of the Marquis of Montrose, while *Galasp,* if any individual was definitely intended, is probably to be identified with the Covenanting clergyman, George Gillespie.

9. *our like mouths; i.e.,* our mouths which are beginning to be like the barbarous names that are too familiar to them.

12. Sir John Cheke, the first Professor of Greek at Cambridge and later tutor to the young King Edward VI, was said by Roger Ascham

April, 1648.   J. M.
*Nine of the Psalms done into Metre, wherein all but what is
in a different Character, are the very words of the Text,
translated from the Original.*

PSAL. LXXX

1 Thou Shepherd that dost Israel *keep*
    Give ear *in time of need,*
Who leadest like a flock of sheep
    Thy loved Joseph's seed,
That sitt'st between the Cherubs *bright*   5
    Between their wings out-spread,
Shine forth, *and from thy cloud give light,*
    And on our foes thy dread.
2 In Ephraim's view and Benjamin's,
    And in Manasse's sight   10
Awake* thy strength, come, and *be seen*   *Gnorera.
    To save us by thy might.
3 Turn us again, *thy grace divine*
    To us O God *vouchsafe;*
Cause thou thy face on us to shine   15
    And then we shall be safe.
4 Lord God of Hosts, how long wilt thou,
    How long wilt thou declare
Thy *smoking wrath, *and angry brow*   *Gnashanta.
    Against thy people's pray'r?   20
5 Thou feed'st them with the bread of tears,
    Their bread with tears they eat,
And mak'st them* largely drink the tears   *Shalish.
    Wherewith their cheeks are wet.
6 A strife thou mak'st us *and a prey*   25
    To every neighbour foe,
Among themselves they* laugh, they* play,   *Jilgnagu.
    And flouts at us they throw.

(*Works,* ed. by Giles, I, p. xxxvii) to have made his subject more
popular than Latin. He had enemies, chief among whom was Bishop
Gardiner, against whom he had to defend Erasmus' way of pronouncing Greek and, indeed, the whole attitude of the Reformers toward the
language.

7 Return us, *and thy grace divine,*
   O God of Hosts *vouchsafe;*   30
Cause thou thy face on us to shine,
   And then we shall be safe.

8 A Vine from Egypt thou hast brought,
   Thy free love made it thine,
And drov'st out Nations *proud and haut*   35
   To plant this *lovely* Vine.

9 Thou did'st prepare for it a place
   And root it deep and fast
That it *began to grow apace,*
   And fill'd the land *at last.*   40

10 With her *green* shade *that* cover'd *all,*
   The Hills were *over-spread,*
Her Bows as *high as* Cedars tall
   Advanc'd their lofty head.

11 Her branches *on the western side*   45
   Down to the Sea she sent,
And *upward* to that river *wide*
   Her other branches *went.*

12 Why hast thou laid her Hedges low
   And brok'n down her Fence,   50
That all may pluck her, as they go,
   With rudest violence?

13 The *tusked* Boar out of the wood
   Upturns it by the roots,
Wild Beasts there browse, and make their food   55
   Her Grapes and tender Shoots.

14 Return now, God of Hosts, look down
   From Heav'n, thy Seat divine,
Behold *us, but without a frown,*
   And visit this *thy* Vine.   60

15 Visit this Vine, which thy right hand
   Hath set, and planted *long,*
And the young branch, that for thyself
   Thou hast made firm and strong.

16 But now it is consum'd with fire,   65
   And cut *with Axes* down,
They perish at thy dreadful ire,
   At thy rebuke and frown.

17 Upon the man of thy right hand
    Let thy *good* hand be *laid,*   70
  Upon the Son of Man, whom thou
    Strong for thyself hast made.
18 So shall we not go back from thee
    To ways of sin and shame,
  Quick'n us thou, then *gladly* wee   75
    Shall call upon thy Name.
  Return us, *and thy grace divine*
    Lord God of Hosts *voutsafe,*
  Cause thou thy face on us to shine,
    And then we shall be safe.   80

PSAL. LXXXI

1 To GOD our strength sing loud, *and clear,*
    Sing loud to God *our King,*
  To Jacob's God, *that all may hear*
    Loud acclamations ring.
2 Prepare a Hymn, prepare a Song,   5
    The Timbrel hither bring,
  The *cheerful* Psaltry bring along
    And Harp *with* pleasant *string.*
3 Blow, *as is wont,* in the new Moon
    With Trumpets' *lofty sound,*   10
  Th' appointed time, the day whereon
    Our solemn Feast *comes round.*
4 This was a Statute *giv'n of old*
    For Israel *to observe,*
  A Law of Jacob's God, *to hold*   15
    From whence they might not swerve.
5 This he a Testimony ordain'd
    In Joseph, *not to change,*
  When as he pass'd through Egypt land;
    The Tongue I heard, was strange.   20
6 From burden, *and from slavish toil,*
    I set his shoulder free;
  His hands from pots, *and miry soil,*
    Deliver'd were *by me.*

7 When trouble did thee sore assail,   25
   On me then didst thou call,
And I to free thee *did not fail,*
   And led thee out of thrall.
I answer'd thee in *thunder deep   **Be Sether ragnam.*
   With clouds encompass'd round;   30
I tried thee at the water *steep*
   Of Meriba *renown'd.*
8 Hear O my people, *heark'n well,*
   I testify to thee
Thou ancient stock of Israel,   35
   If thou wilt list to mee,
9 Throughout the land of thy abode
   No alien God shall be,
Nor shalt thou to a foreign God
   In honour bend thy knee.   40
10 I am the Lord thy God which brought
   Thee out of Egypt land;
Ask large enough, and I, *besought,*
   Will grant thy full demand.
11 And yet my people would not *hear,*   45
   Nor hearken to my voice;
And Israel *whom I lov'd so dear*
   Mislik'd me for his choice.
12 Then did I leave them to their will
   And to their wand'ring mind;   50
Their own conceits they follow'd still
   Their own devices blind.
13 O that my people would *be wise*
   To serve me *all their days,*
And O that Israel would *advise*   55
   To walk my *righteous* ways.
14 Then would I soon bring down their foes
   That now so proudly rise,
And turn my hand against *all those*
   That are their enemies.   60
15 Who hate the Lord should *then be fain*
   To bow to him and bend,
But *they, His people, should remain,*
   Their time should have no end.

16 And he would feed them *from the shock*   65
    With flour of finest wheat,
  And satisfy them from the rock
    With Honey *for their Meat.*

PSAL. LXXXII

1 GOD in the *great *assembly stands   *Bagnadath-el.
    Of Kings and lordly States,
  Among the gods† on both his hands   †Bekerev.
    He judges and debates.
2 How long will ye *pervert the right   *Tishphetu
    With *judgement false and wrong,   gnavel.   5
  Favouring the wicked *by your might,*
    Who thence grow bold and strong?
3 *Regard the *weak and fatherless,   *Shiphtu-dal.
    *Dispatch the *poor man's cause,   10
  And †raise the man in deep distress
    By †just and equal Laws.   †Hatzdiku.
4 Defend the poor and desolate,
    And rescue from the hands
  Of wicked men the low estate   15
    Of him *that help demands.*
5 They know not nor will understand,
    In darkness they walk on,
  The Earth's foundations all are *mov'd   *Jimmotu.
    And *out of order gone.   20
6 I said that ye were Gods, yea all
    The Sons of God most high;
7 But ye shall die like men, and fall
    As other Princes *die.*
8 Rise God, *judge thou the earth *in might,*   25
    This *wicked* earth *redress,   *Shiphta.
  For thou art he who shalt by right
    The Nations all possess.

PSAL. LXXXIII

1 BE NOT thou silent *now at length*
　O God hold not thy peace,
Sit not thou still O God of *strength,*
　We cry and do not cease.

2 For lo thy *furious* foes *now* *swell   5
　And *storm outrageously,   **Jehemajun.*
And they that hate thee *proud and fell*
　Exalt their heads full high.

3 Against thy people they †contrive   †*Jagnarimu.*
　†Their Plots and Counsels deep,   †*Sod.*   10
*Them to ensnare they chiefly strive   **Jithjagnatsu gnal.*
　*Whom thou dost hide and keep.   **Tsephuneca.*

4 Come let us cut them off say they,
　Till they no Nation be,
That Israel's name for ever may   15
　Be lost in memory.

5 For they consult †with all their might,   †*Lev jachdau.*
　And all as one in mind
Themselves against thee they unite,
　And in firm union bind.   20

6 The tents of Edom, and the brood
　Of *scornful* Ishmael,
Moab, with them of Hagar's blood
　That in the Desert dwell,

7 Gebal and Ammon *there conspire,*   25
　And *hateful* Amalec,
The Philistines, and they of Tyre
　Whose bounds the Sea doth check.

8 With them *great* Asshur also bands,
　And doth confirm the knot,   30
All these have lent their armed hands
　To aid the Sons of Lot.

9 Do to them as to Midian *bold*
　That wasted all the Coast,
To Sisera, and as *is told*   35
　Thou didst to Jabin's *host,*

When at the brook of Kishon *old*
　　They were repulst and slain,
10 At Endor quite cut off, and roll'd
　　As dung upon the plain.   40
11 As Zeb and Oreb evil sped
　　So let their Princes speed,
　　As Zeba, and Zalmunna *bled*
　　So let their Princes *bleed.*
12 *For they amidst their pride* have said   45
　　By right now shall we seize
　　God's houses, and *will now invade*
　　†Their stately Palaces.   †*Neoth Elohim*
　　　　　　　　　　　　　　　　　　　　bears both.
13 My God, oh make them as a wheel,
　　No quiet let them find,   50
　　Giddy and *restless* let *them* reel
　　Like stubble from the wind.
14 As *when* an *aged* wood takes fire
　　Which on a sudden strays,
　　The *greedy* flame runs higher and higher   55
　　Till all the mountains blaze,
15 So with thy whirlwind them pursue,
　　And with thy tempest chase;
16 *And till they *yield thee honour due,   *They seek thy*
　　Lord fill with shame their face.   *Name.* Heb.
17 Asham'd and troubl'd let them be,   60
　　Troubl'd and sham'd for ever,
　　Ever confounded, and so die
　　With shame, *and scape it never.*
18 Then shall they know that thou whose name
　　Jehovah is alone,   65
　　Art the most high, *and thou the same*
　　O'er all the earth *art one.*

PSAL. LXXXIV

1 How lovely are thy dwellings fair!
　　O Lord of Hosts, how dear
　　The *pleasant* Tabernacles are
　　Where thou dost dwell so near!

2 My Soul doth long and almost die   5
   Thy Courts O Lord to see,
My heart and flesh aloud do cry,
   O living God, for thee.

3 There ev'n the Sparrow *freed from wrong*
   Hath found a house of *rest,*   10
The Swallow there, to lay her young
   Hath built her *brooding* nest,
Ev'n *by* thy Altars Lord of Hosts
   They find their safe abode,
And home they fly from round the Coasts   15
   Toward thee, My King, my God.

4 Happy who in thy house reside
   Where thee they ever praise,
5 Happy whose strength in thee doth bide,
   And in their hearts thy ways!   20

6 They pass through Baca's *thirsty* Vale,
   That dry and barren ground
As through a fruitful wat'ry Dale
   Where Springs and Show'rs abound.

7 They journey on from strength to strength   25
   With joy and gladsome cheer,
Till all before *our* God *at length*
   In Sion do appear.

8 Lord God of Hosts hear *now* my prayer,
   O Jacob's God give ear,   30
9 Thou God our shield look on the face
   Of thy anointed *dear.*

10 For one day in thy Courts *to be*
   Is better, *and more blest*
Then *in the joys of Vanity,*   35
   A thousand days *at best.*
I in the temple of my God
   Had rather keep a door,
Than dwell in Tents, *and rich abode,*
   With Sin *for evermore.*   40

11 For God the Lord, both Sun and Shield,
   Gives grace and glory *bright,*
No good from them shall be with-held
   Whose ways are just and right.

12 Lord *God* of Hosts *that reign'st on high,*   45
   That man is *truly* blest
Who *only* on thee doth rely.
   And in thee only rest.

PSAL. LXXXV

1 THY Land to favour graciously
   Thou hast not Lord been slack,
Thou hast from *hard* Captivity
   Returned Jacob back.
2 Th' iniquity thou didst forgive   5
   That wrought thy people woe,
And all their Sin, *that did thee grieve*
   Hast hid *where none shall know.*
3 Thine anger all thou hadst remov'd,
   And *calmly* didst return   10
From thy †fierce wrath which we had prov'd †Heb. *The burning heat of thy wrath.*
   Far worse than fire to burn.
4 God of our saving health and peace,
   Turn us, and us restore,
Thine indignation cause to cease   15
   Toward us, *and chide no more.*
5 Wilt thou be angry without end,
   For ever angry thus?
Wilt thou thy frowning ire extend
   From age to age on us?   20
6 Wilt thou not* turn, and *hear our voice*   *Heb. *Turn to quicken us.*
   And us again* revive,
That so thy people may rejoice
   By thee preserv'd alive.
7 Cause us to see thy goodness Lord,   25
   To us thy mercy show,
Thy saving health to us afford
   And life in us renew.
8 *And now* what God the Lord will speak
   I will *go straight and* hear,   30
For to his people he speaks peace
   And to his Saints *full dear,*

To his dear Saints he will speak peace,
    But let them never more
Return to folly, *but surcease*   35
    To trespass as before.
9 Surely to such as do him fear
    Salvation is at hand
And glory shall *ere long appear*
    To dwell within our Land.   40
10 Mercy and Truth *that long were miss'd*
    Now *joyfully* are met;
Sweet Peace and Righteousness have kiss'd
    And hand in hand are set.
11 Truth from the earth *like to a flowr*   45
    Shall bud and blossom *then,*
And Justice from her heavenly bow'r
    Look down *on mortal men.*
12 The Lord will also then bestow
    Whatever thing is good;   50
Our Land shall forth in plenty throw
    Her fruits *to be our food.*
13 Before him Righteousness shall go
    His Royal Harbinger,
Then* will he come, and not be slow,   *Heb. *He will set his steps to the way.*   55
    His footsteps cannot err.

PSAL. LXXXVI

1 THY *gracious* ear, O Lord, incline,
    O hear me *I thee pray,*
For I am poor, and almost pine
    With need, *and sad decay.*
2 Preserve my soul, for† I have trod   †Heb. *I am good, loving, a doer of good and holy things.*   5
    Thy ways, and love the just,
Save thou thy servant O my God
    Who *still* in thee doth trust.
3 Pity me Lord for daily thee
    I call; 4 O make rejoice   10
Thy Servant's Soul; for Lord to thee
    I lift my soul *and voice.*

 5 For thou art good, thou Lord art prone
    To pardon, thou to all
  Art full of mercy, thou *alone*   15
    To them that on thee call.
 6 Unto my supplication Lord
    Give ear, and to the cry
  Of my *incessant* prayers afford
    Thy hearing graciously.   20
 7 I in the day of my distress
    Will call on thee *for aid;*
  For thou wilt *grant* me *free access*
    And answer, *what I pray'd.*
 8 Like thee among the gods is none   25
    O Lord, nor any works
  Of all that other Gods have done
    Like to thy *glorious* works.
 9 The Nations all whom thou hast made
    Shall come, *and all shall frame*   30
  To bow them low before thee Lord,
    And glorify thy name.
10 For great thou art, and wonders great
    By thy strong hand are done,
  Thou *in thy everlasting Seat*   35
    Remainest God alone.
11 Teach me O Lord thy way *most right,*
    I in thy truth will bide,
  To fear thy name my heart unite,
    So shall it never slide.   40
12 Thee will I praise O Lord my God
    Thee honour, and adore
  With my whole heart, and blaze abroad
    Thy name for ever more.
13 For great thy mercy is toward me,   45
    And thou hast freed my Soul,
  Ev'n from the lowest Hell set free
    From deepest darkness foul.
14 O God the proud against me rise
    And violent men are met   50
  To seek my life, and in their eyes
    No fear of thee have set.

15 But thou Lord art the God most mild
　　Readiest thy grace to show,
　　Slow to be angry, and *art styl'd*　　　　55
　　Most merciful, most true.
16 O turn to me *thy face at length,*
　　And me have mercy on,
　　Unto thy servant give thy strength,
　　And save thy hand-maid's Son.　　　　60
17 Some sign of good to me afford,
　　And let my foes *then* see
　　And be asham'd, because thou Lord
　　Dost help and comfort me.

PSAL. LXXXVII

1 AMONG the holy Mountains *high*
　　Is his foundation fast,
　　There Seated in his Sanctuary,
　　His Temple there is plac't.
2 Sion's *fair* Gates the Lord loves more　　　5
　　Than all the dwellings *fair*
　　Of Jacob's *Land, though there be store,*
　　And all within his care.
3 City of God, most glorious things
　　Of thee *abroad* are spoke;　　　　10
4 I mention Egypt, *where proud Kings*
　　Did our forefathers yoke,
　　I mention Babel to my friends,
　　Philistia *full of scorn,*
　　And Tyre with Ethiop's *utmost ends,*　　15
　　Lo this man there was born:
5 But *twice that praise shall in our ear*
　　Be said of Sion *last:*
　　This and this man was born in her,
　　High God shall fix her fast.　　　　20
6 The Lord shall write it in a Scroll
　　That ne'er shall be out-worn
　　When he the Nations doth enroll
　　That this man there was born.

7 Both they who sing, and they who dance   25
    With sacred Songs are there,
  In thee *fresh brooks and soft streams glance,*
    And all my fountains *clear.*

PSAL. LXXXVIII

1 LORD GOD that dost me save and keep,
    All day to thee I cry;
  And all night long before thee *weep,*
    Before thee *prostrate lie.*
2 Into thy presence let my prayer   5
    With sighs devout ascend;
  And to my cries, that *ceaseless are,*
    Thine ear with favour bend.
3 For cloy'd with woes and trouble store
    Surcharg'd my Soul doth lie,   10
  My life *at death's uncheerful door*
    Unto the grave draws nigh.
4 Reck'n'd I am with them that pass
    Down to the *dismal* pit;
  I am a *man, but weak alas   *Heb. *A man*   15
    And for that name unfit.   *without manly*
                   strength.
5 From life discharg'd and parted quite
    Among the dead *to sleep,*
  And like the slain *in bloody fight*
    That in the grave lie *deep;*   20
  Whom thou rememberest no more,
    Dost never more regard,
  Them from thy hand deliver'd o'er
    Death's hideous house hath barr'd.
6 Thou in the lowest pit *profound*   25
    Hast set me *all forlorn,*
  Where thickest darkness *hovers round,*
    In horrid deeps *to mourn.*
7 Thy wrath *from which no shelter saves*
    Full sore doth press on me;   30
  *Thou break'st upon me all thy waves,   *The Heb. *bears*
    *And all thy waves break me.   *. both.*

8 Thou dost my friends from me estrange,
    And mak'st me odious,
  Me to them odious, *for they change,*   35
    And I here pent up thus.

9 Through sorrow, and affliction great
    Mine eye grows dim and dead,
  Lord all the day I thee entreat,
    My hands to thee I spread.   40

10 Wilt thou do wonders on the dead,
    Shall the deceas'd arise
  And praise thee *from their loathsome bed*
    With pale and hollow eyes?

11 Shall they thy loving kindness tell   45
    On whom the grave *hath hold,*
  Or they *who* in perdition *dwell*
    Thy faithfulness *unfold?*

12 In darkness can thy mighty *hand*
    Or wondrous acts be known,   50
  Thy justice in the *gloomy* land
    Of *dark* oblivion?

13 But I to thee O Lord do cry
    Ere yet my life be spent,
  And *up to thee* my prayer *doth hie*   55
    Each morn, and thee prevent.

14 Why wilt thou Lord my soul forsake,
    And hide thy face from me,

15 That am already bruis'd, and †shake   †Heb. *Prae Concus-*
    With terror sent from thee;   *sione.*   60
  Bruised, and afflicted and *so low*
    As ready to expire,
  While I thy terrors undergo
    Astonish'd with thine ire.

16 Thy fierce wrath over me doth flow   65
    Thy threat'nings cut me through:

17 All day they round about me go,
    Like waves they me pursue.

18 Lover and friend thou hast remov'd
    And sever'd from me far.   70
  They *fly me now* whom I have lov'd,
    And as in darkness are.

ON THE LORD GENERAL FAIRFAX *AT THE SIEGE* OF COLCHESTER

FAIRFAX, whose name in arms through Europe rings
   Filling each mouth with envy, or with praise,
   And all her jealous monarchs with amaze
   And rumours loud, that daunt remotest kings,
Thy firm unshak'n virtue ever brings   5
   Victory home, though new rebellions raise
   Thir Hydra heads, and the false North displays
   Her brok'n league, to imp their serpent wings.
O yet a nobler task awaits thy hand;
   For what can War, but endless war still breed,   10
   Till Truth, and Right from Violence be freed,
And Public Faith clear'd from the shameful brand
   Of Public Fraud. In vain doth Valour bleed
   While Avarice, and Rapine share the land.

(1648)

_____

1. Sir Thomas Fairfax's victories over the Royalists at Marston Moor on July 2, 1644, and Naseby, June 14, 1645, decided their fate. When sporadic revolts against the Parliament broke out in 1648, he drove the Royalists of Kent and Essex into Colchester, but his career virtually ended with his capture of that city on August 27, after a siege of seventy-five days.

5. *virtue* keeps the Latin force of "manly courage." Compare Gloucester's praise of Henry V:
     "Virtue he had, deserving to command:
     His brandish'd sword did blind men with his beams."
              (*I Henry VI*, I, i, 10–1.)

7. So Shakespeare used the metaphor comparing civil war to the *Hydra,* the many-headed monster which instantly developed two new heads for every one that was cut off, until Hercules destroyed it. In *II Henry IV,* IV, ii, 38, the rebels speak of their own movement as "this Hydra son of war."

The *false North*—Scotland, which, in spite of having entered into the Solemn League and Covenant with the English Parliament in September, 1645, sent the Duke of Hamilton to Charles's support in 1648. This sonnet must have been written before news of his defeat by Cromwell at Preston, August 17–19, reached London.

8. Imping or grafting feathers to the injured wing of a falcon was once a common practice. Compare Shakespeare's metaphor, to
     "Imp out our drooping country's broken wing."
              (*Richard II*, II, i, 292.)

TRANSLATION FROM *THE TENURE OF KINGS AND MAGISTRATES*

THERE can be slain
No sacrifice to God more acceptable
Than an unjust and wicked king.

(Seneca, *Hercules Mad*, 922–4.)

(1649)

LATIN VERSES FROM *PRO POPULO ANGLICANO DEFENSIO*

IN SALMASII HUNDREDAM

QUIS expedivit Salmasio suam *hundredam*
Picamque docuit verba nostra conari?
Magister artis venter, et Iacobaei
Centum, exulantis viscera marsupii regis.
Quod, si dolosi spes refulserit nummi,   5
Ipse, Antichristi modo qui primatum Papae
Minatus uno est dissipare sufflatu,
Cantabit ultro Cardinalitium melos.

(1651)

---

1. Claude de Saumaise (1588–1653) was a French scholar whose Protestant sympathies cost him the post of Counsellor to the Parliament of Dijon and caused his early migration to Holland. After he became a professor at the University of Leyden in 1631 he was acknowledged the foremost classical scholar in western Europe. In 1649 he was induced to write his *Defensio Regia pro Carolo I ad Regem Carolum II*, to which Milton replied in March, 1651 with *Pro Populo Anglicano Defensio*. Salmasius' challenge to papal supremacy with his *De Primatu Papae* (1645), to which Milton refers in line 6, was sincere; but, because he had shown some sympathy with the English Presbyterians and later declared for a limited episcopacy and for monarchy, Milton regarded him as a traitor to what should have been their common cause.

In the *Defensio Regia* Salmasius had paraded a knowledge of English law and government and had expatiated on the term "hundred," which was applied to the subdivisions of the English counties.

AGAINST THE *HUNDRED* OF SALMASIUS

Who made Salmasius[1] so glib with his "Hundred" and taught the magpie to try our words? His teacher in this art was his stomach and the hundred Jacobuses[3] that were the vitals of the purse of the exiled king. If there were a glimmer of hope of ill-gotten lucre, this very fellow—who recently threatened to blow to pieces the supremacy of the Pope, the Antichrist, with a single puff—would be perfectly willing to sing the song of the Cardinals.

---

3. Rumour had it that Charles II paid Salmasius a hundred Jacobuses (a gold coin worth about 24 shillings) for writing the *Defensio Regia*.

TO THE LORD GENERAL CROMWELL

On the proposals of certain ministers at the Committee for
Propagation of the Gospel

CROMWELL, our chief of men, who through a cloud
    Not of war only, but detractions rude,
    Guided by faith and matchless Fortitude,
    To peace and truth thy glorious way hast plough'd,
And on the neck of crowned Fortune proud   5
    Hast rear'd God's Trophies, and his work pursu'd,
    While Darwen stream with blood of Scots imbru'd,
    And Dunbar field resounds thy praises loud,
And Worcester's laureate wreath; yet much remains
    To conquer still; peace hath her victories   10
    No less renown'd than war, new foes arise
Threat'ning to bind our souls with secular chains:
    Help us to save free Conscience from the paw
    Of hireling wolves whose Gospel is their maw.

                              (May, 1652)

1–4. Newton suggested that *Truth and Peace* were the professed objects of the Parliamentarians, for the words were inscribed on one of their coins in 1651.

7. The battle of Preston was fought on the banks of the river *Darwen.* Compare the note on line 7 in the Sonnet *On the Lord General Fairfax.*

8. On September 3, 1650, Cromwell routed the Scots under Leslie at *Dunbar,* in Scotland, and exactly a year later defeated the Scottish invaders, led by Leslie and Charles II, at Worcester.

10–11. There seems to be a clear allusion to Cicero's balancing of the glories of war against those of peace in the *De officiis,* I, xxii.

12–14. Smart points out that in the debate in 1652 over the limitation of the rights of irregular preachers and the proposal to empower the regularly installed and salaried clergy to license them, Cromwell so far sympathized with Milton as to say that he "had rather that Mahometanism were permitted among us than that one of God's children should be persecuted."

14. Compare the echo in *Lycidas* (114–22) of Christ's warning to "Beware of false prophets, which come to you in sheep's clothing, but inwardly they are ravening wolves." (Mat. vii, 15.)

WHEN I CONSIDER

Wнεn I consider how my light is spent,
 Ere half my days, in this dark world and wide,
 And that one Talent which is death to hide,
 Lodg'd with me useless, though my Soul more bent
To serve therewith my Maker, and present   5
 My true account, lest he returning chide;
 Doth God exact day-labour, light denied,
 I fondly ask; But patience to prevent
That murmur, soon replies, God doth not need
 Either man's work or his own gifts; who best   10
 Bear his mild yoke, they serve him best; his State
Is Kingly. Thousands at his bidding speed
 And post o'er Land and Ocean without rest:
 They also serve who only stand and wait.

             (1652?)

1–2. Total blindness overtook Milton soon after the publication of the *Defence of the English People* in March, 1651, and Mr. Tillyard is surely right in suggesting that this allusion to his life as half spent corresponds better with his age then, forty-two, than it does with the age of forty-six which is implied by the position of this sonnet after that *On the Late Massacre in Piemont* in the Cambridge manuscript. Milton's light *is spent*. It has just failed and he is in poignant doubt over his future as thinker and artist.

3. Again, as he did in his sonnet on arriving at the age of twenty-three, Milton thought of the parable of the servants to whom various numbers of talents were intrusted, but here he identifies himself with the man who received only one talent and by neglecting it deserved the reproof of a "wicked and slothful servant." (Mat. xxv, 26. Compare *How soon hath Time . . . . ,* line 3, note.)

12–13. The *Thousands* are the "huge, mighty and royal armies" of the angels of God, which Hooker described as "rapt with the love of his beauty" and "unweariable and even unsatiable in their longing to do by all means all manner good unto all the creatures of God, but especially unto the children of men." (*Of the Laws of Ecclesiastical Polity,* I, iv, 1.) Compare Milton's picture of the angels,

  "Who in God's presence, nearest to his Throne
  Stand ready at command, and are his Eyes
  That run through all the Heav'ns, or down to th'Earth
  Bear his swift errands over moist and dry,
  O'er Sea and Land."

      (*P.L.* III, 649–53.)

14. Perhaps Milton remembered Beatrice's explanation to Dante in

TO SIR HENRY VANE THE YOUNGER

VANE, young in years, but in sage counsel old,
    Than whom a better Senator ne'er held
    The helm of Rome, when gowns not arms repell'd
    The fierce Epirot and the African bold,
Whether to settle peace, or to unfold   5
    The drift of hollow states, hard to be spell'd,
    Then to advise how war may best, upheld,
    Move by her two main nerves, Iron and Gold,

---

the ninth circle of heaven (*Paradise,* XXVIII, 110) that the highest orders of angels enjoy a knowledge of God which excels even the joy of expressing the love of God in action. In any case, he was content to believe that, "It is good that a man should . . . quietly wait for the salvation of the Lord." (Lam. iii, 26.)

1. Sir Henry Vane was born in 1612. In 1636–7 he was Governor of the Massachusetts Bay Colony, but lost the post by defending the right of the religious enthusiast, Mrs. Anne Hutchinson, to immunity from interference by the civil authorities. In 1640 he entered Parliament and in 1643 took a leading part in negotiating the Covenant with Scotland. On June 4, 1652, when hostilities between Van Tromp's fleet and Blake's had already begun, the Council of State appointed him the first member of a committee to deal with the Dutch ambassadors, who were suspected of protracting negotiations merely in order to stay in London as spies. They received their passports four days before Milton sent this sonnet to Vane.

2–4. Repeatedly in his accounts of the invasion of Italy by Pyrrhus, King of Epirus, early in the third century B.C., and by Hannibal towards its end, Livy lays stress upon the courage of the Senate in such crises as that which followed the Carthaginian victory at Cannae. (*History of Rome,* XXII, lx.)

6. The *hollow states*—Holland. There is a punning suggestion that they are as hollow, or false, in character as their territory is hollow, or low-lying.

8. *nerves*—sinews. Compare the word in *S.A.* 1646.

In all her equipage; besides to know
  Both spiritual power and civil, what each means,   10
  What severs each, thou hast learnt, which few have done.
The bounds of either sword to thee wee owe.
  Therefore on thy firm hand religion leans
  In peace, and reck'ns thee her eldest son.

(July, 1652)

10–12. Smart offers evidence that Vane was one of the leaders in the Westminster Assembly of Divines whom Milton described in *A Treatise of Civil Power in Ecclesiastical Causes* as championing the doctrine that "then both commonwealth and religion will at length, if ever, flourish in Christendom, when either they who govern discern between civil and religious, or they only who so discern shall be admitted to govern." (*P.W.* II, p. 521.)

12. *either sword; i.e.,* the spiritual and temporal swords, the former of which the *N.E.D.* quotes Bishop Latimer as describing as the weapon of the preacher to "teach, improue, amende and instruct in rightwesnes."

PSAL. I

Done into Verse, 1653.

Bless'd is the man who hath not walk'd astray
In counsel of the wicked, and i'th'way
Of sinners hath not stood, and in the seat
Of scorners hath not sat.   But in the great
Jehovah's Law is ever his delight,   5
And in his Law he studies day and night.
He shall be as a tree which planted grows
By wat'ry streams, and in his season knows
To yield his fruit, and his leaf shall not fall,
And what he takes in hand shall prosper all.   10
Not so the wicked, but as chaff which fann'd
The wind drives, so the wicked shall not stand
In judgement, or abide their trial then,
Nor sinners in th'assembly of just men.
For the Lord knows th'upright way of the just,   15
And the way of bad men to ruin must.

PSAL. II

Done Aug. 8. 1653.   *Terzetti.*

Why do the Gentiles tumult, and the Nations
    Muse a vain thing, the Kings of th'earth upstand
    With power, and Princes in their Congregations
Lay deep their plots together through each Land,
    Against the Lord and his Messiah dear?   5
    Let us break off, say they, by strength of hand
Their bonds, and cast from us, no more to wear,
    Their twisted cords: he who in Heaven doth dwell
    Shall laugh, the Lord shall scoff them, then severe
Speak to them in his wrath, and in his fell   10
    And fierce ire trouble them; but I, saith hee,
    Anointed have my King (though ye rebel)
On Sion my holy hill.   A firm decree
    I will declare; the Lord to me hath said,
    Thou art my Son, I have begotten thee   15

This day; ask for me, and the grant is made;
　As thy possession I on thee bestow
　Th'Heathen, and as thy conquest to be sway'd
Earth's utmost bounds: them shalt thou bring full low
　With Iron Sceptre bruis'd, and them disperse   20
　Like to a potter's vessel shiver'd so.
And now be wise at length ye Kings averse,
　Be taught ye Judges of the earth; with fear
　Jehovah serve, and let your joy converse
With trembling; kiss the Son lest he appear   25
　In anger and ye perish in the way,
　If once his wrath take fire like fuel sere.
Happy all those who have in him their stay.

PSAL. III

Aug. 9. 1653.

When he fled from Absalom.

Lord, how many are my foes!
　　How many those
　　That in arms against me rise!
　　Many are they
That of my life distrustfully thus say,   5
No help for him in God there lies.
But thou, Lord, are my shield, my glory,
　　Thee through my story
　　Th' exalter of my head I count,
　　Aloud I cried   10
Unto Jehovah, he full soon replied
And heard me from his holy mount.
I lay and slept, I wak'd again,
　　For my sustain
　　Was the Lord.　Of many millions   15
　　The populous rout
I fear not though incamping round about
They pitch against me their Pavilions.
Rise Lord, save me my God, for thou
　　Hast smote ere now   20

On the cheek-bone all my foes,
        Of men abhorr'd
Hast broke the teeth.   This help was from the Lord;
Thy blessing on thy people flows.

PSAL. IV

Aug. 10. 1653.

ANSWER me when I call,
God of my righteousness;
In straits and in distress
Thou didst me disinthrall
And set at large; now spare,   5
    Now pity me, and hear my earnest pray'r.
Great ones how long will ye
My glory have in scorn?
How long be thus forborne
Still to love vanity,   10
To love, to seek, to prize
    Things false and vain and nothing else but lies?
Yet know the Lord hath chose,
Chose to himself apart,
The good and meek of heart   15
(For whom to choose he knows);
Jehovah from on high
    Will hear my voice what time to him I cry.
Be aw'd, and do not sin,
Speak to your hearts alone,   20
Upon your beds, each one,
And be at peace within.
Offer the offerings just
    Of righteousness and in Jehovah trust.
Many there be that say   25
Who yet will show us good?
Talking like this world's brood;
But Lord, thus let me pray,
On us lift up the light,
    Lift up the favour of thy count'nance bright.   30
Into my heart more joy
And gladness thou hast put

Than when a year of glut
Their stores doth over-cloy,
And from their plenteous grounds   35
   With vast increase their corn and wine abounds.
In peace at once will I
Both lay me down and sleep,
For thou alone dost keep
Me safe where'er I lie: 40
As in a rocky Cell
   Thou Lord alone in safety mak'st me dwell.

PSAL. V

Aug. 12. 1653.

JEHOVAH, to my words give ear,
    My meditation weigh,
  The voice of my complaining hear,
My King and God, for unto thee I pray.
  Jehovah thou my early voice   5
    Shalt in the morning hear,
  I'th'morning I to thee with choice
Will rank my Prayers, and watch till thou appear.
  For thou art not a God that takes
    In wickedness delight,   10
  Evil with thee no biding makes;
Fools or mad men stand not within thy sight.
  All workers of iniquity
    Thou hat'st; and them unblest
  Thou wilt destroy that speak a lie;   15
The bloody and guileful man God doth detest.
  But I will in thy mercies dear,
    Thy numerous mercies go
  Into thy house; I in thy fear
Will towards thy holy temple worship low.   20
  Lord lead me in thy righteousness,
    Lead me because of those
  That do observe if I transgress,
Set thy ways right before, where my step goes.

For in his falt'ring mouth unstable   25
    No word is firm or sooth;
  Their inside, troubles miserable;
An open grave their throat, their tongue they smooth.
  God, find them guilty, let them fall
      By their own counsels quell'd;   30
  Push them in their rebellions all
Still on; for against thee they have rebell'd;
    Then all who trust in thee shall bring
        Their joy, while thou from blame
    Defend'st them, they shall ever sing   35
And shall triumph in thee, who love thy name.
    For thou Jehovah wilt be found
        To bless the just man still,
    As with a shield thou wilt surround
Him with thy lasting favour and good will.   40

PSAL. VI

Aug. 13. 1653.

LORD in thine anger do not reprehend me,
    Nor in thy hot displeasure me correct;
  Pity me, Lord, for I am much deject,
    Am very weak and faint; heal and amend me,
For all my bones, that even with anguish ache,   5
    Are troubled, yea my soul is troubled sore;
And thou, O Lord, how long? turn Lord, restore
    My soul, O save me for thy goodness' sake!
For in death no remembrance is of thee;
    Who in the grave can celebrate thy praise?   10
Wearied I am with sighing out my days,
    Nightly my Couch I make a kind of Sea;
My Bed I water with my tears; mine Eye
    Through grief consumes, is waxen old and dark
I'th' mid'st of all mine enemies that mark.   15
    Depart all ye that work iniquity.
Depart from me, for the voice of my weeping
    The Lord hath heard, the Lord hath heard my pray'r
My supplication with acceptance fair
    The Lord will own, and have me in his keeping.   20

Mine enemies shall all be blank and dash't
  With much confusion; then grow red with shame;
They shall return in haste the way they came,
  And in a moment shall be quite abash't.

PSAL. VII

Aug. 14. 1653.

Upon the words of Chush *the* Benjamite *against him.*

      Lord my God to thee I fly,
      Save me and secure me under
      Thy protection while I cry,
      Lest as a Lion (and no wonder)
      He haste to tear my Soul asunder,   5
      Tearing and no rescue nigh.

      Lord my God, if I have thought
      Or done this, if wickedness
      Be in my hands, if I have wrought
      Ill to him that meant me peace,   10
      Or to him have render'd less,
      And not freed my foe for naught;

      Let th'enemy pursue my soul
      And overtake it, let him tread
      My life down to the earth and roll   15
      In the dust my glory dead,
      In the dust and there outspread
      Lodge it with dishonour foul.

      Rise Jehovah in thine ire
      Rouse thyself amidst the rage   20
      Of my foes that urge like fire;
      And wake for me, their fury assuage;
      Judgement here thou didst engage
      And command which I desire.

So th' assemblies of each Nation   25
Will surround thee, seeking right,
Thence to thy glorious habitation
Return on high and in their sight.
Jehovah judgeth most upright
All people from the world's foundation.   30

Judge me Lord, be judge in this
According to my righteousness
And the innocence which is
Upon me: cause at length to cease
Of evil men the wickedness,   35
And their power that do amiss.

But the just establish fast,
Since thou art the just God that tries
Hearts and reins. On God is cast
My defence, and in him lies,   40
In him who both just and wise
Saves th' upright of Heart at last.

God is a just Judge and severe,
And God is every day offended;
If th' unjust will not forbear,   45
His Sword he whets, his Bow hath bended
Already, and for him intended
The tools of death, that waits him near.

(His arrows purposely made he
For them that persecute.)   Behold   50
He travels big with vanity,
Trouble he hath conceiv'd of old
As in a womb, and from that mould
Hath at length brought forth a Lie.

He digg'd a pit, and delv'd it deep,   55
And fell into the pit he made;
His mischief that due course doth keep,
Turns on his head, and his ill trade
Of violence will undelay'd
Fall on his crown with ruin steep.   60

Then will I Jehovah's praise
According to his justice raise
And sing the Name and Deity
Of Jehovah the most high.

PSAL. VIII

Aug. 14. 1653.

O JEHOVAH, our Lord, how wondrous great
   And glorious is thy name through all the earth!
So as above the Heavens thy praise to set
   Out of the tender mouths of latest birth,

Out of the mouths of babes and sucklings thou   5
   Hast founded strength because of all thy foes,
To stint th'enemy, and slack th'avenger's brow
   That bends his rage thy providence to oppose.

When I behold thy Heavens, thy Fingers' art,
   The Moon and Stars which thou so bright hast set   10
In the pure firmament, then saith my heart,
   O what is man that thou rememb'rest yet,

And think'st upon him? or of man begot
   That him thou visit'st and of him art found?
Scarce be less than Gods, thou mad'st his lot,   15
   With honour and with state thou hast him crown'd.

O'er the works of thy hand thou mad'st him Lord,
   Thou hast put all under his lordly feet,
All Flocks, and Herds, by thy commanding word,
   All beasts that in the field or forest meet.   20

Fowl of the Heavens, and Fish that through the wet
   Sea-paths in shoals do slide, and know no dearth
O Jehovah, our Lord, how wondrous great
   And glorious is thy name through all the earth!

LATIN VERSES FROM *DEFENSIO SECUNDA PRO POPULO ANGLICANO*

IN SALMASIUM

GAUDETE, scombri, et quicquid est piscium salo,
Qui frigida hieme incolitis algentes freta!
Vestrum misertus ille Salmasius Eques
Bonus amicire nuditatem cogitat;
Chartaeque largus apparat papyrinos   5
Vobis cucullos, praeferentes Claudii
Insignia, nomenque et decus, Salmasii;
Gestetis ut per omne cetarium forum
Equitis clientes, scriniis mungentium
Cubito virorum, et capsulis, gratissimos.   10

DE MORO

Galli ex concubitu gravidam te, Pontia, Mori,
  Quis bene moratam morigeramque neget?

(1654)

ON SALMASIUS

REJOICE, ye mackerel and all salt-water fishes which live freezing in the seas in the cold winter![1] The good knight, Salmasius,[3] sympathizing witn you, is meditating how he may clothe your nudity. Prodigal of his stationery, he is preparing paper cowls for you, marked with the insignia, name and dignity of Claudius Salmasius, so that you may promenade through the whole fish-market like a knight's clients—most welcome to the boxes and kegs of the gentlemen who wipe their noses on their elbows.[9]

(ABOUT MORE)

O Pontia, pregnant with More's Gallic lust, who denies that you have played the *mori*gerate fool more than enough?

1–4. The condemnation of bad verses to wrap fish was proverbial. So Martial (III, ii, 1–5) deprecates the untimely end of his book as a garb for sardines, and Persius (I, 45) speaks of verses "which have no dread of mackerel." In an *Apology for Smectymnuus* Milton jeered at the Remonstrant, Bishop Hall, "whose best folios are predestined to no better end than to make winding sheets in Lent for pilchers." (*P.W.* III, p. 144.)

3. *Salmasius Eques*—the salmon knight. Milton punned on the resemblance of Salmasius' name to the Latin *salmo,* a salmon. Salmasius had the doubtful honour of the Order of St. Michael, with which Louis XIII had invested him.

9–10. *mungentium Cubito*—wiping their noses on their elbows. Warton compared Suetonius's reference to Horace's father in the *Vita Horatii:*

"Quoties ego vidi patrem tuum cubito emungentem."

The phrase, Warton explained, "was a cant appellation among the Romans for fishmongers. It was said to Horace, of his father, by way of laughing at his low birth."

ON THE LATE MASSACRE IN PIEMONT

AVENGE, O Lord, thy slaughter'd Saints, whose bones
   Lie scatter'd on the Alpine mountains cold,
   Ev'n them who kept thy truth so pure of old
   When all our Fathers worship't Stocks and Stones,
Forget not: in thy book record their groans   5
   Who were thy Sheep and in their ancient Fold
   Slain by the bloody *Piemontese* that roll'd
   Mother with Infant down the Rocks. Their moans
The Vales redoubl'd to the Hills, and they
   To Heav'n. Their martyr'd blood and ashes sow   10

---

1. The "Piedmontese Easter," as the massacre on April 24, 1655, was called, was carried out with extraordinary cruelty by the soldiers of the Marquis of Pianezza, who had been billeted among the unsuspecting mountaineers. Cromwell immediately voiced English resentment, not only by dispatching a formal protest, which Milton wrote in May, to the Duke of Savoy, but also by successful appeals to Cardinal Mazarin and to many Protestant statesmen throughout Europe to protect the Waldensians. In England a national fast was declared and a subscription of about £80,000 was secured for the refugees.

3–4. The Waldensian heresy arose early in the twelfth century. Its first martyr was Peter of Bruys, who was burned at Saint-Gilles in 1140, which was probably the birth-year of the leader who gave the movement his name, Peter Valdo. At first his followers had no more thought than did those of St. Francis of leaving the Catholic Church, but in 1215 they were formally excommunicated. Their doctrines spread into France and Germany, Hungary and Poland and at the Reformation they joined forces with the Protestant Churches. Exactly a century before the "Piedmontese Easter" they secured local rights of worship in Savoy.

7–8. Sir Samuel Morland, who took Cromwell's protest to the Duke of Savoy, brought back ample, documented evidence of Milton's charges.

O'er all th'*Italian* fields where still doth sway
The triple Tyrant: that from these may grow
A hunderd-fold, who having learnt thy way
Early may fly the *Babylonian* woe.

(1655)

---

12. *The triple Tyrant*—the Pope, "that Priest-king" of whom Phineas Fletcher explained;

"Three mitred crownes the proud Impostor weares,
For he in Earth, in Hell, in Heav'n will raigne."

(*Apollyonists.* Phineas Fletcher's *Poems,* ed. by Grosart, Vol. II, p. 117.)

14. The *Babylonian woe* is a reminiscence of Petrarch's reference to the Papal Court as a modern Babylon and a "fountain of woe" in the first quatrain of Sonnet CXXXVIII (or CVIII in Milton's reference), from which Milton translated the sestet at the close of the First Book of his tract *Of Reformation in England.* (*P.W.* II, 383.) See p. 388 above.

LAWRENCE *OF VIRTUOUS FATHER*

LAWRENCE of virtuous Father virtuous Son,
   Now that the Fields are dank, and ways are mire,
   Where shall we sometimes meet, and by the fire
   Help waste a sullen day; what may be won
From the hard Season gaining: time will run   5
   On smoother, till *Favonius* re-inspire
   The frozen earth; and clothe in fresh attire
   The Lily and Rose, that neither sow'd nor spun.
What neat repast shall feast us, light and choice,

---

1. The *virtuous Father* was Henry Lawrence of St. Ives, in the county of Huntingdon, who became Lord President of the Council under Cromwell. His earlier years were spent among the German and Dutch Protestants and he published several theological works, of which the best known was *Our Communion and War with Angels,* 1646.

The *Son* has been shown by Smart to have been Edward Lawrence, Henry's oldest son. He was born in 1633 and in November, 1656, he became a member of Parliament, but died a year later. A poem addressed to him by Davenant and a reference to him in Milton's letter of August first, 1657, to Henry Oldenburg, who was later the first Secretary of the Royal Society, suggest that he possessed the most solid virtues.

6. The Latin name of the west wind, *Favonius,* suggests the opening line of Horace's famous *Ode* (I, iv) on the coming of spring, with its Epicurean invitation to gather rosebuds.

8. Compare the counsel of Jesus; "Consider the lilies of the field, how they grow; they toil not, neither do they spin." (Mat. vi, 28.)

Of Attic taste, with Wine, whence we may rise   10
To hear the Lute well toucht, or artful voice
Warble immortal Notes and *Tuscan* Air?
He who of those delights can judge, and spare
To interpose them oft, is not unwise.

(1655)

---

10. Attic or Athenian banquets seem always to have been *light and choice*. Even the taste of Epicurus, in his *Symposium,* was abstemious. Milton's sonnet is an example of the grave Epicureanism which Owen Feltham expressed in his *Resolve On the Use of Pleasure,* when he said, "Pleasure that . . . brings detriment . . . was laughed at by Epicurus himself; but a lawful *pleasure,* lawfully used, doubtless, is an Emanation of the *goodness* of the *Deity* to *Man."*

12. *Tuscan* is equivalent to "Italian," for Tuscany and its capital, Florence, were the centre of Italian culture.

13. *spare*—forbear.

14. In *unwise* there seems to be an allusion to the "wise man" of whom the ancient Epicureans as well as the Stoics spoke, meaning one who realized the ethical ideal of his philosophic creed.

CYRIACK, *WHOSE GRANDSIRE*

CYRIACK, whose Grandsire on the Royal Bench
   Of British *Themis,* with no mean applause
   Pronounc't and in his volumes taught our Laws,
   Which others at their Bar so often wrench:
Today deep thoughts resolve with me to drench   5
   In mirth, that after no repenting draws;
   Let *Euclid* rest and *Archimedes* pause,
   And what the *Swede* intend, and what the *French.*
To measure life learn thou betimes, and know
   Toward solid good what leads the nearest way;   10
   For other things mild Heav'n a time ordains,
And disapproves that care, though wise in show,
   That with superfluous burden loads the day,
   And when God sends a cheerful hour, refrains.

(1655)

---

1. Cyriack Skinner was the posthumous son of William Skinner of Thornton Curtis in Lincolnshire and the grandson of Sir Edward Coke, Chief Justice of the King's Bench from 1613 to 1616 and famous as the prosecutor of Essex, Southampton and Raleigh as well as for his support of the Petition of Right in the Parliament of 1628. Cyriack was born in 1627 and became one of Milton's pupils in the house in Aldersgate Street. Their friendship was life-long. "In a letter written in 1654," says Smart, Andrew Marvell "congratulated Milton on the fact that Mr. Skinner has taken a dwelling near his, and may now be more frequently in his society."

2. *Themis*—the Greek goddess of Justice.

3. Coke's *Institutes of the Law of England* ("Coke upon Littleton") and his *Reports* were great legal classics.

7. We know that Skinner was a lawyer and a liberal political thinker, while the references to the Greek mathematicians, *Euclid* and *Archimedes,* imply other interests.

8. Between 1654 and 1660 Charles X of Sweden was conducting his dashing campaigns first against the Poles and later against the Danes. At the same time French policy was being astutely guided by Cardinal Mazarin.
The line is an echo of Horace's invitation to Quintius Hirpinus to forget what "the warlike Cantabrian and the Scyth" may be meditating and to remember that "youth flees fast away." (*Odes,* II, xi, 1–6.) Compare the Horatian echo in *Lawrence of virtuous Father,* 6. The two sonnets are pitched in the same key and may have been invitations to the same entertainment.

CYRIACK, *THIS THREE YEARS' DAY*

CYRIACK, this three years' day these eyes, though clear
  To outward view, of blemish or of spot,
  Bereft of light thir seeing have forgot;
  Nor to thir idle orbs doth sight appear
Of Sun or Moon or Star throughout the year,   5
  Or man or woman.   Yet I argue not
  Against heav'n's hand or will, nor bate a jot
  Of heart or hope; but still bear up and steer
Right onward.   What supports me, dost thou ask?
  The conscience, Friend, to have lost them overplied   10
  In liberty's defence, my noble task,
Of which all Europe talks from side to side.
  This thought might lead me through the world's vain masque
  Content though blind, had I no better guide.

(1655)

---

1. *this three years' day*—throughout the past three years.
Since Milton finally lost his sight shortly after the publication of the
Defence of the English People in March, 1651, this sonnet can hardly
be dated later than 1654-5.

2. In the *Second Defence,* in the spring of 1654, Milton said, in replying to charges which had been brought against his character and
appearance on the score of his blindness: "At this moment I have the
same courage, the same strength, though not the same eyes; yet so little
do they betray any external appearance of injury, that they are as un-
clouded and bright as the eyes of those who most distinctly see."
(*P.W.* I, p. 235.)

7-8. Compare the allusion in the *Second Defence* to "those wise and
ancient bards," Tiresias and Phineus, to whom he referred in *P.L.* III,
36, thinking in both cases that their misfortunes were "compensated
by superior endowments."

"God himself is truth;" he continued, "in propagating which, as
men display a greater integrity and zeal, they approach nearer to the
similitude of God, and possess a greater portion of his love." (*P.W.* I,
p. 236.)

10. *conscience*—consciousness. Compare "the conscience of her
worth" in *P.L.* VIII, 502.

12-14. "Surrounded by congregated multitudes," Milton wrote in the
Second Defence (*P.W.* I, p. 220), "I now imagine that, from the col-
umns of Hercules to the Indian Ocean, I behold the nations of the earth
recovering that liberty which they so long had lost."

METHOUGHT I SAW

METHOUGHT I saw my late espoused Saint
   Brought to me like *Alcestis* from the grave,
   Whom *Jove's* great Son to her glad Husband gave,
   Rescu'd from death by force though pale and faint.
Mine as whom washt from spot of child-bed taint,   5
   Purification in the old Law did save,
   And such, as yet once more I trust to have
   Full sight of her in Heaven without restraint,
Came vested all in white, pure as her mind:
   Her face was veil'd, yet to my fancied sight,   10
   Love, sweetness, goodness, in her person shin'd
So clear, as in no face with more delight.
   But O, as to embrace me she inclin'd,
   I wak'd, she fled, and day brought back my night.

                                 (1658)

---

1. *Saint* is used in its primitive English sense of "a soul in heaven."
Milton thought of his wife as he did of the Marchioness of Winchester,
whom he called in her *Epitaph* (l. 71) a "new welcome Saint" in
heaven. She appears "vested all in white" because he could imagine
her only as one of the throng "which are arrayed in white robes," as
St. John describes the redeemed in heaven, "which came out of great
tribulation, and have washed their robes, and made them white in the
blood of the Lamb." (Rev. vii, 13–4.) He can hardly have seen the
living Katherine Woodcock, whom, as Phillips says, understating the
time, he married "about two or three years after his being wholly de-
prived of sight." She was twenty-eight when they were married and
her child, which was born in October, 1657, survived her by only a
few weeks. She died when she was not quite thirty years old, in
February, 1658.

2–4. Milton thought of the moving scene in Euripides' *Alcestis,* when
Hercules, "the child of Zeus" (l. 1121), wrests the wife who has offered
to die for her husband, Admetus, from the arms of Death himself.
Looking at her veiled figure without recognizing her, Admetus says, "I
seem to see my wife. She stirs my heart and fountains burst from
my eyes." (Ll. 1062–3.)

5–6. Hebrew law regarded a woman as "unclean" after the birth of
a child and provided a ritual of sacrifice before the priest could make
"atonement" for her. (Lev. xii.)

TRANSLATIONS FROM *THE HISTORY OF BRITAIN,*
BOOK I

(Geoffrey of Monmouth says that Brutus the Trojan asked the advice of Diana at her shrine on the forsaken, Mediterranean island
of Leogecia.   The Greek verses of his address to the goddess were
turned by Gildas into the Latin elegiacs which Milton translated.)

> Goddess of Shades, and Huntress, who at will
> Walk'st on the rolling Sphere, and through the deep,
> On thy third Reign, the Earth, look now, and tell
> What Land, what Seat of rest thou bidst me seek,
> What certain Seat, where I may worship thee
> For aye, with Temples vow'd, and Virgin quires.

"To whom sleeping before the Altar," says Milton, *"Diana* in a
Vision that night thus answer'd;"

> Brutus, far to the West, in th' Ocean wide
> Beyond the realm of Gaul, a Land there lies,
> Sea-girt it lies, where Giants dwelt of old,
> Now void, it fits thy People; thither bend
> Thy course, there shalt thou find a lasting seat,
> There to thy Sons another Troy shall rise,
> And Kings be born of thee, whose dreaded might
> Shall awe the World, and Conquer Nations bold.
>   (1645–70)

APOLOGUS DE RUSTICO ET HERO[1]

RUSTICUS ex Malo sapidissima poma quotannis
    Legit, et urbano lecta dedit Domino.
Hic, incredibili fructus dulcedine Captus,
    Malum ipsam in proprias transtulit areolas.
Hactenus illa ferax, sed longo debilis aevo,   5
    Mota solo assueto, protinus aret iners.
Quod tandem ut patuit Domino, spe lusus inani,
    Damnavit celeres in sua damna manus;
Atque ait, 'Heu quanto satius fuit illa Coloni,
    Parva licet, grato dona tulisse animo!   10
Possem Ego avaritiam frenare, gulamque voracem:
    Nunc periere mihi et foetus et ipsa parens.'

---

[1]Beyond the fact that this poem was added to the *Book of Elegies* in
1673, there is no evidence of its date and nothing to indicate whether
it was a schoolboy exercise in translation from William Bullokar's
"fable taken out of Mantuane" (in his *Aesop's Fables in True Orthog-
raphy,* London, 1585), which Mr. MacKellar notes that it resembles, or
whether—as Masson suggested—it was written after 1645 and had "a
touch of political significance."

A FABLE OF A PEASANT AND HIS LANDLORD[1]

A PEASANT gathered most savoury fruit year after year from his apple-tree and gave the choice specimens to his city-dwelling landlord. The latter, pleased with the unbelievable sweetness of the fruit, transferred the tree itself to his own gardens. The tree, though it had long been fruitful, was enfeebled by old age and, when it was moved out of its accustomed soil, it forthwith withered past all bearing. When it was clear at last to the master that he had been tricked by a vain hope, he cursed the hands that were so swift to their own undoing:

"Alas!" he cried, "how much more satisfactory it was to receive my tenant's offerings with a grateful heart, small though they were! If only I might bridle my cupidity and my voracious gullet! Now both the fruit and the parent tree are lost to me."

PARABLE OF A PEASANT AND HIS LANDLORD

PARADISE REGAINED

AND

SAMSON AGONISTES

INTRODUCTION

I. *PARADISE REGAINED*

1. To enjoy *Paradise Regained* as poetry—as a part of Milton's testament of beauty—we need not go to it convinced, like M. Saurat, that he embodied a perfectly coherent philosophy in both his epics of Paradise, nor persuaded, like Herr Mutschmann, that philosophically he was as blind as he was physically. What we do need, when we are confronted by his theme of "one man's firm obedience fully tried Through all temptation," is to be able to feel somewhat as he did about Christ. The poem is an epic of Christ's self-realization. It is a very much more interesting effort to handle that mystery than is Milton's chapter on *The Son* in his treatise *On Christian Doctrine*. Traditional theology had solved the mystery by the doctrine of the Incarnation, which traditional art had popularized in countless paintings of the Annunciation to the Virgin. Milton inherited a new theology, tinged with Platonism and enthusiastically critical of the Bible, yet loyal to its letter. He could draw upon the Neo-Platonism and Kabbalistic scholarship of the Renaissance as well as upon the currents of speculation which flowed from bold, antitrinitarian reformers like the Italians, Faustus and Laelius Socinus, and the Spaniard, Servetus, whom Calvin sent to the stake for heresy. Although he was too independent to be individually indebted to any of these men, he was deeply interested in liberal religious thought and even in the "libertinism" of the famous French jurist, Jean Bodin. Yet, like many of his contemporaries who regarded Jesus in quite unorthodox ways, he believed passionately in the *"Almighty* spirit of Christ," the "very same Spirit, that once *moved* upon *the waters* of the universe at the first Creation, and spreading mighty wings over

them, did hatch the new-born World into this perfection."
The quoted words come from a sermon by the Cambridge
Platonist, Ralph Cudworth, preaching before Parliament at
St. Margaret's, Westminster, on the thirty-first of March, 1647.
He continued, in a sentence very like the opening lines of
Paradise Regained, to explain that, "The *first Adam* . . .
brought in a reall defilement, which like a noisome Leprosie,
hath overspread all mankind: and therefore *the second Adam*
must . . . convey such an *immortall seed* of Grace into the
hearts of true Believers, as may prevaile still more and more in
them, till it have at last, quite wrought out that *poison* of the
Serpent."

2. Most of the humanistic reformers of the Church had regarded Adam as a kind of Platonic ideal, a man actually perfect
until his ruin by the Serpent, the principle of evil or Satan.
Christ's life seemed to them most significant as the reconquest
of that lost perfection. It was not hopelessly lost, for they
thought of it as still potential "in every child, who comes now,
as Adam did, made in the image of God, and with creative
freedom of the will to settle his own destiny."[1] Stoic control of the passions, or obedience to the will of God, or, at
all events, some stern variety of Puritanism is what we today
see in that vanished faith in the creative freedom of the will.
Milton saw more than that. When in the tractate *Of Education* he wrote that the "end . . . of learning is to repair the
ruins of our first parents by regaining to know God aright"
he was sincere in his romantic hope that English schoolboys
might be made to blossom into "the highest perfection." He
was thinking of a life surpassing the idyl of Adam and Eve
in "the happy Garden." Perhaps since Adam very few men,
except Jesus, had had even a glimpse of that life; but the way
to it had been pointed by some ideal figures, the heroes of the
world's great epics, the *Odyssey* and the *Aeneid.* Like most
Renaissance critics, Milton read those poems as biographies of
men in search of perfection. Their meaning crystallized for
him in the word man, which occurs in the first lines of both;

---

[1] Rufus Jones, *Spiritual Reformers,* p. xxxi.

and he crystallized *Paradise Lost* and *Paradise Regained* in the disobedient and obedient men of their respective openings. The essence of an epic poem was an inner conflict of the hero. That is why for the subject of *Paradise Regained* he chose Christ's temptation rather than any of the more familiar dramas of the Gospels—the Nativity, the arrest in the Garden of Gethsemane, the Crucifixion, or the Resurrection—subjects which he had jotted down as possibilities in 1641.

3. Milton was by no means alone in his view of epic poetry. The same idea had inspired Tasso's *Jerusalem Delivered* and in England it had produced *The Faerie Queene*. Indeed, Spenser's hero, Guyon, is most interestingly related to Milton's Christ. The resemblance is close enough to make it worth while for any reader of *Paradise Regained* to compare it with the second book of *The Faerie Queene* or at least with the story of Guyon's temptation in the Cave of Mammon. In Spenser's Legend of Temperance the hero tries to realize an ideal of perfection which is at heart Christian, although, like Milton's conception of Christ, it has striking classical features. Aristotle's principle of continence coloured it, and so did the doctrine of the mastery of anger and sensuality which is found in Plato's *Symposium* and *Phaedrus*. At the climax of Guyon's story in Canto VII his threefold ordeal curiously corresponds with Christ's triple temptation by Satan. Though Mammon first tries to seduce Guyon with the lure of vulgar riches while Satan's first appeal to Christ is much subtler, the two adversaries proceed alike in the second temptations. Both offer the bait of worldly power and glory in varied forms. Superficially the third temptations differ, but they concur in being mysteriously symbolical. Mammon's final bid is the tree that bore the golden apple which plunged Athene, Aphrodite, and Hera into a quarrel, and so, indirectly, brought on the Trojan War.

> On earth like neuer grew, ne liuing wight
> Like euer saw, but they from hence were sold;
> For those, which *Hercules* with conquest bold
> Got from great *Atlas* daughters, hence began.[1]

[1] *Faerie Queene,* II, vii, 54, 3–6.

What the last temptation in Spenser's allegory meant every reader must decide for himself. Whatever it meant, the hero, Hercules, in his conquest of the apples of the Hesperides, seems to have been a symbol of its mastery. Spenser thought of him as mystically identifiable with Christ, for the classic myths were commonly regarded as strange, pagan versions of the true records preserved in the Bible. When Sir Walter Raleigh wrote in *The History of the World* (I, 6, 4) that "the prophecies, that Christ should break the serpent's head, and conquer the power of hell, occasioned the fables of Hercules killing the serpent of Hesperides," he was expressing a general opinion. It was shared by Milton, and that is why, at the climax of *Paradise Regained,* immediately after Christ's victory is complete, he is compared to Hercules vanquishing the giant, Antaeus. Throughout his life Milton instinctively thought of Hercules as symbolically related to Christ. We can trace the idea in *The Passion,* when as a boy following Giles Fletcher's example in *Christ's Victory and Triumph,* he called Christ a

> Most perfect Hero, tried in heaviest plight
> Of labours huge and hard, too hard for human wight.[1]

4. *Paradise Regained* is an attempt to pierce the mystery of Christ's superhumanity by all the imaginative resources at Milton's command. So, with apologies for the irreverence, he compared it to the mythical divinity won by Hercules in the twelve labours. He was charmed by youthful memories of the platonizing art in Italy which represented Hercules in all his labours as an ideal athlete, a figure of titanic strength with a Galahad's purity. The story of the struggle with the giant, Antaeus, had been a favourite subject with the Italian engravers of the sixteenth century, and typical representations of it had been chosen as the emblems of some of the famous Italian academies. Many years before *Paradise Regained* was written, the president of one of them, the *Elevati* in Ferrara, explained their emblem to the members in an oration which was later published in a once popular collection of speeches.

---

[1] Ll. 13–14.

Milton may never have read his words but their purport was a part of his recollection of his great days as a young man in Italy. It was as natural for him as the president of the *Elevati* thought it ought to be for the members, to feel that, "As Hercules, when he fought with the son of earth and perceived whence it was that strength was being imparted to him, lifted him with mighty force aloft and, pressing him against his breast, crushed him with his strong arms until he gave up the ghost; so we constantly fight with our earthly appetites as with an Antaeus, and compress him with the arms of reason, so that he breathes out his venomous life." When he brought the story of Christ's victory to an abrupt close with the line,

> But Satan smitten with amazement fell,[1]

and immediately added the picture of earth's son, Antaeus, thrown by Hercules, Milton used no casual simile. He wished to suggest that the perfection of Christ included the spiritual and physical health of which Hercules was the symbol.

5. Very much more significant than this equation of Christ with a mythical hero is Milton's way of making Christ constantly compare himself with real men in the ancient world. He admires the republican Romans,

> Quintius, Fabricius, Curius, Regulus,[2]

and mentions them with the modest hope that he may

> Accomplish what they did, perhaps and more.[3]

By common consent the greatest figure in the ancient world was Socrates. Comparison of Christ with him was inevitable and, to a greater extent than appears on the surface, that comparison is the basis of the last two books of *Paradise Regained*. He is first mentioned, admiringly, by Christ. It is early in the second temptation and Satan has been describing a career like Caesar's. In lines that are tinged with tragic irony because

---

[1] IV, 562.

[2] II, 446.

[3] II, 452.

they are an outline of his own destiny, Christ prefers to live like Socrates, who

> By what he taught and suffer'd for so doing,
> For truth's sake suffering death unjust, lives now
> Equal in fame to proudest Conquerors.[1]

Much later in the second temptation, when Satan has reluctantly learned that, if any kind of glory is likely to attract Christ, it can only be a thinker's place in history, he proposes that Christ should study the four schools of thought—Academic, Stoic, Epicurean, and Peripatetic—which stemmed from Socrates,

> Whom well inspir'd the Oracle pronounc'd
> Wisest of men.[2]

Christ's answer is, to modern ears, shockingly contemptuous of the four schools, but there is no contempt in his remark that Socrates, the wisest of ancient thinkers, knew nothing except that he knew nothing. The words cap Satan's reference to the story in Plato's *Apology* that the Delphian oracle gave that reason for recognizing Socrates as the wisest man in Greece. Milton remembered the *Apology* and other Platonic dialogues where, as St. Augustine said, Socrates appears to have been inspired by that "incomprehensible light, which contains the causes of all creation." Christ has just claimed inspiration from the "Fountain of Light." Milton seems to have felt, as St. Augustine did, that it was because Socrates shared that inspiration that "in his moral disputations he did with most elegant and acute urbanity tax and detect the ignorance of those overweening fellows that build castles on their own knowledge, either in this, confessing his own ignorance, or dissembling his understanding, whereupon envy taking hold, he was wrecked by a caluminous accusation, and so put to death."[3]

---

[1] III, 97–99.
[2] IV, 275–276.
[3] *The City of God*, VII, iii. Healey's translation.

6. In his "moral disputations" with Satan Christ is all but a professed disciple of Socrates and perhaps most clearly so in his long speech at the end of Book II. The thought there, it is true, is based upon the maxim in Proverbs (xvi, 32.), "he that ruleth his spirit [is greater] than he that taketh a city." The same principle was familiar in Horace's Odes (II, ii, 9–12.) and in the *Meditations* (VIII, lxi.) of Marcus Aurelius. Even the ancient Epicureans agreed with the Stoic, Epictetus, that no man is free who cannot rule himself. Milton knew that his thought was a commonplace too general for any thinker or for any civilization to claim it. Yet his development of it in lines 466–480 is clearly Platonic, and to him that meant Socratic. The passage is one of several, to be found mainly in *Paradise Lost,* where he wrote out of a passionate sympathy with Plato's identification of the problems of politics with those of private character. It compares with Michael's discussion of "rational liberty" with Adam in the twelfth book of *Paradise Lost.* There all Socrates's great principles—the ideas that goodness springs from right thinking, that the angry and lustful passions of the soul must be dominated by Reason, and that tyranny in the government of a state results directly from private lawlessness—are put into the angel's mouth. Michael is as good a Platonist as Christ when he tells Adam that since his disobedience,

> true Liberty
> Is lost, which always with right Reason dwells
> Twinn'd, and from her hath no dividual being:
> Reason in man obscur'd, or not obey'd,
> Immediately inordinate desires
> And upstart Passions catch the Government
> From Reason, and to servitude reduce
> Man till then free.[1]

7. Plato's thought is built into the ethics of Milton's poems as substantially as some parts of the Bible are built into their plots. In the famous passage of the fourth book of *Para-*

---

[1]*P.L.,* XII, 83–90.

dise Regained, where Christ condemns the schools of philosophy which stemmed from Socrates, there is no inconsistency. Milton's admiration for them and for Greek culture
in most of its aspects is no less strong here than it is in the
rhapsody on Greek freedom in *Areopagitica.* No less than
Jeremy Taylor, Milton looked upon Christian literature as "the
great treasure house of those excellent, moral, and perfective
discourses, which with much pains and pleasure, we find
respersed and thinly scattered in all the Greek and Roman
poets, historians, and philosophers." Even in the heat of the
debate he did not make Christ condemn Socrates, and it is the
abuse and degradation of Stoicism rather than Stoicism itself
which he attacks. The same is true of Aristotle's disciples,
the Peripatetics. What Milton, like Bacon, hated in Aristo-
telianism was its scientific pretentiousness, the same vice which
in pre-Socratic philosophy Satan (here echoing Cicero's words
in the *Tusculan Disputations,* V, iv, 10.) said was eradicated
when it descended from vain speculations about heaven to
"Socrates's low-roof'd house." When he made Christ condemn the futilities of the Stoics Milton was unconsciously attacking the bugbear of all enlightened men, the logic-chopping
and grandiose claims to scientific knowledge of the decadent
medieval Scholasticism which was not yet dead in Europe.
His feeling was like Taylor's at the close of his devotional commentary on the Gospels, *The Great Exemplar.* Wisest men,
said Taylor, find more to value in the Greek poets and philosophers and even in "the old Academics and Stoics" than in
"the triflings of many of the latter schoolmen," who "added
nothing to Christianity but trouble, scruple, and vexation."[1]
Most Englishmen of the seventeenth century who thought
about the triumph of Christianity over the philosophical schools
of ancient Greece unconsciously confused those schools with
the degenerate Scholasticism which the Renaissance had inherited from the Middle Ages. In *The Church Militant*

---

[1] *The Whole Works of the Right Reverend Jeremy Taylor, D.D.* edited
by Reginald Heber. Revised edition, London, 1850, Vol. II, p. 36.

George Herbert betrays the same confusion when he describes
Christianity penetrating Greece,

> where arts
> Gave her the highest place in all men's hearts;
> Learning was pos'd, Philosophie was set,
> Sophisters taken in a fisher's net.
> Plato and Aristotle were at a losse,
> And wheel'd about again to spell Christ-Crosse.
> Prayers chas'd syllogismes into their den,
> And Ergo was transform'd into Amen.

8. It is a paradox in the criticism of *Paradise Regained* that
after making Christ condemn Stoicism for its "philosophic
pride" Milton should have been blamed for giving him
"speeches which display . . . the defiant virtue of the Stoic or
the self-conscious righteousness of the pharisee." Indeed the
Stoic element in both *Paradise Lost* and *Paradise Regained* has
seemed to some recent readers, especially in Germany, to out-
weigh the Platonic. Herr Josef Reck says bluntly that Christ
is a purely Stoic figure, an incarnation of obedience to Law,
and of Intellect triumphing over Sensuality. While he recog-
nizes a mighty source of strength in the resulting personality,
he is repelled by its "moral fanaticism." Whether Christ is a
prig or the Christian hero of Milton's own hero-worship may
be a matter of individual taste. But it is marvellous that Milton created nothing at all like the pale saint of Giles Fletcher's
treatment of the Temptation in *Christ's Victorie on Earth*.
Traditionally Christian art had made the temptation a spectacle
of perfect virtue snubbing impudent sin. The Christ of the
Coventry Temptation play is a naïve pharisee. At the end he
solemnly exhorts the audience to

> exaumple take
> By these grete werkys that thou dost se.

In his duel with Satan no such complacency is possible for Milton's Christ. He is no more a Stoic than he is a mere allegorical figure or the bare abstract principle which Mark Pattison
thought him.

9. Both intellectually and emotionally it is hard to feel the full power of the psychological drama in Milton's Christ. We are too far away from the medieval debates between the body and the soul and from the morality plays, where Everyman struggles against the almost infinite force of the devil for his puny soul and yet, thanks to the Grace of God which is never quite distinct from his own conscience, has a chance to win and usually does win. We are too far from the medieval hope of spiritual perfection which had its loveliest expression in the Grail romances. There Milton remembered that

> Knights of Logres, or of Lyones,
> Lancelot or Pelleas, or Pellenore,[1]

encounter the fiend "in likeness of a man of religion," as Malory says, or again, "in woman's likeness." Malory ends his fourteenth book with the picture of a mysterious old man (who is, of course, an angel and like the angelic comforters of Christ after his victory) congratulating Sir Bors on his resistance of a temptress who was really "the master fiend of hell. . . . And that was the champion that thou foughtest withal." The romancers thought of their knights as possessing an enchanted virtue, but Milton made Christ's virtue as human as he could. He stopped short of dogmatic explanation of it, however, and there is not a word of dogma in the address of God to the angels in heaven. Even there Milton did not try to rationalize the mystery of Christ's dual nature. God refers to his virgin birth as a matter of miraculous fact, but He also refers to the defeat of Satan by the Old Testament worthy, Job, as if Satan's imminent defeat by Jesus were analogous.

10. In spite of his embroidery upon the story, Milton accepted the accounts of it in the Gospels, and especially in Luke, whose record he followed in the order of the temptations. For comparison it will be convenient to insert the short passage here. After his baptism by John the Baptist, Luke says in his fourth chapter that

---

[1] *P.R.*, II, 360-361.

Jesus, being full of the Holy Ghost, returned from Jordan, and was led by the Spirit into the wilderness, being forty days tempted of the devil. And in those days he did eat nothing: and when they were ended, he afterward hungered. And the devil said unto him, If thou be the Son of God, command this stone that it be made bread. And Jesus answered him, saying, It is written, That man shall not live by bread alone, but by every word of God. And the devil, taking him up into an high mountain, showed unto him all the kingdoms of the world in a moment of time. And the devil said unto him, All this power will I give thee, and the glory of them: for that is delivered unto me; and to whomsoever I will I give it. If thou therefore wilt worship me, all shall be thine. And Jesus answered and said unto him, Get thee behind me, Satan; for it is written, Thou shalt worship the Lord thy God, and him only shalt thou serve.

And he brought him to Jerusalem, and set him on a pinnacle of the temple, and said unto him, If thou be the Son of God, cast thyself down from hence; For it is written, He shall give his angels charge over thee, to keep thee; and in their hands they shall bear thee up, lest at any time thou dash thy foot against a stone. And Jesus answering said unto him, It is said, Thou shalt not tempt the Lord thy God.

And when the devil had ended all the temptation, he departed from him for a season.

11. Beside these verses from Luke, the reader of *Paradise Regained* should know the accounts of the temptation in Matthew (iv, 1–11.) and Mark (i, 12–13.) and, to imagine the duel between Christ and Satan as Milton did, he should be familiar with the Book of Job. Although in the *Reason of Church Government* Job is called a model "short epic," it is really a drama. In the main, it consists of dialogue between Job and his comforters, as *Paradise Regained* mainly consists of a rather different kind of dialogue between Christ and his tempter, and as *Samson Agonistes* consists of dialogues between the hero and various other persons. The narrative opening of Job brings Satan before God's throne, boasting that he can shake Job's faith by taking away his property and, finally, his children. The attack is on Job's confidence in God

and the value of life itself is at stake. Here perhaps Milton found an impulse towards his treatment of Satan's suggestion that the stones be turned into bread as a temptation of distrust. So Christ calls it (I, 355.), evidently seeing in it both a vulgar appeal to anxiety about his daily bread and a subtler appeal to him to upset the order of nature by relieving the desert folk

> With Food, whereof we wretched seldom taste.[1]

Milton's treatment of the first temptation ends with the close of Book I. In the second temptation (II, 242–IV, 393.) Job's example is still a factor, but now he is a type of Aristotle's supreme virtue of magnanimity, which to Milton meant indifference to money, power, and glory. The patriarch Job had long been a conventional symbol of that Christian interpretation of the proud, Greek quality of high-mindedness. In a popular Italian work on ethics,[2] which was only one among many of its kind, Job's name appears linked with Christ's, in the chapter *On Ambition,* among other instances of magnanimous refusal of earthly glory. The influence of the Book of Job in *Paradise Regained* may not be so great as Milton's frequent allusions to it suggest, but a share of his interest in it will help a modern reader to enjoy his poem.

12. It is important to understand that the gorgeous banquet offered to Christ (II, 337–377.) is a part of the second temptation and not a repetition of the first, as many good Miltonists have supposed. It is a part of that "show of luxury" which is never far from Satan's mind. To the very end of the struggle, he cannot realize that Jesus despises any life which includes "sumptuous gluttonies and gorgeous feasts" (IV, 114.). DeQuincey made the suggestion that the psychological value of the banquet is the sudden contrast of the throng of lovely demon servitors with the solitariness of the desert. Christ is taken unawares by the pleasure which moves almost anyone returning from nature's fastnesses to civilized life. It has its

---

[1] I, 345.
[2] *Selva Nuovissima di Concetti,* by Alessandro Calamato, Venice, 1648.

philosophical side also, for Milton is reverting to the sophistry of Comus when he argues with the Lady against the "lean and sallow Abstinence" of "the budge doctors of the Stoic Fur" and asks:

> Wherefore did Nature pour her bounties forth,
> With such a full and unwithdrawing hand,
> Covering the earth with odours, fruits, and flocks,
> Thronging the Seas with spawn innumerable,
> But all to please, and sate the curious taste?

13. Though he is a less sympathetic tempter than Comus, Satan is a more dramatic figure. True, he is the principle of evil and the embodiment of deceit. His trick of profiting by what he learns of Christ's nature to improve upon his temptations may seem to be a mere reflection of the facts of psychology. Money first, then power, then earthly fame of the noblest kind, is the series of bids made to Spenser's Guyon by Mammon as it is to Christ by Satan. There is an unconscious hierarchy among men which is based upon their various abilities to penetrate these three lures. Those who are blinded by the second fall victims to the first, for, as Satan points out, the sinews of power are wealth. And fame, when it is not sought out of sheer vanity, can be an object only for men who wish to feel their power stretching beyond the grave. So Satan may be regarded as a mere allegory of the self-deception of life and his temptations as symbols of the *maya* of the Hindu philosophers or of the vanity of the world taught by Christian mystics. But Milton did not think of him primarily in any such fashion. Without belief in the Old Nick of popular tradition, he thought of himself and of all Christians as wrestling—to use St. Paul's words (Ephesians, vi, 12.)—against "principalities and powers," or spiritual forces without ourselves which make for unrighteousness. He thought of them as being what Satan called them, "Powers of Air and this wide World" (I, 44–45.), who had escaped from Hades and established themselves here when Adam "fell." Of Satan he thought as their leader, who had stirred them up to their first

revolt against God and who is sure, whenever a heroic man is born, to become his "Adversary." Satan is no longer the glorious rebel of *Paradise Lost,* but he is still dictator in the parliaments of his followers. In *Paradise Regained* there are two councils of the demons, neither of them comparable with the great debate in the second book of *Paradise Lost;* but the first serves admirably to set the stage and let the villain exhibit his character in speeches which are really soliloquies. Like a protagonist in a Greek tragedy, Satan is aware of a prophecy of a "fatal wound" (I, 53.) hanging over him and knows that signs are pointing to Christ as his dangerous enemy. At the baptism in the river Jordan he has heard a voice from heaven call Christ God's son, and the word fills him with foreboding. Can this son be like the first-begotten Son by whom, he reminds his followers, in the struggle for the mastery of heaven, before the creation of the world, they were driven down to hell,

> When his fierce thunder drove us to the deep?[1]

Who this new son is, he tells the demons,

> we must learn, for man he seems
> In all his lineaments, though in his face
> The glimpses of his Father's glory shine.[2]

By his pertinacity in answering that question Satan brings on the catastrophe, his second fall, "smitten with amazement."

14. Early Christian tradition helped to shape Milton's Satan as a spirit inviting his own doom by reckless curiosity about Christ. The source may have been Prudentius or St. Augustine's story that "the prince of devils made question of his deity, and tempted Him for the trial of His deity, trying how far He would suffer Himself to be tempted."[3] From early times the Christian imagination had played around the scene. Some of the fathers of the Church, like Origen, thought of

---

[1] I, 90.
[2] I, 91-93.
[3] *The City of God,* VIII, xxi.

Christ's entire forty days in the wilderness as a continual conflict between him and Satan.   The desert beyond Jordan, as
they imagined it, was not unlike the wilderness in Malory
where the foul fiend tempted knights of utter purity "in likeness of a man of religion."   That disguise became fixed.   In
old Bishop Bale's interlude, *The Temptation of Our Lord,*
Satan first attacks in that guise, for he knows that,

> Subtlety must help; else all will be amiss,
> A godly pretense, outwardly, must I bear,
> Seeming religious, devout and sad in my gear.

In the desert where Spenser's Knights of Holiness and Temperance wander it is really the devil who comes to them in the
person of the enchanter, Archimago, wearing the dress of a
hermit.   So inevitably Satan first appears in the disguise of
a pious old man.   Milton may have been familiar with the
scene in Giles Fletcher's *Christ's Victorie* where Satan is only
a shadow of Spenser's Archimago.   Christ sees an "aged Syre"

> Come slowly footing, everie step he guest
> One of his feete he from the grave did drawe,
> Three legges he had, the woodden was the best,
> And all the waie he went, he ever blest
>   With benedicities, and prayers store,
>   But the bad ground was blessed ne'r the more,
> And all his head with snowe of Age was waxen hore.[1]

15. Satan's nature must correspond with his disguise and it
is only in the short, third temptation (IV, 451–559.) that he
tries at all to resume his dominating character in *Paradise Lost.*
Then on the pinnacle of the temple, in the despair of defeat, he
is all insolence.   Both physically and psychologically Milton is
setting the stage for his downfall.   Elsewhere he is a wise
hypocrite and he has the dignity of that character.   Milton is
"modern" in endowing him with perfect comprehension of the
constraints of evil upon the wicked.   In the long speech which
closes the first book, for example—balancing the speech of

[1]Stanza *1*

Christ at the end of the second—the poignancy of Pirandello's
Clothe the Naked is compressed in the question to Christ,

> where
> Easily canst thou find one miserable,
> And not inforc'd oft-times to part from truth?[1]

A little later, when he claims privileges with Christ like those
permitted to the atheist priests whom God tolerates about his
altars, Satan is fencing with a sceptical idea which must have
disturbed Milton himself. In *Paradise Lost* (V, 117.) he had
recognized evil as entering into the mind of God and here again
he is confronting the old difficulty of all theologians; is evil
indispensable to the existence of good and can it justify itself
as a humble, necessary attendant on good? When the question is put by evil incarnate it becomes its own answer. Milton's prose, especially the *Christian Doctrine,* proves that all his
life he had been harassed by such questions, and the Satan of
Paradise Regained expresses even better than the Satan of
Paradise Lost his haunting sense of their difficulty. In that respect, autobiography can be read into both his Satans. As Professor Dowden pointed out, Jesus' censure of the Greek philosophers for accusing God under the name of Fortune (IV,
316.) is Milton's commentary on the hypocrisy of Satan's
famous lines in Book I (358–360.):

> 'Tis true, I am that Spirit unfortunate,
> Who leagu'd with millions more in rash revolt
> Kept not my happy Station.

16. It is in the rhythms of the poem and particularly of passages like those which have just been quoted that we should
look for autobiography. Here rather than in *Paradise Lost*
the Miltonic blank verse reaches its final form. The charge of
lost grandeur is futile, for the poem is pitched to record the
conquest of the lust of the eye and the pride of life and it can
hardly encourage any lust of the ear. Under severe restraint
the old glory is still there, ready to flame up in sudden remi-

---

[1] I, 470–472.

niscences of young Pompey quelling the "Pontic King" (III, 36.) or in panoramas

> Of Caucasus, and dark Iberian dales.[1]

There is no evidence of decay in the increasing proportion of lines which overflow the strict pattern of the pentameter; *e.g.,*

> To be infring'd, our freedom and our being.[2]

Like the hypermetric lines of Shakespeare's later plays, they indicate the poet's increasing command of his medium.   These later rhythms are more like those of speech, Milton's own personal speech, and of his thought in his last years, after he had escaped from the illusions of a singularly disinterested life of action.   If there is any justice in the charge that his Christ is made in his own image, the resemblance is less in Jesus' recollection of his serious youth than in his decision not

> To rescue Israel from the Roman yoke,[3]

because he

> held it more humane, more heavenly first
> By winning words to conquer willing hearts.[4]

The real Milton transpires less in the Saviour's contempt for the "miscellaneous vulgar" (III, 51.) than it does in the picture of the

> Plain Fishermen . . . .
> Close in a Cottage low together got;[5]

for Christ's last act is to turn his back on both earthly and heavenly glory to resume a life like theirs.   In youth Milton had been preoccupied with the thought that

> Fame is no plant that grows on mortal soil,[6]

---

[1]III, 318.

[2]I, 62.

[3]I, 217.

[4]I, 221–222.

[5]II, 27–28.

[6]*Lycidas,* 78.

and he speaks his final word on that subject, which is the real theme of *Paradise Regained,* in the subdued but confident rhythm of Christ's retort to Satan:

> This is true glory and renown, when God
> Looking on the Earth, with approbation marks
> The just man, and divulges him through Heaven
> To all his Angels.[1]

II. *SAMSON AGONISTES*

17. Again in the rhythms of *Samson Agonistes* we meet Milton's signature. When he wrote the tragedy, probably in close succession to *Paradise Regained* and not very far from the publication of *Paradise Lost* in 1667, he was ready to manipulate his blank verse in some ways more boldly than Shakespeare did even in *The Tempest.* In his choruses he invented measures for which he has had the most various blame and praise, but which—whatever may be said for or against them —certainly bear the form and pressure of his mind. He acknowledged in his introduction that they were written without regard to the stanzaic patterns of strophe, antistrophe, and epode in the choral odes of Greek drama. The measure, he said, was "of all sorts, called by the Greeks monostrophic." Actually, his rhythms drew upon both the spoken and the sung utterances of the Attic choruses; but, perhaps more than has been realized, their occasional rhymes and their long sentences —overflowing with cryptic distortions of normal grammar from one irregular verse to the next—betray how deeply he had learned to admire the irregular though richly rhymed lines of such Italian tragedies as Trissino's *La Sofonisba.* No one should go to *Samson Agonistes* expecting to find lyric strophes like those of Swinburne's *Atalanta in Calydon.* Indeed, any metrical prejudice is fatal here. The flexible, minor music of the choruses subtly offsets Samson's moods, which at the outset are darker than those of his comforters, but become more confident than theirs after the tide within him turns. The

---

[1] III, 60–63.

shifting rhythms are those of the enveloping thought and emotion which created the tragedy. The better we understand it—both intellectually and emotionally—the less likely we are to concur in the opinion that "there is a harshness in the metre of his Chorus . . . such at least as the ear will not patiently endure, nor which any recitation can make harmonious." When Richard Cumberland wrote those words in *The Observer*,[1] in a really able essay replying to Dr. Johnson's criticism of *Samson,* he may not have been unfair to Milton; but today—whatever reasons we may have for subscribing to his opinion—we are quite sure that the metrical prejudices of the eighteenth century, which made him entertain it, are for ever invalid.

18. As for the blank verse, the key to its harmony has been available since Robert Bridges first published his little essay *On the Prosody of* "Paradise Regained" *and* "Samson Agonistes" in 1889. Anarchy rather than harmony is the first impression of a conventional eye scanning these lines where the regular ten syllables are sometimes truncated to eight or six and may be extended to twelve (*e.g.,* in l. 497); and where unstressed, extra-metrical syllables insinuate themselves not merely at the end of the verses, but indiscriminately in any position. In l. 1095,

To have wrought / such won- / ders with / an Ass- / 's Jaw,

the extra syllable is in the first foot and in l. 1109 it is in the second,

Afford / me, assas- / sinat- / ed and / betray'd.

In Milton's flexible iambic pattern one or even two "feet" may drop out of step, as the two opening trochees in l. 170 do,

Uni- / versal- / ly crown'd / with high- / est praises.

The art of reading such a line consists in putting just the right, deliberate stress upon *crown'd* to give it the predominance which it was evidently intended to have, and which marks it

---

as the point of recovery of the iambic rhythm. A similar appreciation of the pivotal importance of the second syllable in *extraordinary* is the key to l. 1383,

> To some- / thing ex- / traordi- / nary / my thoughts.

Against the opinion of many editors but—as it seems to me—rightly, Mr. Bridges[1] insisted upon pronouncing the word *extraordinary* in the normal, correct way here, as a word of five syllables with a very heavy stress upon the second and with the last three enunciated distinctly, but very lightly and rapidly. The result, if we use the terms of classical scansion, is to make the first foot iambic, the second and third trochaic, the fourth a very light trochee and the fifth a heavy iambus with the first element, *my,* given almost as much emphasis as should be laid upon *thoughts,* so that the last foot comes only a little short of being a spondee. Many examples of very light feet which are immediately compensated by spondees might be cited: *e.g.,* in l. 960,

> Ĭ sēe / thŏu ārt / ĭmplă- / căblĕ / mōre dēaf—

or in l. 143,

> Thĕ Jāw / ŏf ă / dēad Āss, / thĭs swōrd / ŏf bōne,

or in l. 1362,

> What act / more ex- / ecrably / unclean / profane.

This is an interesting case, for two heavy feet, which are better treated as spondees than as iambs, close the line after a very light foot of *three* syllables. This third foot would lose its first syllable, *e,* by elision in conventional scansion, which might justify itself by pointing to the elision of the first *i* in *med'cinal* in l. 627, where the spelling with the apostrophe goes back to the first edition and presumably has Milton's own authority. In general, however, I feel that he did not intend to syncopate many syllables and would have

---

[1] In the *Athenaeum* of July 18, 1903, pp. 93–94.

sounded the *u* in *miraculous* in l. 587 and the *e* in *miseries* in l. 65, both of which many editors would like to elide. It is harder to justify such syncopations than it is to sustain Mr. Bridges' bold elision of *atr* in *idolatrous* in l. 443,

> By the / Idol- / *atr*ous rout / amidst / thir wine.

Milton had the art of subduing every word to his metre without violence even to the lightest syllables. Whatever elisions there are, we may be sure, were as a rule made in the best spoken English of his times. It is his voice that we hear in *Samson,* speaking the language of his "sessions of sweet silent thought," often tortured into the Greek and Latin constructions which were a part of the fibre of his brain, but never falsified by the pattern of his verse nor falsifying a word to conform it to that pattern. Unless there is evidence that an elision was made in the spoken English of his times, we should be chary of making it to satisfy a modern ear or a modern theory.

19. There are other personal, or even autobiographical, elements in the tragedy besides its metrical characteristics, but it is easy to overstress them. Nowhere in *Paradise Lost* nor even in the sonnet *On his Blindness* does that subject provoke anything so poignant as Samson's

> O dark, dark, dark, amid the blaze of noon.[1]

The poignancy, however, is the result of Milton's complete mastery and objectification of his own blindness. Samson is less the mouthpiece for his creator's lyric cry than he is the representative of all blind humanity. To some degree he may represent the physically blind Milton, but a more important question is the extent to which Milton applied to himself one of the observations of the Chorus about Samson:

> thy Soul
> (Which Men enjoying sight oft without cause Complain)
> Imprison'd now indeed,

---

[1]L. 80.

In real darkness of the body dwells,
Shut off from outward light
To incorporate with gloomy night;
For inward light, alas,
Puts forth no visual beam.[1]

20. So many recent students have focused attention upon
Samson as a personal document, and as Milton's last defiance
of the triumphant Royalists in the name of his republican
principles, that we are in danger of becoming more concerned
about it as autobiography than as literature. If we accept the
criticism—much of it excellent—which has followed the lead
of Sir Walter Raleigh in *Milton's Last Poems,* the poet's old
age becomes interesting as a psychological problem at the price
of becoming spiritually more remote from us than is necessary.
For Sir Walter *Samson* expressed a personal isolation magnificent but dreadful. Unfortunately for his enjoyment of the
poem, its political principles are a lost cause which has never
been at home in Oxford. In the Edinburgh of the nineteenth
century where, if they were not completely at home, they were
at least very welcome visitors, they did not seem like the self-
justification of a defeated old man living in splendid isolation.
Professor Masson spoke Milton's language when he asked,
"Who are the Philistines but the partisans of the Restoration?
. . . Who are the Philistine lords and ladies, and captains, and
priests, assembled in their seats within the covered part of the
temple of Dagon on the day of festival? Who but Charles
himself, and the Duke of York, and the whole pell-mell of the
Clarendons, Buckinghams, Buckhursts, Killigrews, Castle-
maines, Moll Davises, Nell Gwynns, Sheldons, Morleys, and
some hundreds of others, . . . priests and laymen, . . . that
formed the court-society of England in that most swinish
period of her annals?"[2]

21. There is something to be said for Professor Masson's
point of view. We may, for one thing, be sure that Harapha

---

[1] Ll. 156–163.
[2] *The Life of John Milton,* Vol. VI, p. 676.

stands for what he called "the whole pell-mell." Efforts, which when everything has been said are mere guesswork, have been made to identify this giant with the Duke of York, who is known to have spoken insultingly of Milton, and with his old foe, Salmasius. There can be no doubt, however, that Harapha is what Herr Christian Kreipe calls a *collectivmus,* a collective representative of the whole court party. He is a monstrous, composite portrait standing opposite to the mass of caricatures of the Commonwealth men in Butler's *Hudibras.* There is comedy about him and if Milton's principles of dramatic decorum had been less exacting and his dramatic talent more genial, the giant might have become as comic a personage as some of the representatives of the degenerate Athenian demos in Aristophanes' *Birds.* Plato, says the *Areopagitica,* "commended the reading of Aristophanes" and "holy Chrysostom" learned from him "the art to cleanse a scurrilous vehemence into the style of a rousing sermon." Harapha's scene may be an inartistically vehement attack upon his class, but for that reason he is interesting historically if not dramatically. And as he was created to embody a social group, so his enemy, Samson, was very much more than a mere projection of John Milton sitting alone, defeated but defiant, in the little house in Artillery Walk.

22. Long before he wrote his tragedy, and before he was in danger of losing his sight, we know that Milton thought of Samson as the symbol of a national ideal. In 1641, three years before the first symptoms of failing sight appeared, he ended *The Reason of Church Government* by likening "the state and person of a king . . . to that mighty Nazarite Samson; who being disciplined from his birth in the precepts and the practice of temperance and sobriety, without the strong drink of injurious and excessive desires, grows up to a noble strength and perfection with those his illustrious and sunny locks, the laws, waving and curling about his godlike shoulders." One wonders whether the "illustrious and sunny locks" were not a side-glance at Charles I. The whole passage is pointed in its reference to the King, and it goes on to twist the story of

Samson's exploits in Judges xiv–xvi into a parable against the
bishops. There is sad stuff about the "strumpet flatteries of
the prelates," which are compared to Dalila's betrayal of the
secret of her lover's hair; but the tragedy to be written long
afterward flashes out in the final picture of the King, a modern
Samson, knowing at last "this prelatical razor to have bereft
him of his wonted might," nourishing again "his puissant
hair, the golden beams of law and right; and they sternly
shook, thunder with ruin upon the heads of his evil coun-
cillors, but not without great affliction to himself." When
these words were written Milton had not lost all confidence
in the King. Looking back upon them after twenty-five years
—if he still remembered the peroration to his youthful pamphlet—he must have taken grim pleasure in pouring all the
disillusion and indomitable purpose of the intervening quarter-
century into the Samson of our tragedy.

23. About this same year, 1641, Milton jotted down in the
Cambridge Manuscript the subjects of a very large number of
possible dramas on biblical themes, and among them a group
of five which were to be based upon episodes in Samson's
career: (1) *Samson in Ramoth Lechi,* Judges xv (the episode
which is recalled in lines 142–5), (2) *Samson marrying* (the
episode of Samson's marriage with the woman of Timnath to
which lines 219–226 and 381–7 refer), (3) *Dagonalia,* Judges xvi
(the overthrow of the temple of Dagon in Gaza which is the
subject of our tragedy), (4) *Samson pursophorus* (Samson the
fire-bearer, or Samson when he burned the Philistines' corn by
driving three hundred foxes into it with lighted torches between them, Judges xv, 3–5), and (5) *Samson Hybristes* (the
Insolent Samson, or Samson inviting a tragic fate by some act
of over-confidence like his betrayal of his secret to Dalila).
If the *Dagonalia* had been written when it was planned, we
may be sure that at the outset Samson would have been made
a glorious symbol of the leadership of the English, who are
described in *Areopagitica* as "a knowing people, a nation of
prophets, of sages and of worthies." And his death would
have appealed to Milton's sanguine imagination as a symbol,

not of defeat, but of the act of self-discipline which he was begging his country to perform and so "wax young again, entering the glorious ways of truth and prosperous virtue, destined to become great and honorable in these latter ages." As an individual Samson might have been superficially tragic, but his failure would not have had the dark background of recreancy among the national leaders which embitters his feeling towards

> Israel's Governors, and Heads of Tribes,
> Who, seeing those great acts which God had done
> Singly by me against their Conquerors,
> Acknowledg'd not, or not at all consider'd
> Deliverance offer'd.[1]

Even in prison the Samson of 1641 would probably have been a conventionally heroic figure. Milton was familiar with the traditional conception of him which John Donne recalled in *Biathanatos* (III, v, 4.): "A man so exemplar, that not onely the times before him had him in Prophecy, and the times after him more consummately in Christ, of whom he was a Figure, but even in his own time, other nations may seeme to have had some type, or Copy of him, in Hercules." This traditional identification of Hercules with Samson is responsible for the Chorus's comparison of the two worthies in line 150—a comparison which has been questioned as anachronistic. It was part of an established idealization of Samson, just as the comparison of Christ with Hercules in *Paradise Regained* was a part of His idealization as Milton inherited it from the liberal theologians of the sixteenth century. In 1641 Milton would have had need of extraordinary originality to emancipate himself from the accepted view of his hero as a saint, and even as a type of Christ, sufficiently to make him genuinely tragic. An admirer of the tragedy of *Samson or Sacred Vengeance* (1660) by the Dutch poet, Joost van den Vondel (with whose work Milton was more or less familiar, though it is a question whether he knew this play) insists that beside Milton's demi-

---

[1] Ll. 241–246.

god, who is human only in his implacable hatred for Dalila,
Vondel's Samson is a sympathetic human being who has loved,
suffered, and made a supreme sacrifice. Yet even Vondel
was conventional enough to end his play with a scene where
Samson's mourners are met by the angel who prophesied his
birth, Fadaël, and are forbidden to mourn for a spirit emanci-
pated from its anguish and for a body freed from its blindness.
Samson is at rest with the heroes of the past and, the angel
adds, he is a type of another and greater hero, still unborn,
whose death will mean the conquest, not of the Philistines,
but of enemies more terrible than the grave itself.

24. There is nothing conventional in Milton's treatment of
the story of Samson, yet, like all works of art, his tragedy was
built upon tradition. Broadly speaking, the tradition was the
heroic one which had created the *Franciad,* the *Jerusalem Delivered,* and *The Faerie Queene,* and which had just produced
the tragedies of Corneille and was still producing those of
Racine. Milton has been condemned for making Samson so
noble that his indiscretion with Dalila is absurd. Critics prefer
now to go to the opposite extreme and imagine him as Leonid
Andreev drew him, foul in his prison, a hairy ape of the historical imagination, passionately loved to the end by a no less
primitive Dalila. The difference between Andreev's tradition
and that which Milton inherited is strikingly illustrated by the
contrast between the former's handling of the moment when
Samson gathers all his powers together to pull down the pillars
of Dagon's temple and the treatment of that same scene by a
minor English poet, Francis Quarles, who published *The His-
torie of Samson* in 1631. Andreev was interested in the incident as a case of abnormal power produced by the psychic
stimulus of fanaticism. What it meant to Quarles is indicated
by the prayer which he put into Samson's mouth at the moment of catastrophe:

> Lord, the wrong is thine:
> The punishment is just and onely mine:
> I am thy Champion, Lord; It is not me
> They strike at; Through my sides, they thrust at thee:

> Against thy Glory 'tis, their Malice lies;
> They aym'd at that, when they put out these eyes.[1]

25. This traditional view of the situation as ultimately a struggle between God and Dagon is woven all through *Samson Agonistes*. Manoa first suggests it when he says that the worst consequence of his son's indiscretion is that

> So Dagon shall be magnifi'd, and God,
> Besides whom is no God, compar'd with Idols,
> Disglorifi'd, blasphem'd, and had in scorn
> By th'Idalotrous rout amidst thir wine.[2]

Samson's reply is to say that his only hope consists in the fact that "All the contest is now 'Twixt God and Dagon." And in the end the Chorus chants God's delusion of his enemies with a "mad desire to call in haste for thir destroyer" when they were

> Drunk with Idolatry, drunk with Wine,
> And fat regorg'd of Bulls and Goats,
> Chanting thir Idol, and preferring
> Before our living Dread who dwells
> In Silo his bright Sanctuary.[3]

Milton's proneness to think of Samson as the soldier of a jealous God may be a particularly savage aspect of his "Hebraism" and consequently questionable both as art and as religion. To students with the Freudian conceptions about the artistic temperament which Mr. E. H. Visiak applied to *Paradise Lost* in *Milton Agonistes,* Samson will seem like a savage attempt to compensate in the ideal world for the poet's defeat in old age. Even Masson suspected that he sometimes took a "fell pleasure" in imagining some cruel triumph over his enemies, like that of Samson, for himself; and Mr. Tillyard accuses him of something very like ferocity. There is justice in the charge, but we would be unjust to Milton if we did not remember the

---

[1]Section 23.

[2]Ll. 440–443.

[3]Ll. 1670–1674.

part played by tried and sound tradition in his portrayal of
the champion of God. It will be worth while to compare the
influence of tradition upon his portrayal of Dalila.

26. The third act of his tragedy opens with the Chorus's
first glimpse of her

> this way sailing
> Like a stately Ship
> Of Tarsus.[1]

It ends when they dismiss her with the words,

> She's gone, a manifest Serpent by her sting
> Discover'd in the end, till now conceal'd.[2]

In the whole drama, hers is the only glamorous scene and to
most readers it is very moving. Its dramatic purpose is put
beyond doubt by Samson when he says after she disappears,

> God sent her to debase me,
> And aggravate my folly.[3]

We acquiesce in his refusal of her invitation to leave his slavery
in the mill and go to live with her again mainly because it is an
indispensable step towards the catastrophe. Within the limits
of the act itself our sympathies are divided. They go out to
both Samson and Dalila, but more strongly to her than to
him. We feel a conflict in ourselves something like that felt
in reading Shakespeare's *Antony and Cleopatra*. It would be
odd if Milton's treatment of the situation did not have something suggestive of Shakespeare's play about it, for both poets
were dealing with stories which had been for centuries brack-
eted together as emblems of what Spenser called

> beauties lovely baite, that doth procure
> Great Warriours oft their rigour to represse.[4]

---

[1] Ll. 713–715.
[2] Ll. 997–998.
[3] Ll. 999–1060.
[4] *F.Q.*, V, viii, 1.

In a curious stanza Spenser recalled that

> whylome learnd that mighty Jewish swaine,
> Each of whose lockes did match a man in might,
> To lay his spoiles before his lemans traine:
>
> *   *   *   *
>
> And so did warlike Antony neglect
> The worlds whole rule for Cleopatras sight.[1]

Milton inherited Dalila from Spenser as one of the many daughters of Circe, and to that fact both the starkness and the beauty of his treatment of her are due. The presence of the myth of Circe in the background transpires strangely when Samson calls her invitation to him

> Thy fair enchanted cup, and warbling charms.[2]

Essentially she stands to Samson as Circe's son, Comus, does to the Lady. If Milton had been less of a poet and more of a puritan, he would have drawn her without subtlety and treated the situation as crudely as Phineas Fletcher did when he wrote in *The Apollyonists* that the

> strongest Champion, who with naked hands
> A Lyon tore, who all unarm'd and bound
> Heap't mounts of armed foes on bloody sands,
> By womans art, without or force or wound
> Subdu'd, now in a mill blind grinding stands.[3]

The marvellous thing about Milton's Dalila is that she is both the traditional incarnation of treacherous lust and a subtly characterized woman. We almost believe in her remorse, for it is as eloquent as Cleopatra's denial of a cold heart:

> Ah! dear, if I be so,
> From my cold heart let heaven engender hail,
> And poison it in the source; and the first stone
> Drop in my neck.[4]

---

[1] *F.Q.*, V, viii, 2.
[2] L. 934.
[3] Canto IV, xxiii.
[4] *Antony and Cleopatra*, III, xi, 158–161.

Cleopatra's sincerity comes out of the tragic torture of a complex nature, but Dalila's eloquence is the charming rhetoric of a diabolic temptress. Milton betrayed the working of his imagination about her when he made her plead in her own defence that "to the public good Private respects must yield." When he wrote those words he must have remembered Satan in *Paradise Lost* pleading that

> public reason just,
> Honour and Empire with revenge enlarged,
> By conquering this new World, compels me now
> To do what else though damn'd I should abhor.[1]

Another link with *Paradise Lost* is the simile there which compares Adam's rising from his drugged sleep after eating the forbidden fruit to the awakening of

> the *Danite* strong
> *Herculean Samson* from the Harlot-lap
> Of *Philistean Dalilah.*[2]

Because he thought of Dalila as a temptress in the service of the powers of darkness, Milton made Samson treat her as severely as Spenser made his Knight of Temperance, Guyon, treat the enchantress, Acrasia, when he broke her charms and destroyed her gardens. Yet it was the tradition which placed Dalila in the enchanting tribe of Acrasia and Circe which enriched his limited dramatic talent so that he could endow her with more than a suggestion of the glory of Shakespeare's Cleopatra.

27. No one denies life to Dalila, but—leaving her apart— many readers may agree with Mr. Max Beerbohm that "the *personae* come on, speak, go off, without any swelling or expediting the volume of the idea. . . . All is quite static and marmoreal."[3] A similar verdict is often brought against the Book of Job, for it is a series of actionless dialogues without even a tragic ending to offset the pious protagonist's triumphs

---

[1] *P.L.,* IV, 389–392.
[2] *P.L.,* IX, 1059–1061.
[3] *The Saturday Review of Literature,* LXXXIX, p. 489.

over misfortunes any one of which would threaten an ordinary man with tragedy. Job had some influence upon *Samson.* In the preface to the second book of *The Reason of Church Government* Milton mentioned it as a model for his imitation —not as a drama, it is true, but in close conjunction with the Greek dramas which he admired, "those dramatic constitutions, wherein Sophocles and Euripides reign." His preface to *Samson* leaves no doubt that the Greeks were his models, constantly in his thoughts as he wrote; and his text is sown with their reminiscences. One of the most interesting aspects of the drama and one of the moot questions about it is its relation to the Greeks. Is the play, as Mr. Beerbohm says, void of all Greek dramatic quality, with a hero whose attitude of submission to God is "admirable, edifying, correct, but . . . never for one instant touching drama"?

28. In essence Mr. Beerbohm's objection is the same as Dr. Johnson's in the *Life of Milton,* when he said that although Samson "has a beginning and an end which Aristotle himself could not have disapproved, . . . it must be allowed to have no middle, since nothing passes between the first act and the last, that either hastens or delays the death of Samson. . . . Yet this is the tragedy which ignorance has admired, and bigotry has applauded." For a good many years now the consensus of critical opinion has generally condemned this judgement. The third act, Dalila's, is recognized as complete in itself and vital to Samson's recovery of his power. The fourth, Harapha's, provides the motive for summoning Samson to the temple of Dagon and in itself, especially if its satire is understood, it is dramatic. The second act, which opens with Manoa's first appearance, begins at once to prepare for the catastrophe, and the messenger's report of Samson's death in the fifth act is as moving as the parallel reports of the death of Oedipus and that of Electra by Sophocles. In the second act Samson first unconsciously prophesies the catastrophe when he says that God

> will arise and his great name assert:
> Dagon must stoop, and shall ere long receive

> Such a discomfit as shall quite despoil him
> Of all these boasted Trophies won on me,
> And with confusion blank his Worshippers.[1]

Manoa exclaims that he takes the words as a prophecy. The reader, knowing what is to come, looks forward with a sudden thrill to the collapse of the pillars in the temple. If he is familiar with Euripides, he may be struck by a resemblance between Manoa's words and those of Xuthus in the *Ion* (l. 561), when Ion salutes him as father and he joyfully treats the words as an auspicious omen. There *is* a prophecy in them, but its full import is clear only to the audience. Throughout Milton's drama such tragic irony continually prepares for the catastrophe. It is pathetic when Manoa, confident at last of his hopes for ransoming his son, persuades himself that

> God had not permitted
> His strength again to grow up with his hair,
>
> *   *   *   *   *   *
>
> were not his purpose
> To use him further yet in some great service.[2]

It is terrible when Manoa mentions his confidence that the Philistines will be willing to liberate Samson because he can no longer do them any harm. As Samson recovers his sense of his mission and begins to feel some "rousing motions" in him, his utterances—like his remark that the hatred of the Philistines for him may involve them all in a common ruin— seem almost clairvoyant. When the catastrophe arrives its way has been prepared by every effect of the tragic irony which the Greeks loved. Mr. Tillyard, following Professor Jebb and several other classical scholars, has pointed out that "the essence of the plot in *Samson* is that nearly all the actions should lead whither they had not seemed to lead."[3]

---

[1] Ll. 467–471.
[2] Ll. 1495–1499.
[3] *Milton*, p. 343.

Outward events point to Samson's hopeless degradation until he is seemingly forced to submit to the utter ignominy which is destined to become his utter triumph.

29. Milton's plot is undeniably Sophoclean, but it is hard to tell whether Aeschylus, Sophocles, or Euripides had the greatest influence upon him. The traditional opinion is that it was Euripides. Macaulay, who thought that he should have "taken Aeschylus for his model" and "given himself up to the lyric inspiration," blamed the influence of Euripides for the fact that, "We cannot identify ourselves with the characters, as in a good play. We cannot identify ourselves with the poet, as in a good ode." Macaulay disliked Euripides for what seem to-day to have been wrong reasons. Our objection to him depends upon Nietzsche's criticism that his tragic effects "depended on. . . . the great rhetero-lyric scenes in which the passion and dialectics of the chief hero swelled to a broad and mighty stream. Everything was arranged for pathos, not for action; and whatever was not arranged for pathos was regarded as objectionable."[1] Now it is undeniable that the symmetrically arranged debates of Samson with Dalila and Harapha, with their clever twisting and retorting of ideas, are Euripidean; but their end is action. The choruses, which Milton took care to relate closely to his situations instead of allowing them to speculate at large as Euripides did, are rather Sophoclean. Verbal reminiscences of all three Greeks are scattered broadcast through *Samson,* but it seems to me that those from Aeschylus have more significance than has been recognized. Mr. Wilmon Brewer has suggested that Samson's character owes something to Aeschylus' Prometheus and that the plots of *Samson* and the *Prometheus Bound* are too much alike for the resemblance to be accidental. It is strange that in each drama the three middle acts should consist of three interviews which are mutually so unrelated that both dramatists should have been accused of losing sight of Aris-

---

[1] *The Birth of Tragedy,* translated by W. A. Haussmann, New York, 1924. P. 99.

totle's basic principle of unity of action. Yet in each play the interviews lead straight to the catastrophe, for each hero is "roused successively to hope, resentment, and a confident sense of power, which find expression in three speeches of defiances."[1] After all, however, the question of Milton's relative indebtedness to the Greeks cannot be solved, and it is much less important than the question whether his drama is at bottom Greek at all, or even tragic.

30. The great difficulty with Samson for Mr. Beerbohm and for many modern readers is his perfect submission to God, the sense of sin which Mlle. Stengers rather absurdly complains makes him a "demi-god," and which certainly does make him a religious man. Professor Hanford would like to regard him as an example of classical hybris, but admits that "the cloak of Prometheus . . . refuses to fit the less majestic Hebrew Titan."[2] For real tragic pride or hybris he turns to the Philistines—"Drunk with Idolatry, drunk with Wine"— as they are described in the semi-chorus which has already been quoted. There is no denying that, from the outset, Samson is outspokenly repentant for the sin which has brought him, blind, to the mill in Gaza, or that, passively and actively, he is the servant of God. And in his world God is undisputed lord of Fate. Only once does Milton seem to conceive of him as contending with an all-powerful Destiny. In the Chorus's description of Samson as

> self-kill'd
> Not willingly, but tangl'd in the fold
> Of dire necessity,[3]

Mr. Verity's note objects that there is an inconsistent lapse into the Greek conception of Fate. The phrase, however, seems like a recollection of the Ode (III, xxiv, 6.) where Horace speaks of dire Necessity as having final power to destroy a

---

[1] *P.M.L.A.* XLII, p. 914.
[2] "*Samson Agonistes* and Milton in Old Age," p. 184.
[3] Ll. 1664–1666.

corrupt civilization. In the ancient world Necessity was as vague a force as it is today, but its use by the tragedians can hardly be called irreligious. Plato defined it as the essence of the laws of nature and in that sense he said that there was truth in the adage, "Not even God will ever be seen fighting against Necessity." But when misapplied to the affairs of men he said that it was "of all sayings by far the most fatuous."[1] Although in this chorus Milton may have written "necessity" without a very definite idea, we may be sure that he would not have run foul of Plato. If there is anything fatalistic in *Samson,* it is in the implied Stoicism of some of the choruses, not in their deliberate opinions.

31. The charge that Stoicism vitiates the religious spirit in both *Paradise Regained* and *Samson Agonistes* is often made, but in the latter case it can be almost formally refuted. The essence of Stoicism, Bacon said in *The Advancement of Learning* (II, xx, 10.), is the quest of security through the selfish limitation of our ideas of happiness to things which are within our power. He was thinking of the sacrifice of spiritual integrity to mere well-being, physical and moral. To that he opposed "the wisdom of that heavenly leader . . . who hath affirmed that 'a good conscience is a continual feast.'" Now Samson makes just that distinction when the Philistine officer tells him to regard himself and he answers,

> Myself? my conscience and internal peace.[2]

In quest of that peace he follows the officer to his death.

32. The "calm of mind, all passion spent" on which the Chorus congratulates itself as it takes leave is, of course, the mood to which Milton expected to bring his audience. It is a mood of confidence in a too obviously just God, a very "Hebraic" mood indeed. Yet it is Greek and Christian too. In the end he quite consistently put the broadly religious interpretation upon his tragedy which Euripides put upon the

---

[1] *Laws,* Book VII, 818, B.
[2] L. 1334.

Alcestis, Andromache, Bacchae, and *Helen* by closing them all with the lines which are paraphrased in the last chorus:

> All is best, though oft in doubt,
> What th'unsearchable dispose
> Of highest wisdom brings about,
> And ever best found in the close.[1]

The Chorus does not mean that Samson has in any sense escaped his tragic end. What it does mean is that he has redeemed himself by his last act from the passions which were his spiritual tragedy. In accordance with the conception of Aristotle's principle of tragic "catharsis" as he interpreted it in his preface, Milton expected our pleasure in watching the disease of passion run its course in his hero to work as a kind of homeopathic medicine upon us and "purge" us of the "pity" and "fear" by which we are beset. This view of the Aristotelian principle is far from orthodox, and even in the seventeenth century it was questioned. It makes tragedy a matter of morality and edification rather than primarily of profound aesthetic experience. The result here is a drama which to some degree reconciles genuinely Greek with genuinely Christian elements. Hellenists like Sir Richard Jebb may discount its Greek qualities and Christians like Mr. T. S. Eliot may sense a pagan Stoicism pervading all Milton's work. Both opinions are extreme. When our drama has been read to the end, Samson, even more clearly than Archbishop Thomas à Becket in *Murder in the Cathedral,* has vindicated himself of the sin which Mr. Eliot makes the last chorus in that most Christian tragedy confess, both for itself and for the other actors—the sin of fearing the injustice of men more than the justice of God. Professor Clyde Curry has good reason to rank *Samson* among the tragedies which revolve "about the central idea of the Christian religion, namely sin and its inevitable ravages in the human heart, purification and reconciliation through repentance, self-sacrifice and atonement."[2] For

---

[1] Ll. 1745–1748.
[2] *The Sewanee Review,* XXXII, p. 351.

that very reason *Samson* has seemed to many readers untragic. Certainly, no one is obliged to take sides with Professor Curry in his challenge to Professor Paull Baum's dictum that a "deep religious feeling *paramount* . . . and a high tragic spirit are antithetical." On that point every reader is entitled to his own opinion; but whatever we may think, final revolt against the will of heaven is hardly compatible with a tragic hero's experience—whether he be the Prometheus of Aeschylus or the Oedipus of Sophocles or the Samson of Milton.

BIBLIOGRAPHY

I. PARADISE REGAINED

Excellent discussion of *Paradise Regained* and of *Samson Agonistes* will be found in Mr. E. M. W. Tillyard's *Milton,* in John C. Bailey's *Milton,* Mark Pattison's *Milton,* and Sir Walter Raleigh's *Milton,* though of these only the first is abreast of modern scholarship. The following list of articles and monographs indicates the scope of recent specialized study and mentions some other works of value for the understanding of the two poems. The best modern edition of *Paradise Regained* is by Mr. E. H. Blakeney, London, 1932.

Bridges, Robert, *Milton's Prosody.* Revised edition, Oxford University Press, 1921.

It contains the substance of the privately printed essay *On the Prosody of "Paradise Regained" and "Samson Agonistes."*

Cory, Herbert E., *Spenser, the School of the Fletchers, and Milton.* University of California Publications. Modern Philology, 1912.

Dowden, Edward, *Paradise Regained.* In *Milton Memorial Lectures.* Oxford, 1909.

One of Professor Dowden's most illuminating essays.

Gilbert, Allan H., *The Temptation in "Paradise Regained."* *J.E.G.P.* XV, 599–611.

Notable for its interpretation of the second temptation.

Hanford, James H., *The Temptation Motive in Milton.* *S.P.* XV, 176–94.

Miller, R. D., *Milton's Conception of the Temptation as Portrayed in "Paradise Regained."* M.L.N. XV, 202–5.

The last statement of some traditional misconceptions.

Raleigh, Sir Walter A., *Milton's Last Poems. Living Age,* CCLX, 251–3.

Traeger, E., *Milton's "Paradise Regained."* Werdau, 1900.

II. SAMSON AGONISTES

The best modern edition is by Mr. A. W. Verity in "The Pitt Press Series," issued by the Cambridge University Press most recently in 1931. Professor H. M. Percival's edition, issued by Macmillan and Company, London, 1916, is also excellent.

Baum, Paull F., *"Samson Agonistes" Again.* P.M.L.A. XXXVI, 354–71.

Brewer, Wilmon, *Two Athenian Models for "Samson Agonistes."* P.M.L.A. XLII, 910–20.

Brown, Macmillan, *The "Samson Agonistes" of Milton.* New Zealand and London, 1905.

Clark, E. M., *Milton's Conception of Samson.* University of Texas Studies in English. VIII, 88–99.

Curry, Walter C., *"Samson Agonistes" Yet Again. Sewanee Review,* XXXII, 336–52.

Epps, P. H., *Two Notes on English Classicism.* S.P. XIII, 190–6.

Grierson, H. J. C., *"Samson Agonistes" and "Samson of Heilige Wraeck."* Melanges . . . Baldensperger. Paris. 1930. Vol. I, pp. 332–9.
Milton and Wordsworth. Cambridge University Press. 1937. Chapter VI has a significant treatment of Milton's *Samson.*

Hanford, James H., *"Samson Agonistes" and Milton in Old Age. Studies in Shakespeare, Milton, and Donne.* New York, 1925.

The most scholarly and penetrating interpretation of the drama as a key to Milton's mind.

Jebb, Sir Richard C., *"Samson Agonistes" and the Hellenic Drama*. Proceedings of the British Academy, 1907–8, pp. 341–8.

A fine overstatement of the "Hebraism" in *Samson*.

Knowlton, Edgar C., *Causality in "Samson Agonistes."* M.L.N. XXXVII, pp. 333–9.

Kreipe, Christian E., *Milton's "Samson Agonistes."* Halle, 1926.

Larson, Martin A., *Milton's Puritanism and Stoicism. P.Q.* VI, 201–220.

Mahaffy, John P., *What Have the Greeks Done for Modern Civilization?* New York, 1909.

Parker, W. R., *Milton's Debt to Greek Tragedy in "Samson Agonistes."* Johns Hopkins Press. 1937.

Here Mr. Parker gathers up the results of his many valuable studies of *Samson Agonistes* and presents a final reply to the position of Sir Richard Jebb.

The Kommos of Milton's "Samson Agonistes." S.P. XXXII, 240–4.

Powell, Chilton L., *Milton Agonistes. Sewanee Review,* XXXIV, 169–83.

Thompson, Edward J., *Samson Agonistes. L.Q.R.* CXXV, 244–54.

Thompson, E. N. S., *Milton's Puritanism. P.Q.* VI, 291–4.

Timberlake, P. W., *Milton and Euripides. The Parrott Presentation Volume.* Princeton University Press, 1935.

Tupper, James W., *The Dramatic Structure of "Samson Agonistes."* P.M.L.A. XXXV, 375–89.

PARADISE
REGAIN'D.
A
POEM.

In IV *BOOKS*.

To which is added

SAMSON AGONISTES.

The Author
JOHN MILTON.

LONDON,

Printed by *J. M.* for *John Starkey* at the
Mitre in *Fleetstreet,* near *Temple-Bar.*
MDCLXXI.

PARADISE REGAINED

The First Book

I who erewhile the happy Garden sung,
By one man's disobedience lost, now sing
Recover'd Paradise to all mankind,
By one man's firm obedience fully tried
Through all temptation, and the Tempter foil'd   5
In all his wiles, defeated and repuls't,
And *Eden* rais'd in the waste Wilderness.
   Thou Spirit who led'st this glorious Eremite
Into the Desert, his Victorious Field
Against the Spiritual Foe, and brought'st him thence   10
By proof the undoubted Son of God, inspire,
As thou art wont, my prompted Song, else mute,
And bear through highth or depth of nature's bounds
With prosperous wing full summ'd to tell of deeds

---

1. The allusion to the happy Garden of Eden recalls four spurious lines prefixed to all early editions of the *Aeneid* in which Virgil was supposed to turn regretfully away from his Arcadian theme in the *Georgics*. In opening *The Faerie Queene* Spenser set the example of imitating them.

2–4. For the background of this use of St. Paul's verse (Rom. v, 19); "For as by one man's disobedience many were made sinners; so by the obedience of one shall many be made righteous;" see the Introduction §1–2.

8–12. Milton thought of the Spirit of God, which Luke (iv, 1) says led Jesus into the desert, as "that divine breath or influence by which everything is created and nourished," and he invoked it in *P.L.,* I, 17, because it also signified to him "a divine impulse, or light, or voice, or word, transmitted from above." (*C.D.,* I, vi.)

8. The poetical form *Eremite* derives more directly than *hermit* from the original Greek word, which means a desert-dweller.

14. In falconry a hawk with full grown feathers was called *full summ'd, i.e.,* developed to the sum of perfection.

Above Heroic, though in secret done,   15
And unrecorded left through many an Age,
Worthy t' have not remain'd so long unsung.
  Now had the great Proclaimer with a voice
More awful than the sound of Trumpet, cried
Repentance, and Heaven's Kingdom nigh at hand   20
To all Baptiz'd: to his great Baptism flock'd
With awe the Regions round, and with them came
From *Nazareth* the Son of *Joseph* deem'd
To the flood *Jordan,* came as then obscure,
Unmarkt, unknown; but him the Baptist soon   25
Descried, divinely warn'd, and witness bore
As to his worthier, and would have resign'd
To him his Heavenly Office, nor was long
His witness unconfirm'd; on him baptiz'd
Heaven open'd, and in likeness of a Dove   30
The Spirit descended, while the Father's voice
From Heav'n pronounc'd him his beloved Son.
That heard the Adversary, who roving still
About the world, at that assembly fam'd
Would not be last, and with the voice divine   35

---

15. In *P.L.,* IX, 25, Milton asserted that he had a better "Subject for Heroic Song" than Homer or Virgil, for he thought the warlike deeds of Achilles, Ulysses and Aeneas less truly *heroic* than the spiritual warfare of Adam and Christ.

18. The *Proclaimer* is John the Baptist, who preached "in the wilderness of Judaea, . . . saying, Repent ye: for the kingdom of heaven is at hand. . . . Then went out to him Jerusalem, and all Judaea, and all the region round about Jordan. And were baptized of him in Jordan." (Mat. iii, 1–6.)

26. *divinely* keeps a trace of its Latin meaning of which we are more conscious in the verb *to divine, i.e.,* to guess or know something by supernatural guidance. Compare *P.L.,* VIII, 500 and *S.A.,* 226.

30–32. After Jesus' baptism Matthew describes "the Spirit of God descending like a dove, and lighting upon him: And lo a voice from heaven, saying, This is my beloved Son, in whom I am well pleased." (iii, 16–17.)

33. The Evil One appears as the *Adversary* in Job (i, 6) and frequently in the N.T. as the False Accuser, which is the meaning of the Greek word from which *devil* and *diabolic* are both derived.
  roving: In Job i, 7, Satan tells the Lord that he comes "From going to and fro in the earth, and from walking up and down in it."
  still has its regular early meaning of "always" or "constantly."

Nigh Thunder-struck, th' exalted man, to whom
Such high attest was giv'n, a while survey'd
With wonder, then with envy fraught and rage
Flies to his place, nor rests, but in mid air
To Council summons all his mighty Peers,   40
Within thick Clouds and dark ten-fold involv'd,
A gloomy Consistory; and them amidst
With looks aghast and sad he thus bespake.

   O ancient Powers of Air and this wide world—
For much more willingly I mention Air,   45
This our old Conquest, than remember Hell
Our hated habitation—well ye know
How many Ages, as the years of men,
This Universe we have possest, and rul'd
In manner at our will th' affairs of Earth,   50
Since *Adam* and his facile consort *Eve*
Lost Paradise deceiv'd by me, though since
With dread attending when that fatal wound

39–42. The demonic councils in *P.R.* compare better with those in
the first book of Vida's *Christias*, the fourth canto of Tasso's *Jerusalem
Delivered*, and Alain's *Anticlaudian*, VIII, iii–vii, or with Milton's own
juvenile epic *On the Fifth of November*, than with those in *P.L.* They
were a conventional part of the Christian epic which could hardly be
altogether eliminated from *P.R.*

39–45. Satan's title of "prince of the power of the air" (Eph. ii, 2)
and the tradition that the devils were "rulers of the darkness of this
world" (Eph. vi, 12) were based upon ancient Jewish ideas. Burton
(*Anatomy*, II, ii, 3) records the current belief that the air was "full of
Spirits which inhabit it, as the *Paracelsians* and *Platonists* hold." Compare *P.L.*, I, 516, and X, 185.

43. *bespake* is intransitive, although the prefix *be-* usually made a
verb transitive, as it does in modern English.

46. A part of the judgement upon Adam for his disobedience in
P.L., X, 189, was the promise that Christ should vanquish the powers
of the air,

            "The Realm itself of Satan long usurpt."

50. *In manner at our will:* as if the affairs of earth were at our disposal (instead of being in God's power).

53–55. The judgement upon the serpent, which was generally interpreted as referring to Satan for tempting Eve, was that her "seed"
should bruise its head. (Gen. iii, 15.) Compare the Introduction §13.

53. *attending* has its original French meaning of waiting. *when* is
equivalent to until.

Shall be inflicted by the Seed of *Eve*
Upon my head. Long the decrees of Heav'n   55
Delay, for longest time to him is short;
And now too soon for us the circling hours
This dreaded time have compast, wherein we
Must bide the stroke of that long threat'n'd wound,
At least if so we can, and by the head   60
Broken be not intended all our power
To be infring'd, our freedom and our being
In this fair Empire won of Earth and Air;
For this ill news I bring, the Woman's seed
Destin'd to this, is late of woman born: 65
His birth to our just fear gave no small cause,
But his growth now to youth's full flow'r, displaying
All virtue, grace and wisdom to achieve
Things highest, greatest, multiplies my fear.
Before him a great Prophet, to proclaim   70
His coming, is sent Harbinger, who all
Invites, and in the Consecrated stream
Pretends to wash off sin, and fit them so
Purified to receive him pure, or rather
To do him honour as their King; all come,   75
And he himself among them was baptiz'd,
Not thence to be more pure, but to receive
The testimony of Heaven, that who he is
Thenceforth the Nations may not doubt; I saw
The Prophet do him reverence; on him rising   80

55-58. Milton thought of the psalm (xc, 4) which makes a thousand
years like a day in God's sight and of the thought of fate which was
associated in Homer (*Od.*, XI, 247) and Virgil (*Aen.*, I, 234) with
phrases like "circling months" or "years."

60. Understand *if* as repeated before *by*.

62. *infring'd* keeps its literal Latin force of "broken."

68. Milton remembered Luke's account of Jesus' youth, when he "increased in wisdom and stature, and in favour with God and man."
(Luke ii, 52.)

73. Satan speaks ironically in referring to John's claim to cleanse from
sin as a pretense.

74. The turn of thought seems to follow I John iii, 3; "Every man
that hath this hope in him purifieth himself, even as he is pure."

78-85. Compare the note on 30.

Out of the water, Heav'n above the Clouds
Unfold her Crystal Doors, thence on his head
A perfect Dove descend, whate'er it meant,
And out of Heav'n the Sovran voice I heard,
This is my Son belov'd, in him am pleas'd.   85
His Mother then is mortal, but his Sire,
He who obtains the Monarchy of Heav'n,
And what will he not do to advance his Son?
His first-begot we know, and sore have felt,
When his fierce thunder drove us to the deep;   90
Who this is we must learn, for man he seems
In all his lineaments, though in his face
The glimpses of his Father's glory shine.
Ye see our danger on the utmost edge
Of hazard, which admits no long debate,   95
But must with something sudden be oppos'd,
Not force, but well couch't fraud, well woven snares,
Ere in the head of Nations he appear
Their King, their Leader, and Supreme on Earth.
I, when no other durst, sole undertook   100
The dismal expedition to find out
And ruin *Adam*, and the exploit perform'd
Successfully; a calmer voyage now

---

82. *her* is very frequent in Milton's poetry instead of "its," a form
which was only beginning to be established early in the seventeenth
century.

84. The Italian spelling *Sovran* was Milton's preference, although in
the first edition the French spelling *sovraign* occurs in this line.

86–93. Compare the Introduction §14–15, and Book IV, 501–540.

87. *obtains* keeps its Latin meaning of "possesses."

94–95. Compare Bertram's promise to be loyal "To th' extreme edge
of hazard," in *All's Well that Ends Well*, III, iii, and the pursuit to
"the edge of all extremitie," in *Troilus and Cressida*, IV, v.

97. *couch't* meant "concealed." *N.E.D.* quotes Holinshed as describing "some harquebusiers secretlie couched in couert."

100–102. Satan reminds the demons of the scene in hell when he
undertook to seek "deliverance" for them by exploring the way from
the deep of hell across Chaos to this universe. (*P.L.*, II, 430–466.)

103. The way from the middle "region" of the air down to earth is
calmer than Satan found his voyage through the "warring Winds" of
Chaos. (*P.L.*, II, 905.)

Will waft me; and the way found prosperous once
Induces best to hope of like success.   105
   He ended, and his words impression left
Of much amazement to th' infernal Crew,
Distracted and surpris'd with deep dismay
At these sad tidings; but no time was then
For long indulgence to their fears or grief: 110
Unanimous they all commit the care
And management of this main enterprise
To him their great Dictator, whose attempt
At first against mankind so well had thriv'd
In *Adam's* overthrow, and led thir march   115
From Hell's deep-vaulted Den to dwell in light,
Regents and Potentates, and Kings, yea gods
Of many a pleasant Realm and Province wide.
So to the Coast of *Jordan* he directs
His easy steps, girded with snaky wiles,   120
Where he might likeliest find this new-declar'd,
This man of men, attested Son of God,
Temptation and all guile on him to try,
So to subvert whom he suspected rais'd
To end his Reign on Earth so long enjoy'd: 125
But contrary unweeting he fulfill'd
The purpos'd Counsel pre-ordain'd and fixt
Of the most High, who, in full frequence bright
Of Angels, thus to *Gabriel* smiling spake.

---

104. The fact that the way has been *found prosperous once* gives
ground for hoping that it will prove so again.   Compare "Since first her
Salutation heard" in II, 107.

117. Milton's conception of the demons as having been worshipped
under the names of the pagan deities is found more significantly in the
Nativity ode (197–228) and in *P.L.,* I, 361–521.

120. *girded with snaky wiles* resembles Virgil's phrase to describe
the treacherous Sinon (*Aen.* II, 152) and Homer's to describe Ulysses
(*e.g., Il.,* IV, 339), but Milton's phrase is a contrast to Isaiah's prophecy
(which he understood to refer to Christ) that "righteousness shall be
the girdle of his loins."   (*Isa.* xi, 5.)

126. *unweeting:* unknowingly.

128. *full frequence:* thronged assembly.   The word is used in this
Latin sense again in II, 130.

129. *Gabriel,* whose name means "the strength or champion of God,"
appears as the guardian of Eden in *P.L.,* IV, 549.   His interest in

Gabriel, this day by proof thou shalt behold,   130
Thou and all Angels conversant on Earth
With man or men's affairs, how I begin
To verify that solemn message late,
On which I sent thee to the Virgin pure
In *Galilee,* that she should bear a Son   135
Great in Renown, and call'd the Son of God;
Then told'st her doubting how these things could be
To her a Virgin, that on her should come
The Holy Ghost, and the power of the highest
O'er-shadow her: this man born and now up-grown,   140
To show him worthy of his birth divine
And high prediction, henceforth I expose
To Satan; let him tempt and now assay
His utmost sublety, because he boasts
And vaunts of his great cunning to the throng   145
Of his Apostasy; he might have learnt

Christ as the angel of the annunciation to Mary and of the prophecy of John the Baptist's birth to his father, Zachariah, makes it natural to address him particularly here.

Milton made God speak *smiling* not merely because he remembered Virgil's picture of Jove answering Venus with a smile (*Aen.,* I, 254), but because he had the courage of his belief that, "If God be said 'to have made man in his own image,' it is not beneath the dignity of God to grieve in that for which he is grieved, or to be refreshed in that which refresheth him." (*C.D.,* I, ii.)

131–132. Hesiod's belief that "upon the bounteous earth Zeus has thrice ten thousand spirits, watchers of mortal men," (*Works and Days,* 252–254) is perhaps echoed in Adam's words,

> "Millions of spiritual Creatures walk the Earth
> Unseen."

> (*P.L.,* IV, 677–8.)

134–140. The story of Gabriel's visit to the Virgin is found in Luke i, 26–38.

135. *Galilee* was the most northern part of Palestine, bounded on the east by the Jordan and on the west by Phoenicia and the Mediterranean Sea.

143. *assay,* to put to a test of any kind, is now an archaic form of "essay" (except that we still use "assay" of metals). Compare the noun "assay" in 264 below.

145–146. *the throng Of his Apostasy;* Satan's host of apostate, or rebel angels. So Milton calls Abraham's followers abstractly his "numerous servitude." (*P.L.,* XII, 132.)

Less over-weening, since he fail'd in *Job,*
Whose constant perseverance overcame
Whate'er his cruel malice could invent.
He now shall know I can produce a man   150
Of female Seed, far abler to resist
All his solicitations, and at length
All his vast force, and drive him back to Hell,
Winning by Conquest what the first man lost
By fallacy surpris'd.   But first I mean   155
To exercise him in the Wilderness;
There he shall first lay down the rudiments
Of his great warfare, ere I send him forth
To conquer Sin and Death the two grand foes,
By Humiliation and strong Sufferance: 160
His weakness shall o'ercome Satanic strength
And all the world, and mass of sinful flesh;
That all the Angels and Ethereal Powers,
They now, and men hereafter, may discern
From what consummate virtue I have chose   165
This perfect Man, by merit call'd my Son,
To earn Salvation for the Sons of men.
    So spake the Eternal Father, and all Heaven

---

147. Compare the references to Job in 369 and 425 below and in III, 64, 67 and 95, and in the Introduction, §12.

155. *fallacy;* speciously false reasoning.

157. *rudiments* has its Latin force of "beginnings" and this line and the next may echo Evander's grief over the sad beginnings of his dead son, Pallas, as a warrior. (*Aen.,* XI, 157.)

159. Milton presumes that his reader knows his vivid pictures of *Sin* and *Death* in *P.L.,* II, 648–673 and X, 585–609.

161. Compare I Corinthians i, 27: ". . . God hath chosen the weak things of the world to confound the things which are mighty."

163. The *Ethereal Powers* are the angels, whose bodies Milton imagined as made of the "Ethereal mould" (*P.L.* II, 139) or refined fire which is the substance of heaven.

165–166. In *C.D.,* I, v, Milton denied any "unity of essence" between the Son and God, although there is perfect "intimacy of communion" between them. In *P.L.* the Son, who vanquishes the apostate angels, "by right of merit reigns" (VI, 43); as here, it is his *consummate virtue* which deserves the name Son. Compare the Introduction §10.

165. *chose* was not entirely extinct as a participle for more than a century after Milton's time.

Admiring stood a space, then into Hymns
Burst forth, and in Celestial measures mov'd, 170
Circling the Throne and Singing, while the hand
Sung with the voice, and this the argument.
   Victory and Triumph to the Son of God
Now ent'ring his great duel, not of arms,
But to vanquish by wisdom hellish wiles. 175
The Father knows the Son; therefore secure
Ventures his filial Virtue, though untried,
Against whate'er may tempt, whate'er seduce,
Allure, or terrify, or undermine.
Be frustrate, all ye stratagems of Hell, 180
And devilish machinations come to nought.
   So they in Heav'n their Odes and Vigils tun'd.
Meanwhile the Son of God, who yet some days
Lodg'd in *Bethabara* where *John* baptiz'd,
Musing and much revolving in his breast, 185
How best the mighty work he might begin
Of Saviour to mankind, and which way first

169–171. So in *P.L.*, V, 619, there is "song and dance" when God's Son is first presented to the angels. Compare *P.L.*, V, 178. The circling choirs of angels were a tradition which is most familiar in Dante's *Paradise* (canto xxviii) and Tibullus' description of his vision of Apollo "singing with hands (*i.e.*, on the lyre) and voice" (*Carmina*, III, iv, 41) also flashed into Milton's imagination.

172. *argument:* subject. Compare *P.L.*, I, 24, VI, 84, IX, 13.

174. Compare Michael's prophecy of this *duel* in *P.L.*, XII, 386–400.

175. The scansion is strange, but the accent ought probably not to be shifted from the first syllable of *vanquish*.

176. Compare Jesus' words: "As the Father knoweth me, even so know I the Father." (John x, 15.)
secure keeps its Latin force of "careless," or "justifiably free from all anxiety." So Milton condemned Charles I because "with a bloody surprise (he) falls on our secure forces." (*Eikonoklastes*, xviii.)

180. *frustrate* is equivalent to "frustrated." Compare "instruct" in 439 below. Adjectives derived, like these, from Latin perfect passive participles were often used with something like their Latin grammatical force.

182. *Vigils:* prayers or hymns sung in a service at night.

184. *Bethabara* was the ford of Jordan where John baptized. The town of the same name was just east of the river.

185–186. *much revolving . . . How:* a Latinism, equivalent to our idiom of "turning something over in the mind."

Publish his God-like office now mature,
One day forth walk'd alone, the Spirit leading
And his deep thoughts, the better to converse   190
With solitude, till far from track of men,
Thought following thought, and step by step led on,
He enter'd now the bordering Desert wild,
And with dark shades and rocks environ'd round,
His holy Meditations thus pursu'd.   195
    O what a multitude of thoughts at once
Awak'n'd in me swarm, while I consider
What from within I feel myself, and hear
What from without comes often to my ears,
Ill sorting with my present state compar'd.   200
When I was yet a child, no childish play
To me was pleasing, all my mind was set
Serious to learn and know, and thence to do
What might be public good; myself I thought
Born to that end, born to promote all truth,   205
All righteous things: therefore above my years,
The Law of God I read, and found it sweet,
Made it my whole delight, and in it grew
To such perfection that, ere yet my age
Had measur'd twice six years, at our great Feast   210
I went into the Temple, there to hear
The Teachers of our Law, and to propose
What might improve my knowledge or their own;

---

193. Gilbert quotes Adrichomius as placing Christ's temptation in
the Desert of Quarentana, between Jerusalem and Jericho.

200. *sorting:* corresponding.

200–214. Milton has been blamed for the supposed autobiography
in this passage and also for its representation of Jesus' youth; but,
compared with ideas of Christ's infancy and childhood which medieval
painters took from the apochryphal gospels, it is credible and humane.

205. Compare Jesus' words to Pilate: "To this end was I born, and
for this cause came I into the world, that I should bear witness unto
the truth."   (John xviii, 37.)

208. His "delight is in the law of the Lord" is the description of the
righteous man in Psalm i, 2.

209–214. The account of Jesus' talk with the doctors of the Law is
found in Luke ii, 46–50.

210. The *great Feast* is the Passover.

And was admir'd by all: yet this not all
To which my Spirit aspir'd, victorious deeds   215
Flam'd in my heart, heroic acts; one while
To rescue *Israel* from the *Roman* yoke,
Then to subdue and quell o'er all the earth
Brute violence and proud Tyrannic pow'r,
Till truth were freed, and equity restor'd: 220
Yet held it more humane, more heavenly, first
By winning words to conquer willing hearts,
And make persuasion do the work of fear;
At least to try, and teach the erring Soul
Not wilfully mis-doing, but unware   225
Misled: the stubborn only to subdue.
These growing thoughts my Mother soon perceiving
By words at times cast forth, inly rejoic'd,
And said to me apart, high are thy thoughts
O Son, but nourish them and let them soar   230
To what highth sacred virtue and true worth
Can raise them, though above example high;
By matchless Deeds express thy matchless Sire.
For know, thou art no Son of mortal man;
Though men esteem thee low of Parentage,   235
Thy Father is the Eternal King, who rules
All Heaven and Earth, Angels and Sons of men.
A messenger from God fore-told thy birth
Conceiv'd in me a Virgin; he fore-told
Thou shouldst be great and sit on *David's* Throne,   240
And of thy Kingdom there should be no end.
At thy Nativity a glorious Quire

---

214. *admir'd* has its original, Latin force of "wondered at." Compare Thomas Fuller's aphorism, "Admiration is the daughter of Ignorance."

218–219. Milton intended a contrast with Virgil's famous dictum that Rome's destiny was to impose peace in the world and quell the proud. (*Aen.*, VI, 851–853.)

222. Perhaps the nearest of many vague classical parallels to this line was suggested by Jortin in Xenophon's remark that it is more divine than human to govern men who freely consent. (*Oeconomics*, XXI, 12.)

228. Compare *inly* in 466 below and III, 203.

240–254. The details of Christ's birth are taken from the second chapter of Matthew and the first two chapters of Luke.

Of Angels in the fields of *Bethlehem* sung
To Shepherds watching at their folds by night,
And told them the Messiah now was born,   245
Where they might see him, and to thee they came,
Directed to the Manger where thou lay'st,
For in the Inn was left no better room.
A Star, not seen before, in Heaven appearing
Guided the Wise Men thither from the East,   250
To honour thee with Incense, Myrrh, and Gold,
By whose bright course led on they found the place,
Affirming it thy Star new grav'n in Heaven,
By which they knew thee King of *Israel* born.
Just *Simeon* and Prophetic *Anna,* warn'd   255
By Vision, found thee in the Temple, and spake,
Before the Altar and the vested Priest,
Like things of thee to all that present stood.
This having heard, straight I again revolv'd
The Law and Prophets, searching what was writ   260
Concerning the Messiah, to our Scribes
Known partly, and soon found of whom they spake
I am; this chiefly, that my way must lie
Through many a hard assay even to the death,
Ere I the promis'd Kingdom can attain,   265
Or work Redemption for mankind, whose sins'
Full weight must be transferr'd upon my head.
Yet neither thus dishearten'd or dismay'd,
The time prefixt I waited, when behold
The Baptist (of whose birth I oft had heard,   270

255–259. The prophecies of *just Simeon* and *Anna* about Christ are
in Luke ii, 25–36.

262–263. The eliptical construction, expanded, would be:
". . . I soon found that he of whom they spake I am . . ."

264. Compare the note on *assay* in 143 above.

266–267. Milton applied Isaiah's words—"The Lord hath laid on him
the iniquity of us all" (liii, 6)—to Christ.

268. *neither* . . . *or* for "neither . . . nor" is a result of the
influence of Latin idiom.

270–279. Mark's gospel opens with the account of John the Baptist
as "the voice of one crying in the wilderness, Prepare ye the way of
the Lord, make his paths straight." Details are taken from Matthew
iii, and Luke iii.

Not knew by sight) now come, who was to come
Before Messiah and his way prepare.
I as all others to his Baptism came,
Which I believ'd was from above; but he
Straight knew me, and with loudest voice proclaim'd 275
Me him (for it was shown him so from Heaven)
Me him whose Harbinger he was; and first
Refus'd on me his Baptism to confer,
As much his greater, and was hardly won.
But as I rose out of the laving stream,   280
Heaven open'd her eternal doors, from whence
The Spirit descended on me like a Dove;
And last the sum of all, my Father's voice,
Audibly heard from Heav'n, pronounc'd me his,
Me his beloved Son, in whom alone   285
He was well pleas'd; by which I knew the time
Now full, that I no more should live obscure,
But openly begin, as best becomes
The Authority which I deriv'd from Heaven.
And now by some strong motion I am led   290
Into this Wilderness, to what intent
I learn not yet; perhaps I need not know;
For what concerns my knowledge God reveals.
   So spake our Morning Star then in his rise,
And looking round on every side beheld   295
A pathless Desert, dusk with horrid shades;
The way he came not having mark'd, return

---

281. *eternal doors:* the "everlasting doors" of Psalm XXIV, 7 and 9.

286–7. The belief that "when the fulness of the time was come, God
sent forth his Son" (Gal. iv, 4) is involved in the treatment of both
Christ and Satan.   Compare lines 55–65 above.

291–293. In common with most Protestant commentators on the Gospels, Milton held that, "Even the Son . . . knows not all things
absolutely; there being some secret purposes, the knowledge of which
the Father has reserved to himself alone." (*C.D.,* I, v.)

294. In St. John's Apocalypse (xxii, 16) Jesus appears saying, "I
am . . . the bright and morning star."

296. *horrid* has its Latin meaning of "bristling."   *N.E.D.* cites Evelyn's
description of "a very romantic seate" on a "horrid Alp," *i.e.,* a mountain covered with trees.

297–298. The broken construction seems to mean that return was

Was difficult, by human steps untrod;
And he still on was led, but with such thoughts
Accompanied of things past and to come   300
Lodg'd in his breast, as well might recommend
Such Solitude before choicest Society.
Full forty days he pass'd, whether on hill
Sometimes, anon in shady vale, each night
Under the covert of some ancient Oak,   305
Or Cedar, to defend him from the dew,
Or harbour'd in one Cave, is not reveal'd;
Nor tasted human food, nor hunger felt
Till those days ended, hunger'd then at last
Among wild Beasts: they at his sight grew mild,   310
Nor sleeping him nor waking harm'd, his walk
The fiery Serpent fled, and noxious Worm,
The Lion and fierce Tiger glar'd aloof.
But now an aged man in Rural weeds,
Following, as seem'd, the quest of some stray Ewe,   315
Or wither'd sticks to gather, which might serve
Against a Winter's day when winds blow keen,
To warm him wet return'd from field at Eve,
He saw approach; who first with curious eye

difficult both because Jesus had not marked the way he came and because there were no people in the desert to make beaten paths.

302. Cowley's essay *Of Solitude* opens with the remark that Cicero's aphorism, "Never less alone than when in solitude" (*De Officiis*, III, i, 1), "is now become a very vulgar saying." Compare *P.L.* VIII, 427 and IX, 249.

310–313. Mark's statement (i, 13) that Jesus "was with the wild beasts" in the desert is employed because Christ was regarded as fulfilling Isaiah's prophecy (lxv, 25) that: "The wolf and the lamb shall feed together, and the lion shall eat straw like the bullock: and dust shall be the serpent's meat. They shall not hurt nor destroy in all my holy mountain, saith the Lord." Compare Isaiah, xi, 6–9, and Ezekiel xxxiv, 25.

312. *Worm*—serpent. The clown who brings the asp in *Antony and Cleopatra* (V, ii, 254–5) "makes a very good report o' the worm." Milton's memory was reaching back to the "fiery serpents" (Num. xxi, 6) of the desert experiences of the Israelites.

314. Satan's disguise has a long history, which is sketched in the Introduction §14.

319. Phrases like an "angry, jealous, lickerous," or "wandering eye" are cited by the *N.E.D.* since 1300. Here *curious* means "jealously

Perus'd him, then with words thus utter'd spake.   320
   Sir, what ill chance hath brought thee to this place
So far from path or road of men, who pass
In Troop or Caravan, for single none
Durst ever, who return'd, and dropt not here
His Carcase, pin'd with hunger and with drought?   325
I ask the rather, and the more admire,
For that to me thou seem'st the man whom late
Our new baptizing Prophet at the Ford
Of *Jordan* honour'd so, and call'd thee Son
Of God; I saw and heard, for we sometimes   330
Who dwell this wild, constrain'd by want, come forth
To Town or Village nigh (nighest is far)
Where aught we hear, and curious are to hear,
What happ'ns new; Fame also finds us out.
   To whom the Son of God.   Who brought me hither 335
Will bring me hence, no other Guide I seek.
   By Miracle he may, replied the Swain,
What other way I see not, for we here
Live on tough roots and stubs, to thirst inur'd
More than the Camel, and to drink go far,   340
Men to much misery and hardship born;
But if thou be the Son of God, Command
That out of these hard stones be made thee bread;

---

appraising," as it does in Mercutio's use of the phrase, "curious eye,"
in *Romeo and Juliet,* I, iv, 31.

320. *Perus'd* is similarly used by Adam when he says that on first
coming to himself after his creation he perused himself, "and Limb by
Limb Survey'd." (*P.L.,* VIII, 267–8.)

325. "Pine" is used transitively in *P.L.* XII, 77, where Adam sur-
mises that the "thin Air" on the summit of the tower of Babel would
"pine" the "entrails gross" of the builders.

331. "Dwell" is no longer used transitively, as it is here and again in
P.L., III, 670, and the use was never common.

333–334. aught . . . What: anything that.
Fame keeps its Latin meaning of "rumour" and has a trace of personification, as in Chaucer's *Hous of Fame* and Virgil's *Aeneid.*

339. Commentators have struggled to justify any meaning for *stubs*
which would suggest edibility, but Milton may have intended to suggest the futile search for food in a desert full of
                "stubs of trees,
Whereon nor fruit, nor leafe was euer seene."
              (*F.Q.,* I, ix, 34.)

So shalt thou save thyself and us relieve
With Food, whereof we wretched seldom taste.   345
   He ended, and the Son of God replied.
Think'st thou such force in Bread? is it not written
(For I discern thee other than thou seem'st)
Man lives not by Bread only, but each Word
Proceeding from the mouth of God, who fed   350
Our Fathers here with Manna?   In the Mount
Moses was forty days, nor eat nor drank,
And forty days *Eliah* without food
Wander'd this barren waste, the same I now:
Why dost thou then suggest to me distrust,   355
Knowing who I am, as I know who thou art?
   Whom thus answer'd th' Arch Fiend now undisguis'd.
'Tis true, I am that Spirit unfortunate,
Who, leagu'd with millions more in rash revolt,
Kept not my happy Station, but was driv'n   360
With them from bliss to the bottomless deep,
Yet to that hideous place not so confin'd
By rigour unconniving, but that oft,

---

349. Christ cites from Deuteronomy viii, 3.   The dialogue between him and Satan is based upon the passage in Luke iv, which is found in the Introduction §10, and upon Matthew's parallel account.

352. Exodus xxiv, 18, describes Moses, when he went up Mt. Sinai to receive the Ten Commandments, as being "in the mount forty days and forty nights."

353. *eat,* rather than "ate," was the usual past tense.
Eliah (or *Elijah,* as the name is spelled in II, 268 and 277), after eating the food which an angel brought to him, "went in the strength of that meat forty days and forty nights unto Horeb the mount of God."   (I Kings, xix, 8.)

355. The Introduction, §11, suggests that *distrust* is the essence of the first temptation.

357. The third syllable should have the first stress in this line.   Its odd scansion, with the pause after the spondee, *Arch Fiend,* makes a deliberate transition between the two speeches.

360. Jude (6) calls the devils "Angels which kept not their first estate."

361. Only four stresses are possible, but the pause at the end of the line and the very distinct caesura after *bliss* assimilate it to the five-stress pattern.

363. *unconniving:* literally "unwinking"; *i.e.,* never relaxing vigilance.

Leaving my dolorous Prison, I enjoy
Large liberty to round this Globe of Earth, 365
Or range in th' Air, nor from the Heav'n of Heav'ns
Hath he excluded my resort sometimes.
I came among the Sons of God, when he
Gave up into my hands *Uzzean Job*
To prove him, and illustrate his high worth; 370
And when to all his Angels he propos'd
To draw the proud King *Ahab* into fraud
That he might fall in *Ramoth,* they demurring,
I undertook that office, and the tongues
Of all his flattering Prophets glibb'd with lies 375
To his destruction, as I had in charge;
For what he bids I do. Though I have lost
Much lustre of my native brightness, lost
To be belov'd of God, I have not lost
To love, at least contémplate and admire 380
What I see excellent in good, or fair,
Or virtuous; I should so have lost all sense.
What can be then less in me than desire
To see thee and approach thee, whom I know

366–368. Satan is described (Job i, 6) as presenting himself before
God's throne in heaven with the other "sons of God." Compare the
Introduction §11.

369. *Uz* may have lain somewhere in Arabia Deserta, where Fuller
placed it, but it was "a land . . . obscure" (III, 94) to Milton.

370. *illustrate* keeps its Latin meaning of "add lustre to."

371–377. In I Kings xxii, 19–22, Milton read that "a lying spirit"
volunteered before the throne of God to deceive the prophets, or sooth-
sayers, of the wicked king Ahaz and so lure him to his death at Ramoth
in Gilead.

372. *fraud* keeps a Latin force of "wickedness which is deceitful" in
the doer. So Satan is said to draw Eve (*P.L.,* IX, 643–644) and the
rebel angels (*P.L.* VII, 143) into fraud.

373. *they demurring:* when they hesitated. An absolute construction,
like many others which are a mark of the influence of Latin syntax upon
Milton.

377–378. Tradition identified Satan with Lucifer,
            "brighter once amidst the Host
    Of Angels, than that Star the Stars among."
                (*P.L.,* VII, 132–133.)

Declar'd the Son of God, to hear attent   385
Thy wisdom, and behold thy God-like deeds?
Men generally think me much a foe
To all mankind: why should I? they to me
Never did wrong or violence; by them
I lost not what I lost, rather by them   390
I gain'd what I have gain'd, and with them dwell
Copartner in these Regions of the World,
If not disposer; lend them oft my aid,
Oft my advice by presages and signs,
And answers, oracles, portents and dreams,   395
Whereby they may direct their future life.
Envy they say excites me, thus to gain
Companions of my misery and woe.
At first it may be; but long since with woe
Nearer acquainted, now I feel by proof,   400
That fellowship in pain divides not smart,
Nor lightens aught each man's peculiar load:
Small consolation then, were Man adjoin'd.
This wounds me most (what can it less) that Man,
Man fall'n shall be restor'd, I never more.   405
    To whom our Saviour sternly thus replied.
Deservedly thou griev'st, compos'd of lies

---

385. *attent:* attentively.

393–396. Milton shared the widespread interest of his age in the problem of the ancient oracles, whose answers to questions were as "truthful" as those of modern "mediums"; but, like St. Augustine and all the fathers of the Church, he regarded the spirits which spoke in the oracles as mere pretenders to be divine "messengers and bringers of men's good fortunes." (*The City of God,* VII, xxii.)

397–9. From his first sight of Adam's happiness in Paradise (*P.L.,* IV, 115.) envy is a dominant motive with Satan.

401–403. Milton thought of the tradition represented in the question of Marlowe's Faustus to Mephistophilis as to why Lucifer desires his soul. The answer is, to "enlarge his kingdom," for misery loves company. (*The Tragical History of Doctor Faustus,* II, i.) The thought was a commonplace as far back as Seneca's letter *To Polybius on Consolation* (XII, ii). Like Milton, Sir Thomas Browne challenged "that natural fallacy of Man, to take comfort from Society, and think adversities less, because others also suffer them." (*Christian Morals,* I, xviii.)

407. In John viii, 44, Jesus calls the devil "a liar, and the father of it."

From the beginning, and in lies wilt end;
Who boast'st release from Hell, and leave to come
Into the Heav'n of Heavens; thou com'st indeed,   410
As a poor miserable captive thrall
Comes to the place where he before had sat
Among the Prime in Splendor, now depos'd,
Ejected, emptied, gaz'd, unpitied, shunn'd,
A spectacle of ruin or of scorn   415
To all the Host of Heaven; the happy place
Imparts to thee no happiness, no joy,
Rather inflames thy torment, representing
Lost bliss, to thee no more communicable,
So never more in Hell than when in Heaven.   420
But thou art serviceable to Heaven's King.
Wilt thou impute to obedience what thy fear
Extorts, or pleasure to do ill excites?
What but thy malice mov'd thee to misdeem
Of righteous *Job,* then cruelly to afflict him   425
With all inflictions?   But his patience won.
The other service was thy chosen task,
To be a liar in four hundred mouths;
For lying is thy sustenance, thy food.
Yet thou pretend'st to truth; all Oracles   430
By thee are giv'n, and what confest more true
Among the Nations?   That hath been thy craft,

---

413. *Prime:* first, foremost.

414. *gazed* (at): compare "dwell" without the usual preposition following it in 331 above.

420. When Satan was in Eden,
     "the hot Hell that always in him burns,
     Though in mid Heav'n, soon ended his delight."
                    (*P.L.,* IX, 467–468.)
Compare *P.L.,* I, 255 and IV, 20.

423. In *P.L.,* I, 160, Satan tells Beelzebub that their "sole delight" will be "ever to do ill."

428. The lying prophets of Ahaz mentioned in 475 above, numbered four hundred.

430–432. Robert Burton expressed the prevailing belief of the times when he said that the greater demons which fell from heaven with Satan became "those false gods of the Gentiles, which were adored heretofore in several Idols, and gave Oracles at Delphos, and elsewhere; whose Prince is Beelzebub." (*Anatomy,* I, ii, 1, 2.)

By mixing somewhat true to vent more lies.
But what have been thy answers, what but dark,
Ambiguous and with double sense deluding,   435
Which they who ask'd have seldom understood,
And not well understood as good not known?
Who ever by consulting at thy shrine
Return'd the wiser, or the more instruct
To fly or follow what concern'd him most,   440
And run not sooner to his fatal snare?
For God hath justly giv'n the Nations up
To thy Delusions; justly, since they fell
Idolatrous; but when his purpose is
Among them to declare his Providence   445
To thee not known, whence hast thou then thy truth,
But from him or his Angels President
In every Province, who, themselves disdaining
To approach thy Temples, give thee in command

434–441. Ancient literature contained much sceptical discussion of
the oracles, such as the lost collection of their false, true, and
treacherously ambiguous replies by Chrysippus, which Cicero mentioned (*Of Divination*, II, lvi). The Fathers of the Church, like Lactantius (*Divine Institutes*, II, xvi), attributed the oracles to the demons
posing as gods, and the "words deceiving" of Apollo and the other
pagan deities in Milton's *Nativity* (l. 175) are an expression of that
view. Although scientific thought was moving toward the essentially
modern opinion of that theory which Fontenelle advanced in his *History of Oracles* (1687), thinkers of all schools shared Thomas Hobbes's
lively contempt for "the ambiguous or senslesse answers of the Priests at
Delphi, Delos, Ammon, and other famous oracles." (*Leviathan*, I, xii.)

439. *instruct:* instructed. Compare the note on "frustrate" in l. 180
above.

447–448. Jewish tradition regarded the points of the compass as angelic provinces. Before his fall, Lucifer possessed the "Quarters of the
North" (*P.L.*, V, 689), where he rallied his rebel angels. Gabriel's
post was in the east, where Milton placed him when he was set as a
watchman
                "Against the eastern Gate of Paradise."
                          (*P.L.*, IV, 542.)

449–453. Lactantius (*Institutes*, II, xvi) explained that by virtue of
their experience as God's ministers before they fell the demons could
claim honours not properly theirs by more or less accurately forecasting
the future. Fontenelle interpreted similar passages in Tertullian and
other early Fathers as having contributed to keep pagan superstitions
alive for centuries in the Christian world. (*Histoire des Oracles*, iii.)

What to the smallest tittle thou shalt say   450
To thy Adorers? thou with trembling fear,
Or like a Fawning Parasite obey'st;
Then to thyself ascrib'st the truth fore-told.
But this thy glory shall be soon retrench'd;
No more shalt thou by oracling abuse   455
The Gentiles; henceforth Oracles are ceast,
And thou no more with Pomp and Sacrifice
Shalt be inquir'd at *Delphos* or elsewhere,
At least in vain, for they shall find thee mute.
God hath now sent his living Oracle   460
Into the World, to teach his final will,
And sends his Spirit of Truth henceforth to dwell
In pious Hearts, an inward Oracle
To all truth requisite for men to know.
    So spake our Saviour; but the subtle Fiend,   465
Though inly stung with anger and disdain,
Dissembl'd, and this answer smooth return'd.
    Sharply thou hast insisted on rebuke,
And urg'd me hard with doings, which not will
But misery hath wrested from me; where   470
Easily canst thou find one miserable,
And not inforc'd oft-times to part from truth;
If it may stand him more in stead to lie,
Say and unsay, feign, flatter, or abjure?

454–464. Milton's most interesting use of the tradition that at the
birth of Christ the oracles ceased throughout the world is in *Nativity*,
173–180. It was specifically to attack this tradition in its crude form
that Fontenelle wrote, but he acknowledged its interpretation in Platonic
Christian literature as meaning that after God's Son, or the Logos of
Platonic thought, had been incarnated in the world the impostures of
paganism little by little disappeared. Milton's emphasis here upon the
living Oracle (*i.e.,* Christ as distinguished from the Holy Spirit) suggests that he had in mind St. Augustine's distinction between the
instruction which men supposed that they got from oracles and the
real illumination that comes from God's Son and Holy Spirit. (*The
City of God,* IX, xxiii.)

458. *Delphos* is a form drawn from the Greek accusative plural. The
nominative, *Delphi,* is more usual. Apollo's Delphian oracle, situated
in a magnificent gorge in Phocis, in central Greece, was the most
famous shrine in the Greek world.

462. Jesus promised his disciples that "when he, the Spirit of truth,
is come, he will guide you into all truth." (John xvi, 13.)

But thou art plac't above me, thou art Lord;   475
From thee I can and must submiss endure
Check or reproof, and glad to scape so quit.
Hard are the ways of truth, and rough to walk,
Smooth on the tongue discourst, pleasing to th' ear,
And tuneable as Silvan Pipe or Song;   480
What wonder then if I delight to hear
Her dictates from thy mouth? most men admire
Virtue, who follow not her lore: permit me
To hear thee when I come (since no man comes)
And talk at least, though I despair to attain.   485
Thy Father, who is holy, wise and pure,
Suffers the Hypocrite or Atheous Priest
To tread his Sacred Courts, and minister
About his Altar, handling holy things,
Praying or vowing, and vouchsaf'd his voice   490
To *Balaam* Reprobate, a Prophet yet
Inspir'd; disdain not such access to me.
　　To whom our Saviour with unalter'd brow.
Thy coming hither, though I know thy scope,
I bid not or forbid; do as thou find'st   495
Permission from above; thou canst not more.
　　He added not; and Satan, bowing low

---

476. *submiss:* submissive. Or perhaps the word was felt as equivalent to the Latin participle from which it comes and meant "submitted," *i.e.,* because I am subjected to thee, I must endure, *etc.*

477. *quit* is still used colloquially to mean "rid of" or "free from."

480. So Milton called the prayers of Adam and Eve
　　　"More tuneable than needed Lute or Harp
　　　　To add more sweetness."
　　　　　　　(*P.L.,* V, 151.)

487. *Atheous:* atheistic, unbelieving.

490–492. When Balaam was urged to curse the Israelites by his master, the King of Moab, his answer was that God had commanded him "to bless; and he hath blessed; and I cannot reverse it." (Num. xxiii, 20.)

491. *Reprobate:* alienated from God, "damned" or desperately wicked.

494. *scope:* purpose. Literally the word means the object of a person's view, or a mark to shoot at.

497–499. *gray dissimulation* crystallizes Satan's nature as the great deceiver, disappearing like his own dark delusions in the presence of Truth. There is a resemblance in Milton's scene to the disappearances

His gray dissimulation, disappear'd
Into thin Air diffus'd: for now began
Night with her sullen wing to double-shade   500
The Desert; Fowls in thir clay nests were couch't;
And now wild Beasts came forth the woods to roam.

The End of the First Book

The Second Book

MEANWHILE the new baptiz'd, who yet remain'd
At *Jordan* with the Baptist, and had seen
Him whom they heard so late expressly call'd
Jesus Messiah, Son of God declar'd,
And on that high Authority had believ'd,   5
And with him talkt, and with him lodg'd, I mean
Andrew and *Simon,* famous after known
With others though in Holy Writ not nam'd,
Now missing him thir joy so lately found,
So lately found, and so abruptly gone,   10
Began to doubt, and doubted many days,
And as the days increas'd, increas'd thir doubt:
Sometimes they thought he might be only shown,
And for a time caught up to God, as once
Moses was in the Mount, and missing long;   15
And the great *Thisbite* who on fiery wheels
Rode up to Heaven, yet once again to come.

---

of the gods in Homer, Virgil and Ovid; *e.g.,* Mercury's vanishing into
thin air after an interview with Aeneas. (*Aen.,* IV, 278.)

4. The Hebrew word *Messiah* was translated in the Septuagint by
the Greek word, *Christ.* Both words mean "anointed one."

7. John's Gospel says that about the time of Jesus' baptism Andrew
and Simon Peter went with him "and saw where he dwelt, and abode
with him that day." (John i, 39.)

14–15. Compare the note on I, 352.

16–17. The *great Thisbite:* Eliah or Elijah, as Milton spells the name
in 268 and 277 below. He found the form *Thisbite* in the Vulgate and
in some early English translations of the Bible instead of Tishbite in
the Authorized Version (I Kings xvii, 1). Thisbe was a city east of

Therefore as those young Prophets then with care
Sought lost *Eliah,* so in each place these
Nigh to *Bethabara;* in *Jericho*   20
The City of Palms, *Aenon,* and *Salem* Old,
Machaerus and each Town or City wall'd
On this side the broad lake *Genezaret,*
Or in *Peraea,* but return'd in vain.
Then on the bank of *Jordan,* by a Creek,   25
Where winds with Reeds and Osiers whisp'ring play,
Plain Fishermen, (no greater men them call)
Close in a Cottage low together got,
Thir unexpected loss and plaints out breath'd.

---

the Jordan in Gilead, but in *Elegy IV, 97,* Milton confused it with
Thebez by Mount Ephraim.

In *P.L.* (III, 522) Milton referred to the story in II Kings ii, 11, of
the translation of the prophet Elijah to heaven,

"Rapt in a Chariot drawn by fiery Steeds."

Compare his grimly humorous use of the story in the Epigram (I)
on Guy Fawkes, and the allusion in *The Passion* (36–37).

Malachi (iv, 5) prophesied the return of Elijah "before the coming
of the great and dreadful day of the Lord," and Jesus told the Jews
that, if they would accept him, John the Baptist was "Elias, which
was for to come." (Mat. xi, 14.)

18–19. After Elijah was translated, "fifty strong men" of the "sons
of the prophets" searched for him "three days, but found him not."
(II Kings ii, 15–17.)

20–24. Identification of these places is interesting, but it gives only
a pale suggestion of the delight that was taken in such biblical panoramas as Thomas Fuller drew in *A Pisgah-sight of Palestine and The
Confines thereof.*

20. *Bethabara* has been mentioned in I, 184. *Jericho,* just west of
the Jordan and about five miles from the Dead Sea, is called the "city
of palm trees" in Deuteronomy xxxiv, 3.

21. Beside baptizing at Bethabara, "John also was baptizing in Aenon
near to Salim." (John iii, 23.) Both places seem to have been on the
west bank of the Jordan.

22. *Machaerus* was a tremendous fortress on a wild mountain in
Peraea, in the desert east of the Dead Sea. It was there that legends
fixed the death of John the Baptist.

23. *Genezaret* was an alternative name for the Sea of Galilee, a lake
formed by the widening of the Jordan north of Bethabara.

24. *Peraea* was the region east of the Jordan, opposite the towns on
"this side," *i.e.,* the west bank of the river as Milton visualized it from
his house in London.

27. The words in parentheses seem to be a deliberate reminiscence of

Alas, from what high hope to what relapse   30
Unlook'd for are we fall'n!   Our eyes beheld
Messiah certainly now come, so long
Expected of our Fathers; we have heard
His words, his wisdom full of grace and truth,
Now, now, for sure, deliverance is at hand,   35
The Kingdom shall to *Israel* be restor'd:
Thus we rejoic'd, but soon our joy is turn'd
Into perplexity and new amaze:
For whither is he gone, what accident
Hath rapt him from us? will he now retire   40
After appearance, and again prolong
Our expectation?   God of *Israel,*
Send thy Messiah forth, the time is come;
Behold the Kings of the Earth how they oppress
Thy chosen, to what highth thir pow'r unjust   45
They have exalted, and behind them cast
All fear of thee; arise and vindicate
Thy Glory, free thy people from thir yoke!
But let us wait; thus far he hath perform'd,
Sent his Anointed, and to us reveal'd him,   50
By his great Prophet, pointed at and shown,

Spenser's reference to himself in *The Shepheardes Calendar* (January,
1) as

"A shepheards boye (no better doe him call)."

30–31. *from what high hope . . . are we fall'n!* an odd applica-
tion of a phrase in Terence's comedy, *The Self-tormentor* (II, iii, 9),
which was a by-word with every schoolboy in Milton's England.

34. An echo of John's passage (i, 14); "And the Word was made
flesh, and dwelt among us, . . . full of grace and truth."

35–36. Milton adapted the question put to Christ by the disciples
when they first met him after the Resurrection: "Lord, wilt thou at
this time restore again the kingdom to Israel?" (Acts i, 6.)

38. *amaze:* amazement, stupefaction. Except rarely in poetry, the
word is obsolete.

40. *rapt:* probably from the obsolete verb "rap," which meant "to
snatch" or "to carry away."

43. Milton intended the sense of breathless expectation of the fulfilment of the prophecies about the Messiah to pervade his poem.
Compare I, 55–65 and 286.

50. *Anointed* is the English equivalent of Messiah. Compare the
note on 4 above.

In public, and with him we have convers'd;
Let us be glad of this, and all our fears
Lay on his Providence; he will not fail
Nor will withdraw him now, nor will recall,   55
Mock us with his blest sight, then snatch him hence,
Soon we shall see our hope, our joy return.
    Thus they out of their plaints new hope resume
To find whom at the first they found unsought:
But to his Mother *Mary,* when she saw   60
Others return'd from Baptism, not her Son,
Nor left at *Jordan,* tidings of him none;
Within her breast, though calm, her breast though pure,
Motherly cares and fears got head, and rais'd
Some troubl'd thoughts, which she in sighs thus clad.   65
   O what avails me now that honour high
To have conceiv'd of God, or that salute,
Hail highly favour'd, among women blest!
While I to sorrows am no less advanc't,
And fears as eminent, above the lot   70
Of other women, by the birth I bore,
In such a season born when scarce a Shed
Could be obtain'd to shelter him or me
From the bleak air; a Stable was our warmth,
A Manger his; yet soon enforc't to fly   75
Thence into *Egypt,* till the Murd'rous King
Were dead, who sought his life, and missing fill'd
With Infant blood the streets of *Bethlehem.*
From *Egypt* home return'd, in *Nazareth*
Hath been our dwelling many years, his life   80
Private, unactive, calm, contemplative,

---

60. *to his Mother Mary* is a Latin, dative construction, equivalent to "for his mother, Mary, there were cares," *etc.*

62. The double negative and the detached, or absolute construction are both Latin.

68–69. The salute is in the words of Gabriel at the Annunciation. (Luke i, 28.)

75–78. Herod the Great was *the Murd'rous King* who "slew all the children that were in Bethlehem" (Mat. ii, 16) and drove Joseph and Mary to take refuge in Egypt.

79. Nazareth, in Galilee, is still the site of a church which stands over the traditional place of the Annunciation.

Little suspicious to any King; but now
Full grown to Man, acknowledg'd, as I hear,
By *John* the Baptist, and in public shown,
Son own'd from Heaven by his Father's voice;   85
I look't for some great change; to Honour? no,
But trouble, as old *Simon* plain fore-told,
That to the fall and rising he should be
Of many in *Israel,* and to a sign
Spoken against, that through my very Soul   90
A sword shall pierce, this is my favour'd lot,
My Exaltation to Afflictions high;
Afflicted I may be, it seems, and blest;
I will not argue that, nor will repine.
But where delays he now? some great intent   95
Conceals him: when twelve years he scarce had seen,
I lost him, but so found, as well I saw
He could not lose himself; but went about
His Father's business; what he meant I mus'd,
Since understand; much more his absence now   100
Thus long to some great purpose he obscures.

---

82. *suspicious:* worthy of suspicion.

83–86. The participles, *grown, acknowledg'd, shown* and *own'd,* stand apart from the main verb, *look'd,* in a kind of Latin absolute construction. Before every one of them Milton felt an unexpressed phrase like "since he is."

87–91. Simeon's prophecy has been recalled in I, 255–256. The words here closely paraphrase Luke ii, 34–35.

95. *intent:* intention. Compare the "sincere intent" of *P.L.,* III, 192.

97. *as:* that. This use occurs frequently in Shakespeare, *e.g.,*
            "You shall be so received
    As you shall deem yourself lodged in my heart."
            (*Love's Labour's Lost,* II, i, 174.)

98–99. Jesus' justification of himself, to Mary, when, aged twelve, he left her to talk for three days in the Temple with the scribes, was, "Wist ye not that I must be about my Father's business?" (Luke ii, 49.)

99–104. Luke's account adds that "his mother kept all these sayings in her heart." (ii, 51. Compare Luke ii, 19.)

99. *mus'd:* wondered.

101. *obscures:* hides. The word often kept its Latin meaning of "make dark" or "conceal."

But I to wait with patience am inur'd;
My heart hath been a store-house long of things
And sayings laid up, portending strange events.
    Thus *Mary* pondering oft, and oft to mind   105
Recalling what remarkably had pass'd
Since first her Salutation heard, with thoughts
Meekly compos'd awaited the fulfilling:
The while her Son tracing the Desert wild,
Sole, but with holiest Meditations fed,   110
Into himself descended, and at once
All his great work to come before him set;
How to begin, how to accomplish best
His end of being on Earth, and mission high:
For Satan with sly preface to return   115
Had left him vacant, and with speed was gone
Up to the middle Region of thick Air,
Where all his Potentates in Council sat;
There without sign of boast, or sign of joy,
Solicitous and blank he thus began.   120
    Princes, Heaven's ancient Sons, Ethereal Thrones,
Demonian Spirits now, from the Element

_____

102. *inur'd:* accustomed, used (in the colloquial sense of "using to do
something" or "being used to something").

109. *trace:* traverse.

111. *Into himself descended:* perhaps a reminiscence of similar language in Persius' fourth *Satire,* l. 23.

116. *vacant:* unoccupied, at leisure.

117. An accepted scientific theory divided the air into three levels
or regions, in the middle of which Bacon said that "Rains [are con-
densed] by the Cold" (*Silva,* §81). The middle region was thought to
be the special haunt of demons, which, as Burton pointed out
(*Anatomy,* II, ii, 3) are called "Princes of the Air" because they cause
storms and all portents in the sky. It is, of course, a demonic storm
which sweeps the desert in IV, 409–425. Compare *P.L.,* I, 516.

120. *Solicitous:* disturbed and excited.
    blank: at a loss what to say. Milton used the word in *Eikonoklastes*
(xxi) to describe the Duchess of Burgundy when in open council her
own letters proved her guilty of a lie.

122–124. Milton's interest in the belief that the devils were attached
to the four elements was expressed in *Il Penseroso* (93–96). He found
it in the writings of alchemists like Cornelius Agrippa and of Neo-
Platonists like Michael Psellus, and in Jewish tradition it went back to
the Book of Enoch (lx, 11–21). To some extent it was implicit in

Each of his reign allotted, rightlier call'd,
Powers of Fire, Air, Water, and Earth beneath,
So may we hold our place and these mild seats   125
Without new trouble; such an Enemy
Is ris'n to invade us, who no less
Threat'ns than our expulsion down to Hell.
I, as I undertook, and with the vote
Consenting in full frequence was impow'r'd,   130
Have found him, view'd him, tasted him, but find
Far other labour to be undergone
Than when I dealt with *Adam* first of Men,
Though *Adam* by his Wife's allurement fell,
However to this Man inferior far,   135
If he be Man by Mother's side, at least
With more than human gifts from Heav'n adorn'd,
Perfections absolute, Graces divine,
And amplitude of mind to greatest Deeds.
Therefore I am return'd, lest confidence   140
Of my success with *Eve* in Paradise
Deceive ye to persuasion over-sure
Of like succeeding here; I summon all
Rather to be in readiness with hand
Or counsel to assist; lest I who erst   145
Thought none my equal, now be over-match'd.

---

the interpretation of the gods by the mythologists of the Renaissance
as sovereigns of the elements, Vulcan of the fire,
       "Ops, of the earth; and Juno, of the ayre;
          Neptune, of seas."
                    (*F.Q.*, VII, vii, 26.)

125. *So may we hold* may express a hope that the devils will keep
their rule of the elements or a fear that, if prophecy is fulfilled, they
will lose it.

131. *tasted:* examined. Basically the word means "to investigate by
touching."

136. In the original editions the comma did not precede, but followed, *at least.*

139. Milton had in mind an ideal that stemmed from Aristotle's
great-souled man, whose supreme virtue of magnanimity consisted in
honourable ambition. (*Nicomachean Ethics*, IV, iii.) He thought of
Christ as magnanimous in the way that he himself defined the term;
"Magnanimity is shown, when in seeking or avoiding . . . riches, advantages, or honours, we are actuated by a regard to our own dignity,
rightly understood." (*C.D.*, II, ix.)

So spake the old Serpent doubting, and from all
With clamor was assur'd thir utmost aid
At his command; when from amidst them rose
Belial the dissolutest Spirit that fell,   150
The sensuallest, and after *Asmodai*
The fleshliest Incubus, and thus advis'd.
   Set women in his eye and in his walk,
Among daughters of men the fairest found;
Many are in each Region passing fair   155
As the noon Sky; more like to Goddesses
Than Mortal Creatures, graceful and discreet,
Expert in amorous Arts, enchanting tongues
Persuasive, Virgin majesty with mild
And sweet allay'd, yet terrible to approach,   160
Skill'd to retire, and in retiring draw
Hearts after them tangl'd in Amorous Nets.
Such object hath the power to soft'n and tame
Severest temper, smooth the rugged'st brow,
Enerve, and with voluptuous hope dissolve,   165
Draw out with credulous desire, and lead
At will the manliest, resolutest breast,

---

150. The word *Belial,* in the Old Testament, was simply an abstract noun meaning "worthlessness" and was used in the Hebraic phrase "sons of Belial" to mean, as Milton said, "the draff of men." In late Jewish and in medieval tradition it began vaguely to mean Satan or a distinct demon, but as such Milton first gave it real character in the great appearances in *P.L.* I, 490, II, 109, 226, and VI, 620.

151. *Asmodai,* or Asmodeus, as Milton called him in *P.L.,* IV, 168, is the lustful angel of the apochryphal Book of Tobit. He loved Tobit's wife, Sara, and on their wedding nights killed seven men who married her.

152. In the Middle Ages belief in *incubi* was universal enough to be the basis of established criminal laws and it persisted in the notion that witches "use venerie with a divell called Incubus." (Reginald Scot, *Discoverie of Witchcraft,* II, ix.)

160. *allay'd:* tempered, softened.

164. *temper:* temperament, character. Compare *P.L.,* II, 218.
rugged'st: very corrugated, frowning. Compare the nightingale's song "Smoothing the rugged brow of Night" in *Il Penseroso,* 58. For the comparison of the adjective see Abbott, §473.

165. *Enerve:* enervate.

166. There seems to be a deliberate allusion to Horace's "credulous hope" of response from his mistress in a lover's heart. (*Odes,* IV, i, 30.)

As the Magnetic hardest Iron draws.
Women, when nothing else, beguil'd the heart
Of wisest *Solomon,* and made him build,   170
And made him bow to the Gods of his Wives.
　　To whom quick answer Satan thus return'd.
Belial, in much uneven scale thou weigh'st
All others by thyself; because of old
Thou thyself doat'st on womankind, admiring   175
Thir shape, thir colour, and attractive grace,
None are, thou think'st, but taken with such toys.
Before the Flood thou with thy lusty Crew,
False titl'd Sons of God, roaming the Earth,
Cast wanton eyes on the daughters of men,   180
And coupl'd with them, and begot a race.
Have we not seen, or by relation heard,
In Courts and Regal Chambers how thou lurk'st,
In Wood or Grove by mossy Fountain side,
In Valley or Green Meadow, to way-lay   185
Some beauty rare, *Calisto, Clymene,*
Daphne, or *Semele, Antiopa,*
Or *Amymone, Syrinx,* many more
Too long, then lay'st thy scapes on names ador'd,

---

168. *Magnetic:* magnet. The word was often used as a noun.

170. In *P.L.,* I, 444–446, there is a similar allusion to the story of Solomon's worship of the gods of his wives in I Kings xi, 1–8.

178–181. Here and in *P.L.,* III, 463–465 (in contrast with the interpretation in *P.L.,* XI, 574–592) the strange story of the "sons of God" who took wives of the "daughters of men" (Gen. vi, 2) is interpreted as if it referred to the fallen angels. As far back as Clement of Alexandria Christian apologists had treated the pagan myths of the amours of the gods as Milton does here, but the charm of his passage betrays his admiration of Ovid's handling of those stories in the *Metamorphoses.*

186–188. All these nymphs figure in Ovid's *Metamorphoses;* some of them famous, like Daphne, whom Apollo loved (see *Comus,* 661, note), and others mentioned for their amours with the sylvan gods. Professor Osgood suggests (p. 10.) that Milton was influenced here by patristic arraignments of the gods for their incontinence, like that in the *Protrepticus* (27 P, ff.) of Clement of Alexandria.

189. *scapes*—escapades. The word was common in this sense. *N.E.D.* cites Wilson's *Arte of Rhetorique:* "Maydens that haue made a scape are commonly called to be nurses."
　　too long; i.e., to mention all of them. Compare *P.L.* III, 473.

Apollo, Neptune, Jupiter, or *Pan,*   190
Satyr, or Faun, or Silvan?   But these haunts
Delight not all; among the Sons of Men,
How many have with a smile made small account
Of beauty and her lures, easily scorn'd
All her assaults, on worthier things intent?   195
Remember that *Pellean* Conqueror,
A youth, how all the Beauties of the East
He slightly view'd, and slightly over-pass'd;
How hee surnam'd of *Africa* dismiss'd
In his prime youth the fair *Iberian* maid.   200
For *Solomon,* he liv'd at ease, and full
Of honour, wealth, high fare, aim'd not beyond
Higher design than to enjoy his State;
Thence to the bait of Women lay expos'd.
But he whom we attempt is wiser far   205
Than *Solomon,* of more exalted mind,
Made and set wholly on the accomplishment
Of greatest things; what woman will you find,
Though of this Age the wonder and the fame,
On whom his leisure will vouchsafe an eye   210
Of fond desire? or should she confident,
As sitting Queen ador'd on Beauty's Throne,
Descend with all her winning charms begirt
To enamour, as the Zone of *Venus* once
Wrought that effect on *Jove,* so Fables tell;   215
How would one look from his Majestic brow,

---

196. Alexander the Great was born at Pella, the capital of Macedonia. In his Life by Plutarch, Milton read that after the battle of Issus
he treated the wife and daughters of Darius as "ladies, not only of high
rank, but also of great modesty and virtue, and took care that they
should not hear an indecent word, nor have the least cause to suspect
any danger to their honour."

199–200. Livy's *History of Rome* (xxvi, 50) says that Scipio—who,
Milton later recalls, "brought down The Carthaginian pride" (III, 35)
and so won the title of Africanus—treated one of his beautiful Spanish
prisoners at the capture of Cartagena with distinguished respect. Livy's
candid avowal of his diplomatic motive in doing so makes it a little
hard to understand why "the praise of . . . Scipion" (Spenser, *Virgils
Gnat,* 613) should have been as cordial as it was in Renaissance poetry.

214–215. Homer describes Jove's surrender to Juno when she came

Seated as on the top of Virtue's hill,
Discount'nance her despis'd, and put to rout
All her array; her female pride deject,
Or turn to reverent awe! for Beauty stands   220
In the admiration only of weak minds
Led captive; cease to admire, and all her Plumes
Fall flat and shrink into a trivial toy,
At every sudden slighting quite abasht:
Therefore with manlier objects we must try   225
His constancy, with such as have more show
Of worth, of honour, glory, and popular praise;
Rocks whereon greatest men have oftest wreck'd;
Or that which only seems to satisfy
Lawful desires of Nature, not beyond;   230
And now I know he hungers where no food
Is to be found, in the wide Wilderness;
The rest commit to me, I shall let pass
No advantage, and his strength as oft assay.
    He ceas'd, and heard thir grant in loud acclaim;   235

---

to him wearing the girdle of Venus. It was decorated with all the
symbols of passion, Homer says (*Il.*, XIV, 214–218), for Venus'

> "husband Vulcan whylome for her sake,
> When first he loved her with heart entire,
> This pretious ornament, they say, did make."
>   (*F.Q.*, IV, v, 4.)

217. The subject of *seated* is implied in *his*. Compare "the Prison of
his Tyranny who Reigns." (*P.L.*, II, 59.)

Newton suggested that Milton had in mind the hill to which the
allegorical figure of Virtue points in the illustrations of Prodicus' famous
apologue, *The Judgment of Hercules*, and mentioned particularly that
by Annibal Caracci in the Farnese palace in Rome. Compare Sonnet,
Lady that in the prime, 4, note.

220–222. Milton shared the contempt which Bacon expressed (*Essay*
X) for a lover who can "do nothing but kneel before a little idol, and
make himself a subject, though not of the mouth (as beasts are), yet
of the eye; which was given him for higher purposes."

222–223. Milton certainly was thinking of a peacock and probably,
as Dunster suggested, of a passage in Ovid's *Art of Love*, I, 627, which
says that the bird of Juno shows its plumes only to an admiring audience.

235. *grant:* assent. The first meaning of the word is "consent" or
"permission."

Then forthwith to him takes a chosen band
Of Spirits likest to himself in guile
To be at hand, and at his beck appear,
If cause were to unfold some active Scene
Of various persons, each to know his part;   240
Then to the Desert takes with these his flight;
Where still from shade to shade the Son of God
After forty days fasting had remain'd,
Now hung'ring first, and to himself thus said.

    Where will this end? four times ten days I have pass'd, 245
Wand'ring this woody maze, and human food
Nor tasted, nor had appetite: that Fast
To Virtue I impute not, or count part
Of what I suffer here; if Nature need not,
Or God support Nature without repast   250
Though needing, what praise is it to endure?
But now I feel I hunger, which declares,
Nature hath need of what she asks; yet God
Can satisfy that need some other way,
Though hunger still remain: so it remain   255
Without this body's wasting, I content me,
And from the sting of Famine fear no harm,
Nor mind it, fed with better thoughts that feed
Mee hung'ring more to do my Father's will.

    It was the hour of night, when thus the Son   260
Commun'd in silent walk, then laid him down
Under the hospitable covert nigh

    236–240. The lovely forms which these spirits assume are comparable
with the beauty of Spenser's false Florimell, which was assumed by
        "A wicked Spright yfraught with fawning guile,
         And faire resemblance aboue all the rest,
         Which with the Prince of Darknesse fell somewhile,
         From heauens blisse and euerlasting rest."
                        (*F.Q.*, III, viii, 8.)
    240. *persons . . . part;* dramatic terms.
    246. *Wand'ring* is transitive, as it is in I, 354.
    255. *so:* provided that.
    258. Compare Milton's reference to himself as feeding on the
thoughts out of which he wrote in *P.L.*, III, 37.
    259. In John iv, 34, Jesus says, "My meat is to do the will of him
that sent me."

Of Trees thick interwoven; there he slept,
And dream'd, as appetite is wont to dream,
Of meats and drinks, Nature's refreshment sweet.   265
Him thought, he by the Brook of *Cherith* stood
And saw the Ravens with thir horny beaks
Food to *Elijah* bringing Even and Morn,
Though ravenous, taught to abstain from what they brought:
He saw the Prophet also how he fled   270
Into the Desert, and how there he slept
Under a Juniper; then how awakt,
He found his Supper on the coals prepar'd,
And by the Angel was bid rise and eat,
And eat the second time after repose,   275
The strength whereof suffic'd him forty days;
Sometimes that with *Elijah* he partook,
Or as a guest with *Daniel* at his pulse.
Thus wore out night, and now the Herald Lark
Left his ground-nest, high tow'ring to descry   280
The morn's approach, and greet her with his Song.
As lightly from his grassy Couch up rose
Our Saviour, and found all was but a dream,
Fasting he went to sleep, and fasting wak'd.
Up to a hill anon his steps he rear'd,   285
From whose high top to ken the prospect round,
If Cottage were in view, Sheep-cote or Herd;
But Cottage, Herd or Sheep-cote none he saw,

---

264. *appetite:* a hungry man. The abstract is put for the concrete
as it is in the word *Apostasy* in I, 146.

266. *Him* is used instead of the nominative form because *thought*
is not the preterite of "think" but of an obsolete verb meaning "to
seem."

266–276. In I Kings xvii, 5–6, Milton found the account of Elijah's
retreat to the "brook Cherith, that is before Jordan," where "the ravens
brought him bread and flesh," and in I Kings xix, 4–8, the story of
the angel and the food which lasted him forty days. Compare I, 353.

269. The only excuse for the pun on *ravenous* is the fact that contemporary taste approved paronomasia, or plays on words, as the ornament of epic poetry which Abraham Fraunce called them in his *Arcadian
Rhetorike*, xxiv.

277. *that* connects the following clause with *thought* in l. 266.

278. The story of Daniel's refusal of King Nebuchadnezzar's meat
to live on his usual diet of pulse is found in the Book of Daniel i, 8–19.

Only in a bottom saw a pleasant Grove,
With chant of tuneful Birds resounding loud.   290
Thither he bent his way, determin'd there
To rest at noon, and enter'd soon the shade
High rooft and walks beneath, and alleys brown
That open'd in the midst a woody Scene;
Nature's own work it seem'd (Nature taught Art)   295
And to a Superstitious eye the haunt
Of Wood-Gods and Wood-Nymphs; he view'd it round,
When suddenly a man before him stood,
Not rustic as before, but seemlier clad,
As one in City, or Court, or Palace bred,   300
And with fair speech these words to him address'd.
   With granted leave officious I return,
But much more wonder that the Son of God
In this wild solitude so long should bide
Of all things destitute, and well I know,   305
Not without hunger.   Others of some note,
As story tells, have trod this Wilderness:
The Fugitive Bond-woman with her Son
Outcast *Nebaioth,* yet found he relief
By a providing Angel; all the race   310

---

289. *bottom:* low-lying land, dell or valley.

293. *alleys:* paths.
brown: dusky, dark. This is the primitive meaning of the word.
Compare its use to describe foliage "broad and brown as Evening" in
P.L., IX, 1088.

295. It seems that Milton intended to suggest that the scene, which
looked "natural," was really raised by Satan's art. Like the Garden of
Eden, this enchanted grove was "sweet" because "Wild above rule or
art" (*P.L.,* V, 296–297), but its contrast with the desert was an artistic
effect which Tasso recommended when he said in his essay *On the
Heroic Poem* (Book III) that "the view of deserts and of the rugged-
ness and sternness of mountains is agreeable in contrast with the amenity
of lakes and gardens."

302. *officious* had none of its modern, unpleasant connotation, but
kept its Latin force of "anxious to please."

306–310. The *Bond-woman* is Hagar, whose son, Ishmael, would
have died in the desert if "the angel of God" had not shown her "a
well of water." (Gen. xxi, 17–19.) It is not clear why Milton should
have called Ishmael by the name of his oldest son, Nebaioth.   (Gen.
xxv, 13.)

310–312. In the wilderness of Sin (or Zin) "the children of Israel did

Of *Israel* here had famish'd, had not God
Rain'd from Heaven Manna; and that Prophet bold
Native of *Thebez* wand'ring here was fed
Twice by a voice inviting him to eat.
Of thee these forty days none hath regard,   315
Forty and more deserted here indeed.
    To whom thus Jesus; what conclud'st thou hence?
They all had need, I as thou seest have none.
    How hast thou hunger then? Satan replied.
Tell me, if Food were now before thee set,   320
Would'st thou not eat? Thereafter as I like
The giver, answer'd Jesus. Why should that
Cause thy refusal, said the subtle Fiend,
Hast thou not right to all Created things,
Owe not all Creatures by just right to thee   325
Duty and Service, nor to stay till bid,
But tender all their power? nor mention I
Meats by the Law unclean, or offer'd first
To Idols, those young *Daniel* could refuse;
Nor proffer'd by an Enemy, though who   330
Would scruple that, with want opprest? behold
Nature asham'd, or better to express,
Troubl'd that thou shouldst hunger, hath purvey'd
From all the Elements her choicest store
To treat thee as beseems, and as her Lord   335
With honour; only deign to sit and eat.
    He spake no dream, for as his words had end,
Our Saviour lifting up his eyes beheld

---

eat manna forty years, until they came to a land inhabited." (Exod.
xvi, 35.)

312. The *Prophet* is Elijah the Thisbite. Compare the note on 16–17
above.

324–327. Satan is challenging Jesus as God's "Son, whom he hath
appointed heir of all things, by whom also he made the worlds."
(Heb. i, 2.)

328–329. The "king's meat" which Daniel refused must have included the flesh of many animals forbidden by the Mosaic law in
Deuteronomy xiv, 3–20, and Leviticus xi. The selling of meat that
had been offered to idols disturbed some tender consciences, which
St. Paul reassured. (I Cor. x, 28.)

331. *scruple,* used transitively, did not become rare until the nineteenth century.

In ample space under the broadest shade
A Table richly spread, in regal mode,   340
With dishes pil'd, and meats of noblest sort
And savour, Beasts of chase, or Fowl of game,
In pastry built, or from the spit, or boil'd,
Gris-amber-steam'd; all Fish from Sea or Shore,
Freshet, or purling Brook, of shell or fin,   345
And exquisitest name, for which was drain'd
Pontus and *Lucrine* Bay, and *Afric* Coast.
Alas how simple, to these Cates compar'd,
Was that crude Apple that diverted *Eve!*
And at a stately side-board by the wine   350
That fragrant smell diffus'd, in order stood
Tall stripling youths rich-clad, of fairer hue

---

340. Milton remembered Armida's extravagant banquet in the open air to tempt her lovers, for she offered

> "All Beasts, all Birds beguil'd by Fowler's Trade,
> All Fish were there in Floods or Seas that pass,
> All Dainties made by Art, and at the Table
> An hundred Virgins serv'd, for Husbands able."
> (*J.D.*, X, 64.)

Such "regal" luxury would seem to Jesus as burdensome as Cowley's essay *Of Liberty* says that his table is to the rich man who "seems to be the Lord of All Nature; the Earth affords him her best Metals for his Dishes, her best Vegetables and Animals for his Food; the Air and Sea supply him with their choicest Birds and Fishes."

regal mode seems to be an echo of Virgil's description of the banquet with which Pirithous was tormented in Taratarus. (*Aen.*, VI, 605.)

344. *Gris-amber:* ambergris, which was used as a sauce. *N.E.D.* quotes Sedley's *Bellamira* (IV, i): "Breakfast . . . upon new-laid eggs, ambergrease and gravy."

347. *Pontus,* the Black Sea. The *Lucrine Bay* was a lagoon near Naples. Juvenal mentions connoisseurship of its oysters as a mark of one of his decadent Romans. (*Satires*, IV, 141.)

348. *Cates:* delicacies.

349. *diverted* keeps its literal, Latin meaning, which is close to that of "pervert" in modern English.

352–361. In Michael Psellus' dialogue, *Timothy, or about Demons,* (18, 19), or in some similar work, Milton may have found the theory that the devils could assume any form at pleasure by the working of their imagination upon their subtle, airy bodies, and that the demons inhabiting the water resembled women and were called by the Greeks Naïades and Nereids.

Than *Ganymede* or *Hylas;* distant more
Under the Trees now tripp'd, now solemn stood
Nymphs of *Diana's* train, and *Naiades*   355
With fruits and flowers from *Amalthea's* horn,
And Ladies of th' *Hesperides,* that seem'd
Fairer than feign'd of old, or fabl'd since
Of Fairy Damsels met in Forest wide
By Knights of *Logres,* or of *Lyones,*   360
Lancelot or *Pelleas,* or *Pellenore;*
And all the while Harmonious Airs were heard
Of chiming strings, or charming pipes, and winds
Of gentlest gale *Arabian* odours fann'd
From their soft wings, and *Flora's* earliest smells.   365
Such was the Splendor, and the Tempter now
His invitation earnestly renew'd.
    What doubts the Son of God to sit and eat?
These are not Fruits forbidden; no interdict

---

353. *Ganymede.* Compare *Elegy VII,* 21, note.
Apollonius Rhodius (*Argonautica,* I, 127, ff.) tells the story of the
kidnapping of Hylas, the friend of Hercules, by the nymphs who admired his beauty.

356. *Amalthea's horn:* the cornucopia or horn of plenty. Ovid (*Fasti,*
V, 115, ff.) says that Amalthea was a goat which nursed Jove when he
was an infant on Mount Ida, and that the marvellous horn was her
reward.

357. The *Hesperides,* or daughters of Hesperus, were not "feign'd of
old" to be particularly beautiful, but Milton had the authority of the
mythologist, Natale Conti (VII, vii) for representing them so. He
thought of them as resembling the fairy mistresses of knights like
Lancelot, Pelleas and Pellenore. Compare the Introduction §9.

360. *Logres:* according to Geoffrey of Monmouth, England east of
the Severn and south of the Humber.
Lyones: Lyonesse was the land from which Arthur was supposed to
have come. It lay somewhere near Cornwall and is sometimes said to
be the submerged region between Land's End and the Scilly Isles.

363. *charming* keeps its Latin meaning of "singing." Compare the
use of "charm" for the song of birds in *P.L.,* IV, 642.

364. Compare the "Odours from the spicy shore of *Araby* the blest"
in *P.L.,* IV, 162–163.

365. *Flora:* the goddess of flowers.

368. *What doubts:* why hesitates? The Latin neuter, interrogative
pronoun is used in this way and *doubts* has its Latin meaning of "to
be in two minds."

Defends the touching of these viands pure;   370
Thir taste no knowledge works, at least of evil,
But life preserves, destroys life's enemy,
Hunger, with sweet restorative delight.
All these are Spirits of Air, and Woods, and Springs,
Thy gentle Ministers, who come to pay   375
Thee homage, and acknowledge thee thir Lord:
What doubt'st thou Son of God? sit down and eat.

   To whom thus Jesus temperately replied:
Said'st thou not that to all things I had right?
And who withholds my pow'r that right to use?   380
Shall I receive by gift what of my own,
When and where likes me best, I can command?
I can at will, doubt not, as soon as thou,
Command a Table in this Wilderness,
And call swift flights of Angels ministrant   385
Array'd in Glory on my cup to attend:
Why shouldst thou then obtrude this diligence,
In vain, where no acceptance it can find,
And with my hunger what hast thou to do?
Thy pompous Delicacies I contemn,   390
And count thy specious gifts no gifts but guiles.

   To whom thus answer'd Satan malcontent:
That I have also power to give thou seest;
If of that pow'r I bring thee voluntary
What I might have bestow'd on whom I pleas'd,   395

---

370. *Defends:* forbids. The word retains the meaning which it has in French.

382. *likes me:* a construction like our "it pleases me!" Milton says that Spirits "as they please

. . . . Limb themselves, and colour, shape or size
    Assume, as likes them best."
          (*P.L.,* VI, 351–353.)

384. There may be an allusion to the blasphemy of the Israelites in the desert of Sin, when they asked, "Can God furnish a table in the wilderness?" (Psalm lxxviii, 19.)

385. Perhaps there is an echo of the "flights of angels" which Horatio invokes to sing Hamlet to his rest. (*Hamlet,* V, ii, 347.)

391. The proverb that the gifts of enemies are no gifts is in Sophocles' *Ajax,* 664.

394. *voluntary:* voluntarily. For the adverb without the suffix -ly see Abbott §23.

And rather opportunely in this place
Chose to impart to thy apparent need,
Why shouldst thou not accept it? but I see
What I can do or offer is suspect;
Of these things others quickly will dispose   400
Whose pains have earn'd the far-fet spoil.   With that
Both Table and Provision vanish'd quite
With sound of Harpies' wings and Talons heard;
Only the importune Tempter still remain'd,
And with these words his temptation pursu'd.   405
    By hunger, that each other Creature tames,
Thou art not to be harm'd, therefore not mov'd;
Thy temperance invincible besides,
For no allurement yields to appetite,
And all thy heart is set on high designs,   410
High actions; but wherewith to be achiev'd?
Great acts require great means of enterprise,
Thou art unknown, unfriended, low of birth,
A Carpenter thy Father known, thyself
Bred up in poverty and straits at home;   415
Lost in a Desert here and hunger-bit:
Which way or from what hope dost thou aspire
To greatness? whence Authority deriv'st,
What Followers, what Retinue canst thou gain,
Or at thy heels the dizzy Multitude,   420

---

399. *suspect:* suspected.   Compare the note on "frustrate" in I, 180.

401. *far-fet:* far-fetched.   "Fet" for "fetched" was not unusual; *e.g.,* Spenser's "brasse from Corinth fet" (*Muiopotmos, 77*).

403. In the *Aeneid* (III, 225–228) the Trojans' meal is interrupted
        "When from the mountain-tops, with hideous cry,
        And clatt'ring wings, the hungry harpies fly:
        They snatch the meat, defiling all they find."
                (Dryden's translation, 293–5.)
The scene suggests the stage direction in *Tempest* (III, iii): "Enter Ariel like a harpy; claps his wings upon the table; and with a quaint device, the banquet vanishes."

404. *importune:* importunate.

416. Satan's words may echo those of one of Job's comforters; "His strength shall be hunger-bitten." (Job xviii, 12.)

420–421. The thought is too typically Miltonic to make it certain that the language owes anything to Horace's *Epistles,* I, xix, 37, which it closely resembles.

Longer than thou canst feed them on thy cost?
Money brings Honour, Friends, Conquest, and Realms;
What rais'd *Antipater* the *Edomite,*
And his Son *Herod* plac'd on *Judah's* Throne
(Thy throne) but gold that got him puissant friends?   425
Therefore, if at great things thou wouldst arrive,
Get Riches first, get Wealth, and Treasure heap,
Not difficult, if thou hearken to me,
Riches are mine, Fortune is in my hand;
They whom I favour thrive in wealth amain,   430
While Virtue, Valour, Wisdom sit in want.

   To whom thus Jesus patiently replied:
Yet Wealth without these three is impotent,
To gain dominion or to keep it gain'd.
Witness those ancient Empires of the Earth,   435
In highth of all thir flowing wealth dissolv'd;
But men endu'd with these have oft attain'd
In lowest poverty to highest deeds:
Gideon and *Jephtha,* and the Shepherd lad,
Whose off-spring on the Throne of *Judah* sat   440

---

422. The entire scene resembles the temptation of Spenser's Knight of
Temperance in the cave of Mammon, and here the thought recalls Mam-
mon's appeal to Guyon to purchase honour with riches:
   "Here is the fountaine of the worldes good:
   Now therefore, if thou wilt enriched bee,
   Auise thee well, and chaunge thy wilfull mood."
                              (*F.Q.* II, vii, 38, 6–8).

423. Milton found the story of the rise of Antipater, "who was very
rich, and in his nature an active and seditious man," in Josephus
Antiquities of the Jews, XIV, i.

427. Here there is certainly the memory of Horace's line, "O citizens, citizens, money should be the first object."   (*Epistles,* I, i, 53.)

439. When God called Gideon to be the champion of Israel against
the Midianites, he answered, "Lord, wherewith shall I save Israel? be-
hold, my family is poor in Manasseh." (Judges vi, 15.)
Jephthah, who delivered Israel from the Ammonites, was disinherited
and banished in his youth. (Judges xi, 2.)
The *Shepherd lad:* David, whom God "took from the sheep-folds.
From following the ewes great with young he brought him to feed
Jacob his people, and Israel his inheritance." (Psalm lxxviii, 70–71.)

440–442. The last of many prophecies of the endurance of David's
line is in the message of Gabriel to Mary; that her son should "be called
the Son of the Highest: and the Lord God shall give unto him the
throne of his father David." (Luke i, 32.)

So many Ages, and shall yet regain
That seat, and reign in *Israel* without end.
Among the Heathen, (for throughout the World
To me is not unknown what hath been done
Worthy of Memorial) canst thou not remember   445
Quintius, Fabricius, Curius, Regulus?
For I esteem those names of men so poor
Who could do mighty things, and could contemn
Riches though offer'd from the hand of Kings.
And what in me seems wanting, but that I   450
May also in this poverty as soon
Accomplish what they did, perhaps and more?
Extol not Riches then, the toil of Fools,
The wise man's cumbrance if not snare, more apt
To slacken Virtue, and abate her edge,   455
Than prompt her to do aught may merit praise.
What if with like aversion I reject
Riches and Realms; yet not for that a Crown,
Golden in show, is but a wreath of thorns,
Brings dangers, troubles, cares, and sleepless nights   460
To him who wears the Regal Diadem,
When on his shoulders each man's burden lies:

---

446. *Quintius:* better known as Cincinnatus, the Roman Dictator who, after holding power for sixteen days, defeated the Aequians in 456 B.C. and went back to his ploughing in the Alban hills.

Milton remembered *Fabricius'* reply to Pyrrhus: "If I am dishonest, I am not worth a bribe; if honest, you know I will not take one."

Curius Dentatus, a hero of the Samnite wars, was said to have been found cooking turnips by some Samnites who came to bribe him and discovered that he wanted nothing which their money could buy. The scene figures in several books of emblems.

Regulus, who was conquered in Africa in the First Punic War, preferred death in Carthage to the dishonour of breaking his word to the Carthaginians. "Those old *Fabritii* and *Curii,*" Milton said in the conclusion of *The Reason of Church Government,* knew that God "delights most to work from within himself, and not by the heavy luggage of corporeal instruments." (*P.W.* II, 504.)

458-465. The implication is that Jesus, if he were not convinced of the futility of violence, would be willing to forego the "infinite heart's ease" which Shakespeare's *Henry V* (IV, i, 256-257) says that kings must neglect and "private men enjoy." Milton regarded kings as mere "entrusted servants of the commonwealth" who could not make any personal sacrifice too large "in discharge of their public duty." (*Eikonoklastes,* xiii.)

For therein stands the office of a King,
His Honour, Virtue, Merit and chief Praise,
That for the Public all this weight he bears.   465
Yet he who reigns within himself, and rules
Passions, Desires, and Fears, is more a King;
Which every wise and virtuous man attains:
And who attains not, ill aspires to rule
Cities of men, or head-strong Multitudes,   470
Subject himself to Anarchy within,
Or lawless passions in him which he serves.
But to guide Nations in the way of truth
By saving Doctrine, and from error lead
To know, and knowing worship God aright,   475
Is yet more Kingly; this attracts the Soul,
Governs the inner man, the nobler part;
That other o'er the body only reigns,
And oft by force, which to a generous mind
So reigning can be no sincere delight.   480
Besides to give a Kingdom hath been thought
Greater and nobler done, and to lay down
Far more magnanimous than to assume.
Riches are needless then, both for themselves,
And for thy reason why they should be sought,   485
To gain a Sceptre, oftest better miss't.

The End of the Second Book.

The Third Book

So SPAKE the Son of God, and Satan stood
A while as mute confounded what to say,
What to reply, confuted and convinc't
Of his weak arguing, and fallacious drift;

466–480. Compare the Introduction §6.

481–483. Milton's conception of magnanimity (see the note on 139
above) could best be illustrated by the refusal of a crown. "Carolus
Martellus," wrote Sir Richard Barckley in *The Felicitie of Man* (1631),
"shewed great magnanimitie in refusing principalitie."

3. *convinc't:* convicted, vanquished in debate. Compare *Comus,* 792:
"Thou art not fit to hear thyself convinc'd."

At length collecting all his Serpent wiles,   5
With soothing words renew'd, him thus accosts.
    I see thou know'st what is of use to know,
What best to say canst say, to do canst do;
Thy actions to thy words accord, thy words
To thy large heart give utterance due, thy heart   10
Contains of good, wise, just, the perfect shape.
Should Kings and Nations from thy mouth consult,
Thy Counsel would be as the Oracle
Urim and *Thummim,* those oraculous gems
On *Aaron's* breast; or tongue of Seers old   15
Infallible; or wert thou sought to deeds
That might require th' array of war, thy skill
Of conduct would be such, that all the world
Could not sustain thy Prowess, or subsist
In battle, though against thy few in arms.   20
These God-like Virtues wherefore dost thou hide?
Affecting private life, or more obscure
In savage Wilderness, wherefore deprive
All Earth her wonder at thy acts, thyself
The fame and glory, glory the reward   25

---

11. *shape:* ideal form or pattern. When Milton wrote "Virtue in her shape how lovely" (*P.L.,* IV, 848), and made the Lady in *Comus* (215–216) speak of seeing the "unblemish't form of Chastity . . . visibly," he was influenced by the Platonic doctrine that "the very form and shape of Moral Goodness, if it could be seen with the physical eye, would"—as Cicero said to his son, Marcus (*De officiis,* I, v. 15)— "awaken a marvellous love of wisdom." So in *The Reason of Church Government,* II, iii, he spoke of "the very shape and visage of truth," which is obscured by "the subtle imposture of these sensual mistresses, that keeps the ports and passages between her and the object."

14. It is not certain what the urim and thummim worn by Aaron in his high-priestly breastplate (Lev. viii, 8) were, but the Urim were used by Eleazar the priest to "ask counsel . . . before the Lord." (Num. xxvii, 21. Divination of some kind seems to have been meant.)

18. *conduct:* leadership, direction.

22. *Affecting:* aspiring to, preferring. Both meanings were often combined in the word, as the corresponding meanings may be in the abstract noun "affection."

23. *savage* keeps its Latin meaning of "pertaining to woodland," *i.e.,* uncultivated, wild.

25–30. Compare the Introduction, §16. Perhaps there is a trace here of Cicero's observation that "in the greatest minds and the most

That sole excites to high attempts the flame
Of most erected Spirits, most temper'd pure
Ethereal, who all pleasures else despise,
All treasures and all gain esteem as dross,
And dignities and powers all but the highest?   30
Thy years are ripe, and over-ripe, the Son
Of *Macedonian Philip* had ere these
Won *Asia* and the Throne of *Cyrus* held
At his dispose; young *Scipio* had brought down
The *Carthaginian* pride, young *Pompey* quell'd   35
The *Pontic* King and in triumph had rode.
Yet years, and to ripe years judgement mature,
Quench not the thirst of glory, but augment.
Great *Julius,* whom now all the world admires,
The more he grew in years, the more inflam'd   40
With glory, wept that he had liv'd so long
Inglorious: but thou yet art not too late.
　　To whom our Saviour calmly thus replied.
Thou neither dost persuade me to seek wealth
For Empire's sake, nor Empire to affect   45
For glory's sake by all thy argument.

---

splendid spirits is found the greatest passion for honour, empire, power
and glory." (*De officiis,* I, viii, 26.)

27. *erected:* upright, noble. Mammon is called "the least erected
Spirit that fell From heav'n." (*P.L.,* I, 679–680.)

32–36. Alexander was twenty-five when he won his first victory over
the Persians at Arbela (331 B.C.).
Scipio was about twenty-seven when he drove the Carthaginians out
of Spain. Compare the note on II, 199–200.
Pompey did not conquer the Pontic king, Mithridates, until he was
forty years old (in 66 B.C.), but he was distinguished for his part in
the Social War and against Marius before he was thirty.

34. *dispose:* disposal.

37. *to:* in addition to.

39–42. In his *Life of Caesar* Plutarch related how, when he was commanding in Spain, Caesar happened to read the history of Alexander's
wars and burst into tears because he did not have "one glorious
achievement to boast."

44–59. Even when he began *The Tenure of Kings and Magistrates* in
February, 1649, and felt himself "endued with fortitude and heroic
virtue to fear nothing but the curse written against those 'that do the
work of the Lord negligently,' " Milton shrank from the sweat and
labour "amidst the throng and noises of vulgar and irrational men."

For what is glory but the blaze of fame,
The people's praise, if always praise unmixt?
And what the people but a herd confus'd,
A miscellaneous rabble, who extol   50
Things vulgar, and well weigh'd, scarce worth the praise?
They praise and they admire they know not what;
And know not whom, but as one leads the other;
And what delight to be by such extoll'd,
To live upon thir tongues and be thir talk,   55
Of whom to be disprais'd were no small praise?—
His lot who dares be singularly good.
Th' intelligent among them and the wise
Are few, and glory scarce of few is rais'd.
This is true glory and renown, when God   60
Looking on the Earth, with approbation marks
The just man, and divulges him through Heaven
To all his Angels, who with true applause
Recount his praises; thus he did to *Job,*
When to extend his fame through Heaven and Earth,   65
As thou to thy reproach mayst well remember,
He ask'd thee, hast thou seen my servant *Job?*
Famous he was in Heaven, on Earth less known;
Where glory is false glory, attributed
To things not glorious, men not worthy of fame.   70
They err who count it glorious to subdue
By Conquest far and wide, to over-run
Large Countries, and in field great Battles win,
Great Cities by assault: what do these Worthies,
But rob and spoil, burn, slaughter, and enslave   75
Peaceable Nations, neighbouring, or remote,
Made Captive, yet deserving freedom more
Than those thir Conquerors, who leave behind

60–63. Compare *Lycidas,* 78–84.

62. *divulges:* publishes, proclaims.   Compare *S.A.,* 1248.

64–68. Compare the Introduction, §12.   The quoted words in line 67
are paraphrased from Job i, 8.

71–87. This passage is an expansion of the attack in *P.L.,* XI, upon
the conquerors who are styled
      "Patrons of Mankind, Gods, and Sons of Gods,
        Destroyers rightlier call'd and Plagues of men."
                    (696–697.)

Nothing but ruin wheresoe'er they rove,
And all the flourishing works of peace destroy,   80
Then swell with pride, and must be titl'd Gods,
Great Benefactors of mankind, Deliverers,
Worship't with Temple, Priest and Sacrifice?
One is the Son of *Jove,* of *Mars* the other,
Till Conqueror Death discover them scarce men,   85
Rolling in brutish vices, and deform'd,
Violent or shameful death thir due reward.
But if there be in glory aught of good,
It may by means far different be attain'd,
Without ambition, war, or violence;   90
By deeds of peace, by wisdom eminent,
By patience, temperance; I mention still
Him whom thy wrongs with Saintly patience borne,
Made famous in a Land and times obscure;
Who names not now with honour patient *Job?*   95
Poor *Socrates* (who next more memorable?)
By what he taught and suffer'd for so doing,
For truth's sake suffering death unjust, lives now
Equal in fame to proudest Conquerors.
Yet if for fame and glory aught be done,   100
Aught suffer'd; if young *African* for fame
His wasted Country freed from *Punic* rage,
The deed becomes unprais'd, the man at least,
And loses, though but verbal, his reward.
Shall I seek glory then, as vain men seek   105

81–84. The Roman emperors generally were granted the title of
"Divine" by the Senate. Ptolemy III enjoyed the title of "Benefactor"
and similar titles were taken by several of Alexander's successors.
Alexander himself posed as the son of Jupiter Ammon, and Romulus
was called the son of Mars. Romulus died violently and Alexander's
ambition and miserable death in Babylon made him a by-word as the
man who

> "would as *Ammons* sonne be magnifide,
> Till scornd of God and man a shamefull death he dide."
> (*F.Q.,* I, v, 48.)

96–99. For this parallel of Socrates with Job see the Introduction, §6.

101. *young African;* Scipio Africanus Major, the Scipio already mentioned in 34 above. In the Second Punic War his campaigns in Spain
finally delivered Italy from Hannibal's invasion.

Oft not deserv'd?   I seek not mine, but his
Who sent me, and thereby witness whence I am.
   To whom the Tempter murmuring thus replied.
Think not so slight of glory: therein least
Resembling thy great Father; he seeks glory,   110
And for his glory all things made, all things
Orders and governs, nor content in Heaven
By all his Angels glorifi'd, requires
Glory from men, from all men good or bad,
Wise or unwise, no difference, no exemption;   115
Above all Sacrifice, or hallow'd gift
Glory he requires, and glory he receives
Promiscuous from all Nations, Jew, or Greek,
Or Barbarous, nor exception hath declar'd;
From us his foes pronounc't glory he exacts.   120
   To whom our Saviour fervently replied.
And reason; since his word all things produc'd,
Though chiefly not for glory as prime end,
But to show forth his goodness, and impart
His good communicable to every soul   125
Freely; of whom what could he less expect
Than glory and benediction, that is thanks,
The slightest, easiest, readiest recompense

106–107. Jesus said to the Pharisees (John viii, 50), "I seek not mine own glory"; and appealed to the witness of his Father to justify himself. (John v, 31–32.)

110–120. The sophistry is based upon the doctrine in the Westminster Shorter Catechism that the chief end of man is "to glorify God," and upon scriptures like the words of the four and twenty elders before the throne of God, "Thou art worthy, O Lord, to receive glory and honour and power: for thou hast created all things, and for thy pleasure they are and were created." (Rev. iv, 11.)

119. *Barbarous* is used with its Greek meaning to signify all the nations outside of the Greek world, as "gentile" is used to signify all nations outside of Israel.

122. In passages like II Peter iii, 5, "by the word of God the heavens were of old," and in the opening statement of John's Gospel that the Word was in the beginning with God, Milton found justification for his conception in *P.L.,* VII, 163–167, of God's Word as identical with his Son, who is sent out into Chaos to create the universe.

123–131. Orthodox Catholic doctrine taught that God's object in the creation of the universe was to provide means for the expression of his love.

From them who could return him nothing else,
And not returning that would likeliest render   130
Contempt instead, dishonour, obloquy?
Hard recompense, unsuitable return
For so much good, so much beneficence.
But why should man seek glory? who of his own
Hath nothing, and to whom nothing belongs   135
But condemnation, ignominy, and shame?
Who for so many benefits receiv'd
Turn'd recreant to God, ingrate and false,
And so of all true good himself despoil'd,
Yet, sacrilegious, to himself would take   140
That which to God alone of right belongs;
Yet so much bounty is in God, such grace,
That who advance his glory, not thir own,
Them he himself to glory will advance.

    So spake the Son of God; and here again   145
Satan had not to answer, but stood struck
With guilt of his own sin, for he himself
Insatiable of glory had lost all,
Yet of another Plea bethought him soon.

    Of glory as thou wilt, said he, so deem,   150
Worth or not worth the seeking, let it pass:
But to a Kingdom thou art born, ordain'd
To sit upon thy Father *David's* Throne;
By Mother's side thy Father, though thy right
Be now in powerful hands, that will not part   155
Easily from possession won with arms;
Judaea now and all the promis'd land

---

136. *ignominy* should have the accent distinctly on the first syllable
while the others have very light but about equal stress.

138. *recreant:* unfaithful, apostate.

147–148. Raphael, speaking of the rebel angels to Adam, explained
that

      "strength from Truth divided and from Just,
   Illaudable, naught merits but dispraise
   And ignominy, yet to glory aspires
   Vain-glorious, and through infamy seeks fame."
           (*P.L.*, VI, 381–384.)

157–160. Judaea became a Roman province in A.D. 6, when Jesus was
a boy of ten, if modern computation is trustworthy. Tiberius, who
was emperor from A.D. 24 to 37, kept Pilate in office from 26 to 36,

Reduc't a Province under Roman yoke,
Obeys *Tiberius;* nor is always rul'd
With temperate sway; oft have they violated 160
The Temple, oft the Law with foul affronts,
Abominations rather, as did once
Antiochus: and think'st thou to regain
Thy right by sitting still or thus retiring?
So did not *Maccabaeus:* he indeed 165
Retir'd unto the Desert, but with arms;
And o'er a mighty King so oft prevail'd.
That by strong hand his Family obtain'd,
Though Priests, the Crown, and *David's* Throne usurp'd,
With *Modin* and her Suburbs once content. 170
If Kingdom move thee not, let move thee Zeal,
And Duty; Zeal and Duty are not slow;
But on Occasion's forelock watchful wait.
They themselves rather are occasion best,
Zeal of thy Father's house, Duty to free 175

in spite of many acts of tyranny like the massacre of "the Galileans, whose blood Pilate had mingled with their sacrifices." (Luke xiii, 1.)

161. Pompey violated the Holy of Holies in the Temple at Jerusalem in B.C. 63.

162–163. Antiochus Epiphanes "entered proudly into the sanctuary, and took away the golden altar, and the candlestick of light, and all the vessels thereof. . . . And when he had taken all away, he went into his own land, having made a great massacre, and spoken very proudly." (I Maccabees, i, 21–24.)

165–170. In 166 B.C., Judas surnamed Maccabaeus, or the Hammerer, a scion of a Levite family in the obscure Judaean town of Modin, began the struggle with Antiochus Epiphanes which ended by putting his family on the throne of David as the Asmonean Dynasty.

171. *Kingdom:* kingship.

173. Renaissance literature abounded in references to Occasion; sometimes represented [as Milton may have seen it in Alciati's *Emblemata* (cxxii)] as an old woman whose

"lockes, that loathly were and hoarie gray,
Grew all afore, and loosely hong vnrold,
But all behind was bald, and worne away,
That none thereof could euer taken hold."
(*F.Q.,* II, iv, 4.)

175. Christ's whipping of the money-changers out of the Temple was interpreted by his disciples (John ii, 17) as fulfilling a prophecy in Psalm lxix, 9: "For the zeal of thine house hath eaten me up."

Thy Country from her Heathen servitude;
So shalt thou best fullfil, best verify
The Prophets old, who sung thy endless reign,
The happier reign the sooner it begins.
Reign then; what canst thou better do the while?   180
   To whom our Saviour answer thus return'd.
All things are best fulfill'd in their due time,
And time there is for all things, Truth hath said:
If of my reign Prophetic Writ hath told
That it shall never end, so when begin   185
The Father in his purpose hath decreed,
He in whose hand all times and seasons roll.
What if he hath decreed that I shall first
Be tried in humble state, and things adverse,
By tribulations, injuries, insults,   190
Contempts, and scorns, and snares, and violence,
Suffering, abstaining, quietly expecting
Without distrust or doubt, that he may know
What I can suffer, how obey? who best
Can suffer, best can do; best reign, who first   195
Well hath obey'd; just trial e'er I merit
My exaltation without change or end.
But what concerns it thee when I begin
My everlasting Kingdom, why art thou
Solicitous, what moves thy inquisition?   200

---

183. "The first of those attributes which show the inherent nature of God," Milton wrote in *C.D.*, I, ii, "is *Truth.*" He thought of the Bible as containing God's truth, even in so worldly-wise a book as *Ecclesiastes,* a verse of which (iii, 1) is paraphrased here.

187. "It is not for you," Jesus said to his disciples, "to know the times or the seasons, which the Father hath put in his own power." (Acts i, 7.)

194–197. The antithesis between suffering and doing great things was a commonplace in ancient literature; *e.g.,* Caius Mucius' famous retort to Porsena that, "To act and to suffer with fortitude is the behaviour of a Roman," and the amusing comic twist of the maxim in Plautus' *Comedy of Asses* (324), of which the present line might serve as a translation.

The principle that obedience is the best discipline for rule goes back at least as far as Plato's doctrine that "the ministration of the laws must be assigned to that man who is most obedient to the laws." (*Laws,* IV, 715, C.)

Know'st thou not that my rising is thy fall,
And my promotion will be thy destruction?
  To whom the Tempter inly rackt replied.
Let that come when it comes; all hope is lost
Of my reception into grace; what worse?   205
For where no hope is left, is left no fear;
If there be worse, the expectation more
Of worse torments me than the feeling can.
I would be at the worst; worst is my Port,
My harbour and my ultimate repose,   210
The end I would attain, my final good.
My error was my error, and my crime
My crime; whatever for itself condemn'd,
And will alike be punish'd; whether thou
Reign or reign not; though to that gentle brow   215
Willingly I could fly, and hope thy reign,
From that placid aspect and meek regard,
Rather than aggravate my evil state,
Would stand between me and thy Father's ire,
(Whose ire I dread more than the fire of Hell)   220
A shelter and a kind of shading cool
Interposition, as a summer's cloud.
If I then to the worst that can be haste,
Why move thy feet so slow to what is best,
Happiest both to thyself and all the world,   225
That thou who worthiest art shouldst be thir King?
Perhaps thou linger'st in deep thoughts detain'd
Of the enterprise so hazardous and high;
No wonder, for though in thee be united
What of perfection can in man be found,   230
Or human nature can receive, consider
Thy life hath yet been private, most part spent
At home, scarce view'd the *Galilean* Towns,

204–211. Here Satan speaks with no less fortitude, though with less
insolence, than in the soliloquy in *P.L.,* IV, 108–110:
        "So farewell Hope, and with Hope farewell Fear,
          Farewell Remorse: all Good to me is lost;
          Evil be thou my Good."
  213–214. Whatever the crime, its punishment is within itself. In the
soliloquy in *P.L.,* IV, 75, Satan realizes that he is his own hell, regardless where he may be.

And once a year *Jerusalem,* few days'
Short sojourn; and what thence couldst thou observe?   235
The world thou hast not seen, much less her glory,
Empires, and Monarchs, and thir radiant Courts,
Best school of best experience, quickest in sight
In all things that to greatest actions lead.
The wisest, unexperienc't, will be ever   240
Timorous and loth, with novice modesty,
(As he who seeking Asses found a Kingdom)
Irresolute, unhardy, unadvent'rous:
But I will bring thee where thou soon shalt quit
Those rudiments, and see before thine eyes   245
The Monarchies of the Earth, thir pomp and state,
Sufficient introduction to inform
Thee, of thyself so apt, in regal Arts,
And regal Mysteries; that thou mayst know
How best their opposition to withstand.   250
      With that (such power was giv'n him then) he took
The Son of God up to a Mountain high.
It was a Mountain at whose verdant feet
A spacious plain outstretcht in circuit wide

234–235. Luke says (ii, 41) that Jesus' "parents went to Jerusalem
every year at the feast of the passover."

242. I Samuel ix, tells the story of Saul's quest of his father's lost
asses, which ended in his meeting with the prophet, Samuel, who "took
a vial of oil, and poured it upon his head, . . . and said, Is it not
because the Lord hath anointed thee to be captain over his inheritance?"   (I Sam. x, 1.)

244–245. *quit Those rudiments:* go beyond that elementary knowledge. Compare *rudiments* in I, 157.

249. *Mysteries* may be used, with a touch of irony, as it is in Christ's
words to the disciples, "It is given to you to know the mysteries of
the kingdom."   (Mat. xiii, 11.)

252–258. The Mountain was probably Mount Niphates, where Milton
made Satan land when he first reached this world (*P.L.,* III, 742); but
it is hardly more definitely located than the mountain of Adam's final
vision of the future, which is compared with it in *P.L.,* XI, 381–384.
Luke and Matthew both say simply that Satan took Jesus up into a high
mountain, and the instantaneousness of his vision suggests that he saw
with the mind's rather than the body's eye.   The two rivers are the
Tigris and Euphrates and they correspond with the situation of Mount
Niphates in the Taurus range on the Assyrian border of Armenia.

Lay pleasant; from his side two rivers flow'd,   255
Th'one winding, the other straight, and left between
Fair Champain with less rivers intervein'd,
Then meeting join'd thir tribute to the Sea:
Fertile of corn the glebe, of oil and wine,
With herds the pastures throng'd, with flocks the hills,   260
Huge Cities and high tow'r'd, that well might seem
The seats of mightiest Monarchs; and so large
The Prospect was, that here and there was room
For barren desert fountainless and dry.
To this high mountain top the Tempter brought   265
Our Saviour, and new train of words began.
    Well have we speeded, and o'er hill and dale,
Forest and field, and flood, Temples and Towers
Cut shorter many a league; here thou behold'st
Assyria and her Empire's ancient bounds,   270
Araxes and the *Caspian* lake, thence on
As far as *Indus* East, *Euphrates* West,
And oft beyond; to South the *Persian* Bay,
And inaccessible the *Arabian* drouth;
Here *Ninevee,* of length within her wall   275

---

255. *his: i.e.,* the mountain's. Compare the note on "her" in I, 82.

267–344. Virgil's survey of the regions and races of Italy which sent troops to the support of Turnus against Aeneas (*Aen.* VII, 641–782) has fine panoramic quality, but it was tuned to the theme of Roman glory and flattered the parochial traditions of the Italians; Milton's outlook was as wide as the entire ancient world with the dimension of time deepened by the perspective of a really profound and critical student of history who read the records in the light of his Christian faith.

271. The river Araxes flows eastward from near Erzerum in Armenia and falls into the Caspian. With this use of *lake* compare the "lake Genezaret" in II, 23, and the "Galilean lake" in *Lycidas,* 109.

273. *Persian Bay:* the arm of the Indian ocean between Persia and Arabia which receives the Tigris and Euphrates.

274. *drouth:* desert. The abstract for the concrete.

275–279. Nineveh was supposed, at least by the Greeks, to be named for its mythical founder, Ninus. All ancient writers speak of its *length* (*i.e.,* circuit) with wonder, like the Old Testament writers, who called it "an exceeding great city of three days journey" (Jonah iii, 3) to walk the length of the circumvallations. Salmanassar (Shalmaneser) carried the ten northern tribes of Israel into captivity in 726 B.C.

Several days' journey, built by *Ninus* old,
Of that first golden Monarchy the seat,
And seat of *Salmanassar,* whose success
Israel in long captivity still mourns;
There *Babylon* the wonder of all tongues,   280
As ancient, but rebuilt by him who twice
Judah and all thy Father *David's* house
Led captive, and *Jerusalem* laid waste,
Till *Cyrus* set them free; *Persepolis*
His city there thou seest, and *Bactra* there;   285
Ecbatana her structure vast there shows,
And *Hecatompylos* her hunderd gates,
There *Susa* by *Choaspes,* amber stream,
The drink of none but Kings; of later fame
Built by *Emathian,* or by *Parthian* hands,   290
The great *Seleucia, Nisibis,* and there

280–283. The new Babylonian empire was founded in 625 B.C. and
its second king, Nebuchadnezzar, who was an even greater builder than
conqueror, attacked Jerusalem in 605 B.C. and again in 597, when he
carried away King Jehoiachin "and all the princes, and all the mighty
men of valour, even ten thousand captives." (II Kings xxiv, 14.)

284–288. *Cyrus,* the founder of the Persian empire, seized Ecbatana,
the capital of Media, and in 538 B.C. took Babylon. His capital,
Persepolis, lay in southern Persia, but he transferred it to Susa on the
river Choaspes. Herodotus (I, 188) says that on all his marches the
Great King "took with him water of the Choaspes boiled, . . . of which
alone and of no other river the king drinks."
Bactra, modern Balkh in Afghanistan, was the capital of the Persian
province of Bactria. *Hecatompylos,* "the city of a hundred gates,"
was a city in Parthia, the site of which is unknown.

289–293. After the death of Alexander the Great *Seleucia* (or Se-
leuceia) was founded by the Emathian (*i.e.,* Macedonian) general
Seleucus Nicator and became one of the greatest cities in the ancient
world. It was on the Tigris about fifty miles from the site of Babylon
on the Euphrates.
Nisibis was a city in northern Mesopotamia, near the Armenian
border, which became important in the struggle of the Parthians with
Rome.
Artaxata was the ancient capital of Armenia.
Teredon, somewhere near the mouth of the river formed by the confluence of the Tigris and Euphrates, became known to the Greeks
when it was visited by Alexander's admiral, Nearchus, on his voyage
from the mouth of the Indus to the mouth of the Euphrates.
Ctesiphon was built by the Parthians on the Tigris close to Seleucia
and for some time it was their capital.

Artaxata, Teredon, Ctesiphon,
Turning with easy eye thou mayst behold.
All these the *Parthian,* now some Ages past,
By great *Arsáces* led, who founded first   295
That Empire, under his dominion holds
From the luxurious Kings of *Antioch* won.
And just in time thou com'st to have a view
Of his great power; for now the *Parthian* King
In *Ctesiphon* hath gather'd all his Host   300
Against the *Scythian,* whose incursions wild
Have wasted *Sogdiana;* to her aid
He marches now in haste; see, though from far,
His thousands, in what martial equipage
They issue forth, Steel Bows and Shafts their arms,   305
Of equal dread in flight, or in pursuit;
All Horsemen, in which fight they most excel;
See how in warlike muster they appear,
In Rhombs and wedges, and half-moons, and wings.
    He look't and saw what numbers numberless   310
The City gates out pour'd, light armed Troops
In coats of Mail and military pride;
In Mail thir horses clad, yet fleet and strong,

294-297. About 250 B.C. *Arsaces* broke the Seleucid dynasty whose capital was then at Antioch on the river Orontes, in Syria, about twenty miles from its mouth.

301-302. The barbarians living east and north of the Caspian Sea were known as *Scyths* and the Parthian province adjacent to them was *Sogdiana.* It was roughly divided into halves by the river Oxus, the modern Amu-Daria.

309. *Rhombs:* formations of infantry in the shape of a rhombus, really a double wedge with points in two directions. Milton's interest in the art of war made him think often in terms of the geometrical arrangements of troops which his contemporaries admired in ancient military practice. His interest found expression in the squared regiments of *P.L.* I, 758 and VIII, 232, the "Globe of fiery Seraphim" of II, 512, and the "cubic Phalanx" of the angels in VI, 399.

311-314. Milton shared Montaigne's interest in Ammianus Marcellinus' account of the Parthian arms; "they had (saith he) their horses stiffe and strong, covered with thicke hides and themselves armed from head to foot, with massie iron plates so artificially contrived, that where the joynts are, there they furthered the motion, and helped the stirring. A man would have said, they had been men made of yron." Florio's *Montaigne,* II, ix.

Prancing their riders bore, the flower and choice
Of many Provinces from bound to bound;   315
From *Arachosia,* from *Candaor* East,
And *Margiana* to the *Hyrcanian* cliffs
Of *Caucasus,* and dark *Iberian* dales;
From *Atropatia* and the neighbouring plains
Of *Adiabene, Media,* and the South   320
Of *Susiana* to *Balsara's* hav'n.
He saw them in thir forms of battle rang'd,
How quick they wheel'd, and flying behind them shot
Sharp sleet of arrowy showers against the face
Of thir pursuers, and overcame by flight;   325
The field all iron cast a gleaming brown,
Nor wanted clouds of foot, nor on each horn,
Cuirassiers all in steel for standing fight;

316–321. *Arachosia* was a province west of the Indus, in modern Beluchistan.

Candaor, now called Candahar, was not an ancient name. It is a province of Afghanistan.

Margiana corresponds with modern Khorasan.

Hyrcania bordered on the Caspian Sea not far from the Caucasus, but Milton was probably thinking of Virgil's lines where Dido, in language already conventional, vituperates Aeneas with being the son of the rugged Caucasus mountains and the nursling of Hyrcanian tigers. (*Aen.,* IV, 366–367.)

This *Iberia* is not Spain but a region of the Caucasus lying near the Caspian Sea. Purchas (*Pilgrimes,* 3, 110) speaks of its "palpable darkness" and mysterious inhabitants.

Atropatia was a province of Media south of the river Araxes.

Adiabene is mentioned by Strabo (XVI, i, 1) as one of the great plains around Nineveh.

Susiana was the most southerly province of the Persian and Parthian realms. It bordered on the Persian Gulf.

Balsara, the modern Bassora, on the Chatt-el-Arab or united Tigris and Euphrates, was a great port which Milton's contemporaries identified with the ancient Teredon.

323–324. Horace (*Odes,* II, xiii, 17–18) spoke of the arrows and swift flight of Parthians as the terror of the Roman soldiers, and Virgil (*Georgic,* III, 31) called Augustus' victory over the Parthian, whose reliance is on flight and his backward arrows, a supreme triumph. A "Parthian shot" originally meant more than "the last word."

326. Compare the note on *brown* in II, 293.

327. A "cloud of foot" was a phrase inherited from Homer (*Il.,* IV, 274) and Virgil (*Aen.,* VII, 793).

Chariots or Elephants indorst with Towers
Of Archers, nor of labouring Pioners   330
A multitude with Spades and Axes arm'd
To lay hills plain, fell woods, or valleys fill,
Or where plain was raise hill, or over-lay
With bridges rivers proud, as with a yoke;
Mules after these, Camels and Dromedaries,   335
And Waggons fraught with Utensils of war.
Such forces met not, nor so wide a camp,
When *Agrican* with all his Northern powers
Besieg'd *Albracca,* as Romances tell,
The City of *Gallaphrone,* from thence to win   340
The fairest of her Sex, *Angelica,*
His daughter, sought by many Prowest Knights,
Both *Paynim,* and the Peers of *Charlemagne.*
Such and so numerous was thir Chivalry;
At sight whereof the Fiend yet more presum'd,   345

329. "Indorse" first entered English as a legal word with essentially its modern meaning. *N.E.D.* calls Milton's use of the literal, Latin sense of "put on the back" pedantic, but to him it seemed perhaps a bit playfully ornate, as it must have seemed to Ben Jonson when he wrote his epigram saying of the Earl of Newcastle's horse that his master's "seat his beauties did endorse."
Elephants carrying howdahs with archers were familiar to the Greeks from the time when Alexander faced them in the armies of Darius.

334. There may be a shadow here of the prophetic picture of the river Araxes reluctantly submitting to a Roman bridge, which was a part of the decoration of the shield which Vulcan made for Aeneas. (*Aen.,* VIII, 728.)

338-343. In Boiardo's *Orlando Innamorato* (I, x–xiv) *Angelica* is responsible for involving Astolfo, Roland, and other less famous of Charlemagne's Twelve Peers of France in the fighting around *Albracca,* a fabulous fortress of her father, *Gallaphrone,* the king of Cathay (China), when it is besieged by her lover, *Agrican,* the king of Tartary. The exploits of the knights were as fantastic as their numbers— twenty-two hundreds of thousands in the investing army alone. (I, x, 26.)

342. *Prowest:* hardiest. The derivation is from the Old French word *prou,* meaning "knightly."

343. *Paynim:* pagan. Compare the *"Paynim* chivalry" of *P.L.,* I, 765, and the other passage in *P.L.,* I, 581–587, where Milton evoked his early reading of the Italian romances.

344. *Chivalry* was "applied by early translators to the horsemen of ancient Greece and Rome, for which 'cavalry' is the modern equivalent." *N.E.D.* The word stands for the whole army indiscriminately.

And to our Saviour thus his words renew'd.
    That thou mayst know I seek not to engage
Thy Virtue, and not every way secure
On no slight grounds thy safety; hear, and mark
To what end I have brought thee hither and shown   350
All this fair sight: thy Kingdom though foretold
By Prophet or by Angel, unless thou
Endeavour, as thy Father *David* did,
Thou never shalt obtain; prediction still
In all things, and all men, supposes means,   355
Without means us'd, what it predicts revokes.
But say thou wert possess'd of *David's* Throne
By free consent of all, none opposite,
Samaritan or *Jew;* how couldst thou hope
Long to enjoy it quiet and secure,   360
Between two such enclosing enemies
Roman and *Parthian?* therefore one of these
Thou must make sure thy own, the *Parthian* first
By my advice, as nearer and of late
Found able by invasion to annoy   365
Thy country, and captive lead away her Kings,
Antigonus, and old *Hyrcanus* bound,
Maugre the *Roman:* it shall be my task
To render thee the *Parthian* at dispose;
Choose which thou wilt, by conquest or by league.   370
By him thou shalt regain, without him not,
That which alone can truly reinstall thee
In *David's* royal seat, his true Successor,

---

358. *opposite:* opposing.

359. An alliance of Samaritans with Jews would be almost impossible, for the Jews had "no dealings with the Samaritans." (John iv, 9.)

367–368. Josephus (*Antiquities,* XIV) recounts the consolidation of *Antigonus'* brief power by Parthian support against his uncle, the High Priest, *Hyrcanus,* who had been confirmed in his position by Julius Caesar. Although he carried Hyrcanus captive to Seleucia, Antigonus reigned only three years when his shameful execution by Herod the Great ended the Asmonean dynasty about 37 B.C. Hyrcanus returned to Jerusalem, but was degraded by Herod and at last executed treacherously at the age of eighty, in 30 B.C.

Maugre: in spite of. From French *malgré.*

373–380. About 722 B.C. Shalmaneser IV and his successor Sargon,

Deliverance of thy brethren, those ten Tribes
Whose off-spring in his Territory yet serve   375
In *Habor,* and among the *Medes* dispers't,
Ten Sons of *Jacob,* two of *Joseph* lost
Thus long from *Israel;* serving as of old
Thir Fathers in the land of *Egypt* serv'd,
This offer sets before thee to deliver.   380
These if from servitude thou shalt restore
To thir inheritance, then, nor till then,
Thou on the Throne of *David* in full glory,
From *Egypt* to *Euphrates* and beyond
Shalt reign, and *Rome* or *Caesar* not need fear.   385
    To whom our Saviour answer'd thus unmov'd.
Much ostentation vain of fleshly arm,
And fragile arms, much instrument of war
Long in preparing, soon to nothing brought,
Before mine eyes thou hast set; and in my ear   390
Vented much policy, and projects deep
Of enemies, of aids, battles and leagues,
Plausible to the world, to me worth naught.
Means I must use thou say'st, prediction else
Will unpredict and fail me of the Throne: 395
My time I told thee, (and that time for thee

---

crushed the ten northern tribes of Israel (including the two named after Ephraim and Manasseh, the sons of Joseph) and placed them "in Habor [*i.e.,* the land adjacent to river Habor, a tributary of the Euphrates] by the river of Gozan, and in the cities of the Medes." (II Kings xvii, 6.)

384. God's covenant with Abraham was to give his descendants the whole region "from the river of Egypt, unto the great river, the river Euphrates" (Gen. xv, 18), and David's son, Solomon, actually reigned over all the kingdoms from the Euphrates "unto the border of Egypt." (I Kings iv, 21.)

387. There is an allusion to the curse in Jeremiah xvii, 5, on the "man that trusteth in man, and maketh flesh his arm."

391. *policy:* shrewd statecraft. Satan's purpose in hell was to found a

> "nether Empire, which might rise
> By policy, and long process of time,
> In emulation opposite to Heav'n."
>
> (*P.L.,* II, 296–298.)

Compare *politic* in 400 below.

396–397. *My time . . . is not yet come:* the words of Jesus to his

Were better farthest off) is not yet come;
When that comes think not thou to find me slack
On my part aught endeavouring, or to need
Thy politic maxims, or that cumbersome   400
Luggage of war there shown me, argument
Of human weakness rather than of strength.
My brethren, as thou call'st them, those Ten Tribes,
I must deliver, if I mean to reign
David's true heir, and his full Sceptre sway   405
To just extent over all Israel's Sons;
But whence to thee this zeal, where was it then
For Israel, or for David, or his Throne,
When thou stood'st up his Tempter to the pride
Of numb'ring Israel, which cost the lives   410
Of threescore and ten thousand Israelites
By three days' Pestilence? such was thy zeal
To Israel then, the same that now to me.
As for those captive Tribes, themselves were they
Who wrought their own captivity, fell off   415
From God to worship Calves, the Deities
Of Egypt, Baal next and Ashtaroth,
And all the Idolatries of Heathen round,
Besides thir other worse than heathenish crimes;
Nor in the land of their captivity   420
Humbled themselves, or penitent besought

---

unfriendly "brethren" in a context (John vii, 6) that rebuked worldly
standards.

409–412. "Satan stood up against Israel, and provoked David to
number Israel." (I Chron. xxi, 1.) Why the taking of the census
should have displeased God is not indicated clearly, but, perhaps as a
punishment for confidence in numbers, "the Lord sent pestilence upon
Israel, and there fell of Israel seventy thousand men."

414–417. Jeroboam, who divided the Ten Tribes from Judah and
Benjamin, and founded the northern kingdom of Samaria, "made two
calves of gold, and said unto them, . . . behold, thy gods, O Israel,
which brought thee up out of the land of Egypt." (I Kings xii, 28.)
Compare P. L., I, 482–489.

417–418. Jeroboam also "went and served Baal and worshipped
him" (I Kings xvi, 31) after his marriage with the daughter of Ethbaal, king of Zidon. Baal was a name common to many local gods
worshipped under local names like Baal-Peor and Baal-hammon. Ashtoreth (plural Ashtaroth) was the Phoenician Venus. Compare P.L.,
I, 422 and 438.

The God of their fore-fathers; but so died
Impenitent, and left a race behind
Like to themselves, distinguishable scarce
From Gentiles, but by Circumcision vain,   425
And God with Idols in their worship join'd.
Should I of these the liberty regard,
Who freed, as to their ancient Patrimony,
Unhumbl'd, unrepentant, unreform'd,
Headlong would follow; and to thir Gods perhaps   430
Of *Bethel* and of *Dan?* no, let them serve
Thir enemies, who serve Idols with God.
Yet he at length, time to himself best known,
Rememb'ring *Abraham,* by some wond'rous call
May bring them back repentant and sincere,   435
And at their passing cleave the *Assyrian* flood,
While to their native land with joy they haste,
As the Red Sea and *Jordan* once he cleft,
When to the promis'd land thir Fathers pass'd;
To his due time and providence I leave them.   440
    So spake *Israel's* true King, and to the Fiend
Made answer meet, that made void all his wiles.
So fares it when with truth falsehood contends.

The End of the Third Book.

427–431. The thought is a doubt whether, if they were repatriated,
the Ten Tribes would not return to the worship of the pagan deities
whose cults their kings had established in the cities of *Bethel* and *Dan.*
(I Kings xii, 29.)

429. The three negative adjectives give an effect of stubborn wickedness which is exactly the reverse of the picture of Abdiel's loyalty to
God,
                    "unmov'd,
     Unshak'n, unseduc'd, unterrifi'd"
       (*P.L.*, V, 898–899. Compare II, 185.)
It is natural to compare Hamlet's description of his father as sent into
the other world,
         "Unhousel'd, disappointed, unanel'd."
          (*Hamlet,* I, v, 77.)
Probably Milton remembered many similar effects in Greek literature,
such as Hector's wish that Paris had been unbegotten or at least unwed
(*Il.,* III, 40).

436–439. Isaiah (xi, 16) had prophesied a "highway for the remnant
of his people, which shall be left, from Assyria; like as it was to
Israel in the day that he came up out of the land of Egypt."

The Fourth Book

PERPLEX'D and troubl'd at his bad success
The Tempter stood, nor had what to reply,
Discover'd in his fraud, thrown from his hope,
So oft, and the persuasive Rhetoric
That sleek't his tongue, and won so much on *Eve,*   5
So little here, nay lost; but *Eve* was *Eve,*
This far his over-match, who self-deceiv'd
And rash, before-hand had no better weigh'd
The strength he was to cope with, or his own:
But as a man who had been matchless held   10
In cunning, over-reach't where least he thought,
To salve his credit, and for very spite
Still will be tempting him who foils him still,
And never cease, though to his shame the more;
Or as a swarm of flies in vintage time,   15
About the wine-press where sweet must is pour'd,
Beat off, returns as oft with humming sound;
Or surging waves against a solid rock,
Though all to shivers dash't, the assault renew,
Vain batt'ry, and in froth or bubbles end;   20
So Satan, whom repulse upon repulse

---

1. *success:* outcome, result. Compare the pertinacity of Satan who, "by success untaught" (*P.L.,* II, 9) conspired to attack heaven after being cast into hell.

3. *Discover'd:* exposed.
thrown from his hope: an idiom common in Latin; *e.g.,* Cicero's description of Catiline as fallen from his hope of subverting the state. (Second Catilinarian oration, §7.)

4–5. In *P.L.,* IX, 532–732, Milton tried to realize that *persuasive Rhetoric.*

10–20. In *P.L.* the similes are often chained together as they are in the Homeric poems. Homer's comparison of the warriors around the body of Sarpedon to flies around the milk cans in a peasant's hut (*Il.* XVI, 641), and of the courage of Menelaus to the boldness of a persistent fly (*Il.* XVII, 570), may have suggested the first simile here. Tasso had set the example of likening the demons to flies or bees, as Milton did in *P.L.* I, 768, and Spenser compared the illusions of temptation to buzzing flies. (*F.Q.* II, ix, 51.) The cunning man of the first simile has been identified with Salmasius; but, if a real counterpart for him must be found in history, Charles I, as he is represented in *Eikonoklastes,* is a possibility.

Met ever, and to shameful silence brought,
Yet gives not o'er though desperate of success,
And his vain importunity pursues.
He brought our Saviour to the western side   25
Of that high mountain, whence he might behold
Another plain, long but in breadth not wide;
Wash'd by the Southern Sea, and on the North
To equal length back'd with a ridge of hills
That screen'd the fruits of the earth and seats of men   30
From cold *Septentrion* blasts, thence in the midst
Divided by a river, of whose banks
On each side an Imperial City stood,
With Towers and Temples proudly elevate
On seven small Hills, with Palaces adorn'd,   35
Porches and Theatres, Baths, Aqueducts,
Statues and Trophies, and Triumphal Arcs,
Gardens and Groves presented to his eyes,
Above the highth of Mountains interpos'd:
By what strange Parallax or Optic skill   40
Of vision multiplied through air, or glass
Of Telescope, were curious to enquire:
And now the Tempter thus his silence broke.
    The City which thou seest no other deem
Than great and glorious *Rome,* Queen of the Earth   45
So far renown'd, and with the spoils enricht
Of Nations; there the Capitol thou seest,

27–31. The *plain* washed by the southern (*i.e.,* Mediterranean) sea
is Latium, with Rome in the centre and the Apennines screening it
from the *Septentrion blasts* or north winds. The Septentrion is the
group of seven stars constituting the constellation of the Great Bear.

37. *Arcs:* triumphal arches. The three great arches of Titus, Trajan,
and Constantine were, of course, not yet in existence, but Augustus
had erected an arch to commemorate his victory over Antony at Actium.
In general it seems to be imperial Rome of the first or even of a later
century which Milton visualized.

40. *Parallax:* any displacement of vision. The word is not used in its
astronomical sense, although Milton was thinking of the wizardry of the
new science of optics and the newly invented telescope.

44–45. Satan's first words evoke the proud picture of Rome in the
Apocalypse (xviii, 7): "for she saith in her heart, I sit a queen, and am
no widow, and shall see no sorrow."

47. The *Capitol* meant to Milton the temple of Jupiter, Juno, and
Minerva on the Capitoline hill. At the close of the Punic wars it was

Above the rest lifting his stately head
On the *Tarpeian rock,* her Citadel
Impregnable, and there Mount *Palatine*   50
The Imperial Palace, compass huge, and high
The Structure, skill of noblest Architects,
With gilded battlements, conspicuous far,
Turrets and Terraces, and glittering Spires.
Many a fair Edifice besides, more like   55
Houses of Gods (so well I have dispos'd
My Aery Microscope) thou mayst behold
Outside and inside both, pillars and roofs
Carv'd work, the hand of fam'd Artificers
In Cedar, Marble, Ivory or Gold.   60
Thence to the gates cast round thine eye, and see
What conflux issuing forth, or ent'ring in,
Praetors, Proconsuls to thir Provinces
Hasting or on return, in robes of State;
Lictors and rods, the ensigns of thir power,   65
Legions and Cohorts, turms of horse and wings:
Or Embassies from Regions far remote
In various habits on the *Appian* road,

---

reconstructed at an expense which has been estimated at $20,000,000.00 and it was crowded with splendid trophies of Roman victories.

49. The *Tarpeian rock* was the steepest precipice of the Capitoline hill and was famous because condemned men were thrown down there.

50–54. Perhaps Milton intended to suggest Nero's famous Golden House, which stood on the Palatine hill.

57. *Aery;* the spelling was Milton's preference. Compare *P.L.,* I, 430, 775, *etc.,* in all a dozen times in that poem.

63. The powers of the *Praetors,* which were originally those of a judge within the city of Rome, had been extended to imply a year of provincial government like the proconsular year as a colonial governor to which the consuls looked forward, and their number had been increased to sixteen.

65. *Lictors:* the ceremonial attendants of the higher Roman officials. Twelve of them followed a consul and twenty-four a dictator, carrying bundles of rods to signify his power to punish criminals.

66. A *Cohort* was, technically, the tenth part of a legion. Because the cavalry fought on the flanks of the Roman armies its units were called *wings,* and the tenth part of a *wing* was a *turm.*

68. The *Appian* Way was constructed from Rome to Brindisi by Appius Claudius in 312 B.C. It is still lined for several miles outside of Rome by the ruins of monumental tombs.

Or on the *Aemilian,* some from farthest South,
Syene, and where the shadow both way falls,   70
Meroe, Nilotic Isle, and more to West,
The Realm of *Bocchus* to the Black-moor Sea;
From the *Asian* Kings and *Parthian* among these,
From *India* and the golden *Chersonese,*
And utmost *Indian* Isle *Taprobane,*   75
Dusk faces with white silken Turbants wreath'd:
From *Gallia, Gades,* and the *British* West,
Germans and *Scythians,* and *Sarmatians* North
Beyond *Danubius* to the *Tauric* Pool.
All Nations now to *Rome* obedience pay,   80

---

69. Various extensions of the *Aemilian* Way connected Rome with Dertona in Cis-Alpine Gaul and with Aquileia, near the head of the Adriatic Sea, and points east as far as Bononia.

70–86. The romantic imperialism here is like Claudian's in his picture of the Roman Empire as uniting Colchian and Iberian, mitred Arab and coifed Armenian, painted Sacian and dyed Mede, dark Indians in their jewelled pavilions and warriors from the Rhone and Atlantic shores. (*On Stilicho's Consulship,* I, 152–160.)

70. *Syene:* the modern Assouan, lying at the foot of the Great Falls of the Nile. It was a Roman frontier post.

71. The Nile, the Blue Nile, and the Atbara partly surrounded the "Isle" of *Meroe.* The city of Meroe was the Ethiopian capital, famous for mysterious temples and a sacred dynasty of queens, and famous also because "twice in the yeere the shadowes are gone, and none at all seene, to wit, when the summer is in the 18 degree of Taurus, and in the 14 of Leo." (Pliny's *Natural History,* Book II, Cap. 73, Sec. 75. Holland's translation.) The latitude is 14° north.

72. *Bocchus,* who was king of what is now Mauretania and western Algeria, was famous for his betrayal of his son-in-law, Jugurtha, to the Romans in 106 B.C.
Black-moor Sea: the part of the Mediterranean off the coast of Mauretania.

74. Sumatra and Malacca were rivals for identification with "the land called Ophir, but now the *Aurea Chersonesus,* which belongs to India," where Josephus (*Antiquities,* VIII, vi, 4) says that Solomon sent for gold. Compare *P.L.,* XI, 392.

75. *Tapróbane* (four syllables): the ancient name for Ceylon.

77. Gallia: Gaul, modern France.
Gades: modern Cadiz.

78. *Scythians* was a general name for the barbarians of central *Asia.* The *Sarmatians* occupied most of modern Poland and Russia west of the Volga.
The *Tauric Pool,* or Pool Maeotis of *P.L.,* IX, 78; the Sea of Azof.

To *Rome's* great Emperor, whose wide domain
In ample Territory, wealth and power,
Civility of Manners, Arts, and Arms,
And long Renown thou justly mayst prefer
Before the *Parthian;* these two Thrones except,   85
The rest are barbarous, and scarce worth the sight,
Shar'd among petty Kings too far remov'd;
These having shown thee, I have shown thee all
The Kingdoms of the world, and all thir glory.
This Emperor hath no Son, and now is old,   90
Old, and lascivious, and from *Rome* retir'd
To *Capreae,* an Island small but strong
On the *Campanian* shore, with purpose there
His horrid lusts in private to enjoy,
Committing to a wicked Favourite   95
All public cares, and yet of him suspicious,
Hated of all, and hating; with what ease
Indu'd with Regal Virtues as thou art,
Appearing, and beginning noble deeds,
Might'st thou expel this monster from his Throne   100
Now made a sty, and in his place ascending
A victor people free from servile yoke?
And with my help thou mayst; to me the power
Is given, and by that right I give it thee.
Aim therefore at no less than all the world,   105
Aim at the highest, without the highest attain'd
Will be for thee no sitting, or not long
On David's Throne, be prophesi'd what will.

---

83. *Civility:* the spirit of civilized people. *N.E.D.* cites Sir Thomas
Browne anent bees and ants; "The civility of these little citizens . . .
neatly sets forth the wisdom of their maker."

90–94. Tiberius (42 B.C.–A.D. 37) was attracted to *Capri* in the Bay
of Naples, off the *Campanian* shore, "because," as Suetonius says, "it
was accessible only by one small beach and was girt about everywhere else
by sheer rocks and deep water"; but the crimes of which he was traditionally accused in his retirement there seem exaggerated. (*Lives of
the Caesars,* III, xl.)

95–97. The *Favourite* was Sejanus. Though Suetonius says that he
moderated Tiberius' cruelty, the pictures of him in Juvenal's Tenth
Satire and Ben Jonson's play are in general not unjust.

104. "And the devil said unto him, All this power will I give thee,
and the glory of them; for that is delivered unto me." (Luke iv, 6.)

To whom the Son of God unmov'd replied.
Nor doth this grandeur and majestic show   110
Of luxury, though call'd magnificence,
More than of arms before, allure mine eye,
Much less my mind; though thou should'st add to tell
Thir sumptuous gluttonies, and gorgeous feasts
On *Citron* tables or *Atlantic* stone,   115
(For I have also heard, perhaps have read)
Their wines of *Setia, Cales,* and *Falerne,*
Chios and *Crete,* and how they quaff in Gold,
Crystal and Murrhine cups imboss'd with Gems
And studs of Pearl, to me should'st tell who thirst   120
And hunger still: then Embassies thou show'st
From Nations far and nigh; what honour that,
But tedious waste of time to sit and hear
So many hollow compliments and lies,
Outlandish flatteries? then proceed'st to talk   125
Of the Emperor, how easily subdu'd,
How gloriously; I shall, thou say'st, expel
A brutish monster: what if I withal
Expel a Devil who first made him such?
Let his tormentor Conscience find him out,   130
For him I was not sent, nor yet to free

115–116. The suggestion in parentheses is a reminder that Milton thought of Christ's knowledge of the world as human, not divine. He himself was familiar with Roman records of extravagant feasting like Juvenal's attack on those who "search every element for the delicacies that they love" and whose pleasure in food depends on nothing but its cost. (*Satire* XI, 14–16.)

115. The African citrus furnished a perfumed wood which Pliny (*Natural History,* XIII, xxix, Sec. 15) says was used for expensive furniture.

The Atlas mountains in Algeria gave their name to the marble from their slopes as well as to the ocean beyond them.

117. *Setia* lay near Rome, while *Cales* and the *Falernian* region, which were still more famous for their wines, were in Campania, in the neighbourhood of Mount Vesuvius.

118. The islands of *Chios* and *Crete* furnished expensive Greek wines.

119. *Murrhine cups* were made of a rare earth and seem to have been first brought from Parthia. Juvenal speaks of a huge diamond, and of crystal and murrhine cups as the three great objects of a spoiled woman's wishes. (*Satire* VI, 155–156.)

That people victor once, now vile and base,
Deservedly made vassal, who once just,
Frugal, and mild, and temperate, conquer'd well,
But govern ill the Nations under yoke,   135
Peeling thir Provinces, exhausted all
By lust and rapine; first ambitious grown
Of triumph, that insulting vanity;
Then cruel, by thir sports to blood inur'd
Of fighting beasts, and men to beasts expos'd,   140
Luxurious by thir wealth, and greedier still,
And from the daily Scene effeminate.
What wise and valiant man would seek to free
These thus degenerate, by themselves enslav'd,
Or could of inward slaves make outward free?   145
Know therefore when my season comes to sit
On *David's* Throne, it shall be like a tree
Spreading and over-shadowing all the Earth,
Or as a stone that shall to pieces dash
All Monarchies besides throughout the world,   150
And of my Kingdom there shall be no end:
Means there shall be to this, but what the means,
Is not for thee to know, nor me to tell.

132–145. The thought is a reinforcement of that in Book II, 446–480.
In *Of Reformation in England* (Book II, *P.W.*, III, p. 178) Milton spoke
of the civil government of Republican Rome as so "divinely and
harmoniously tuned" that no nation except reformed England might
excel it, but he thought of Imperial Rome as an example of a powerful state enslaved by the passions of its citizens.

136. *Peeling:* pillaging. Milton thought of the systematic robbery of
the provinces by the proconsuls, such as the stripping of Sicily as Cicero
described it in his invective *Against Verres*.

138–142. Lactantius (*Divine Institutes,* VI, xx, 12–13 and 27–29) attacked the gladiatorial sports for dehumanizing the Romans and the
corrupt mimes in the theatres for making them effeminate. Milton was
deliberately recalling one of the great charges of the early Church
against the civilization of Rome.

142. *Scene:* stage, theatre.

147–150. Jesus appropriates Nebuchadnezzar's vision of a tree which
"reached unto heaven, and the sight thereof to the end of all the
earth." (Dan. iv, 11.)   And he sees a prophecy of his own destiny in
Daniel's vision of a stone which smote the image of worldly power and
"became a great mountain, and filled the whole earth." (Dan. ii, 35.)

To whom the Tempter impudent replied.
I see all offers made by me how slight   155
Thou valu'st, because offer'd, and reject'st:
Nothing will please the difficult and nice,
Or nothing more than still to contradict:
On the other side know also thou, that I
On what I offer set as high esteem,   160
Nor what I part with mean to give for naught;
All these which in a moment thou behold'st,
The Kingdoms of the world to thee I give;
For giv'n to me, I give to whom I please,
No trifle; yet with this reserve, not else,   165
On this condition, if thou wilt fall down,
And worship me as thy superior Lord,
Easily done, and hold them all of me;
For what can less so great a gift deserve?
     Whom thus our Saviour answer'd with disdain.   170
I never lik'd thy talk, thy offers less,
Now both abhor, since thou hast dar'd to utter
The abominable terms, impious condition;
But I endure the time, till which expir'd,
Thou hast permission on me. It is written   175
The first of all Commandments, Thou shalt worship
The Lord thy God, and only him shalt serve;
And dar'st thou to the Son of God propound
To worship thee accurst, now more accurst
For this attempt bolder than that on *Eve*,   180
And more blasphémous? which expect to rue.
The Kingdoms of the world to thee were giv'n,
Permitted rather, and by thee usurp't,
Other donation none thou canst produce:

----

157. *nice:* fastidious. So Raphael, when Adam offers him food in
Eden, accepts it with the words; "to taste Think not I shall be nice."
(*P.L.,* V, 432–433.)

163–169. Compare the Introduction, §10.

176–177. Jesus is quoting from Deuteronomy vi, 13: "Thou shalt
fear the Lord thy God, and serve him."

184. *donation* has its legal force—as in Latin—of bestowal of property or privilege by a superior authority upon an individual or institution.

If given, by whom but by the King of Kings,   185
God over all supreme? if giv'n to thee,
By thee how fairly is the Giver now
Repaid?   But gratitude in thee is lost
Long since.   Wert thou so void of fear or shame,
As offer them to me the Son of God,   190
To me my own, on such abhorred pact,
That I fall down and worship thee as God?
Get thee behind me; plain thou now appear'st
That Evil one, Satan for ever damn'd.

    To whom the Fiend with fear abasht replied.   195
Be not so sore offended, Son of God,
Though Sons of God both Angels are and Men;
If I to try whether in higher sort
Than these thou bear'st that title, have propos'd
What both from Men and Angels I receive,   200
Tetrarchs of fire, air, flood, and on the earth
Nations besides from all the quarter'd winds,
God of this world invok't and world beneath;
Who then thou art, whose coming is foretold
To me so fatal, me it most concerns.   205
The trial hath indamag'd thee no way,
Rather more honour left and more esteem;
Me naught advantag'd, missing what I aim'd.
Therefore let pass, as they are transitory,
The Kingdoms of this world; I shall no more   210
Advise thee, gain them as thou canst, or not.
And thou thyself seem'st otherwise inclin'd

185–186. St. Paul gave the title "King of kings" to God (I Tim.
vi, 15), and St. John gave it to the risen Christ. (Rev. xvii, 14 and
xix, 16.)

197. In Job i, 6, Satan is included among the other "sons of God"
who appear in heaven. Hosea (i, 10) anticipated the Christian teaching that all men who "are led by the spirit of God, are sons of God."
(Rom. viii, 14.)

201–203. Compare the note on II, 122–124. *Tetrarch* was a Greek
and Roman title given to a ruler of a fourth part of a country and it
is given here to the demons because they were supposed to be assigned
respectively to their individual elements among the traditional four.
Satan means that his subordinate devils give him control of the elements,
while the blindness of men to the truth makes him "the god of this
world." (II Cor. iv, 4.)

Than to a worldly Crown, addicted more
To contemplation and profound dispute,
As by that early action may be judg'd,   215
When slipping from thy Mother's eye thou went'st
Alone into the Temple; there wast found
Among the gravest Rabbies disputant
On points and questions fitting *Moses'* Chair,
Teaching not taught; the childhood shows the man,   220
As morning shows the day.   Be famous then
By wisdom; as thy Empire must extend,
So let extend thy mind o'er all the world,
In knowledge, all things in it comprehend.
All knowledge is not couch't in *Moses'* Law,   225
The *Pentateuch* or what the Prophets wrote,
The *Gentiles* also know, and write, and teach
To admiration, led by Nature's light;
And with the *Gentiles* much thou must converse,
Ruling them by persuasion as thou mean'st,   230
Without thir learning how wilt thou with them,
Or they with thee hold conversation meet?
How wilt thou reason with them, how refute
Thir Idolisms, Traditions, Paradoxes?
Error by his own arms is best evinc't.   235

215–220. Jesus has already mentioned his youthful talks in the Temple (I, 209–214) with the Scribes and Pharisees who pretended to interpret the Law and "sit in Moses' seat."   (Mat. xxiii, 2.)

226. *Pentateuch:* the first five books of the Old Testament, in which the Mosaic law is embodied.

228. Like Richard Hooker, Milton was struck by the belief of many pagan thinkers who found proof in natural law that "nature hath some director of infinite knowledge to guide her in all her ways."   (*Laws of Ecclesiastical Polity,* I, iii, 4.)

230. Compare I, 221–3.

234. *N.E.D.* mentions *Idolism*—meaning the practice of idolatry—as having been used first by Sylvester in his translation of Du Bartas' *The Divine Weekes.*
Milton may have been thinking of the five Stoic *paradoxes,* which dealt in such doctrines as the proposition that wise men are the only kings, or of sceptical paradoxes, like Carneades' proof that assent to an idea is impossible because judgement involves thought processes for which we have no criterion.   Compare the note on ll. 300–308.

235. *evinc't* keeps its Latin force of "conquered."

Look once more ere we leave this specular Mount
Westward, much nearer by Southwest, behold
Where on the *Aegean* shore a City stands
Built nobly, pure the air, and light the soil,
Athens, the eye of *Greece,* Mother of Arts   240
And Eloquence, native to famous wits
Or hospitable, in her sweet recess,
City or Suburban, studious walks and shades;
See there the Olive Grove of *Academe,*
Plato's retirement, where the *Attic* Bird   245
Trills her thick-warbl'd notes the summer long;
There flow'ry hill *Hymettus* with the sound
Of Bees' industrious murmur oft invites
To studious musing; there *Ilissus* rolls
His whispering stream; within the walls then view   250
The schools of ancient Sages; his who bred
Great *Alexander* to subdue the world,

---

236. *specular Mount:* mountain of wide outlook. The Latin *specula*
means "watch-tower."

239. Athenian intelligence was, at least from the time of Plato
(*Timaeus,* 24, C), explained by the clear air of Athens and the temperate living appropriate to its light soil.

240. Justinus (*Epitome,* 5, 8, 4) spoke of Athens and Sparta as the
eyes of Greece.

241–242. Milton remembered that Socrates and Plato were almost
the only natives of Athens who became great philosophers, while
Aristotle and a host of other famous thinkers came to enjoy the city's
hospitality.
wits: wise (rather than witty) men. In *Areopagitica* Milton spoke of
Athens as a place where "wits were ever busier than in any other part
of Greece."
recess: asylum, retreat.

243. *studious:* study-inviting.

244–246. The *Olive Grove* in the suburbs of Athens where Plato met
his disciples was called the Academy.

247–250. The mountain range to the southeast of Athens was famous
for its bees. Roman, as well as Greek, poets often called it "flowery
Hymettus." The river *Ilissus,* which Plato made the setting of some of
his dialogues, rises there and flows through the city of Athens.

251–253. The *Lyceum* was a park with covered walks to the east of
Athens and gave its name to Aristotle's school because his disciples
were in the habit of walking with him there.
Zeno, the founder of the Stoic school, taught in a colonnade in the
market-place of Athens which Pausanias (1, 3, 1; 14, 6, 3) described in

Lyceum there, and painted *Stoa* next;
There thou shalt hear and learn the secret power
Of harmony in tones and numbers hit
By voice or hand, and various-measur'd verse,
Aeolian charms and *Dorian Lyric* Odes,
And his who gave them breath, but higher sung,
Blind *Melesigenes* thence *Homer* call'd,
Whose Poem *Phoebus* challeng'd for his own.
Thence what the lofty grave Tragoedians taught
In *Chorus* or *Iambic,* teachers best
Of moral prudence, with delight receiv'd
In brief sententious precepts, while they treat
Of fate, and chance, and change in human life;
High actions, and high passions best describing:
Thence to the famous Orators repair,
Those ancient, whose resistless eloquence
Wielded at will that fierce Democraty,
Shook the Arsenal and fulmin'd over *Greece,*
To *Macedon,* and *Artaxerxes'* Throne;
To sage Philosophy next lend thine ear,

255

260

265

270

---

the second century, A.D. as having been decorated with frescos by famous painters like Micon and Polygnotus.

257. *charms* keeps its Latin meaning of "songs," as it does in *P.L.,* IV, 642; "charm of earliest Birds." *Aeolian* lyric poetry is best represented by Sappho's songs and *Dorian* by Pindar's odes and hymns.

259–260. The epics of Homer, who, according to one tradition, was born near the river Meles in Ionia, are in the Ionic dialect. An epigram in the Greek Anthology (found in the *Palatine Anthology,* 9, 455) suggested that Apollo admired the Homeric epics enough to lay claim to them: "It was I who sang, but divine Homer wrote it down."

262. Aside from the choral odes, Greek tragedy was mainly written in iambic meter.

269. *Democraty:* democracy.

270–271. Perhaps Milton was thinking of Aristophanes' satire of the Athenian democracy for crying up good government and the virtue of temperance when what it really desired was control of the arsenal and of the treasury. (*Birds,* 1540.) Pericles, the leader of the democratic party in Athens, "thundered and lightened and confounded Hellas" (Aristophanes' *Acharnians,* 530), when its troops were involved in the Peloponnesian War against Sparta and its fleet was challenging the ships of the Persian king, Artaxerxes. Demosthenes' greatest orations were efforts to arouse public opinion in Athens against Philip of Macedon.

272–294. See the Introduction, §5.

From Heaven descended to the low-rooft house
Of *Socrates,* see there his Tenement,
Whom well inspir'd the Oracle pronounc'd   275
Wisest of men; from whose mouth issu'd forth
Mellifluous streams that water'd all the schools
Of Academics old and new, with those
Surnam'd *Peripatetics,* and the Sect
Epicurean, and the *Stoic* severe;   280
These here revolve, or, as thou lik'st, at home,
Till time mature thee to a Kingdom's weight;
These rules will render thee a King complete
Within thyself, much more with Empire join'd.
    To whom our Saviour sagely thus replied.   285
Think not but that I know these things; or think
I know them not; not therefore am I short
Of knowing what I ought: he who receives
Light from above, from the fountain of light,
No other doctrine needs, though granted true;   290
But these are false, or little else but dreams,
Conjectures, fancies, built on nothing firm.
The first and wisest of them all profess'd
To know this only, that he nothing knew;
The next to fabling fell and smooth conceits;   295
A third sort doubted all things, though plain sense;
Others in virtue plac'd felicity,
But virtue join'd with riches and long life;
In corporal pleasure he, and careless ease;
The Stoic last in Philosophic pride,   300

---

295. *The next* is Plato, whose myths evidently seemed the most
vulnerable part of his thought to Milton when the college exercise *On
the Platonic Idea* was written.

The word *conceits* is used as Spenser used it when he called *The
Faerie Queene* a "continued Allegory or darke conceit."

296. Pyrrho was the founder of the sceptical school and Carneades
(see the note on 234 above) was its leader in the second century, B.C.

297-298. *Others:* Aristotle's followers, the Peripatetics.

299. *he:* Epicurus. In spite of the slurring tone of the line, Milton
may not have meant to do an injustice to the Epicurean principle of
tranquillity of mind got by means of a life of controlled physical
pleasure.

300-308. From boyhood Milton was familiar with the famous debate
in Cicero's *De finibus* where the Aristotelian ethic prevails over the

By him call'd virtue; and his virtuous man,
Wise, perfect in himself, and all possessing
Equal to God, oft shames not to prefer,
As fearing God nor man, contemning all
Wealth, pleasure, pain or torment, death and life,   305
Which when he lists, he leaves, or boasts he can,
For all his tedious talk is but vain boast,
Or subtle shifts conviction to evade.
Alas! what can they teach, and not mislead;
Ignorant of themselves, of God much more,   310
And how the world began, and how man fell
Degraded by himself, on grace depending?
Much of the Soul they talk, but all awry,
And in themselves seek virtue, and to themselves
All glory arrogate, to God give none,   315
Rather accuse him under usual names,
Fortune and Fate, as one regardless quite
Of mortal things.   Who therefore seeks in these
True wisdom, finds her not, or by delusion
Far worse, her false resemblance only meets,   320
An empty cloud.   However, many books
Wise men have said are wearisome; who reads
Incessantly, and to his reading brings not

Stoic ideal of the perfectly virtuous man, utterly self-sufficient in his
impossible realization of the five paradoxes (see the note on 234 above),
indifferent to wealth and honour and even insensible to pain. In *C.D.*,
II, x, he condemns this insensibility to pain or "stoical apathy, for
sensibility to pain, and even lamentations, are not inconsistent with
true patience; as may be seen in Job and the other saints, when under
the pressure of affliction." By making the devils in hell (*P.L.*, II, 564)
argue about "apathy" he indicated his opinion of the ingenuity of the
Stoics in defending their paradoxes.

314–315. Editors cite Cicero's argument (*On the Nature of the Gods*,
III, 36) that, to be genuine, virtue must be rooted in the human heart
and not be, like outward possessions, a gift of the gods.

316–318. Compare the Introduction, §15.

320–321. Milton refers to the myth that Jove made a cloud-image
of Juno for her lover, Ixion, to embrace.

321–322. "Of making many books there is no end; and much study
is a weariness of the flesh." (Eccl. xii, 12.)

322–330. It is just possible that Sir Isaac Newton's confession that he
was like a child playing with pebbles on the shore of the ocean of
science was an allusion to this passage.

A spirit and judgment equal or superior,
(And what he brings, what needs he elsewhere seek)   325
Uncertain and unsettl'd still remains,
Deep verst in books and shallow in himself,
Crude or intoxicate, collecting toys,
And trifles for choice matters, worth a sponge;
As Children gathering pebbles on the shore.   330
Or if I would delight my private hours
With Music or with Poem, where so soon
As in our native Language can I find
That solace?   All our Law and Story strew'd
With Hymns, our Psalms with artful terms inscrib'd, 335
Our Hebrew Songs and Harps in *Babylon,*
That pleas'd so well our Victors' ear, declare
That rather *Greece* from us these Arts deriv'd;
Ill imitated, while they loudest sing
The vices of their Deities, and thir own   340
In Fable, Hymn, or Song, so personating
Thir Gods ridiculous, and themselves past shame.
Remove thir swelling Epithets thick laid

---

328. *Crude* has its Latin meaning of "surfeited."

329. *worth a sponge* probably means "fit to be expunged."

334. *Story:* history.   Compare II, 307.

335. *artful:* full of art.   The reference is to the terms at the beginning of the psalms to indicate their poetical classification or the instruments to be used with them.

336–337. "By the rivers of Babylon, there we sat down. . . . For there they that carried us away captive required of us a song." (Psalm cxxxvii, 1–3.)

338. "Poesy," said Ben Jonson in *Timber,* inheriting a belief which went back to the Fathers of the Church, "had her original from heaven, received thence from the Hebrews, and had in prime estimation among the Greeks, transmitted to the Latins and all nations that professed civility."   See the Introduction, §3.

340–342. Compare II, 178–191.   Milton was influenced by the Church Fathers who, like St. Augustine (*City of God,* VI, vii) attacked the "fabulous, scenical, filthy and ridiculous" divinities of the pagans as betraying the hearts of the men who invented them.

341. *personating:* impersonating, *i.e.,* presenting the gods on the stage, or scene, as they were in both the Greek tragedies and—with the utmost indecency—in the Roman mimes, and even in a play like Plautus' *Amphitruo.*

343. Milton had in mind epithets like "the far-darter" of Apollo,

As varnish on a Harlot's cheek, the rest,
Thin sown with aught of profit or delight, 345
Will far be found unworthy to compare
With *Sion's* songs, to all true tastes excelling,
Where God is prais'd aright, and Godlike men,
The Holiest of Holies, and his Saints;
Such are from God inspir'd, not such from thee; 350
Unless where moral virtue is express'd
By light of Nature not in all quite lost.
Thir Orators thou then extoll'st, as those
The top of Eloquence, Statists indeed,
And lovers of thir Country, as may seem; 355
But herein to our Prophets far beneath,
As men divinely taught, and better teaching
The solid rules of Civil Government
In thir majestic unaffected style
Than all the Oratory of *Greece* and *Rome*. 360
In them is plainest taught, and easiest learnt,
What makes a Nation happy, and keeps it so,
What ruins Kingdoms, and lays Cities flat;
These only, with our Law, best form a King.
    So spake the Son of God; but Satan now 365
Quite at a loss, for all his darts were spent,
Thus to our Saviour with stern brow replied.
    Since neither wealth, nor honour, arms nor arts,
Kingdom nor Empire pleases thee, nor aught

"the saviour" of Zeus or Jupiter, and "the golden" and "the crowned"
of Aphrodite or Venus.

346–350. These lines should be read in the light of the Introduction,
§7, and of the widespread opinion to which Sir Philip Sidney gave
classical expression when he said in *An Apologie for Poetrie* that the
best poets were the biblical writers who "did imitate the inconceiuable
excellencies of GOD. Such were *Dauid* in his Psalmes, Salomon in his
song of Songs, in his Ecclesiastes, and Prouerbs, *Moses* and *Debora* in
theyr Hymnes, and the writer of *Iob*."

351–352. *Unless* qualifies *unworthy* in 346. Milton refers to thinkers
like Socrates. Compare line 228 above.

354. *Statists:* statesmen. Sir Thomas Browne said that "Statists that
labour to contrive a Commonwealth without poverty, take away the
object of charity." (*Religio Medici,* II, xiii.)

366. Perhaps there is an allusion to "the fiery darts of the wicked"
(Eph. vi, 16) which are turned by "the shield of faith."

By me propos'd in life contemplative,   370
Or active, tended on by glory, or fame,
What dost thou in this World? the Wilderness
For thee is fittest place; I found thee there,
And thither will return thee; yet remember
What I foretell thee, soon thou shalt have cause   375
To wish thou never hadst rejected thus
Nicely or cautiously my offer'd aid,
Which would have set thee in short time with ease
On *David's* Throne; or Throne of all the world,
Now at full age, fulness of time, thy season,   380
When Prophecies of thee are best fullfill'd.
Now contrary, if I read aught in Heaven,
Or Heav'n write aught of Fate, by what the Stars
Voluminous, or single characters,

370–371. St. Augustine made a distinction which had fundamental importance in the Middle Ages and the Renaissance when he said that "the study of wisdom is either concerning action or contemplation, and thence assumes two several names, active and contemplative, the active consisting in the practice of morality in one's life, and the contemplative in penetrating into the abstruse causes of nature, and the nature of divinity." (*The City of God,* VII, iv.)

377. *Nicely:* squeamishly, fastidiously. Compare *nice* in l. 157.

380–381. Compare the note on I, 286.

382–393. In *P.L.* (especially in X, 656–672) Milton betrays a scientifically rationalized interest in judicial astrology. Its basis was the belief that the heavenly bodies

"Not only enlighten, but with kindly heat
Of various influence foment and warm,
Temper or nourish, or in part shed down
Thir stellar virtue on all kinds that grow
On Earth."

(*P.L.* IV, 668–672.)

This belief came down both through "Ptolemaic" channels such as Pontano's cosmic poem in Latin, the *Urania* (1490), and also through the writings of such English pioneers of the Copernican astronomy as Robert Record and Leonard Digges. It was not at all incompatible with Pico della Mirandola's theories in his *Confutation* of the astrologers nor with John Calvin's treatise against astrology (1561). Even Bishop Carleton, whose great book on *the madness of the astrologers* (1624) attacked them on definitely modern scientific grounds, regarded them as being victims and tools of the devil. Newton suggested that in this passage Milton was satirizing the Italian astrologer and physician, Jerome Cardan (1501–1576), for his famous attempt to cast the horoscope of Jesus.

In their conjunction met, give me to spell,   385
Sorrows, and labours, opposition, hate,
Attends thee, scorns, reproaches, injuries,
Violence and stripes, and lastly cruel death.
A Kingdom they portend thee, but what Kingdom,
Real or Allegoric I discern not,   390
Nor when, eternal sure, as without end,
Without beginning; for no date prefixt
Directs me in the Starry Rubric set.
    So saying he took (for still he knew his power
Not yet expir'd) and to the Wilderness   395
Brought back the Son of God, and left him there,
Feigning to disappear.   Darkness now rose,
As day-light sunk, and brought in louring night,
Her shadowy off-spring, unsubstantial both,
Privation mere of light and absent day.   400
Our Saviour meek and with untroubl'd mind
After his aery jaunt, though hurried sore,
Hungry and cold betook him to his rest,
Wherever, under some concourse of shades
Whose branching arms thick intertwin'd might shield 405
From dews and damps of night his shelter'd head,
But shelter'd slept in vain, for at his head

---

385. *conjunction:* the apparent near approach of two stars or planets.
It was one of the unfavourable "aspects" of astrology.   Compare the
Synod unbenign of *P.L.* X, 661.
    spell: decipher, unriddle.

391. *eternal sure,* in the light of l. 472 below, seems certainly ironical.

393. *Rubric:* a calendar or a document containing laws of any kind.
The term was derived from the red coloring of the captions in ancient
Roman law books and in medieval liturgical works.

397–400. Through Boccaccio's *Genealogy of the Gods* (I, v) and
similar mythological works Milton inherited his interest in Hesiod's
personification of Night as the wife and sister of Erebus or Darkness.
(*Theogony,* 748–757.)   His faith in the essential goodness of matter
and of life made him allegorize Night as the wife of Chaos and contrast it as "unessential" (*P.L.* II, 439) with the Light which is coeternal
with God.

402. *jaunt* originally meant a tiring or difficult journey.

404. *Wherever:* anywhere where rest could be found.

407–409. So in *P.L.* IV, 799–809 Satan is found "close at the ear
of Eve," inspiring evil dreams.

The Tempter watch'd, and soon with ugly dreams
Disturb'd his sleep; and either Tropic now
'Gan thunder, and both ends of Heav'n; the Clouds   410
From many a horrid rift abortive pour'd
Fierce rain with lightning mixt, water with fire
In ruin reconcil'd: nor slept the winds
Within thir stony caves, but rush'd abroad
From the four hinges of the world, and fell   415
On the vext Wilderness, whose tallest Pines,
Though rooted deep as high, and sturdiest Oaks
Bow'd thir Stiff necks, loaden with stormy blasts,
Or torn up sheer: ill wast thou shrouded then,
O patient Son of God, yet only stood'st   420
Unshaken; nor yet stay'd the terror there.
Infernal Ghosts, and Hellish Furies, round
Environ'd thee, some howl'd, some yell'd, some shriek'd,
Some bent at thee thir fiery darts, while thou
Sat'st unappall'd in calm and sinless peace.   425
Thus pass'd the night so foul till morning fair

409. *Tropic* is used loosely to mean opposite parts of the sky.

412–413. *ruin* has the Latin meaning of "fall." The phrasing suggests
Aeschylus' storm in which "fire and sea, those old enemies, leagued
together to hurl pitiless destruction upon the Greek fleet" returning
from Troy. (*Agamemnon*, 659–661.)
Milton thought of this tempest as the work of demons, rulers of "the
middle air" (*P.L.* I, 516; compare *P.R.* I, 39–45); but it is a symbol
also, like "the hideous storme of raine" before the encounter of
Spenser's Redcross Knight with the monster, Error, when a dark sky
deluged the plain so fast
                "That euery wight to shrowd it did constrain."
                        (*F.Q.* I, i, vi, 8.)

414. Milton thought of the vast cave in which Virgil (*Aen.* I, 52–64)
describes the god Aeolus as confining the winds between the storms
which devastate the sea.

415. We derive the term "cardinal" (as in cardinal points of the
compass) from Latin *cardo,* which means a hinge.

419. *sheer:* completely, absolutely.

420. *only:* pre-eminent. Compare Shakespeare's "your onely Iigge-
maker." (*Hamlet*, III, ii, 131.)

426–430. Milton makes artistic use of the superstition that the fiends
lose their power to torment men
                "Ere the first Cock his Matin rings."
                        (*L'Allegro*, 114.)

Came forth with Pilgrim steps in amice gray;
Who with her radiant finger still'd the roar
Of thunder, chas'd the clouds, and laid the winds,
And grisly Spectres, which the Fiend had rais'd   430
To tempt the Son of God with terrors dire.
And now the Sun with more effectual beams
Had cheer'd the face of Earth, and dried the wet
From drooping plant, or dropping tree; the birds
Who all things now behold more fresh and green,   435
After a night of storm so ruinous,
Clear'd up their choicest notes in bush and spray
To gratulate the sweet return of morn.
Nor yet amidst this joy and brightest morn
Was absent, after all his mischief done,   440
The Prince of darkness; glad would also seem
Of this fair change, and to our Saviour came,
Yet with no new device, they all were spent;
Rather by this his last affront resolv'd,
Desperate of better course, to vent his rage,   445
And mad despite to be so oft repell'd.
Him walking on a Sunny hill he found,
Back'd on the North and West by a thick wood;
Out of the wood he starts in wonted shape,
And in a careless mood thus to him said.   450
    Fair morning yet betides thee, Son of God,
After a dismal night; I heard the rack
As Earth and Sky would mingle; but myself
Was distant; and these flaws, though mortals fear them
As dangerous to the pillar'd frame of Heaven,   455

---

427. *amice:* a hood or cape, lined with grey fur, worn by some religious orders.

436. *ruinous:* compare the note on *ruin* in l. 413.

438. *gratulate:* give thanks for. Compare *Comus,* 949.

449. *wonted shape:* usual form, *i.e.,* undisguised.

452. *rack:* ruin, destruction. Compare *P.L.* XI, 821:
    "A World devote to universal rack."

453. Here the reminiscence of Virgil's account of the storm on the Mediterranean mingling earth and sky (*Aen.* I, 133–134) seems deliberate.

455. Here, as in *Comus,* 598, the allusion is to *Job* xxvi, 11. "The pillars of heaven tremble and are astonished at his reproof."

Or to the Earth's dark basis underneath,
Are to the main as inconsiderable,
And harmless, if not wholesome, as a sneeze
To man's less universe, and soon are gone;
Yet as being oft times noxious where they light   460
On man, beast, plant, wasteful and turbulent,
Like turbulencies in the affairs of men,
Over whose heads they roar, and seem to point,
They oft fore-signify and threaten ill:
This Tempest at this Desert most was bent;   465
Of men at thee, for only thou here dwell'st.
Did I not tell thee, if thou didst reject
The perfet season offer'd with my aid
To win thy destin'd seat, but wilt prolong
All to the push of Fate, pursue thy way   470
Of gaining *David's* Throne no man knows when,
For both the when and how is nowhere told,
Thou shalt be what thou art ordain'd, no doubt;
For Angels have proclaim'd it, but concealing
The time and means: each act is rightliest done,   475
Not when it must, but when it may be best.
If thou observe not this, be sure to find,
What I foretold thee, many a hard assay
Of dangers, and adversities and pains,
Ere thou of *Israel's* Scepter get fast hold;   480
Whereof this ominous night that clos'd thee round,
So many terrors, voices, prodigies
May warn thee, as a sure fore-going sign.

---

457. *main:* the entire universe.

458–459. In medicine, Bacon observed (*Advancement of Learning,*
II, x, 2), "the ancient opinion that man was *microcosmus,* an abstract
or model of the world, hath been fantastically strained by Paracelsus
and the alchemists, as if there were to be found in man's body certain
correspondences and parallels, which should have respect to all varieties
of things, as stars, planets, minerals, which are extant in the great
world." The conception went back beyond Plato, and Milton may have
been thinking of the passage in the *Timaeus* (81, A) which says that in
the body "the processes of filling and evacuating take place just as the
motion of everything in the Universe takes place."

468. *perfet:* Milton's usual spelling of "perfect," although no other
instance is found in *P.R.*

478. *assay:* compare the note on l. 264 in Book I.

So talk'd he, while the Son of God went on
And stay'd not, but in brief him answer'd thus.   485
    Mee worse than wet thou find'st not; other harm
Those terrors which thou speak'st of, did me none;
I never fear'd they could, though noising loud
And threat'ning nigh; what they can do as signs
Betok'ning, or ill-boding, I contemn   490
As false portents, not sent from God, but thee;
Who, knowing I shall reign past thy preventing,
Obtrud'st thy offer'd aid, that I accepting
At least might seem to hold all power of thee,
Ambitious spirit, and wouldst be thought my God,   495
And storm'st refus'd, thinking to terrify
Mee to thy will; desist, thou art discern'd
And toil'st in vain, nor me in vain molest.
    To whom the Fiend now swoln with rage replied:
Then hear, O Son of *David,* Virgin-born;   500
For Son of God to me is yet in doubt:
Of the Messiah I have heard foretold
By all the Prophets; of thy birth at length
Announc't by *Gabriel* with the first I knew,
And of the Angelic Song in *Bethlehem* field,   505
On thy birth-night, that sung thee Saviour born.
From that time seldom have I ceas'd to eye
Thy infancy, thy childhood, and thy youth,
Thy manhood last, though yet in private bred;
Till at the Ford of *Jordan* whither all   510
Flock'd to the Baptist, I among the rest,
Though not to be Baptiz'd, by voice from Heav'n
Heard thee pronounc'd the Son of God belov'd.
Thenceforth I thought thee worth my nearer view
And narrower Scrutiny, that I might learn   515
In what degree or meaning thou art call'd
The Son of God, which bears no single sense;
The Son of God I also am, or was,
And if I was, I am; relation stands;
All men are Sons of God; yet thee I thought   520
In some respect far higher so declar'd.
    Therefore I watch'd thy footsteps from that hour,

501–521. See the Introduction, §13.

And follow'd thee still on to this waste wild;
Where by all best conjectures I collect
Thou art to be my fatal enemy.   525
Good reason then, if I before-hand seek
To understand my Adversary, who
And what he is; his wisdom, power, intent,
By parle, or composition, truce, or league
To win him, or win from him what I can.   530
And opportunity I here have had
To try thee, sift thee, and confess have found thee
Proof against all temptation as a rock
Of Adamant, and as a Centre, firm;
To the utmost of mere man both wise and good,   535
Not more; for Honours, Riches, Kingdoms, Glory
Have been before contemn'd, and may again:
Therefore to know what more thou art than man,
Worth naming Son of God by voice from Heav'n,
Another method I must now begin.   540
  So saying he caught him up, and without wing
Of *Hippogrif* bore through the Air sublime

---

524. *collect:* draw an inference, gather.

525. *fatal* keeps its Latin meaning of "established by fate." Compare
Moloch's confession that God's "fatal throne" is inaccessible. (*P.L.*
II, 104.) From the opposite point of view, the word means "un-
escapable" or "loaded with evil destiny"—as it does in l. 205 above.

529. *parle:* parley, negotiation. All the terms in this line have military connotations.

530. *win . . . win:* compare *drooping . . . dropping* in l. 434 above
and the note on II, 269.

534. *Adamant,* Milton remembered, is etymologically the same word
as "diamond." *Rock of Diamond* is similarly used in *P.L.* VI, 364,
and in VI, 110, Satan wears arms of *Adamant.* The word keeps its
Greek force of "unconquerable."
Centre: point of a body's equilibrium. *N.E.D.* cites Sir William
Temple: "Things drawn out of their center are not to be moved without much force, or skill; . . . but, to make them return to their center
again, there is required but little of either."

542. Milton probably thought of Ariosto's tale of Astolfo's journey to
the moon on a *Hippogrif:*
   "Only the Beast he rode was not of art,
   But gotten of a Griffeth on a Mare,
   And like a Griffeth had the former part,
   As Wings and Head, and Claws that hideous are,

Over the Wilderness and o'er the Plain;
Till underneath them fair *Jerusalem,*
The holy City, lifted high her Towers,   545
And higher yet the glorious Temple rear'd
Her pile, far off appearing like a Mount
Of Alabaster, top't with golden Spires:
There on the highest Pinnacle he set
The Son of God; and added thus in scorn: 550
    There stand, if thou wilt stand; to stand upright
Will ask thee skill; I to thy Father's house
Have brought thee, and highest plac't, highest is best,
Now show thy Progeny; if not to stand,
Cast thyself down; safely if Son of God: 555
For it is written, He will give command
Concerning thee to his Angels, in thir hands
They shall up lift thee, lest at any time
Thou chance to dash thy foot against a stone.
    To whom thus Jesus: also it is written,   560
Tempt not the Lord thy God; he said and stood.
But Satan smitten with amazement fell
As when Earth's Son *Antaeus* (to compare

    And passing strength and force, and ventrous Heart,
    But all the rest may with a Horse compare."
    (*Orlando Furioso,* IV, 13.   Harington's translation.)

sublime keeps its Latin meaning of "raised aloft." In *P.L.* VI, 771, Milton says that the Messiah "on the wings of Cherub rode sublime."

546. This was the vast temple built by Herod the Great on the site where Solomon had erected the first temple in Jerusalem.

549. *Pinnacle* suggests the spire of a European church rather than the "little wing" or projection which is indicated by St. Luke's word in the Greek N.T.

554. *Progeny:* birth, descent, parentage.

556–559. The lines paraphrase Psalm xci, 11–12.

561. The verse to which Jesus alludes, "Ye shall not tempt the Lord your God" (Deut. vi, 16), was a warning to the Jews not to try the patience of God.
The emphatic word *stood* marks the moment of Satan's recognition of Christ's full power and identity, and the catastrophe of his own fall is the consequence. Compare the Introduction, §15.

563–571. Hercules was called *Alcides* after his grandfather, Alceus, and the myth represented Jove (Zeus) as his father. Milton seems to have remembered Pindar's account of his struggle with the giant,

Small things with greatest) in *Irassa* strove
With *Jove's Alcides,* and oft foil'd still rose,   565
Receiving from his mother Earth new strength,
Fresh from his fall, and fiercer grapple join'd,
Throttl'd at length in the Air, expir'd and fell;
So after many a foil the Tempter proud,
Renewing fresh assaults, amidst his pride   570
Fell whence he stood to see his Victor fall.
And as that *Theban* Monster that propos'd
Her riddle, and him, who solv'd it not, devour'd;
That once found out and solv'd, for grief and spite
Cast herself headlong from th' *Ismenian* steep,   575
So strook with dread and anguish fell the Fiend,
And to his crew, that sat consulting, brought
Joyless triumphals of his hop't success,
Ruin, and desperation, and dismay,
Who durst so proudly tempt the Son of God.   580
So Satan fell and straight a fiery Globe
Of Angels on full sail of wing flew nigh,
Who on their plumy Vans receiv'd him soft
From his uneasy station, and upbore
As on a floating couch through the blithe Air,   585
Then in a flow'ry valley set him down
On a green bank, and set before him spread

Antaeus, as having occurred in *Irassa* in Cyrenaica, or what is now Libya.
Compare the Introduction, §3–4.

572–575. The *Monster* was the sphinx which threw itself from the
acropolis of Thebes into the river Ismenus when Oedipus found the
answer, "Man," to her question which animal walks first on four, then
on two, and finally on three legs. Milton was familiar with many
interpretations of the myth such as Bacon suggested when he said
that "the riddle proposed to Oedipus . . . related to the nature of
man, for whoever has a thorough insight into the nature of man may
shape his fortune almost as he will, and is born for empire." (*Wisdom
of the Ancients,* xxviii.)

576. *strook* had not given way entirely to "struck." Milton uses the
latter form in III, 146.

578. *triumphals:* celebrations. Ironical, of course.

581. *Globe:* a solid body of soldiers. So Satan is surrounded by a
"Globe of fiery Seraphim" in *P.L.* II, 512.

583. *Vans:* wings. In *P.L.* II, 927, Satan spreads "his Sail-broad
Vans."

A table of Celestial Food, Divine,
Ambrosial, Fruits fetcht from the tree of life,
And from the fount of life Ambrosial drink,   590
That soon refresh'd him wearied, and repair'd
What hunger, if aught hunger had impair'd,
Or thirst; and as he fed, Angelic Quires
Sung Heavenly Anthems of his victory
Over temptation, and the Tempter proud.   595
   True Image of the Father whether thron'd
In the bosom of bliss, and light of light
Conceiving, or remote from Heaven, enshrin'd
In fleshly Tabernacle, and human form,
Wand'ring the Wilderness, whatever place,   600
Habit, or state, or motion, still expressing
The Son of God, with Godlike force indu'd
Against th' Attempter of thy Father's Throne,
And Thief of Paradise; him long of old
Thou didst debel, and down from Heav'n cast   605
With all his Army; now thou hast aveng'd
Supplanted *Adam,* and by vanquishing

---

589. Although *Ambrosia,* the food of the Olympian gods, was supposed to give immortality, Milton used the word without that connotation when he described the trees of life in heaven as bearing "ambrosial fruitage" (*P.L.* V, 427). There the word means "divinely delicious," as it does here, and does again in *P.L.* II, 245, where Mammon mentions God's altar as breathing "Ambrosial Odours and Ambrosial Flowers."

589–590. Milton thought of the symbolic *well of life* from which Spenser's Knight of Holiness drank at the crisis of his combat with a satanic dragon (*F.Q.,* I, xi, 29), and perhaps of the place
     "Where *Tigris* at the foot of Paradise
     Into a Gulf shot under ground, till part
     Rose up a Fountain by the Tree of Life."
                    (*P.L.* IX, 71–73.)

591–592. *repair'd . . . impair'd:* compare the note on l. 530.

596–597. The lines allude to the opening verses of John's gospel, where Christ, the Word, is said to have been from the beginning with God, who is Light and Life, and to have declared Him to men, because He "is in the bosom of the Father." (Verse 18.)

604. Perhaps Milton remembered his description of Satan when he entered Eden to seduce Eve as "this first grand Thief." (*P.L.* IV, 192.)

605. *debel:* war down. Milton thought of Anchises' prophecy that it should be Rome's destiny to debel proud lawlessness throughout the world. (*Aen.* VI, 853.)

Temptation, hast regain'd lost Paradise,
And frustrated the conquest fraudulent:
He never more henceforth will dare set foot   610
In Paradise to tempt; his snares are broke:
For though that seat of earthly bliss be fail'd,
A fairer Paradise is founded now
For *Adam* and his chosen Sons, whom thou
A Saviour art come down to re-install,   615
Where they shall dwell secure, when time shall be
Of Tempter and Temptation without fear.
But thou, Infernal Serpent, shalt not long
Rule in the Clouds; like an Autumnal Star
Or Lightning thou shalt fall from Heav'n trod down 620
Under his feet: for proof, ere this thou feel'st
Thy wound, yet not thy last and deadliest wound
By this repulse receiv'd, and hold'st in Hell
No triumph; in all her gates *Abaddon* rues
Thy bold attempt; hereafter learn with awe   625
To dread the Son of God: he all unarm'd
Shall chase thee with the terror of his voice
From thy Demoniac holds, possession foul,
Thee and thy Legions; yelling they shall fly,
And beg to hide them in a herd of Swine,   630
Lest he command them down into the deep
Bound, and to torment sent before thir time.
Hail Son of the most High, heir of both worlds,
Queller of Satan, on thy glorious work

---

611. *broke,* for "broken," was already obsolete in the seventeenth century. There is an echo of Psalm cxxiv, 7: "the snare is broken, and we are escaped."

612. *be fail'd:* have disappeared. "To be absent or wanting" is the first meaning of the word.

620–621. Jesus' words, "I beheld Satan as lightning fall from heaven" (Luke x, 18) are involved with prophecies like Malachi's promise that "ye shall tread down the wicked." (Mal. iv, 3.)

622. Milton refers to Satan's final destruction at the end of time as St. John foresaw it in the Apocalypse. (Rev. xx, 10.)

624. *Abaddon* is a name of hell in Job xxvi, 6, xxviii, 22, and xxxi, 12.

629–632. The legion of devils which Jesus cast out of the Gergesene madmen and allowed to take refuge in a herd of swine asked him, "Art thou come hither to torment us before the time?" (Mat. viii, 29.)

Now enter, and begin to save mankind.   635
   Thus they the Son of God our Saviour meek
Sung Victor, and from Heavenly Feast refresht
Brought on his way with joy; hee unobserv'd
Home to his Mother's house private return'd.

The End.

---

639. *private* has become a colourless word, but we can recover some
appreciation of the meaning that it had for Milton and of its significance
in this characteristic closing line, if we recall Satan's sneer at Jesus
for "affecting private life" (III, 22) and his contempt for the life which
Jesus lived in Nazareth,
> "Private, unactive, calm, contemplative."
> (II, 81.)

SAMSON AGONISTES[1]

A DRAMATIC POEM

Aristot. Poet. Cap. 6

Τραγῳδία μίμησισ πράξεωσ σπουδαίασ, etc.

Tragoedia est imitatio actionis seriae, etc. per misericordiam et metum perficiens talium affectuum lustrationem.

OF THAT SORT OF DRAMATIC POEM WHICH IS CALL'D TRAGEDY

Tragedy, as it was anciently compos'd, hath been ever held the gravest, moralest, and most profitable of all other Poems: therefore said by *Aristotle*[2] to be of power by raising pity and fear, or terror, to purge the mind of those and such like passions, that is to temper and reduce them to just measure with a kind of delight, stirr'd up by reading or seeing those passions well imitated. Nor is Nature wanting in her own effects to make good his assertion: for so in Physic things of melancholic hue and quality are us'd against melancholy, sour

---

[1]*Agonistes,* in the title, transliterates the Greek name for the amateur athletes who competed in the public games, and it refers to Samson's appearance at the festival of the Philistines in the temple of Dagon at the climax of the tragedy, when he wrestles with the pillars there. Milton used the epithet to point to that particular incident in his hero's life as Aeschylus used the epithets "Bound" and "Freed" in the titles of two of the tragedies in his Promethean trilogy to indicate the particular events in the life of Prometheus on which his plots were based.

[2]Milton is paraphrasing the Aristotelian definition of tragedy which he partly quotes in the original Greek and in Latin translation as an epigraph.

against sour, salt to remove salt humours.[1] Hence Philosophers and other gravest Writers, as *Cicero, Plutarch* and
others, frequently cite out of Tragic Poets, both to adorn and
illustrate their discourse. The Apostle *Paul* himself thought
it not unworthy to insert a verse of *Euripides* into the Text
of Holy Scripture,[2] 1 Cor. 15. 33. and *Paraeus,*[3] commenting on
the *Revelation,* divides the whole Book as a Tragedy, into
Acts distinguisht each by a Chorus of Heavenly Harpings
and Song between. Heretofore Men in highest dignity have
labour'd not a little to be thought able to compose a Tragedy.
Of that honour *Dionysius*[4] the elder was no less ambitious,

---

[1]In his *Art of Poetry* (1564) the Italian critic, Minturno, had applied
the homeopathic, medical theory that "like cures like" to Aristotle's
theory of tragic catharsis, saying that, "Medicine has no greater power,
by means of poison, to expel poison from an afflicted body than tragedy
has to purge the soul of its impetuous passions by the skilful expression
of strong emotion in poetry."

Contemporary physicians sometimes applied homeopathic remedies in
direct relation to the four humours of the body—blood, phlegm,
choler or bile, and melancholy or black bile—as saffron is still popularly used for the liver, because its colour is like that of bile. Burton,
in the *Anatomy* (I, i, 3, 3), recognized "diversity of melancholy matter"
which appeared internally as a black humour and might cause black
jaundice, scurvy, quartan ague or leprosy; or, "if it trouble the mind,
as it is diversely mixed, it produces several kinds of madness and
dotage." "But most commonly," he thought, "fear, grief, and some
sudden commotion or perturbation of the mind, begin it, in such bodies
especially as are ill-disposed." (*Ibid.,* I, ii, 5, 4. Compare lines 600–
601 below.)

[2]The verse, "Evil communications corrupt good manners," was proverbial when St. Paul quoted it. Although Milton attributed it to
Euripides, both here and in *Areopagitica* (*P.W.,* II, 63), the fragment
in which it has come down has been doubtfully assigned both to him
and to Menander.

[3]Milton had long been interested in the commentaries of the German Calvinist, David Paraeus, whose work on Revelation was translated into English in 1644. Its eighth chapter, "Touching the Forme
of the Revelation," suggested his description of the Apocalypse of
St. John, in the Preface to Book II of *The Reason of Church Government,* as "the majestic image of a high and stately tragedy, shutting
up and intermingling her solemn scenes and acts with a sevenfold chorus
of hallelujahs and harping symphonies: and this my opinion the grave
authority of Paraeus . . . is sufficient to confirm."

[4]Dionysius (431–367 B.C.), tyrant of Syracuse, consolidated the cities

than before of his attaining to the Tyranny. *Augustus Caesar*
also had begun his *Ajax*,[1] but unable to please his own judgement with what he had begun, left it unfinisht. *Seneca* the
Philosopher is by some thought the Author of those Tragedies[2] (at least the best of them) that go under that name.
Gregory Nazianzen a Father of the Church, thought it not
unbeseeming the sanctity of his person to write a Tragedy,
which he entitl'd *Christ Suffering*.[3] This is mention'd to
vindicate Tragedy from the small esteem, or rather infamy,
which in the account of many it undergoes at this day with
other common Interludes; happ'ning through the Poet's error
of intermixing Comic stuff with Tragic sadness and gravity;
or introducing trivial and vulgar persons, which by all judicious hath been counted absurd; and brought in without dis-
cretion, corruptly to gratify the people. And though ancient
Tragedy use no Prologue,[4] yet using sometimes, in case of
self defence, or explanation, that which *Martial* calls an Epistle;
in behalf of this Tragedy coming forth after the ancient

---

of Magna Graecia and stopped the Carthaginian expansion in Sicily.
He patronized all the arts and wrote a tragedy himself, *The Ransom of
Hector*, to which the Athenians gave the first prize at the Dionysiac
festival.

[1]Milton was familiar with the story about Augustus Caesar which
Suetonius told (II, 85): "Though he began a tragedy with much enthusiasm, he destroyed it because his style did not satisfy him."

[2]The ten tragedies which are probably rightly attributed to Seneca
were published in Newton's English translation in 1581.

[3]Like all his contemporaries, Milton believed that the tragedy called
Christ Suffering, which now seems to have been written by a Byzantine
Greek about the end of the twelfth century, was the work of Gregory
Nazianzen (325?–390?), Bishop of Constantinople. He undoubtedly
admired its many Euripidean echoes and must have been interested in a
long-standing controversy as to whether the "Playe of Christ" by
Nazianzenus, as Stephen Gosson called it in his *Schoole of Abuse*, was
intended for acting on the stage or was composed "dialoguewise, as
Plato and Tullie did their Philosophye, to be reade, not to be played."

[4]Milton used the word *Prologue* to mean an apology for a work of
art, standing first, like the epistle to the reader prefixed to Martial's
first book of *Epigrams*, or like the "epistles dedicatory" of some Restoration plays—disregarding the fact that Aristotle described "the whole
of that part of a tragedy which precedes the entrance of the chorus"
as the prologue. (*Poetics*, xii.)

manner, much different from what among us passes for best, thus much before-hand may be Epistl'd; that *Chorus* is here introduc'd after the Greek manner, not ancient only but modern, and still in use among the *Italians*. In the modeling therefore of this Poem, with good reason, the Ancients and *Italians*[1] are rather follow'd, as of much more authority and fame. The measure of Verse us'd in the Chorus is of all sorts, call'd by the Greeks *Monostrophic,* or rather *Apolely-menon,*[2] without regard had to *Strophe, Antistrophe* or *Epode,* which were a kind of Stanzas fram'd only for the Music, then us'd with the Chorus that sung; not essential to the Poem, and therefore not material; or being divided into Stanzas or Pauses, they may be call'd *Allaeostropha.*[3] Division into Act and Scene referring chiefly to the Stage (to which this work never was intended) is here omitted; it suffices if the whole Drama be found not produc't beyond the fift Act.

Of the style and uniformity, and that commonly call'd the Plot, whether intricate or explicit, which is nothing indeed but such economy,[4] or disposition of the fable as may stand best with verisimilitude and decorum; they only will best judge

---

[1] So in *Of Education* Milton spoke of the Italians as the best representatives, after the ancients, of "that sublime art which in Aristotle's poetics, in Horace, and the Italian commentaries of Castelvetro, Tasso, Mazzoni, and others, teaches what the laws are of a true epic poem, what of a dramatic, what of a lyric, what decorum is, which is the grand masterpiece to observe." Milton was thinking of the great Senecan dramas in Italy of which Tasso's *Torrismondo* is a good example.

[2] *Apolelymenon* transliterates a Greek term meaning "free" in the sense that the choruses are not bound by the strict divisions into the elaborate stanzaic patterns of the strophe, antistrophe and epode which, in Greek classical tragedies, were distinctly marked off by being sung respectively as the singers moved from right to left, then from left to right, and finally as they stood stationary.

[3] *Allaeostropha:* having strophes or stanzas of irregular length.

[4] First and most important among the six elements of tragedy Aristotle named plot or the arrangement of incidents, which is what Milton meant by *economy*. Aristotle called plots in which there was no sudden reversal in the fortune of the hero from happiness to misery, or from misery to happiness and back again, simple, as contrasted with those in which such changes occur; and criticized them as likely to be episodic and disunited.

who are not unacquainted with *Aeschylus, Sophocles,* and *Euripides,* the three Tragic Poets unequall'd yet by any, and the best rule to all who endeavour to write Tragedy. The circumscription of time[1] wherein the whole Drama begins and ends, is according to ancient rule, and best example, within the space of 24 hours.

THE ARGUMENT

Samson *made Captive, Blind, and now in the Prison at* Gaza,[2] *there to labour as in a common work-house, on a Festival day, in the general cessation from labour, comes forth into the open Air, to a place nigh, somewhat retir'd, there to sit a while and bemoan his condition. Where he happens at length to be visited by certain friends and equals[3] of his tribe, which make the Chorus, who seek to comfort him what they can; then by his old Father* Manoa, *who endeavours the like, and withal tells him his purpose to procure his liberty by ransom; lastly, that this Feast was proclaim'd by the* Philistins[4] *as a day of Thanksgiving for thir deliverance from the hands of* Samson, *which yet more troubles him.* Manoa *then departs to prosecute his endeavour with the*

---

[1]The "unity of time," or principle that a drama ought not to exceed twelve, or at most twenty-four hours in the ideal duration of its action, was unconsciously observed by Aeschylus, Sophocles, and Euripides because it was almost inevitable on a stage without a drop curtain to mark long pauses between the acts. It was not, however, a part of Aristotle's doctrine, but was read into the *Poetics* by neoclassical critics.

[2]Milton seems to have visualized Gaza as Sandys described it in his *Travels* (p. 116): "But now return we unto Gaza, one of the five Cities, and that the principal that belonged to the Palestines, called Philistins in the Scripture, a warlike and powerful people . . . Gaza or Aza signifieth strong." It lay near the Mediterranean coast in southwestern Palestine. Compare the note on l. 1605.

[3]*equals* has its Latin meaning of "contemporaries," persons of about the same age.

[4]The *Philistins* seem to have been a Semitic people, for the name is derived from a Semitic root meaning "to wander," and Milton had the authority of Jeremiah (xlvii, 4) and Deuteronomy (ii, 23) for calling them "sons of Caphtor" in l. 1713. Caphtor has been very uncertainly identified with Crete, with the Nile delta, with Caria on the southwestern shore of Asia Minor and with Cappodocia in west-central Asia Minor.

Philistian *Lords* for Samson's *redemption; who in the meanwhile
is visited by other persons; and lastly by a public Officer to require his coming to the Feast before the Lords and People, to
play or show his strength in thir presence; he at first refuses, dis-
missing the public Officer with absolute denial to come; at length
persuaded inwardly that this was from God, he yields to go along
with him, who came now the second time with great threatenings
to fetch him; the Chorus yet remaining on the place,* Manoa
*returns full of joyful hope to procure ere long his Son's de-
liverance: in the midst of which discourse an Ebrew comes in
haste; confusedly at first and afterward more distinctly relating
the Catastrophe,*[1] *what* Samson *had done to the* Philistins, *and by
accident to himself; wherewith the Tragedy ends.*

THE PERSONS

Samson.
Manoa *the Father of* Samson.
Dalila *his Wife.*
Harapha *of* Gath.
Public Officer.
Messenger.
Chorus *of* Danites.

The Scene before the Prison in Gaza.

SAMSON AGONISTES

Samson. A little onward lend thy guiding hand
To these dark steps, a little further on;
For yonder bank hath choice of Sun or shade,
There I am wont to sit, when any chance
Relieves me from my task of servile toil,   5
Daily in the common Prison else enjoin'd me,

---

[1]Milton thought again of Aristotle's *Poetics* (xviii), where the catastrophe or denouement is the name given to the final part of a tragedy,
beginning at the point where the fortunes of the hero take their final
turn.

1–2. The situation is like that in the opening scene of Sophocles'
Oedipus at Colonus, where Antigone leads her blind father forward, and
also like that in the *Phoenissae* (834–835) of Euripides, where the
"blind feet" of Tiresias are guided forward by his daughter.

Where I a Prisoner chain'd, scarce freely draw
The air imprison'd also, close and damp,
Unwholesome draught: but here I feel amends,
The breath of Heav'n fresh-blowing, pure and sweet,   10
With day-spring born; here leave me to respire.
This day a solemn Feast the people hold
To *Dagon* thir Sea-Idol, and forbid
Laborious works, unwillingly this rest
Thir Superstition yields me; hence with leave   15
Retiring from the popular noise, I seek
This unfrequented place to find some ease,
Ease to the body some, none to the mind
From restless thoughts, that like a deadly swarm
Of Hornets arm'd, no sooner found alone,   20
But rush upon me thronging, and present
Times past, what once I was, and what am now.
O wherefore was my birth from Heaven foretold
Twice by an Angel, who at last in sight
Of both my Parents all in flames ascended   25
From off the Altar, where an Off'ring burn'd,
As in a fiery column charioting
His Godlike presence, and from some great act
Or benefit reveal'd to *Abraham's* race?

---

11. *day-spring*—day-break. Compare *P.L.* V, 139, and VI, 521.

13. Milton's conception of Dagon as a "Sea Monster, upward Man And downward Fish" (*P.L.* I, 462–3) corresponds with the most usual derivation of his name from a Semitic root meaning "fish." He is very doubtfully identified with an Assyrian deity, Dagan. In Phoenicia his name was connected with the word for corn, *dagan,* and he seems to have been an agricultural deity. His cult, as Judges xvi, 23, and I Samuel v, indicate, was centred in the Philistine cities of Ashdod and Gaza.

19–20. The simile was a commonplace. Compare l. 623 and *P.R.* I, 196–7, and IV, 15, note.

20. *found* anticipates *me* in l. 21.

22. Compare Satan's "bitter memory Of what he was, what is." (*P.L.* IV, 24–5.)

24. Samson's birth was foretold to his mother (Judg. xiii, 3–5) and later to her and to Manoa (*Ibid.,* 10–20).

27–28. Milton thought of Elijah's translation to heaven in a chariot of fire. Compare the note on *P.R.* II, 16–7. Josephus (*Antiquities,* V, viii) says that after Manoa had sacrificed "the angel ascended openly, in their sight, up to heaven, by means of the smoke as by a vehicle."

Why was my breeding order'd and prescrib'd   30
As of a person separate to God,
Design'd for great exploits; if I must die
Betray'd, Captiv'd, and both my Eyes put out,
Made of my Enemies the scorn and gaze;
To grind in Brazen Fetters under task   35
With this Heav'n-gifted strength?   O glorious strength
Put to the labour of a Beast, debas't
Lower than bondslave!   Promise was that I
Should *Israel* from *Philistian* yoke deliver;
Ask for this great Deliverer now, and find him   40
Eyeless in *Gaza* at the Mill with slaves,
Himself in bonds under *Philistian* yoke;
Yet stay, let me not rashly call in doubt
Divine Prediction, what if all foretold
Had been fulfill'd but through mine own default,   45
Whom have I to complain of but myself?
Who this high gift of strength committed to me,
In what part lodg'd, how easily bereft me,
Under the Seal of silence could not keep,
But weakly to a woman must reveal it,   50
O'ercome with importunity and tears.
O impotence of mind, in body strong!
But what is strength without a double share
Of wisdom?   Vast, unwieldy, burdensome,

---

30. *breeding*—training, education (*i.e.,* as a Nazarite. Compare Judges xiii, 7).

31. The root meaning of "Nazarite" was "to separate," in the sense that a man or woman who should "separate themselves to vow a vow of a Nazarite, to separate themselves unto the Lord; He shall separate himself from wine and strong drink." (Num. vi, 2–3.)

34. *gaze*—gazing stock. So Macduff threatens to make Macbeth "the shew, and gaze o'th'time." (*Macbeth,* V, viii, 24.)

37. L. 1162 says that asses worked at the mills with the slaves.

38–39. Compare the angel's prophecy that Samson should "begin to deliver Israel out of the hand of the Philistines." (Judg. xiii, 5.)

47. *gift* is the object of *keep* in l. 49.

53–54. Editors quote the saying that "strength without wisdom falls by its own weight" from Horace (*Odes,* III, iv, 65), but the commonplace goes back as far as Pindar (*Pythian Odes,* viii, 15). Samson was a proverbial example of unreasonable strength. Compare 208–209 below. *Ingenium Superat vires* was a familiar maxim.

Proudly secure, yet liable to fall 55
By weakest subtleties, not made to rule,
But to subserve where wisdom bears command.
God, when he gave me strength, to show withal
How slight the gift was, hung it in my Hair.
But peace, 1 must not quarrel with the will 60
Of highest dispensation, which herein
Haply had ends above my reach to know:
Suffices that to me strength is my bane,
And proves the source of all my miseries;
So many, and so huge, that each apart 65
Would ask a life to wail, but chief of all,
O loss of sight, of thee I most complain!
Blind among enemies, O worse than chains,
Dungeon, or beggary, or decrepit age!
Light the prime work of God to me is extinct, 70
And all her various objects of delight
Annull'd, which might in part my grief have eas'd,
Inferior to the vilest now become
Of man or worm; the vilest here excel me,
They creep, yet see; I dark in light expos'd 75
To daily fraud, contempt, abuse and wrong,
Within doors, or without, still as a fool,
In power of others, never in my own;
Scarce half I seem to live, dead more than half.
O dark, dark, dark, amid the blaze of noon, 80
Irrecoverably dark, total Eclipse

---

55. *secure* keeps its Latin meaning of "careless," or "heedless of danger." Compare *P.R.* I, 176, note.

60. The first meaning of *quarrel* is "to find fault" or "to raise objections."

66. *ask*—require, need.

70. Milton thought of the conception of light as the "offspring of Heav'n first-born" which is the basis of the opening passage of *P.L.*, III.

extinct keeps its Latin meaning as the past participle of a verb meaning "extinguish."

73. *Inferior* refers to *me* in l. 70.

74. *Of man or worm*—of men or of worms.

77. *still*—always.

Without all hope of day!
O first created Beam, and thou great Word,
Let there be light, and light was over all;
Why am I thus bereav'd thy prime decree?   85
The Sun to me is dark
And silent as the Moon,
When she deserts the night,
Hid in her vacant interlunar cave.
Since light so necessary is to life,   90
And almost life itself, if it be true
That light is in the Soul,
She all in every part; why was the sight
To such a tender ball as th' eye confin'd?
So obvious and so easy to be quench't,   95
And not as feeling through all parts diffus'd,
That she might look at will through every pore?
Then had I not been thus exil'd from light;
As in the land of darkness yet in light,
To live a life half dead, a living death,   100
And buried; but O yet more miserable!
Myself my Sepulchre, a moving Grave,
Buried, yet not exempt

---

82. *all*—any. Compare Lady Macbeth's words: "Things without all remedie Should be without regard." (*Macbeth,* III, ii, 11–12.)

83–84. A reminiscence of God's command, "Let there be light," in the story of the creation in Genesis (i, 3), which Milton expanded in *P.L.* VII, 243–260.

85. *bereav'd*—robbed of. In earlier English the preposition was often omitted. *N.E.D.* cites Elyot's *Boke of the Governour:* "Enuy had . . . bireft hym his lyfe."

87–89. *silent* has its Latin meaning of "inactive" or "quiet," a use of the word which Pliny explains (*Natural History,* XVI, 74) was regular in referring to the moon between its waning and its crescent phases.

89. *vacant* has its Latin force of "empty" or "at leisure."

93. Milton thought of the theory that the soul was diffused throughout every part of the body and perhaps of the contrast which he puts into Raphael's mouth between human bodies and those of the angels:
　　　"All Heart they live, all Head, all Eye, all Ear,
　　　　All Intellect, all Sense."
　　　　　　　(*P.L.,* VI, 350–351.)

100. Compare Adam's dread of a "living death" in *P.L.* X, 788.

By privilege of death and burial
From worst of other evils, pains and wrongs,   105
But made hereby obnoxious more
To all the miseries of life,
Life in captivity
Among inhuman foes.
But who are these? for with joint pace I hear   110
The tread of many feet steering this way;
Perhaps my enemies who come to stare
At my affliction, and perhaps to insult,
Thir daily practice to afflict me more.
   Chorus. This, this is he; softly a while;   115
Let us not break in upon him;
O change beyond report, thought, or belief!
See how he lies at random, carelessly diffus'd,
With languish't head unpropt,
As one past hope, abandon'd,   120
And by himself given over;
In slavish habit, ill-fitted weeds
O'erworn and soil'd;
Or do my eyes misrepresent? Can this be hee,
That Heroic, that Renown'd,   125
Irresistible *Samson?* whom unarm'd
No strength of man, or fiercest wild beast could withstand;
Who tore the Lion, as the Lion tears the Kid,
Ran on embattled Armies clad in Iron,
And weaponless himself,   130

---

106. *obnoxious* keeps its Latin meaning of "exposed to."

115–116. The first appearance of the chorus, which in Greek tragedy usually numbered twelve or fifteen persons, was termed the parados, and the same name was given to its first song. Here the rhythm and the situation evidently are a reminiscence of the scene in Euripides' *Orestes* (140–145) where Electra warns the chorus of maidens not to disturb her Fury-possessed brother.

118. *diffus'd* keeps its literal Latin meaning of "poured out." Editors compare Ovid's picture of himself in exile, his "languid limbs poured out upon his bed." (*From Pontus,* III, iii, 8.)

119. *languish't*—relaxed. The two words are etymologically related.

122. *habit*—dress. *weeds*—clothes.

128. Judges xiv, 5–6, tells the story of Samson's finding honey in the carcase of a young lion which "roared against him: . . . and he rent him as he would have rent a kid."

Made Arms ridiculous, useless the forgery
Of brazen shield and spear, the hammer'd Cuirass,
Chalybean temper'd steel, and frock of mail
Adamantean Proof;
But safest he who stood aloof,   135
When insupportably his foot advanc't,
In scorn of thir proud arms and warlike tools,
Spurn'd them to death by Troops.   The bold *Ascalonite*
Fled from his Lion ramp, old Warriors turn'd
Thir plated backs under his heel;   140
Or grov'ling soil'd thir crested helmets in the dust.
Then with what trivial weapon came to hand,
The Jaw of a dead Ass, his sword of bone,
A thousand fore-skins fell, the flower of *Palestine,*
In *Ramath-lechi* famous to this day: 145

---

131. *forgery* has the active meaning of "forging."

133. *Chalybean* is now accented on the third syllable, but Milton may have intended the stress to fall on the second.   The usual Elizabethan accentuation of words ending in -ean was on the syllable preceding the ending.

The Chalybes lived in Pontus, on the southern shore of the Black Sea, and were famous for their skill in forging iron.

134. *Adamantean.*   In the ancient world the word meant steel of the hardest kind, but in early English "the properties ascribed to it show a confusion of ideas between the diamond and the loadstone or magnet." (*N.E.D.*) Milton described Satan's shield as made of adamant. (*P.L.* VI, 254.)

136. *insupportably*—irresistibly.

137. *tools*—weapons.   The word often meant "sword," as in *Romeo and Juliet,* I, i, 28–9; "Draw thy toole, here comes two of the house of the Montagues."

138. Ascalon, Askalon, or Ashkelon, was one of the five great Philistine cities and lay on the Mediterranean coast near Gaza.   The reference is to Samson's raid when he "went down to Ashkelon, and slew thirty men of them, and took their spoil." (Judg. xiv, 19.)

140. *plated*—armour-clad.   Shakespeare describes Antony as "like plated Mars." (*Antony and Cleopatra,* I, i, 4.)

142. The *trivial weapon* was the jawbone of an ass which Samson found "and slew a thousand men therewith.   And Samson said, With the jawbone of an ass, heaps upon heaps, with the jaw of an ass have I slain a thousand men." (Judg. xv, 15–16.)

144. *Palestine* refers to Philistia.   Compare note 4 on the Argument.

145. Samson "called that place Ramath-lechi." (Judg. xv, 17.)   The

Then by main force pull'd up, and on his shoulders bore
The Gates of *Azza,* Post, and massy Bar
Up to the Hill by *Hebron,* seat of Giants old,
No journey of a Sabbath day, and loaded so;
Like whom the Gentiles feign to bear up Heav'n.   150
Which shall I first bewail,
Thy Bondage or lost Sight,
Prison within Prison
Inseparably dark?
Thou art become (O worst imprisonment!)   155
The Dungeon of thyself; thy Soul
(Which Men enjoying sight oft without cause complain)

---

margin translates the Hebrew words as "the casting away or the lifting up of the jawbone."

146–149. Samson's last great exploit, before his betrayal by Dalila, was his midnight surprise of the Gazites, when he "took the doors of the gate of the city, and the two posts, and went away with them, bar and all, . . . and carried them up to the top of an hill, that is before Hebron." (Judg. xvi, 3.)

Milton remembered the account of the first Hebrew spies who penetrated Palestine and at Hebron saw "the giants, the sons of Anak, which come of the giants; and so we were in our own sight as grasshoppers, and so we were in their sight." (Num. xiii, 33.)

147. *Azza* was a variant form of *Gaza.* Compare note 2 on the Argument.

148. *Hebron* lay about twenty miles south of Jerusalem, and about forty miles from Gaza; while the limit for a Sabbath day's journey in the Mosaic law (Exod. xvi, 29) was less than one mile.

150. It is odd to find the Hebrews casually referring to the Gentile (*i.e.,* Graeco-Roman) myth of the giant Atlas who was supposed to support the sky on his shoulders. Such allusions may not have seemed to Milton to be justified merely by poetic convention, for, like Sandys (*Travels,* p. 116), he thought of Samson as living "in the time of the Trojan Wars, an Age that produced Worthies, whose force and fortunes are said to have given to the Poets their inventions of Hercules, who lived not long before him." One of the poets' "inventions of Hercules" was the tale that he relieved Atlas temporarily of his load. Compare the Introduction, §23.

156. The First Brother puts the thought into this same metaphor in *Comus,* 383–5, and in *P.L.* IV, 20–23, it inspires the picture of Satan unable to fly from "The Hell within him."

157. *Which* refers to the entire thought following in lines 157 to 163. The blind man's soul cannot generate its own light for physical, or even spiritual vision. Compare *That Nature is not subject to old Age,* 3, note.

Imprison'd now indeed,
In real darkness of the body dwells,
Shut up from outward light   160
To incorporate with gloomy night;
For inward light, alas,
Puts forth no visual beam.
O mirror of our fickle state,
Since man on earth unparallel'd!   165
The rarer thy example stands,
By how much from the top of wondrous glory,
Strongest of mortal men,
To lowest pitch of abject fortune thou art fall'n.
For him I reckon not in high estate   170
Whom long descent of birth
Or the sphere of fortune raises;
But thee whose strength, while virtue was her mate,
Might have subdu'd the Earth,
Universally crown'd with highest praises.   175
    Samson. I hear the sound of words, thir sense the air
Dissolves unjointed ere it reach my ear.
    Chorus. Hee speaks, let us draw nigh.   Matchless in might,
The glory late of *Israel,* now the grief;
We come thy friends and neighbours not unknown   180
From *Eshtaol* and *Zora's* fruitful Vale
To visit or bewail thee, or, if better,

---

163. *visual beam,* like the *visual ray* of *P.L.* III, 620, means the
faculty of sight, which was imagined as a kind of ray of light emanat-
ing from the eye.

164. *mirror*—reflection or pattern. The reference to "the sphere of
fortune" in l. 172 indicates that Milton was thinking of the medieval
conception of the tragic hero as a man first raised high on Fortune's
wheel and then swept down, but he seems also to have been trying to
suggest—by his stress on Samson's sometime possession of strength combined with virtue—that he had a better hero than even Aristotle's ideal
tragic figure. (*Poetics,* xiii.)

175. For the scansion refer to the Introduction, §18.

181. The story of Samson opens in Judges (xiii, 2) with the statement that his father, Manoah, was a citizen of *Zora.* The town lay in
the coastal plain of Sorec (mentioned in l. 229), west of Jerusalem,
and in the list of cities in that valley in Joshua xv, 33, it is mentioned
as next in order after *Eshtaol.*

182. *if better*—if (we may do) better (than merely visit and bewail

Counsel or Consolation we may bring,
Salve to thy Sores; apt words have power to swage
The tumours of a troubl'd mind,   185
And are as Balm to fester'd wounds.
  Samson. Your coming, Friends, revives me, for I learn
Now of my own experience, not by talk,
How counterfeit a coin they are who friends
Bear in their Superscription (of the most   190
I would be understood); in prosperous days
They swarm, but in adverse withdraw their head
Not to be found, though sought.   Yee see, O friends,
How many evils have enclos'd me round;
Yet that which was the worst now least afflicts me,   195
Blindness, for had I sight, confus'd with shame,
How could I once look up, or heave the head,
Who like a foolish Pilot have shipwrack't
My Vessel trusted to me from above,
Gloriously rigg'd; and for a word, a tear,   200
Fool, have divulg'd the secret gift of God
To a deceitful Woman: tell me, Friends,
Am I not sung and proverb'd for a Fool

---

thee, we come to bring counsel). The comma before *if* is not found
in the original editions.

  184. *Salve to . . . Sores* was a proverbial phrase and is illustrated
by Britomart's refusal in *F.Q.* III, ii, 36–37, to accept "idle wordes" as
salve to her sores.

  184–185. Of the many parallels to the thought one of the most
interesting is the question of Ocean in Aeschylus' *Prometheus Bound*
(l. 379)—which was famous because Cicero quoted it in the *Tusculan
Disputations* (III, 31):
           "Know'st thou not this, Prometheus, that mild words
           Are medicines of fierce wrath?"

  185. *Tumour* was often used to mean a swelling of passion in the
mind. *N.E.D.* quotes Sir Henry Wotton: "There is in him no tumour,
no sowrenesse, . . . but a quiet mind."

  190. *Superscription*—stamp denoting the value of a coin; on a counterfeit it would hardly correspond with the real value.

  191. Editors compare Ovid's lines from the *Tristia* (I, ix, 5–6):
"Whilst thou art happy, thou numberest countless friends; once skies
are overcast, thou art alone."

  197. *heave* was equivalent to "lift." The Spirit in *Comus* (885)
called upon Sabrina to "rise, and heave thy rosy head."

  203. David, in despair over his "foolishness," says (Psal. lxix, 11) that

In every street; do they not say, how well
Are come upon him his deserts? yet why?   205
Immeasurable strength they might behold
In me, of wisdom nothing more than mean;
This with the other should, at least, have pair'd,
These two proportion'd ill drove me transverse.

    Chorus. Tax not divine disposal; wisest Men   210
Have err'd, and by bad Women been deceiv'd;
And shall again, pretend they ne'er so wise.
Deject not then so overmuch thyself,
Who hast of sorrow thy full load besides;
Yet truth to say, I oft have heard men wonder   215
Why thou shouldst wed *Philistian* women rather
Than of thine own Tribe fairer, or as fair,
At least of thy own Nation, and as noble.

    Samson. The first I saw at *Timna,* and she pleas'd
Mee, not my Parents, that I sought to wed,   220

---

he has become "a proverb" to his enemies, and Job's worst chagrin is
the fact that he is "a byword to the people." (Job xvii, 6.) In Milton's England many an unpopular person was "sung" in ballads on the
streets.

207. *mean*—ordinary, average.

208. *pair'd*—equalled. In this essentially Latin meaning the word is
obsolete, but its root survives in "peer" and "compeer," both of which
mean "an equal," and in verbs like "impair" and "compare."

209. *transverse*—off the straight course (*i.e.,* of Samson's intended
career).

210. Both the English verb *tax* and the Latin verb from which it is
derived meant "to blame" or "to complain against."
    disposal often denoted divine control of events. *N.E.D.* cites
Tenure of Kings: "God, out of his providence and high disposal," etc.

210–212. In *Tetrachordon* Milton had argued that only Adam, in his
first perfection, "had the gift to . . . apprehend at first sight the true
fitness of that consort which God provided him, while "the best and
wisest men, amidst the sincere and most cordial designs of their hearts,
do daily err in choosing."

212. *pretend* probably keeps its frequent, sixteenth century meaning
of "intend" and the clause means, "however wisely they may intend,"
rather than, "however wise they pretend to be."

213. *Deject* survives only in the past participial form, "dejected."

219–225. The account of Samson's resolve to marry the woman of
Timnath which Milton found in Judges xiv, 1–4, does not suggest that
his motive was passion, and his reply to his parents' protest against his

The daughter of an Infidel: they knew not
That what I motion'd was of God; I knew
From intimate impulse, and therefore urg'd
The Marriage on; that by occasion hence
I might begin *Israel's* Deliverance,   225
The work to which I was divinely call'd;
She proving false, the next I took to Wife
(O that I never had! fond wish too late)
Was in the Vale of *Sorec, Dalila,*
That specious Monster, my accomplisht snare.   230
I thought it lawful from my former act,
And the same end; still watching to oppress
Israel's oppressors: of what now I suffer
She was not the prime cause, but I myself,
Who vanquisht with a peal of words (O weakness!)   235
Gave up my fort of silence to a Woman.
    Chorus. In seeking just occasion to provoke
The *Philistine,* thy Country's Enemy,
Thou never wast remiss, I bear thee witness:
Yet *Israel* still serves with all his Sons.   240
    Samson. That fault I take not on me, but transfer

---

marriage with a Philistine woman—"Get her for me; for she pleaseth
me well"—is justified by the statement that "his father and mother
knew not that it was of the Lord, that he sought an occasion against
the Philistines."

223. *intimate* has its literal, Latin meaning of "inward."

226. *divinely*—by divine or supernatural summons. Compare the
same word in *P.R.* I, 26.

229. There is no suggestion of divine guidance in the statement that
"it came to pass afterward that" Samson "loved a woman in the valley
of Sorek, whose name was Delilah." (Judg. xvi, 4.)

231–232. *lawful*—permissible because of the precedent of the former
marriage and because the *end,* or object in view was the same.

235. It was only when Dalila "pressed him daily with her words,
and urged him, so that his soul was vexed unto death, that he told
her all his heart, and said unto her, There hath not a razor come upon
mine head; for I have been a Nazarite unto God from my mother's
womb: if I be shaven, then my strength will go from me." (Judg.
xvi, 16–17.)

peal is used again in this sense in l. 906 below.   Compare the "hideous
Peal" from the mouths of the Hell Hounds in *P.L.* II, 656.   Milton
thought of a peal of cannon discharged at a fort.

240. *serves*—is in subjection (*i.e.,* to the Philistines).

On *Israel's* Governors, and Heads of Tribes,
Who seeing those great acts which God had done
Singly by me against their Conquerors
Acknowledg'd not, or not at all consider'd   245
Deliverance offer'd: I on th' other side
Us'd no ambition to commend my deeds,
The deeds themselves, though mute, spoke loud the doer;
But they persisted deaf, and would not seem
To count them things worth notice, till at length   250
Thir Lords, the *Philistines,* with gather'd powers
Enter'd *Judea* seeking mee, who then
Safe to the rock of *Etham* was retir'd,
Not flying, but fore-casting in what place
To set upon them, what advantag'd best;   255
Meanwhile the men of *Judah* to prevent
The harass of thir Land, beset me round;
I willingly on some conditions came
Into thir hands, and they as gladly yield me
To the uncircumcis'd a welcome prey,   260
Bound with two cords; but cords to me were threads

---

245. *consider'd*—esteemed, appreciated.

247. *ambition* keeps its primitive Latin meaning of going about or
canvassing for public support. *N.E.D.* cites Houssaie's *Government of
Venice:* "This bartering and ambition of Office was forbidden."

248. Samson's attitude is that of Shakespeare's Coriolanus, who, like
a good soldier, "rewards His deeds with doing them." (*Coriolanus,* II,
ii, 142–143.)

249. *persisted deaf; i.e.,* persisted in refusing to hear.

251. *powers*—forces, troops.

253–264. It was seemingly to consider his next step after smiting
the Philistines "hip and thigh with a great slaughter," that Samson
"went and dwelt in the top of the rock Etam." (Judg. xv, 8.) There
he hoped that the Hebrews would rally to him, but the "three
thousand men of Judah" who came to him asked him to allow them
to bind him and deliver him to the Philistines. "And Samson said
unto them, Swear unto me, that ye will not fall upon me yourselves.
And they spake unto him, saying, No; but we will bind thee fast, and
deliver thee into their hand. . . . And when he came unto Lehi, the
Philistines shouted against him: and the Spirit of the Lord came
mightily upon him, and the cords that were upon his arms became
as flax that was burnt with fire, and his bands loosed from off his
hands." (*Ibid.,* 12–14.) The story of what followed has already been
mentioned in 142–145 above.

Toucht with the flame: on thir whole Host I flew
Unarm'd, and with a trivial weapon fell'd
Their choicest youth; they only liv'd who fled.
Had *Judah* that day join'd, or one whole Tribe,   265
They had by this possess'd the Towers of *Gath,*
And lorded over them whom now they serve;
But what more oft in Nations grown corrupt,
And by thir vices brought to servitude,
Than to love Bondage more than Liberty,   270
Bondage with ease than strenuous liberty;
And to despise, or envy, or suspect
Whom God hath of his special favour rais'd
As thir Deliverer; if he aught begin,
How frequent to desert him, and at last   275
To heap ingratitude on worthiest deeds?
   Chorus. Thy words to my remembrance bring
How *Succoth* and the Fort of *Penuel*
Thir great Deliverer contemn'd,
The matchless *Gideon* in pursuit   280
Of *Madian* and her vanquisht Kings:
And how ingrateful *Ephraim*
Had dealt with *Jephtha,* who by argument,

---

266. *by this*—by this time.
Gath stands here for the whole country of Philistia, one of whose five great cities it was.

268–271. For the part played by this principle in *P.L.* and *P.R.* see the Introduction, §6.

273–276. Perhaps as he wrote these lines Milton thought of the dashing, Puritan cavalry leader, General Lambert, whose resistance to the movement which eventuated in the restoration of Charles II was finally checked at York by the renegade Cromwellian officers, General Monk and Fairfax.

278–281. The *vanquisht Kings* were "Zebah and Zalmunna, kings of Midian," in whose pursuit the men of the Hebrew cities of Succoth and Penuel refused to aid Gideon. (Judg. viii, 4–9.)
Madian is found only once in the Bible (in Acts vii, 29), but it is usual as the Greek rendering of the regular form in the Old Testament, *Midian,* in the Septuagint.

282–289. Jephthah's diplomatic and military victory over the Ammonites is recorded in Judges xi, 12–33. Later he and his Gileadite supporters quarreled with the Ephraimite Hebrews, who had refused to help him against the Ammonites. The successful Gileadites seized the fords of the Jordan and, "when those Ephraimites which were

Not worse than by his shield and spear
Defended *Israel* from the *Ammonite,*   285
Had not his prowess quell'd thir pride
In that sore battle when so many died
Without Reprieve adjudg'd to death,
For want of well pronouncing *Shibboleth.*

  Samson. Of such examples add mee to the roll,   290
Mee easily indeed mine may neglect,
But God's propos'd deliverance not so.

  Chorus. Just are the ways of God,
And justifiable to Men;
Unless there be who think not God at all: 295
If any be, they walk obscure;
For of such Doctrine never was there School,
But the heart of the Fool,
And no man therein Doctor but himself.

  Yet more there be who doubt his ways not just,   300
As to his own edícts, found contradicting,
Then give the reins to wand'ring thought,

---

escaped said, Let me go over; . . . the men of Gilead said unto him,
Art thou an Ephraimite? If he said, Nay;
  "Then said they unto him, Say now Shibboleth; and he said Sib-
boleth: for he could not frame to pronounce it right. Then they . . .
slew him . . . : and there fell . . . of the Ephraimites forty and
two thousand." (Judg. xii, 5–6.)

  291. *mine: i.e.,* my people. Compare the parallel Latinism in *thine*
in l. 1169. Samson forgives his people for neglecting him, but reproaches them for forgetting the cause of God's deliverance of Israel.

  293. There is an echo of the song of the triumphant host on the fiery
sea of glass in Revelation xv, 3: ". . . just and true are thy ways,
thou King of saints."

  295. *think not God at all*—disbelieve absolutely in God. Milton used
a Greek construction here which was familiar to him in many authors,
from Herodotus to Plato, in expressions of disbelief in the gods.

  298. Milton began his chapter "Of God" in *C.D.* with the acknowl-
edgment that "there be not a few who deny the existence of *God,* for
'the fool hath said in his heart, There is no God,' Psalm xiv, 1"; but
he rejoined immediately that "the Deity has imprinted upon the human
mind so many unquestionable tokens of himself, and so many traces of
him are apparent throughout the whole of nature, that no one in his
senses can remain ignorant of the truth."

  299. *Doctor* has its Latin meaning of "authoritative teacher."

  300–301. Milton thought of the ancient question to which Plutarch's
essay *On the Delay of the Divine Justice* was the best pagan answer.

Regardless of his glory's diminution;
Till by thir own perplexities involv'd
They ravel more, still less resolv'd,   305
But never find self-satisfying solution.
    As if they would confine th' interminable,
And tie him to his own prescript,
Who made our Laws to bind us, not himself,
And hath full right to exempt   310
Whomso it pleases him by choice
From National obstriction, without taint
Of sin, or legal debt;
For with his own Laws he can best dispense.
    He would not else who never wanted means,   315
Nor in respect of the enemy just cause
To set his people free,
Have prompted this Heroic *Nazarite,*
Against his vow of strictest purity,
To seek in marriage that fallacious Bride,   320
Unclean, unchaste.
    Down Reason then, at least vain reasonings down,
Though Reason here aver
That moral verdit quits her of unclean:

---

305. *ravel* is used in its primitive meaning of "become tangled" or
"confused."
resolv'd—decided. Compare the use in Luke xvi, 4: "I am resolved
what to do."

307. *interminable*—infinite (*i.e.,* God). The thought is like that put
into God's mouth in Job xl, 3: "Wilt thou also disannul my judgement?
wilt thou condemn me, that thou mayest be righteous?"

312. *obstriction*—a legal bond or obligation. Here the word, which
was first used, seemingly, by Milton, refers to the Mosaic law against
gentile marriages in Deuteronomy vii, 3.

313. *legal debt*—any liability incurred by having broken the law.

319. *strictest purity* did not imply celibacy, according to Mosaic law,
even for a Nazarite; but any infraction of the law constituted impurity
and Samson had broken it by his gentile marriages.

320. *fallacious*—deceitful. *N.E.D.* quotes Cowley's *The Complaint:*
"Teach me not then, O thou fallacious Muse, The Court . . . to
accuse."

321. *Unclean* is used in an almost technical sense, for by the Mosaic
law all gentiles were unclean.

324. *quits*—acquits. *verdit*—verdict.

Unchaste was subsequent, her stain not his.   325
   But see here comes thy reverend Sire
With careful step, Locks white as down,
Old *Manoa:* advise
Forthwith how thou ought'st to receive him.
   Samson. Ay me, another inward grief awak't,   330
With mention of that name renews th' assault.
   Manoa. Brethren and men of *Dan,* for such ye seem,
Though in this uncouth place; if old respect,
As I suppose, towards your once gloried friend,
My Son now Captive, hither hath inform'd   335
Your younger feet, while mine cast back with age
Came lagging after; say if he be here.
   Chorus. As signal now in low dejected state,
As erst in highest, behold him where he lies.
   Manoa. O miserable change! is this the man,   340
That invincible *Samson,* far renown'd,
The dread of *Israel's* foes, who with a strength
Equivalent to Angels' walk'd thir streets,
None offering fight; who single combatant
Duell'd thir Armies rank't in proud array,   345
Himself an Army, now unequal match
To save himself against a coward arm'd
At one spear's length. O ever failing trust
In mortal strength! and oh, what not in man
Deceivable and vain! Nay, what thing good   350
Pray'd for, but often proves our woe, our bane?
I pray'd for Children, and thought barrenness
In wedlock a reproach; I gain'd a Son,

---

327. *careful* keeps its literal force of "full of care." Compare Spenser's refrain in his dirge in the November Eclogue in *The Shepheards Calendar:* "O heavie herse! O carefull verse!"

328. *advise*—take thought, consider.

333. *uncouth*—unknown, strange. Compare Raphael's "voyage uncouth and obscure" in *P.L.* VIII, 230.

334. *gloried* may mean either "honoured" or "boasted."

335. *inform'd*—guided. So the Lady in *Comus,* 179-180, asks, ". . . where else, Shall I inform my unacquainted feet?"

338. *signal*—eminent, conspicuous.

345. *Duell'd*—fought duels with.

And such a Son as all Men hail'd me happy;
Who would be now a Father in my stead?   355
O wherefore did God grant me my request,
And as a blessing with such pomp adorn'd?
Why are his gifts desirable; to tempt
Our earnest Prayers, then, giv'n with solemn hand
As Graces, draw a Scorpion's tail behind?   360
For this did the Angel twice descend? for this
Ordain'd thy nurture holy, as of a Plant;
Select, and Sacred, Glorious for a while,
The miracle of men: then in an hour
Ensnar'd, assaulted, overcome, led bound,   365
Thy Foes' derision, Captive, Poor, and Blind,
Into a Dungeon thrust, to work with Slaves?
Alas! methinks whom God hath chosen once
To worthiest deeds, if he through frailty err,
He should not so o'erwhelm, and as a thrall   370
Subject him to so foul indignities,
Be it but for honour's sake of former deeds.
    Samson. Appoint not heavenly disposition, Father,
Nothing of all these evils hath befall'n me
But justly; I myself have brought them on,   375
Sole Author I, sole cause: if aught seem vile,
As vile hath been my folly, who have profan'd
The mystery of God giv'n me under pledge
Of vow, and have betray'd it to a woman,
A *Canaanite,* my faithless enemy.   380

---

354. *as* was often used to mean "that."   Compare *Richard III*, III, iv, 38–40:

> "Catesby . . . finds the testy gentleman so hot
> As he will lose his head ere give consent."

360. *Graces*—favours. Perhaps the line was influenced by Luke xi, 12. "If a son shall ask of his father an egg, will he offer him a scorpion?"

368. *methinks*—it seems to me.

373. *Appoint*—pin down to a fixed course of action. Compare *Areopagitica* (*P.W.* II, 98): "Neither is God appointed and confined where his chosen shall be first heard to speak."

377. *profan'd* has the Latin meaning of "disclose a sacred secret."

380. *Canaanite:* the Philistines might be called Canaanites because they had conquered and occupied the land of Canaan before the advent of the Hebrews.

This well I knew, nor was at all surpris'd,
But warn'd by oft experience: did not she
Of *Timna* first betray me, and reveal
The secret wrested from me in her highth
Of Nuptial Love profest, carrying it straight   385
To them who had corrupted her, my Spies,
And Rivals?   In this other was there found
More Faith? who also in her prime of love,
Spousal embraces, vitiated with Gold,
Though offer'd only, by the scent conceiv'd   390
Her spurious first-born; Treason against me?
Thrice she assay'd with flattering prayers and sighs,
And amorous reproaches to win from me
My capital secret, in what part my strength
Lay stor'd, in what part summ'd, that she might know: 395
Thrice I deluded her, and turn'd to sport
Her importunity, each time perceiving
How openly, and with what impudence
She purpos'd to betray me, and (which was worse
Than undissembl'd hate) with what contempt   400
She sought to make me Traitor to myself;
Yet the fourth time, when must'ring all her wiles,

382–387. At Samson's wedding with the woman of Timna he challenged his thirty Philistine groomsmen to solve the riddle: "Out of the eater came forth meat, and out of the strong came forth sweetness." Unable to solve it, "they said unto Samson's wife, Entice thy husband, that he may declare unto us the riddle. . . . And she wept before him the seven days, while their feast lasted; and . . . on the seventh day . . . he told her . . . and she told the riddle to the children of her people. And the men of the city said unto him . . . What *is* sweeter than honey? and what *is* stronger than a lion? And he said unto them, if ye had not plowed with my heifer, ye had not found out my riddle." (Judg. xiv, 11–18.) The story to which the riddle referred is in Judges xiv, 5–8.

390. The offer of the lords of the Philistines to Dalila, if she could extract Samson's secret, was "eleven hundred pieces of silver" from every one of them. (Judg. xvi, 5.)

394. Here and in the allusion to the Serpent's "capital bruise" (*P.L.* XII, 383) there is probably an overtone of the word's literal, Latin meaning of "pertaining to the head" from which the meaning "fatal" is derived.

402. *must'ring*—assembling (like troops)—is the first of several military metaphors suggesting that Samson was veritably besieged by Dalila.

With blandisht parleys, feminine assaults,
Tongue-batteries, she surceas'd not day nor night
To storm me over-watch't, and wearied out. 405
At times when men seek most repose and rest,
I yielded, and unlock'd her all my heart,
Who with a grain of manhood well resolv'd
Might easily have shook off all her snares:
But foul effeminacy held me yok't 410
Her Bond-slave; O indignity, O blot
To Honour and Religion! servile mind
Rewarded well with servile punishment!
The base degree to which I now am fall'n,
These rags, this grinding, is not yet so base 415
As was my former servitude, ignoble,
Unmanly, ignominious, infamous,
True slavery, and that blindness worse than this,
That saw not how degenerately I serv'd.
    Manoa. I cannot praise thy marriage choices, Son, 420
Rather approv'd them not; but thou didst plead
Divine impulsion prompting how thou might'st
Find some occasion to infest our Foes.
I state not that; this I am sure; our Foes
Found soon occasion thereby to make thee 425
Thir Captive, and thir triumph; thou the sooner
Temptation found'st, or over-potent charms
To violate the sacred trust of silence
Deposited within thee; which to have kept

---

405. *over-watch't*—tired out with keeping awake. Compare the "seafaring men o'er-watcht" of *P.L.* II, 288.

414–419. In The Conclusion of *Reason of Church Government* Milton wrote a little allegory in which the prelates were represented by Dalila and the English Church by Samson, who "laying down his head among the strumpet flatteries of prelates, while he sleeps and thinks no harm, they wickedly shaving off all those bright and weighty tresses of his laws, . . . which were his ornament and strength, deliver him over to indirect and violent counsels, which, as those Philistines, put out the fair and far-sighted eyes of his natural discerning." Compare the Introduction, §22.

417. Compare the note on *P.R.,* III, 429.

422. *prompting* modifies *impulsion.*

423. *infest*—annoy, molest.

424 *state*—make a statement about. We still say "to state a case."

Tacit, was in thy power; true; and thou bear'st   430
Enough, and more the burden of that fault;
Bitterly hast thou paid, and still art paying
That rigid score.   A worse thing yet remains.
This day the *Philistines* a popular Feast
Here celebrate in *Gaza;* and proclaim   435
Great Pomp, and Sacrifice, and Praises loud
To *Dagon,* as their God who hath deliver'd
Thee, *Samson,* bound and blind into thir hands,
Them out of thine, who slew'st them many a slain.
So *Dagon* shall be magnifi'd, and God,   440
Besides whom is no God, compar'd with Idols,
Disglorifi'd, blasphem'd, and had in scorn
By th' Idolatrous rout amidst thir wine;
Which to have come to pass by means of thee,
Samson, of all thy sufferings think the heaviest,   445
Of all reproach the most with shame that ever
Could have befall'n thee and thy Father's house.
    Samson. Father, I do acknowledge and confess
That I this honour, I this pomp have brought
To *Dagon,* and advanc'd his praises high   450
Among the Heathen round; to God have brought
Dishonour, obloquy, and op't the mouths
Of Idolists, and Atheists; have brought scandal

---

430. *tacit* keeps the force of the Latin participle from which it comes;
"covered in silence," "not mentioned."

433. *score*—record of a debt.

434–439. After Samson's betrayal, "the lords of the Philistines
gathered them together for to offer a great sacrifice unto Dagon their
god, and to rejoice: for they said, Our god hath delivered Samson
our enemy into our hand."   (Judg. xvi, 23.)

439. *them* is in the dative case and *slain* is the direct object of
slew'st; i.e., "slew many to their disadvantage."

442. *disglorifi'd*—robbed of glory.   Compare "disenchant," and "dis-
burden."

446. *reproach*—dishonour, shame.

450. *advanc'd*—raised.   Compare Christ's words in *P.R.* III, 142–
144:

> ". . . so much bounty is in God, such grace,
> That who advance his glory, not thir own,
> Them he himself to glory will advance."

453. "Idolists" seems to have been first used by Sylvester. *N.E.D.*

To *Israel,* diffidence of God, and doubt
In feeble hearts, propense enough before   455
To waver, or fall off and join with Idols:
Which is my chief affliction, shame and sorrow,
The anguish of my Soul, that suffers not
Mine eye to harbour sleep, or thoughts to rest.
This only hope relieves me, that the strife   460
With me hath end; all the contést is now
'Twixt God and *Dagon; Dagon* hath presum'd,
Me overthrown, to enter lists with God,
His Deity comparing and preferring
Before the God of *Abraham.* He, be sure,   465
Will not connive, or linger, thus provok'd,
But will arise and his great name assert:
Dagon must stoop, and shall ere long receive
Such a discomfit, as shall quite despoil him
Of all these boasted Trophies won on me,   470
And with confusion blank his Worshippers.

   Manoa. With cause this hope relieves thee, and these words
I as a Prophecy receive: for God,
Nothing more certain, will not long defer
To vindicate the glory of his name   475
Against all competition, nor will long
Endure it, doubtful whether God be Lord,
Or *Dagon.* But for thee what shall be done?
Thou must not in the meanwhile here forgot
Lie in this miserable loathsome plight   480
Neglected. I already have made way

---

quotes from *Bethulia's Rescue,* II, 498: "You shall . . . make ruddy
Mocmur's Floud, With Idolist Assyrian Armies bloud."

   454. *diffidence*—distrust, absolute want of confidence.

   455. *propense*—having a propensity, inclined.

   463. *Me overthrown*—since my overthrow.

   466. *connive,* here as in *P.L.* X, 624, has the Latin sense of "shut the
eyes," or "ignore."

   469. *discomfit*—discomfiture, crushing defeat.

   470. *won on*—won over.

   471. *blank*—confound. Compare Satan in *P.R.* II, 119–120; "without
sign of boast, or sign of joy, Solicitous and blank."

   472–473. See the Introduction, §28.

To some *Philistian* Lords, with whom to treat
About thy ransom: well they may by this
Have satisfi'd thir utmost of revenge
By pains and slaveries, worse than death inflicted   485
On thee, who now no more canst do them harm.

    Samson. Spare that proposal, Father, spare the trouble
Of that solicitation; let me here,
As I deserve, pay on my punishment;
And expiate, if possible, my crime,   490
Shameful garrulity.   To have reveal'd
Secrets of men, the secrets of a friend,
How heinous had the fact been, how deserving
Contempt, and scorn of all, to be excluded
All friendship, and avoided as a blab,   495
The mark of fool set on his front?   But I
God's counsel have not kept, his holy secret
Presumptuously have publish'd, impiously,
Weakly at least, and shamefully: A sin
That Gentiles in thir Parables condemn   500
To thir abyss and horrid pains confin'd.

    Manoa. Be penitent and for thy fault contríte,
But act not in thy own affliction, Son;
Repent the sin, but if the punishment
Thou canst avoid, self-preservation bids;   505
Or th' execution leave to high disposal,

---

489. *pay on*—go on paying.   Compare Acts xiii, 15: "If ye have any
word of exhortation, . . . say on."

493. *fact*—deed.   Adam, referring to the sin in Eden, says, "perhaps
the Fact Is not so heinous now."   (*P.L.* IX, 928–929.)

499–501. Milton thought of the myth of Tantalus, who, Euripides
says (*Orestes*, l. 10), was punished in Hades for revealing the secrets
of the gods.   Natale Conti, in whose *Mythology* (VI, xviii) several
allegorical interpretations of the myth are represented, preferred this of
Euripides, and in support of it he cited Pindar's reference to Tantalus
as suffering for giving nectar and ambrosia from the table of his father,
Zeus, to his mortal friends.   In a number of classical references to
Tantalus, in which nothing is said definitely about his crime (*e.g.*,
Ovid's *Met.* IV, 457), Conti found evidence that he was condemned for
his "loquacity, because he divulged the secrets of the gods."

503–508. In *C.D.* II, viii, Milton defines *righteousness* as justice to a
man's self.   "Opposed to this is, first, a perverse hatred of self.   In
this class are to be reckoned those who lay violent hands on themselves."

And let another hand, not thine, exact
Thy penal forfeit from thyself; perhaps
God will relent, and quit thee all his debt;
Who evermore approves and more accepts   510
(Best pleas'd with humble and filial submission)
Him who imploring mercy sues for life,
Than who self-rigorous chooses death as due;
Which argues over-just, and self-displeas'd
For self-offence, more than for God offended.   515
Reject not then what offer'd means, who knows
But God hath set before us, to return thee
Home to thy country and his sacred house,
Where thou mayst bring thy off'rings, to avert
His further ire, with prayers and vows renew'd.   520
    Samson. His pardon I implore; but as for life,
To what end should I seek it? when in strength
All mortals I excell'd, and great in hopes
With youthful courage and magnanimous thoughts
Of birth from Heav'n foretold and high exploits,   525
Full of divine instinct, after some proof
Of acts indeed heroic, far beyond
The Sons of *Anak,* famous now and blaz'd,
Fearless of danger, like a petty God
I walk'd about admir'd of all and dreaded   530
On hostile ground, none daring my affront.
Then swoll'n with pride into the snare I fell

---

509. *quit thee all his debt*—remit or cancel all your debt to him.   Compare *Merchant of Venice,* IV, i, 381: "To quit the fine for one half of his goods, I am content."

514. *argues over-just*—proves a person excessively just or rigorous toward himself. Compare Satan's words to Gabriel: "But still thy words . . . Argue thy inexperience." (*P.L.* IV, 930–931.)

516–517. *what offer'd means, who knows But God hath set*—the means which are offered, and which—for aught anyone may know— God has provided.

526. *instinct*—inward knowledge or impulse. Compare *P.L.* X, 262–263:

> "Nor can I miss the way, so strongly drawn
> By this new felt attraction and instinct."

528. For the *Sons of Anak* see the note on ll. 147–148 above.

531. *none daring my affront*—no one daring to encounter me.

Of fair fallacious looks, venereal trains,
Soft'n'd with pleasure and voluptuous life;
At length to lay my head and hallow'd pledge   535
Of all my strength in the lascivious lap
Of a deceitful Concubine who shore me
Like a tame Wether, all my precious fleece,
Then turn'd me out ridiculous, despoil'd,
Shav'n, and disarm'd among my enemies.   540
    Chorus. Desire of wine and all delicious drinks,
Which many a famous Warrior overturns,
Thou couldst repress, nor did the dancing Ruby
Sparkling, out-pour'd, the flavour, or the smell,
Or taste that cheers the heart of Gods and men,   545
Allure thee from the cool Crystálline stream.
    Samson. Wherever fountain or fresh current flow'd
Against the Eastern ray, translucent, pure,
With touch ethereal of Heav'n's fiery rod

---

533. *venereal trains*—appeals to physical passion.

535–540. Milton remembered the scene in Judges xvi, 19, when Dalila made Samson "sleep upon her knees: and she called for a man, and she caused him to shave off the seven locks of his head; and she began to afflict him, and his strength went from him." Compare *P.L.* IX, 1059–1062.

537–538. *me* is indirect and *fleece* direct object of *shore*.

541–546. For the Nazarite vow of abstinence see the note on l. 31. Here there is a reminiscence of Jotham's parable of the trees which asked the vine to be their king. "And the vine said unto them, Should I leave my wine, which cheereth God and man, and go to be promoted over the trees?" (Judg. ix, 13.)

547–549. Here Thyer compared Tasso's verses in *The Seven Days of the World's Creation* (III, 133–40) which say that of all pleasant waters the most wholesome is that which springs out of clayey soil directly in the face of the rising sun. Professor Percival traces this idea, which is paralleled in Burton's *Anatomy*, II, ii, 1, 1, back as far as Ezekiel's vision of the waters which "issue out toward the east country, and go down into the desert, and go into the sea; which being brought forth into the sea, the waters shall be healed." (Ezek. lvii, 8.)

549. Milton thought of *Heav'n's fiery rod* (*i.e.,* the sun's rays) as a
      "Magnetic beam, that gently warms
    The Universe, and to each inward part
    With gentle penetration, though unseen,
    Shoots invisible virtue."
            (*P.L.* III, 583–586.)

I drank, from the clear milky juice allaying   550
Thirst, and refresht; nor envied them the grape
Whose heads that turbulent liquor fills with fumes.
   Chorus. O madness, to think use of strongest wines
And strongest drinks our chief support of health,
When God with these forbidd'n made choice to rear   555
His mighty Champion, strong above compare,
Whose drink was only from the liquid brook.
   Samson. But what avail'd this temperance, not complete
Against another object more enticing?
What boots it at one gate to make defence,   560
And at another to let in the foe,
Effeminately vanquish't? by which means,
Now blind, disheart'n'd, sham'd, dishonour'd, quell'd,
To what can I be useful, wherein serve
My Nation, and the work from Heav'n impos'd,   565
But to sit idle on the household hearth,
A burdenous drone; to visitants a gaze,
Or pitied object, these redundant locks
Robustious to no purpose clust'ring down,
Vain monument of strength; till length of years   570

---

550. *milky juice,* like the "milky stream" of *P.L.* V, 306, is used for sweet or fresh water.

551. *Thirst* is the object both of *allaying* and of *refresht.*

552. *fumes*—influences from food or drink penetrating the body and brain, like the "unkindly fumes" of *P.L.* IX, 1050, which bred a gross sleep in Adam and Eve after they had eaten the fruit of the Tree of Knowledge.

553–557. "The rule of not too much, by temperance taught,
            In what thou eat'st and drink'st,"
                        (*P.L.* XI, 531–532.)
which was revealed to Adam by Michael, corresponds with these lines. In *C.D.* II, ix, Milton defined Temperance as consisting first in *Sobriety* or "abstinence from immoderate eating and drinking."

557. *liquid* is used in the Latin sense of "translucent" or "transparent." Compare the "liquid Light" of *P.L.* VII, 362, and the "liquid Air" of *Comus,* 980.

560. *What boots it*—what good does it do? Compare *Lycidas,* 64–65.

568. *redundant* is used in the Latin sense of "waving" or "flowing."

569. *Robustious* is used without any unfavourable connotation, and means strong or healthy looking. *N.E.D.* cites Daniel's *Hymen's Triumph:* "Not degenerate From my robustious manly Ancestors."

And sedentary numbness craze my limbs
To a contemptible old age obscure?
Here rather let me drudge and earn my bread,
Till vermin or the draff of servile food
Consume me, and oft-invocated death   575
Hast'n the welcome end of all my pains.
   Manoa. Wilt thou then serve the *Philistines* with that gift
Which was expressly giv'n thee to annoy them?
Better at home lie bed-rid, not only idle,
Inglorious, unimploy'd, with age out-worn.   580
But God who caus'd a fountain at thy prayer
From the dry ground to spring, thy thirst to allay
After the brunt of battle, can as easy
Cause light again within thy eyes to spring,
Wherewith to serve him better than thou hast;   585
And I persuade me so; why else this strength
Miraculous yet remaining in those locks?
His might continues in thee not for naught,
Nor shall his wondrous gifts be frustrate thus.
   Samson. All otherwise to me my thoughts portend,   590
That these dark orbs no more shall treat with light,
Nor th' other light of life continue long,
But yield to double darkness nigh at hand:
So much I feel my genial spirits droop,
My hopes all flat, nature within me seems   595

---

571. *craze*—to impair or render infirm. *N.E.D.* cites Heywood's *Dialogue;* "Craz'd . . . or in health."

574. *draff*—offal. Compare the "draff and filth" of *P.L.* X, 630.

578. *annoy* keeps its basic meaning of "injure" or "damage."

581–583. The story is told, but not very clearly, in Judges xv, 18–19. Josephus says (*Antiquities,* V, viii, 9) that God, moved by Samson's entreaties when he was a-thirst after his victory at Ramath-lechi (see the note on l. 145 above), "raised him up a plentiful fountain of sweet water at a certain rock; whence it was that Samson called the place *The Jaw-bone.*" It seems that the rock itself resembled a jaw-bone.

586. *I persuade me*—I persuade myself. Compare l. 1495 below.

589. Because *frustrate* is directly derived from a Latin perfect passive participle, Milton used it as equivalent to "frustrated."

593. *double darkness*—darkness of blindness and of death.

594. *genial*—arising from a man's "genius" or natural character. *N.E.D.* cites Sir Thomas Browne's *Psuedodoxia Epidemica:* "Naturall incapacity, and geniall indisposition."

In all her functions weary of herself;
My race of glory run, and race of shame,
And I shall shortly be with them that rest.
   Manoa. Believe not these suggestions which proceed
From anguish of the mind and humours black,   600
That mingle with thy fancy. I however
Must not omit a Father's timely care
To prosecute the means of thy deliverance
By ransom or how else: meanwhile be calm,
And healing words from these thy friends admit.   605
   Samson. O that torment should not be confin'd
To the body's wounds and sores
With maladies innumerable
In heart, head, breast, and reins;
But must secret passage find   610
To th' inmost mind,
There exercise all his fierce accidents,
And on her purest spirits prey,
As on entrails, joints, and limbs,
With answerable pains, but more intense,   615
Though void of corporal sense.
   My griefs not only pain me
As a ling'ring disease,
But finding no redress, ferment and rage,
Nor less than wounds immedicable   620
Rankle, and fester, and gangrene,
To black mortification.
Thoughts my Tormentors arm'd with deadly stings

599–601. Compare the note on ll. 8–11 in the Preface.

605. The traditional metaphor in *healing words* has occurred in l. 184 above, but the use of the same phrase in *P.L.* IX, 290, suggests that in both cases Milton may have remembered the misused "healing words" of the nurse in Euripides' *Hyppolitus,* l. 478.

609. *reins*—kidneys.

612. *accidents* was regularly used to mean symptoms of disease of any kind. Burton mentions "Old age, from which natural melancholy is almost an inseparable accident." (*Anatomy,* I, i, 3, 2.)

615. *answerable*—corresponding. So Milton prays (*P.L.* IX, 20) Urania to give him, for his epic, an "answerable style" to that which Homer's Muse gave to him.

Mangle my apprehensive tenderest parts,
Exasperate, exulcerate, and raise   625
Dire inflammation which no cooling herb
Or med'cinal liquor can assuage,
Nor breath of Vernal Air from snowy *Alp*.
Sleep hath forsook and giv'n me o'er
To death's benumbing Opium as my only cure,   630
Thence faintings, swoonings of despair,
And sense of Heav'n's desertion.
    I was his nursling once and choice delight,
His destin'd from the womb,
Promis'd by Heavenly message twice descending.   635
Under his special eye
Abstemious I grew up and thriv'd amain;
He led me on to mightiest deeds
Above the nerve of mortal arm
Against the uncircumcis'd, our enemies.   640
But now hath cast me off as never known,
And to those cruel enemies,
Whom I by his appointment had provok't,
Left me all helpless with th' irreparable loss
Of sight, reserv'd alive to be repeated   645
The subject of thir cruelty, or scorn.
Nor am I in the list of them that hope;
Hopeless are all my evils, all remediless;
This one prayer yet remains, might I be heard,
No long petition, speedy death,   650
The close of all my miseries, and the balm.

---

624. *apprehensive*—sensitive. *N.E.D.* quotes Puttenham: ". . . disproportion to the partes apprehensiue, as . . . when a sound is either too loude or too low."

628. *Alp*—any high mountain. *P.L.* II, 620, describes the devils passing "many a Frozen, many a Fiery Alp."

635. *message*—messenger. Milton often used an abstract noun for a concrete thing. Compare "frequence" meaning "an assembly" in *P.R.* I, 128, and II, 130.

639. *nerve*—sinew or muscle. Compare the use of the word in l. 1646 below.

643. *appointment:* compare *appoint* in l. 373 above.

645. *repeated*—made to repeat the experience of being over and over (the subject, *etc.*).

Chorus. Many are the sayings of the wise
In ancient and in modern books enroll'd,
Extolling Patience as the truest fortitude,
And to the bearing well of all calamities,   655
All chances incident to man's frail life
Consolatories writ
With studied argument, and much persuasion sought
Lenient of grief and anxious thought,
But with th' afflicted in his pangs thir sound   660
Little prevails, or rather seems a tune,
Harsh, and of dissonant mood from his complaint,
Unless he feel within
Some source of consolation from above;
Secret refreshings, that repair his strength,   665
And fainting spirits uphold.
    God of our Fathers, what is man!
That thou towards him with hand so various,

652–656. A good example of these traditional *sayings of the wise* is Henry More's chapter in *An Account of Virtue* (II, vii) which quotes from Aristotle, Andronicus of Rhodes, and Cicero in its consideration of *"Fortitude"* as "a Branch of *Patience."* Elsewhere (II, iii) More calls Christian patience "the highest Perfection of Man's Will." Compare the note on ll. 1287–1291 below.

659. *lenient*—softening, allaying. Milton felt the word as grammatically almost equivalent to the Latin present, active participle from which it is derived; and he may have remembered Horace's use of that verb in a famous assertion of the power of philosophy to heal suffering. (*Epistles*, I, i, 34.)

662. *mood* is obviously the musical term. In *P.L.* I, 550, Milton alludes to the Platonic doctrine that Dorian music inspires courage, and here perhaps he recalled the ideal personality described in Plato's *Laches* (188, d), whose spirit is constantly attuned to the Dorian mood and never to the effeminate Ionian, the passionate Phrygian, or the "soft Lydian." Compare *L'Allegro,* 136.

667. Milton repeats the question, "What is man, that thou art mindful of him?" which is echoed in Hebrews ii, 6, from Psalm viii, 4, and varied in Job vii, 17, to "What is man, that thou shouldest magnify him?" Probably he remembered the same question as put to Prometheus in the second choral hymn of Aeschylus' *Prometheus Bound:*

"What is man? behold!
Can he requite thy love—child of a day—
Or help thy extreme need?"
(Blackie's translation.)

Or might I say contrarious,
Temper'st thy providence through his short course,   670
Not evenly, as thou rul'st
The Angelic orders and inferior creatures mute,
Irrational and brute.
Nor do I name of men the common rout,
That wand'ring loose about   675
Grow up and perish, as the summer fly,
Heads without name no more remember'd,
But such as thou hast solemnly elected,
With gifts and graces eminently adorn'd
To some great work, thy glory,   680
And people's safety, which in part they effect:
Yet toward these, thus dignifi'd, thou oft,
Amidst thir highth of noon,
Changest thy countenance and thy hand, with no regard
Of highest favours past   685
From thee on them, or them to thee of service.
    Nor only dost degrade them, or remit
To life obscur'd, which were a fair dismission,
But throw'st them lower than thou didst exalt them high,
Unseemly falls in human eye,   690
Too grievous for the trespass or omission,

----

672. The subdivision of the nine orders of the angels into three
hierarchies was made in the anonymous *Angelic Hierarchy*, which,
though it was probably written in the fifth century, was attributed to
St. Paul's convert, Dionysius the Areopagite. The conception of angelic orders went back into early Christian and Jewish tradition.
Compare the angels
            "Under thir Hierarchs in orders bright."
                        (*P.L.* V, 587.)

677. *Heads*—persons.

682. *dignifi'd*—raised to dignities or positions of power and distinction.

684–686. Perhaps there is a reference to the reverse of fortune which
God permitted to overtake the Puritan party when Charles II returned
to the throne in 1660, even though Milton thought that they might
have expected better things after God's favours to them when the party
was in power under the Cromwells and after the service which it had
done in reforming the English Church.

687. *remit*—return, send back.

688. *obscur'd*—disgraced.

Oft leav'st them to the hostile sword
Of Heathen and profane, thir carcases
To dogs and fowls a prey, or else captív'd:
Or to the unjust tribunals, under change of times,   695
And condemnation of the ingrateful multitude.
If these they scape, perhaps in poverty
With sickness and disease thou bow'st them down,
Painful diseases and deform'd,
In crude old age;   700
Though not disordinate, yet causeless suff'ring
The punishment of dissolute days: in fine,
Just or unjust, alike seem miserable,
For oft alike, both come to evil end.
    So deal not with this once thy glorious Champion,   705
The Image of thy strength, and mighty minister.
What do I beg? how hast thou dealt already?
Behold him in this state calamitous, and turn
His labours, for thou canst, to peaceful end.
    But who is this, what thing of Sea or Land?   710
Female of sex it seems,
That so bedeckt, ornate, and gay,
Comes this way sailing
Like a stately Ship

693–694. Milton may have had in mind the insult to the bodies of
Cromwell, Ireton, and Bradshaw. They were exhumed and publicly
hanged on the gallows at Tyburn on the twelfth anniversary of
Charles I's execution—worse treated than the Greeks whose bodies
Homer says were thrown to the dogs and birds. (*Il.* I, 4–5.)

694–696. The surviving judges who were responsible for Charles's
death were condemned to die; Sir Henry Vane was executed and General Lambert was imprisoned until his death in 1694.

697–700. Milton thought of the poverty and sickness to which he
was reduced when he wrote, partly as a result of the loss of his in-
come from the state and partly in consequence of the loss of his home
in the fire of 1666.

700. *crude*—premature.

701. *Though not disordinate*—though they have not been intemperate in their lives.

706. *minister*—agent. The angels who pursue the falling demons
in *P.L.* I, 170, are called God's "Ministers of vengeance."

714–715. Ships of Tarshish are often mentioned in the O.T. when
proud ships of any kind are intended, and usually they are made objects

Of *Tarsus,* bound for th' Isles   715
Of *Javan* or *Gadire*
With all her bravery on, and tackle trim,
Sails fill'd, and streamers waving,
Courted by all the winds that hold them play,
An Amber scent of odorous perfume   720
Her harbinger, a damsel train behind;
Some rich *Philistian* Matron she may seem,
And now at nearer view, no other certain
Than *Dalila* thy wife.
     Samson. My Wife, my Traitress, let her not come near
          me.   725
     Chorus. Yet on she moves, now stands and eyes thee fixt,
About t' have spoke, but now, with head declin'd
Like a fair flower surcharg'd with dew, she weeps
And words addrest seem into tears dissolv'd,
Wetting the borders of her silk'n veil;   730
But now again she makes address to speak.
     Dalila. With doubtful feet and wavering resolution
I came, still dreading thy displeasure, *Samson,*

---

of God's anger; *e.g.,* "Thou breakest the ships of Tarshish with an east
wind." (Psalm xlviii, 7. Compare Isa. xxiii, 1 and 14.) Milton, like
Josephus (*Antiquities,* VIII, vii, 2), seems to have identified *Tarsus* on
the River Cydnus in Cilicia with the Tarshish of the O.T., but he
probably thought of it as a Phoenician city with its navy held in
common with Tyre.

715–716. Noah's grandson, *Javan* (see Gen. x, 2), was the traditional
ancestor of the Ionians or of the Greeks generally, as Milton implies
in *P.L.* I, 508. One of Ezekiel's taunts of the fallen city of Tyre was
the reminder that "Javan, Tubal, and Meshech, they were thy mer-
chants." (Ezek. xxvii, 13.)
     Gadire (modern Cadiz) was a Phoenician city.

717. *bravery*—finery. *N.E.D.* cites the *Remains* of Sir Walter Raleigh:
"Exceed not in the humour of rags and bravery."

719. *hold them play*—hold them in play, play with them.

720. *amber* originally meant *ambergris,* which was used in the seventeenth century, as it now is, in perfumes.

728. The simile corresponds with the root meaning of the name
"Dalila"—feeble or declining. Editors compare Homer's picture of
the young Gorgythio, pierced by Teucer's arrow and drooping like a
poppy—a comparison which Virgil (*Aen.* IX, 436) and Tasso (*J.D.*
V, 85) borrowed to describe the deaths of boyish warriors.

729. *addrest*—ready for utterance. Compare *address* in l. 731.

Which to have merited, without excuse,
I cannot but acknowledge; yet if tears   735
May expiate (though the fact more evil drew
In the perverse event than I foresaw)
My penance hath not slack'n'd, though my pardon
No way assur'd.   But conjugal affection,
Prevailing over fear and timorous doubt,   740
Hath led me on desirous to behold
Once more thy face, and know of thy estate.
If aught in my ability may serve
To light'n what thou suffer'st, and appease
Thy mind with what amends is in my power,   745
Though late, yet in some part to recompense
My rash but more unfortunate misdeed.
    Samson. Out, out *Hyaena;* these are thy wonted arts,
And arts of every woman false like thee,
To break all faith, all vows, deceive, betray,   750
Then as repentant to submit, beseech,
And reconcilement move with feign'd remorse,
Confess, and promise wonders in her change,
Not truly penitent, but chief to try
Her husband, how far urg'd his patience bears,   755
His virtue or weakness which way to assail:
Then with more cautious and instructed skill
Again transgresses, and again submits;
That wisest and best men full oft beguil'd,
With goodness principl'd not to reject   760
The penitent, but ever to forgive,

736–737. *fact* and *event* keep their respective Latin meanings of "deed" and "outcome."

738. *penance*—penitence.

738–739. *though my pardon No way assur'd* is a Latin absolute construction. "Be" must be read in after *pardon.*

742. *estate*—condition.

748. Milton's readers were familiar with the belief that the hyaena was "a wilde beaste that counterfaiteth the voyce of men, and so entiseth them out of their houses and devoureth them." (Gloss of the Geneva Bible to Ecclesiasticus xiii, 18, quoted by *N.E.D.*)

752. *move*—propose.

760. *principl'd*—actuated by the principle (*i.e.,* that they ought not to reject, *etc.*).

Are drawn to wear out miserable days,
Entangl'd with a pois'nous bosom snake,
If not by quick destruction soon cut off
As I by thee, to Ages an example.   765
    Dalila. Yet hear me *Samson;* not that I endeavour
To lessen or extenuate my offence,
But that on th' other side if it be weigh'd
By itself, with aggravations not surcharg'd,
Or else with just allowance counterpois'd,   770
I may, if possible, thy pardon find
The easier towards me, or thy hatred less.
First granting, as I do, it was a weakness
In me, but incident to all our sex,
Curiosity, inquisítive, importúne   775
Of secrets, then with like infirmity
To publish them, both common female faults:
Was it not weakness also to make known
For importunity, that is for naught,
Wherein consisted all thy strength and safety?   780
To what I did thou show'd'st me first the way.
But I to enemies reveal'd, and should not.
Nor shouldst thou have trusted that to woman's frailty:
Ere I to thee, thou to thyself wast cruel.
Let weakness then with weakness come to parle   785
So near related, or the same of kind,
Thine forgive mine; that men may censure thine
The gentler, if severely thou exact not
More strength from me, than in thyself was found.
And what if Love, which thou interpret'st hate,   790
The jealousy of Love, powerful of sway

---

763. The treacherous snake cherished in the breast was proverbial.
In *Richard II* (III, ii, 131) the king calls his unfaithful favourites
    "Snakes, in my heart-blood warm'd, that sting my heart!"

775. *Curiosity* is in apposition with *weakness* in 773, while the two
adjectives following it modify *sex* in 774.
    importune—persistently bent upon an object. Satan, returning per-
sistently to his temptation of Christ, is called "the importune Tempter."
(*P.R.* II, 404.)

777. *publish*—make public, betray.

785. *parle*—parley, discussion.

786. *kind*—nature.

In human hearts, nor less in mine towards thee,
Caus'd what I did?   I saw thee mutable
Of fancy, fear'd lest one day thou wouldst leave me
As her at *Timna,* sought by all means therefore   795
How to endear, and hold thee to me firmest:
No better way I saw than by importuning
To learn thy secrets, get into my power
Thy key of strength and safety: thou wilt say,
Why then reveal'd?   I was assur'd by those   800
Who tempted me, that nothing was design'd
Against thee but safe custody, and hold:
That made for me, I knew that liberty
Would draw thee forth to perilous enterprises,
While I at home sat full of cares and fears   805
Wailing thy absence in my widow'd bed;
Here I should still enjoy thee day and night
Mine and Love's prisoner, not the *Philistines',*
Whole to myself, unhazarded abroad,
Fearless at home of partners in my love.   810
These reasons in Love's law have pass'd for good,
Though fond and reasonless to some perhaps:
And Love hath oft, well meaning, wrought much woe,
Yet always pity or pardon hath obtain'd.
Be not unlike all others, not austere   815

---

794. *fancy*—affection, love. Compare "maiden meditation, fancy-free," in *Midsummer Night's Dream,* II, i, 161.

794-795. Samson seems to have been a neglectful husband, for, when he visited his first wife after an absence, "her father said, I verily thought that thou hadst utterly hated her; therefore I gave her to thy companion." (Judg. xv, 2.)

796. *endear: s.v.,* myself.

800-802. Milton could count upon his readers to recognize a lie here because they would remember that the Philistines asked Dalila to entice his secret from Samson so that they might "bind him to afflict him." (Judg. xvi, 5.)

803. *That made for me*—that seemed to be for my advantage.

808. *Mine,* for "my," was regularly used when the word was separated from its noun.

811. Milton thought of the law of Love as traditionally administered in the medieval Courts of Love, such as Chartier's *Parliament of Love,* where Hope was judge, Desire was lawyer, and Sweet Thought was sergeant-at-arms.

As thou art strong, inflexible as steel.
If thou in strength all mortals dost exceed,
In uncompassionate anger do not so.
    Samson. How cunningly the sorceress displays
Her own transgressions, to upbraid me mine!   820
That malice not repentance brought thee hither,
By this appears: I gave, thou say'st, th' example,
I led the way; bitter reproach, but true,
I to myself was false ere thou to me;
Such pardon therefore as I give my folly,   825
Take to thy wicked deed: which when thou seest
Impartial, self-severe, inexorable,
Thou wilt renounce thy seeking, and much rather
Confess it feign'd.   Weakness is thy excuse,
And I believe it, weakness to resist   830
Philistian gold: if weakness may excuse,
What Murtherer, what Traitor, Parricide,
Incestuous, Sacrilegious, but may plead it?
All wickedness is weakness: that plea therefore
With God or Man will gain thee no remission.   835
But Love constrain'd thee; call it furious rage
To satisfy thy lust: Love seeks to have Love;
My love how couldst thou hope, who took'st the way
To raise in me inexpiable hate,
Knowing, as needs I must, by thee betray'd?   840
In vain thou striv'st to cover shame with shame,
Or by evasions thy crime uncover'st more.
    Dalila. Since thou determin'st weakness for no plea
In man or woman, though to thy own condemning,

---

820. In *upbraid me mine* (instead of "upbraid me with mine") *me* is a dative, and the direct object of the verb is *mine.*

826. *which* refers to *pardon* in l. 825. The compressed thought means that when he feels an impulse to pardon himself he is inexorable with himself.

828. *thy seeking*—what thou seekest.

835. *remission*—forgiveness.

837. There are many classical parallels to the thought, such as Cicero's definition of love as nothing less than the cherishing of the loved person without ceasing and without thought of advantage of any kind. (*On Friendship,* xxvii, 100.)

840. *knowing . . . betray'd*—knowing myself to have been betrayed.

Hear what assaults I had, what snares besides,   845
What sieges girt me round, ere I consented;
Which might have aw'd the best resolv'd of men,
The constantest to have yielded without blame.
It was not gold, as to my charge thou lay'st,
That wrought with me: thou knowst the Magistrates   850
And Princes of my country came in person,
Solicited, commanded, threat'n'd, urg'd,
Adjur'd by all the bonds of civil Duty
And of Religion, press'd how just it was,
How honourable, how glorious to entrap   855
A common enemy, who had destroy'd
Such numbers of our Nation: and the Priest
Was not behind, but ever at my ear,
Preaching how meritorious with the gods
It would be to ensnare an irreligious   860
Dishonourer of *Dagon:* what had I
To oppose against such powerful arguments?
Only my love of thee held long debate,
And combated in silence all these reasons
With hard contest: at length that grounded maxim   865
So rife and celebrated in the mouths
Of wisest men, that to the public good
Private respects must yield, with grave authority
Took full possession of me and prevail'd;
Virtue, as I thought, truth, duty so enjoining.   870
    Samson. I thought where all thy circling wiles would end;
In feign'd Religion, smooth hypocrisy.
But had thy love, still odiously pretended,
Been, as it ought, sincere, it would have taught thee
Far other reasonings, brought forth other deeds.   875

850-851. Compare the note on ll. 800-802 above.

854. *press'd*—urg'd. *N.E.D.* cites *Merchant of Venice,* IV, i, 425: "You press mee farre, and therefore I will yeeld."

866. *rife*—widespread, prevalent. Compare Satan's reference to "new Worlds; whereof so rife There went a fame in Heav'n." (*P.L.* I, 650-651.)

868. *respects*—interests, considerations. The reasoning is like Satan's justification of his attempt upon Eve on grounds of "public reason." (*P.L.* IV, 389.)

871. *circling*—devious, prevaricating, indirect in coming to the point.

I before all the daughters of my Tribe
And of my Nation chose thee from among
My enemies, lov'd thee, as too well thou knew'st,
Too well, unbosom'd all my secrets to thee,
Not out of levity, but over-pow'r'd   880
By thy request, who could deny thee nothing;
Yet now am judg'd an enemy.   Why then
Didst thou at first receive me for thy husband,
Then, as since then, thy country's foe profest?
Being once a wife, for me thou wast to leave   885
Parents and country; nor was I their subject,
Nor under their protection but my own,
Thou mine, not theirs: if aught against my life
Thy country sought of thee, it sought unjustly,
Against the law of nature, law of nations,   890
No more thy country, but an impious crew
Of men conspiring to uphold thir state
By worse than hostile deeds, violating the ends
For which our country is a name so dear;
Not therefore to be obey'd.   But zeal mov'd thee;   895
To please thy gods thou didst it; gods unable
To acquit themselves and prosecute their foes
But by ungodly deeds, the contradiction

---

880. Milton thought of levity as a serious vice, opposed, as he says in
C.D. II, xiii, to the virtue of gravity, which "consists in an habitual self-
government of speech and action, . . . befitting a man of holiness and
probity."

884. *profest*—avowed, declared.

885–886. Adam's words after the creation of Eve were, "Therefore
shall a man leave his father and his mother, and shall cleave unto
his wife: and they shall be one flesh."   (Gen. ii, 24.)

890. To a contemporary ear the line would recall the title—*Of the
Law of Nature and of Nations*—of "that noble volume written by our
learned Selden," as Milton called the book in *Doctrine of Divorce*,
II, xxii.

891. Milton often used *crew* in this derogatory sense in *P.L.* to refer
to the devils. *N.E.D.* compares II *Henry VI*, II, ii, 72: "Winke at the
Duke of Suffolkes insolence, At Beaufords Pride, at Somersets ambition,
At Buckingham, and all the Crew of them."

895. *But zeal mov'd thee:* the words refer ironically to Dalila's plea
in ll. 857–861 above.

897. *acquit*—clear one's self of any obligation. Here the word
means "to pay off a score against an enemy."

Of their own deity, Gods cannot be:
Less therefore to be pleas'd, obey'd, or fear'd.   900
These false pretexts and varnish'd colours failing,
Bare in thy guilt how foul must thou appear?
   Dalila. In argument with men a woman ever
Goes by the worse, whatever be her cause.
   Samson. For want of words no doubt, or lack of breath, 905
Witness when I was worried with thy peals.
   Dalila. I was a fool, too rash, and quite mistaken
In what I thought would have succeeded best.
Let me obtain forgiveness of thee, *Samson,*
Afford me place to show what recompense   910
Towards thee I intend for what I have misdone,
Misguided: only what remains past cure
Bear not too sensibly, nor still insist
To afflict thyself in vain: though sight be lost,
Life yet hath many solaces, enjoy'd   915
Where other senses want not their delights
At home in leisure and domestic ease,
Exempt from many a care and chance to which
Eye-sight exposes daily men abroad.
I to the Lords will intercede, not doubting   920
Thir favourable ear, that I may fetch thee

---

901. *colours* was frequently used in this sense. So Prospero in *The
Tempest* (I, ii, 143), speaking of the excuses for their treachery made
by his brother's confederates, says that they "With colours fairer
painted their foul ends."

904. *goes by,* like the modern colloquialism, "come by," means
"gets."

906. *Witness when*—witness the times when. So to prove his
charges against the Sons of Belial Milton wrote,
      "Witness the Streets of *Sodom,* and that night
      In *Gibeah,* when the hospitable door
      Expos'd a Matron to avoid worse rape."
             (*P.L.* I, 503–505.)
   peals: compare "a peal of words" in 235 above.

913. *sensibly*—sensitively, acutely. *N.E.D.* cites Bunyan; "When he
doth sensibly, and with heart-humiliation, thus think, then hath he
good thoughts."

915. *enjoy'd*—capable of being enjoyed.

916. *want*—lack.

920–921. *not doubting Thir favourable ear:* not doubting that I shall
be favourably heard.

From forth this loathsome prison-house to abide
With me, where my redoubl'd love and care
With nursing diligence, to me glad office,
May ever tend about thee to old age   925
With all things grateful cheer'd, and so supplied,
That what by me thou hast lost thou least shalt miss;
   Samson. No, no, of my condition take no care;
It fits not; thou and I long since are twain;
Nor think me so unwary or accurst   930
To bring my feet again into the snare
Where once I have been caught; I know thy trains
Though dearly to my cost, thy gins, and toils;
Thy fair enchanted cup, and warbling charms
No more on me have power, their force is null'd,   935
So much of Adder's wisdom I have learn't
To fence my ear against thy sorceries.
If in my flower of youth and strength, when all men
Lov'd, honour'd, fear'd me, thou alone could hate me,
Thy Husband, slight me, sell me, and forego me;   940
How wouldst thou use me now, blind, and thereby
Deceivable, in most things as a child
Helpless, thence easily contemn'd, and scorn'd,
And last neglected? How wouldst thou insult
When I must live uxorious to thy will   945

924. *office*—responsibility, task.

930. *accurst*—under a divine curse or possessed by a hostile, supernatural power. Milton used the word in a Greek sense, as Homer did
in describing Lycurgus as "A wretch accursed, and hated by the gods."
(Pope's *Il.* VI, 177.)

933. *gins and toils*—traps and nets.

934–935. The allusion is to Circe,
                "whose charmed Cup
    Whoever tasted lost his upright shape,
    And downward fell into a grovelling Swine."
              (*Comus,* 51–53.)
The word *charms* has the Latin meaning of "songs" as it does in *P.R.*
IV, 257, where Satan mentions "Aeolian charms" as one of the amenities
of Greek civilization, but it also means "spells."

935. *null'd*—annulled, destroyed.

936. The popular superstition that adders are deaf is as old as the
account in Psalm lviii, 4–5, of "the deaf adder *that* stoppeth the ear;
Which will not hearken to the voice of the charmers, charming never
so wisely."

In perfet thraldom, how again betray me,
Bearing my words and doings to the Lords
To gloss upon, and censuring, frown or smile?
This Gaol I count the house of Liberty
To thine whose doors my feet shall never enter.   950
    Dalila. Let me approach at least, and touch thy hand.
    Samson. Not for thy life, lest fierce remembrance wake
My sudden rage to tear thee joint by joint.
At distance I forgive thee, go with that;
Bewail thy falsehood, and the pious works   955
It hath brought forth to make thee memorable
Among illustrious women, faithful wives:
Cherish thy hast'n'd widowhood with the gold
Of Matrimonial treason: so farewell.
    Dalila. I see thou art implacable, more deaf   960
To prayers, than winds and seas, yet winds to seas
Are reconcil'd at length, and Sea to Shore:
Thy anger, unappeasable, still rages,
Eternal tempest never to be calm'd.
Why do I humble thus myself, and suing   965
For peace, reap nothing but repulse and hate?
Bid go with evil omen and the brand
Of infamy upon my name denounc't?
To mix with thy concernments I desist
Henceforth, nor too much disapprove my own.   970
Fame if not double-fac't is double-mouth'd,

---

948. *gloss*—make remarks about. *censuring*—judging.

950. *To*—in comparison with.

953. Samson's wish is less ferocious than Polymestor's impulse to tear Hecuba limb from limb (Euripides' *Hecuba*, l. 1125), with which it is compared. His behaviour in this entire scene is an expression of Milton's belief that "Hatred . . . is in some cases a religious duty. . . We are to hate even our dearest connexions, if they endeavor to seduce or deter us from the love of God." (*C.D.* II, xi.)

954. *go with that*—go content with that.

967. The *evil omen* is Samson's warning of the kind of reputation and life in store for her (in ll. 956–959 above).

969. *concernments*—interests, affairs.

971. *double-fac't*—having two opposite faces (like "a subtile Janus," as Milton—in *Animadversions*, II—called the Roman god of gates whom he is comparing here with the goddess Fame). (*P.W.* III, 53.)

971–974. Here and in his picture of Fame flying through the clouds

And with contrary blast proclaims most deeds;
On both his wings, one black, th' other white,
Bears greatest names in his wild aery flight.
My name perhaps among the Circumcis'd   975
In *Dan*, in *Judah*, and the bordering Tribes,
To all posterity may stand defam'd,
With malediction mention'd, and the blot
Of falsehood most unconjugal traduc't.
But in my country where I most desire,   980
In *Ekron*, *Gaza*, *Asdod*, and in *Gath*
I shall be nam'd among the famousest
Of Women, sung at solemn festivals,
Living and dead recorded, who to save
Her country from a fierce destroyer, chose   985
Above the faith of wedlock-bands, my tomb
With odours visited and annual flowers.
Not less renown'd than in Mount *Ephraim*,

---

on multi-coloured wings in *On the Fifth of November* (205–212)
Milton was influenced by Boccaccio's interpretation (*Genealogy of the
Gods*, I, x) of the earth-born goddess in the *Aeneid* (IV, 173–190),
who flies through the night sky with sinister news. Milton gives
Fame one black wing and one white because he was familiar with
symbolism like that which led Ben Jonson to introduce Good Fame
in the *Masque of Queens* as a goddess "attired in white, with white
wings." Milton's Fame is the author of mixed reports, like Chaucer's
"femynyne creature" in the third book of *The House of Fame* who,
when men asked her for glory, summoned the god, Eolus, to bring his
golden trumpet, Clear Laud, and his black trumpet, Slander, and blow
them indiscriminately. Why Milton should make Fame masculine is
not easy to surmise, unless he partly confused her with her trumpeter,
Eolus.

975. *the Circumcis'd*—the Jews.

976. The territory of *Dan*, Samson's own tribe, lay immediately
northwest of that of the tribe of *Judah* and extended as far as the
Mediterranean.

981. Beginning with the most northern Philistine city, *Ekron*, Dalila
next names the southernmost, *Gaza*, and then two other principal
cities of her countrymen, to suggest that she will be known everywhere in Philistia.

987. *odours*—spices. The promise is like that made by Jeremiah to
Zedikiah: "But thou shalt die in peace: and with the burnings of thy
fathers, the former kings which were before thee, so shall they burn
odours for thee." (Jer. xxxiv, 5.)

988–990. The Song of Deborah (Judg. v) celebrates the death of the

Jael, who with inhospitable guile
Smote *Sisera* sleeping through the Temples nail'd.   990
Nor shall I count it heinous to enjoy
The public marks of honour and reward
Conferr'd upon me, for the piety
Which to my country I was judg'd to have shown.
At this who ever envies or repines   995
I leave him to his lot, and like my own.
    Chorus. She's gone, a manifest Serpent by her sting
Discover'd in the end, till now conceal'd.
    Samson. So let her go, God sent her to debase me,
And aggravate my folly who committed   1000
To such a viper his most sacred trust
Of secrecy, my safety, and my life.
    Chorus. Yet beauty, though injurious, hath strange power,
After offence returning, to regain
Love once possest, nor can be easily   1005

Canaanite leader, *Sisera,* whom *Jael* lured to take refuge with her
after his defeat by the Hebrews. "Then Jael, Heber's wife, took a
nail of the tent, and took an hammer in her hand, . . . and smote
the nail into his temples: . . . for he was fast asleep and weary: so he
died." (Judg. iv, 21.)   In the Song the tribe of Ephraim is mentioned
(Judg. v, 14) as if it was foremost in the attack on the Canaanites.
Deborah lived "between Ramah and Bethel in Mount Ephraim."
(Judg. iv, 5.)

993. *piety* is used in the Latin sense of devotion to one's country.
Tamora, the Gothic queen, in *Titus Andronicus* (I, i, 114-115), replies
to Titus' refusal of mercy to her sons who are his captives:
      "O! if to fight for king and commonweal
        Were piety in thine, it is in these."

995-996. There may be a reminiscence of the scene in Sophocles'
Ajax (1038-1039) where Teucer tells his opponents to love their
opinions, as he intends to love his own.

1000. *aggravate* is used in the literal, Latin sense of "add to the
gravity, or weight, of anything."

1003-1005. Here and in Adam's reconciliation with Eve in *P.L.* X,
937-946, Milton may have recalled his own reconciliation with Mary
Powell; but he also regarded Dalila symbolically, as Tasso did Armida
when he described the wizard, Hidraort, sending her to deceive the
Christian host:
      "Shed brinish Tears, Sob, Sigh, Entreat and Pray,
      Wring thy fair Hands, cast up thine Eyes above,
      (For Mourning Beauty hath much Power [Men say]
      The stubborn Hearts with Pity frail to move)."
        (*J.D.* IV, 25. Fairfax's translation.)

Repuls't, without much inward passion felt
And secret sting of amorous remorse.
  Samson. Love-quarrels oft in pleasing concord end,
Not wedlock-treachery endangering life.
   Chorus. It is not virtue, wisdom, valour, wit,   1010
Strength, comeliness of shape, or amplest merit
That woman's love can win or long inherit;
But what it is, hard is to say,
Harder to hit,
(Which way soever men refer it)   1015
Much like thy riddle, *Samson,* in one day
Or seven, though one should musing sit;
  If any of these or all, the *Timnian* bride
Had not so soon preferr'd
Thy Paranymph, worthless to thee compar'd, 1020
Successor in thy bed,
Nor both so loosely disallied
Thir nuptials, nor this last so treacherously
Had shorn the fatal harvest of thy head.
Is it for that such outward ornament   1025
Was lavish't on thir Sex, that inward gifts
Were left for haste unfinish't, judgement scant,
Capacity not rais'd to apprehend
Or value what is best
In choice, but oftest to affect the wrong?   1030

1006. *passion*—emotion.

1007. *remorse*—pity. "It was your own pleasure and your own remorse," Celia tells her father in *As You Like It,* I, iii, 73, which permitted Rosalind to remain behind when her father was banished.

1008. A paraphrase of a famous line in Terence's *Andria,* 554–5.

1012. *inherit*—keep, possess. Compare Luke xviii, 18: "what shall
I do to inherit eternal life?"

1014. *hit* means "strike a target."

1016–1017. Compare the note on ll. 382–387 above.

1020. *Paranymph*—groomsman. For the story, see the note on ll. 794–
795 above.

1025. *for that*—because.

1030. *affect* has the Latin meaning of "aim at," or "ardently desire."
The construction is elliptical, for *to affect* must be understood as dependent on "such as" or "so low as" or some other unexpressed phrase
following *but* and modifying *Capacity* in 1028.

Or was too much of self-love mixt,
Of constancy no root infixt,
That either they love nothing, or not long?
  Whate'er it be, to wisest men and best
Seeming at first all heavenly under virgin veil,   1035
Soft, modest, meek, demure,
Once join'd, the contrary she proves, a thorn
Intestine, far within defensive arms
A cleaving mischief, in his way to virtue
Adverse and turbulent, or by her charms   1040
Draws him awry enslav'd
With dotage, and his sense deprav'd
To folly and shameful deeds which ruin ends.
What Pilot so expert but needs must wreck
Embark'd with such a Steers-mate at the Helm?   1045
  Favour'd of Heav'n who finds
One virtuous, rarely found,
That in domestic good combines:

1034–1037. These lines and, less definitely, the entire chorus are related to Hippolytus' outburst against women in Euripides (*Hippolytus*,
ll. 616–617, and the entire speech to l. 668, which contributed also to
Adam's invective against women in *P.L.* X, 888–899). Euripides asks,
     "Why should a place in the light of the sun, O Zeus,
     Be granted to women, that specious curse upon men?"

1037. *Once join'd*—once married.

1037–1038. *a thorn Intestine* suggests St. Paul's phrase, "a thorn in
the flesh," but *Intestine* is here equivalent to "domestic," as it is in
Milton's reference to marital unhappiness as "an intestine evil." (*C.D.*,
I, x.)

1038–1039. *far within defensive arms A cleaving mischief* seems like
a reminiscence of "th'envenom'd robe" (*P.L.* II, 543) which fatally
poisoned Hercules by its mere contact. Against it all defensive
armour would be worthless.

1046–1047. Perhaps there are allusions here to the maxim in Proverbs (xix, 14) that, "A prudent wife is from the Lord," and to the
cry of the chorus in Euripides' *Alcestis* (473–475) that it is a rare lot
in life to find a wife good like their lady.

1048. *That in domestic good combines*—that unites herself perfectly with her husband for the sake of domestic happiness. Here
and in *P.L.* IX, 232–234, Milton may have been thinking of the virtuous woman in Proverbs (xxxi, 10–11) whose "price is far above
rubies. The heart of her husband doth safely trust in her." His ideal
resembles Sir Thomas Overbury's in *A Good Woman*: "Now she is
given fresh and alive to a husband, and she doth nothing more than

Happy that house! his way to peace is smooth:
But virtue which breaks through all opposition,   1050
And all temptation can remove,
Most shines and most is acceptable above.
  Therefore God's universal Law
Gave to the man despotic power
Over his female in due awe,   1055
Nor from that right to part an hour,
Smile she or lour:
So shall he least confusion draw
On his whole life, not sway'd
By female usurpation, nor dismay'd.   1060
   But had we best retire, I see a storm?
  Samson. Fair days have oft contracted wind and rain.
  Chorus. But this another kind of tempest brings.
  Samson. Be less abstruse, my riddling days are past.
  Chorus. Look now for no enchanting voice, nor fear   1065
The bait of honied words; a rougher tongue
Draws hitherward, I know him by his stride,
The Giant *Harapha* of *Gath,* his look
Haughty as is his pile high-built and proud.
Comes he in peace? what wind hath blown him hither   1070
I less conjecture than when first I saw
The sumptuous *Dalila* floating this way:
His habit carries peace, his brow defiance.
  Samson. Or peace or not, alike to me he comes.

---

love him, for she takes him to that purpose. So his good becomes the
business of her actions, and she doth herself kindness upon him. After
his, her chiefest virtue is a good husband. For she is he."

  1053–1060. In *Doctrine of Divorce,* II, xv, Milton protested against
the "female pride" which claims any domestic equality and he quoted;
" 'I suffer not,' saith St. Paul, 'the woman to usurp authority over the
man.' "   Corresponding passages are found in *P.L.* IV, 295–299, and
X, 145–156.

  1062. *contracted* has the Latin meaning of "drawn together," or
"assembled."

  1064. For the allusion in *riddling days* see ll. 382–387 and ll. 1017–1033
above and ll. 1199–1200 below.

  1068. The name *Harapha* is composed of the Hebrew definite article,
ha, and of the word for giant, *raphah.*

  1069. *his pile*—his enormous body, which is like a tremendous tower.

Chorus. His fraught we soon shall know, he now arrives.

Harapha. I come not, *Samson,* to condole thy chance,   1076
As these perhaps, yet wish it had not been,
Though for no friendly intent.   I am of *Gath;*
Men call me *Harapha,* of stock renown'd
As *Og* or *Anak* and the *Emims* old   1080
That *Kiriathaim* held: Thou knowst me now
If thou at all art known.   Much I have heard
Of thy prodigious might and feats perform'd
Incredible to me, in this displeas'd,
That I was never present on the place   1085
Of those encounters, where we might have tried
Each other's force in camp or listed field;
And now am come to see of whom such noise
Hath walk'd about, and each limb to survey,
If thy appearance answer loud report.   1090

Samson. The way to know were not to see but taste.

Harapha. Dost thou already single me; I thought

1075. *fraught*—freight, *i.e.,* charge or business.

1076. *condole,* as a transitive verb, is obsolete, but *N.E.D.* quotes
from Cranley's *Amanda:* "A grieved soule, That with repentance doth
his sinnes condole."

1077. *these* refers to the chorus. *yet wish, etc.*: Though he does not
sympathize with Samson, he regrets his mischance, for it has prevented them from meeting on equal terms.

1080. *Og,* king of Bashan, is described in Deuteronomy (iii, 11) as
alone remaining "of the remnant of the giants; behold, his bedstead
. . . . Nine cubits was the length thereof."
The *Emims* were "a people great, and many, and tall, as the Ana-
kims; which also were accounted giants." (Deut. ii, 10–11.) In
Genesis (xiv, 5) they are said to have been crushed by their enemies
in the town of Kiriathaim, east of the Jordan.

1081–1082. So Satan says to Ithuriel and Zephon,
        "Not to know mee argues yourselves unknown."
                        (*P.L.* IV, 830.)

1087. *camp* keeps the Italian meaning of "field" (*i.e.,* of battle).
listed—furnished with lists such as those in which knights met in
tournament.

1088. *noise*—rumour, fame.

1091. *taste*—try, examine. So Satan reports having found Jesus,
"view'd him, tasted him." (*P.R.* II, 131.)

1092. *single*—challenge to single combat. *N.E.D.* quotes Richard's

Gyves and the Mill had tam'd thee?   O that fortune
Had brought me to the field where thou art fam'd
To have wrought such wonders with an Ass's Jaw;   1095
I should have forc'd thee soon wish other arms,
Or left thy carcase where the Ass lay thrown:
So had the glory of Prowess been recover'd
To *Palestine,* won by a *Philistine*
From the unforeskinn'd race, of whom thou bear'st   1100
The highest name for valiant Acts; that honour
Certain to have won by mortal duel from thee,
I lose, prevented by thy eyes put out.
 Samson. Boast not of what thou wouldst have done, but do
What then thou wouldst, thou seest it in thy hand.   1105
 Harapha. To combat with a blind man I disdain,
And thou hast need much washing to be toucht.
 Samson. Such usage as your honourable Lords
Afford me assassinated and betray'd,
Who durst not with thir whole united powers   1110
In fight withstand me single and unarm'd,
Nor in the house with chamber Ambushes
Close-banded durst attack me, no not sleeping,
Till they had hir'd a woman with their gold,
Breaking her Marriage Faith to circumvent me.   1115
Therefore without feign'd shifts let be assign'd
Some narrow place enclos'd, where sight may give thee,
Or rather flight, no great advantage on me;
Then put on all thy gorgeous arms, thy Helmet

---

challenge: "Now, Clifford, I have singled thee alone."   (III *Henry VI,*
II, iv, 1.)

 1096. *wish* is the prevailingly accepted editorial emendation for the
reading "with" of the original editions.

 1102. *mortal duel*—duel to the death of one of the parties.

 1105. *in thy hand*—in thy power (*i.e.,* to fight man to man).

 1109. *afford*—allow, grant. *assassinated*—treacherously attacked, not
actually slain. An *N.E.D.* example, dated 1683, is: "William of Orange
was twice Assasinated, and lost his Life the Second time."

 1113. *close-banded*—secretly banded. A man practices closeness and
secrecy, said Bacon (Essay VI) when he "leaveth himself without observation, or without hold to be taken, what he is."

 1116. *feign'd shifts*—delusive tricks.

And Brigandine of brass, thy broad Habergeon,   1120
Vant-brass and Greaves, and Gauntlet, add thy Spear
A Weaver's beam, and seven-times-folded shield,
I only with an Oak'n staff will meet thee,
And raise such out-cries on thy clatter'd Iron,
Which long shall not with-hold me from thy head,   1125
That in a little time, while breath remains thee,
Thou oft shalt wish thyself at Gath to boast
Again in safety what thou wouldst have done
To *Samson,* but shalt never see *Gath* more.
  Harapha. Thou durst not thus disparage glorious arms 1130
Which greatest Heroes have in battle worn,
Thir ornament and safety, had not spells
And black enchantments, some Magician's Art
Arm'd thee or charm'd thee strong, which thou from Heaven
Feign'd'st at thy birth was giv'n thee in thy hair,   1135
Where strength can least abide, though all thy hairs
Were bristles rang'd like those that ridge the back
Of chaf't wild Boars, or ruffl'd Porcupines.

1120. *Brigandine*—Body armour of metal plates or rings sewed between layers of cloth or leather.
  Habergeon—a sleeveless coat of mail.

1121. *Vant-brass*—vambrace, armour for the forearm.

1121–1122. *thy Spear, A Weaver's* beam is a reminiscence of the description of Goliath in I Samuel xvii, 7; "the staff of his spear was like a weaver's beam."

1122. Milton may have thought of the shield of the gigantic Ajax, which was made of seven layers of bull's hide (*Il.* VII, 220) or of the seven-fold shield of Turnus which Aeneas pierced in their mortal duel. (*Aen.* XII, 925.)

1134. *Arm'd thee or charm'd thee strong:* gave thee magically powerful arms or a charm of personal strength. For the jingle compare *P.R.* II, 269, note, and l. 1278 below.

1134–1135. *which* implies an unexpressed antecedent, "strength."
  It is hard to understand why Milton should have represented Samson's story that his strength depended on his hair as incredible to Harapha, for he knew that ancient literature abounded with parallels, such as the myth of Nisus, whose daughter, Scylla, was able to betray him because his life and fortune depended on a purple lock in his hair. It would be natural, however, for the Philistines to explain Samson's strength by black magic.

1138. With the *ruffl'd Porcupines* compare the Ghost's words to Hamlet (I, v, 19–20): ". . . each particular hair to stand an end, Like quills upon the fretful porpentine."

   Samson. I know no spells, use no forbidden Arts;
My trust is in the living God who gave me   1140
At my Nativity this strength, diffus'd
No less through all my sinews, joints and bones,
Than thine, while I preserv'd these locks unshorn,
The pledge of my unviolated vow.
For proof hereof, if *Dagon* be thy god,   1145
Go to his Temple, invocate his aid
With solemnest devotion, spread before him
How highly it concerns his glory now
To frustrate and dissolve these Magic spells,
Which I to be the power of *Israel's* God   1150
Avow, and challenge *Dagon* to the test,
Offering to combat thee his Champion bold,
With th' utmost of his Godhead seconded:
Then thou shalt see, or rather to thy sorrow
Soon feel, whose God is strongest, thine or mine.   1155
   Harapha. Presume not on thy God, whate'er he be,
Thee he regards not, owns not, hath cut off
Quite from his people, and delivered up
Into thy Enemies' hand, permitted them
To put out both thine eyes, and fetter'd send thee   116c
Into the common Prison, there to grind
Among the Slaves and Asses thy comrades,
As good for nothing else, no better service
With those thy boist'rous locks, no worthy match
For valour to assail, nor by the sword   1165

1139–1144. Todd compared the oath taken by the champions in
medieval judicial combats: "I do swear that I have not upon me, nor
on any of the arms I shall use, words, charms, or enchantments, to
which I trust for help to conquer my enemy, but that I do only trust
in God, in my right, and in the strength of my body and arms."

1143. *while*—as long as.

1147. *spread*—lay.

1157. The language is like that of the sanctions pronounced against
disobedient Hebrews in the O.T.: "that soul shall be cut off from
Israel." (Exod. xii, 15.)

1164. *boist'rous*—thick-growing. *N.E.D.* compares George Wither's
Mistress of Philarete: the pool "overgrown with boystrous Sedge."

1165. *valour*—a brave man. Another case of an abstract noun used
for a concrete.

1165–1166. *nor by the sword, etc.,* follows loosely upon *worthy*

Of noble Warrior, so to stain his honour,
But by the Barber's razor best subdu'd.
    Samson. All these indignities, for such they are
From thine, these evils I deserve and more,
Acknowledge them from God inflicted on me   1170
Justly, yet despair not of his final pardon
Whose ear is ever open; and his eye
Gracious to re-admit the suppliant;
In confidence whereof I once again
Defy thee to the trial of mortal fight,   1175
By combat to decide whose god is God,
Thine or whom I with *Israel's* Sons adore.
    Harapha. Fair honour that thou dost thy God, in trusting
He will accept thee to defend his cause,
A Murtherer, a Revolter, and a Robber.   1180
    Samson. Tongue-doughty Giant, how dost thou prove me
    these?
    Harapha. Is not thy Nation subject to our Lords?
Thir Magistrates confest it, when they took thee
As a League-breaker and deliver'd bound
Into our hands: for hadst thou not committed   1185
Notorious murder on those thirty men
At *Askalon,* who never did thee harm,
Then like a Robber stripp'dst them of thir robes?
The *Philistines,* when thou hadst broke the league,
Went up with armed powers thee only seeking,   1190
To others did no violence nor spoil.

---

match; *i.e.,* not worthy of a noble warrior's sword, for it would be a
stain upon the honour of a warrior to attack you.

    1168. *indignities* means unjust taunts; unjust, that is, from the Philis-
tines.

    1169. For *thine* used to mean Harapha's people generally see the
note on *mine* in l. 291 above.

    1175–1176. Again, as in 1139–1144 above, there is a reference to
the medieval trials of the justice of various kinds of causes by combat
between champions representing the parties.

    1182–1185. For the original story of this incident see the note on
253–264 above.

    1185–1188. After the betrayal of his riddle by the woman of Timna,
Samson "went down to Ashkelom, and slew thirty men of them, and
took their spoil, and gave change of garments to them which ex-
pounded the riddle." (Judg. xiv, 19.)

Samson. Among the Daughters of the *Philistines*
I chose a Wife, which argu'd me no foe;
And in your City held my Nuptial Feast:
But your ill-meaning Politician Lords,   1195
Under pretence of Bridal friends and guests,
Appointed to await me thirty spies,
Who, threat'ning cruel death, constrain'd the bride
To wring from me and tell to them my secret,
That solv'd the riddle which I had propos'd.   1200
When I perceiv'd all set on enmity,
As on my enemies, wherever chanc'd,
I us'd hostility, and took thir spoil
To pay my underminers in thir coin.
My Nation was subjected to your Lords.   1205
It was the force of Conquest; force with force
Is well ejected when the Conquer'd can.
But I a private person, whom my Country
As a league-breaker gave up bound, presum'd
Single Rebellion and did Hostile Acts.   1210
I was no private but a person rais'd
With strength sufficient and command from Heav'n
To free my Country; if their servile minds
Me their Deliverer sent would not receive,
But to thir Masters gave me up for nought,   1215
Th' unworthier they; whence to this day they serve.
I was to do my part from Heav'n assign'd,
And had perform'd it if my known offence
Had not disabl'd me, not all your force:

1194. After Manoa had arranged for his marriage with the woman of
Timna, his first wife, "Samson made there a feast; for so used the
young men to do." (Judg. xiv, 10.)

1195–1197. Josephus (*Antiquities,* V, viii, 6) says that "the people
of Timnath, out of dread of the young man's strength, gave him
during the time of the wedding feast, . . . thirty of the most stout
of their youth, in pretense to be his companions, but in reality to be
a guard upon him."

1198–1200. After Samson had propounded his riddle the thirty men
"desired the damsel (*i.e.,* his wife) to discover it by the means of her
husband, and tell it them; and they threatened to burn her if she did
not tell it them." (*Ibid.*) For the substance of the riddle see the
note on ll. 382–387 above.

1217. *I was to do*—I was under obligation to do.

These shifts refuted, answer thy appellant,   1220
Though by his blindness maim'd for high attempts,
Who now defies thee thrice to single fight,
As a petty enterprise of small enforce.
    Harapha. With thee a Man condemn'd, a Slave enroll'd,
Due by the Law to capital punishment?   1225
To fight with thee no man of arms will deign.
    Samson. Cam'st thou for this, vain boaster, to survey me,
To descant on my strength, and give thy verdict?
Come nearer, part not hence so slight inform'd;
But take good heed my hand survey not thee.   1230
    Harapha. O *Baal-zebub!* can my ears unus'd
Hear these dishonours, and not render death?
    Samson. No man with-holds thee, nothing from thy hand

1220. *appellant*—challenger. *N.E.D.* quotes Caxton's *Chronicle of England:* "A great batayll . . . by twene two squyers, . . . Gloucestre that was the appellaunt and Arthur the defendaunt."

1221. *high attempts*—great enterprises. The words belonged to the language of romance and heraldry. *N.E.D.* quotes Guillim's *Heraldry:* "His noble courage and high attempts atchieved."

1222. *thrice*—for the third time. The medieval custom of challenging three times in judicial combats was familiar to Milton's contemporaries through the coronation ceremonies. When Charles II was crowned, a herald proclaimed that "if any dare deny Charles Stewart to be lawful King of England, here was a champion that would fight with him." "And with these words," Pepys says (under date of April 23rd, 1661), "the Champion flings down his gauntlet, and all this he do three times in his going up towards the King's table."

1224–1226. Todd quoted from the treatise on duelling (published in 1595) of Vincentio Saviolo, the London fencing master who suggested Touchstone's quarrelling "by the book" (*As You Like It,* V, iv, 94) to Shakespeare, a passage denying the right of single combat to traitors, robbers, "excommunicate persons, hereticks, vsurers, and all other persons, not liuing as a gentleman or a souldier."

1228. *descant* was often used in the sense of "make unfavourable comments," as Milton used it in *Eikonoklastes:* "To descant on the misfortunes of a Person fall'n from dignity is not commendable." (Quoted by *N.E.D.*)

1231. The god's name is regularly spelled "Beelzebub" in *P.L.* (*e.g.*, in I, 81), but here Milton may have wished to stress its formation from its elements. Baal was the great sun-god of the Philistines, Canaanites and Phoenicians, but he was worshipped under many local and attributive names, of which Baal-zebub (literally "Baal" or "god of flies") was his title in his splendid temple at Ekron.
    unus'd—unaccustomed (*i.e.*, to insults).

Fear I incurable; bring up thy van,
My heels are fetter'd, but my fist is free.   1235
   Harapha. This insolence other kind of answer fits.
   Samson. Go baffl'd coward, lest I run upon thee,
Though in these chains, bulk without spirit vast,
And with one buffet lay thy structure low,
Or swing thee in the Air, then dash thee down   1240
To the hazard of thy brains and shatter'd sides.
   Harapha. By *Astaroth,* ere long thou shalt lament
These braveries in Irons loaden on thee.
   Chorus. His Giantship is gone somewhat crestfall'n,
Stalking with less unconsci'nable strides,   1245
And lower looks, but in a sultry chafe.
   Samson. I dread him not, nor all his Giant-brood,
Though Fame divulge him Father of five Sons
All of Gigantic size, *Goliah* chief.
   Chorus. He will directly to the Lords, I fear,   1250
And with malicious counsel stir them up
Some way or other yet further to afflict thee.
   Samson. He must allege some cause, and offer'd fight
Will not dare mention, lest a question rise
Whether he durst accept the offer or not,   1255
And that he durst not plain enough appear'd.
Much more affliction than already felt

   1234. *bring up thy van*—bring up thy advance-guard, begin the fight.

   1239. Compare *structure* with *pile* in 1069.

   1242. In *P.L.* I, 338–339, Milton mentions "Astoreth, whom the Phoenicians call'd *Astarte,* Queen of Heav'n," and in *P.L.* I, 422, he explains that the form *Ashtaroth* is plural. It was a general name for the many manifestations of the supreme goddess who stood opposite to Baal and represented fertility and passion, and seems to have been equivalent to the great goddess Ishtar of the Assyro-Babylonians.

   1243. *braveries*—boasts.

   1245. *unconsci'nable*—unreasonable, absurdly insolent.

   1248. *divulge*—proclaim, announce. Compare *P.R.* III, 62. II Samuel xxi, tells the story of four sons who "were born to the giant in Gath, and fell by the hand of David, and by the hand of his servants." The giant is called in Hebrew simply "Rapha," the word from which Milton derived the name "Harapha." See l. 1068, note. His fifth son was Goliath.

   1250. *he will*—he will go.

   1253. *offer'd fight, i.e.,* my offer to fight.

They cannot well impose, nor I sustain;
If they intend advantage of my labours,
The work of many hands, which earns my keeping   1260
With no small profit daily to my owners.
But come what will, my deadliest foe will prove
My speediest friend, by death to rid me hence,
The worst that he can give, to me the best.
Yet so it may fall out, because thir end   1265
Is hate, not help to me, it may with mine
Draw thir own ruin who attempt the deed.
      Chorus. Oh how comely it is and how reviving
To the Spirits of just men long opprest!
When God into the hands of thir deliverer   1270
Puts invincible might
To quell the mighty of the Earth, th' oppressor,
The brute and boist'rous force of violent men
Hardy and industrious to support
Tyrannic power, but raging to pursue   1275
The righteous and all such as honour Truth;
He all thir Ammunition
And feats of War defeats
With plain Heroic magnitude of mind
And celestial vigour arm'd,   1280
Thir Armories and Magazines contemns,
Renders them useless, while
With winged expedition
Swift as the lightning glance he executes
His errand on the wicked, who surpris'd   1285
Lose thir defence, distracted and amaz'd.
      But patience is more oft the exercise

1263. The thought that "Though death be poor, it ends a mortal woe," (*Richard II,* II, i, 152) is too widespread to suggest a "parallel" here.

1277. *Ammunition*—munitions of war.

1278–1280. It is worth while to compare the sonnets to Fairfax, Cromwell and Sir Henry Vane the Younger.

1283. *expedition*—speed. Compare "The banded Powers of *Satan* hasting on With furious expedition." (*P.L.* VI, 85–86.)

1285. *errand*—mission or commission (*i.e.,* of vengeance).

1286. *defence*—power to defend themselves.

1287–1291. Compare the sentiment in 652–659. where Milton was

Of Saints, the trial of thir fortitude,
Making them each his own Deliverer,
And Victor over all   1290
That tyranny or fortune can inflict.
Either of these is in thy lot,
Samson, with might endu'd
Above the Sons of men; but sight bereav'd
May chance to number thee with those   1295
Whom Patience finally must crown.
This Idol's day hath been to thee no day of rest,
    Labouring thy mind
More than the working day thy hands.
And yet perhaps more trouble is behind,   1300
For I descry this way
Some other tending, in his hand
A Sceptre or quaint staff he bears,
Comes on amain, speed in his look.
By his habit I discern him now   1305
A Public Officer, and now at hand.
His message will be short and voluble.
    Officer. Ebrews, the Pris'ner *Samson* here I seek.
    Chorus. His manacles remark him, there he sits.

---

thinking of Stoic virtue rather than of Christian patience, the Patience
which spoke and resolved his own difficulty in the sonnet *On his
Blindness.*

1294. *sight bereav'd*—loss of sight. This Latin construction was a
favourite with Milton. Compare "never since created man" (*P.L.* I,
573), which means "never since the creation of man."

1296. Compare "the crown that Virtue gives." (*Comus,* 9.)

1303. *quaint,* curiously made or decorated, like the wands of office
which Greek heralds and messengers carried.

1307. *voluble*—swift and pointed. Milton illustrates the word in
Eikonoklastes, 32, with "A discours, voluble anough, and full of sentence."

1308. Milton's apparent inconsistency in spelling *Ebrews* here and
in ll. 1319 and 1540 below, while in *P.R.* IV, 336, and Psalm cxxxvi,
50, he spelled the word *Hebrew,* must at least in part be due to his
familiarity with the unaspirated form of the word in Greek and Italian.
In the Latin Vulgate, however, he found it regularly spelled with initial
H and he knew that in the Hebrew Bible its initial vowel was
aspirated.

1309. *remark*—distinguish. *N.E.D.* compares Jeremy Taylor: "Those

Officer. Samson, to thee our Lords thus bid me say;   1310
This day to *Dagon* is a solemn Feast,
With Sacrifices, Triumph, Pomp, and Games;
Thy strength they know surpassing human rate,
And now some public proof thereof require
To honour this great Feast, and great Assembly;   1315
Rise therefore with all speed and come along,
Where I will see thee heart'n'd and fresh clad
To appear as fits before th' illustrious Lords.
  Samson. Thou knowst I am an *Ebrew,* therefore tell them,
Our Law forbids at thir Religious Rites   1320
My presence; for that cause I cannot come.
  Officer. This answer, be assur'd, will not content them.
  Samson. Have they not Sword-players, and ev'ry sort
Of Gymnic Artists, Wrestlers, Riders, Runners,
Jugglers and Dancers, Antics, Mummers, Mimics,   1325
But they must pick me out with shackles tir'd,
And over-labour'd at thir public Mill,
To make them sport with blind activity?
Do they not seek occasion of new quarrels
On my refusal to distress me more,   1330
Or make a game of my calamities?
Return the way thou cam'st, I will not come.
  Officer. Regard thyself, this will offend them highly.

---

blessings and separations with which God hath remarked your family
and person."

1312. *Triumph*—public festivity. Compare the note on *Pomp* in
L'Allegro, 127.

1320. The Mosaic law commanded, "Thou shalt not bow down to
their gods, nor serve them; . . . but thou shalt utterly overthrow them,
and quite break down their images." (Exod. xxiii, 24.)

1323. Though *Sword-players* usually meant Roman gladiators, in this
passage, where Milton's contempt for the sports of Restoration London
made him abandon historical consistency, it must refer to professional
fencers.

1324. *Gymnic Artists*—gymnasts.

1325. *Antics*—grotesquely dressed participants in a pageant or carni-
val of any kind.
  Mummers—actors in a dumb show or in street entertainments such as
still go by that name in Philadelphia.

1333. *Regard thyself*—watch yourself, look to your own interests.

Samson. Myself? my conscience and internal peace.
Can they think me so broken, so debas'd   1335
With corporal servitude, that my mind ever
Will condescend to such absurd commands?
Although thir drudge, to be thir fool or jester,
And in my midst of sorrow and heart-grief
To show them feats, and play before thir god,   1340
The worst of all indignities, yet on me
Join'd with extreme contempt?   I will not come.

Officer. My message was impos'd on me with speed,
Brooks no delay: is this thy resolution?

Samson. So take it with what speed thy message needs. 1345

Officer. I am sorry what this stoutness will produce.

Samson. Perhaps thou shalt have cause to sorrow indeed.

Chorus. Consider, *Samson;* matters now are strain'd
Up to the highth, whether to hold or break;
He's gone, and who knows how he may report   1350
Thy words by adding fuel to the flame?
Expect another message more imperious,
More Lordly thund'ring than thou well wilt bear.

Samson. Shall I abuse this Consecrated gift
Of strength, again returning with my hair   1355
After my great transgression, so requite
Favour renew'd, and add a greater sin
By prostituting holy things to Idols;
A *Nazarite* in place abominable
Vaunting my strength in honour to thir *Dagon?*   1360
Besides, how vile, contemptible, ridiculous,
What act more execrably unclean, profane?

1334. Compare "the sweet peace that goodness bosoms ever" of *Comus,* 368, and the Introduction, §31.

1342. *Join'd*—enjoined, imposed.

1344. *brooks*—permits, bears.

1346. *sorry what*—sorry to imagine what.
stoutness—pride, arrogance.

1355. The expectation that Samson's strength would return with his hair, which Manoa first expresses (in ll. 586–587), rests upon the statement that, "Howbeit the hair of his head began to grow again after he was shaven." (Judg. xvi, 22.)

1360. *Vaunting*—displaying proudly.

1362. *unclean* is used in the Jewish, legal sense in which Samson's

Chorus. Yet with this strength thou serv'st the *Philistines,*
Idolatrous, uncircumcis'd, unclean.

Samson. Not in thir Idol-Worship, but by labour   1365
Honest and lawful to deserve my food
Of those who have me in thir civil power.

Chorus. Where the heart joins not, outward acts defile not.

Samson. Where outward force constrains, the sentence
 holds;
But who constrains me to the Temple of *Dagon,*   1370
Not dragging? the *Philistian* Lords command.
Commands are no constraints. If I obey them,
I do it freely; venturing to displease
God for the fear of Man, and Man prefer,
Set God behind: which in his jealousy   1375
Shall never, unrepented, find forgiveness.
Yet that he may dispense with me or thee
Present in Temples at Idolatrous Rites
For some important cause, thou needst not doubt.

Chorus. How thou wilt here come off surmounts my reach.

Samson. Be of good courage, I begin to feel   1381
Some rousing motions in me which dispose

Philistine bride is called "unclean" (in l. 321), *i.e.,* bearing the taint of
association with the gentiles.

1366. *deserve*—earn. N.E.D. quotes *Henry VII,* Act II: "Artificers
. . . waste moch part of the day and deserve not their wagis."

1368. The maxim may refer to Aristotle's great doctrine that "it is
only voluntary feelings and actions for which praise and blame are
given; those that are involuntary are condoned, and sometimes even
pitied." (*Nicomachean Ethics,* III, i, 1.)

1369. *sentence*—maxim.

1374–1375. The Second Commandment forbids any kind of worship
of idols: "Thou shalt not bow down thyself to them, nor serve them:
for I the Lord thy God am a jealous God." (Exod. xx, 5.)

1377. *dispense with*—arrange to remit a penalty for a person so that
he may do a forbidden act. N.E.D. quotes Latimer's Sermons: "God
had dispensed wyth theym to haue many wyues."

1377–1379. In *C.D.* II, v, Milton raises the question "whether it be
lawful for a professor of the true religion to be present at idol-worship,
in cases where his attendance is necessary for the discharge of some
civil duty. The affirmative seems to be established by the example of
Naaman the Syrian, II Kings v, 17–19, who was permitted . . . to con-
struct for himself a private altar of Israelitish earth."

To something extraordinary my thoughts.
I with this Messenger will go along,
Nothing to do, be sure, that may dishonour   1385
Our Law, or stain my vow of *Nazarite*.
If there be aught of presage in the mind,
This day will be remarkable in my life
By some great act, or of my days the last.
    Chorus. In time thou hast resolv'd, the man returns.   1390
    Officer. Samson, this second message from our Lords
To thee I am bid say.   Art thou our Slave,
Our Captive, at the public Mill our drudge,
And dar'st thou at our sending and command
Dispute thy coming? come without delay;   1395
Or we shall find such Engines to assail
And hamper thee, as thou shalt come of force,
Though thou wert firmlier fast'n'd than a rock.
    Samson. I could be well content to try thir Art,
Which to no few of them would prove pernicious.   1400
Yet knowing thir advantages too many,
Because they shall not trail me through thir streets
Like a wild Beast, I am content to go.
Masters' commands come with a power resistless
To such as owe them absolute subjection;   1405
And for a life who will not change his purpose?
(So mutable are all the ways of men)
Yet this be sure, in nothing to comply
Scandalous or forbidden in our Law.
    Officer. I praise thy resolution; doff these links: 1410
By this compliance thou wilt win the Lords
To favour, and perhaps to set thee free.
    Samson. Brethren farewell, your company along
I will not wish, lest it perhaps offend them
To see me girt with Friends; and how the sight   1415
Of me as of a common Enemy,
So dreaded once, may now exasperate them
I know not.   Lords are Lordliest in thir wine;

    1396. *Engines*—probably "engines of torture."
    1397. *hamper*—fetter, confine. *of force*—by force.
    1400. *pernicious* has the Latin meaning of "deadly."
    1402. *because*—so that.

And the well-feasted Priest then soonest fir'd
With zeal, if aught Religion seem concern'd: 1420
No less the people on thir Holy-days
Impetuous, insolent, unquenchable.
Happ'n what may, of me expect to hear
Nothing dishonourable, impure, unworthy
Our God, our Law, my Nation, or myself;   1425
The last of me or no I cannot warrant.
    Chorus. Go, and the Holy One
Of *Israel* be thy guide
To what may serve his glory best, and spread his name
Great among the Heathen round: 1430
Send thee the Angel of thy Birth, to stand
Fast by thy side, who from thy Father's field
Rode up in flames after his message told
Of thy conception, and be now a shield

1419–1420. The lines resume the attack upon "such as for their
bellies' sake, Creep and intrude, and climb into the Fold" (*Lycidas,*
114–115), the clergy whom Milton called in *Animadversions,* xiii, a
"race of Capernaïtans, senseless of divine doctrine, and capable only of
loaves and belly-cheer!" "Show us any one point in your Remonstrance," he challenged them (*Ibid.,* i), "that does not more concern
superiority, pride, ease, and the belly, than the truth and glory of God."

1421–1422. In his controversial writing Milton fully sympathized with
the Puritan condemnation of Sabbath-breaking as equivalent to idolatry.
In *Of Reformation* (Book II, *P.W.* II, 402) he attacked the bishops
who "took the ready way to despoil us both of manhood and grace at
once, and that in the shamefullest and ungodliest manner, upon that
day which God's law, and even our own reason hath consecrated;
. . . at such a time that men should be plucked from their soberest
and saddest thoughts, and by bishops, the pretended fathers of the
church, instigated, by public edict, and with earnest endeavour pushed
forward to gaming, jigging, wassailing, and mixed dancing, is a horror
to think! Thus did the reprobate hireling priest Balaam seek to
subdue the Israelites to Moab, if not by force, then by his devilish
policy, to draw them from the sanctuary of God to the luxurious and
ribald feasts of Baal-peor."

1426. The thought is: "Whether you see me for the last time now or
not, I cannot positively say."

1431–1435. The *Angel* has been mentioned in ll. 24, 361, and 635
above and his fiery ascent to heaven in ll. 27–28. Milton's belief that
there are "Angels conversant on Earth With Man or men's affairs"
(*P.R.* I, 131–2) is stated clearly in *C.D.* I, ix.

1433. *after his message told:* after the delivery of his message. Compare the note on l. 1294 above.

Of fire; that Spirit that first rusht on thee   1435
In the camp of *Dan*
Be efficacious in thee now at need.
For never was from Heaven imparted
Measure of strength so great to mortal seed,
As in thy wond'rous actions hath been seen.   1440
But wherefore comes old *Manoa* in such haste
With youthful steps? much livelier than erewhile
He seems: supposing here to find his Son,
Or of him bringing to us some glad news?
    Manoa. Peace with you brethren; my inducement hither 1445
Was not at present here to find my Son,
By order of the Lords new parted hence
To come and play before them at thir Feast.
I heard all as I came, the City rings,
And numbers thither flock; I had no will,   1450
Lest I should see him forc't to things unseemly.
But that which mov'd my coming now, was chiefly
To give ye part with me what hope I have
With good success to work his liberty.
    Chorus. That hope would much rejoice us to partake   1455
With thee; say reverend Sire, we thirst to hear.
    Manoa. I have attempted one by one the Lords
Either at home, or through the high street passing,
With supplication prone and Father's tears
To accept of ransom for my Son thir pris'ner.   1460

1435–1436. In the biblical story, Samson's first inkling of his strength
came when "the Spirit of the Lord began to move him at times in the
camp of Dan between Zorah and Eshtaol." (Judg. xiii, 25.)

1445. *Peace with you* is a constant greeting in the O.T.: *e.g.,* Samuel's
salute: "Peace be to thee, peace be to thy house, peace be to all."
(I Sam. xxv, 6.)

1447. *new parted*—just departed.

1453. *To give ye, etc.,* to share whatever hope I have with you.
ye is a dative here.

1454. *success*—effect, consequence. The word seldom had the modern force which would make *good* unnecessary. Compare Belial's
"Ominous conjecture on the whole success" (*P.L.* II, 123) of the devils'
purposes.

1457. *attempted*—appealed to, tried to win the sympathies of.
N.E.D. compares *Merchant of Venice,* IV, i, 421; "Deare sir, of force
I must attempt you further."

Some much averse I found and wondrous harsh,
Contemptuous, proud, set on revenge and spite;
That part most reverenc'd *Dagon* and his Priests:
Others more moderate seeming, but thir aim
Private reward, for which both God and State   1465
They easily would set to sale: a third
More generous far and civil, who confess'd
They had enough reveng'd, having reduc't
Thir foe to misery beneath thir fears,
The rest was magnanimity to remit,   1470
If some convenient ransom were propos'd.
What noise or shout was that? it tore the Sky.
   Chorus. Doubtless the people shouting to behold
Thir once great dread, captive, and blind before them,
Or at some proof of strength before them shown.   1475
   Manoa. His ransom, if my whole inheritance
May compass it, shall willingly be paid
And number'd down: much rather I shall choose
To live the poorest in my Tribe, than richest,
And he in that calamitous prison left.   1480
No, I am fixt not to part hence without him.
For his redemption all my Patrimony,
If need be, I am ready to forego
And quit: not wanting him, I shall want nothing.
   Chorus. Fathers are wont to lay up for thir Sons, 1485
Thou for thy Son are bent to lay out all;
Sons wont to nurse thir Parents in old age,
Thou in old age car'st how to nurse thy Son,
Made older than thy age through eye-sight lost.
   Manoa. It shall be my delight to tend his eyes,   1490

1461–1470. Perhaps there is a reminiscence here of the treatment of Milton's champions by various parties on the King's side after the Restoration. His anti-episcopal tracts had deserved the special hostility of the Anglican clergy, who may be intended in l. 1463, and the magnanimous group (l. 1469) may correspond to the liberal men in Parliament who kept Milton from being excepted from the benefit of the Indemnity Bill.

1470. *The rest etc.*: the rest of their revenge, they said, it would be only magnanimous to let go.

1480. *And he . . . left*—while he is left.

1484. *wanting*—lacking.

1487. *wont*—are wont.

And view him sitting in the house, ennobl'd
With all those high exploits by him achiev'd,
And on his shoulders waving down those locks,
That of a Nation arm'd the strength contain'd:
And I persuade me God had not permitted   1495
His strength again to grow up with his hair
Garrison'd round about him like a Camp
Of faithful Soldiery, were not his purpose
To use him further yet in some great service,
Not to sit idle with so great a gift   1500
Useless, and thence ridiculous about him.
And since his strength with eye-sight was not lost,
God will restore him eye-sight to his strength.
   Chorus. Thy hopes are not ill-founded, nor seem vain,
Of his delivery, and thy joy thereon   1505
Conceiv'd, agreeable to a Father's love,
In both which we, as next, participate.
   Manoa. I know your friendly minds and—O what noise!
Mercy of Heav'n! what hideous noise was that?
Horribly loud, unlike the former shout.   1510
   Chorus. Noise call you it or universal groan
As if the whole inhabitation perish'd?
Blood, death, and deathful deeds are in that noise,
Ruin, destruction at the utmost point.
   Manoa. Of ruin indeed methought I heard the noise,   1515
Oh it continues, they have slain my Son.
   Chorus. Thy Son is rather slaying them; that outcry
From slaughter of one foe could not ascend.
   Manoa. Some dismal accident it needs must be;
What shall we do, stay here or run and see?   1520

   1494. In Ovid's version of the story of Nisus (see ll. 1134–5, note)
there is a similar line, which describes the hope of a mighty kingdom
as dependent upon his hair. (*Met.* VIII, 10.)

   1495. *had not; i.e.,* would not have permitted. Before *were* in 1498
understand "if it."

   1503. *to his strength*—in addition to his strength.

   1506. *agreeable to*—corresponding to.

   1507. *next; i.e.,* of kin, because the chorus, like Samson, are Danites.

   1515. *ruin* has the Latin meaning of "downfall" or "collapse." Compare "Heav'n ruining from Heav'n" in *P.L.* VI, 868.

   1520–1522. So, in moments of crisis, Euripides' choruses sometimes

Chorus. Best keep together here, lest, running thither,
We unawares run into danger's mouth.
This evil on the *Philistines* is fall'n,
From whom could else a general cry be heard?
The sufferers then will scarce molest us here,   1525
From other hands we need not much to fear.
What if his eye-sight (for to *Israel's* God
Nothing is hard) by miracle restor'd,
He now be dealing dole among his foes,
And over heaps of slaughter'd walk his way?   1530
   Manoa. That were a joy presumptuous to be thought.
   Chorus. Yet God hath wrought things as incredible
For his people of old; what hinders now?
   Manoa. He can, I know, but doubt to think he will;
Yet Hope would fain subscribe, and tempts Belief.   1535
A little stay will bring some notice hither.
   Chorus. Of good or bad so great, of bad the sooner;
For evil news rides post, while good news baits.
And to our wish I see one hither speeding,
An *Ebrew,* as I guess, and of our Tribe.   1540
   Messenger. O whither shall I run, or which way fly
The sight of this so horrid spectacle
Which erst my eyes beheld and yet behold?

---

question whether they should leave the scene.   When Phaedria's death-
cry is heard, the chorus divides:
Semi-chorus 1. "What shall we do, friends? Deem ye we should pass
   The doors, and from the halter loose the queen?"
Semi-chorus 2. "Wherefore? Are no young handmaids at her side?
   The busy meddler treadeth perilous paths."
                    (*Hippolytus,* 782–785.)

1529. *dole*—grief, pain. Perhaps there is a play on the homonym
which means "something dealt," for it was familiar in phrases like
Shakespeare's "dole of blows."   (*II Henry IV,* I, i, 169.)

1538. *baits*—delays, travels slowly. The meaning arose from the use
of "bait" to mean "to stop in a journey to feed horses."

1541. So the messengers in Greek tragedies, when they have dreadful
news, often enter with distracted cries.   "Wretch that I am!" exclaims
the messenger who brings Creon the news of his nephews' fatal strife
in Euripides' *Phoenissae* (1336–1338), "What language can I find? . . .
Ah, wretched me, I yet again exclaim."

1543. *erst*—not long ago. The word was a favourite with Spenser;
e.g., "the armes, that earst so bright did show."   (*F.Q.* I, v, 9.)

For dire imagination still pursues me.
But providence or instinct of nature seems,   1545
Or reason though disturb'd, and scarce consulted,
To have guided me aright, I know not how,
To thee first, reverend *Manoa,* and to these
My Countrymen, whom here I knew remaining,
As at some distance from the place of horror,   1550
So in the sad event too much concern'd.
   Manoa. The accident was loud, and here before thee
With rueful cry, yet what it was we hear not;
No Preface needs, thou seest we long to know.
   Messenger. It would burst forth, but I recover breath   1555
And sense distract, to know well what I utter.
   Manoa. Tell us the sum, the circumstance defer.
   Messenger. Gaza yet stands, but all her Sons are fall'n,
All in a moment overwhelm'd and fall'n.
   Manoa. Sad, but thou knowst to *Israelites* not saddest   1560
The desolation of a Hostile City.
   Messenger. Feed on that first, there may in grief be surfeit.
   Manoa. Relate by whom.
   Messenger.   By *Samson.*
   Manoa.   That still lessens
The sorrow, and converts it nigh to joy.
   Messenger. Ah *Manoa,* I refrain too suddenly   1565
To utter what will come at last too soon;
Lest evil tidings with too rude irruption
Hitting thy aged ear should pierce too deep.
   Manoa. Suspense in news is torture, speak them out.
   Messenger. Then take the worst in brief, *Samson* is dead.1570

   1554. *No Preface needs*—no introduction is necessary. Compare "here needs no account." *P.L.* IV, 235.

   1556. *distract*—distracted. Compare *extinct* in l. 70, note.

   1557. *the sum*—the main thing, the gist. Compare *Henry V,* III, vi, 172; "the sum of all our answer is but this."
   circumstance—circumstances. *N.E.D.* quotes Tourneur's *Atheist's Tragedy,* I, iv; "Time cuts off circumstance; I must be briefe."

   1562. Compare Valentine's words in *Two Gentlemen of Verona,* III, i, 220–221:
         "O, I have fed upon this woe already,
          And now excess of it will make me surfeit."

   1570. In the *Electra* (673) of Sophocles, Todd noticed that the death

Manoa. The worst indeed!   O all my hope's defeated
To free him hence! but death who sets all free
Hath paid his ransom now and full discharge.
What windy joy this day had I conceiv'd
Hopeful of his Delivery, which now proves   1575
Abortive as the first-born bloom of spring
Nipt with the lagging rear of winter's frost.
Yet ere I give the reins to grief, say first,
How died he? death to life is crown or shame.
All by him fell thou say'st, by whom fell he,   1580
What glorious hand gave *Samson* his death's wound?
    Messenger. Unwounded of his enemies he fell.
    Manoa. Wearied with slaughter then or how? explain.
    Messenger. By his own hands.
    Manoa. Self-violence? what cause
Brought him so soon at variance with himself   1585
Among his foes?
    Messenger.   Inevitable cause
At once both to destroy and be destroy'd;
The Edifice where all were met to see him
Upon thir heads and on his own he pull'd.
    Manoa. O lastly over-strong against thyself!   1590
A dreadful way thou took'st to thy revenge.
More than enough we know; but while things yet
Are in confusion, give us if thou canst,
Eye-witness of what first or last was done,
Relation more particular and distinct.   1595
    Messenger. Occasions drew me early to this City,
And as the gates I enter'd with Sun-rise,
The morning Trumpets Festival proclaim'd

---

of Orestes is announced in just this way, with the bare words, "Orestes is dead."

1573. Manoa's dearest wish has been to ransom Samson.   Compare ll. 483, 604, 1460 and 1476 above.

1574. *windy*—vain. *N.E.D.* quotes Gabriel Harvey: "A wan or windy Hope, is a notable breake-necke vnto itselfe."

1576–1577. The clear Shakespearian quality of the lines has led editors to compare *Love's Labour's Lost,* I, i, 100–101: "Like an envious sneaping frost, That bites the first-born infants of the spring."

1596. *Occasions*—affairs, business.

Through each high street: little I had dispatch't
When all abroad was rumour'd that this day   1600
Samson should be brought forth to show the people
Proof of his mighty strength in feats and games;
I sorrow'd at his captive state, but minded
Not to be absent at that spectacle.
The building was a spacious Theatre   1605
Half round on two main Pillars vaulted high,
With seats where all the Lords and each degree
Of sort, might sit in order to behold,
The other side was op'n, where the throng
On banks and scaffolds under Sky might stand;   1610
I among these aloof obscurely stood.
The Feast and noon grew high, and Sacrifice
Had fill'd thir hearts with mirth, high cheer, and wine,
When to thir sports they turn'd.   Immediately
Was *Samson* as a public servant brought,   1615
In thir state Livery clad; before him Pipes
And Timbrels, on each side went armed guards,
Both horse and foot before him and behind,
Archers, and Slingers, Cataphracts and Spears.

1599. *little . . . dispatch't; i.e.,* had dispatched little business.

1603. *minded*—resolved. Compare the noun in *P.L.* V, 452: "sudden mind arose, In *Adam,* not to let th'occasion pass."

1605–1610. In Judges xvi, 27, the building is described as a "house full of men and women; and all the lords of the Philistines were there; and there were upon the roof about three thousand men and women, that beheld while Samson made sport." There seems to be good ground for Mr. Verity's suggestion that by putting the common people outside his "theatre" and laying stress upon the destruction of
"Lords, Ladies, Captains, Counsellors, or Priests"
(l. 1653.)
Milton intended the scene to adumbrate the ruin of the Royalist nobles, soldiers and clergy.

1607–1608. *degree . . . sort*—social rank of high quality. *N.E.D.* quotes *Measure for Measure,* IV, iv, 20: "Give notice to such men of sort and suite as are to meete him."

1610. *banks*—benches.

1616. *Livery*—uniform of public or private retainers of any kind.

1619. *Cataphracts*—mounted soldiers whose horses, like themselves, were heavily protected with armour. The word is a Greek military term.
Spears—spearmen.

At sight of him the people with a shout   1620
Rifted the Air clamouring thir god with praise,
Who had made thir dreadful enemy thir thrall.
He patient but undaunted where they led him,
Came to the place, and what was set before him
Which without help of eye might be assay'd,   1625
To heave, pull, draw, or break, he still perform'd
All with incredible, stupendious force,
None daring to appear Antagonist.
At length for intermission sake they led him
Between the pillars; he his guide requested   1630
(For so from such as nearer stood we heard)
As over-tir'd to let him lean a while
With both his arms on those two massy Pillars
That to the arched roof gave main support.
He unsuspicious led him; which when *Samson*   1635
Felt in his arms, with head a while inclin'd,
And eyes fast fixt he stood, as one who pray'd,
Or some great matter in his mind revolv'd.

1621. *rifted*—rent, tore.

With *clamouring* N.E.D. compares Evelyn's use of the verb transitively: "Legions of women went down to clamour the House for his enlargement."

1626. *still*—constantly.

1627. *stupendious,* for "stupendous," is found in *P.L.* X, 351. It was the prevailing form of the word.

1630–1634. The account in Judges (xvi, 25–26) says that Samson was set between the pillars for his performance, and that he "said unto the lad that held him by the hand, Suffer me that I may feel the pillars whereupon the house standeth, that I may lean upon them."

1634. Milton may have been influenced by the account of the contemporary appearance of the ruins of Gaza in Sandys' *Travels* (p. 116): "On the North-East Corner and summity of the Hill are the ruines of huge Arches sunk low in the Earth, and other foundations of a stately Building. . . . The Jews do fable this place to have been the Theatre of Sampson pulled down on the heads of the Philistines." Sandys adds that in his opinion the ruins belonged to a Roman structure, and Milton may have known that the arch was a Roman invention, and have described the building as *arched* with no more definite an idea of it than Quarles had when he spoke of its "arched roofe" as all "Builded with massie stone" and yet as being sustained by "mighty Rafters." (*The History of Samson,* Sec. 23.)

1637–1638. *eyes fast fixt . . . revolv'd;* the phrasing recalls Virgil's picture of Aeneas with eyes fast bent downward and sad countenance

At last with head erect thus cried aloud,
Hitherto, Lords, what your commands impos'd   1640
I have perform'd, as reason was, obeying,
Not without wonder or delight beheld.
Now of my own accord such other trial
I mean to show you of my strength, yet greater;
As with amaze shall strike all who behold.   1645
This utter'd, straining all his nerves he bow'd;
As with the force of winds and waters pent
When Mountains tremble, those two massy Pillars
With horrible convulsion to and fro
He tugg'd, he shook, till down they came, and drew   1650
The whole roof after them with burst of thunder
Upon the heads of all who sat beneath,
Lords, Ladies, Captains, Counsellors, or Priests,
Thir choice nobility and flower, not only
Of this but each *Philistian* City round   1655
Met from all parts to solemnize this Feast.
Samson with these immixt, inevitably
Pull'd down the same destruction on himself;
The vulgar only scap'd who stood without.
    Chorus. O dearly-bought revenge, yet glorious! 1660
Living or dying thou hast fulfill'd
The work for which thou wast foretold
To *Israel,* and now li'st victorious
Among thy slain self-kill'd
Not willingly, but tangl'd in the fold   1665

---

as he left the cave of the Sibyl, revolving sad events in his mind.
(*Aen.* VI, 156–8.)

1642. The sense is, "and I have been beheld by you with wonder
and delight."

1645. *amaze*—confusion. Compare *amaz'd* in l. 1286.

1647–1648. Two great similes in *P.L.* (I, 230–7, and VI, 195–8)
arise from the belief that earthquakes are caused by "Winds under
ground or waters forcing way Sidelong."

1659. *vulgar*—the throng of ordinary spectators. Compare ll. 1604–
1610, note.

1664–1665. *self-kill'd Not willingly:* although, as Donne observed
(*Biathanatos,* III, v, 4) Samson's "fact of selfe-killing is celebrated by
the Church . . . as the act of a Martyr," it seemed perilously like
suicide. "The very Text," said Donne, is against those who, like St.
Augustine, "equally zealous of Samson's honour and his own con•

Of dire necessity, whose law in death conjoin'd
Thee with thy slaughter'd foes in number more
Than all thy life had slain before.
    Semichorus. While thir hearts were jocund and sublime,
Drunk with Idolatry, drunk with Wine,   1670
And fat regorg'd of Bulls and Goats,
Chaunting thir Idol, and preferring
Before our living Dread who dwells
In *Silo* his bright Sanctuary:
Among them he a spirit of phrenzy sent,   1675
Who hurt thir minds,
And urg'd them on with mad desire
To call in haste for thir destroyer;
They only set on sport and play
Unweetingly importun'd   1680
Thir own destruction to come speedy upon them.
So fond are mortal men
Fall'n into wrath divine,
As thir own ruin on themselves to invite,
Insensate left, or to sense reprobate,   1685

---

science," argue that he acted simply by divine prompting, "for *Samson* dyed with these words in his mouth, *Let mee lose my life with the Philistins.*"

1666. *dire necessity:* see the Introduction, §30.

1667–1668. From Judges xvi, 30; "the dead which he slew at his death were more than they which he slew in his life."

1669. *sublime* is used in the Latin sense of "uplifted." Compare Adam's "fair large Front and Eye sublime." (*P.L.* I, 502.)

1674. It was at *Silo* (in the Authorized Version, Shiloh) that "the whole congregation of the children of Israel . . . set up the tabernacle of the congregation there." (Josh. xviii, 1.) Milton thought of it as it is described in Exodus xl, 34: "the glory of the Lord filled the tabernacle."

1675. *phrenzy* was a spelling frequently used to indicate the supposed Greek etymology of the word. "Some writers show a tendency to prefer it when the reference is to . . . demoniacal possession." *N.E.D.*

1676. Homer often describes a god as hurting or distracting men's minds, as Ate, the goddess of wrath, does in *Iliad,* IX, 503.

1680. *Unweetingly*—unwittingly, unknowingly.

1683. *wrath divine*—wrath divinely inspired. "Whom the gods would destroy they first make mad."

1685. So St. Paul says of perverted men that "God gave them over

And with blindness internal struck.
   Semichorus. But he though blind of sight,
Despis'd and thought extinguish't quite,
With inward eyes illuminated
His fiery virtue rous'd   1690
From under ashes into sudden flame,
And as an ev'ning Dragon came,
Assailant on the perched roosts,
And nests in order rang'd
Of tame villatic Fowl; but as an Eagle   1695
His cloudless thunder bolted on thir heads.
So virtue giv'n for lost,
Deprest, and overthrown, as seem'd,
Like that self-begott'n bird
In the *Arabian* woods embost,   1700

---

to a reprobate mind" (Rom. i, 28), and "the object which reprobation has in view," Milton wrote in *C.D.* I, iv, "is the destruction of unbelievers."

1692. *Dragon*—serpent.

1695. *villatic Fowl*—barndoor fowls. To Milton's mind the word *villa* kept its Italian meaning of "a farmhouse."

1696. Perhaps Milton thought of Horace's professed conversion by the portent of a thunderclap from a clear sky (*Odes,* I, xxxiv, 6) to a belief that the gods concern themselves in the affairs of men.

1697. *giv'n for lost*—given up as lost.

1699. *that self-begott'n bird*—the Phoenix, which Ovid describes (*Met.* XV, 391–402) as completing five secles (whence *secular* in l. 1707) or centuries of life and then building a nest of spices in the top of a nodding palm tree to be its own funeral pyre. "But from the father's body, it is said, a little phoenix will arise, destined to live an equal number of years." In Tasso's poem, *The Phoenix,* Milton could find a Christianized version of the myth drawn from sources as various as Herodotus (II, 73), Pliny (X, ii) and the *Song of the Phoenix* attributed to Lactantius. His rhythm here is strikingly like Shakespeare's in *The Phoenix and the Turtle,* and he may also have felt the influence of symbolism like Vaughan's in *Resurrection and Immortality,* where the intrinsic virtue in all created things,

> "Phenix-like renew'th
>   Both life and youth;
> For a preserving spirit doth still passe
>   Untainted through this Masse,
> Which doth resolve, produce, and ripen all."

Compare *Damon's Epitaph,* 181, note.

1700. *embost*—hidden, sheltered.

That no second knows nor third,
And lay erewhile a Holocaust,
From out her ashy womb now teem'd,
Revives, reflourishes, then vigorous most
When most unactive deem'd,   1705
And though her body die, her fame survives,
A secular bird ages of lives.
    Manoa. Come, come, no time for lamentation now,
Nor much more cause: *Samson* hath quit himself
Like *Samson,* and heroicly hath finish'd   1710
A life Heroic, on his Enemies
Fully reveng'd hath left them years of mourning,
And lamentation to the Sons of *Caphtor*
Through all *Philistian* bounds.   To *Israel*
Honour hath left, and freedom, let but them   1715
Find courage to lay hold on this occasion;
To himself and Father's house eternal fame;
And which is best and happiest yet, all this
With God not parted from him, as was fear'd,
But favouring and assisting to the end.   1720
Nothing is here for tears, nothing to wail
Or knock the breast, no weakness, no contempt,
Dispraise, or blame, nothing but well and fair,
And what may quiet us in a death so noble.
Let us go find the body where it lies   1725
Soak't in his enemies' blood, and from the stream
With lavers pure and cleansing herbs wash off
The clotted gore.   I with what speed the while

1701. *That no second knows;* because only one phoenix is alive at a time.

1702. *Holocaust*—a sacrifice completely consumed by the fire.

1703. *her* must refer to *virtue* in l. 1697, and at this point the simile ends, although the comparison with the phoenix emerges in the metaphor which makes virtue a *secular bird*.
    teem'd—delivered, brought forth.

1709. *quit*—acquitted.

1713. *Sons of Caphtor*—the Philistines. Compare the Argument, l. 10, note.

1728. *with what speed;* i.e., with what speed I can.

(*Gaza* is not in plight to say us nay)
Will send for all my kindred, all my friends   1730
To fetch him hence and solemnly attend
With silent obsequy and funeral train
Home to his Father's house: there will I build him
A Monument, and plant it round with shade
Of Laurel ever green, and branching Palm,   1735
With all his Trophies hung, and Acts enroll'd
In copious Legend, or sweet Lyric Song.
Thither shall all the valiant youth resort,
And from his memory inflame thir breasts
To matchless valour, and adventures high: 1740
The Virgins also shall on feastful days
Visit his Tomb with flowers, only bewailing
His lot unfortunate in nuptial choice,
From whence captivity and loss of eyes.
　　Chorus. All is best, though we oft doubt,   1745
What th' unsearchable dispose
Of highest wisdom brings about,
And ever best found in the close.
Oft he seems to hide his face,

1729. *plight*—state or condition. Compare "sweetest, saddest plight" in *Il Penseroso*, 57.

1730–1733. "Then his brethren and all the house of his father came down, and . . . brought him up, and buried him between Zorah and Eshtaol, in the burying-place of Manoah his father." (Judg. xvi, 31.)

1736. *Trophies*—spoils of his enemies.

1737. *Legend*—either an inscription over the tomb or a literary record like the lives of the saints in the Golden Legend.
　　Lyric Song—a paean like the Song of Deborah in Judges v.

1745–1748. Compare the closing choruses—identical in every case—with which Euripides ended the *Alcestis, Andromache, Bacchae* and *Helen:*

　　　"In many forms the gods appear,
　　　　And many things unhoped they do;
　　　Forecasts of men they bring not to pass;
　　　What is unforecast they bestow.
　　　So happens this marvel now."

1746. *dispose*—dispensation. *N.E.D.* compares "Such is the dispose of the sole disposer of empires, that they have their risings, their fuls, and their fals." (Speed, *History of Great Britain,* VII, xxxi, 2.)

1749. *hide his face; i.e.,* in anger. Compare the prayer, "Hide not

But unexpectedly returns   1750
And to his faithful Champion hath in place
Bore witness gloriously; whence *Gaza* mourns
And all that band them to resist
His uncontrollable intent;
His servants he with new acquist   1755
Of true experience from this great event
With peace and consolation hath dismist,
And calm of mind, all passion spent.

THE END

---

thy face far from me; put not thy servant away in anger." (Psalm
xxvii, 9.)

1751. *in place*—"on the spot, then and there." *N.E.D.*

1755. *acquist*—increase, acquisition. *N.E.D.* quotes Isaac Barrow;
"In the gifts of fortune, or in the acquists of industry."

1758. *passion* is used in the strong sense that it is in the quotation
from Minturno in the note to ll. 8–11 of the Preface.

INDEX OF FIRST LINES

INDEX OF BOOKS AND HISTORICAL PERSONS

References are to the introductions and footnotes to the poems. References to Milton's works in the footnotes and to works from which verbal parallels are cited are not included.